The Book of
the Thousand Nights
and One Night

The Book of
the Thousand Nights
and One Night

RENDERED INTO ENGLISH FROM
THE LITERAL AND COMPLETE
FRENCH TRANSLATION OF
DR J. C. MARDRUS
BY POWYS MATHERS

Volume I

Routledge
Taylor & Francis Group

LONDON AND NEW YORK

Reprinted ten times
Second edition 1964
Reprinted 1972
First published as a paperback in 1986
by Routledge & Kegan Paul plc

Reprinted 1989, 1993, 1994, 1995, 1996, 1999, 2001 by
Routledge
2 Park Square, Milton Park, Abingdon, Oxon, OX14 4RN
270 Madison Ave, New York, NY 10016

Reprinted 2003, 2008

Routledge is an imprint of the Taylor & Francis Group, an informa business

Printed & bound in Great Britain by
TJ International Ltd, Padstow, Cornwall

ISBN 10: 0-415-04539-8 (vol 1)
ISBN 10: 0-415-04543-6 (set)

ISBN 13: 978-0-415-04539-1 (vol 1)
ISBN 13: 978-0-415-04543-8 (set)

Contents of Volume I

v

CONTENTS OF VOLUME I

CONTENTS OF VOLUME I

Note

For this revised edition of The Book of the Thousand Nights and One Night all names of persons and places and all Arabic words retained in the text have, where necessary, been compared with and corrected by Macnaghten's Calcutta Edition of the original (1839–42). As the object of the present translation was in the first place, and still is, to parallel Dr. Mardrus' ideal of a simple and unannotated version of the complete work for the entertainment of the casual reader, the system of transliteration adopted here, though it gives a consistency lacking in my first edition and in the French of Dr. Mardrus, has been simplified almost beyond the approval of scholars. I have taken this course because I have been assured by experts on the subject that the Anglo-Saxon eye, when reading for pleasure, invariably shies at and side-steps any foreign word decorated with diacritical points or such sound-signs as '(for 'ain) and' (for aliph). The long vowels are marked in order that the reader may have some idea of the rhythm intended, but all other signs are omitted lest they should spoil his enjoyment of the text. Such a simplification allows, of course, of misunderstanding; it does not, for instance, show that Abū Ishāk, Hārūn's musician, should be pronounced Is-hāk; but such occasional losses seem, when we bear in mind the purpose of the translation, more than counterbalanced by the gain in ease of reading and to the eye.

P. M.

As Allāh Wills!
In the Name of Allāh,
The Merciful, The Compassionate!

Praise be to Allāh, master of the Universe! And prayer and peace upon the Prince of Messengers, Muhammad, our lord paramount! And upon all his people prayer and peace together for ever until the judgment day!

And afterwards! may the legends of the men of old be lessons to the people of our time, so that a man may see those things which befell others beside himself: then he will honour and consider carefully the words and adventures of past peoples, and will reprove himself.

Also glory be to him who preserved the tales of the first dwellers to be a guide for the purposes of the last!

Now it is from among these lessons that the stories called The Thousand Nights and One Night are taken; together with all that there is in them of wonder and instruction.

The Tale of King Shahryār and of his Brother, King Shahzamān

IT is related—but Allāh is all wise and all knowing, all powerful and all beneficent—that there was, in the tide and show of ancient time and the passage of the age and of the moment, a king among the kings of Sāsān, in the isles of India and China. He was master of armies and auxiliaries, of slaves and of a great following; and he had two sons, one tall and the other small. Both were heroic horsemen; but the taller was the greater in this exercise and reigned over lands and governed with justice among men, so that the peoples of the land and of the kingdom loved him. His name was King Shahryār. The smaller brother was called King Shahzamān and ruled over Samarkand al-Ajam.

Both lived in their countries and were just rulers of the people for a space of twenty years; by the end of which time each was at the height of his splendour and his growth.

This was the way with them until the tall king was seized by a violent longing to see his brother. Then he commanded his wazīr to depart and return with him: and the wazīr answered: 'I hear and I obey.'

The wazīr set out and, arriving in all security by the grace of Allāh, entered the presence of the brother, wished him peace, and told him the purpose of his journey.

King Shahzamān answered: 'I hear and I obey.' Then he made preparations for his departure and for the going out of his tents, his camels, and mules; his slaves and fighting-men. Lastly he raised his own wazīr to the governorship, and departed to seek the lands of his brother.

But, in the middle of the night, he recalled a thing which he had left forgotten at the palace. Returning and entering, he found his wife stretched on her bed and being embraced by a black slave. At this sight, the world darkened before his face and he said within his soul: 'If such a thing has come to pass when I have hardly left the city, what would the conduct of this wanton be if I were absent for long at my brother's house?' So he drew his sword and with one stroke killed them upon the carpets of the bed. Then he returned and, ordering his camp to move forward, journeyed through the night till he came to his brother's city.

His brother rejoiced at his approach, went out to meet him and, greeting him, wished him peace; also he adorned the city for him, and began to speak with him jovially. But King Shahzamān remembered the affair of his wife, and a cloud of grief veiled him; his cheeks became sallow and his body frail. King Shahryār, seeing him in this pass and thinking it was due to his exile from lands and kingdom, questioned him no further on the subject and let him be. But, on a later day, he said: 'My brother, I know not! and yet I see your body grow frail and your cheeks sallow.' Shahzamān answered: 'My brother, I am stricken in the heart of my heart.' But he did not reveal what he had seen happen to his wife. So King Shahryār continued: 'Then come hunting and coursing with me, for in that pursuit perhaps your breast may throw off this trouble.' But King Shahzamān had no wish to do so; and his brother went out to hunt alone.

Now there were in the King's palace certain windows that looked on to the garden, and, as King Shahzamān leaned there and looked out, the door of the palace opened and twenty women slaves with twenty men slaves came from it; and the wife of the King, his brother, was among them and walked there in all her bright beauty. When they came to the pool of a fountain they all undressed and mingled one with another. Suddenly, on the King's wife crying: 'O Masud! Yā Masud!', a gigantic negro ran towards her, embraced her, and, turning her upon her back, enjoyed her. At this signal, all the other men slaves did the same with the women and they continued thus a long while, not ceasing their kisses and embraces and goings in and the like until the approach of dawn.

At this sight the King's brother said within himself: 'By Allāh, mine is even a lighter misfortune than his.' So he let his grief and discontent slip from him, saying to himself: 'Truly, this is more terrible than all which happened to me.' And from that moment he began to drink again and to eat without pause.

Meanwhile the King, his brother, came back from hunting, and the two wished each other peace. Then King Shahryār, observing his brother Shahzamān, saw that colour and life had come back to him and further that he, who had so long dealt sparingly with his food, now ate abundantly. So, in his astonishment, he asked him the explanation of this; and the other answered: 'Listen and I will tell you the cause of my former pallor. When you sent your wazīr to me to require my presence at your side, I made my preparation for departure and left my city. But afterwards, remembering the present which

2

I destined for you and which I gave you at the palace, I went back and found my wife lying with a black slave, the two sleeping upon the carpets of my bed. I killed the pair of them and made my way to you, thrice wretched in my thought for what had happened. That was the cause of my former paleness and loss of strength. As for the return of colour to my cheeks, spare me, I pray, from speaking of it.'

When his brother heard these words, he said: 'By Allāh, I conjure you to tell me the other half of the matter!' So King Shahzamān told him all he had seen. And King Shahryār exclaimed: 'First must I see this with my own eyes!' To this his brother answered: 'Make it appear, then, that you are going out to hunt and course; but hide instead with me, and you shall be witness of the sight and see the truth of it!'

Immediately the King proclaimed his departure by the public crier and the soldiers went out beyond the city with their tents. The King went forth also and, settling himself in his tents, said to his young slaves: 'Let no one enter!' Then he disguised himself and, leaving secretly, went towards the palace where his brother was. On his arrival he stationed himself at the window giving on to the garden. Scarcely had an hour passed when the women slaves, circling about their mistress, came into the garden with the men slaves; and they did all that Shahzamān had told of them and passed the time in these diversions until asr, the beginning of the sun's decline.

When King Shahryār saw these things, reason fled from her seat in his mind and he said to his brother Shahzamān: 'Let us go hence and fare forth to seek our destiny upon the road of Allāh; for we have no right in royalty, nor shall have, until we have found someone who has met a fate like ours: without that, in truth, death would be better than our lives.' To this his brother made the fitting answer and both went out by a secret door of the palace. They travelled night and day until they came to a tree in the middle of a lonely meadow near the salt sea. In this meadow there was an eyelet of fresh water at which they drank and afterwards sat down to rest. An hour had hardly passed when the sea began to be troubled and suddenly a column of black smoke came up out of it which rose to the sky and moved towards the meadow. Seeing this, they became afraid and climbed as high as they were able into the tall tree, and began to consider what this might mean. Then, behold! the smoke column changed to a Jinnī of great size, vast-shouldered, gigantically-breasted, and carrying on his head a box. He put foot to the earth, came towards the tree in which they were, and stopped below it. Then he lifted the lid of the box and took from it a large coffer which he also opened; and thereupon appeared a desirable young girl, bright in her beauty, shining like the sun. As the poet says:

> She comes, a torch in the shadows, and it is day;
> Her light more brightly lights the dawn.
> Suns leap from out her beauty
> And moons are born in the smiling of her eyes.
> Ah, that the veils of her mystery might be rent
> And the folk of the world lie ravished at her feet.
> Forced by the great light of her sweet glancing
> Wet tears smart forth from every watching eye.

When the Jinnī had looked long at the beauty of the girl, he said to her: 'O Queen of every silky thing! O you whom I ravished away upon your bridal night! I would sleep a little.' And the Jinnī, resting his head upon the knees of the young girl, went to sleep.

Then the child raised her head and saw the two kings hidden in the tree-top. At once she lifted the head of the Jinnī from her knees, rested it upon the ground, and stood up beneath the tree, saying to them by signs: 'Come down. Have no fear of this Ifrīt.' They also answered by signs: 'Allāh be with you! Pray excuse us from such a dangerous undertaking!' She said: 'I conjure you by Allāh! Come down quickly, or I will warn the Ifrīt and he shall kill you with the worst of deaths!' Then they were afraid and came down beside her; and she said at once: 'Come, pierce me violently with your lances; if not, I will wake the Ifrīt.' Then Shahryār said fearfully to Shahzamān: 'You, my brother, do first what she requires!' To which the other answered: 'I will do nothing until you have given me an example, my elder brother!' And each began to coax the other, making with their eyes gestures of coupling. Then she said: 'Why do I see you working your eyes in this way? If you do not come forward and do it to me at once, I will wake the Ifrīt.' So, in their fear of the Jinnī, they both did to her as she had commanded, and when they were well wearied, she said: 'You are indeed experienced riders!' Then, drawing from her pocket a little bag, she took from it a necklace of five hundred and seventy seal-rings, saying: 'Know you what these are?' And they answered: 'We do not know.' Then she said: 'The givers of these seal-rings have all coupled with me on the unwitting horns of this Ifrīt. So now, O brothers, give me yours!'

Then they gave her their seal-rings, taking them off their hands. Whereon she said: 'Know that this Ifrīt carried me off on the night of my marriage, prisoned me in a coffer and placed that coffer in a box and fastened about the box seven chains, yes, and then laid me at the bottom of the moaning sea that wars and dashes with its waves. But he did not know that whenever any one of us women desires a thing, nothing can prevent her from it. And the poet said, besides:

> Friend, trust not at all in women, smile at their promising,
> For they lower or they love at the caprice of their parts.
> Filled to the mouth with deceit, they lavish a lying love
> Even while the very floss fringing their silks is faithless.
> Respect and remember the words of Yūsuf. Forget not
> Iblīs worked all Adam's woe with one woman.
> Rail not, my friend. At this house, at whom you are railing,
> Mild love tomorrow will give place to madness.
> Say not: "If I love, I'll escape the follies of loving,"
> But rather: "Only a miracle brings a man safe from among them."

At these words the brothers marvelled even to the limits of marvelling and said to each other: 'If this be a Jinnī and in spite of his power much more terrible things have happened to him than to us, it is an adventure which ought to console us!'

So at that same hour they left the young woman and returned each to his own city.

When King Shahryār entered his palace, he caused his wife's head to be cut off at the neck, and in the same way the heads of the slaves, both men and women. Then he ordered his wazīr to bring him every night a young and virgin girl, whom he ravished and, when the night had passed, caused to be slain. This he did for three long years; so that the people were all one cry of grief, one tumult of horror. They fled away with such daughters as remained to them; and in all the city there remained not one girl who retained the state to serve for this assault.

At last the King, as was his custom, ordered the wazīr to bring him a young girl; and the wazīr went forth and hunted, but found no girl at all. So he returned to his own home, dejected and wretched, and with his soul full of his fear of the King.

Now this wazīr had himself two daughters who in the matters of beauty, charm, brilliance, perfection, and delicate taste, were each unrivalled save by the other. The name of the elder was Shahrazād, and that of the younger Dunyazād. Shahrazād had read the books, the annals, and the legends of old kings, together with the histories of past peoples. Also she was credited with possessing a thousand books of stories telling of the peoples, the kings, and the poets of bygone ages and of past time. She was sweetly eloquent of speech and to listen to her was music.

When she had looked at her father, she said: 'Why do I see you so bowed and changed with care and sorrow? Know, my father, that the poet says: "Thou who art sad, oh be comforted; for nothing endures and as every joy vanishes away so also vanishes every sorrow!" '

When the wazīr heard these words, he told his daughter from beginning to end all that had happened concerning the King. Then Shahrazād said: 'By Allāh, father, you must marry me to this king; for either I shall live or, dying, I shall be a ransom for the daughters of the Mussulmāns and the cause of their deliverance out of the hands of the King.' Then said he: 'Allāh be with you! You shall never expose yourself to such a danger.' And she answered: 'It is necessary that I do this.' So he said to her: 'Take care that the fate of the ass with the bull and the husbandman befall not you also. Listen':

The Fable of the Ass, the Bull and the Husbandman

K NOW, my daughter, that there was once a merchant, master of riches and cattle, married and the father of children; to whom Allāh had also given understanding of the tongues of beasts and birds. The place of this merchant's house was in a fertile land on the bank of a river, and in his farm there were an ass and a bull.

One day the bull came to the stable where the ass was lodged and found it well swept and watered, with well-winnowed barley in the manger and on the ground well-sifted straw, and the ass lying there at his ease. (For when his master mounted him it would only be for some short ride that chance demanded, and the ass would quickly return to his rest.) Now on that day the merchant heard the bull say to the ass: 'Give you joy of your food, and may you find it healthy, profitable, and of a good digestion! I myself am weary; but you are rested. You eat well-winnowed barley and are cared for; and if, on occasion, your master mounts you, he brings you quickly back. As for me I am but used to labour and to work the mill.' And the ass said: 'When you go out into the field and they put the yoke upon your neck, throw yourself to the earth and do not rise, even if they beat you; also, when you do get up, fall down again immediately. And after, if they let you back to the byre and give you beans to eat, leave them, as if you were ill. Force yourself in this way not to eat or drink for a day or two or even three. Thus you will rest from your labour and your weariness.'

Remember that the merchant was there and heard their words.

When the husbandman came to give forage to the bull, he saw that he ate very little; and when in the morning he took him out to work he found him to be ill. Then the merchant said to the husbandman: 'Take the ass and make him work in the bull's place for the whole day!' So the man returned and took the ass in place of the bull and made it labour during the whole day.

When the ass came back to the stable at the end of the day, the bull thanked him for his goodness of heart and for having let him rest from his fatigue. But the ass answered nothing and, instead, repented very bitterly.

Next day the husbandman came and took the ass again and made him work till the fall of day; so that the ass returned with a galled neck and broken by fatigue. Then the bull, seeing the state he was in, began to thank him with effusion and load him with praises. To which the ass replied: 'How restful were the days before this, when nothing but luxury was my lot,' and added: 'Meanwhile I will give you a piece of good advice; I heard our master say: "If the bull does not get up from his place, we must hand him over to the slaughterer to kill and to make a leather cloth for the table!" I am much afraid for your safety.'

When the bull heard the ass's words, he thanked him and said: 'To-morrow I will go with them freely and attend to my labours.' With that he began to eat and swallowed all the forage and even licked the bushel clean with his tongue.

Remember their master saw and heard all this.

When the day came the merchant went out with his wife towards the byres and both of them sat down. Then the husbandman came and took out the bull who, at the sight of his master, began to frisk his tail and loudly break wind and gallop wildly in all directions. The merchant was seized with such a laughter that he rolled on his back. His wife asked: 'What are you laughing at?' He answered: 'At a thing which I have seen and heard, but of which I may not tell you without dying.' And she said: 'You must tell me the reason of your laughter, even if you have to die for it.' He said: 'I cannot tell you, because I fear to die.' Then said she: 'I know, you are laughing at me.' After this she did not cease to quarrel and confound him with wilful words until she drove him into great perplexity. Finally, he made his children come to him and sent to call the kādī and witnesses, wishing to make his will before he should tell the secret to his wife and die. For he greatly loved his wife, since she was the daughter of his father's brother and the mother of his children, and since he had lived with her for one hundred and twenty years. Further, he invited all his wife's relatives and the folk of the district and, relating the story, told them how he would die on the instant of revealing his secret. Then all who were present said to the wife: 'Allāh be with you! Leave this matter on one side lest your husband, the father of your children, die.' But she answered: 'I will never leave him in peace until he tells me, even if he has to die for it.' So they stopped reasoning with her; and the merchant rose from among them and went, by the side of the stable, towards the garden, in order that he might first make his death ablution there and then return to tell his secret and to die.

Now the merchant had a valiant cock which could satisfy fifty hens, and also a dog. And he heard the dog calling to the cock and scolding it, saying: 'Are you not ashamed of being so gay when our master is on the point of death?' Then the cock asked the dog how this was so, and, when the dog had told him the story, he exclaimed: 'By Allāh, our master is extraordinarily lacking in intelligence! I myself have fifty wives, and I succeed very well by contenting one and scolding another, while he, who has only one wife, does not know the way of dealing even with her. It is quite simple; he has but to cut himself some good mulberry twigs, go back in strength to his private room, and beat her until she either dies or repents. She will not importune him with any questions on any subject after that, I do assure you.' So the cock spoke, and when the merchant heard him, light returned to his reason and he resolved to beat his wife.

Here the wazīr paused in his story and said to his daughter Shahrazād: 'It may be I shall do to you as the merchant did to his wife.' She asked him: 'What did he do?' And the wazīr continued:

The merchant entered his wife's chamber, after having cut and hidden about him certain mulberry twigs, and called to her, saying: 'Come into my private room that I may tell you my secret, out of the sight of all, and then die.' So she entered with him and he shut the door of the private room and fell upon her with redoubled blows until she swooned away. Finally, when she could speak, she cried: 'I repent! I repent!' and, beginning to caress her husband's hands and feet, did repent in very truth. Afterwards she walked out with him, and all the relatives and those gathered there rejoiced. Happy and prosperous were the fortunes of them all until their deaths.

Thus he spoke, and when Shahrazād, the wazīr's daughter, heard her father's story, she said: 'Even so, my father, I wish you to do what I have asked you.' So the wazīr, without insisting further, had the wedding garments of his daughter Shahrazād made ready, and then went to tell the matter to King Shahryār.

Meanwhile, Shahrazād gave these instructions to her young sister: 'When I am with the King I will send to fetch you; then when you have come and when you see the King finish his act with me, you must say: "Tell me, my sister, some of your stories of marvel that the night may pass pleasantly." Then will I tell you tales which, if Allāh wills, shall be the deliverance of the daughters of the Mussulmāns.'

After this the wazīr, her father, came to take her and went up with her into the presence of the King. And the King, being overborne with happiness, said to him: 'Is the needful thing indeed present?' And respectfully the wazīr answered: 'Yes!'

But when the King wished to take the young girl, she began to weep, so that he asked: 'What ails you?' She answered: 'O my King, I have a little sister and I would say my farewells to her.' So the King sent for the little sister, who came and threw herself upon the neck of Shahrazād, and lastly cowered down beside the bed.

Then the King rose and, taking the maiden Shahrazād, ravished her virginity.

Afterwards they spoke together and Dunyazād said to Shahrazād: 'Allāh be with you! Tell us, my sister, some of your tales of marvel, that the night may pass pleasantly.' And Shahrazād answered: 'Gladly and as a duty, if the great and courteous King permits.' When the King heard these words, and being moreover unable to sleep, he was in no way averse to listening to the tale of Shahrazād.

And Shahrazād, this first night, began the following tale:

HERE BEGIN THE
THOUSAND NIGHTS AND ONE NIGHT

The Tale of the Merchant and the Ifrīt

SHAHRAZĀD SAID:

IT has come to me, O auspicious King, that there was once a merchant of the merchants, master of many riches and of affairs of commerce in all lands.

One day he mounted on horseback and left for certain places whither his business called him. As the heat became too vexing, he sat down under a tree and, putting his hand into his food-bag, took from it a snack and also some dates. When he had finished eating the dates, he threw the stones to a distance; but suddenly an enormous Ifrīt appeared who approached him, brandishing a sword and crying: 'Rise up, that I may slay you as you have slain my child!' On this the merchant asked: 'How have I slain your child?' The other said: 'When you threw the stones of the dates you had eaten, they struck my boy in the breast and he died forthwith.' Then said the merchant to the Ifrīt: 'Know, O great Ifrīt, that I am a Believer and know not how to lie. Now I have many riches and children and a wife, also I have at my home deposits which have been trusted to me. Give me leave to go to my house that I may render each his due and, when I have done this, I will return to you. Indeed, indeed, you have my promise and my oath that I will return to you forthwith. Then you shall do to me as you wish. And Allāh is a witness of my words.' So the Jinnī had trust in the merchant and let him depart.

The merchant returned to his own land, rid himself of his obligations, rendered each his due, and lastly revealed to his wife and his children the fate that had overtaken him. So they all, relations, women and children, began to weep. Then the merchant made his will and rested with his folk until the year's end; after which, taking his winding-sheet beneath his arm, he bade farewell to his nearest, to his neighbours, and to the folk of his house, and went forth, as it were, in spite of his nose. Then indeed was lamentation made and grief cried over him.

As for the merchant, he continued to journey until he came to the garden where he was due on the first day of the new year. Now, while he sat down to weep over his fate, behold a venerable sheikh came towards him leading a gazelle by a chain. He saluted the merchant, wishing him a life of prosperity and saying to him: 'What is the reason of your staying alone upon this Jinn-haunted spot?' Then the merchant told him of his adventure with the Ifrīt. And the sheikh, master of the gazelle, being greatly astonished, said: 'By Allāh, your faith, my brother, is indeed a rare faith! And your story is so prodigious that, were it only written with a needle on the inner corner of an eye, it would yet be a matter of reflection to the circumspect.' Then he sat down by the merchant's side, saying: 'By Allāh! I shall certainly stay here with you, my brother, until I have seen what happens between you and the Ifrīt.' So he stayed, conversing with the merchant, and beheld him swooning with fear and horror, a prey to deep sorrow and to stormy thoughts. Suddenly, as the master of the gazelle waited, there came a second sheikh, who advanced towards them leading two dogs of greyhound breed which were both black. He came up to them, wishing them peace and asking the reason of their stay upon that Jinn-haunted spot. So they told him the story from beginning to end. But hardly had he seated himself, when a third sheikh came towards them, leading a bay-coloured she-mule, and he also wished them peace and asked them the reason of their stay. Again they told the story from beginning to end; but nothing is to be gained by repeating it in this place.

In a little while a sand-devil lifted and a great wind blew heavily, coming towards the middle of the grassland. Then, the dust dispersing, the self-same Jinnī appeared, a fine-sharpened blade in his hand and sparks of fire storming from his eyes. He came to them and, seizing the merchant from among them, said: 'Come, that I may kill you as you killed my child, who was the breath of my life and the fire of my heart.' Then the merchant began to weep and lament, and the three sheikhs also set themselves most conspicuously to weep and groan and sob.

But the first sheikh, master of the gazelle, at last plucked up his courage and kissed the hand of the Jinnī, saying: 'O Jinnī, O chief among the Kings of the Jinn and their crown also, if I relate to you the tale of myself and this gazelle and it is such that you marvel at it, oh grant me in return mercy for a third of the blood of this merchant!' The Jinnī answered: 'Assuredly, O venerable sheikh. If you tell me the story and I find it indeed extraordinary, I will grant you mercy for a third of this blood!'

The Tale of the First Sheikh

THE FIRST SHEIKH SAID:

O GREAT Ifrīt, know that this gazelle was my uncle's daughter and my own flesh and blood. I married her when she was quite young and lived with her for nearly thirty years; but Allāh granted me no child by her. So I took a concubine who, by Allāh's favour, gave me a man-child as beautiful as the rising moon, with fine eyes, meeting brows, and perfect limbs. When he had grown to be a boy of fifteen, I was obliged to journey to a far city on an important matter of business.

You must know that my uncle's daughter, this gazelle, had been initiated since childhood into sorcery and the lore of enchantment. By the art of magic she changed my son into a calf and the slave his mother into a cow, and put both of them under the care of our herd.

A long time afterwards I came back from my journey and asked for my son and his mother. Then my wife said: 'Your slave is dead and your son has fled I know not whither!'

For a year I remained broken by my heart's grief, with the tears ever in my eyes.

Then, when the yearly feast of the Day of Sacrifice came round, I sent to bid my herd choose a well-fattened cow for me, and he brought me one, but she was my concubine bewitched by this gazelle. Then I pulled up the sleeves and skirts of my garments and, knife in hand, prepared to sacrifice the cow; but suddenly she began to moan and weep abundant tears. So I stopped and ordered the herd to sacrifice her. He did so; but when he had flayed her, we found neither fat nor flesh on her but only skin and bone. Then I repented that I had sacrificed her—though my repentance was of no avail—and gave her to the herd, saying: 'Bring me a well-fatted calf.' So he brought me my son in the likeness of a calf.

When the calf saw me, he broke the cord that held him and running to me rolled at my feet with groans and tears. Then I had pity on him and said to the herd: 'Bring me another cow and let this be.'

At this point in her tale, Shahrazād saw the approach of morning and discreetly fell silent. Then her sister Dunyazād said: 'Sister, your words are sweet and gentle and pleasant to the taste.' And Shahrazād answered: 'Indeed they are nothing to that which I would tell both of you tomorrow night if I were still alive and the King thought good to spare me.' On this, the King said to himself:

12

'By Allāh, I will not kill her until I have heard the rest of her tale!'

Then the King and Shahrazād passed the rest of the night in each other's arms, till the King departed to sit in judgment. When he saw the wazīr approach, carrying under his arm the winding-sheet destined for his daughter Shahrazād whom he believed already dead, the King said nothing to him but continued to administer justice, raising some to office and debasing others, until the fall of day. So that the wazīr was plunged into perplexity and the extreme of astonishment.

When the dīwān was over, King Shahryār returned to his palace.

And when the second night had come

DUNYAZĀD SAID TO SHAHRAZĀD: 'Sister, I pray you finish for us the tale of the merchant and the Jinnī.' To this Shahrazād answered: 'With all my heart and as my duty is, if the King permits.' Then the King said: 'You may speak.'

AND SHE SAID:

It is related, O favoured King and lover of justice, that, when the merchant saw the calf weeping, his heart was softened and he said to the herd: 'Leave this calf to graze among the cows.'

The Jinnī was mightily astonished at this strange tale and the sheikh, master of the gazelle, continued:

O master of the Kings of the Jinn, my uncle's daughter, this gazelle, was looking on and said to me: 'Certainly we must sacrifice this calf; he is fattened to perfection.' But for very pity I could not make up my mind to sacrifice him and at my order the herd took him again and went away with him.

On the next day, as I was sitting in my house, the herd came to me, saying: 'Master, I have a joyful thing to tell you, good news worthy of recompense.' 'Surely,' I answered. Then he said: 'Great merchant, my daughter is a sorceress and has learnt magic from an old woman who lodges with us. Yesterday, when you gave me that calf, I brought him with me into the presence of my daughter, and scarcely had she set eyes on him when she covered her face with her veil, first weeping and then laughing. Finally she said to me: "Has my worth so fallen in your eyes that you let strange men like this come into my presence?" "Where are these strange men?" I answered. "And why have you wept and then laughed?" Then she said: "This

13

calf with you is the son of our master, the merchant, but he is be-witched; yes, both he and his mother, bewitched by his step-mother; and it was the calf expression of his face at which I laughed. And if I wept it was for the mother of this poor calf, slain by his father." I was greatly astonished by these words of my daughter and waited with impatience for the dawn that I might come to tell you.'

Then, mighty Jinnī, continued the sheikh, hearing the herd's words, I went out with him, drunken without wine for joy of seeing my son again. When I came to the herd's house, his young daughter welcomed me, kissing my hand, and the calf came and rolled at my feet. Then I asked the herd's daughter: 'Is what you say of this calf true?' And she answered: 'Yes, master, indeed! He is your son, your heart's delight.' Then said I: 'My gentle, helpful child, if you deliver my son I will give you all the cattle and the goods your father holds for me.' She smiled at my words and said: 'Master, I would only be willing to take these riches on two conditions; the first that I marry your son, and the second that I have your leave to bewitch and confine whomsoever I wish. Without these things I cannot answer for the good of my interference against the evil arts of your wife.'

Mighty Jinnī, when I heard the words of the herd's daughter, I answered: 'Be it so! And further you shall have the riches which your father holds for me. As for my uncle's daughter, you may dispose of her life as you wish.'

When she heard me say this, she took a small copper basin and filled it with water, speaking magic incantations over it. Then she sprinkled the calf with the water and conjured him in these words: 'If Allāh made thee a calf, remain a calf; but if thou art bewitched, return to thy former shape, by the grace of Allāh the Most High!' Even as she spoke, the calf, beginning to tremble and dislimn, re-turned to human form. I threw myself upon him in a long embrace and then I asked him in the name of Allāh to tell me what my uncle's daughter had done to him and to his mother. So he told me all that had happened, and I said: 'My son, Allāh, Master of Destinies, has raised up one to save you and restore your rights.'

After this, good Jinnī, I married my son to the herd's daughter; and she by magic arts bewitched my wife, turning her into this gazelle which you now see. Passing by here I saw this excellent merchant and, asking him what he did and hearing what had hap-pened, sat down to watch the event. Such is my story.

Then the Jinnī cried: 'Your tale is marvellous enough and I grant you mercy for a third of this blood.'

After this the second sheikh, master of the two greyhounds, came forward and said: 'O mighty Ifrīt, if I tell you the adventure which befell me from these two hounds, which are my brothers, and if you find it more marvellous than the tale you have just heard, will you grant me mercy for another third of this man's blood?' 'Assuredly, venerable sheikh,' answered the Jinnī, 'if your adventure be indeed more marvellous.'

So the second sheikh began:

The Tale of the Second Sheikh

KNOW, O Lord of the Kings of the Jinn, that these two hounds are my brothers, and I am the third. When our father died, he left us an inheritance of three thousand dīnārs and with my share I opened a shop and began to trade in it. My brothers did the same, but soon one of them set out on a commercial venture and was away with the caravans for over a year. When he returned, he had lost all his money and I was moved to say to him: 'Brother, did I not counsel you against this journey?' Then he wept and said: 'Allāh, the All-powerful, allowed this loss of mine, and your words cannot help me now that I have nothing left.' Then I brought him up into my shop and afterwards conducted him to the baths and gave him a fine robe of rare workmanship. When at last we were sitting down to eat together, I told my brother that I was about to compute the yearly gains from my shop and that, leaving the capital untouched, I would divide whatever profit there might be equally between us. When, on making my accounts, I found that I had a profit of a thousand dīnārs for the year, I gave thanks to the power and greatness of Allāh and rejoiced exceedingly. Then I divided the sum equally between my brother and myself, and we dwelt together for many days.

But at length both my brothers made up their minds to go on a second journey and wished me to set out with them. When I declined this invitation, pointing out that the result of the first journey did not tempt me to imitate them, they began to reproach me. But their words were of no avail and we stayed buying and selling, each in our respective shops, for a whole year. At the end of the year they again proposed a journey, and again I refused, and this went on for six whole years. But at last I acceded to their request to set out with them and suggested that we should count up what money we had. We did so and found that it came in all to six thousand dīnārs. Then said I: 'Let us hide the half of this in the earth to be a help if we encounter ill fortune and let us each take with us a thousand dīnārs to trade with.' 'May Allāh favour your advice,' they answered. So, taking the money and dividing it, I hid three thousand dīnārs and divided the other three thousand between us three. Then we bought merchandise of many kinds, hired a ship and, placing all we had on board her, set sail.

After a month's voyage we dropped anchor at a certain city, where we sold our goods at a profit of ten dīnārs for one. Then we left the city.

When we came down to the sea side, we found there a woman dressed in old and tattered garments who approached me and kissed my hand, saying: 'Master, can you help me and save me? Well I know how to repay your goodness!' I answered: 'Certainly I will help and save you, but you must not think it necessary to repay me.' 'Marry me then, Master,' she said, 'carry me with you to your country and I will pledge my soul to you. Do this for me, for I am of those who know the value of an obligation. Also, I pray, do not be ashamed of my poor condition.' When I heard her speak, I pitied her from the bottom of my heart, for nothing comes to pass but Allāh wills it. I carried her with me, clothed her in rich garments and stretched fine carpets for her on the ship. Then, when I had given her a full and cordial welcome, we set sail.

As time went on I grew to love her and would not be parted from her day or night, preferring her company to that of my brothers. So they grew jealous of me, envying me my riches and the beauty of my possessions. They cast greedy eyes on all that I had, and plotted my death and the theft of my money. Satan made this plan seem good to them.

One day, as I lay sleeping by my wife's side, they stole up to us and cast us both into the sea. My wife woke in the water and suddenly, changing her shape, became an Ifrītah. Then she took me upon her shoulders and, carrying me to an island, left me and disappeared for the whole night. In the morning she returned and said: 'Do you not know me? I am your wife. It was I who held you up and saved you from death by Allāh's grace. Know now that I am a

Jinnīyah and that when first I saw you my heart loved you, for Allāh willed it so, and I am a believer in Him and in His prophet, whom may He bless and keep. Even when I came to you in poor estate you were willing to marry me, and now, in my turn, I have saved you from death in the water. As for your brothers, I am enraged against them and must kill them.'

Astonished by her words, I thanked her heartily. 'But as for killing my brothers, this thing must not be,' I said, and told her all that had happened between us from beginning to end. When she had heard me out, she said: 'To-night I will fly to them and sink their ship so that they die.' Then said I: 'Allāh be with you! do not do this thing. The Master of Proverbs has said: "You who have helped the unworthy, know that the wicked man has in his wickedness punishment enough!" And whatever they have done, they are still my brothers.' 'No! I must kill them,' she said, and I begged her clemency in vain; she took me on her shoulders and, flying through the air, set me down upon the terrace of my house at home.

I opened the door of my house and lifted the three thousand dīnārs from their hiding place. Then, after making the customary visits of greeting, I opened my shop and stocked it anew with goods.

When night came, I shut my shop and, entering my own house, found these two hounds tied up in a corner. When they saw me, they rose weeping and caught hold of my garments. At that moment my wife ran up to me, saying: 'These are your brothers.' And when I asked her who had done this thing to them, she answered: 'I did! I asked my sister, who is far more deeply learned in enchantments than I am, and she changed them into these forms, out of which they cannot come again until ten years have passed.'

That is why, O powerful Jinnī, I happen to be in this place, because I am on my way to my sister-in-law to beg her to deliver these poor creatures now that ten years have passed. When I came here, I saw this good merchant and, after hearing his tale, wished to remain and witness what would happen between him and you. This is my story.

'Truly a remarkable tale!' the Jinnī said. 'For it I grant you mercy on a third of this blood which is forfeit to me.'

Then the third sheikh, master of the mule, came forward and said to the Jinnī: 'I will tell you a tale more marvellous than either of these, if you will grant me mercy for the rest of the blood which is forfeit to you.' 'Let it be so!' answered the Jinnī.

And the third sheikh said:

The Tale of the Third Sheikh

O THOU Sultān, O thou Chief of the Jinn, this mule, which you see, was once my wife. A time came when I had been far away on a journey for a whole year. When at last my business was finished, I returned by night and found her lying with a black slave on the carpets of my bed. They were talking, laughing, and kissing, and exciting each other with little games. As soon as my wife saw me, she sprang up and came towards me, snatching up a pitcher of water. She whispered a few words over the pitcher and sprinkled some of the water upon me, saying: 'Come out from thy proper shape and put on the form of a dog!' At once I became a dog and she chased me from the house. I wandered about the city and, coming at last to a butcher's shop, went near and began eating the bones. When the master of the shop saw me, he lifted me and took me with him to his house.

When the butcher's daughter saw me, she veiled her face because of me, saying to her father: 'Is this the way to behave? To bring a man with you into my presence?' 'Where is this man you speak of?' asked her father, and she answered: 'This dog is a man. It is a woman who has bewitched him and I am able to save him.' 'Save him then, my daughter, in Allāh's name!' said her father. She took a pitcher of water and, after speaking certain words over it, sprinkled a few drops upon me: 'Come out from this shape and return to thy former appearance!' So I returned to my former appearance and, kissing the young girl's hand, I told her that I ardently wished to bewitch my wife, as she had bewitched me. Then the butcher's daughter gave me a little of the water telling me, if I found my wife asleep, to sprinkle her and that she would then become whatever I wished. So, finding her asleep, I sprinkled her with the water, saying: 'Leave this shape and put on the form of a mule!' And forthwith she became a mule, as you may see with your own eyes, O Sultān and Chief of all the Kings of the Jinn!

Then the Jinnī, turning to the mule, asked her: 'Is this true?' At which she nodded her head, as if to say: 'Yes, yes, it is true!'

This tale made the Jinnī tremble with pleasurable emotion . . .

Here Shahrazād saw the approach of morning and discreetly fell silent. Then her sister Dunyazād said: 'Sister, your words are sweet and gentle and pleasant to the taste.' And Shahrazād answered: 'Indeed they are nothing to that which I would tell both of you to-morrow night if I were still alive and the King thought good to spare me.' On this, the King said to himself: 'By Allāh, I will not kill her until I have heard the rest of her remarkable tale!'

Then the King and Shahrazād spent the remainder of the night in each other's arms, till the King departed for the Council. The wazīr and the officers of the court came in and, when the dīwān was full of people, the King gave judgment, raising some and abasing others, concluding cases and giving commands, until the fall of day. At length the dīwān rose and King Shahryār returned to his palace.

And when the third night had come

DUNYAZĀD SAID: 'Sister, I pray you finish your tale.' To this Shahrazād answered: 'Gladly and with all my heart!' Then she continued:

It is related, O auspicious King, that when the third sheikh had told the most wonderful tale of the three, the Jinnī was stricken with wonder and trembled with pleasurable emotion. At last he said: 'I grant you the rest of the forfeit and here relinquish this merchant to you.'

Then the merchant in an ecstasy of happiness came and thanked the sheikhs and they, in their turn, congratulated him on his safe deliverance.

After this, each returned to his own country.

But, continued Shahrazād, these tales are in no way more wonderful than the tale of the fisherman. 'What is the tale of the fisherman?' asked the King.

And Shahrazād said:

The Fisherman and the Jinnī

IT is related, O auspicious King, that there was once a fisherman, very old and poor, who was married and had three children.

He used to cast his net four times a day, never more often. Now once, when he had gone to the shore at noon, he set down his basket and, casting his net, waited for it to sink to the bottom. When it had done so he twitched the cords and found it so heavy that he could not pull it in. So, bringing the ends to shore, he made them fast to a wooden stake. Then he undressed and, diving into the sea, laboured till he had hauled the net ashore. Dressing himself again in high good humour he examined the net and found that it contained a dead ass. Disgusted at this sight, he exclaimed: 'Be it as Allāh wills!' and added: 'Yet it is a strange gift that Allāh has seen good to send me.' Then he recited this verse:

> Blind diver in the dark
> Of night and loss,
> Luck delights not in energy;
> Cease, and be still.

After he had freed the net and squeezed the water out of it, he waded into the sea and cast it again, invoking the name of Allāh. When the net had sunk to the bottom, he again tried to pull it ashore but this time it was even heavier and harder to shift. Thinking that he had caught some great fish, he fastened the ends to the stake, and, undressing again, dived in and carried the net to shore. This time he found a great earthen jar full of mud and sand. In his disappointment at this sight, he proclaimed these verses:

> I said I wished that fortune would die or fly away,
> Who lets a man be virtuous and then keep back his pay.
> I left my house to look for luck
>   (A search I now abandon);
> She dropped the wise man in the muck
>   For all the fools to stand on,
> And, having fixed this state of things,
> She either died or sprouted wings.

Then he threw away the jar and cleaned his net, asking pardon from Allāh the while for his lack of submission to the divine will. And finally, coming down to the sea, he cast for the third time and waited for the net to sink. When he hauled in this time, the net was full of broken pots and pieces of glass. Seeing this, he recited the stanza of a certain poet:

> Be not astonished that the golden wind
> Blows the world forward, leaving you behind;
>   There are no dīnārs in a rose-wood pen
> For any but a merchant's hand to find.

Then lifting his face to the sky, he cried: 'Allāh, Allāh! Thou knowest that I cast my net but four times in the day, and see! I have already cast it thrice.' After this, he once more cast his net into the sea, again invoking the name of Allāh, and waited for it to sink. This time, in spite of all his efforts, he could not move the net an inch, so hard was it held against the rocks below the water. Again he undressed, crying: 'Be it as Allāh wills!' and, diving for the fourth time, began to work the net until he had freed it and brought it to shore. This time he found in it a great jar of yellow copper, heavy and unhurt, its mouth stopped with lead and sealed with the seal of the Lord Sulaimān, son of Dāūd. Seeing this, the fisherman was delighted and said: 'Here is something that I can sell at the market of the coppersmiths. It must be worth at least ten dīnārs of gold.' Then, after trying to shake the jar and finding it too heavy, he continued: 'First I had better open the jar and hide whatever it contains in my basket; then I shall be able to sell the thing itself to the coppersmiths.' So he took his knife and began to work the lead until he had removed it. Then he turned the jar over and shook it, but nothing came out except a cloud of smoke, which rose to the blue sky and also spread along the earth. Finally the smoke, to the utter amazement of the fisherman, came clear of the vase and, shaking and thickening, turned to an Ifrīt whose top reached to the clouds while his feet were on the ground. The head of this Ifrīt was like a dome, his hands like pitchforks, his legs like the masts of a ship, and his mouth like a cave in which the teeth had the appearance of great stones. His nostrils were like jugs, his eyes like torches, and his hair was dusty and matted. At the appearance of this being the fisherman was so frightened that his muscles quivered, his teeth chattered together, and he stood with burning mouth and eyes that could not see the light.

When the Jinnī, in his turn, saw the fisherman, he cried: 'There is no other God but Allāh, and Sulaimān is Allāh's prophet!' Then, speaking directly to the fisherman, he said: 'O great Sulaimān, O thou prophet of Allāh, slay me not. Never again will I be disobedient or mutiny against thy just decrees.' Then said the fisherman: 'Darest thou, O blasphemous giant, to call Sulaimān the prophet of Allāh? Sulaimān has been dead for eighteen hundred years and we have come to the end of the world's time. What tale is this? How did you come to be in the jar?' At these words the Jinnī altered his tone and said: 'There is no other God but Allāh. I bring good news, O fisherman!' 'What news is that?' asked the poor man. And the Jinnī answered: 'News of your death, instant and most horrible.'

'Let Allāh be far from rewarding you for such news, Prince of the Afārīt! Why do you wish my death and how have I deserved it? I delivered you out of your jar, breaking your long imprisonment in the sea.' But the Ifrīt only answered: 'Consider and choose the manner of death you would prefer and the way that I shall kill you.' 'But what is my fault? What is my fault?' repeated the wretched fisherman. 'Listen to my story and you shall know,' said the Ifrīt. 'Speak then, and make your tale a short one,' said the fisherman, 'for my soul is ready to run out of my feet for very fear.' So the Ifrīt began:

Know that I am Sakhr al-Jinnī, one of the rebel Afārīt who mutinied against Sulaimān, son of Dāūd. There was a time when Sulaimān sent his wazīr Asāf ibn Barakhyā against me, who overpowered me in spite of all my strength and led me into the presence of Sulaimān. You may believe that at that moment I humbled myself very very low. Sulaimān, seeing me, prayed to Allāh and conjured me both to take that faith and to promise him obedience. When I refused, he had this jar brought before him and imprisoned me within it. Then he sealed it with lead and impressed thereon the Most High Name. Lastly, certain faithful Jinn took me upon their shoulders at his order and cast me into the middle of the sea. I stayed in the water for a hundred years and kept on saying: 'I shall give eternal riches to him who sets me free!' But the hundred years passed and no one set me free. So, when I was entering on the second hundred years, I swore: 'To him who sets me free will I both show and give all the treasures upon earth!' But no one freed me, and four hundred years passed away, and I said: 'To him who frees me I will give the three wishes of his heart!' But still no one set me free. So I flew into a heat of passion in my jar and swore: 'Now I will kill the man who frees me, my only gift being the choice of the death!' And it is you, O fisherman, who have set me free; therefore I let you choose the death you die.

Hearing the Ifrīt speak in this way, the fisherman could not help exclaiming: 'O Allāh, the bad luck of it! It would have been left for me to do this freeing! Spare me, O Jinnī, and Allāh will spare you; kill me, and be very sure that He will raise up one to slay you also.' Then said the Ifrīt: 'I shall kill you because you freed me. There is no help for it.' On this the fisherman exclaimed: 'Prince of the Afārīt indeed! Is this how you repay good with evil? The proverb does not lie which says:

If you would know the taste of bitterness
Seek sorrow out and comfort her distress,
You need not feed a jackal cub to see
Just how ungrateful gratitude can be.'

But the Ifrīt said: 'You have used words enough. Prepare to meet your end.' Then the fisherman reasoned with himself in this way: 'Though I am a man and he is a Jinnī, yet Allāh has given me my share of brains. I think I see a trick, a stroke of subtlety, which may undo him yet.' Then aloud to the Ifrīt he said: 'You are determined that I shall die?' And when the other said: 'No doubt of that!' the fisherman solemnly addressed him thus: 'I conjure you by the Most High Name graved on the seal of Sulaimān to answer me one question truthfully!' And when the Ifrīt, dashed by hearing the Most High Name, promised that he would answer truthfully, the fisherman asked: 'How could this jar, which, as it is, scarcely could hold a foot or hand of yours, have ever held the whole of you?' 'Can it be that you doubt this thing?' asked the Ifrīt. And the other answered: 'Never would I believe it unless I saw you with my own eyes entering the jar!'

But at this point Shahrazād saw the coming of morning and fell silent.

And when the fourth night had come

SHE SAID:

It is related, O auspicious King, that, when the fisherman told the Ifrīt that he would not believe the thing unless he saw it with his own eyes, the Ifrīt began to shake and waver to and fro until he became a smoke again. This smoke, after first sweeping to the sky, began to condense and creep little by little into the jar until it had all disappeared. Immediately the fisherman snatched up the leaden cap, sealed with the seal of Sulaimān, and stoppered the neck of the jar with it. Then he called to the Ifrīt, saying: 'You there! Consider and choose the manner of death you would prefer, otherwise I am going to throw you into the sea and build a house for myself upon the shore of it. I will prevent anyone from fishing by saying: "An Ifrīt is in the water there. If anyone pulls him out he will give them a choice of deaths as a reward!"' When the Ifrīt heard the jeers of the fisherman, he tried to get out, but could not; and he felt that he was

fastened down again with the seal of Sulaimān above him, that seal
no Jinnī might prevail against. Feeling also that the fisherman was
carrying him down to the sea, he called out: 'No, no, no, I say!' To
which the fisherman only answered: 'Yes, yes, yes!' So the Jinnī
began to smooth his words and asked humbly what was to be done
with him. 'I am going to throw you into the sea!' said the fisherman.
'Eighteen hundred years you have lain there, and I shall see to it
that you lie there until the Judgment Day. Did I not beg you to
spare me that Allāh might spare you, not to slay me that Allāh might
slay you not? But you spurned my prayer and used me wickedly.
Therefore Allāh has delivered you into my hands and I have bested
you.' Then wailed the Ifrīt: 'Open the jar and I will heap benefits
upon you!' 'You lie, O thing of treachery!' answered the fisherman.
'It is between you and me as it passed between the wazīr of King
Yūnān and Rayyān the doctor.'

'What passed between the wazīr of King Yūnān and Rayyān the
doctor?' asked the Ifrīt. 'And what tale is this?'

The Tale of the Wazīr of King Yūnān
and Rayyān the Doctor

THE fisherman said: Know, O Ifrīt, that there was, in the tide
and show of ancient time and the passage of the age and of
the moment, a king called Yūnān in the city of Fārs in the land of
Rūm. He was a rich and powerful king, master of armies, strong in
his ways and allied with many a royal house. But his body was
marred by a leprosy which baffled every doctor and learned man.
Drugs, pellets, and ointments were of no avail and no physician
could find out a cure for it. Now one day an old and famous doctor,
whose name was Rayyān, came to King Yūnān's city. He had read
books written in Greek, Persian, Latin, Arabic, and Syriac; he had
studied the craft of medicine and of the stars and knew the principles
and rules of each, their good and ill effects. Also he knew the virtues
of all plants and of all herbs both fresh and dry, their good and ill
effects. Moreover he had studied philosophy and all the sciences of
healing and other sciences. When this doctor had come into the
city and stayed there some days he heard of the leprosy with which
Allāh had seen good to plague the body of the King and of the utter

unsuccess which all the doctors and sages had met with in their treatment. Hearing these things the doctor pondered for a night, but when he woke at morning (when light shone high and Allāh's bountiful jewel, the bright sun, kissed all the earth) he clothed himself in his richest garments and entered the King's palace. Kissing the earth between King Yūnān's hands, he called down upon him power and pride everlasting and the richest blessings of Allāh. After this he told him who he was and said: 'My lord, I have been told of the evil which has eaten into your body and that no physician may find a way to remove it. So I have come to cure you, nor will I give you any drug to drink in my cure nor salve to rub upon you.' 'How will you do that?' asked King Yūnān in astonishment. 'For, as Allāh lives, if you cure me I will enrich you, and the sons of your sons after you. I will grant you wishes and realise them for you, and you shall be my cupman and my friend.' Then the King gave him a fair robe and other gifts and asked again: 'Is it really true that you will cure this ill of mine without drugs or salves?' 'Indeed it is true,' the other answered. 'Also the cure shall be without weariness or pain.' Then the King, being even more astonished, asked eagerly: 'Great doctor, what day, what hour shall see this thing come to pass? Make haste with it, my child.' 'I hear and I obey!' said the other. 'It shall be to-morrow.'

Rayyān went down out of the palace and hiring a house filled it with his books, his cures, and aromatic plants. Then he made extracts of his drugs and simples, and, carving a short, curved, hollow mallet, placed them inside and then fitted a handle. Also he made a ball as skilfully as he was able. The next day, when his labours were completed, he went up into the palace and kissed the earth between the King's hands. Then he prescribed to the King that he should ride on his horse to the maidan, the polo-ground, and exercise there with the mallet and the ball.

The King went there accompanied by his amīrs, chamberlains, wazīrs, and the chiefs of his kingdom, and was met at the maidan by Rayyān, the doctor, who gave him the mallet, saying: 'Take this mallet and grip it in this way; then strike the ball as hard as you can. Go on doing this until both your palm and all your body sweat. In this way my cure will go in through your palm and travel throughout all your body. When you have sweated and the cure has had time to work, return to your palace and go at once to bathe at the hammām. So shall you be cured. And in the meantime, peace be with you!'

Then King Yūnān took the mallet, gripped it closely and, when his chosen cavaliers had mounted their horses and set the ball in motion, began to gallop after it, come up with it, hit it forward as hard as he could and gallop after it again. He did this until both his palm and all his body sweated, and the cure went in by his palm and travelled about his body. When the wise Rayyān saw that the cure had impregnated the whole body of the King, he ordered him back to the palace. King Yūnān therefore returned and ordered the hammām to be prepared. When the carpet-spreaders had made haste and the slaves hurried to prepare the linens and towels, the King bathed and, dressing himself at the hammām, rode back to the palace and went to sleep.

In the meanwhile, Rayyān the physician slept in his house. As soon as he woke in the morning, he went up to the palace and, having gained admission, kissed the earth between the King's hands and began very solemnly to intone these lines:

> O chosen father of the sweet speech of kings,
> Bright burning face that cools the red of the fire,
> Face of young light, that shall behold undimmed
> Time putting wrinkles in the face of time,
> As a cool cloud covers a parched hill
> So you have covered me over with love-presents,
> Who are yourself the peak of glory's hill,
> Destiny's darling. She can refuse you nothing.

Hearing him say these verses, the King rose and threw himself upon the doctor's neck, made him sit by his side, and gave him robes of honour, magnificently worked.

For you must know that, when the King came out of the hammām on the previous day, he looked upon his body and found no trace of the leprosy there, but rather that his skin had become pure and stainless as virgin silver. Therefore he had rejoiced as if his heart would break, walking with broadened breast and head held high. So it was that, with the coming of morning, when the King had entered the dīwān with his chamberlains and the great ones of his kingdom and Rayyān, the doctor, had presented himself, he rose hastily and made him sit by his side. Then slaves brought meats and draughts of good drink for these two throughout the day, and at nightfall the King gave the physician two thousand dīnārs over and above the robes of honour and the other presents he had made him, and set him upon his own horse. In such happy fashion the physician took leave and returned to his own house.

As for the King, he was continuous in his admiration for the art of this physician and many times he said: 'He has cured me from the outside of my body, not even smearing me with a salve. By Allāh, so wonderful a science has he shown that the least of my duties is to overwhelm him with gifts and take him for my companion and great friend for ever.' And that night King Yūnān lay down to sleep in an ecstasy of joy, knowing that he was clean in body and cured of his evil.

Next morning when the King sat down upon his throne with the chiefs of the kingdom standing about him and the amīrs and wazīrs seated on his right and left, he called for Rayyān, who came and kissed the earth between his hands. Then the King rose as before and made the doctor sit down by him, eat with him, and gave him more robes of honour with other rich things, wishing him long life as he gave them. After, he talked with him until nightfall and gave him as a further fee five robes of honour and a thousand dīnārs. That night also the doctor returned to his house calling down blessings upon the King.

When the sun rose the next morning, the King came down and entered the dīwān, the amīrs, wazīrs and chamberlains clustering about him as before. Now among the wazīrs there was one of repellent face and sinister expression, a cruel man of evil omen, grossly avaricious, an envious fellow, eaten out with jealousy. When this wazīr saw the King raise up Rayyān to sit by him and give presents to him, he became jealous and vowed the fall of this good man. The proverb says: 'Each man envies, the strong openly, the weak in secret.' The wazīr came to the King and, kissing the earth, said to him: 'King of this hundred years and of all time, you who wrap all men in the garment of your benefits, I have in my heart a counsel of prodigious weight, nor would I be aught but a bastard and no true servant were I to hide it from you.' Disturbed by these sinister words, the King commanded him to explain himself, and he went on: 'O glorious King, the ancients had a saying: "He who regards not the end and the consequence shall never thrive." Now I have seen, and that even now, my lord failing to regard the end and the consequence in making gifts to his enemy, to a man who desires the cutting off of his reign; yes, heaping him with generosities, smothering him with favours. Indeed, my lord, this makes me fear for the

King's safety.' At these words the King became pale and agitated. At length he asked: 'Who is this man you feign to be my enemy?' 'If you are asleep, O King, I pray you wake. I speak of Rayyān the doctor,' said the wazīr. 'He is my friend,' answered the King angrily, 'nearer to me than all men; for he gave me a thing to hold in my hand which took away my leprosy, and delivered me from an evil which no other physician might touch. In this time, in this world, neither in the East nor in the West, is there another like him. How dare you say these things of him? I tell you that from to-day I shall make him a salary and allowances so that he has a thousand dīnārs every month. Even if I gave him the half of my kingdom it would be a little thing for such as he. No, no, I am convinced that you have said all this out of jealousy, just as it happened in a tale they told me once about King Sindbād!'

At this point Shahrazād saw the approach of morning and fell silent. Then Dunyazād said to her: 'Your words are sweet and pleasant to the taste.' 'But this is nothing,' Shahrazād answered, 'to that which I would tell you to-morrow night, if I were still alive and the King wished to preserve me.' Then the King said in his soul: 'By Allāh, I will not kill her until I have heard the rest of this truly marvellous tale!' They passed the remainder of the night in each other's arms, and in the morning the King went down to the Hall of Justice. When the dīwān was filled with people, the King sat in judgment, giving power and taking it away, guiding the people and making an end of the cases that were brought before him until the fall of day. Then, when the dīwān rose, he went back to his palace and did as was his wont with Shahrazād, the daughter of the wazīr.

And when the fifth night had come

SHAHRAZĀD SAID:

It is related, O auspicious King, that King Yūnān said to his wazīr: 'You have let envy steal into your heart, my wazīr, against this good physician. You are desirous that I should kill him and then repent, as King Sindbād repented after he had killed his falcon.' 'How did that come to pass?' asked the wazīr.

So King Yūnān began:

The Tale of King Sindbād and the Falcon

THEY say that there was a king among the Kings of Fārs who was a great lover of sport, of riding through the great gardens, and of all kinds of hunting. He had a falcon which he had trained himself and which never left him by day or night; for even during the night he carried it upon his fist and when he went hunting and coursing took it with him. He had also a little cup of gold hung from her neck at which she used to drink. One day, as he was sitting in his palace, his chief falconer approached him, saying: 'King of the ages, the weather is just right for hunting.' The King made ready and, taking his falcon, set out with a great company and came at length to a valley where they spread the hunting nets. Suddenly a gazelle fell into the nets, and the King said: 'I will kill him who lets her pass.' Then they began to narrow the hunting net about the gazelle so that she came near the King and, standing on her hind legs, brought her forelegs close to her chest, as if she wished to salute him. On this the King clapped his hands to frighten the gazelle and she leapt over his head and fled far away over the plain. Turning to his huntsmen, the King saw them winking at each other, so he asked his wazīr why they were winking and the other answered: 'I think they are reminding each other of what you said, that you would put anyone to death who let the gazelle pass.' Then the King cried out: 'By my life, we must follow this gazelle and bring her back!' So he galloped at full speed on her track, and when he came up to her, the falcon struck her above the eyes with his beak, blinding and bewildering her, and the King took his mace and rolled her over with one blow. Then he dismounted to disembowel and flay the animal, and afterwards hung the carcase on his saddle-bow. By this time, both the King and his horse had become faint from thirst, the day being very hot and the place a dry waterless desert; but, chancing to look round, the King saw a tree, down whose trunk water was falling as thick as butter. The King, who had his hands covered with leather gloves, took the cup from the falcon's neck, filled it with this water and placed it before the bird. But the falcon hit the cup with his claw and knocked it over. Again the King filled it and, still thinking that the bird was thirsty, placed it before him, but the falcon knocked it over a second time. Then the King became angry with the bird and, filling the cup a third time, held it out to his horse, but the falcon fluttered forward and knocked it over with his wing.

'Allāh entomb you, you ill-omened bird!' cried the King. 'You have prevented me from drinking and the horse also, to say nothing of your silly self!' So he struck at the falcon with his sword, and cut both her wings. Then the falcon lifted her head up, as she were saying by signs: 'Look into the tree!' The King looked up and saw in the tree a knot of serpents, dripping their venom-like water down the trunk. Seeing this, he was sorrowful for what he had done and, mounting his horse, rode back to his palace. Arrived there, he threw the carcase of the gazelle to the cook, telling him to prepare it. Then he sat down, still with the falcon on his hand: but no sooner had he done so than the bird gave a sob and fell dead. At this sight, the King uttered cries of lamentation and repentance that he had killed the bird who had saved him from a frightful death.

This is the tale of King Sindbād.

When the wazīr heard the tale of King Yūnān, 'Great King, dignified Majesty,' he said, 'what evil have I ever done that had so sad an ending? Only out of love for my King have I spoken as I have; later you shall see the truth of my words. Hear me, and you are saved; regard me not, and I fear that you will perish as perished a certain treacherous wazīr who harmed the son of a king.'

The Tale of the Prince and the Ogress

THIS king had a son much given to hunting and coursing, and he had also a wazīr whom he had commanded to accompany his son wherever he went. One day the prince went out to hunt and course, taking his father's wazīr with him, and both as they went saw a miraculous beast rise in their path. The wazīr, who knew what manner of thing it was, yet shouted to the prince: 'Forward, forward, after this noble beast and take her!' So the prince rode after the animal until it disappeared from view somewhere in the desert; and the prince was at a loss, not knowing which way to go, until he saw a young girl weeping above the track which he followed. He asked her who she was and she answered: 'I am the daughter of one of the Kings of Hind. While I journeyed over the desert with a caravan, sleep overcame me and I fell from my beast without any noticing. Now I am lost and alone and very sorrowful.' When the prince heard this, he pitied her and, setting her on his saddle-bow, rode away with her. As they were passing a little deserted ruin, the girl said: 'Master, I must obey a call of nature.' She went down into the ruin and the prince, after waiting and noticing that she was taking longer than was natural, went in after her without attracting her notice and behold! she had become an ogress and was saying to her brood: 'To-day, my dears, I have brought you a fine fat youth!' On this they shouted: 'Bring him in, mother, bring him in, that we may eat our bellyful!' When the prince heard these terrifying words, he gave himself up for lost. His muscles relaxed for very terror and he crawled from the ruin. When the ogress came out in her turn, she noticed his fear and trembling and said: 'Why are you afraid?' He answered that he had an enemy and the ogress asked: 'Did you not tell me that you were a prince?' 'That is true,' he replied, and she continued: 'If you are a prince, why do you not give money to your enemy and satisfy him?' 'He would never be satisfied with money,' answered the prince, 'never, I fear, with anything but my death. Thus it is I go in fear of my life and am the victim of an evil chance.' To this she said: 'If that is so, you have only to ask the help of Allāh against your enemy and He will save you and deliver you from the malice of those you fear.' Then the prince lifted up his head and prayed, saying: 'O Thou, who answerest the oppressed when they call upon Thee, give me to triumph over my enemy and in Thy might remove him from about my way!' When the ogress heard this prayer, she disappeared; and the prince, returning to his father the King, told him of the evil counsel of his wazīr, and the King put the wazīr to death.

After this tale the wazīr of King Yūnān continued in these subtle terms:

'But I fear, O King, that if you put your trust in this doctor, he will make you die the worst of deaths. Even while you cover him with favours and make him your friend he is plotting your death. Do you not see why he has cured your illness from the outside of your body by means of a thing to hold in the hand? Do you not see that it is simply that he may later cause your death with another thing held in the hand?' 'Indeed what you say is true,' agreed Yūnān. 'Let all be done as you advise, O wazīr of good counsel! It is more than likely that this doctor has come in secret as a spy, to cause my death. Since he cured me with a thing held in the hand, what is to prevent him killing me with some other thing, perhaps some scent that he will give me to smell? What should I do, O wazīr?' 'Send someone to fetch him at once,' answered the wazīr, 'and, when he

comes, have his head cut off at the neck; only thus can you put a stop
to his evil plans and be carefree as you were before. Strike before he
strikes, that is my advice!' 'You have spoken well, O wazīr!' said
King Yūnān, and he sent to fetch the doctor, who came quickly and
cheerfully, not knowing what the Compassionate had in store for
him. A poet has written these verses:

> Go on your way and be comforted,
>   Child of the Faithful;
> He who has moulded the world in His hands
> Holds it and us in His hands forever.
> What He has written you cannot alter,
> What He has not written never shall be,
> So go on your way and be comforted,
>   Child of the Faithful.
>
> I keep the sweetness of my voice to sing to Him,
>   I make my fairest verses in His praise.
> Rare and more rare fall His gifts about me,
> Granted before I have the wit to ask them,
> His kindness to me is greater than I can bear;
> My voice is not sweet enough to sing of Him
>   And my verses are too little to hold His praise.
>
> Walk on light-hearted, caring and carrying nothing
>   Leaving all to Him;
> Fear not what man may do, grieve not at sorrow,
> Especially plan not, for He has planned all things;
> Walk on light-hearted, caring and carrying nothing,
>   Leaving all to Him.

When Rayyān, the physician, presented himself before the King,
the latter asked him: 'Do you know why I have sent for you?' And
the physician answered: 'None knows the unknown save Allāh!'
Then said the King: 'I have sent for you that you may die.' At these
words Rayyān was struck as by thunder and exclaimed: 'Why
should you kill me, O King? What harm have I done?' 'They say
you are a spy and have come here to kill me,' answered the King.
'Therefore will I strike the blow first!' Then raising his voice he
cried to his executioner: 'Strike through the neck of this traitor and
rid me of his wiles!' 'Spare me, and so shall Allāh spare you!' cried
the unfortunate doctor. 'Kill me not, lest He also rise up and slay!'

He cried this prayer again and again, O Ifrīt, just as I did with you. And you had no mercy upon me but continued hot for my death.

King Yūnān said to the doctor: 'Never will I have trust or peace again until I have killed you; for if you cured me with a thing held in the hand, doubtless you would kill me with a thing to smell, or in some other way.' 'Is this how you reward me?' asked the doctor. 'Is this how you return me evil for my good?' But the King said: 'You must die, there are no two ways about it.' When the physician saw that the King was resolute for his death, he wept and repented bitterly of all the services he had done to those not worthy to receive them. Bearing on this subject, the poet said:

> Although Maimunah was a fool
> Her father kept the golden rule;
> He had a torch to guide his feet
> Through all the perils of the street.

After this the executioner advanced, bandaged the doctor's eyes, and, freeing his blade, asked leave of the King. But the doctor continued to weep and to reiterate: 'Spare me, and so shall Allāh spare you! Kill me not, lest He also rise up and slay!' Also he intoned these lines of the poet:

> Fools take the prize
>   And cruelty lives on,
> While wisdom dies
>   And kindness is undone.
> If I come free
>   I'll swear to change my ways,
> And practise ignorance and cruelty
>   Through all my days.

Then he said to the King: 'Is this my reward? You are treating me after the manner of a certain crocodile.' Then the King asked: 'What is this tale of the crocodile?' And the doctor answered: 'Indeed, indeed, I cannot tell you tales while I am in this sorry state. I conjure you, by Allāh, save me and so shall Allāh preserve you at the last.' Then he began to weep again, very sorrowfully.

At this point some of the King's favourites rose and said to him: 'Spare, we beseech you, O King, the life of this great and good physician, for we have seen no fault in him against you; but rather have we seen him cure you of an evil which neither doctors nor sages were able to touch.'

But the King answered them: 'You know not the reason of this doctor's death; if I spared him I should myself be lost, for he who has cured me by a thing held in the hand might well kill me by giving me something to smell. Also I fear that he would kill me for some reward set upon my life, for he is probably a spy come here for no other reason but to kill me. His death is necessary. I shall have peace again.' Then the doctor called out again: 'Spare me, and so shall Allāh spare you! Kill me not, lest He also rise up and slay!'

Now know, O Ifrīt, that when the physician was finally certain that the King would kill him, he said: 'King, if my death is really necessary, at least allow me a delay for going down to my house. I must put my affairs in order, instruct my family and my neighbours to arrange my funeral, and, above all, I must give away my books of medicine. Also, now that I think of it, I have indeed a book that is the extract of extracts, the rarity of rarities in science, and I would offer it to you that you may keep it carefully for ever among your chests of books.' So the King asked him what this book might be, and he made answer: 'It holds devices that are above price, the least of its secrets being this: if, when my head is off, you turn three pages of the book, then read three lines upon the left-hand page, my severed head will speak and answer any manner of question!' The King trembled with joyful amazement at these words, and said: 'Doctor, is this true? Even if I cut your head off will you speak?' 'Indeed it is true, my King,' he answered. 'It is one of the prodigies of my science.' After this, the King let him go down to his house between guards; and on that day and the next he wound up his affairs. When he came back to the dīwān, it was like a garden full of flowers with the coloured clothes of the amīrs, the wazīrs, the chamberlains, the nawwābs and all the chief persons of the kingdom. First the physician stood before the King, holding a very old book and a little kohl box in which there was a powder. Then he sat down and said: 'Let someone bring me a plate!' A plate was brought to him, and he poured the powder on to it, smoothing it over the surface with his fingers. Finally he said: 'Take this book, my King, but do not use it until you have cut off my head. When my head is off, set it upon this plate and have it pressed down firm upon the powder to stop the bleeding. After that open the book.'

But the King in his haste hardly listened to him. He took the book and, opening it, found that the pages were stuck together; so he put his finger to his mouth, wetted it with his spittle, and succeeded in opening the first leaf. He did the same with the second and the third, experiencing great difficulty each time. When six single sheets had been opened in this way, he tried to read but could find no manner of writing in the book. 'There is nothing written here,' he cried, and the doctor answered: 'Go on turning.' So the King went on turning the leaves but hardly had a minute passed when the venom (for the leaves of the book were indeed poisoned) began to work in the blood and body of the King. He fell back in terrible convulsions, crying: 'Poisoned! Poisoned!' And Rayyān, the physician, addressed him, extemporising these lines:

> When the unjust judge
> Without justice judges,
> Horrible, horrible things are done;
> But more horrible things are done
> When justice judges
> The unjust judge.

As Rayyān made an end of his verses, the King fell back dead.

Learn from this, O you Ifrīt, that if King Yūnān had preserved Rayyān, the physician, Allāh would have preserved him in his turn. But he refused and brought about his own death. And you, if you had wished to preserve me, Allāh would have preserved you.

At this point Shahrazād saw the coming of morning and discreetly fell silent. Then her sister Dunyazād said: 'How pleasant are your words!' 'They are nothing,' she answered, 'to that which I would tell you to-morrow night if I were still alive and the King wished to spare me.' After this, they spent the night in complete joy and happiness until the morning. Finally the King went up to his dīwān; also, when the dīwān had risen, he returned to his own palace and his people.

And when the sixth night had come

SHAHRAZĀD SAID:

It is related, O auspicious King, that the fisherman said to the Ifrīt: 'If you had preserved me I would now preserve you, but, as you wished my death, I shall throw you into the sea and leave you to die imprisoned in this jar.' Then the Ifrīt cried: 'For the love of Allāh, do not do this thing! Release me, out of your generosity, not blaming me too much for what I did. If I was evil, be thou good. Does not the proverb say: "He who requites a fault with kindness at the same time pardons the evil"? Do not to me as Uman did to Atīkah.' 'What was their story?' asked the fisherman. 'This jar is no place for telling tales in,' answered the Ifrīt. 'When you let me out I will tell you what happened between them.' 'No, no,' said the fisherman, 'I must cast you into the sea, so that you shall never come up out of it again. For, by your way of treating me, I know that you come of an evil race.' But the Ifrīt cried: 'Release me, and I will not only tell you the story, but I will promise never to do you hurt and, moreover, I will bring you into the way of great riches.' Then the fisherman trusted him and, being assured of his good faith, after making him swear in the name of Allāh, opened the jar.

Out rose the smoke from the jar and again became an Ifrīt of immortal ugliness, who with a mighty kick sent the jar flying out to sea. When he saw the jar disappearing in the water, the fisherman piddled his garments in an ecstasy of fear, saying: 'This is no good sign!' Then to reassure himself he thus addressed the Jinnī: 'Allāh the Most-High has said, O Ifrīt: "Stand by your oaths or I will call you to account!" You both promised and swore that you would not harm me. Be certain, then, that if you do harm me, Allāh will punish you; for He is a jealous God and if He bides His time yet does He not forget. Remember I said to you, as Rayyān the physician said to King Yūnān: "Spare me, and Allāh shall spare you!"'

At these words the Ifrīt burst out laughing and walked away, telling the fisherman to follow him. Still in uncertainty the fisherman walked behind, and in this order they left the city behind till it was out of sight and, climbing a mountain, came down over the other side into a great deserted valley, in the middle of which was a lake. Here the Ifrīt stopped and ordered the fisherman to cast his net, and the latter, looking down into the water, saw fish, white, red, blue, and yellow, swimming about in it. Marvelling at this sight, he cast his net and caught four fish, each of a different colour. As he was rejoicing at his good fortune, the Ifrīt said: 'Take these fish to the Sultān's palace and he will make you a rich man. In the meantime, I must ask you to excuse me; I fear I have forgotten my manners during my long sojourn below the sea, never looking upon the land for eighteen hundred years. I advise you to come and fish here every day, but only once a day. Finally, Allāh be good to you, and farewell!' With this the Ifrīt stamped both his feet against the earth, which opened and swallowed him up.

Marvelling at all that had befallen him, the fisherman returned towards the city and, coming to his house with the fish, filled an earthen pot with water and placed them in it. When they began to swim about in the water, he put the pot upon his head and walked with it to the palace, as the Ifrīt had told him. When the fisherman came into the presence of the King and offered him the fish, the King, who had never seen the like either in size or colour, marvelled exceedingly and commanded that they should be given to the black cook-maid. You must know that this slave had been given him as a present three days before by the King of Rūm and that so far he had had no occasion to sample her cookery. So the wazīr took the fish to the cook-maid and told her to fry them, adding: 'Excellent negress, the King my master sent you this message: "I have reserved you specially, O tear of mine, for some great day. Give us proof, now, of your excellence with the cookpots and the luxury of your dishes, for to-day the Sultān entertains one who brings gifts to him."' Then the wazīr returned to the King, who ordered him to give the fisherman four hundred dīnārs. Having received this sum, the fisherman placed it in the tail of his robe and returned contentedly to his wife at home. We will leave him buying all manner of necessities for his children.

In the meanwhile the cook-maid cleaned the fishes, put them in the pan and, when they were well cooked on one side, turned them over. But suddenly the wall of the kitchen opened and through it entered a young and slender girl with full smooth cheeks and delightful features. Her eyelids were darkened with black kohl and her body bent daintily with the weight of her breasts. On her head she wore a kerchief of blue silk from which her hair escaped about her ears; she had gold bracelets round her wrists, and on her fingers rich and coloured stones sparkled from rings. She came forward to the fire and, thrusting a bamboo wand she carried in her hand into the pan, said: 'Fish, fish, are you faithful?' Seeing this the cook-maid fainted away, and the young girl repeated her question a second and third time. Then all the fish lifted their heads from inside the pan and cried: 'Yes, yes, we are!' Then in chorus they intoned these lines:

> Come back and so will we,
>   Keep faith and we'll keep faith,
> But if you show us treachery
>   It shall be to your scathe.

At these words the young girl upset the pan and passed out by the way she had come, the wall of the kitchen coming together again after her. When the cook-maid came out of her swoon, she saw that the four fishes had fallen into the fire and been burnt to black cinders. And calling out: 'Oh, even at the first assault his vigour ebbed away!' she continued to lament until the wazīr came back and told her to carry the fishes to the Sultān. At this the cook-maid burst into tears, and told the wazīr all that had happened. The wazīr, utterly amazed at the strangeness of the thing, sent for the fisherman and commanded him to bring four other fishes of the same kind. So the fisherman made his way to the mountain lake and, casting his net, brought four more fish to land. These he took to the wazīr who, in his turn, took them to the cook-maid and said: 'Stir yourself now and fry these in my presence, that I may see what there is in this story of yours.' The negress cleaned the fish and set them in a pan on the fire, but hardly had she done so when the wall opened and the young girl appeared a second time, dressed as before and still holding the wand in her hand. She thrust the wand into the pan, saying: 'Fish, fish, are you faithful?' whereupon the fishes lifted their heads and intoned these lines in chorus:

> Come back and so will we,
>   Keep faith and we'll keep faith,
> But if you show us treachery
>   It shall be to your scathe.

At this point Shahrazād saw the approach of morning and discreetly fell silent.

And when the seventh night had come

SHE SAID:

It is related, O auspicious King, that when the fishes spoke in this manner the young girl upset the pan with her wand and departed by the fissure in the wall, which closed after her. 'This is a thing that we can in no wise keep from the King!' exclaimed the wazīr, so he sought out the King and told him the whole circumstances. 'This is a thing that I must see for myself!' cried the King and, sending for the fisherman, he commanded him to fetch four other fish of the like kind, allowing him three days in which to complete the matter. But the fisherman hurried to the lake and came back immediately with four more fish, for which he was given four hundred dīnārs at the King's command. Then the King ordered his wazīr to prepare the fish himself in the royal presence. 'I hear and I obey,' answered the wazīr and, conducting the King to the kitchen, he carefully cleaned the fish and, in the King's sight, set them in the pan to fry. When they were cooked on one side, he turned them; immediately the kitchen wall opened and through it entered a negro, as ugly as a great buffalo or one of the giants of the tribe of Hād. He carried a green branch in his hand and said in a distinct and terrible voice: 'Fish, fish, are you faithful?' Then all the fish lifted their heads from inside the pan and cried: 'Yes, yes, we are!' and in chorus they intoned these lines:

> Come back and so will we,
>   Keep faith and we'll keep faith,
> But if you show us treachery
>   It shall be to your scathe.

Then the negro came up to the pan and upset it with his branch, so that the fish fell out and were burnt to black cinders. Finally he departed by the way he had come, and the King said: 'Here is a matter on which it is impossible to keep silent. Surely there is some strange tale connected with these fishes!' So he sent for the fisherman and asked him where the fishes came from. 'From a lake between four hills,' he answered, 'behind the mountain which looks down upon your city.' 'How many days' journey is it?' asked the King. 'My lord, it is not more than half an hour away,' the other answered. So the Sultān set out forthwith, taking his soldiers with him, and also the fisherman, who went along in a confused state of mind, secretly cursing the Ifrīt. At length the King's party passed over the mountain and came down into a desert valley, such as they had never seen before. They marvelled at it, and at the lake, and at the fish of different colours, red, white, yellow and blue, which swam within it. Halting his men, the King asked if anyone there had ever seen a lake in that place and, when all answered that they had not, he said: 'As

Allāh lives, I will never more go back to my city or sit upon my throne until I have found out the truth about this lake and these strange fishes!' Then, sending out his men to inspect the mountains round about, he called his wazīr to him, who was a scholar and a sage, an eloquent man of great learning. To him the King said: 'There is a thing that I mean to do and I must tell you of it. I have determined to go forth alone to-night and seek out unaided the answer to the mystery of this lake. Your part will be to stand guard at the door of my tent and tell any wazīrs, amīrs or chamberlains who may seek audience, that I am ill and have given order that none may be admitted. Above all tell no one of my plan.' The wazīr promised to obey and the King, having disguised himself and girt on his sword, slipped out unperceived from among his bodyguard. All that night and through the next morning he journeyed on, stopping only to sleep through the noonday heat. Then he continued his quest throughout the rest of that day and the following night. On the second morning he saw a black object far off and joyfully exclaimed: 'Surely yonder I shall find someone to tell me the story of the lake!' Coming nearer, he saw that the thing was a palace, built all of black stones fastened together with great clamps of steel. Stopping at the mighty double door, one half of which was open, he knocked softly, once, twice, and again, without receiving any answer. The fourth time, he knocked with great violence and still no one came. So, supposing the palace to be deserted, he plucked up his courage and entered. 'O masters of this palace, I am a stranger, a wayfarer, and I come to ask a little refreshment in my journey!' He repeated this twice more and, getting no reply, became emboldened to go along the corridor as far as the very centre of the palace. Here he found no one, though all the place was splendid with star-wrought tapestries and, in the middle of the inner court, four lions of red gold held up a fountain, spraying so fair a water that it had the appearance of diamonds and white pearls. About the court were many birds, which could not fly away because of a great golden net stretched above the palace. The King marvelled at all these things and yet he grieved in his heart to find no one there who could explain the riddle of the lake, the mountain, the fish, and the palace. Soon he sat down between two of the doors in a profound reverie, which was suddenly cut short by a feeble voice of complaint, rising it seemed from a surcharged heart. He heard these lines sung in a sweet whisper:

> I could not keep love down:
> He rose and pinned my sleepy eyes awake,
> He crept into my voice and made it break,
>   My heart, and made it ache.
>
> I could not keep love down:
> He rose and lighted fires within my brain,
> And all the waters of the world are vain
>   To put them out again.

Moving towards the sound of this low plaining, the King found a door covered by a curtain. Lifting the curtain, he saw a young man lying upon his elbow on a great bed in a mighty hall. He was fair and supple, dowered with the very voice of music; his brow was like a flower, and his cheeks like the flowers of roses. Also, on one of these cheeks there lay a mole like a fragment of black amber. The poet has said:

> Sweet and slim is the boy
> With hair of shadows paling the night
> And a brow of light
> Making the stars seem grey.
> My eyes have turned his way
> And found a joy
> Of which I dare not speak
> In a nut-brown beauty spot
> Which he has got
> Below his dark eye on his rose-leaf cheek.

The King rejoiced at the sight of the young man and said to him: 'Peace be with you!' But the youth, who wore a robe of golden-embroidered silk, did not move from his position on the bed and it was with great sorrow both of voice and feature that he greeted the King, saying: 'Excuse me, my lord, for not rising.' Thereupon the King said: 'Tell me, O fair young man, the story of the lake and the coloured fishes, and also the reason of this palace and of your solitude and your tears.' At these words the youth wept even more sorely and answered: 'What is there in the evil fate that has come upon me that I should not weep?' So saying, he moved his thin hand towards the skirts of his garment and lifted them away from his body. Then the King saw that the lower half of this youth was all of marble, while the upper half of his body, from his navel to the hair upon his head, remained that of a man. As he stood there astonished, the young man said to him: 'You must know, my lord, that the tale of the fishes is indeed a strange tale. Were it written with a bodkin on the inner corner of an eye, yet would it be a lesson for a man of mind.'

And the youth told this story:

The Tale of the Young Man and the Fishes

Know, my Lord, that my father was the King of a city which you see not and yet it was here. His name was Mahmūd and he was master of the Black Isles, which are now four mountains. He reigned for seventy years before passing to the mercy of Allāh, Remunerator of the world. After his death I became Sultān and took to wife my cousin, the daughter of my uncle, who so well loved me that if I left her even for a short while she neither ate nor drank till my return. For five years I cherished her until a day came when she went to the hammām, after having ordered an alluring supper for us from the cook. Then I entered this hall of my palace and lay down to sleep in my accustomed place, bidding two of my girl slaves to move their fans above me as I slept. One sat at my head and the other at my feet, but I could not sleep for thinking of my wife and, though my eyelids closed, my wits remained alert. Thus it was that I heard the slave at my head say to the other at my feet: 'How ill-starred is the youth of our poor lord, Masūdah. How sad it is that he should have married our mistress, that bitch, that unclean whore.' 'God's curse on all adulteresses!' the other replied, 'this bastard who spends her nights in every vagabond bed is a millionfold too evil to be the wife of our master.' 'And yet,' said the first slave, 'he must be very innocent not to notice the woman's goings on.' 'How can you say that?' objected the other. 'What chance does she give him to suspect her? Why, every night she puts something into the wine he drinks before he sleeps. She mixes banj with the drink and he sleeps like the dead. How then can he know what she does or where she goes? After making him drink the drugged wine, she dresses and goes out and stays away till morning. When she comes back, she burns a scented something below his nose and he wakes fresh from his sleep.'

My lord, when I heard the conversation of these slaves, light became darkness before my eyes, and yet in my impatience I thought that night would never fall. At last, however, my wife came back from the hammān, and, spreading the cloth, we ate for an hour, giving each other drink as was our custom. When I asked for the final cup which I drank every night before my sleep, and she handed it to me, I put it to my lips, but instead of drinking spilled it secretly into the upper fold of my robe. At once I lay down on my bed and feigned to go to sleep. Then I heard her saying: 'Sleep, you devil, sleep, and never wake. As Allāh lives, I hate you, yes, every inch of you, and my soul sickens when you are near!' After this she rose, dressed herself in her finest garments, perfumed herself, girt on my sword and left the palace. Instantly I rose and followed her. She crossed all the markets of the city and, coming at last to the outer gates, spoke to them in a tongue I did not understand and lo! the locks fell from their places, the gates swung open of themselves and she went out beyond the city. I followed her unnoticed till she came to certain mounds formed by the heaping up of refuse, in the middle of which was a round house built of dry mud and topped by a dome of the same. This place she entered by a door, and I, climbing up into the balcony of the dome, lay still to watch. I saw her enter below into the room of a hideous coal-black negro, whose upper lip was like the lid of a stew-pot and his lower lip like the stew-pot itself; great pendulous lips they were, that could have sorted pebbles from the sand of the floor. He was rotten with diseases and lay on a heap of refuse of sugar-cane. Seeing him, my wife, the daughter of my uncle, kissed the earth between his hands, and he, lifting up his head, addressed her thus: 'Curse you, why are you so late? I have had other black men here, drinking wine and having their girls. But I had not the heart to drink because you were not here.' 'Master, darling of my heart, do you not know that I am now married to my cousin, the son of my uncle, that I hate the least detail of his face and am filled with horror to be near him? Ah, if it were not for fear that you would come to harm, I should long ago have destroyed his city, from pinnacle to base, leaving but the voices of owls and of crows to be heard in her streets, hurling the stones of her ruin beyond the mountain of Kāf!' 'You lie, you bitch,' the negro answered, 'and I swear to you on the honour and the great virility of black men, on our mighty superiority over all whites, that if you are late once again after to-day I will throw you aside and never lay my body above yours again. Unfaithful whore, filth, foulest of white girls, you are only late because you have been sating your lust with someone else.'

My lord, continued the prince, you can believe that, when I heard with my own ears this fearful conversation and saw with my own eyes what followed between the two, the world grew very black before my face and I knew not where I was. Then my wife, my cousin, wept in terrible humility before the negro, saying: 'Lover, fruit of my heart, there is none but you; dear boy, dear light of life, send me not away!' When at last he pardoned her because of her weeping, she was filled with joy and, rising, took off all her clothes, even to her petticoat-trousers, and stood before him quite naked. Then she said: 'Master, have you no refreshment for your slave?' 'Look in the pot,' answered the other, 'you will find a stew of rat's bones, and there is some beer in the jerry which you may drink.' When she had eaten and drunken, she washed her hands, and came and lay with the negro on the bed of trash. She was naked and cuddled against him under the unclean rags.

When I saw this, I could contain myself no longer; jumping from the dome, I rushed into the room and snatched the sword which my wife was carrying, determined to kill them both. First I slashed the negro across his neck and thought that I had killed him.

At this point Shahrazād saw the approach of morning and discreetly fell silent. When day had come, King Shahryār entered his hall of justice, and the dīwān sat until nightfall. Then the King returned to his palace, and Dunyazād said to her sister: 'I pray you go on with your story.' 'With all my heart and as in duty bound,' she answered.

And when the eighth night had come

SHE CONTINUED:

It is related, O auspicious King, that the young man who was bewitched went on with his story in this fashion:

When I slashed the negro across his neck, I severed his windpipe, both the skin and flesh of it, and thought that I had killed him, because a high and terrible cry came from him. I rushed away, and my wife, daughter of my uncle, who had been sleeping, rose, took up and sheathed the sword and, returning to the city, stole into the palace and lay down by me in my bed till morning. Next day I saw that she had cut off her hair and put on mourning garments. This she explained to me by saying: 'Husband, son of my uncle, do not blame me for what I have done. I have just heard that my mother is dead, that my father has been killed in the holy war, that one of my brothers had been stung to death by a scorpion and the other buried alive by the fall of a huge building. It is only right that I should weep and mourn.' Not wishing to seem as if I had noticed anything untoward, I answered: 'Do what you think necessary; I shall not stop you.' So it came about that she stayed shut in with her tears, her insane ecstasy of grief for a whole year. At the end of that time, she said: 'Husband, I wish a tomb built in your palace, in the form of a pillared dome. There I can shut myself, in solitude and tears, and call the name of it the House of Mourning.' 'Do what you think necessary,' I answered. So she had her House of Mourning built with the dome above it and a tomb as big as a water-ditch inside. To this place she had the negro carried. For he was not dead, though very ill and feeble, and quite unable to be of any delight to my wife. Still this did not prevent him from drinking both wine and beer at all hours of the day. From the moment of his wound he had not been able to speak, and now he lived on in the tomb because his time had not yet come. Each day my wife would go in under the dome, at dawn and twilight, and fall to raving and weeping. Also she gave soups and strong broths to the man inside. She behaved in this way, morning and night, for the whole of a second year, while I abode here patiently. But one day, coming upon her unawares, I found her weeping and striking her face and in a sad voice saying these verses:

> When you passed on by my tent door
> I said goodbye to all the world,
> Forgetting how to love for ever more
> When you passed on.
>
> If you come back the way you went
> I pray you take my body up,
> And set it in a calm grave near your tent
> When you come back.
>
> If your dear voice recall the tones,
> The sweetness of the way you said my name,
> Kneel down, dear love, and say the same;
> I'll answer with the clicking of my bones.

When she had finished this plaint of hers, I drew my sword and cried: 'O you unfaithful, these are the words of a naughty passion and not of grief! I was the more deceived.' I raised my arm and was about to strike, when she jumped to her feet and, understanding it would seem for the first time that it was I who had wounded her negro, muttered strange unknown words which must have meant: 'By my dark power, God turn you half to stone!' And at that moment, my lord, I became as you see me now. I could not move about, nay, could not stir myself an inch; but I lie here, neither dead nor alive. After she had done this horrible thing to me, she bewitched the four isles of my kingdom, turning them to mountains with a lake between and all my people into fishes in the lake. But this is not all. Every day she comes to torture me and give me a hundred lashes with a leather thong. After she has done this she puts a shirt of hair next to my skin under my clothes, all over the upper sentient part of me.

At this stage in his tale the young man burst into tears and moaned these lines:

> I have waited upon His justice,
> I have tarried for the pleasure of my God
> And the time of His coming to judgment.
> Though my afflictions rise about me like trees,
> I look for the deliverance of the sword of Allāh
> With patient eyes.

The King turned to the young man and said: 'Your story has added a sorrow to my sorrows. Tell me, where is this woman?' 'With the negro in the tomb under the dome,' he answered. 'Each day she comes to me, beating me as I have said, and I cannot stir an inch to help myself. Then she goes back to her negro, night and morning, with wines and broth.' 'As Allāh lives, my brave young man,' exclaimed the King, 'now must I do you a service that will be remembered, a benefit that shall pass into the books of history!' After talking with the prince till nightfall, the King rose and, on the striking of the night hour of wizardry, undressed, girt on his sword, and stole towards the negro's tomb. In it he saw lighted candles and hanging lamps, incense and perfumes and all unguents. Without delay he smote the negro with his sword and, when he was dead, lifted him upon his back and hurled his body to the bottom of a certain well which was in the palace. Then he came back, put on the negro's clothes, and walked up and down below the dome, waving his great and naked sword.

After an hour, the wanton sorceress came into the young prince her husband and, baring his body, lashed him cruelly. When he cried out: 'Ay, ay, enough, for pity's sake enough!' she answered: 'Pity? What pity had you for me and for my lover?' After this she wrapped him in a goat's-hair shirt, replacing his other clothes on top of it, and went to visit her negro, carrying a cup of wine and a bowl of vegetable soup. Entering under the dome, she wept, saying: 'Speak to me, O my master, let me hear your voice!' Then in deep grief she intoned these lines:

> If you desire these sweet fain limbs of mine
> To comfort you like wine,
> Turn not aside;
> But if you lust after my misery,
> My torment, and not me,
> Be satisfied.

Finishing, she burst into sobs and repeated: 'Speak to me, O my master!' Then the supposed negro, putting his tongue across his mouth, so that he should sound like a black man, called out: 'Aha, there is no strength nor power save in Allāh!' When she heard him speak who had so long been silent, she shouted with joy and fainted away. But coming to herself she said: 'Praise be, praise be, my master is himself again!' Then said the King in a disguised and feeble voice: 'O curse of mine, you have not merited a word from me!' 'How is that?' she said. And the King answered: 'You lash your husband every day, so that his groans and cries for help take all my sleep away from me at night; he weeps for mercy, so that I cannot sleep. If it had not been so I should have been cured long before this.' 'Since you order it,' she said, 'I am willing to save him from his present state.' 'Do so,' said the King, 'and let us have a little peace.' Murmuring: 'I hear, and I obey!', she rose and left the dome. Arrived at the great hall, she took a copper bowl filled with water and said magic words over it. When the water began to boil and bubble as if it had been in a fiery cauldron, she sprinkled the prince with it, saying: 'By these words that I have uttered, by this spell that I have muttered, turn to what you were before!' At this the young man shivered and rose upright upon his feet, shouting for joy and crying: 'There is no other God but Allāh, and Muhammad is His prophet, whom Allāh bless and keep!' 'Go,' shrieked his wife in his very face, 'and never return, or I shall kill you!' The young man slipped away

from the palace and his wife, going back to the dome, called softly:
'Rise up, my master, that I may look upon you!' In a very feeble
voice came this answer : 'You have done nothing yet; you have hardly
restored a twentieth of my peace, for the main cause of my trouble
still remains.' 'What is this main cause, my darling?' she asked. 'The
fish in the lake, the people of this ancient city and of the Four Isles,'
he answered. 'At midnight every night they lift their heads out of
the lake and pray down curses upon you and me. I cannot get well
while this goes on. Deliver them, my dear, and afterwards come
back to take me by the hand and help me rise, for surely then I shall
be whole and well.' Thinking he was the negro, she answered cheerfully: 'Master, your wish is as the law of my head and the object of
my eye. Bismillāh!' Saying this, she rose and ran and coming to the
lake, took up a little of the water and . . .

At this point Shahrazād saw the approach of morning and discreetly fell silent.

And when the ninth night had come

SHE SAID:

It is related, O auspicious King, that when the young witch took
up a little water out of the lake and said over it certain words, the
fishes wriggled and trembled in the water and lifted their heads and
became men again. The magic that had held them slacked off from
the bodies of the people, and their place became again a great and
flourishing city with mighty markets, and each man in it went about
his business and concern. The mountains became again the islands of
old time, and the woman ran back to the King. Still thinking him the
negro, she said: 'Give me your generous hand, my darling, that I
may kiss it.' 'Come near me, then,' answered the King, in a low voice.
So she came near and he, lifting his good sword, pierced her through
the breast so that the point came out behind her back. He struck her
again, and cut her into two halves; which done, he went out of that
place and found the young man who had been bewitched waiting
for him. He congratulated him on his deliverance, and the young
man kissed his hands and thanked him heartily. Later the King asked:
'Do you wish to stay in your own city, or come with me to mine?'
'King of all time,' answered the young man, 'do you know how far
your city is from here?' 'Two and a half days' journey,' said the
King. Then the young man laughed and said: 'If you are sleeping, my

King, wake up. Even with Allāh speeding the journey, it would take you a year to get to your own city. If you came here in two days and a half it was because my kingdom was contracted and bewitched. As for your question, know that I shall never leave you again, even for the winking of an eye.' The King rejoiced at this and cried: 'Praise be to Allāh who set you upon my road! Henceforth you shall be my son, for He has not blessed me with a child of my own.' So they fell upon each other's necks and rejoiced exceedingly.

Going up to the palace, the King who had been spellbound made proclamation to the chief men of his kingdom that he was about to set out upon the sacred pilgrimage to Mecca. When all the necessary preparations had been made, he and the Sultān set forth, the heart of the latter burning for his kingdom from which he had been absent for a whole year. They journeyed with a troop of fifty mamelūks charged with gifts and rarities, and halted not night or day for a whole year, until they came in sight of the Sultān's city. On their approach the wazīr and all the fighting men came out to meet their King, whom they had never thought to see again. They came near and kissed the earth between his hands, giving him welcome. The King went up into his palace, sat upon his throne and, calling the wazīr to him, told him all that had happened. Hearing the strange adventures of the young man, the wazīr congratulated him upon his deliverance and present safety.

After he had given audience and gifts to many, the King said to his wazīr: 'Send quickly for the fisherman who brought the fishes which were the cause of all these things.' The wazīr sent and fetched the fisherman, who had in truth delivered the inhabitants of that other city, and the King presented him with robes of honour, questioning him about his manner of life and asking him if he had any children. When the fisherman answered that he had one son and two daughters, the King straightway married one of the two daughters himself, and the prince married the other. Their father the King kept in his train and made treasurer-in-chief of all the kingdom. The wazīr he appointed Sultān of the prince's city and of the Black Islands, sending him thither with the same fifty mamelūks and many robes of honour for all the amīrs of that land. The wazīr kissed his King's hand and departed to take over his own kingdom, while the Sultān and the prince lived together in joy and contentment. As for the fisherman, thanks to his position as treasurer-in-chief, he soon became the richest man of all that century, and his daughters were the wives of kings even till the days of their death.

But do not believe, said Shahrazād, that this tale is at all more wonderful than the tale of the Porter.

The Tale of the Porter and the Young Girls

THERE WAS ONCE a young man in the city of Baghdād, who was by faith a bachelor and by trade a porter.

One day, as he was leaning idly against his basket in the marketplace, a woman, wearing a full veil of Mosul silk, tasselled with gold and turned with rare brocade, stopped before him and raised the veil a little from her face. Above it there showed dark eyes with long lashes of silk and lids to set a man dreaming. Her body was slight, her feet were very small, and clear perfection shone about her. She said, and oh, but her voice was sweet: 'Take up your basket, porter, and follow me.' Hardly believing that so exquisite words could have been said to him, the porter took up his basket and followed the girl, who stopped eventually before the door of a house. She knocked at the door and immediately a Christian opened to her, who gave her, in exchange for a dīnār, a great measure of olive-clear wine which she put into the basket, saying to the porter: 'Lift and follow me.' 'By Allāh, this is a day of days!' exclaimed the porter, as he lifted his basket and followed the girl. Arrived at the stall of a fruiterer, she bought Syrian apples, Osmāni quinces, peaches from Uman, jasmine of Aleppo, Damascene nenuphars, cucumbers from the Nile, limes from Egypt, Sultāni citrons, myrtle berries, flowers of henna, blood-red anemones, violets, pomegranate bloom, and the narcissus. All these she put into the porter's basket, and said: 'Lift!'; so he lifted and followed her until she came to a butcher's stall. Here she said: 'Cut me ten pounds of mutton.' So they cut her ten pounds which she wrapped in banana leaves and put into the basket, and said: 'Lift!' He lifted and followed her to an almond seller, from whom she bought every kind of almond that there is. Then the porter followed her to a sweetmeat seller from whom she bought a great platter which she covered with things from the stall: openwork sugar tarts with butter, velvet pastries perfumed with musk and stuffed deliciously, sābūnīyah biscuits, small cakes, lime tarts, honey-tasting jam, those sweets called mushabbak, little soufflèd patties called lukaimātal-Kādī, and those others named combs of Zainab which are made with butter and mingled with milk and honey. All these pleasant things she put upon the platter and then placed the platter in the basket. 'If you had told me, I would have brought a mule,' said the porter. Smiling at his jest, she stopped at the stall of a distiller of perfumes and bought ten sorts of waters, rose water, water of orange flowers, willow flower, violet and other kinds; she bought also a spray of rose-musk-scented water, grains of male incense, aloe wood, ambergris and musk; finally she selected candles of Alexandrian wax and put all in the basket, saying: 'Lift and follow!' Obediently the porter took up his basket and followed the young lady until she came to a splendid palace, having a great court set in an inner garden; it was tall, magnificent and four-square, and the door had two leaves of ebony, plated with plates of red gold.

The young girl rapped gently upon the door and it flew wide open. Then the porter looked at her who had opened the door and saw that she was a child having a slim and gracious body, the very model of all a young girl should be, not only for her round and prominent breasts, not only for her beauty and her air of breeding, but also for the perfection of her waist and of her carriage. Her brow was as white as the first ray fallen from the new moon, her eyes were the eyes of a gazelle, and the brows above them were as the crescent moons of Ramadān. Her cheeks were anemones, her mouth the scarlet seal of Sulaimān, her face pale as the full moon when she first rises above the grasses, her breasts twin passion-fruit. As for her young white pliant belly, it lay hid beneath her robe like some precious love letter in a silken case. Seeing her, the porter felt that he was losing his wits and nearly let the basket slip from his shoulders. 'As Allāh lives, this is the most blessed day of all my life!' he said. Standing within, the young portress said to her sister the cateress and also to the porter: 'Enter, and be your welcome as great as it is good!'

They went in and came at last to an ample hall giving on the central court, hung over with silk brocade and gold brocade, and full of fair gold-crusted furniture. There were vases and carved seats, curtains and close-shut presses all about it, and in the middle a marble couch, inlaid with pearl and diamond, covered with a red satin quilt. On the bed lay a third girl who exceeded all the marvel that a girl can be. Her eyes were Babylonian, for all witchcraft has its seat in Babylon. Her body was slim as the letter alif, her face so fair as to confuse the bright sun. She was as a star among the shining of the stars, a true Arabian woman, as the poet says:

> Who sings your slender body is a reed
>   His simile a little misses,
> Reeds must be naked to be fair indeed
>   While your sweet garments are but added blisses.
>
> Who sings your body is a slender bough
>   Also commits a kindred folly,
> Boughs to be fair must have green leaves enow
>   And you, my white one, must be naked wholly.

The young girl got up from the bed, moved a few paces into the middle of the hall until she was near her two sisters and then said to them: 'Why are you standing still like this? Take the basket from the porter's head.' Then the cateress came in front of the porter, the portress came behind him and, helped by their third sister, they relieved him of his burden. When they had taken everything out of the basket, they arranged all neatly and gave two dīnārs to the porter, saying: 'Turn and be gone, O porter!' But he looked at the young girls, admiring the perfection of their beauty, and thought that he had never seen the like. He noticed that there was no man with them and, marvelling at all the drinks, fruits, perfumed flowers, and other good things, had no desire to go away.

The eldest of the girls said: 'Why do you not go? Do you find your payment too little?' and then, turning to her sister the cateress: 'Give him a third dīnār.' But the porter said: 'As Allāh lives, fair ladies, my ordinary pay is but two half dīnārs; you have paid me well enough and yet all my heart and the inner parts of my soul are troubled about you. I cannot help asking myself what this life of yours is, that you live alone and have no man here to bear you human company. Do you not know that a minaret is of no value unless it be one of the four minarets of a mosque? You are but three, my ladies, you need a fourth. Women cannot be truly happy without men. The poet has said: "There can be no harmony save with four joined instruments: the lute, the harp, the cithern and flagiolet." Now you are only three, my ladies; you need a flagiolet, a fourth instrument, a man of discretion, full both of sentiment and intellect, a gifted artist with sealed lips!'

'But, porter,' said the young girls, 'do you not know that we are virgins and so are fearful of confiding ourselves to the indiscretion of a man? We also have read the poets, and they say: "Confide in none; a secret told is a secret spoiled." '

Hearing this, the porter cried: 'I swear on your dear lives, my ladies, that I am a man sure, faithful and discreet, one who has studied the annals and read books. I speak of only pleasing things and am carefully silent about all the rest. I act up always to the saying of the poet:

> I know the duties of high courtesy,
> Your dearest secrets shall be safe with me;
>   I'll shut them in a little inner room
> And seal the lock and throw away the key.

Their hearts were much moved towards the porter when they heard his verses and all the rhymes and rhythms he recited, and in jest they said: 'You must know that we have spent a great sum of money on this place. Have you the silver to pay us back? For we would not ask you to sit with us unless you paid the reckoning. We take it you desire to stay here, to become our companion in the wine and, above all, to keep us waking all the night until the shadow of the dawn fall on our faces.' 'Love without gold is a poor make-weight in the scales,' added the eldest of the girls, the mistress of the house; and the portress said: 'If you have nothing, get you gone with nothing!' But here the cateress interrupted, saying: 'Let us leave this joke, my sisters. As Allāh lives, this boy has not spoiled our day and another might not have been so patient. I myself will undertake to pay for him.'

At this the porter rejoiced with all his heart and said to the cateress: 'By Allāh, I owe this wonderful bargain all to you!' 'Stay with us, then, brave porter,' she replied, 'and rest assured that you shall be the darling of our eyes.' So saying, she rose and, after clasping his waist, began to arrange the flasks, to clarify and pour the wine, and to set places for the feast near a pool of water in the centre of the hall. She brought in everything of which they might have need, handed the wine, and saw that all were seated. The porter with these girls on every hand thought that he was dreaming in his sleep.

Soon the cateress took the wine flagon and filled a cup from which each drank three times. Then she filled it afresh and passed it to her sisters and then to the porter, who drank and said these lines:

In this red wine is liveliness
        And strength and well-being,
In this red wine is all caress
        And every wanton thing;
Drink deep and you will find, I trust,
In this red wine is very lust.

On this he kissed the hands of the three girls and drained the cup. Then he went up to the mistress of the house, saying: 'Mistress, I am your slave, your thing, your chattel!' and he recited, in her honour, this stanza of a certain poet:

I stand most like a slave
        Outside your door,
Must I an entrance crave
        In vain for ever more?
There is one gift I have—
I stand most like a slave.

Then, 'Drink, my friend,' said she, 'and may the wine be sweet and wholesome in its going down: may it give you strength to set out upon that road where lies all bodily well-being.' The porter took the cup, kissed the girl's hand and, in a sweetly-modulated voice, sang very low these verses of the poet:

I gave my love a wine
    Splendidly red as are her cheeks, I said;
Then she: 'I cannot drink these cheeks of mine.'
    'Ah, let me speak,' I said,
'Thou can'st not drink those cheeks of thine;
Then drink these tears and blood of mine!'

Again the young girl took the cup to the porter and, after holding it to his lips, sat down beside her sister. Soon they began to dance and sing and to play with the wonderful petals, the porter all the time taking them in his arms and kissing them, while one said saucy things to him, another drew him to her, and the third beat him with flowers. They went on drinking until the grape sat throned above their reason, and, when her reign was fully established, the portress rose and stripped off all her clothes until she was naked. Jumping into the water of the fountain, she began to play with it, taking it in her mouth and blowing it noisily at the porter, washing all her body, and letting it run between her childish thighs. At length she got out of the fountain, threw herself on the porter's lap, stretched out on her back and, pointing to the thing which was between her thighs, said:

'My darling, do you know the name of that?' 'Aha,' answered the porter, 'usually that is called the house of compassion.' Then she cried: 'Yū, yū! Are you not ashamed?' and taking him by the neck she began to slap him. 'No, no!' he cried. 'It is called the thing.' But she shook her head, and 'Then it is your behind piece,' said the porter. Again she shook her head, and 'It is your hornet,' said he. At these words she began to slap him so hard that she abraded his skin. 'You tell me its name!' he shouted, and she told him: 'Basil of the bridges.' 'At last,' cried the porter. 'Praise be to Allāh for your safety, O my basil of the bridges!'

After that, they let the cup go round and round; and the second girl, taking off her clothes, jumped into the basin. There she did as her sister had done and then, getting out, threw herself on to the porter's lap. Pointing to her thighs and the thing between them, she said: 'Light of my life, what is the name of that?' 'Your crack,' he answered. 'O listen to his naughty word!' she cried, and slapped him so hard that the hall echoed with the sound. 'Then it is basil of the bridges,' he hazarded, but she again cried that it was not and went on slapping his neck. 'Well, what is its name?' he yelled, and she answered: 'The husked sesame.'

Now the third girl, in her turn, got up, undressed, and went down into the basin, where she did as her sisters had done. Afterwards she put on some of her clothes and stretched herself over the thighs of the porter. 'Guess the name of that,' she said, pointing to her delicate parts. The porter tried this name and that and ended by asking her to tell him and cease her slapping. 'The khān of Abu-Mansūr,' she replied.

Then, in reprisal, the porter rose, undressed and went down into the water, and lo! his blade swam level with the surface. He washed as the girls had done, came out of the basin, and, throwing himself into the lap of the portress, rested his feet in that of the cateress. Pointing to his organ, he asked the mistress of the house: 'What is his name, my queen?' At this all the girls laughed till they fell over on their backs, and cried together: 'Your zabb!' 'No,' he said, and took a little bite at each by way of forfeit. Then they cried: 'Your tool, then!' But he said: 'No,' and pinched their breasts. 'But it is your tool,' they cried in astonishment, 'for it is hot. It is your zabb, because it moves.' Each time the porter shook his head and kissed and bit and pinched and hugged them until they laughed again. In the end they had to ask him to tell them; and the porter reflected a moment, looked between his thighs, and winking, said: 'Ladies, this child, my zabb, says for himself:

"My name is the Mighty Ungelt Mule who feeds on the basil of bridges, feasts on husked sesame, and stays the night in father Mansūr's khān." '

At these words, the girls laughed so much that they fell over on their bottoms; and afterwards all four went on drinking from the same cup until the approach of evening. When night fell, they said to the porter: 'Be gone, now, turn your face and let us see the width of your shoulders.' But the porter cried: 'By Allāh, it is easier for my soul to quit my body than for me to quit your house, my ladies! Let us make the night continue the sweet day, and to-morrow all can part and follow their destiny upon the road of Allāh.' The young cateress then spoke up saying: 'By my life, sisters, let us ask him to pass the night with us; we will have many good laughs at the naughty fellow who is so shameless and yet so gentle.' The others agreed, and said to the porter: 'Very well, you can stay with us this night on condition that you obey implicitly and ask no reason or explanation of anything you see.' 'I agree to that, ladies,' he said. 'Get up, then, and read what is over the door,' they commanded; so he rose, and found over the door these words lettered in gold:

'Speak not of that which concerns you not or you will hear that which shall please you not.'

Reading this, the porter said: 'Ladies, I call you to witness that I will never speak of that which concerns me not.'

At this point Shahrazād saw the approach of morning and discreetly fell silent.

But when the tenth night had come

DUNYAZĀD SAID: 'Finish your tale, dear sister.'

So Shahrazād answered: 'Gladly and as in duty bound,' and thus continued:

It is related, O auspicious King, that when the porter had made his promise to the girls, the cateress rose and set meat before them all, which they ate with good appetite. After the meal, candles were

lighted, perfumed wood and incense burned, and all began to drink
again and to eat the various delicacies from the market; especially
the porter who also recited well-formed verses all the time, shutting
his eyes and shaking his head. Suddenly they heard a knocking on
the door, which, though it did not interrupt their pleasure, caused
the portress to rise. She came back, saying: 'Indeed, to-night's
pleasure is to be perfect, for there are three strangers at the door
with shaved beards and each blind of the left eye, which is a strange
coincidence. It is easy to see that they come from the lands of Rūm,
each has different features and yet their faces all match in their
fittingness for being laughed at. If we let them in, we can have much
fun at their expense.' She persuaded her companions, who said:
'Tell them that they may come in, but be sure they understand the
condition: "Speak not of that which concerns you not or you will
hear that which shall please you not." ' So the young girl ran joyously to the door and came back leading the three one-eyed men,
who indeed had shaved beards, moustaches twisted back, and all the
signs of that brotherhood of beggars called kalandars. As soon as
they came in, they wished peace to the company, backing one by one
as they did so; on which the girls stood up and invited them to be
seated. The three men, after they had sat down, looked at the
porter, who was very drunk, and supposing him to belong to their
brotherhood, said among themselves: 'Here is another kalandar; he
is sure to bear us friendly company.' But the porter, who had heard
what they said, jumped to his feet and, eyeing them sternly and a
little squintingly, said: 'All right, all right, my friends, make yourselves at home; and begin by digesting those words written above
the door.' The girls burst out laughing at his words and said to each
other: 'We are going to have fun with these kalandars and the porter.'
They set food before the kalandars—who ate like kalandars!—then
wine—and the kalandars drank turn and turn about, reaching out
again and again for the cup. When the drink was passing round at a
rare pace, the porter said: 'Come, brothers, have you not some good
tale of marvellous adventure in your scrips to amuse us?' Cheered
by this suggestion, the kalandars asked for musical instruments and,
when the portress had fetched out a Mosul drum fitted with crotals, a
lute of Irāk, and a Persian flagiolet, they stood up and began to play
while the girls sang with them. The porter became frenzied with
pleasure and kept on shouting: 'Ha! yā Allāh!', so struck was he by
the harmonious voices of the singers.

In the middle of all this, knocking was again heard upon the door and the portress rose to see who was there.

Now this was the reason for the second knocking on the door:

That night the Khalīfah, Hārūn al-Rashād, had gone down to wander about his city to see and hear for himself what might be going on there. He was accompanied by his wazīr, Jafar al-Barmaki, and by Masrūr, his sword-bearer, the instrument of his justice. You must know that it was a habit of his to disguise himself as a merchant and make such expeditions.

While he was walking through the streets of the city, he passed that palace and heard the sounds of music and gaiety which issued from it. Then said the Khalīfah to Jafar: 'I wish to enter that place to see those singers.' Jafar answered: 'They must be a crowd of drunkards. If we go in some hurt may come to you.' But the Khalīfah said: 'Certainly we must go in. I wish to find a way in which we can enter and take them by surprise.' 'I hear and I obey,' said Jafar at this command and, going up to the door, he knocked.

When the young portress opened the door, the wazīr said to her: 'My mistress, we are merchants from Tiberias. Ten days ago we came to Baghdād with our goods and took lodging in the khān of the merchants. One of the other traders at the khān asked us to his house to-night to eat with him. After the meal, which lasted an hour in which we ate and drank excellently, he gave us leave to depart. We came out but, the night being dark and we strangers, lost our way to the khān where we lodge. So now we beg you of your great goodness to let us come in and pass the night at your house. Allāh will reward your kindness.' The portress looked at them closely and, seeing that they had the appearance of most respectable merchants, went in to ask the advice of her two companions. The other two said: 'Let them come in!' So she returned to the door, crying: 'Enter!' On this invitation the Khalīfah and Jafar and Masrūr came in and the girls rose, putting themselves at their service and saying: 'Be very welcome. Take your ease here, dear companions; but accept, we pray, this one condition: "Speak not of that which concerns you not or you will hear that which shall please you not."'

The newcomers answered: 'Be it so,' and sat down with the others. While they were being invited to drink and to send round the cup, the Khalīfah looked at the three kalandars and was astonished to see that each was blind of the left eye; then at the girls and was overcome with surprise at all their beauty and grace. When the girls, in their ministrations to the guests, offered the Khalīfah a cup of the rarest wine, he refused, saying: 'I am vowed to pilgrimage.' So the portress got up and placed a little table of finest inlay before him on which she set a cup of Chinese porcelain into which she poured spring water refreshed with snow, mingling sugar and rose-water within it. The Khalīfah accepted this, thanking her cordially and saying to himself: 'To-morrow I shall reward her for her kindness.'

The girls continued to act the hostess and pass about the wine till the wits of the companions were dancing dizzily. Then she who was the mistress of the house rose up and, having asked if any wanted more, took the cateress by the hand saying: 'Rise, my sister, that we may do that which we have to do.' 'Be it as you say,' the other answered. On this the portress also rose and, telling the kalandars to get up from the centre of the hall and seat themselves by the door, herself cleared and tidied the central space. The other two called to the porter: 'By Allāh, your friendship is of but little use! You are no stranger here but belong to the house.' On this the porter stood up, lifted the skirts of his robe and tightened his belt, saying: 'Tell me what to do and I shall do it.' 'Follow me,' said the portress. So he followed her out of the hall and saw two black bitches with chains round their necks, which, as he was bid, he led back into the middle of the hall. Then the eldest pulled up her sleeves, took a whip, and told the porter to lead forward one of the bitches. When he had done so, dragging her by the chain, the animal began to weep, rais-ing its head piteously towards the girl; but the latter, without seem-ing to notice, fell upon it, beating it over the head with her whip till the bitch yelled and wept and she herself could strike no more. Then she threw down the whip and, taking the bitch in her arms, clasped it to her breast, wiped away its tears, and kissed its head which she held between her hands. After a little, she said to the porter: 'Bring me the other, and take this one back.' So the porter brought the other bitch forward and the girl treated it as she had the first.

The Khalīfah felt his heart filled with pity at this sight; his breast shook with grief and he signed with his eye to Jafar to question the young woman. But Jafar signed to him that it were better to keep silent. Soon the mistress of the house turned to her sisters saying: 'Come, let us do as is our custom.' They answered: 'Yes'; so she got up on to the marble bed which was plated with gold and silver and said to the other two: 'Let it be done!' Then the portress also got up on to the bed; but the cateress went into her own room and brought back a satin bag fringed with green silk. Halting before the other two, she opened the bag and drew a lute from it. First tuning this and then playing upon it, she sang these lines of love and all the sadness of love:

> Love at my door
> Knocked and I gave him bed.
> When sleep saw this
> He took offence and fled.
> 'Give me back sleep;
> Where has he gone?' I said.

> They said: 'Our friend
> That kept the sure straight way,
> Who has done this
> To send you so astray,
> To lead you blind
> Into the sand?' said they.

> I said: 'Not I,
> But she must answer make.
> I could but cry:
> My blood, which is hers to take,
> Lies heavily
> Not spilled yet for her sake.

> I chose a girl
> To put my thought in her;
> She is my thought,
> My thought's her imager;
> Now she is gone
> Fire is my comforter.

> See for yourselves!
> Even Allāh like a lover
> From molten threads
> Of the syrup of life wove her;
> Then made all gems
> And fruits with what was over.'

But they said: 'Fool,
Small joy and, for the rest,
    Torture and tears
And hugging to the breast
    Shades on a pool.
The first drink is the best.'

'If I am drunk
I came not so by drinking,
    It was enough
To see the ruby winking
    There in the glass—
Sleep saw it too, I'm thinking.

It's not that time
Has passed, but that so has she,
    It's not that love
Won't last, but that nor will she,
    Not that life's gone,
But that she's gone from me.

My soul is bound
By the scents of her body,
    Jasmine and musk
And rose of her body,
    Amber and nard,
The scents of her body.'

'Allāh comfort you, my sister,' cried out the portress, when the song was finished; then, tearing all her clothes in an ecstasy of grief, she fell in a faint upon the floor.

Her body being in some sort bared, the Khalīfah was able to see upon it the prints of whips and rods, a circumstance which astonished and appalled him. But the cateress came and cast water in her sister's face until she recovered consciousness; then she brought her a new robe and helped her into it.

The Khalīfah whispered to Jafar: 'You do not seem moved by this. Do you not see the marks of the scourge on the woman? I can hardly keep silent and I will know no rest until I have found out the truth of all this and of the matter of the two bitches.' 'Lord and Master,' answered Jafar, 'remember the condition: "Speak not of that which concerns you not or you will hear that which shall please you not." '

While they were talking thus, the cateress again took up the lute and, pressing it against her rounded breast, sounded the chords and sang:

> If one came to us plaining of love,
>   What would we answer?
> Seeing that we also are drowned in love,
>   What would we do?
> If we charged a speaker to speak for us,
>   What would he know of it?

He has brought us within two fingers of the pit of death,
He has cut our heart-strings that they might hold him no more,
Has he kept one withered seed of all our love?
Does he think at all that we are stricken and with what disease?
All that he has forgotten we shall call upon God to remember.

> If one came to us plaining of love,
>   What would we answer?
> Seeing that we also are drowned in love,
>   What would we do?
> If we charged a speaker to speak for us,
>   What would he know of it?

Again the portress wept at this sad song and tore her robe and fell back fainting; and again the cateress cast water in her face, raised her up and put another robe on her, while the eldest oft hem said to her: 'Courage, courage, for the final song! It is our duty.' So the cateress tuned the lute afresh and sang:

> Cease this parting as of years,
> I have no more tears.
>
> Your absence is no longer needed,
> It has succeeded.
>
> Men have the months and years alway,
> Women but a day.
>
> How shall I call a murder on
> You, when the body's nearly gone
> That showed what you had done?

How cry a debt when the wet
White cheek hardly remaineth yet
Where was written the debt?

My sighs fan up your flame,
That would be well if the game
You hunted were still the same.

Mussulmāns, make a feud,
Cover him with the rude
Hates of a multitude.

Yet do not—for all that he
Felt of your cruelty
Would be felt by me.

Rather crush me beneath your feet
And he'll not feel his pulses beat
At the other side of the street.

Again the portress fell fainting and again her naked body showed
the marks of whips and rods.

The three kalandars began whispering together when they saw
this: 'It had been better for us we had never come into this house,
even though we had to sleep on the naked ground; for what we
have just seen is enough to melt the marrow in our spines.' The
Khalīfah turned to them and said: 'Why is that?' 'We are afraid of
what has happened,' they answered. 'Is that so?' said the Khalīfah,
'then you are not of this house?' 'We are not,' they answered, 'we
imagined it belonged to that man beside you.' 'By Allāh, it does not!'
cried the porter.   'This is the very first time that I have entered
here. Also, God knows, it would have been better for me to have
slept on the rubbish heaps among the ruins.'

So they concerted with each other and said: 'We are seven men
to three women, let us demand an explanation of these things and, if
they will not answer willingly, we can use force.' They all agreed to
this except Jafar, who said: 'Do you think that right and equitable?
Remember, we are their guests and that they laid down certain conditions which we swore to keep. The night is nearly over; it would
be better for each of us to go forth and seek his destiny upon the
road of Allāh.' Then, winking at the Khalīfah and drawing him
aside, he continued: 'We have but one more hour to stay here. To-

morrow I promise that I will bring them up before you, and then we can compel them to tell their story.' But the Khalīfah said: 'I have not the patience to wait till to-morrow.' The others continued their planning, some saying this and some saying that, but it all came back to the question: 'Who is to ask them?' At last it was decided that the porter should do so.

So, when the girls said: 'Good folk, what are you talking about?', the porter rose to his feet and, standing up straight before the lady of the house, addressed her courteously: 'My queen, I ask and pray you in the name of Allāh, on behalf of all us jolly fellows, to tell us the tale of those two bitches and why you so beat them and then weep over them and kiss them. Tell us, too, for we wait to hear it, the cause of the marks of whips and rods on the body of your sister. This we ask of you; that is all, my queen.' Then the lady of the house questioned them: 'Is this that the porter has said asked in the name of all?' And each, with the exception of Jafar, answered: 'Yes.' Jafar said nothing.

The eldest girl, hearing this answer of theirs, exclaimed: 'As Allāh lives, you who are our guests have done us here the most grievous of wrongs. We bound you to this condition: "Speak not of that which concerns you not or you will hear that which shall please you not." Was it not enough for you to come into our house and eat our good food? Perhaps, though, it was less your fault than the fault of our sister who let you in.'

So saying, she pulled the sleeves of her robe away from her wrist and beat the floor with her foot three times, calling: 'Come quick, come quick!' The door of one of the great curtained presses opened and out glided seven strong negroes carrying sharpened swords. To these she said: 'Bind the arms of these prattling guests and fasten them one to the other.' This the negroes did, saying: 'O mistress, O hidden flower beyond the sight of men, may we cut off their heads?' 'Have patience for an hour,' she answered. 'I wish to know what sort of men they are before they die.'

On this the porter cried: 'By Allāh, mistress queen, do not kill me for the crime of others. All these have sinned, committing a notable crime against you, but not I. As God lives, how happy, how paradisal would our night have been if we had never set eyes on these ill-omened kalandars. I have always said that kalandars could lay waste the loveliest of cities just by coming into it.' And he added these lines:

> The fairest gift of strength is clemency
>   If the weak offend;
> So do not, for our love's sake, punish me
>   For the fault of a friend.

The eldest girl burst out laughing when the porter had finished speaking.

At this point Shahrazād saw the approach of day and discreetly fell silent.

But when the eleventh night had come

SHE SAID:

It is related, O auspicious King, that when the eldest girl burst out laughing after having been angry, she came down to the company and said: 'Tell me all that there is to tell, for you have but one hour to live. I give you this indulgence because you are poor folk. If you were among the most noble, great ones of your tribes or even governors, it is true that I would hurry on your punishment.'

'Jafar, we are in sorry case,' said the Khalīfah, 'tell her who we are or she may kill us.' 'Which is exactly what we deserve,' said Jafar. Then said the Khalīfah. 'There is a time for being witty and a time for being serious, there is a time for everything.'

Now first of all the eldest girl approached the kalandars and asked them: 'Are you brothers?' To this they answered: 'No, by Allāh, we are only poor men of the poorest who live by cupping and scarifying.' Then she turned to one of them and said: 'Were you born without one eye?' 'As God lives, I was not,' he answered, 'but the tale of the way I lost my eye is so extraordinary that, if it were written with a needle in the corner of another eye, yet would it be a lesson to the circumspect.' The second and the third made the same kind of answer; then all three said: 'Each of us was born in a different country; the stories of our lives are strange and our adventures pass the marvellous.' 'Well, then,' said the girl, 'each of you must tell his story and the reason of his coming to our house. Should the tale seem good to us, each then may make his bow and go his way.'

The first who came forward was the porter; and he said: 'My queen, I am a porter, nothing more. Your cateress here gave me things to carry and led me to you. You know well what happened to me after I got here and, if I refuse to be more particular, you know why. That is all my tale. I will not add another word to it, and Allāh bless you.' Then said the eldest girl: 'Get you gone, make your bow and let us see the last of you.' 'But,' said the porter, 'no, by God, I will not stir until I have heard the tales of these friends of mine.'

Then the first kalandar came forward to tell his tale, and said:

Tale of the First Kalandar

MISTRESS, I am going to tell you the things which led up to the shaving of my beard and the loss of my eye.

Know that my father was a king and that he had a brother who was king over another city. Also it was fated that, on the day of my birth, a son was born to my uncle.

Years passed, and my cousin and I grew to manhood. I must tell you that it was my custom from time to time to visit my uncle and stay some months with him. The last time I visited him, my cousin gave me great and generous welcome, killed the finest sheep for me, clarified the rarest wines in my honour. When we had drunken and the wine had somewhat got the better of us, my cousin said to me: 'Dear friend and best loved cousin, I have a favour to ask of you which I beg you not to refuse.' 'I grant it with all my heart,' I answered, and also, at his request, swore on our sacred Religion that I would do as he bid me. Thereon he went away and came back in a few minutes with a sumptuously dressed, delicately-perfumed lady, accoutred in everything with great expense. Pointing her out to me, he begged me to take her and to precede him to a certain tomb, lying in the middle of many others, whose exact situation he pointed out to me. As I could not refuse because of my oath, I led the lady with me to the tomb, under the dome of which we entered and sat down to wait for my cousin. Soon he joined us, bringing with him a vessel of water, a sack containing plaster, and a little axe. With this axe he lifted the stones of the slab of the tomb one by one and dug in the earth beneath till he exposed a cover about the size of a small door. This he opened, and below it I saw a vaulted stairway. Turning to the woman, my cousin said: 'It is for you to choose,' and without a word the lady went down the stairs and disappeared. Then said my cousin to me: 'Cousin, this is what you must do to complete your vow: when I have gone, put back the cover and the earth, mix the plaster, and so plaster down the stones that none can say:

"Someone has been opening this old tomb." It is quite possible, for I have been working here a year and only Allāh knows it.' Then, adding: 'My only grief is that I am going away from you, dear cousin,' he went down the stairs and was lost in the depths of the tomb. When he had gone from sight, I fastened down the cover and worked at the tomb till it appeared untouched.

Returning to my uncle's palace, I found that he was away hunting; so I lay down and slept all night. But when morning came I thought over all that my cousin and I had done and repented bitterly but uselessly. I went back to the tombs and searched all day till nightfall without being able to find the one I sought; so, when I returned to the palace, I could neither eat nor drink for thinking of my cousin. I lay all night in pain and at daybreak returned to the burial ground, grieving that I had hearkened to my cousin and searching in vain among all the tombs. Having hunted for seven days without finding the one into which he had gone down, I grew almost mad and, both to rest my mind and to distract my grief, set out on the return journey to my father's country.

No sooner had I come to the gates of the city than a rabble rushed out at me and bound my arms to my sides. I was utterly astonished, seeing I was the prince of that place, and that among those men were servants of my father and my own young slaves. 'Alas, alas, what has happened to my father?' I said to myself, and then began to question those who had bound me, without receiving any reply. But finally one of my young slaves who was among them said to me: 'Fate has gone up against your father, his soldiers have mutinied and his wazīr has killed him; we were set here in ambush to wait your coming.'

They took me up, more dead than alive with grief at the death of my father, and brought me into the presence of the wazīr who had killed him. Now there was an ancient enmity between me and this wazīr, which had come about through my passion for shooting with the arbalest. For one day, while I was on the terrace of our palace, a great bird lit on the terrace of the wazīr's palace, where the wazīr happened to be walking. I fired and, missing the bird, hit the wazīr in the eye and put it out, as had been ordained by Allāh. As it is written:

> God writes for eternity, this is not given to men;
> But even He cannot rewrite it again,
> And we walk in the wake of His pen.

We have followed the tracing of the letters of God, my friend,
The outline was not ours to mar or to mend;
Sit quiet and wait for the end.

When I knocked out the wazīr's eye, he dared not say anything because my father was the King of the city; but now, when I stood before him with arms bound to my sides, he ordered my head to be cut off. 'For what crime?' I asked, and, 'What crime is greater than this?' he answered, pointing to his eye-socket. 'I did it by accident,' I said. 'Yes,' he replied, 'you did it by accident and I will do it on purpose.' Then, ordering me to be brought within his reach, he put forward his finger and pulled out my left eye.

Since then I have been one-eyed, as you all see.

Not content with this, the wazīr had me bound completely and put in a chest, which he delivered to his sword-bearer, saying: 'This is your affair. Draw your sword, take him out beyond the city, kill him, and leave him as food for the wild beasts.'

So the sword-bearer carried me outside the city, lifted me out of the chest and was about to bind my eyes, when I began to weep and intone these lines:

> When you wept apart,
> In the days of my power I regarded your tears;
> I thought you a steel shield proof against spears,
> And you are the lance-head pressed against my heart.
>
> You had proved your aim,
> The great bowman I had looked for to confound my foes;
> I knew yours from the arrows of all bows;
> True-flying to my heart I see the same.

When the sword-bearer heard these lines, he remembered that he had been my father's sworder also and that I had been very good to him; so he exclaimed: 'How can I kill you, I who am your slave?' Then he said to me: 'Flee, for I spare your life; but never return to this land or you will die and be the cause of my death also. The poet has said:

> Go, my friend, you shall not die,
>   Leave the houses;
> There are other lands to try
>   Full of free carouses.

Is it not a silly thing
  To be put on,
When the whole world breaks in Spring
  For you to set your foot on?

Somewhere, somehow, you will pass,
  That is certain;
But when you'll see the under-grass
  Lies still behind the curtain.

The lion grows each yellow thew
  Near Samarkand;
Remember that his soul grows too
  In the freedom of the sand.'

I kissed his hands, when he had said these lines, and could hardly believe that I was safe until I had fled forward a long way.

As I went, I consoled myself for the loss of my eye by thinking on my deliverance from death, and so proceeded until I reached my uncle's city again. When I found my uncle and told him of the fate of my father and how I had lost my eye, he wept bitterly, crying: 'Nephew, nephew, you add another grief to all my griefs, another sorrow to my sorrows. My own boy has been missing for many days and none can tell me what has happened to him.' He swooned and, coming out of his swoon, continued: 'My child, I was grieving bitterly for my son, now I must grieve for you and your father. But remember, my boy, it is better to have lost an eye than to have lost life itself.'

At this, I could no longer keep silent as to what had happened to my cousin; so I told my uncle the whole truth and he rejoiced exceedingly at my story. 'Take me quickly to the tomb!' he cried, and I was forced to admit I could not find it.

Nevertheless, we went together to the burial ground and this time, after a long search, I recognised the tomb. We both rejoiced and, after entering the dome and displacing the stones, the earth and the cover, made our way down fifty steps of the staircase. At the bottom we were met by a great smoke which blinded us, but my uncle said that word which takes away all fear: 'There is no power and dominion save in Allāh, Almighty, Most High!'

We journeyed through the smoke and came to a great hall, filled with flour and every kind of grain and provision of all sorts. In the middle of the hall we saw a curtain draped above a bed, and, when we looked into the interior of the bed, my uncle recognised his son who was lying there in the arms of the woman who had gone down with him. But they were both nothing save black cinders, just as if they had been thrown into a pit of fire.

My uncle, seeing this, spat in his son's face, crying: 'This is your reward, O wicked youth, the punishment of this world. There yet remains the punishment of another world, more terrible and lasting longer.' So saying, my uncle took off his slipper and struck his dead son's face with the heel of it.

At this point Shahrazād saw the approach of day and discreetly fell silent.

But when the twelfth night had come

SHE SAID:

It is related, O auspicious King, that, while the Khalīfah and Jafar and all who were there listened intently, the kalandar continued his tale to the girl who was the mistress of the house:

When my uncle slippered his son's face, I was sore astonished and wept for my cousin and the girl lying there in the likeness of charcoal. So I cried: 'Uncle, as Allāh lives, restrain yourself! I am in the throes of grief at what has happened to your son, yes, for both him and her, lying there like charcoal; but most at seeing you, his father, beating his dead face with a slipper.' Then my uncle explained to me saying: 'Nephew, you must know that this child of mine was inflamed with love for his own sister. I kept him away from her and used to console myself with the thought that they were so young. But nothing of the sort! Hardly had they become pubic when they did evil together and I found them out. I was scarcely able to believe my eyes, and scolded him with a terrible scolding, saying: "Beware of these filthy actions which none ever did before and none will ever do after. Otherwise we shall become shamed and despicable among kings. Riders will carry the tale about the earth. Take care then that you do not do this again, or I will first curse you and then slay you!" Afterwards I kept them sedulously apart, but the wretched girl also loved him with an inordinate love and Satan completed his work within them.

'When my son saw that he was kept away from his sister, he secretly prepared this chamber underground, filled it with food and, taking advantage of my absence at the hunt, came down here with her.

'Then the wrath of the Highest kindled against them, and the fire of the Highest burned them both together. But their punishment in the next world will be more terrible and lasting.'

Then my uncle wept and I wept and he said to me: 'Henceforward you shall be my son in the place of this one.'

When I had sat there for an hour, considering the sorry ways of the world, my father's death and usurped throne, the loss of my eye which you all have seen, and that strange end which had come to my cousin, I wept again from the bottom of my heart.

Eventually we came up out of the tomb, heaped earth upon it and, leaving it exactly as it had been before, made our way home.

But hardly had we gone in and seated ourselves than we became aware of sounds of war, drums and trumpets, and the galloping of soldiers in the streets. The city became full of noise and shouting and dust raised by horses' hoofs. We were at a loss to understand what these things might mean until the king, my uncle, asked an attendant, who said: 'The wazīr, who has killed your brother, has massed all his troops of soldiers and come against us in forced marches to take the city by assault. And the people, seeing that they were not in a state to resist him, have opened the gates and given him the city.'

I was thrown into great despondency at these words, coming as they did on top of all the trials and sufferings which had visited us. I did not know what to do, considering that, if I showed myself, the people of the city as well as the soldiers who had been my father's would recognise me and kill me out of hand. So, not being able to think of any other expedient, I shaved my beard, put on these rags and left the city. By tedious stages I reached Baghdād, hoping to find safety and also someone who would admit me into the presence of the Prince of Believers, Hārūn al-Rashīd, the Khalīfah of God, that I might tell him my story and all my sorrows.

It was only to-night that I arrived in the city and I did not know my way about it. By chance I met this other kalandar and, while we were talking together, we were joined by our third companion, also a kalandar. Recognising each other as strangers, we wended our way in the darkness together till the kind hand of Destiny led us to your house, my mistress.

That is the story of my shaved beard and my lost eye.

When she had heard the tale of the first kalandar, the mistress of the house said to him: 'That is well, make your bow and depart with all speed.'

The first kalandar answered: 'Indeed, mistress, I shall not stir from here until I have heard the tales of all the other companions.'

So, while all were marvelling at the story and the Khalīfah was even whispering to Jafar: 'Never in all my life have I heard a like adventure,' the first kalandar sat down cross-legged on the floor and the second kalandar, advancing, kissed the earth between the hands of the young mistress of the house and said:

Tale of the Second Kalandar

INDEED, mistress, neither was I born with one eye only; and the story which I am going to tell you is so marvellous that, if it were written with a needle on the inner corner of any eye, yet would it serve as a lesson to the circumspect.

Though you see me thus, I am a king and the son of a king, a man of education beyond the ordinary. I have read the Koran with all its seven narratives, I have read all essential books and the writings of the masters of science, I have studied the lore of the stars and the starlike lore of the poets. So rapidly did I learn that I surpassed in knowledge all the men of my time.

Especially did my fame spread abroad as a calligrapher; I became renowned in all countries and my worth was known among kings. So it happened that the King of Hind heard tell of me and sent begging my father to let me visit him. This invitation he accompanied with sumptuous gifts and presents meet for us; so my father consented and fitted out six ships for me with all manner of luxuries, and I departed.

After a month's voyage, we came to land and, unshipping the horses and camels we had with us, loaded them with presents for the King of Hind and set out on our journey. But hardly had we started than a great dust storm rose, filling all the sky and the earth with sand for the space of an hour. When it died down, we found close upon us a troop of sixty armed men, raging like lions, desert Arabs, cutpurses of the highway. We turned and fled, but, when they saw our ten camels loaded with gifts for the King of Hind, they pursued us at a gallop. So we signed to them with our finger that we were envoys to the mighty King and should not be molested. But they answered: 'We know nothing of kings,' and forthwith killed some of my slaves. The rest of us took to flight in all directions, I with a great and terrible wound, while the Arabs contented themselves with pillaging our rich belongings.

I fled and I fled, despairing bitterly at my change of fortune, till I came to the top of a mountain, where I found a cave in which I passed the night.

Next morning I left the cave and journeyed on until I came to a great and beautiful city, whose air was of such potent balm that Winter might not lay hand upon her but the Spring covered her with his roses all the year. I wept with joy when I reached this city, being fatigued and broken by my journey, worn and pale from my wound and utterly changed from my former state.

I was wandering ignorantly about the streets when I passed a tailor sewing in his shop, whom I greeted and who greeted me. He cordially invited me to seat myself, embraced me, and asked me generous questions about my wanderings. I told him all that had befallen me from beginning to end and he was much moved at my recital, saying to me: 'My sweet young man, you must on no account tell this story to any other person here; for the king of this city is a deadly enemy of your father, having an old grudge against him, and I fear for your safety.'

He gave me food and drink, and we ate and drank together. After a long conversation, he brought out a mattress and a quilt for me, and let me sleep that night in a corner of his shop. I stayed with him for three days, and at the end of that time he asked if I knew any trade by which I could earn a livelihood. 'Certainly I do,' I answered, 'I am deeply read in the law, I am a past-master of all sciences, literature and computation are thoroughly well known to me.' 'My friend,' he answered "all that is not a trade, or rather, if you wish, it is a trade' (for he saw that I was annoyed), 'but it is not of very much account in the markets of our city. No one here knows anything of study or of writing or of reading, they simply know how to make money.' I could only answer that I knew nothing beside these things. Said he: 'Come, my son, pull yourself together, take an axe and a cord, go out and cut wood in the countryside till Allāh show you a better occupation. Above all, tell your story to no one or they will kill you.' With this the good man bought me an axe and a rope, and sent me out in charge of a gang of woodcutters, under whose special care he placed me.

I went out with the woodcutters and, when I had chopped sufficient faggots, loaded them on my head and sold them in the streets of the city for half a dīnār. With a little of this money I bought food, and the rest I carefully put aside. I laboured in this way for a full year, visiting my friend the tailor in his shop every day and resting there in my corner without having to pay him anything.

One day, straying away from the others, I came to a thickly-wooded glade where there were many faggots to be had. I chose a dead tree and was beginning to loosen the earth about her roots when the head of my axe was caught in a copper ring. I removed the earth all about this ring and, coming to a wooden cover in which it was fastened, lifted it and found an underground staircase. In my curiosity I went down the stairs to the bottom and, opening a door, entered the mighty hall of a most marvellous palace. In this hall there was a young girl, more beautiful than all the pearls of history; I had endured much and yet at the sight of her all my troubles were left behind and I knelt down in adoration before Allāh who had moulded so perfect a beauty out of the centuries.

She looked at me and said: 'Are you a man or a Jinnī?' 'A man,' I answered, and she asked: 'Who then has led you to this hall where for full twenty years I have not seen a human face?' I found her words and herself so sweet that I answered: 'Lady, it was Allāh who led me to your home that all my troubles and my sorrows might be forgotten.' I told her my story from beginning to end; she wept for me and told me her story likewise:

'I am the daughter of King Ifītāmūs, latest of the Kings of Hind and master of the Isle of Ebony. I was to be married to my cousin, but on my wedding night, even before my virginity had been taken, the Ifrīt Jurjīs, son of Rajmūs, son of the Foul Fiend himself, carried me off and put me in this place, which he had provisioned with all I could desire of sweet things and of jams, of robes and precious stuffs, of furniture and meat and drink. Since then he has come to see me every ten days and lies one night with me, going away in the morning. Also he has told me that if I have need of him during the ten days that he is away I have nothing to do but to touch with my hand two lines which are written under the cupola of that little room. If I but touch them he will appear at once. It is four days since he has been here, so that there will be six more before he comes again. Therefore you can stay with me for five days and go away on the day before he comes.'

'Most certainly I can,' I answered, and she was filled with joy. She got up from where she was lying and, taking me by the hand, led me through many arched arpartments to a warm agreeable hammām where all the air was scented. Here we both undressed naked and bathed together. After our bath, we sat side by side on the hammām couch and she regaled me with musk-sweetened sherbert and delicious cakes. We talked for a long time and ate unsparingly of the provisions of the Ifrīt who had ravished her.

At last she said: 'For this evening you had better sleep and rest after all your toil; you will be the more ready for me then.'

I was indeed weary, so I thanked her and lay down to sleep, forgetting all my cares. When I woke I found her by my side, pleasantly massaging my limbs and my feet. So I called down all the blessings of Allāh upon her, and we sat together for an hour saying sweet things to each other. 'As God lives,' she sighed at last, 'before you came I was all alone in this underground palace for twenty years, no one to speak to, with no companion save sorrow and a bosom filled by sobs, but now glory be to Allāh that He has brought you to me!'

Then in a sweet voice she sang this song:

> For your feet,
> If we had known of your coming,
> We would have been weaving
> Our heart's blood,
> The velvet of our eyes
> To a red and black carpet.

> For your couch,
> If we had known of your coming,
> We would have been spreading
> Our cool cheeks,
> The young silk of our thighs,
> Dear stranger in the night.

Hand on heart I thanked her for her song, my love for her increased in me and all my sorrows fell away. We drank together from the same cup till nightfall, and all night I lay with her in a heaven of bliss. Never was such a night; and, when morning came, we rose in love with each other and with happiness.

I was still all passion and, thinking to prolong my rapture, I said: 'Shall I not take you from this underground place and free you from the Jinni?' 'Be quiet,' she answered, laughing, 'and be content with what you have. The poor Ifrīt has only one night in ten; I promise you all the other nine.' But I, lifted by passion and by wine, spoke thus extravagantly: 'Not so! I am going to destroy that alcove with its magic inscription, and then the Ifrīt will come and I shall kill him. For a long time it has been my custom to amuse myself by killing Ifrīt.'

To calm my frenzy she recited these lines:

> You who would bind love
> Thinking to make us
> Yours by the binding
> Soon shall discover
> Ever a lover
> Finishes finding
> Love will forsake us,
> The bound and unkind love;
> But if you unbind love
> He'll wrap us and take us
> In nets of his winding
> And never be over.

But, paying no attention to the lines, I gave a violent kick with my foot at the wall of the alcove.

At this point Shahrazād saw the approach of morning and discreetly fell silent.

And when the thirteenth night had come

SHE SAID:

It is related, O auspicious King, that the second kalandar continued telling his story to the young mistress of the house in these words:

Mistress, when I kicked down the alcove, the woman cried: 'The Ifrīt is upon us! Did I not warn you? As Allāh lives, you have destroyed me! Flee by the way you came and save yourself!'

I rushed to the staircase, forgetting my sandals and my axe in the hurry of my terror. When I had climbed a few steps, I remembered them and went back to look for them; but the earth opened and an Ifrît of terrible size and ugliness sprang from it, crying to the woman: 'What does all this violence mean? It frightened me. What harm has befallen you?' 'No harm,' she answered, 'save that, just now, I felt my heart heavy with solitude and, rising to get some drink to lighten it, I fell against the alcove.' But the Ifrît, who had looked about the hall and seen my sandals and my axe, cried: 'Oh, and what are these things, you lying whore? Tell me, what man do they belong to?' 'I never saw them before you showed them to me,' she answered, 'probably they were hanging to the back of your clothes and you brought them here yourself.' 'Weak and tortuous and foolish words!' exclaimed the furious Jinnî. 'They will not take me in, you wanton.'

On this, he stripped her naked, crucified her between four pegs fastened in the earth, and, putting her to the torture, began to question her. I could not bear to see this or to hear her sobs, so I ran trembling up the stairs and, reaching the outer air, put back the cover and removed all traces of the entrance. I repented bitterly of the foolish thing I had done, thinking of the girl's beauty and of all the torture which the wretch who had kept her there for twenty years had inflicted on her for my sake. From this I fell to lamenting my father, my own lost kingdom, and the miserable descent I had made to be a woodcutter. So I wept and recited a suitable verse. Making my way to the city, I found that my friend the tailor had been, as the saying is, on coals of fire at my absence. In his anxiety, he called to me: 'When you did not come yesterday, my heart lay awake all night because of you. I feared that a savage beast or other mischance had destroyed you in the forest. Praise be to Allâh that you are safe!' Thanking him and sitting down in my accustomed corner, I began to brood on what had happened and to curse myself for the unlucky kick that I had given the alcove. All of a sudden my good friend the tailor came to me, saying: 'There is a man at the shop door, a Persian, who has your axe and your sandals and is asking for you. He has been going round all the woodcutters in the street, saying that he found them in the road when he went out to pray at dawn at the call of the muezzin. Some of the woodcutters recognised them and directed the Persian to come here. He is outside the door; go and thank him for his trouble, and take your sandals and your axe again.' I paled and nearly fainted at his words and, while I stayed prostrate where I was, the ground in front of my corner opened and the Persian leapt from it, showing himself to be the Ifrît.

You must know that he had put the young woman to terrible tortures without getting her to admit anything, and so, taking up my axe and sandals, had said: 'I will show you that I am indeed Jurjīs of the true seed of the Evil One. You shall see whether or no I can find the owner of these things.' And, as I have told you, he tracked me among the woodcutters by a trick.

Swiftly he came to me, swiftly lifted me, and flew with me high into the air. When I had lost consciousness, he plunged with me down through the earth to the palace where I had tasted so much lustful bliss. When I saw the girl, naked and with blood flowing from her flanks, I wept bitterly. But the Ifrīt, going to her and seizing her arm, said: 'Here is your lover, you licentious bitch.' The girl looked me straight in the face, saying: 'I do not know him; I have never seen him before.' 'What,' shrieked the Ifrīt, 'here is the very body that you sinned with and you deny it!' But she continued, saying: 'I do not know him. I have never seen him in my life, nor would it be right for me to lie in the face of God.' 'If that is so,' said the Ifrīt, 'take this sword and cut off his head.' She took the sword and stopped before me. Yellow with fear and weeping copiously, I signed to her with my eyebrows to spare me. She winked at me, saying at the same time in a loud voice: 'You are the cause of all our troubles.' I signed to her again with my eyebrows, at the same time reciting these ordinary lines, whose inner significance the Ifrīt could not understand:

> I could not say I had a secret for your ears,
>   But my eyes said so.
> I could not say that you had caused my tears,
>   But my eyes said so.
> I could not say my fingers mean I love you,
> I could not say my brows are meant to move you,
> I could not say my heart is here to prove you,
>   But my eyes said so.

The poor girl understood my signs and my verses, and therefore threw the sword at the feet of the Ifrīt, who picked it up and handed it to me. 'Cut off her head,' he said, 'and you shall depart free and unharmed.' 'Certainly,' I answered, grasping the sword, stepping forward and raising my arm; but she said with her brows: 'Did I betray you?' So I wept and threw away the sword, saying to the Ifrīt: 'Great Jinnī, robust unconquerable hero, if she, who being a woman has neither faith nor reason, found it unlawful to cut off my head and threw away the sword, how can I, who am a man, find it lawful to cut off her head, especially as I have never seen her before? Even if you make me drink the bitterest cup of death I shall not do so.' 'Ah, now I know that there is love between you,' said the Ifrīt.

Then, mistress, that devil cut off both the hands and both the feet of the poor girl with four strokes of the sword, so that I thought I should die of grief at the sight.

But even so she looked at me sideways and winked at me and, alas, the Ifrīt saw the wink. 'O harlot's daughter,' he cried, 'would you commit adultery with your eyes?' So saying, he cut off her head with the sword and, turning to me, addressed me in these words: 'Learn, O human, that among us Jinn it is allowed, and even praiseworthy, to kill an adulteress. I bore away this girl on her wedding night, when she was but twelve years old and still unknown of man. I brought her here and visited her every tenth day, coupling with her in the form of a Persian. Finding her unfaithful, I have killed her. For she was unfaithful, even if it was only with her eye. As for you, since I am not sure that you have fornicated with her, I will not kill you. But, so that you may not laugh at me behind my back, I shall inflict some evil upon you to bring down your pride. Now choose what evil you would prefer.'

Naturally, good lady, I rejoiced to the utmost when I saw that I should escape with my life, and this encouraged me to take advantage of the Ifrīt's clemency. Therefore I said: 'I find it very hard to choose one out of all the evils that there are. I think I would prefer none.'

The Ifrīt stamped in vexation and said: 'I told you to choose; choose quickly, then, into what form I shall change you. What, an ass, a dog, a mule, a crow, an ape?' I answered still facetiously, hoping for pardon: 'As Allāh lives, master Jurjīs of the great tribe of the Evil One, if you spare me Allāh will spare you. Well He knows how to reward one who pardons a good Moslem that has done no harm.' I went on praying and humbling myself in vain, until he cut me short, saying: 'No more words, or I shall kill you. Do not try to take advantage of my goodness, for I am fully determined to bewitch you in some way.'

Straightway he caught me up, broke all the palace and the earth about us, and flew so high with me up into the air that the earth appeared below me in the likeness of a little dish of water. At last he set me down on the top of a high mountain, and, taking a handful of earth, mumbled some words over it; then he muttered: 'Hum, hum, hum,' and threw it over me, crying: 'Come out of that shape and be an ape!' On the instant I became an ape, at least a hundred years old and as foul-faced as hell itself. Seeing myself in this form, I jumped about in grief and found myself capable of prodigious leaps. But these did me no good, so I sat down and wept; whereat the Ifrīt laughed in a terrible fashion and disappeared.

After I had remained there for some time, thinking on the injustice of fate and how it regards not any man, I leapt and gambolled from the top of the mountain to its base; then I set out, walking by day and sleeping by night in the trees, until after a month I came to the beach of the salt sea. I had rested there for an hour when I saw a ship coming up with a favourable breeze out of the sea. I hid behind a rock and waited. After there had been much coming and going among the men, I screwed up my courage and leapt into the ship. 'Chase the ill-omened beast out of that!' cried one of the men. 'No, kill it!' cried another. 'Yes, kill it with a sword!' cried out a third. At this I caught the sword with my paw and burst into bitter tears.

Because of my tears the captain had pity on me and said to those about him: 'This ape has asked for my protection and I give it him. Let no one take hold of him or chase him or interfere with him.' Then he called me to him and spoke kind words to me, all of which I understood; finally he made me his servant on the boat, and in this duty I did everything correctly for him throughout the voyage.

Favouring winds carried us, after fifty days, to a city so great and so populous that Allāh alone could count the people of it. As we cast anchor, certain officers of the King of that place came and welcomed the merchants we had aboard and gave them, with the kind greetings of the King, a roll of parchment on which each man was commanded to inscribe a line in his fairest writing. For the King's wazīr, a great calligraphist, had died and the King had sworn to appoint no one in his place who could not write as well as he.

Ape that I was, I snatched the parchment from their hands and fled away with it, so that they were afraid that I would tear it and throw it into the water. Some were trying to coax me and some to kill me, when I made a sign that I wished to write. Then said the captain: 'Let him write. If he only scribbles and messes we can stop him, but if he writes with a fair writing I shall adopt him as my son, for never in my life have I seen an ape so learned.'

I took the reed pen and, pressing it upon the pad of the inkpot, carefully spread ink on both its faces, and began to write.

I improvised four stanzas, each in a different character and style: the first in rikāī.

> The Giver has been sung since time was new
> But Givers with a hand like yours are few,
>> So first and foremost we will look to God
> And when He fails us we will look to You.

The second in raihānī:

> I'll tell you of this Pen. It is of those
> Pens that are mightier than cedar bows,
>> He holds it in five fingers of his hand
> And from it pour five rivers of pure Prose.

The third in thuluthī:

> I'll tell you of his Immortality.
> He is so certain of eternity,
>> It is his aim to write such things of Him
> As that last Critic shall not blush to see.

And the fourth in muhakkak:

> Ink is the strongest drug that God has made,
> If you can write of beauty unafraid
>> You will be praising Him who gave the ink
> More than all prayers unlearned men have prayed.

When I had finished writing, I handed back the parchment and each of the others, marvelling at what I had done, also wrote a line in the fairest script that he could compass.

Slaves bore the parchment back to the King and of all the writings he was only satisfied with mine, inscribed as they were in four different styles for which, when I had been a prince, I had been famed throughout the whole world.

So the King said to his friends and to his slaves: 'Go all of you to this master of fair writing, give him this robe of honour to put on, mount him on the most magnificent of my mules, and bring him to me in a triumph of musical instruments.'

They all smiled when he said this, so the King became angry and cried: 'How is this? I give you an order and you laugh at me?'

'King of all time,' they answered, 'we would never dare to laugh at any word you said, but we must tell you that the writer of these splendid characters is no man at all but an ape belonging to a ship's captain.' The King was first astonished at their words and then convulsed with spacious laughter. 'I shall buy that ape,' he said, and he ordered all the people of his court to go down to the boat and fetch the ape ashore, taking with them both the mule and the robe of honour. 'Yes, yes,' he added, 'certainly you must clothe him in this robe and bring him to me mounted on the mule.'

All of them came down straightway to the boat and bought me at a great price from the captain, who found it hard to let me go. Then they dressed me in the robe of honour, after I had signed to the captain all my grief at leaving him, set me upon the mule, and conducted me through the city to the noise of harmonious instruments. You may imagine that every soul in those streets was stricken with wonder and admiration at such an unusual sight.

When I was brought before the King, I kissed the earth between his hands three times and stood still in front of him. He invited me to sit down and I did so with such grace that all who were there, but especially the King, marvelled at my fine education and the politeness of my behaviour. When I was seated, the King sent all away except his chief eunuch, a certain young favourite slave, and myself.

Then, to my delight, he ordered food, and slaves brought a cloth laid with all such meats and delicacies as the soul could possibly desire. The King signed to me to eat. So, after rising and kissing the earth between his hands according to seven different schools of politeness, I sat down again in my best manner and began to eat, diligently recalling the education of my youth at every point.

Finally, when the cloth was drawn, I rose, washed my hands and, returning to the King, took up an inkpot, a reed and a sheet of parchment. On the last I inscribed these few lines, celebrating the excellence of Arabian pastries:

Sweet fine pastries
Rolled between white fingers,
Fried things whose fat scent lingers
On him who in his haste tries
To eat enough!
Pastries, my love!

> Kunāfah swimming in butter,
> Bearded with right vermicelli,
> God has not given my belly
> Half of the words it would utter
> Of kunāfah's sweetness
> And syrup'd completeness.
>
> Kunāfah lies on the table
> Isled in a sweet brown oil,
> Would I not wander and toil
> Seventy years to be able
> To eat in Paradise
> Kunāfah's subtleties?

Finishing, I put down the reed and the sheet and, while the King looked in astonishment at what I had written, sat respectfully at a distance. 'But how can an ape compass such a thing?' asked the King. 'As Allāh lives, it surpasses all the marvels of history.'

Just then they brought the King his chess board, and, when he had asked me by signs if I played and I had nodded my head to show him that I did, I arranged the pieces and we settled down to play. Twice I beat him, and he did not know what to think of it, saying: 'If this was a man, he would be the wisest man of all our time.' And to his eunuch he continued: 'Go to our daughter and tell her to come quickly to us, for I wish your mistress to enjoy the sight of this remarkable ape.'

The eunuch went out and soon returned with the princess, his young mistress, who as soon as she set eyes on me covered her face with her veil, saying: 'Father, what has possessed you to send for me into the presence and sight of a strange man?' 'Daughter,' answered the King, 'here are only my young slave who is still a little boy, the eunuch who brought you up, this ape, and your father. Why do you cover your face?' Then she said: 'Know, my father, that this ape is a prince, his father is the King Ifitamarus, ruler of a land far in the interior. The ape is bewitched by the Ifrīt Jurjīs, of the line of Iblīs, who has also killed his own wife, daughter of King Ifītāmūs, master of the Isle of Ebony. This which you think an ape is not only a man, but a learned, wise, and educated man as well.'

'Is it true, what my daughter says of you?' asked the King, looking at me fixedly in his astonishment. I nodded and began to weep; so the king, turning to his daughter, asked her how she knew that I was bewitched. 'Father,' she answered, 'when I was little there was an old woman in my mother's house, a sorceress knowing all the shifts and formulas of witchcraft, who taught me magic. Since then I have studied even more deeply and now know nearly a hundred and seventy codes of necromancy, by the least of which I could remove your palace, with all its stones, even the whole city itself, to the other side of Mount Kāf and turn your country to a sheet of water in which the people should swim in the form of fishes.'

'Then by the truth of the name of Allāh,' cried the King, 'take off the witchcraft from this poor young man and I will make him my wazīr. It is strange indeed that you should have such art and I did not know it. Take off the witchcraft quickly, for he is both polite and wise.'

'With all my heart and as in duty bound,' answered the princess.

At this point Shahrazād saw the approach of morning and discreetly fell silent.

But when the fourteenth night had come

SHE SAID:

It is related, O auspicious King, that the second kalandar thus continued his say to the mistress of the house:

The princess took in her hands a knife on which were graved words in the Hebrew tongue and with it traced a circle in the middle of the palace which she filled with names of power and talismanic lines. This preparation completed, she stood in the middle of the circle murmuring words of magic import and reading from a book so old that none might understand it. After a few minutes of this, the palace became dark with shadows, so thick that we thought to be buried alive under the ruins of the world. Suddenly the Ifrīt Jurjīs stood before us in his most frightful and repellent guise, with hands like hayforks, legs like masts, and eyes like crucibles of fire. We were all driven to the confines of terror except the princess, who said: 'I have no welcome for you, I have no greeting.' Then said the Ifrīt: 'How can you break your word, O traitress? Did we not swear together that neither would use power against the other, nor interfere with the other's doings? Perfidious one, well have you deserved the fate which is about to overtake you—thus!' On the instant he turned into a savage lion which opened wide its throat and hurled itself upon the princess. But as quick as light she plucked a

hair from her head and whispered magic words to it, so that it became a sharp sword, with which she cut the lion in two. Then we
saw the lion's head become a scorpion which scuttled towards the
young girl's heel to bite it, but in the nick of time she changed to a
mighty serpent which threw itself upon the naughty scorpion and
battled with it for a long while. The scorpion, escaping, turned
into a vulture, and the snake became an eagle, which flew at the
vulture and put it to flight. The pursuit lasted for an hour, until the
vulture became a black cat and the girl turned suddenly to a wolf.
Long and long in the middle of the palace the cat and the wolf were
locked in deadly strife, till the cat, seeing that it was being vanquished, turned into a very large red pomegranate, which leapt into
the basin of the fountain in the courtyard. The wolf jumped in after
it and was about to seize it when the pomegranate rose up into the
air. But it was too heavy to be sustained there, and so fell with a
thump on to the marble and broke in pieces, the seeds of it escaping
one by one and covering the whole floor of the courtyard. On this
the wolf changed to a cock who pecked at the seeds and swallowed
them one by one, till only a single seed remained. Just as the cock
was about to swallow this last one, it fell from his beak—in this you
may perceive the hand of Destiny and the will of Fate—and lodged
in a crack of the marble near the basin, so that the cock could not
find it. Thereupon the cock crowed, beat his wings, and signed to
us with his beak; but we did not understand what he would say to
us. At last he gave so terrible a cry that we, who could not understand what he wished, thought that the palace was falling about us.
Round and round, in the middle of the courtyard, trotted the cock
until it found the last seed in the crack near the basin. But, when the
cock had fetched it out and was about to eat it, the seed fell into the
water and became a fish which swam to the bottom. So the cock
turned to a whale of prodigious size which leapt into the water and
sank in pursuit of the fish, so that we did not see it again for a whole
hour. At the end of this time we heard agonised cries coming from
the water and trembled for fear. Out of the basin appeared the Ifrīt
in his own form, but all on fire, as if he were a burning coal, with
smoke leaping from his eyes and mouth and nose. Behind him appeared the princess in her own form, but she also was all on fire as
if she were made of molten metal; and she ran after the Ifrīt who was
now bearing down on us. We were all terrified of being burnt alive
and were on the point of throwing ourselves into the water, when

the Ifrīt halted us with a terrible cry and leaping upon us, in the midst of the hall which gave upon the courtyard, blew fire in our faces. But the princess caught up with him and blew fire in his face, so that flames fell on us from both of them. Those coming from her were harmless to us, but a spark, shooting off from him, destroyed my left eye for ever, another burnt all the lower part of the King's face, his beard and his mouth, making his lower teeth fall out, while a third, falling upon the eunuch's breast, burnt him to death upon the instant.

All this time the young girl was pursuing the Ifrīt and blowing fire at him. Suddenly we heard a voice calling: 'Only Allāh is great! Only Allāh is strong! He breaks and destroys the renegade who denies Muhammad, master of the world!' It was the princess who spoke, pointing at the same time to the Ifrīt who had been reduced to a mass of cinders. Coming to us, the princess said: 'Quick, fetch me a glass of water!' When this was brought, she chanted certain incomprehensible words over it, and sprinkled me with water, saying: 'Be freed, in the name and by the truth of the only Truth! Yea, by the truth of the name of Almighty Allāh, return to your first shape!'

On this I became a man as I had been before, except that I was still blind of one eye. 'Poor youth,' said the princess by way of consolation, 'fire will be fire.' She said the same also to her father on account of his burnt beard and lost teeth, and finally she said: 'Father, I must die; for it is written. Had the Ifrīt been but a man I could have killed him at the first attempt. It was the spilling of the pomegranate seed that was my undoing, for the grain I could not eat was that which held the whole soul of the Jinnī. If only I could have found it he would have been dead upon the instant, but, alas, I could not. It was written. So I was obliged to fight terrible battles below the earth and in the air and under the water, and each time he opened a door of safety I opened a door of danger, until at last he opened the terrible door of fire. When that door is opened there is death toward. Fate allowed me to burn him before I was burnt myself. Before I killed him I tried to make him embrace our Faith, the blessed Law of Islām; but he would not and I burnt him. Now I die. May Allāh fill my place for you.'

After this she wrestled with the fire till black sparks sprang up and mounted to her breast and to her face. When they reached her face, she cried out weeping: 'I bear witness that there is no God but

Allāh! I bear witness that Muhammad is His messenger!' and fell, a heap of cinders, by the side of the Ifrīt.

We mourned for her, and I wished that I could have died in her place rather than see her radiant form go down in ashes, this little princess who had freed me; but the word of Allāh may not be gainsaid.

When the King saw his daughter fall down in cinders, he tore away the little remnant of his beard, beat his cheeks, and rent his garments. I did the same and we both wept over her, until the chamberlains and the chief men of the court came and found their Sultān fainting and weeping beside two piles of ashes. For an hour, in great stupefaction, they walked round and round the King not daring to speak, until at last he recovered himself a little and told them all that had happened to his daughter. Then they cried: 'Allāh, Allāh, the great grief! The great calamity!'

Lastly came the women and the women slaves, who mourned for seven days and lamented over her in due form.

When the week was past, the King ordered a mighty tomb to be built over the ashes of his child, and this was done by forced labour at the same hour, and candles and lanterns were lighted by it both day and night. But the ashes of the Ifrīt were committed to the air, under the curse of Allāh.

Worn out by these griefs and duties, the Sultān fell into a sickness which looked to be mortal and lasted for a whole month. When his strength had come back to him a little, he called me to him and said: 'Young man, before you came we lived here in eternal happiness, safe harboured from the assaults of fortune, but with your coming came also the bitterest of all afflictions. Would we had never seen your ill-omened face, your face which brought down desolation on us. First, you have caused the death of my daughter whose life was worth the lives of a hundred men; second, you were the reason of my being burnt and of the loss and spoiling of my teeth; third, through you my poor eunuch, that faithful servant who had reared my daughter, was killed outright. And yet it is not your fault, nor is the remedy yours; what came to us and to you, came from Allāh. Praise be to Him, then, who allowed my daughter to free you even at the price of her own life. Yes, it is Destiny, it is Destiny. Leave our country, my child, for we have suffered enough because of you. Yet it was all written before by Allāh, so go your way in peace.'

Mistress, I went out from before the King, hardly believing that I was still alive and not knowing at all where to go. In my heart I pondered all that had happened to me from beginning to end: how I had escaped safe from the desert robbers, how I had entered as a stranger into a city and met the tailor there, my sweet amour with the young girl below the earth, my deliverance from the hands of the Ifrīt, my life as an ape, servant to a ship's captain, my purchase at a great price by the King because of my excellent handwriting, my freeing from the spell, and, last and most piteous, the adventure that had lost me my eye. Nevertheless I thanked Allāh, saying: 'Better an eye than a life,' and went down to the hammām to bathe before leaving the city. It was there, my lady, that I shaved my beard so that I might travel in safety in the guise of a kalandar. Each day since then I have not ceased to weep and think of my wrongs, especially the loss of my left eye, and so thinking I have felt my right eye blinded by tears so that I could not see, and have not been able to resist saying over the following stanzas of the poet:

> It was only after the blow
> I knew my sorrow could hurt me so,
> How then could Allāh know?

> I will abide those whips of His
> That the world may know iniquities
> More bitter than patience is.

> Patience has beauty, I've understood,
> When it is practised by one of the Good;
> But Fate is a thing more rude.

> For Fate was probably setting a snare
> When you were born, wherever you were,
> To take your old feet there.

> She knew the secrets of my bed
> And more than so, but she lay dead,
> The Jinnī cut off her head.

> To him who prates of joy down here
> Say: soon you'll taste a day bitter
> As the quick sap of the myrrh.

I left that city and journeyed through many lands, aiming ever for Baghdād, the city of Peace, where I hoped to tell all my tale to the Prince of Believers. To-night I reached Baghdād after many long and weary days. By chance I met this other kalandar, and while we were talking together we were joined by our third companion, also a kalandar. Recognising each other as strangers, we wended our way in the darkness together till the kind hand of Destiny led us to your house, my mistress.

That is the story of my shaved beard and lost eye.

When she had heard the tale of the second kalandar, the mistress of the house said to him: 'Your tale is truly strange; make your bow and depart with all speed.'

But he answered: 'Indeed, I shall not stir from here until I have heard the tale of my third companion.'

So the third kalandar advanced and said:

Tale of the Third Kalandar

GLORIOUS lady, do not think that my tale will be as marvellous as those of my two companions, for it is infinitely more so!

Upon these other two, misfortunes fell solely through the workings of Destiny and Fate; but with me it was not so. The reason of my shaved beard and my lost eye lies in myself, who, through my own fault, was led to the end of fatality and filled to the overflowing of my heart with cares and disappointments.

I am a king and the son of a king. When my father whose name was Kasīb died, I inherited his throne and reigned with justice and to the advantage of my people.

But I had a great love of seafaring which I was able to indulge since my city lay by the sea and many fortified islands in the ocean were under my protection. Wishing one day to visit all my islands, I prepared ten great ships and, victualling them for a month, set sail. My voyage of inspection lasted for twenty days, at the end of which time contrary winds were unloosed against us, blowing throughout the night until the morning. At sunrise, when the wind fell and the sea became calm, we saw a little island, and there we landed and ate and rested for two days. When the tempest was quite abated, we set sail again and voyaged for another twenty days, until we lost our way in unknown waters, strange even to the captain. When he confessed that he did not know that sea at all, we sent a lookout man to the mast-head, who returned, saying to the captain: 'On my right I saw fishes swimming upon the surface of the sea, and in the middle of the sea I could distinguish far off a thing which showed black and white by turns.' The captain seemed thunderstruck by these words of the lookout; he threw his turban on the deck and snatched at his beard, crying: 'Here is death for all! Not one of us will come out alive!' Seeing him weeping, we also wept for ourselves and I asked him to explain his words and those of the lookout man. Then said the captain: 'My lord, for eleven days we have been lost and there is no favouring wind that may bear us back into our course. The appearance of that black and white object and of the fish means that to-morrow we will come to an isle of black rocks called the Magnetic Mountain, against which the force of the water will dash us and destroy our ship. All her nails will fly from her and cleave to the sides of the Magnetic Mountain, for Allāh has made it so that it draws all things of iron to itself. He alone knows what mass of iron things are clinging to those rocks. On the top of the mountain there is a dome of brass lifted on ten columns, and upon this dome stands a rider mounted upon a brazen horse, with a brazen spear in his hand and a plate of graven lead upon his breast bearing unknown and talismanic names. Know, O King, that so long as that rider stays upon his horse all ships which pass below shall be broken to pieces, their sailors drowned, and all their nails and ironwork drawn to the mountain. Until that rider is thrown from his horse there can be no safety.' After telling me this the captain burst into tears, and we, having resigned ourselves to death, said our farewells to each other.

Hardly had morning come when, as he had said, we reached the mountain of black magnetic rocks; the waves drove us alongside, and all the thousands of nails on our ten ships were suddenly wrenched away and flew to join themselves to the mountain. The ships opened out and fell asunder, and we were thrown into the sea.

All day we floated at the mercy of the waves; most of us were drowned and the few survivors never met again, for the billows and terrible winds dispersed them in every direction.

But Allāh, Who is Almighty, preserved me, Madam, for greater evils and for greater pain. I clung to a plank and the waves threw me ashore at the foot of the Magnetic Mountain.

I found a path leading upwards, made of steps hewn in the rock; so I called on the name of Almighty Allāh and . . .

At this point Shahrazād saw the approach of morning and discreetly fell silent.

And when the fifteenth night had come

SHE SAID:

It is related, O auspicious King, that while his companions sat round with folded arms, brooded over by the seven negroes with drawn swords, the third kalandar thus continued his tale to the young mistress of the house:

I called on the name of Almighty Allāh and prayed to him with very great fervour; therefore He stayed the wind and I was able to climb by juts and clefts to the top of the mountain. Here I rejoiced at my deliverance and, reaching the brass dome, knelt down and gave thanks to Him.

Broken by fatigue, I fell where I was upon the earth and slept, and in my sleep I heard a voice saying to me: 'When you wake, O son of Kasīb, dig beneath your feet and you will find a brazen bow and three leaden arrows carved with talismans. Take the bow and shoot the rider who is above this dome; so shall you deliver the world from a great scourge. When you have shot the rider, he will fall from his horse into the sea and the bow will fall from your hand upon the earth. Bury it where it has fallen and straightway the sea will begin to boil and rise up to this summit where you are. When this happens, you will see a boat coming from the ocean with a man in it who shall be like the rider, and yet not he. He will be carrying sculls in his hand, and it will be safe for you to get into the boat with him if you do not name the sacred name of Allāh. This you must not do at any price. Once in the boat, that man will row you for ten days until you come to the sea of Safety, where you will find one to convey you to your own country; but remember that none of this can happen unless you abstain from naming the Holy Name.'

So I woke and did as I had been told in my dream. With the bow and arrows that I found I shot the rider and he fell into the sea. I buried the bow where it had dropped, and at once the sea began to boil and rose up to the top of the mountain. In a few moments I saw a boat coming to me out of the sea, at the sight of which I secretly thanked Allāh. In it was a man of brass bearing on his breast a plate of lead graven with names and talismans. Without a word I climbed aboard, and the man of brass rowed me for one, for two, for three, for ten whole days until, in the evening, islands appeared that were to be my safety. I rejoiced with the extreme of joy and, in the fulness of my gratitude to the Most High, I named and glorified the name of

Allāh, saying: 'In the name of Allāh! There is no God but Allāh!'
Hardly had I breathed the sacred words than the man of brass caught
hold of me and threw me into the sea, himself making off swiftly in
the boat. I was a good swimmer and so kept myself afloat all day
until nightfall, when, my arms and shoulders being dead and weary,
I made my peace with Allāh and prepared to die. But a wave higher
than all the waves of the sea ran up beneath me like a mighty mosque
and threw me far on to the shore of one of the islands which I had
seen. Thus Allāh's will was done.

I climbed up the beach and, spreading my clothes to dry upon the
sand, slept by them all night. When I awoke, I put on my dry garments and, looking about me, beheld a little fertile valley. Wandering round and throughout this place, I found that I was on the
smallest of islets lying alone in the sea. I was sitting, buried in sad
reflections, saying to myself: 'Never am I delivered from one misfortune but I fall into a greater!' and wishing earnestly for death,
when I saw a ship beating up towards the island. Fearing that there
might still be some unpleasant fate awaiting me, I climbed into a
tree and, sitting hidden among the leaves, saw the ship anchor and
ten slaves come out of her, each carrying a spade. They walked to the
middle of the island and dug there until they had discovered a trap-
door, which they opened. Then they returned to the ship and took
out of her a great quantity of things which they loaded on their
shoulders: bread and corn, honey and butter, sheep and bursting
sacks, even down to the least thing which a master of a house might
require. They kept on coming and going from the ship to the trap-
door and back again, until all the heavy things had been transported.
Afterwards they brought out beautiful robes and exquisitely tailored
garments which they carried on their arms, and, this time, I saw
walking among the slaves a venerable old man all eaten up by time,
so that he might no longer be called a man at all. He led by the hand
a boy of surprising beauty, cast from that very mould in which
Allāh had made perfection; his beauty was at once amorous and
pure, his body being as slender and as pliant as a young green
branch, so that he bewitched the heart out of my bosom and made
all the texture of my flesh tremble in love. They all descended by
the trap-door, but returned in a few minutes without the boy and,
going down to the ship, set sail and left the shore.

When they were out of sight, I came down from my tree and ran
to the place where they had heaped the earth over the trap-door.

I dug the earth away again and, though the trap which I discovered was as great and heavy as a millstone, by Allāh's grace I lifted it, and, descending a vaulted stone stair which I saw below, came at last to the bottom. Walking forward I found a great hall, richly-carpeted and hung with silks and velvets, and on a low couch, between lighted candles, flower vases, and pots of fruits and sweetmeats, I saw the boy sitting and fanning himself with a costly fan. He was terrified at the sight of me, but I wished him peace and, when he had answered me, said: 'Have no fear, my lord, I am a man, a king's son, and a king myself. Allāh has guided me here to free you from this sunless place where they have left you to die. I will deliver you and you shall be my friend, for but by looking at you I have lost my head.'

The boy smiled at me with those sweet lips of his and invited me to sit down beside him on the couch, saying: 'My lord, I have not been left in this place to die, but to avoid death. You must know that I am the son of a jeweller, famed throughout all the world for the amount and quality of his riches, his name having gone out into all lands, borne by the caravans he sends afar to sell jewels to the kings and princes of the earth. Though I was born late in his life, my father was warned by the masters of prophecy that I should die before either of my parents, so that, in spite of his joy at my birth and the great happiness of my mother who, by the grace of God, had brought me into the world at the full end of her nine months, he grieved bitterly on my account. And the more so did he do this when the sages who read my destiny in the stars told him that I would be killed by a king, son of a king named Kasīb, forty days after he had cast the brass rider of the Magnetic Mountain into the sea. Because of his forebodings my father, the jeweller, tended me carefully at home until I was fifteen years of age. When he heard that the rider had been thrown into the sea, he wept so sorely (and my mother with him) that his colour failed him, his body pined, and he became suddenly a very old man broken by years and by sorrows. Then it was that he fetched me to this subterranean place, which he had made ready since my birth, to hide me from the king who was to kill me after he had thrown down the brass rider. Both my father and I were certain that the son of Kasīb could not find me on this unknown island. That is the reason of my staying here.'

Then I thought in my heart: 'What liars are these men who read the stars, for by Allāh I would rather kill myself than kill this boy who has become, as it were, a flame about my heart.' Aloud I said:

'My child, the Almighty would never allow a flower like you to be cut down. I will defend you and stay with you here all my life.' Then said he: 'My father will be coming at the end of the fortieth day to take me away, for after that there will be no more danger.' 'Then, dear youth,' I answered, 'I will stay with you for the forty days and afterwards ask your father to let you come with me to my kingdom to be my friend and heir.'

The jeweller's son thanked me with gentle words, and I rejoiced at his air of breeding and at the love which had sprung up between us. We talked for a long while and ate of all those delicacies and provisions, which were enough to last a hundred guests for a year. Afterwards I proved the greatness of my love for his charms, and then we lay down and slept all night. Rising at dawn, I washed and carried the boy a copper basin filled with perfumed water, in which he made his ablutions. I prepared food and we ate together, passed the day in talk and laughter and games until the evening and then, when night fell, spread the cloth. We feasted on mutton stuffed with almonds, dried grapes and muscat nuts, cloves and pepper; we drank fair fresh water and ate both water-melons and melons, with cakes of butter and honey, pastries sweet and light as the hair of a girl, in which neither butter nor honey, almonds nor cinnamon were lacking. Then, as on the night before, we lay down together and I proved how great our friendship had become. So we stayed in alternate pleasure and rest until the fortieth day.

Now when that day came on which we expected the jeweller, the boy wished to take a full bath; so I warmed water for him in a great cauldron heated over a wood fire and poured it into a large copper bath. I added cool water until the heat was pleasant and, when the boy got in, I washed him myself, rubbing, kneading, and perfuming him, and finally carrying him back to the bed where I covered him with a quilt, swathed his head in silver-embroidered silks, and gave him a delicate sherbert to drink.

When he rose from a peaceful sleep, he wished to eat, so I chose the finest and largest of the water-melons, putting it on a plate by his side, and climbed on the bed to reach a large knife which was hung on the wall above his head. But the boy began to tickle my leg in sport and I felt his tickling so much that I fell forward on top of him, the knife being driven right through his heart. There and then he died under my hand.

Mistress, you can imagine how I beat my face, weeping and groaning and tearing my garments, and throwing myself upon the earth in floods of tears; but my friend was dead, his destiny was accomplished to prove that the astrologers had not lied. I lifted my eyes and hands to heaven, crying: 'Master of the world, if this is my crime I am ready for punishment.' I was full of courage to face my death; but whether one asks a good thing or a bad it is never granted.

Not being able to bear the sight of the place any more and knowing also that the jeweller would be coming at the end of the day, I climbed the stairs, shut the trap, and covered it over with earth as before.

Now that I was out in the free air, I said to myself: 'It is quite necessary that I see what happens, but at the same time I must hide or be put to the worst of deaths by the ten slaves.' So I climbed into a great tree near the trap and waited, hiding myself in the leaves. An hour afterwards the same ship came in from the sea, and the old man with his slaves landed and hastened inshore until they came beneath my tree. Seeing that the earth had been freshly moved they were suddenly stricken with fear; the old man looked as if he had lost his wits, but the slaves feverishly cleared the earth away, and all went down through the trap. I heard the old man calling his son by name in a high voice, but the boy did not answer and, when they looked for him, lo! he was dead upon the bed, pierced to the heart with a knife.

At this terrible sight the old man fainted away, and the slaves, sobbing and sighing, bore him on their shoulders up the stairs, and went back for the dead boy whom they wrapped in a winding-sheet and buried in the earth. Lastly, they carried the old man and all the provisions and riches that were left in the hall down to the ship, and sailed away until they were out of sight.

I climbed from my tree and walked round and round the little island all that day and the next night, companioned only by my tears and the desolation of my heart. In a few days I saw that the sea was falling hour by hour, leaving dry sand between the isle and the mainland. I thanked Allāh that he had at last delivered me from that ill-omened island and, crossing over the sand, came to the opposite coast and climbed up on to firm ground. I wandered till sunset, invoking His name, and suddenly saw afar off a great red fire towards which I made my way, thinking that there must be men there cooking a sheep. But when I drew near I saw that the red fire was really the sun at his setting shining on a mighty palace all of brass.

I was astonished to see so great a palace of brass and was admiring the great strength of its construction when ten young men came out of its gate. They were all of surpassing beauty both of face and form, but, marvellous to relate, each was blind of his left eye; a tall and venerable old man, who walked with them, alone had two.

As I was considering the coincidence of all these lost left eyes, the ten young men came up and greeted me and I, greeting them likewise, told them all my adventure. But, since you know it, it would be useless to tell it to you a second time, my mistress.

When they had ceased marvelling at my tale, they bade me a spacious welcome to their palace. We entered it, crossing many halls with costly hangings, and came at last to the central court which was greater and more beautiful than any of the halls. In its midst were ten carpets spread on mattresses, and an eleventh carpet without a mattress lay between them. On this the old man sat down, while the young men stretched themselves on their couches, saying to me: 'My lord, be seated higher up the hall and ask no question, we pray you, on anything you may see pass.'

After he had rested a little, the old man rose and, moving backwards and forwards, brought meat and drink to the ten and to me. When we had finished eating and drinking, he cleared away the remains and was about to seat himself again when the youths cried out: 'Why do you seat yourself before bringing us the things necessary for our vows?' The old man left the court without speaking and in ten journeys brought back as many basins covered over with satin and as many little lanterns. These he set beside the young men, but for me he brought nothing. When each had lifted the stuff which covered his basin I saw with surprise that they contained ashes, lampblack, and kohl, with which the young men, weeping and wailing and crying: 'It was our own fault!' abased themselves. They sprinkled the ashes on their heads, rubbed the lampblack on their faces, and smeared their right eyes with the kohl. At dawn, after washing in other basins which the old man brought them, they changed their clothes and became as they had been the day before.

Though I almost died with astonishment at what I had seen, I dared ask no question either then or on the next three nights when the same performance was repeated. But at last I could contain myself no longer and called out to them: 'My lords, I would rather die than not hear the cause of the loss of your eyes and the reason of what you do with the ashes, the lampblack, and the kohl.' 'Why do you ask that, unhappy man?' they answered. 'You are lost, you are lost!' Then said I: 'I would rather be lost than endure this curiosity.' 'Beware for your left eye!' they said, and I answered: 'What use is my left eye to me if I have to live all my life in curiosity?' 'On your own head be it then,' they said. 'What has happened to us will happen to you and it will be your own fault. Also, when you have lost your left eye, you will not be able to come back here, for we are already ten and there is no place for an eleventh.'

While the old man brought in a live sheep, which he slew and flayed, they went on: 'You will be sewn in this sheep skin and put out on the brass terrace of our palace. Then the mighty bird, the rūkh, who can lift an elephant, will take you for a sheep, swoop down on you, and bearing you into the clouds carry you to the top of a high mountain, inaccessible to men, in order to eat you at his ease. But you must slit the skin with a knife that we shall give you and come out of it, for the terrible rūkh does not eat humans: therefore when he sees you he will fly away. You must walk from that place till you come to a palace ten times larger than ours and a thousand times more lovely. It is plated with plates of gold and all its walls are crested with emeralds and pearls. Enter by the open door, as each of us has entered, and you shall see what you shall see. All of us have lost our left eyes and now spend each night in expiation. That is the chief point of all our stories; were they told in detail they would fill the pages of a great folio. Be it on your own head.'

Seeing that I was fixed in my intention, they gave me the knife, sewed me up in the sheep's skin, and laid me on the terrace. Suddenly I was snatched up by that terrible bird, the rūkh, who flew away with me and set me down on the top of a mountain. I ripped the skin up with my knife and jumped out, crying: 'Kash, kash!' to frighten the rūkh. As it flew heavily away, I saw that it had the appearance of a great white bird as broad as ten elephants and as tall as twenty camels.

I lost no time in setting out and, walking in a fever of impatience, came at noon to the palace of which I had been told. In spite of the description given of it by the ten young men I had not looked for a hundredth part of the marvel of that palace. I went through its great gate which was all of gold, and found that there were about it ninety-nine aloe and sandal wood doors, and that the doors of all the halls of the palace were of ebony inlaid with gold and diamonds.

Each led to halls and gardens in which I caught glimpses of the massed treasures of earth and sea.

In the first hall I found myself surrounded by forty young girls, of such transcendent beauty that it was impossible to make a choice among them or to look on them without faintness.

They rose when they saw me and in the sweetest voices said: 'May our house be as your house, joyful companion; may you be as the apple of our eyes!' They set me upon a dais and, sitting below me on a rich rug, called to me: 'Dear lord, we are your slaves, your things; you are our master, and your presence is as a crown about our heads!'

One brought me water and warm linens and washed my feet; one poured perfumed water from a ewer over my hands; one robed me in a silken garment with a belt of gold and silver threads; one gave me a cup holding a delicate drink perfumed with flowers; one looked at me; one smiled at me; one winked at me; one said verses to me; one lifted her arms above her head for me to see; one twisted her body above her thighs before me; one said: 'Ah!' and another said: 'Oh!'; one said: 'Dear!' and one said: 'Sweet!'; one said: 'Darling!' and one said: 'Love!' and one said: 'Fire above my heart!'

They clustered round me, stroking and caressing me, saying: 'Tell us your story, dear companion. We have been here for many weary days without a man, but now our happiness is complete.' Managing to calm myself a little, I told them part of my tale until the approach of evening.

As the light failed they brought in so many candles that the hall was lighted as if the sun himself had come down into it. They laid cloths and served the most exquisite meats, the most exciting drinks; they played on instruments of music, sang in magic voices, and danced sensuously about me as I ate.

After the amusements they said: 'Dear one, the time has come for bed and the more solid pleasures; choose one of us and do not fear to offend any of us, for each of us forty sisters will have our turn of pleasure with you in the bed, on every fortieth night as it comes round.'

As all were so desirable, I shut my eyes and stretching out my arm seized hold of one; I opened my eyes and then shut them again quickly at the blaze of the beauty of the girl I had caught. She took my hand and led me to her bed, and I stayed with her there all night. I charged her forty times and forty times she charged me, calling at each assault: 'Yū! My darling! Yū! My soul!' First she would caress me, then I would bite her, and then she would pinch me. So the night wore away.

This was the life I led, my lady, one of the sisters being with me each night, and each night showing many assaults on both sides. Thus in passion and in rest a year slipped by, and after every night, the girl of the next night would take me in the morning to the bath, wash me, rub me, and perfume me with all the perfumes that Allāh has given to his servants.

On the morning of the last day of the year all the girls ran to my bed, weeping, dishevelling their hair, and lamenting. 'Light of our eyes,' they said, 'we must leave you as we have left others before you. For you are not the first and many a rider has ridden us before. But you are the mightiest rider of them all, having a lance both broad and long; you are the naughtiest and gentlest of them all. Truly we cannot live without you.' 'Tell me why you must leave me,' I exclaimed, 'for all the joy of my life is centred upon you!' 'We are all the daughters of a king by different mothers,' they answered. 'Since we came to development we have lived in this palace and each year Allāh has sent some rider upon our road to take joy in mounting us. But every year we have to go away for forty days to see our father and our mothers, and now the time has come.' 'Sweetest creatures,' I said, 'I will stay in the house thanking Allāh for what he has given me, until you come back.' 'Be it so!' they said. 'Here are all the keys of all the doors of the palace. It is your home, you are its master; but beware of opening the copper door at the bottom of the garden, for if you do so you will never see us again and a great evil will befall you. Beware of opening the copper door.'

One by one they clung to me weeping and saying farewell. Then all gave me a last sad look and went away.

When they had gone, I left the hall with the keys in my hand and began a tour of inspection throughout the palace. For so chained had my body and soul been to the beds of these girls that I had not had time to visit it before.

Opening the first door with the first key, I saw a garden filled with fruit trees finer than I had ever seen in all the world. They were watered with little runlets and their fruits were of immortal size and loveliness. I ate of them all, especially bananas, finger-long dates, pomegranates, apples, and peaches. When I had finished, I gave thanks to Allāh, and made my way to the second door.

opened it, and at once the senses of my eyes and nose were charmed by a multitude of flowers, filling a great garden and refreshed by little streams. All flowers that may be found in princes' gardens were there; jasmine, narcissus, rose, and violet; jacinth, anemone, carnation, and tulip, with the ranunculus and every flower of every clime. When I had smelt a jasmine and thrust it up my nose, leaving it there so that I might go on breathing its sweetness, I thanked Allāh for his goodness and went to the third door.

No sooner had I opened it than my ears were ravished with the notes of coloured birds, every kind that there is upon the earth. They were held in a vast cage made from aloe and sandal wood rods. The water for their drinking was held in little saucers, some of jade and some of delicately-tinted jasper. The seed for them to eat lay in little gold cups, the floor of the cage was sanded and sprinkled, and the birds all sang in praise of their Creator. I listened to their notes till nightfall, and then slept.

Next morning I went quickly out and opened the fourth door with the fourth key. Then, mistress, I saw things which no man ever beheld before even in a dream. In the middle of a great court I saw a pavilion with porphyry staircases, each leading up to one of forty ebony doors inlaid with gold and silver. These doors stood open, each showing a spacious hall within, holding a different treasure worth more than all the value of my kingdom. The first held ordered mounds of great and little pearls; the great were the more in number, and each as large as a dove's egg and shining like the moon at her full. The second hall was richer than the first, being filled to the roof with diamonds, red rubies, blue rubies which are sapphires, and glittering carbuncles. The third hall was heaped with emeralds; the fourth with masses of unwrought gold; the fifth with gold coins minted over all the earth; the sixth with virgin silver; the seventh with silver coins from every land. All precious stones from the bosom of the earth and of the seas fulfilled the other halls. There were topaz, turquoise, hyacinth, Yemen stones and every colour of cornelian, there were jade vases, and necklaces, bracelets and belts, and every example of jewelwork that may be seen at the courts of kings.

I lifted my hands and gave thanks to Allāh for all these good things, and every day I opened one, two, or three doors until the fortieth day, being more and more astonished by each new marvel. When there remained only the key of the copper door and the end of the separation was at hand, I fell to thinking of my forty girls. I rejoiced in their sweet behaviour, the fresh skin of their bodies, their firm thighs, their narrow parts, their round voluminous buttocks, and their little cries of: 'Yū! my darling! Yū! my soul!', and I cried aloud: 'As Allāh lives, to-night will be a blessed night, a white night!'

But the Evil One drove into my mind a thought of the key to the copper door. I was greatly tempted and I fell. I opened the copper door and could see nothing, but a blast of scent came out at me, so strong that I fell down in a faint outside the door which shut of itself. When I came to, I persisted in my hell-born resolution and, opening the door afresh, noticed that the odours were less strong. Entering, I found another spacious hall. It was strewn with saffron and lighted candles perfumed with ambergris and incense, and by splendid gold and silver lamps burning aromatic oils which filled the hall with a sweet heaviness. Among gold torches and gold lamps I saw a marvellous black horse with a white star on his forehead. His left hindleg and his right foreleg were stockinged in white, his saddle was brocaded, and his bridle was a gold chain. His manger was filled with well-winnowed sesame and barley, his trough held fresh water perfumed with roses. One of my great delights lay in handsome horses and I was considered the finest rider in all my kingdom, so I thought that this beast would suit me well enough. I took him by the bridle and, leading him into the garden, mounted. As he did not go, I slashed him over the neck with the gold chain and at once he spread two mighty black wings which I had not seen, cried out with a terrible voice and, stamping the earth four times with his foot, shot up into the air.

The earth turned sickeningly beneath me, but I pressed my thighs together and kept my seat. At length the horse sank to earth on the terrace of that brass palace from which I had set out. At once he began to buck and sidle so violently that he threw me; then, as I lay on the ground, he ran at me, and lowering one of his wings, thrust out my left eye with the point of it. At last he rose into the air and disappeared.

I walked all about the terrace, holding one hand over my injured eye and clenching the other in grief. Soon the ten young men came out and saw me. 'You would not listen to us,' they cried, 'now behold the fruit of your rashness! We cannot receive you back among us, for we are already ten, but if you follow such and such a road, you will come to the city of Baghdād, where dwells Hārūn al-Rashīd, Prince of Believers, whose fame has reached even to us. Your fate will be in his hands.'

I set out, and, travelling day and night with a shaved beard and in the garments of a kalandar, came this night to Baghdād, the home of peace. Coming upon these other two, who had lost their left eyes, I greeted them saying: 'I am a stranger.' They answered that they too were strangers, and so it was that the three of us came to your hospitable house.

That is the story of my lost eye and my shaved beard.

The young mistress of the house, when she had heard this extraordinary tale, said to the third kalandar: 'Make your bow, and go your ways for you are pardoned.'

But he answered: 'As Allāh lives, I shall stay here till I have heard the stories of these others.'

The young girl then turned to the Khalīfah, Jafar and Masrur, asking for their stories. So Jafar went up and told her the fable that he had already told the portress at the door. After she had heard him, the girl said: 'I will pardon you all. Depart quickly and in peace.'

When they were safely out in the road, the Khalīfah asked the kalandars whither they were going and, when they answered that they did not know, instructed Jafar to take them to his home and bring them before him in the morning, so that he might see what could be done for them.

After Jafar had done his bidding, the Khalīfah returned to his palace, where he tried in vain to sleep. Early in the morning he rose and, mounting his throne, held audience of all the chief men of his empire. When these had departed, he turned to Jafar, saying: 'Bring to me the three young girls and the two bitches and the three kalandars.' Jafar brought them all forthwith and, when they stood before the Khalīfah, the girls being heavily veiled, addressed these words to them: 'We hold you free of any unkindness; you knew not who we were and yet you pardoned us and treated us well. Now learn that you have come into the hands of the fifth of the line of Abbās, Hārūn al-Rashīd, the Khalīfah. It is unwise to tell him aught but the truth.'

When Jafar had thus spoken for the Prince of Believers, the eldest girl came forward, saying: 'Prince of Believers, my story is so strange that if it were written with a needle on the corner of an eye yet would it serve as a lesson to the circumspect!'

At this point Shahrazād saw the approach of morning and discreetly fell silent.

But when the sixteenth night had come

SHE SAID:

It is related, O auspicious King, that the eldest of the young girls stood up before the Prince of Believers and told this story:

The Tale of Zubaidah, the First of the Girls

PRINCE of Believers; my name is Zubaidah, my sister who opened the door for you is Amīnah, and our youngest is called Fahīmah. We were all three born of the same father but not of the same mother; these two bitches, on the other hand, are full sisters to me, being born of the same father and the same mother. When our father died, leaving five thousand dīnārs to be divided equally among us, Amīnah and Fahīmah left us to live with their mother, while I and my two sisters lived together. I was the youngest of the three, though I am older than Amīnah and Fahīmah.

Soon after our father's death, my two elder sisters married and, in a little while, their husbands fitted out commercial ventures with their wives' inheritances and set sail, each taking his wife with him and leaving me alone.

My sisters were away for four years, and during that time their husbands, becoming bankrupt, lost all their goods and made off, abandoning them among strangers in strange lands. After bitter sufferings they managed to make their ways back to me, but they looked so like beggars that at first I did not recognise them. Yet when they spoke to me I knew who they were and questioned them tenderly as to what had happened. 'Sister, words cannot help us now,' they answered. 'Allāh took the reed pen and wrote that it was to be.' I pitied them from the bottom of my heart, sent them to the bath, and put fair new garments upon them, saying: 'Sisters, you are the elder, while I am the younger; you stand to me in the place of both father and mother. My inheritance, by Allāh's grace, has prospered and increased. Come, use the profit of it as your own and live with me in honour and in peace.'

I loaded them with benefits and they stayed with me for a year, sharing my substance. But one day they said: 'Marriage would be better for us, we cannot do without it any longer, we have no more patience with living alone.' 'I fear that you will get little good from marriage,' I said, 'for an honest man is hard to come by in these days. You tried marriage once; have you forgotten how you found it?'

But they would not listen to me, being set on marrying without my consent; so I married them to husbands, giving them money and the necessary clothes. And the new husbands took them away as before.

It was not long, however, before the new husbands deceived them and decamped with all the dowry which I had provided. Naked and full of excuses, they returned to me, saying: 'Do not blame us, we are older than you but you are wiser than we. We promise never to say a word again on the subject of marriage.' 'Sweet welcome to you, my sisters,' I answered, 'there are none dearer to me in the world than you.' So I kissed them and behaved bountifully towards them as before.

After they had lived with me for another year, it came into my head to fit out a ship with merchandise and to voyage in it to do business at Basrah. So I got ready a vessel, filling it with merchandise and goods of all kinds as well as necessaries for the voyage. I asked my sisters whether they would rather stay at home while I was away or come with me. They decided to accompany me, so I took them with me and we set sail. But first I divided my money into two halves, one of which I took with me and one of which I hid at home in case some misfortune befell the ship and we escaped with our lives.

We sailed on night and day, but by ill-luck the captain lost his course, so that we were driven to the outer ocean and into a sea quite other than the one we had designed to reach. Driving before the wind for ten days, we saw at last a city far off and asked the captain what its name might be. 'As Allāh lives, I do not know,' he answered. 'I have never seen it in my life, nor the sea in which we are. But the important thing is that we are now out of danger. It only remains for you to enter that city and offer your merchandise. I suggest that you should sell it there if you can.'

An hour later he came to us again, saying: 'Disembark now and go into the city to see the marvels of Allāh there. Call on His name and you shall go in safety.'

We entered the city and saw to our stupefaction that all the inhabitants had been turned into black rocks, but that, while they had been petrified, everything else in the markets and the streets was as it had been, goods of every kind and appointments of gold and silver all about the place. We were delighted with what we saw and, saying to each other: 'Surely there must be some extraordinary reason for all this,' separated, each going in different directions about the streets, to collect as much as might be conveniently carried of gold, silver and precious fabrics.

It was towards the citadel that I made my way. There I found the King's palace and, entering by a great door of solid gold and lifting a velvet curtain, I saw that all the furniture and everything else there was of fine gold or silver. In the courtyard and in all the rooms soldiers and chamberlains stood or sat, all turned to stone; and in the central hall, filled with chamberlains, lieutenants and wazīrs, I saw the King sitting on his throne, petrified also but arrayed in such noble and costly garments as took my breath away. Fifty silk-clad mamelūks holding naked swords stood there in stone about the King. His throne was encrusted with great pearls lying among other jewels. And each pearl shone so like a star that I thought I should lose my wits in gazing on them.

Going on, I reached the harīm, which I found to be more wonderful than all the rest, built even to the window-bars of solid gold and with silken hangings on the walls and with velvet and satin curtains hanging before the doors and windows. In the midst of a group of women, all turned to stone, I saw the Queen herself dressed in a robe sewn with noble pearls, crowned with a mass of great jewels, with collars and necklaces about her throat of pleasantly carved gold; but herself changed to black stone.

Wandering further, I came to an open door made with two leaves of virgin silver, and beyond it I saw a porphyry staircase of seven steps. Mounting this, I came to a white marble hall, covered with a carpet of gold thread, in the middle of which there rose, between great golden torches, a dais also of solid gold picked out with emeralds and turquoises. An alabaster bed, studded with pearls and upholstered with precious embroidery, stood on the dais with a great light shining by it. I came near and found that the light proceeded from a diamond, as large as an ostrich's egg, lying on a stool by the bedside and shining from all its facets so that the whole hall was filled with radiance.

Although the diamond outshone them utterly, the torches were lighted; therefore I deduced that some human hand was near and went on searching among the other halls, marvelling at all I saw and hunting everywhere for a human being. I was so entranced that I forgot all about my voyage, my ship, and my sisters. Night fell sud denly while I was still in a dream at all that beauty, and when I tried to leave the palace I could not find my way. In my search I came again to the hall with the alabaster bed, the diamond, and the lighted torches. Lying down, I half covered myself with a blue satin quilt wrought with silver and pearl, and took up a copy of our Koran, that sacred book. It was written out in stately gold characters with red devices and illuminations in all colours. From it I read a few verses to the glory of Allāh and to reprove myself that my sleep might be holy. I meditated on the words of the Prophet, whom may Allāh bless, and tried to sleep.

When the middle of the night had come and I was still awake, I heard a sweet and learned voice reciting the Koran. I rose in haste and, going in the direction of the voice, came to a little room with an open door. I entered softly, leaving the torch which I had caught up outside, and saw that the place was a kind of sanctuary. It was lighted by little green glass lamps and on its floor, facing the East, lay a prayer-rug upon which a very beautiful young man was reading the Koran aloud with grave attention and perfect eloquence. In my astonishment I asked myself how this young man alone could have escaped the fate of all the city. I came towards him and wished him peace. When he turned his eyes upon me and wished me peace, I said: 'I conjure you by the truth of the sacred words which you are reading from the book of Allāh to answer my question truly.'

Calmly and sweetly he smiled at me, saying: 'First, O woman, tell me how it is that you have come into this place where I pray, and then I will answer any question you like to put to me.' When he had listened in astonishment to my story, I questioned him concerning the extraordinary appearance of the city. He shut the sacred book and, placing it in a satin bag, bade me sit at his side. I did so and, gazing attentively at him, found in him that full perfection which is in the moon: sympathy, beauty of face, proportioned elegance of body. His cheeks were as clear as crystal, his face had the delicate tint of the fresh date, as if it had been he of whom the poet was thinking when he wrote these lines:

A watcher of the stars at night
Looked up and saw so rose and white
A boy, with such delicious grace,
Such brilliant tint of breast and face,
So curved and delicate of limb,
That he exclaimed on seeing him:
'Sure it was Saturn gave that hair,
A black star falling in the air;
Those roses were a gift from Mars;
The Archer of the seven stars
Gave all his arrows to that eye;
While great sagacious Mercury
Did sweet intelligence impart;
Queen Venus forged his golden heart
And . . . and . . .' But here the sage's art
Stopped short; and his old wits went wild
When the new star drew near and smiled.

Red flames were lighted in my heart when I looked at him and, in the violent trouble of my senses, I regretted that I had not met him long before. 'Master and sovereign,' I said, 'I pray you answer me.' 'I hear and I obey,' he replied, and told me the following remarkable story:

Honourable lady, this was my father's city, filled with his subjects and the people of his kin. He it was whom you saw petrified upon his throne, the Queen you saw was my mother. Both were magicians, worshippers of terrible Nardūn, who swore by fire and light, by shade and heat, and all the turning stars.

For a long time my father had no children. I was the child of his age and he reared me carefully throughout my boyhood, that I might be bred up to the true happiness of kingship.

Now in the palace there was a very old woman who in secret was a Believer in Allāh and his Messenger, though in public she pretended to fall in with the creed of my parents. My father had great confidence in her as a faithful and chaste woman, he heaped benefits upon her and firmly believed that she was of his own faith. When I began to grow up, he put me in her charge, commanding her to give me a good education and a grounding in the laws of Nardūn.

The old woman took me into her charge and at once declared to me the religion of Islām, from its rites of purification and ablution to the sacred forms of its prayers. She taught and expounded the Koran to me in the Prophet's own tongue and, when she had taught me all that she knew, warned me to keep my knowledge sedulously from my father lest he should kill me. I did so and, when a short time afterwards that saintly old woman died breathing her last words into my ear, I continued a secret believer in Allāh and His Prophet. Far different were the inhabitants of this city who hardened their hearts and dwelt in darkness. But one day, while they continued their idolatry, a voice like thunder spoke from an invisible muezzin to far and near, saying: 'O people of the city, leave the worship of fire and Nardūn, and turn to the one Almighty King.'

Terrified by this voice the inhabitants of the city sought the King, my father, and asked the meaning of these awful words. But my father told them not to be frightened or amazed, and bade them stand firm in their old beliefs.

So for another year they blindly worshipped fire, until the day came round again on which the voice had been heard. Then the voice boomed out once more, and this it did on the same day for the next three years. But the people continued to worship their false god until one morning, out of the clear sky of dawn, wrath and sorrow fell upon them and they were suddenly turned to black stone, they and their horses, their mules and their camels, and all their beasts. I alone, who was the sole Believer in the city, escaped the doom.

Since then I have remained here, praying, fasting, and reciting from the Book, but I have been very lonely, lovely lady, with no one to bear me human company.

On this I said to him: 'Youth of every perfection, will you not come with me to the city of Baghdād, where are sages and venerable old men steeped in the teachings of our Religion? There your learning and your faith will be increased together, and I, though I am a woman of some account, will be your slave there. In Baghdād I am mistress among my people, with a following of men, servants and young boys; also I have a ship here full of all necessary goods. Fate threw me upon your coast and Destiny has seen fit to bring us together.' I did not cease from fanning his desire to go with me until he consented to do so.

At this point Shahrazād saw the approach of morning and discreetly fell silent as was her custom.

But when the seventeenth night had come

SHE SAID:

It is related, O auspicious King, that the girl Zubaidah did not cease from fanning the desire of the young man to go with her until he consented to do so.

They talked long together until sleep overcame them, and Zubaidah slept that night at the feet of the young man. I leave you to imagine whether she was happy or no.

(Zubaidah continued her story to the Khalīfah Hārūn al-Rashīd, in the hearing of Jafar and the three kalandars in these words:)

When morning broke, we chose out from all the treasures of the palace the best we could carry, and went down towards the city, where we met my slaves and the captain who had been looking for me a long time. They were delighted to see me again and more than a little astonished when I gave them the outline of my story and of the young man's tale concerning the doom which had fallen upon the city. But hardly had my sisters seen the handsome young man than they were filled with violent jealousy and began in their hatred secretly to plot my hurt.

We all went aboard, I in great joy because I loved the youth, and, taking advantage of a favourable wind, sailed away. My sisters never left us alone, and one day they asked me directly what I intended to do with the youth. I told them that I meant to marry him and, turning towards him, I said: 'Master, I desire to become your slave. Do not refuse me this.' 'Indeed, I do not refuse,' he answered and, our troth being thus plighted, I said to my sisters: 'This young man is enough property for me. All else I have I give to you.' 'Your wish is law,' they answered, but at the same time they schemed against me in their hearts.

We came with favouring winds from the Dread Sea to the Sea of Safety, across which we sailed for several days till we saw the buildings of Basrah rising from the water. That night we cast anchor and all slept.

While we slept, my sisters rose and, lifting the youth and myself, cast us, mattresses and all, into the sea. The poor young man, who could not swim, was drowned. It was written by Allāh that he should become one of the martyrs, just as it was written that I should be saved. For, when I fell into the water, Allāh sent me a spar of wood to which I clung and supported by which I was carried by the waves to the shore of a nearby island. There I dried my clothes and slept, rising in the morning to look for some track which should lead me to safety. Soon I found a road worn by human feet which I followed into the interior of the island, until I had gone right across it and came out on the other side, opposite the city of Basrah. Suddenly I saw a little snake hurrying towards me, hotly pursued by a much larger snake who was trying to kill it. I felt pity for the little snake which was so weary that its tongue hung out. So I lifted a great stone and smashed in the head of the large snake, killing it on the spot. Immediately to my surprise the little snake spread two wings and, flying up into the air, disappeared from my sight.

Being broken by fatigue, I lay down where I was and slept for about an hour. When I woke, I found a beautiful young negress seated at my feet, rubbing and kissing them. I snatched them away in considerable shame, not knowing whether her intentions towards me were honourable or not, and asked her sharply who she was and what she wanted. 'I hastened to come to you,' she said, 'because of the great service you have done me in killing my enemy. I am a Jinnīyah and was in the likeness of that little snake. The big snake was my enemy, a Jinnī who wished to rape me and to kill me. You saved me, so I flew at once to the ship from which your two sisters threw you. I changed them into black bitches and have brought them to you.' Sure enough, there were two black bitches tied to the tree behind me. 'Lastly,' went on the Jinnīyah, 'I transported all your riches to your house in Baghdād and then sank the ship. As for your young man, he is drowned. I can do nothing against death. Allāh alone is Almighty.'

With these words she took me in her arms together with my sisters, the bitches, and, flying with us through the air, set us down safely on the terrace of my house here in Baghdād.

Looking about me I found all the treasures and the goods that had been in my ship ranged in careful order round the rooms, not one having been lost or spoiled. Before she left, the Jinnīyah said to me: 'I command you by the sacred symbol on the Seal of Sulaimān to give each of these bitches three hundred strokes of the whip every day. If you forget even once I shall be obliged to come back and change you also into the same shape.'

What could I answer save: 'I hear and I obey'?

Ever since then, O Prince of Believers, I have beaten them and then pitifully caressed them as you have seen. That is my story.

But my sister Amīnah, my lord, could tell you a stranger tale than mine.

The Khalīfah Hārūn al-Rashīd marvelled exceedingly at this story and then, in the haste of his curiosity, turned to the young Amīnah, who had opened the door on the previous night, and said: 'Now tell me, gracious girl, what caused the marks on your body.'

The Tale of the Portress Amīnah

AT these words of the Khalīfah, the young Amīnah came forward and said:

Prince of Believers, I will not repeat what our sister Zubaidah has told you of our parents; suffice it to say that, when they died, I and our little sister Fahīmah, the youngest of us five, went to live with our mother, while Zubaidah and the other two continued to reside together.

Soon my mother married me to a rich old man, the most wealthy in all the city at that time, and a year later Allāh took my husband to his peace, leaving me with a fortune of eighty thousand dīnārs in gold.

I made haste to order ten dresses of such splendour that they cost a thousand dīnārs each, and in other ways denied myself nothing.

One day, as I was sitting in comfort, an old woman whom I had never seen before was ushered into my presence. She was in every way hideous. Her face was like any other old person's bottom, her nose was broken, her brows moth-eaten, her eyes full of senile lechery, her teeth a wreck. She bubbled at the nose and her neck was thrawn like a hen's. The poet made a fair picture of her when he said:

> This old foul hag could teach
> Things out of the Devil's reach,
> And without speaking show the Devil
> All that he did not know of evil.
> Suppose a thousand mules were tied
> In a soft cobweb's black inside,
> She could set free each struggling beast
> Nor break the cobweb in the least.
> However lewd and gross an act is
> She had it pat by constant practice;

She taught a little girl to sin
By pressing her old finger in,
She coupled with a child who was
Just turning to a full-fledged lass,
She acted quite the lewdest crime
With a fine woman in her prime,
Her quick hand lit a flame, by God,
In a beldam of a hundred odd;
In fact this crapulous old woman
Seemed positively more than human.

She saluted me and said: 'Gracious and accomplished dame, I have an orphan girl at home who is going to be married to-night. I have come to ask you—Allāh will know how to reward you, dear gracious lady—to honour with your presence the marriage of this poor humble girl, who has no powerful person upon her side, unless it may be Allāh.' She wept and kissed my feet so that I, who knew nothing of the blackness of her heart, had pity on her and consented. 'With your dear gracious permission I will now leave you,' she said. 'If you will dress and prepare yourself I will come back for you in the evening.' Then she kissed my hand and went away.

I bathed and perfumed myself, chose the fairest of my ten new gowns and, dressing myself in it, put on my noble pearl necklace, my bracelets, my pendants, and all my jewels. I wound my brocaded belt round my waist, threw my large veil of blue silk and gold over my head and, after continuing the direction of my eyes with kohl, put on my little face veil and was ready. Soon the old woman came for me and said: 'Mistress, the house is already full of the bride-groom's folk, all the most noble ladies in the city. I have told them that you are coming and they are on the tiptoe of happy expectation.' I called some of my slaves to accompany us and we walked till we came to a great well-watered street in which a gentle breeze was playing. Soon we reached a large marble gate, roofed with an alabaster dome held up by arches, through which we saw a palace towering even up to the sky. The old crone knocked and we were admitted into the palace, where we found ourselves in a gaily-arrassed corridor, its ceiling hung with coloured lamps, its walls lighted by torches and covered with gold and silver trophies, with jewel work and warlike arms. We passed along this corridor and came into a hall furnished with such splendour that it is useless to try to tell you of it. In its midst, all spread about with silk stuffs on the floor, stood a bed of alabaster, crusted with monstrous pearls and jewels of great price, and having a satin quilt thrown over it. Seeing us, a young girl as beautiful as a slip of the moon, rose from the bed, saying to me: 'Cordial, friendly and easy welcome to you, my sister; you have done us the greatest of all honours. Welcome, welcome, for you are our consolation and our pride!' She recited these verses in my honour:

> Even the stones of which the house is made
>   Rejoiced when they had heard that you were coming;
> And when you came they bowed and swayed
>   Behind your steps and made a pleasant humming,
> Stone rubbing against stone with this whisper:
> She's here, she's here, she's here, she's here, she's here!

Then she sat down, saying: 'Sister, I must tell you that I have a brother, a well-made youth and fairer far than I, who saw you one day at a marriage feast and has loved you and fainted for you ever since. It was he who gave money to this old woman to visit you and bring you here by an innocent trick, so that he might meet you in all honour in my house. He has no desire but to marry you immediately in this blessed year of Allāh and his Prophet, and therefore he has no shame in making an honest proposal.'

When I heard her and realised that I was both known and esteemed in this house, I said to the girl: 'I hear and I obey!' at which she was filled with great joy and clapped her hands. A door opened at this signal and through it stepped a young man who might have put to shame the moon of Spring. As the poet says:

> He is so dear, we might surmise
> That every heart
> Would surely break apart,
> And when he fixed it with his eyes
> The broken heart go up in ardencies.
>
> He is so fair, we could aver
> That Allāh had
> Made him, and we could add
> That even on such a Jeweller
> Such making did a certain fame confer.

As he came and sat down by his sister my heart was drawn towards him, so that I was not grieved at all at the entrance of the kādī with four witnesses, who saluted and sat down. The kādī wrote out my contract with the young man and, when the witnesses had set their seals to the contract, all departed.

The young man came to me, first saying: 'May our night be blessed!' and then: 'Mistress, I will, if you are agreeable, bind you with a condition.' 'Speak, my lord,' I said, 'and tell me what it is.' He rose and brought the sacred book to me, saying: 'I wish you to swear on the Koran never to choose another than I, never to incline towards another.' When to his great contentment I had taken this oath, he threw his arms about my neck and I felt his blood throbbing in all my veins and about the palace of my heart.

Slaves served us with food and drink, and, when we had eaten and drunken to satiety and the night had come, he stretched me with him upon the bed and all night long we leapt and lay in each other's arms.

We lived together for a month in unclouded happiness, and then, one day, I asked my husband's leave to go to the market to buy some fabrics which I needed. He gave me permission, so I dressed and, taking the old woman with me, went down to the market. I stopped at last before the shop of a young silk merchant whom the old crone had strongly recommended to me for the quality of his goods and because, as she said, she had known him for a long time. As I was examining the wares, she whispered to me: 'This is a youth who by his father's death has come into much money.' Then, turning to the merchant, she said: 'Bring out the best and dearest of all your silks, because they are for this beautiful child.' 'Willingly,' he said, and, while he unrolled bale after bale for my inspection, the old woman went on praising him to me and detailing his beauties and his qualities. At last I answered her: 'I have nothing to do with his beauties or his qualities. My business is but to buy what I need from him and then go home.'

When I offered him the price of the fabric I had chosen, the merchant refused to touch the money, saying: 'I am not taking money today; this silk is but a small return for the pleasure and honour you have done my shop.' 'If he will not accept the money,' I exclaimed to the old woman, 'give him back the silk!' But he cried out: 'As Allāh lives, I will take nothing; this is a present. But if, O glorious girl, you care to give me a single kiss in return, I will value it more highly than all the goods in my shop.' The old crone rallied him, saying: 'Handsome young man, surely you are no great merchant to think a kiss so valuable!' Then to me she continued: 'Do you not hear what the young man says, my daughter? Do not worry, there is no harm in a little kiss. Think, you will be able to choose to your heart's desire among all these pretty stuffs.' 'Do you not know,' I answered sternly, 'that I am bound by oath to my lord?' 'Let him have one little kiss,' she answered, 'if you do not speak of it no one will be hurt, and you will be able to carry back your money and all the pretty silks as well.' The old woman went on persuading me until I put my head, as it were, in the bag. When I had covered my eyes and stretched my veil behind my head, so that no passer-by should see anything, the young man passed his head under my veil and bringing his mouth to my cheek kissed me. But at the same time, since he loved me and wished to make me his, he bit my cheek so violently that the flesh was broken.

I fainted with pain, and when I came to, found myself stretched on the knees of the old woman who was mourning over me. The shop was shut up and the young merchant had disappeared. Presently the old woman said: 'Praise be to Allāh that it is nothing worse! Come, we must get back to the house. When we are there, you had better pretend to be ill, and I will bring you a salve to heal the bite.' I rose and walked as quickly as I could to my husband's house, my terror of him increasing all the way. Arrived there, I went at once to my room and lay down as if I were ill.

It was not long before my husband came in looking very worried, and said: 'My dear, what evil overtook you while you were out?' 'Nothing, I am quite well,' I answered. He looked at me closely and said: 'But what is that wound on your cheek, in its tenderest part?' 'When, with your permission, I went out to-day,' I answered, 'a camel piled with firewood crushed against me in the street so that one of the bits of wood tore my veil and wounded me as you see. Oh, the terrible streets of Baghdād!' 'To-morrow,' he exclaimed angrily, 'I will complain to the governor and he will hang every last one of the camel-men in the city!' Feeling compassion for all these folk, I said: 'By Allāh, do not charge yourself with so great a sin! The thing was my own fault; I was riding on an ass which ran away and threw me, so that by ill-chance a piece of wood on the ground ran into my cheek.' 'To-morrow,' my husband cried, 'I will go and tell this story to Jafar al-Barmaki, who will surely kill all the donkey-

boys in the city!' 'Do you want to kill all the world because of me?'
I answered. 'It was only an accident, decreed by Allāh and allowed
by Fate.'

But at this excuse my husband could not hold his fury any longer.
'No more lies, you traitress!' he cried, 'prepare for punishment!'
He stamped on the ground, cursing me all the time in a terrible
voice, and at once a door opened through which seven great negroes
ran into the room. They dragged me from my bed, threw me into
the middle of the floor and then, by my husband's orders, one held
me by my shoulders and sat on my head, a second sat across my
knees and held my feet and a third stood over me, sword in hand.
Then said my husband: 'Cut her in two and bear her up and throw
her into the Tigris to be food for fishes. That is the punishment for
one who breaks an oath.' Further he recited this stanza:

> If I had known I nightly deepenèd
> Another's dint in your delightful bed,
>   'Come out from her, my soul, and cleanly die,
> Rather than bear this taint,' I would have said.

When he had spoken this stanza, my husband called to the negro
with the sword: 'Come, brave Saad, cut this unfaithful one in two.'
Saad lifted the blade, but just then my husband bethought him and
said to me: 'First say your prayers, then run over all your goods and
clothes and will them to someone, for your time has come to die.'
'Yes, give me time for that,' I said and, lifting my head towards the
sky, fell to considering the ignominy of my fate until the tears came
to my eyes and I wept, intoning these stanzas:

> Your heart lit mine and now your heart is cold,
> You taught me how to wake till night was old,
>   Now your desire has fallen fast asleep
> And all the golden sands of love are told.
>
> You made me swear eternal constancy
> And then with your next heaving of a sigh
>   You puffed the oath I had not made you take
> Down the night wind, to drown in the night sky.
>
> When you have killed me with your foolery
> Write on my foolish tomb for all to see:
>   'This fool was fool enough to fall in love,'
> And fools of the same sort will pity me.

I wept again, but both my tears and my verses only drove my husband to greater fury, so that he countered me with these lines:

> My love was not the love of common air,
> It only died when I became aware
>   That your white body was a compromise,
> A heaven cut in halves for two to share.

When he had finished, I wept again to touch his heart and lessen my punishment, for I hoped that he might spare my life and give me quittance at the price of all my jewels. Gently I recited these lines:

> I whose pale shoulders hardly could uplift
> The lightest parti-coloured silken shift
>   Have to bear up the vessel of distrust
> Which your too jealous hand has set adrift.
>
> I feel no wonder that you do me ill,
> It is a frightened lover's part to kill;
>   No, the sole thing at which I am surprised
> Is that my dying body loves you still.

Again I wept, but he pushed me violently away from him and cursed me in this wise:

> You lay in a strange bed and now give birth
> To a new measure. If I mete the earth
>   With your new measure, surely everything
> Will show the record of your guilty mirth.
>
> I'll lie with others while I measure Faith,
> I'll measure Constancy in terms of Breath,
>   I'll take the height of virtue with a Sin
> And find the limit of your life in Death.

With this he called again to the negro: 'Cut her in two! She is no more to us.' The negro advanced, but just as I was desperately confiding my lot to Allāh, being certain of death, the old woman rushed into the room and threw herself at the feet of my husband, fondling them and saying: 'My child, I conjure you on my rights as your nurse to pardon this girl for she has done nothing worthy of death. Besides, you are young and I fear that her life will be required of you.' With repeated tears and prayers she so worked on my husband that he said: 'For your sake I will pardon her. But I must mark her for all time.' So the negroes stripped me naked and my husband, taking up a pliant quince branch, beat me about the back and breast and flanks so furiously that I fell unconscious at his feet. Thereon he bade his slaves leave me as I was until nightfall and then to take me and throw me down before my own house.

This the slaves did, and when I recovered consciousness it was a long time before I could even crawl into the house. When I managed to do so, I anointed my stripes with various unguents, and little by little they healed. But, as you have all seen, I still bear scars as of whips and canes upon my body.

After four months, when I was quite cured, I wished to see the palace where I had suffered such violence, but I found it a ruin and the street in which it stood a ruin also. Over all that place of marvels there was nothing to be found save heaps of dung and the refuse of the city and in spite of all my enquiries I was not able to hear tidings of my husband.

So I sought out my little sister Fahīmah, who was still a virgin, and we both went to visit Zubaidah, our sister who told you the story of the bitches. We exchanged greetings and narratives, and at last Zubaidah said: 'Dear sister, no one in the world is free from trouble. Thanks be to Allāh we are all alive. Let us stay together from now on and never let the word marriage be heard between us.'

Since then we have lived happily together, little Fahīmah being our cateress who went down every day into the market to buy what we needed, I looking after the door, and Zubaidah ordering all things in the house.

We enjoyed ourselves sufficiently without men until the day on which Fahīmah brought back the porter with all the things she had bought, and we asked him to remain with us a little. After that the three kalandars entered and then you others in the guise of merchants. You know what happened then and how you caused us to be brought before you, Prince of Believers.

Such is my story.

Then the Khalīfah rejoiced at all the marvels he had heard and . . .

At this point, Shaharazād saw the approach of morning and discreetly fell silent.

But when the eighteenth night had come

SHAHRAZĀD CONTINUED IN THIS WISE:

It is related, O auspicious King, that, on hearing the stories of the girls Zubaidah and Amīnah, who with their little sister Fahīmah, the two black bitches, and the three kalandars, had been brought before him, the Khalīfah Hārūn al-Rashīd rejoiced at the marvel of the two tales and ordered them to be written out in fair calligraphy by his scribes.

When the manuscripts had been deposited among the records, the Khalīfah said to Zubaidah: 'Now, noble girl, have you no news of the Ifrītah who bewitched your two sisters?' 'Prince of Believers,' answered Zubaidah, 'I can easily find her, for she gave me a lock of her hair, telling me that if ever I needed her I had but to burn one of the hairs and she would come to me, were it from the other side of Kaf.' 'Give me that hair,' said the Khalīfah and when she had done so he burnt one thread of it. No sooner had they smelt the smell of burning hair than the palace shook as at a great blow and the Jinnīyah stood before them in the likeness of a richly-habited young girl. Being a Believer, she said to the Khalīfah: 'Peace be with you, O vicar of Allāh!' 'Peace light on you!' answered the Khalīfah, 'together with the mercy and blessing of God!' Then said the Ifrītah: 'This girl, who has just called me at your desire, once rendered me so great a service that I can never repay it. I changed her sisters into bitches, only sparing their lives since their deaths might have caused her too great pain. But I do not forget that I am a Believer; if you wish it I will free them from their present shapes, for your sake and the sake of their sister.' 'In truth I wish them to be freed,' answered the Khalīfah. 'After that we will look into the case of the other young woman and her scars. If her story be true, I will bitterly avenge her on him who acted so unjustly.' Then said the Ifrītah: 'Prince of Believers, I can show you in the twinkling of an eye the man who treated young Amīnah so, who beat her and deprived her of her goods, for he is very near us as we stand here.' First she took a glass of water and, speaking magic words over it, sprinkled the bitches until they turned again to young girls, so beautiful that He who made them should be glorified therefor, and then she turned to the Khalīfah, saying: 'The husband of young Amīnah is your own son, al-Amīn.'

When the Khalīfah heard the second story confirmed and that

by no human lips, he called his son to him and asked for an explanation. Al-Amīn told the story from his point of view and the Khalīfah ordered kādīs and witnesses to be brought into the hall.

Then al-Amīn was remarried to the young Amīnah, Zubaidah to the first kalandar who was a king's son, the other two sisters to the other two kalandars, princes both, and the Khalīfah himself wedded the youngest of the five sisters, the maiden Fahīmah, the witty and agreeable cateress.

Hārūn al-Rashīd had a palace built for each couple and endowed them with riches that they might live happily. Also, hardly had night fallen when he himself hastened to bed with the young Fahīmah, and they passed the sweetest of nights together.

But, continued Shahrazād to King Shahryār, do not believe, my Sovereign, that this story is in any way more astonishing than the one I am about to tell you.

The Tale of the Woman Cut in Pieces, the Three Apples & the Negro Raihān

SHAHRAZĀD SAID:

ONE night the Khalīfah Hārūn al-Rashīd said to Jafar al-Barmaki: 'I wish us to go down into the city to-night to inform ourselves of the acts of the governors and the walīs. Those against whom I hear complaint I shall most certainly remove from office.' Jafar answered: 'I hear and I obey.'

So the Khalīfah, Jafar, and Masrūr the sword-bearer, disguised themselves and went down to wander through the streets of Baghdād. In a byway they saw a very old man, carrying a net and creel on his head and a stick in his hand. He was going along very slowly, murmuring these lines:

> They said:
> Your cultured head
> Shines on the black
> Of learning's lack
> In other men.
>
> Pray cease,
> (I answered then)

My girth's increase
And daily peace
Would be maintained
More by the earning
Of an harlot's hour
Than by the power
Of all my learning.

My books and ink,
With all I know and think,
In this world's mart
Would kick the beam
Against a salted bream
And a stale tart.

Learning may have some worth
Below the earth,
So I will roam
Till I have found
The single home
We beggars have,
A shallow grave
Beneath the ground.

The Khalīfah, after listening to these lines, said to Jafar: 'Both the song and the appearance of this poor man would seem to indicate most grievous misery.' Then going up to the old man he said: 'Father, what is your trade?' 'Master, I am a fisherman,' the other answered, 'also I am very old and have a large family. From noon until now I have laboured beyond my strength and yet Allāh has not seen good to provide me with even a morsel of bread for my children. I am tired of myself and tired of life, and death is all I wish for.' Then said the Khalīfah: 'Can you come back with us to the riverside and cast your net once more into the Tigris on my behalf, that I may try my luck? I will buy the catch of that casting for a hundred dīnārs.'

The old man joyfully accompanied them back to the Tigris and, casting his net, brought it to shore in a few moments with a heavy locked chest inside it. Having hefted it and found it of a great weight, the Khalīfah gave the hundred dīnārs to the fisherman who went on his way rejoicing, while Jafar and Masrūr lifted the chest

and carried it to the palace. The Khalīfah lit torches while Jafar
and Masrūr broke open the chest. Inside was a large basket of
palm leaves, sewn with a red cord. This cord they cut and found
in the basket, first a carpet, then a woman's white veil, and last
the woman herself, as pale as virgin silver, murdered and cut in
pieces.

The Khalīfah wept at this sight and then turned in a fury to Jafar,
shouting: 'Dog of a wazīr! This is how men go murdering and
drowning about my city, and the blood they shed will lie heavy
against me on the judgment day. By Allāh, I will not be equal with
this murderer until I have slain him. As for you, Jafar, I swear by
my descent from the children of Abbās·that unless you bring me the
man who has killed this woman I will crucify you on my palace
door and forty of your relatives, the Barmakids, to keep you company.' Thus the Khalīfah exploded in wrath, but when Jafar begged
for a delay of three days he granted it to him.

Poor Jafar wandered about the city in great grief, saying to himself: 'How, in God's name, can I find the murderer and bring him
to the Khalīfah? And if I bring another to die instead of him it will
lie heavy on my conscience. I am in a very sad dilemma.' So saying,
he went up to his house and stayed there for three days in a lethargy
of despair. On the fourth day he appeared before the Khalīfah, who
asked him for the murderer. 'Can I see the invisible or search out the
hidden?' answered Jafar. 'Can I find an unknown assassin in a whole
cityful of people?' Furious at this answer, the Khalīfah ordered Jafar
to be crucified on the gate of the palace and commanded the public
crier to make this proclamation throughout the city:

'All who desire to see Jafar al-Barmaki, wazīr of the Khalīfah,
crucified upon the palace gate, and forty Barmakids crucified upon
the palace gate, are cordially invited to attend the spectacle.'

All the people of Baghdād flocked from every quarter to see the
crucifixion of Jafar and his cousins, not knowing the reason for it
and weeping and wailing because both Jafar and all the Barmakids
were loved for their kindness and generosity.

When the platforms had been erected for the execution and the
captains were only waiting for the word of the Khalīfah, suddenly
a richly-dressed and very beautiful young man burst through the
weeping crowd and threw himself at Jafar's feet, crying: 'Master and
greatest of great lords, O sanctuary of the poor, I come to deliver
you! It was I who killed the woman and hid her remains in the chest

which you recovered from the Tigris. Kill me now, that she may be avenged!'

When Jafar heard the young man's words he grieved for him, though he could not help rejoicing for himself. He was on the point of asking for details when an old man also made his way through the crowd and hurrying up saluted Jafar and the young man with these words:

'Do not believe what this youth has said, O wazīr, for I alone am the slayer of the young woman. I alone should pay the penalty!' 'O wazīr,' broke in the other, 'this old man is in his dotage. He does not know what he says. I alone killed her and must pay the penalty.' To this the old man replied: 'My child, you are young and life is sweet to you; I am old and have quite finished with the world. Gladly will I act as ransom for you, the wazīr, and his cousins. I repeat that I did the murder and should be punished for it.'

Greatly perplexed by these two self-accusers, Jafar obtained leave from the chief of the guard and hurried them both into the presence of the Khalīfah. When he stood before him, he said: 'Prince of Believers, here is the murderer of the young woman!' and when Hārūn asked which was the murderer, he answered: 'This young man says that he is; but the old man denies it and says that he himself did the deed.' Looking at both of them, the Khalīfah said: 'Which of you killed the woman?' 'I did!' they both answered, so the Khalīfah said to Jafar: 'Crucify them both!' 'But if only one of them did the thing, to kill the other would be a great injustice,' said Jafar. At this the young man burst forth: 'I swear by Him Who has stretched out the skies like curtains and laid out the earth below them like a garden, that I alone did the thing. I can prove it to you.' Then he described all the circumstances of the packing away of the body which were only known to the Khalīfah, Jafar, and Masrūr; so that the Khalīfah, being convinced of his guilt, asked in astonishment: 'Why did you do it? Why, having done it, do you confess it without having been beaten about the feet for that end? And why do you come here begging for punishment?' So the young man told this story:

Prince of Believers, that young woman was my wife, daughter of this good old man. She came to me young and clean and Allāh blessed us with three male children. She loved me and waited on me in all docility, and I, for my part, saw nothing of evil in her.

At the beginning of this month she fell sick; but I called in learned doctors and eventually, with the help of Allāh, they cured her. I had not lain with her since the beginning of her illness, and wishing to do so again, suggested that she should go to bathe at the hammām. But she told me that she had a certain queasy longing to bite and smell an apple before she went to the bath. At once I went down into the city to buy her an apple, whatever might be the cost of one. But not one of the fruiterers had such a thing, so I was forced to return empty-handed. Not wishing to see my wife in her disappointment, I studied all night how I might come by the fruit and at dawn made my way to the market-gardens, visiting them one by one, and tree by tree. At last I met an old gardener who said: 'My child, an apple is a very difficult thing to come by for the simple reason that there are none in these parts, save in the orchard of the Commander of the Faithful at Basrah. But even there you will not find it easy to lay hands on one, because they are kept strictly for the Khalīfah.'

I returned home and told my wife what I heard. Then, as my love for her was very great, I set out for Basrah, taking fifteen days on the journey there and back. Luck favoured me and I returned to her with three apples which I had managed to buy at a dīnār each from the keeper of the orchard at Basrah.

Joyfully I went in to my wife and gave her the three apples. But she did not appear delighted at the sight of them and simply laid them carelessly by her side. From this and other signs I saw that the fever had very violently come back to her while I was away. For ten days she was so ill that I never left her side for a moment; but after that, thanks be to Allāh, she became better again, so that I was able to leave her and return to my shop.

Towards noon, while I was sitting in my shop, a negro passed who was throwing an apple from hand to hand. 'Friend,' I called to him, 'tell me where you got that apple. I should like to buy some.' At this he laughed and said: 'I got it from my wench. I went to see her to-day and found that she had been ill for some time. Three apples were lying by her side and when I asked her about them she said: "Just imagine, my dear, my poor cuckold of a husband went all the way to Basrah and bought them for three golden dīnārs!" Then she gave me this apple.' Prince of Believers, the world turned black about me when I heard what the negro said; I shut my shop and went raving through the streets until I came to my house. I looked at the bed and seeing that the third apple had gone I asked my wife where it was. She said that she did not know, thus proving to my mind the negro's story. I leapt upon her, knife in hand, and kneeling on her belly hacked her in pieces. Then hastily I put her into the basket, covering the top with the veil and the carpet and enclosing the basket in the chest, loaded the chest on my mule and later, with my own hands, threw it into the Tigris.

Hasten my death, O Commander of the Faithful, for, unless I expiate now, I have fears for the day of Resurrection.

So I threw her into the Tigris and returned to my house without any having seen me. There I found my eldest little son in tears and, being certain that he knew nothing of his mother's death, I asked him why he wept. He answered: 'Because I took one of mother's apples and ran into the street to play with my brothers. A big negro came by and snatched the apple from my hand, asking where I had got it. I told him that father had gone to Basrah and bought it with two others for three gold pieces; but even then he would not give it back. He beat me and went off with it. Now I am afraid that mother will beat me for taking the apple.'

When the child said this I knew that the negro had told base lies about my wife and that I had killed her for no reason. My father-in-law and I sat side by side and wept till midnight. For five days we kept up the observance of grief, wailing and lamenting even up to to-day.

Prince of Believers, I conjure you by the sacred memory of your ancestors to hasten my death that I may expiate this foul murder!

The Khalīfah was astonished at this story and cried out: 'As Allāh lives, I will slay none except that wicked negro!'

At this point, Shahrazād saw the approach of morning and discreetly fell silent.

But when the nineteenth night had come

SHE SAID:

It is related, O auspicious King, that when the Khalīfah, seeing that there was much excuse for the young man, swore that he would kill only the negro, he turned to Jafar, saying: 'Bring me that wretched black who was the cause of all this tragedy. If you cannot find him, you shall die in his place.'

Jafar went out weeping, and exclaiming: 'How can I bring him the negro? My first escape was as lucky as if a jug having once fallen should not break. Now there is no hope for me save in Allāh. I shall not waste the three days that are left to me in vain searchings but abide in my house the wishes of the Most High.'

So he went up to his house and stayed there for three days. On the fourth, hearing that the Khalīfah was still minded to slay him if he could not produce the negro, he sent for the kādī and, having made his will, bade a tearful farewell to all his children. As he was embracing the smallest of his daughters for the last time, straining her against his breast and weeping, he felt some round thing in her pocket and asked her what it was. 'It is an apple, father,' she answered, 'which our negro, Raihān, sold me four days ago for two dīnārs.'

Hearing the words negro and apple, Jafar gave a great cry of joy and sent straightway for Raihān. On being questioned about the apple, the slave replied: 'Five days ago, master, as I was walking through the city I saw some children playing in a by-street and one of them had this apple in his hand. I took it away from him and beat him; on which he burst out crying and told me that it had been bought with two others for three dīnārs at Basrah by his father for his mother, who was ill and had a longing for the fruit. I took no notice of his tears, but brought the apple here and sold it to my little mistress for two dīnārs.'

Jafar was exceedingly concerned when he saw how all these troubles had come about through the folly of his own slave. He ordered Raihān to be put under arrest and himself made haste to the palace, rejoicing at his narrow escape from death and reciting these lines to himself:

> If your slave gets you into trouble,
> Then scruple not to have him slain;
> A pair of slaves can double and redouble,
> But your lost soul can never come again.

Arrived at the palace, he told the whole story to the Khalīfah, who was so astonished at the circumstances of it that he ordered it to be written out and placed among the annals to be a lesson for the men of all time.

But Jafar said: 'There is no need to be too astonished at this tale, Commander of the Faithful; it is far from equalling that of the wazīr Nūr al-Dīn, and his brother Shams al-Dīn.'

'What tale is that?' asked the Khalīfah, and Jafar answered:

'Prince of Believers, I will not tell it to you unless you pardon my slave, Raihān, for his foolish act.' 'Be it so,' answered the Khalīfah. 'I spare his life on condition that you tell me the tale.'

The Tale of the Wazīr Nūr al-Dīn, his Brother the Wazīr Shams al-Dīn, and Hasan Badr al-Dīn

SAID JAFAR AL-BARMAKI:

KNOW, O Commander of the Faithful, that there was once a just and benevolent sultān in the land of Egypt who had a learned wazīr, skilled in sciences and letters. This wazīr was a very old man but he had two sons as fair as twin moons, called Shams al-Dīn and Nūr al-Dīn. Though Shams al-Dīn, the elder, had been exceptionally gifted with beauty and character, the younger, Nūr al-Dīn, exceeded his brother in every way and had not his equal on the whole earth. Many persons journeyed to Egypt at that time from far countries solely for the pleasure of feasting their eyes on the beauty of Nūr al-Dīn.

When in the fullness of time his wazīr died, the Sultān who had dearly loved him called the two sons and presented each with a robe of honour, saying: 'From now on you shall occupy your father's position at my court.' The brothers humbled themselves before the Sultān in thanks, and after they had prolonged the funeral rites of their father for a month, jointly took over the duties of wazīr, acting week and week about, and he who was wazīr at the time accompanying the Sultān on any journeys he might make.

On the night before one such journey of the Sultān, in which it was Shams al-Dīn's turn to accompany him, the brothers were passing the evening in conversation. In the course of their talk the elder said: 'It seems to me that we should marry, and do so on the same night.' 'Be it as you say, brother,' answered Nūr al-Dīn. When this first point had been agreed between them, Shams al-Dīn said again: 'When we have lain with our wives on the same night and they, if Allāh allows, have given birth on the same day, mine to a girl, yours to a boy, then we should marry the children to each other.' 'And what dowry would you expect my son to give your daughter?' asked Nūr al-Dīn. 'I think I should ask three thousand

golden dīnārs and three of the best farms and villages in Egypt,'
answered Shams al-Dīn. 'That will not be much for a daughter of
mine, and if your son is not willing to give it the matter need not go
further.' 'Do not believe it!' exclaimed Nūr al-Dīn. 'What is all this
talk of a dowry? We are brothers and wazīrs; you should be only
too pleased to let my son have your daughter for nothing: a boy is of
infinitely more worth than a girl. You talk like a merchant doubling
and then redoubling the price of butter because he does not want to
sell.' Said Shams al-Dīn: 'You seem to think that your son is nobler
than my daughter. It just proves my contention that you are absolutely
lacking in both good sense and gratitude. You talk of our wazīrship;
do you not realise that you owe your high estate to me, because I
pitied you and wished someone to help me in the work? You can
say what you like now; your son shall never marry my daughter,
even if he bring with him his weight in gold!' Nūr al-Dīn became
very angry at this and cried: 'Indeed your daughter shall never have
my son!' 'There is no need for more,' said Shams al-Dīn. 'As I have
to set out to-morrow with the Sultān I cannot make you feel just
yet how ill-considered your words have been; when I come back, as
Allāh lives, you shall see what you shall see!'

Nūr al-Dīn straightway left his brother and went home to sleep, a
prey to consuming anger and grief.

Next morning after the Sultān and Shams al-Dīn had set out along
the banks of the Nile, intending to cross over by boat to Jīzah and
continue thence as far as the Pyramids, Nūr al-Dīn rose in a very
bad humour. When he had washed and prayed, he went to his store-
rooms and filled a saddle-bag with gold, thinking all the time of his
brother's harsh words and his own humiliation. He recalled these
stanzas:

> Go out from the city;
> There are friends and life
> In being under black tents.

> Let your soul
> Take root in the brown earth
> And make your friends of strangers.

> Is not water rotten
> Until it wanders?
> Is the moon remarkable
> Until it wanes?

What virtue has a lion in the wood;
Or an arrow
Hiding against the bow?

What is gold in the rock;
Or aloe-wood in the tree?

Go out from the city;
There are friends and life
In being under black tents.

Recalling these lines, he ordered one of his young slaves to saddle his dapple-grey mule, the swiftest and the fairest that he had. The slave put a gold-brocaded saddle on her with Indian stirrups and a saddle-cloth of Isfahān gold, tending her so carefully that she seemed like a bride clothed for her wedding. Nūr al-Dīn had a great silk carpet and a little prayer-rug spread on her and between them he fastened the saddle-bag filled with gold.

'I am going to ride beyond the city,' he said to his slaves, 'as far as Kalyib, where I shall lie for three nights in hope of curing an oppression of the chest with the fine air there. I forbid anyone to follow me.'

He took provisions for his journey and rode away on the mule. Once quit of Cairo he galloped so well that he reached Bulbais by noon. Here he dismounted to rest himself and his animal, and after eating went into the city and bought all of which he had a need. Two days afterwards at noon he arrived at the sacred city of Jerusalem where, having eased his mule and eaten, he lay down on the silken carpet with his head on the saddle-bag and slept. But his dreams were still troubled with anger against his brother. At dawn the next morning he was in the saddle and did not slacken speed until he came to Aleppo, where he stayed in one of the khāns for three days, enjoying the healthy air of the place. On the third day, after having bought some of those excellent sweets which they know so well how to make at Aleppo and which had been favourites with him since childhood—the kind which are stuffed with pistachios and almonds and have a sugar crust—he mounted and again took the road.

Once outside Aleppo he let the mule have her head as he was no longer certain of the country. She carried him night and day until on a certain sunset he reached the city of Basrah, though he did not know what its name was until he had put up at the nearest khān. When he had dismounted all his belongings from the mule, he commanded the stable-boy of the khān to lead her up and down the street a little, so that she should not catch cold by stopping work too suddenly. He himself sat down on his carpet in the khān to rest.

While the stable-boy was leading the mule up and down it chanced that the wazīr of Basrah was looking out on the street from one of the windows of his palace. Seeing so fine an animal so richly caparisoned, he thought that it must belong to some wazīr or even some king. So he sent one of his slaves to fetch the stable-boy to him. The wazīr, who was a very old and honourable man, asked the stable-boy, when he came, who and of what rank the master of the mule might be. 'My lord,' said the stable-boy, 'he is a very beautiful young man, a true heart-breaker, richly dressed like some great merchant's son. His face inspires both trust and admiration.'

The wazīr hearing this mounted one of his horses and rode to the khān. When Nūr al-Dīn saw him coming, he rose and running to meet him helped him from his horse. They greeted each other cordially and the wazīr, sitting down by Nūr al-Dīn's side, asked him whence and why he had come to Basrah. 'I come from Cairo where I was born,' answered Nūr al-Dīn. 'My father was wazīr to the Sultān of Egypt, but now Allāh has had mercy on him and he is dead.' Continuing, the young man told the wazīr all his tale and added: 'I am determined never to return to Egypt until I have visited every city of every country in the world.'

'My child,' said the wazīr gravely, 'such a determination can come to no good. Continuous travel through strange countries leads to ruin and the end of everything. Take my advice in this, dear lad, for I am fearful of what life and time may have in store for you.'

The wazīr then ordered his slaves to bring the mule and all Nūr al-Dīn's other belongings to his own house, where he provided the strange young man with a room and all else he might require.

Nūr al-Dīn stayed some time with the wazīr, who gave him audience every day, heaped favours upon him, and ended by loving him dearly. 'My child,' he said to him one day, 'I am an old man and I have no son: but Allāh has given me one daughter who is both as beautiful and as excellent in all her ways as you are. So far I have refused all offers for her hand, but I have grown so to love you that if you consent I will make her your wife and your slave. Also, if you marry her, I will go to the Sultān and tell him that you are my nephew newly come out of Egypt to Basrah in order to ask my daughter in marriage. For my sake the Sultān will make you wazīr instead of me. I am very old and need rest. It will be a great joy to me when I can go up into my house and never leave it again.'

Nūr al-Dīn sat silent for a little with lowered eyes and then said: 'I hear and I obey!' The wazīr was overjoyed at his consent and ordered all his slaves to prepare a feast, lighting and decorating his greatest hall, which was reserved for the entertaining of the most important amīrs.

When all his friends had come at his invitation, and among them the greatest personages and merchants of Basrah, the wazīr explained the choice which he had made of Nūr al-Dīn, saying: 'I have a brother who was wazīr in the court of Egypt to whom Allāh gave two sons. Before he died he begged me to marry my daughter to one of them and I promised to do so. This young man is one of my nephews and has come here that I may fulfil my promise by him. I desire to have his marriage contract drawn up and for him to come to live with me.'

All were in cordial agreement with this plan and sat down in great good humour to drink every kind of wine and eat prodigious quantities of sweets and pastries. Later, when they had been sprinkled with ceremonial rose-water, they took their leave.

After they had gone, the wazīr ordered his boy slaves to take Nūr al-Dīn to the hammām and give him a luxurious ritual bath. He himself provided a beautiful robe of his own, towels, copper basins, perfume-braziers and all else that he might need. When he had bathed, Nūr al-Dīn put on the new robe and rode back through the streets of the city as the full moon rides through the fairest of the nights of summer. He spurred his dapple mule towards the wazīr's palace and all the people in the streets cried out on Allāh in praise of the fair young man whom He had made. When he had dismounted and entered the palace, he kissed the wazīr's hand and . . .

At this point, Shahrazād saw the approach of morning and discreetly fell silent.

But when the twentieth night had come

SHE SAID:

It is related, O auspicious King, that the wazīr rose and joyfully embraced Nūr al-Dīn, saying: 'Now, my son, go up to your wife and be happy. To-morrow I will take you to the Sultān. For to-night Allāh has so filled this old heart with joy that I have no more to ask of Him.'

Kissing his father-in-law's hand a second time, Nūr al-Dīn went up to the chamber of his bride and there happened that which happened.

So much for Nūr al-Dīn!

As for his brother Shams al-Dīn at Cairo . . . when he had returned from his journey to the Pyramids with the Sultān of Egypt he was disturbed at not finding his brother Nūr al-Dīn. The slaves of whom he asked news could only say that on the morning of the Sultān's setting forth he had had his mule magnificently equipped, saying that he intended to go to Kalyib to cure himself there of an oppression of the chest, and forbidding anyone to follow him. 'Since that day,' they added, 'we have had no further news of him.'

Then Shams al-Dīn began to mourn bitterly because of his brother's absence, becoming each day more certain that it must have been his own harsh words on the eve of the Sultān's setting forth which had caused him to flee the city. 'If I can only find him,' he thought, 'I will handsomely repair my ill-treatment of him.'

So Shams al-Dīn went to the Sultān who, when he had heard the whole tale, wrote dispatches over his own seal to the effect that Nūr al-Dīn had disappeared and must be found; and these he sent by swift horsemen to all his viceroys in other countries.

But all the couriers returned without news, for not one of them had been to Basrah. 'It is my fault,' wept Shams al-Dīn, 'nothing of the sort would have happened if I had shown a little tact and understanding!'

But everything has an end; and at last Shams al-Dīn forgot his grief and married the daughter of one of the greatest merchants in Cairo. That which happened between them happened.

Now it so chanced that it was on the same night that both the brothers, one in Cairo and one in Basrah, lay with their wives for the first time. Allāh allowed it, that it might be shown that He is the master of His creatures' destinies.

Just as the brothers had agreed before their quarrel, their wives not only conceived on the same night but brought forth on the same day: to Shams al-Dīn, wazīr of Egypt, a daughter more beautiful than any in all the land and to Nūr al-Dīn, at Basrah, a son whose beauty had no peer among any who were alive upon the earth at that time. The poet has said:

> Drink at his mouth,
> Forgetting the full red cups and reeling bowls.
>
> Drink at his eyes,
> Forgetting the purple scent of the vine.
>
> Drink at his cheeks,
> Forgetting the life of roses poured in crystal.
>
> Drink at his heart,
> Forgetting everything.

Because of his beauty Nūr al-Dīn's son was named Hasan Badr al-Dīn, the beauty of faith's moon. His birth was the occasion of great public rejoicing and, on the seventh day after his coming into the world, banquets were given in his honour on a royal scale, as if he had been a little prince. When all the feasting was over Nūr al-Dīn was conducted by the wazīr of Basrah into the presence of the Sultān and, as he was a man of great eloquence, learned in the beauties of poetry, he recited, as he kissed the earth between the Sultān's hands, the following impromptu:

> Each thing he does is a new pearl to bless
> The holy throat of his bride, Righteousness;
>   And if my lips adventure to his hand
> They kiss the five white keys of happiness.

Ravished by this well-turned compliment, the Sultān graciously received Nūr al-Dīn, though he did not know who he was; and after he had praised his literary skill asked the wazīr who this eloquent young man might be.

The wazīr told him the whole story from beginning to end; and the Sultān asked: 'How is it that I have never heard you speak of your nephew?' 'Sovereign and Over-lord,' answered the wazīr, 'I had a brother who was wazīr in the court of Egypt. He died leaving two sons, the elder of whom succeeded to his wazīrship, while the younger came to visit me in furtherance of a promise which I had made to his father that I would marry one of my nephews to my daughter. I married him to my dear child as soon as he arrived in Basrah. He is a young man, as you see, and I am old, a little deaf, and inattentive to the business of the state. I come to beg my lord to name this nephew and son-in-law of mine as my successor. I can assure you that he is in every way fit to be your wazīr. He is a man of excellent counsel, fertile in expedient ideas, and well versed in the business of government.' Before replying the Sultān looked long and closely at young Nūr al-Dīn and, finding all about him as it should be, fell in with the aged wazīr's plan and named Nūr al-Dīn grand wazīr on the spot. He gave him a robe of honour wrought by a thousand cunning needles, a mule from his own stables, and appointed guards and chamberlains to be ever about him.

Nūr al-Dīn kissed the Sultān's hand and left the presence with his father-in-law. They went home rejoicing and hastened at once to kiss the week-old Hasan Badr al-Dīn, saying: 'The little one has brought good fortune with him.'

Next day Nūr al-Dīn went up to the palace to take over his new duties and, when he had greeted the Sultān, said:

> Silence were meet, and yet I cry aloud
> In my great sovereign's praise:
> Your days are whiter than a morning cloud,
> And all your nights are days.

With the Sultān's permission Nūr al-Dīn then sat down on the dīwān of the wazīrs and began to deal with the current affairs of the city, doing justice as if he had been a wazīr for many years, and in all acquitting himself so well beneath the eyes of the Sultān that the other marvelled at his intelligence, his business understanding, and his admirable justice.

The Sultān loved him more and more, and admitted him to his closest friendship. But, while he continued to fulfil his difficult duties in the most approved fashion, Nūr al-Dīn did not for a moment neglect the upbringing of his son, Hasan Badr al-Dīn. At the same time he became more powerful and more in favour every day, so that the Sultān increased the number of his chamberlains, slaves, guards, and couriers. Soon Nūr al-Dīn became so rich that he was able to traffic on the grand scale: to fit out argosies, to build great houses, to set up mills and water-wheels, to plant mighty gardens and orchards.

When Hasan Badr al-Dīn was four years old, the aged wazīr died and Nūr al-Dīn gave him a great and solemn funeral at which all the chief men of the land attended.

After this Nūr al-Dīn devoted himself with single purpose to the religious and artistic education of his son. He caused a venerable sage to come each day to teach young Hasan Badr al-Dīn in his home; and this old man little by little initiated him into the teaching of the Koran until he could say the whole of it by heart and after, year by year, grounded him in all branches of secular knowledge. Hasan grew in beauty and in all accomplishments. In the words of the poet:

> He is a moon to whom the sun bequeaths
> Light for his cheek's scarlet anemone sheaths;
> He is a king who has beneath his power
> All the warm meadows and each coloured flower.

During all this time young Hasan never left his father's house for an instant, because his old tutor demanded every moment of his time for lessons. But when he reached his fifteenth year and had nothing more to learn from the old man, his father Nūr al-Dīn put on him the most magnificent of all his robes and setting him on his finest mule went forth with him to visit the Sultān. All the people in the streets of Basrah cried out at the sight of young Hasan Badr al-Dīn, commenting on the beauty of his face and of his body, the rarity of his manner and of his carriage, and exclaiming: 'Yā Allāh! how beautiful! A moon! Allāh preserve him!'

As for the Sultān, when he saw Badr al-Dīn he lost his breath and could not regain it for a whole minute. He bade him approach and, falling in love with him at first sight, made him his favourite, showered gifts upon him and said to his father Nūr al-Dīn: 'Dear wazīr, bring him to me every day, for I cannot live without him.' So Nūr al-Dīn was forced to answer: 'I hear and I obey!'

About the time that Hasan Badr al-Dīn became firmly established as the friend and favourite of the Sultān, Nūr al-Dīn fell seriously ill and knowing that the time was not long before he would be called to Allāh, sent for Hasan and said to him: 'My child, this world is as it were a house falling about our ears, but the world to come will prove an eternal abiding place. Before I die I have certain precepts to give you to which I require you to open both your ears and your heart.' Then Nūr al-Dīn gave Hasan rules of inestimable value for his conduct among his equals and for every occasion in life.

After he had done so, Nūr al-Dīn fell silent and began to think of his brother Shams al-Dīn wazīr of Egypt, of his native land, the people of his house and all his friends in Cairo; until he wept because he would never see them more. Then he said to Hasan: 'My boy, remember the words that I am going to say to you, because they are very important. I have a brother, Shams al-Dīn, who is wazīr of Cairo in Egypt. I left your uncle after an unimportant quarrel and came here to Basrah. Now I would dictate my last instructions to you. Take paper and reed and write as I say.'

Choosing a sheet of paper, Hasan Badr al-Dīn opened the pencase which hung at his belt, chose the finest of his reed pens, and plunged it in the ink-soaked oakum which lay in the middle of the case. He sat down, folded the paper over his right hand and, taking the pen in his left, said: 'Father, I am waiting for your words.' Nūr al-Dīn began to dictate: 'In the name of Allāh, the Merciful, the Compassionate . . .' and went on until he had told all his story from beginning to end. He gave the date of his arrival at Basrah, of his marriage with the wazīr's daughter; he set down all his genealogy with the name of his forbears both direct and indirect, together with the origin of each, the rank that each had acquired; and all the tree of his family both on his father's and on his mother's side. When all was finished, he said: 'Keep this writing safely and if ever evil befall you return to the land of your fathers, even to Cairo the fair city of your father Nūr al-Dīn; seek out your uncle the wazīr and tell him that I died grieving in a strange land that I might not look upon his face again. Forget not, my son Hasan, either this paper or the counsels I have given you.'

Hasan carefully folded the paper, after sanding it and sealing it with his father's seal. Then he enclosed it in waxed cloth to keep it from the damp and sewed it between the sash and bonnet of his turban.

This done he had no other thought but to kiss his father's hand and weep over him; while Nūr al-Dīn whispered counsels in his ear until his soul took flight.

This death cast not only Hasan Badr al-Dīn down into the mire of grief, but the Sultān also, with all the amīrs of the land both great and small.

They buried Nūr al-Dīn according to his rank and Hasan mourned for him for two months with such real grief that he even forgot to go up to the palace to see the Sultān as had been his custom.

The Sultān, not understanding that it was grief alone which kept the beautiful boy from him, but thinking that Hasan avoided him deliberately, became very angry, named another in the place of Nūr al-Dīn which he had sworn that Hasan should have, and took another young chamberlain under his protection.

He did more. He ordered all Hasan's goods, his houses, and everything that his father had left him to be sealed up and confiscated, and commanded the boy himself to be brought before him in chains. The new wazīr took some of the chamberlains with him and set out for Hasan's house where the lad sat, not dreaming of the misfortune so soon to come upon him.

Now among the slaves of the palace there was a certain young mamelūk who loved Hasan Badr al-Dīn. Hearing what was about to happen, he ran at top speed and told everything to the grieving youth. 'Is there time for me to get some money?' asked Hasan. 'Time presses,' answered the mamelūk, 'go now if you would save your life!'

So Hasan rushed out, dressed as he was and empty-handed, with his robe lifted over his head so that he should not be recognised, and hurried towards the outskirts of the city.

All about him the people of Basrah who had heard of the evil intentions of the Sultān were crying: 'Allāh have mercy on his beauty!' Hasan heard them, but he hastened on till chance led him to his father's tomb. He lifted his robe from about his face and went in under the dome of the sepulchre to pass the night there.

While he was seated in bitter reflection, a certain Jew, a well-known merchant in Basrah, passed by on his return to the city from a neighbouring village. He recognised Hasan at once and approached him respectfully, saying: 'Indeed, my lord, your beautiful face is changed. Has some new misfortune befallen you since the death of your father, whom I loved? May Allāh have mercy on his soul!' Not wishing to tell him the whole truth, Hasan answered: 'While I was asleep at home this afternoon my father's spirit came to me and reproached me for not having visited his tomb. I jumped up as I was and ran here in a state of terror and regret. I have not yet recovered my proper looks.'

'My lord,' said the Jew, 'for a long time I have meant to come to speak to you on a matter of business; now that chance has brought us together I will tell you what I have in my mind. I used to do business with your father and know that there are still many ships on the sea bearing back merchandise for him. If you are willing, I will buy one of their cargoes for a thousand dīnārs and pay you on the spot.'

Hasan could not but accept this offer in which he saw the hand of Allāh; so the Jew counted out a thousand dīnārs from his purse and gave them to the young man, asking for a sealed receipt. Hasan took the paper which the Jew offered him, dipped his reed in the other's copper writing-case, and wrote as follows:

'I, Hasan Badr al-Dīn, son of the wazīr Nūr al-Dīn (who is dead and may Allāh have mercy on his soul) have sold to the Jew so-and-so, son of such-and-such, merchant of Basrah, the cargo of the first of my father's boats to reach the city, for the sum of one thousand dīnārs only.'

He sealed the paper with his father's seal and gave it to the Jew, who left him with many expressions of respect.

Hasan sat there mourning and weeping until nightfall when sleep overtook him on his father's grave and he lay as one dead until the rising of the moon. Then, his head having rolled off the stone, he was obliged to turn over and lie out on his back, full in the moonlight in all his beauty.

Now that burial-ground was the resort of benevolent Jinn, Mussulmāns and Believers. By chance a charming Jinnīyah was taking the air at that time under the moonlight, and happening to pass by the sleeping Hasan she halted on seeing his surpassing beauty. 'As Allāh lives,' she exclaimed, 'here is indeed a lovely boy! I feel that I could fall in love with his eyes if they were open; they must be very black and fine. I think I will fly about a little until he wakes and then come back.' So saying she flew off and mounted very high to find the fresh air. In the course of her circling she was delighted to meet a friend, a Jinnī who was also a Believer. She greeted him sweetly and he returned her salutations in proper form. 'Where have you come from?' she asked. 'From Cairo,' he answered. 'How do all the good Believers in Cairo?' she questioned, and he replied: 'Thanks be to Allāh, they do very well.' Then said she: 'Would you like to come with me to look on the beauty of a young man who is lying asleep in the burial ground of Basrah?' 'Certainly,' said the Jinnī; so they took hands and, swooping down, alighted before the young

Hasan. 'Was I not right?' asked the Jinnīyah, winking, and the Jinnī
answered: 'Allāh, Allāh! There is not his like anywhere! Many a
female organ shall, as it were, explode because of him. And yet,' he
went on, 'now that I come to think of it, my sister, I have seen one
with whom this pretty youth might be compared, the daughter of
the wazīr Shams al-Dīn of Cairo.' 'I do not know her,' said the
Jinnīyah. 'Listen, then,' said the Jinnī, 'and I will tell you all about
her.' And he told the following tale:

Her father Shams al-Dīn is very troubled about his daughter; for
the Sultān of Egypt, hearing his women speak of her unparalleled
beauty, asked her in marriage. Shams al-Dīn, who had other views
for his daughter, was thrown into great perplexity and said to the
Sultān: 'My master and my lord, I pray you both to excuse and
pardon me. You know the story of my poor brother Nūr al-Dīn
who was joint wazīr with me; how he left the city after a trivial
quarrel and has never been heard of since. My lord, when my
daughter was born, I swore before Allāh that I would never marry
her to any but the son of my brother Nūr al-Dīn. That was eighteen
years ago. Now only a few days ago I heard to my great delight that
my brother had married the wazīr's daughter of Basrah and had a
son by her; it is written in the stars that my child should marry her
cousin. You, my lord, can choose any young girl you will, and
Egypt is full of many who are not unworthy of kings.'

But the Sultān flew into a great rage and cried: 'Dog of a wazīr, I
have come down even as low as you, willing to do you the honour of
marrying your daughter, and you dare for some cold and silly reason
to refuse me! Be it so. Now I swear that she shall marry the lowest
cur about my palace.' The Sultān had a little horse-groom who was
contorted and hunchbacked, with a hump behind and a pigeon-
breast in front. This little wretch he sent for and contracted to the
daughter of Shams al-Dīn, in spite of all her father's entreaties. He
ordered a great wedding with all manner of music and bade the little
hunchback sleep with the girl this very night.

When I left Cairo the young slaves were all gathered about the
hunchback, shooting off very amusing Egyptian pleasantries at him
and wreathing the marriage candles about his head. I left them when
they were about to take him to the bath, mocking him and calling
out: 'We would rather take the tool of a flayed ass in our hands than
the miserable little zabb of this hunchback!' Indeed, my sister, he is a
most disgusting ugly little thing.

(Here the Jinnī made a horrible face, remembering all the ugliness of the hunchback, and spat on the ground. Then he continued:)

The poor young girl, who is the most beautiful creature I have ever seen, yes, more beautiful even than this youth of yours, is called Sitt al-Husn; and indeed she is the queen of beauty. She was weeping bitterly, denied even her father's presence, for he had been forbidden to go to the marriage. Even now she is sitting there all alone in the middle of the festival, surrounded by musicians, dancers and singers. In a few minutes the disgusting horse-groom will be coming out of the hammām; they are only waiting for that before they begin the ceremony.

At this point, Shahrazād saw the approach of morning, and discreetly fell silent.

And when the twenty-first night had come

SHE SAID:

It is related, O auspicious King, that the Jinnīyah answered the Jinnī in these words: 'I think you must be mistaken in saying that Sitt al-Husn is more beautiful than this youth; it is impossible, because he is the most beautiful human of all time.' 'I assure you that the girl is more beautiful still,' said the Ifrīt, 'come and see for yourself; and at the same time we can prevent the evil hunchback from polluting so marvellous a piece of flesh. The two young people are worthy of each other; you would say that they were brother and sister or cousins at the least. Also it would be a horrible thing for a hunchback to copulate with Sitt al-Husn.'

'You are right, brother,' said the Jinnīyah, 'it will be a good work, and also we can then examine them and determine which is the more beautiful.' So the Ifrīt placed the young man on his back and, helped by the Jinnīyah, flew with all possible speed to Cairo. They set down the lovely Hasan on a stone bench in a street near the palace, which was all full of people, and then woke him. Hasan was excessively disturbed at not finding himself stretched out on his father's tomb at Basrah. He looked to right and left, and everything was unknown to him. It was not even the same city. So surprised was he that he opened his mouth to cry out; but before he could do so he saw a tall, bearded man standing in front of him, who winked and commanded silence.

Hasan controlled himself and the Jinnī, for it was he, gave him a lighted candle and told him to mix with the crowd of candle-bearers, who were gathered to attend the marriage. 'I am a Jinnī, a true Believer,' said the tall man. 'This city is Cairo; I brought you here while you were asleep in order to do you a service, both for the love I bear to Allāh and for your own exceeding beauty. Take this lighted candle, mingle with the crowd, and make your way to the hammām. You will see a sort of little hunchback coming out of it, whom the people will conduct to the palace. Follow, or rather get so near him that you walk by his side. He is newly married: your business is to enter the great hall of the palace with him, as if you belonged to the place. Each time you see a singer or a musician or a dancer stop before the marriage party, plunge your hand into your pocket, which through my art will be always full of gold, and throw great handfuls of coin to all of them. Do not fear that your store will become exhausted; I will see to that. Give a handful to all that come, strike an attitude, and above all fear nothing. Trust in Allāh Who made you so beautiful, and in me who love you. What comes to pass will be through the will and power of Allāh.'

With these words the Jinnī disappeared and Hasan Badr al-Dīn said to himself: 'What can all this mean? What service can this strange Ifrīt be going to render me?' Nevertheless he went forward with his lighted candle and came to the hammām just as the hunchback was leaving in a new robe and on a fine horse.

Hasan mingled with the crowd and threaded his way so well that he came to the head of the procession and walked by the side of the hunchback. His beauty appeared in all its wonderful splendour. He was dressed in the fine robes which he had worn at Basrah, on his head was a tarbūsh wound in the mode of Basrah, with a wide silk turban embroidered in silver and little tinted flowers; he wore a cloak enriched with falls of silk and broad decorations in gold thread. All this only added to his beauty.

Each time a singer or a dancer came out of the group of players and postured before the hunchback, Hasan threw her a handful of gold which fell before her, or filled her little tambourine to overflowing. This he did with an air of perfect grace.

Soon all the women and even all the men of the crowd were giving their full attention to his beauty. At last the procession arrived at the palace, and there the chamberlains drove back the crowd, only allowing the troupe of musicians, dancers, and singers to enter behind the hunchback.

Then the singers and the dancers called to the chamberlains with one voice and said: 'By Allāh, you were right enough not to let men into the harīm to help us with the habiting of the bride. But now we refuse to come in unless you let this young man enter with us. He has loaded us with gold and is our friend; we will make no festivity for you unless he also is there.'

The women took hold of Hassan and dragged him into the great hall of the harīm so that he and the little hunchback were the only two men there, much to the latter's disgust. All the wives of the amīrs, the wazīrs, and the chamberlains of the palace were ranged in two rows up the centre of the hall, each holding a great candle and having her face covered with a little white silk veil because of the presence of the men. Hasan and the hunchback passed between the two files, which stretched right from the hall to the nupital chamber, and seated themselves on a dais.

Now all of the women when they saw the beauty of Hasan Badr al-Dīn, the charms of his figure and the moonlit glory of his face, caught their breath for love. Each burned to clasp the youth, to throw herself on his lap and to rest there for a year, a month, an hour, or even the little time of one assault, just that she might feel him inside her.

Unable to contain themselves any longer they lifted their veils, forgetting the presence of the hunchback, and clustered round Hasan to look at him, to speak a word or two of love, or to express with their eyes the desire they felt for him. All the time the dancers and singers were going about among them, telling of Hasan's generosity and encouraging the ladies to favour him as much as possible; so that soon the fair guests were all crying: 'Allāh, Allāh, what a man! If only he could lie with Sitt al-Husn! They are made for each other! Allāh confound the wicked hunchback!'

While the guests were still praising Hasan and calling down curses on the hunchback, suddenly the musicians struck gaily on their instruments, the door of the bridal chamber opened, and Sitt al-Husn, surrounded by slaves and eunuchs, entered the hall. Shams al-Dīn's daughter shone there like a hūrī and had the appearance among her women of a moon leaving a cloud accompanied by stars. She was scented with musk, with amber, with roses; her delicately-combed hair shone under silk; her slender shoulders showed valiantly beneath the richness of their covering. She was royally clad in a robe of red gold on which beasts and birds were portrayed in jewellery work; and beneath this were so many lighter under-robes that Allāh alone could tell you of them or compute the value of each. I know not how many thousands of dīnārs had been paid for the collar about her little neck; there is no single man alive to-day, no not even a king, who owns one jewel the like of any of those thousands. To put the matter in a few words the bride was as beautiful as is the full moon on her fourteenth night.

Sitt al-Husn moved towards Hasan Badr al-Dīn of Basrah, since he was still seated on the dais, undulating her gracious body from left to right. When the hunchback groom would have leapt up and greeted her, she thrust him back with horror and with one lithe movement stood again before Hasan. To think that he was her cousin and that neither of them knew it!

All the ladies began to laugh at what they saw, especially when the bride so obviously fell in love with Hasan that she cried: 'O Allāh, let this lovely boy be my husband and free me from the importunate hunchback!'

Hasan again plunged his hand into his pocket as he had been told to do and threw showers of gold among Sitt al-Husn's slaves, among the dancers, and the singers, until they all shouted: 'To you the bride!' and Badr al-Dīn smiled graciously upon them at this wish.

The hunchback sat alone through all this scene as ugly and as angry as an ape, chattering and cursing to himself. Each time a woman came near him she blew out her candle in mockery and all of the guests grinned at him and mocked him with full-flavoured witticisms. One said: 'Masturbate, little ape, and then you can marry the air!' another: 'You are no taller than our fair master's zabb; its eggs are as big as your two humps!' a third: 'If his zabb but touched you it would send you flying on your backside into the stable!' and all laughed at the poor fellow.

Seven times, dressed in different fashion, the bride made progress round the hall followed by her ladies, and at the end of each circle halted before Hasan. Each robe was more perfectly in keeping than the last: each set off jewels increasingly more rare and beautiful. All the time that she was walking round and round, the musicians excelled themselves, the singers sang songs progressively more amorous and exciting, and the dancers beating on their tambourines footed it like birds. Hasan went on throwing gold among them, and ladies of rank struggled to pick it up because it had touched his hand. Some of them even profited by the general mirth and excitement, the music and the heady singing, to lie one on top of the other in pretended copulation, their eyes fixed all the time on Hasan. Imagine the chagrin of the hunchback when one woman turning to Hasan brought her stretched hand down sharply inviting him to her parts, another winking pushed her middle finger up and down, a third twisting and swaying her hips clapped her opened right hand over her closed left, or a fourth with a more unbridled gesture still slapped her buttocks, saying to the hunchback himself: 'You can have a taste in apricot time.'

At the end of the bride's seventh circling of the room the festivities, which had lasted a great part of the night, were considered to be over. The music ceased; the players and the dancers and the singers and all the ladies passed before Hasan on their way out, kissing his hand or touching his robe and looking over their shoulders for a last glance. When all had disappeared save Hasan and the bridegroom, her own followers took the bride into the undressing chamber and there took off her garments one by one, saying as each was removed: 'In the name of Allāh!' to avert the evil eye. Then they left her with her old nurse whose duty it was to lead her to the bridal chamber when the hunchback should have gone there.

When they were alone, the hunchback got up from his dais and said dryly to Hasan: 'Indeed, my lord, you have greatly honoured us with your presence and overwhelmed us with your charities. Can it be that you are waiting for someone to throw you out?' Not knowing what to answer or what to do, Hasan rose and exclaiming: 'In the name of Allah!' left the hall. But at the door he was met by the Jinnī, who said: 'Where are you away to, Badr al-Dīn? Stay and listen to my instructions. The hunchback is just going to the closet, and there I will look after him. What you have to do is to enter the bridal chamber and when the bride comes in say to her: "I am your husband; the hunchback is but the most wretched of our grooms. He is now back in the stable drinking a bowl of curdled milk to our good health. His introduction to your marriage was but a trick of the Sultān and your father to ward off the evil eye." Then take her without fear, lift her veil, and do what you shall find to do.' With this the Jinnī disappeared.

In a short time the hunchback went to the closet to make a motion before visiting his bride. He had just squatted down on the marble and begun, when the Jinnī, in the likeness of a huge rat, jumped up through the hole of the privy, calling: 'Zik, zik!' as a rat does. The hunchback crying out: 'Hash, hash!' clapped his hands to frighten the animal away. At once the rat became a large cat with very bright eyes, which mewed at him. The hunchback continued what he was at, so the cat turned into a big dog which barked: 'Hau, hau!' The hunchback became frightened and called out: 'Get away, you beast!' Then the dog swelled and turned into an ass which brayed: 'Hak! hi hak!' into the hunchback's face and also broke wind with a noise like thunder. Filled with terror, the hunchback felt all his belly dissolve in a diarrhœa and had hardly the strength to cry for help. But fearing that he might yet escape, the ass expanded and became a buffalo which completely blocked up the privy door. This time the Jinnī spoke with a human voice and the hunchback heard the buffalo say: 'Woe to you, hunchback of my arse, filthiest of grooms!' Hereupon the hunchback felt the cold of death assail him and slipped down, diarrhœa and all, to the ground, half undressed, with his teeth chattering, and messing himself for very terror.

'Dwarf of the gutter!' cried the buffalo. 'Could you find no other woman but my mistress to harbour your ignoble tool?' Then, as the groom was too horrified to answer, he continued: 'Answer me, or I will make you eat your dung!' On this the hunchback managed to gasp out: 'Before Allāh, it is not my fault; I was forced to the business. And besides, my lord of the buffaloes, I had no idea that the girl had a lover among you. I swear that I repent and ask pardon both from Allāh and from you.' 'Swear then by Him,' said the Jinnī, 'that you will obey my orders.' The bridegroom swore to be obedient and the Jinnī gave him these instructions: 'You must stay where you are till sunrise and then be gone. If you say a word of all this to anyone I will break your head into a thousand pieces, and if ever again you set foot on the woman's side of the palace I will wrench it off and throw it into the common drain. Now to find a suitable position for you!' So saying, the buffalo took up the hunchback in his teeth and thrust him head first into the stinking hole of the privy so that only his legs remained outside. 'Do not dare to move,' he repeated and then vanished. We must now leave the hunchback and return to Hasan Badr al-Dīn.

He stole through the private apartments and sat down in the depths of the marriage-chamber, leaving the hunchback and the Jinnī to fight it out together. Hardly had he done so when the old nurse led in Sitt al-Husn and, herself remaining at the door, cried out to the hunchback whom she supposed to be there: 'Rise, valiant hero, and do shiningly by your wife! Allāh be with you, my children!' Then the old trot withdrew.

Sitt al-Husn, her heart beating feebly, came forward murmuring: 'I would rather die than give myself to this deformed little wretch.' But when she had taken two or three steps she recognised the radiant Badr al-Dīn and gave a small cry of happiness, saying: 'My dear, my dear, how kind of you to have waited for me! Are you alone? What happiness! I swear I thought that you meant to share me with the hunchback and that I would have the two of you about me.' 'Shame, my dear mistress!' answered Badr al-Dīn. 'How can you have thought so?' 'Then which of you is my husband?' asked Sitt al-Husn. 'I am, sweet child,' said Badr al-Din, 'the whole business about the hunchback was only a joke to make you laugh and a precaution against the evil eye. Your father hired him for ten dīnārs, and he is now back in his own stable drinking our health in curdled milk!'

Reassured by what he said, Sitt al-Husn smiled, then sweetly laughed, and finally broke out: 'Darling, in Allāh's name, take me, hold me, fix me to your lap!' And so saying she lifted her garments, showing that she was quite naked below her robe. This she raised with her last words, displaying to him all her rose, together with delightful thighs and jasmine-scented moon. Seeing the desirable details of this hūrī's body, Badr al-Dīn felt the blood rush through his veins and the sleeping child awaken. In all haste he rose to undress: he undid the innumerable rolls of his great trousers and placed them on the dīwān with his purse of gold beneath them; he put his elegant turban on a chair, covering his head with the light night-cap which had been placed ready for the hunchback, and stood up in his gold-embroidered silken shirt and in blue silk drawers fastened with a heavy gold cord.

Sitt al-Husn had stretched all her body out for him, so with one brisk movement he undid the golden cord and threw himself upon her. He knelt between her open thighs, pressed them further apart with his hands and, bringing the battering-ram against the fortress, with one stroke made the breach. Hasan rejoiced when he felt that the pearl had not been pierced before, that no other ram had ever been there even with the tip of its nose. The same happy state of virginity he discovered on the other side and took advantage of its sweet youth with all delight. Fifteen separate times the ram moved up to the walls and then retreated taking no hurt by the way.

It must have been at this time that Sitt al-Husn conceived, as you will hear later on, O Prince of all Believers.

Badr al-Dīn said after the fifteenth assault: 'This will be enough for the time being.' He lay down by the girl's side, pillowing her head gently upon his hand; she clasped him in her arms and so they lay. There is a poem which says:

> Go to it with a will, my dears,
> This is no time for fears;
> God made one picture better far
> Than painters' pictures are:
> A naked boy and girl in bed,
> His arm holding her head,
> His face bent forward on her breast,
> And all the tinted rest:
> Wishing this picture to be duplicated
> And all the young world mated.

So Hasan Badr al-Dīn and Sitt al-Husn slept.

The Jinnī had hurried from the privy to find the Jinnīyah and both of them were now looking down in admiration on the sleeping pair, after having been invisibly present at their games and counting up the number of the points. 'You see that I was right,' said the Jinnī, and then added: 'Now we must take the young man up again and carry him to the place where we found him, by his father's tomb at Basrah. Lift quickly and I will help you, for morning is at hand.' So the Ifrītah lifted young Hasan upon her back, dressed only in his shirt (for his drawers had not kept up during his exercises), and flew away with him, followed closely by the Ifrīt. While they were flying through the air the Ifrīt was seized with libidinous thoughts and attempted to violate the Ifrītah, burdened as she was by the weight of Hasan. At any other time she would have been willing enough, but now she feared for the boy and was pleased enough when Allāh intervened by hurling a thunderbolt at the Ifrīt and dashing him to the earth. An Ifrīt is terrible in copulation and I think the two had a lucky escape. The Ifrītah sank to earth beside the burning Ifrīt; and it was written by Destiny that the place where she set Hasan down should be near one of the gates of Damascus in the land of Syria.

When day rose, the gates of the city were opened and the people who came forth for their business were astonished to see a lovely youth lying on the ground dressed only in his shirt, with a nightcap on his head and wearing no drawers. 'Ah, how awake he must have been,' some said, 'to be so deep asleep!' But others exclaimed: 'By Allāh, he is fair! Lucky the woman who lay with him last night! But why is he naked?' 'Probably,' answered a third group, 'the poor young man was at a tavern longer than he should be and drank beyond his strength. Finding the gates shut he must have laid down to sleep outside them.'

While they were speculating in this sort the morning wind came to kiss the lovely Hasan and lifted up his shirt so that all saw a belly, a navel, thighs, and legs wrought of crystal, and a zabb with eggs of a surprising beauty.

As they were enjoying all these splendours, Badr al-Dīn woke and seeing himself outside an unknown gate and surrounded by strangers, cried out: 'Tell me where I am, good people, and why you stand about me in this way? What has happened?' 'We stopped to look at you,' they answered, 'simply because you are beautiful. But do you not know that this is the gate of Damascus? Where have you passed the night that you should be lying naked here like this?' 'What is this you tell me, my friends?' cried Hasan. 'I passed the night at Cairo and you tell me that I am at Damascus!' All laughed aloud at this, one saying: 'A great eater of hashīsh, surely!' another: 'Certainly he is mad! It is a pity that so peerless a boy should be mad.' And a third: 'What tale is this you tell us?' 'As God lives, I am not lying, good people,' said Hasan. 'I passed last night in Cairo just as surely as I spent yesterday at Basrah, my native city!' A great babble arose on these words, one saying that it was strange and another that he was mad and the most reeling with laughter and clapping their hands, crying: 'Though it is a pity that this peerless boy has lost his wits, yet does he not make a delightful fool?'

One wiser than the rest said: 'Try to clear your wits, my son, and do not say such foolish things.' 'I know what I am talking about,' said Hasan. 'Last night I was a bridegroom in Cairo and had a delicious time.' More convinced of his folly than ever, the crowd cried out: 'He has been married in his dreams!' 'What was it like?' 'How many times?' 'Was she a hūrī or a harlot?' Beginning to be angry Badr al-Dīn answered them in earnest: 'She was a hūrī, and I did not couple in my dreams but between her legs full fifteen times.

I took the place of a diseased hunchback and even wore the nightcap which was meant for him. Here it is!' Then looking down at himself, he cried: 'But, by Allāh, good people, where are my turban and my drawers, my robe and my trousers? Yes, by Allāh, where is my purse?'

Hasan jumped up and was starting to hunt about him for his clothes when all the assembly fell into such an ecstasy of winking that he made up his mind to enter the city as he was.

Poor Hasan was obliged to walk through all the streets and markets followed by a crowd of children, who yelled: 'Look at the madman!' He was indeed at his wits' end when Allāh, fearing that he might come to harm, led him by a certain baker's shop just as its master was opening for the day. Hasan leapt into the shop and hid himself, and, as the pastrycook was a brawny fellow with a certain reputation in the city, the crowd retired.

The Hajj Abdallāh—for so was the cook named—looked over young Hasan Badr al-Dīn carefully and at once fell in love with his beauty and his natural gifts. 'Where do you come from, dear youth?' he asked of Hasan. 'Tell me your story, for I already love you more dearly than my life.' So Hasan told all his story to Abdallāh the cook, who was greatly surprised by it and said when it was ended: 'My young lord Badr al-Dīn, your tale is indeed a marvellous one, but I would counsel you, my child, not to tell it to anyone else, because it is a dangerous thing to confide in one's fellow men. All my shop is at your disposal, and I beg you to live here with me until Allāh sees fit to make an end of your misfortunes. I have no children and will be rejoiced if you will accept me as a father. Yes, I will adopt you as my son.' 'Let it be as you wish, dear uncle,' answered Badr al-Dīn.

Straightway the pastrycook went to the market and bought fine robes to put on Hasan; and afterwards he took him before the kādī and adopted him as his son in the presence of witnesses.

Hasan stayed in the shop of the pastrycook as his son, taking the money and selling pastries, jars of jam, china pots of cream, and all those sweetmeats which the people of Damascus love. Having had lessons from his mother, the wife of the wazīr Nūr al-Dīn of Basrah, he soon picked up the art of making pastry, for which he had a considerable aptitude.

The beauty of Hasan, the fair young man from Basrah, the son of the pastrycook, was soon a byword throughout Damascus, and the shop of Abdallāh became the most famous of all the pastry shops in the city.

Now we will leave Hasan Badr al-Dīn and return to the bride, Sitt al-Husn, the daughter of the wazīr Shams al-Dīn, at Cairo. When she woke on the first night of her marriage and did not find Hasan beside her, she imagined that he had gone to the privy.

While she was waiting for him, her father Shams al-Dīn came to ask her how the night had passed. He was in much confusion of spirit, revolting in his soul against the injustice of the Sultān who had married his daughter by force to a humpbacked slave. Before he entered he said: 'Surely I will kill the girl if she has given herself to that gross freak of nature.'

He knocked at the door and Sitt al-Husn rose in haste to open to him. She had become more beautiful even than was her wont. Her face was lighted from within and all her soul was on a tiptoe of joy at the love her fair stag had given her. When she came blushing to her father and kissed his hands, he was the more distressed to see her glad instead of sad, and cried: 'Shameless child, how dare you come before me in such a sprightly fashion from the bed of a diseased and malformed slave?' Sitt al-Husn smiled knowingly: 'By Allāh, father, the joke has gone far enough. Believe me I was sufficiently laughed at by all of the guests on account of my pretended husband, that hunchback, who was not worth one nail-clipping of my fair lover, the real husband of my night. Ah, what a night it was, filled to the brim by the sweetness of my well-beloved! You have had your joke, my father, now speak no more of the hunchback.' The wazīr was so angry at these inexplicable words of his daughter that his eyes blazed blue with fury and he cried: 'What is all this, unhappy one? Do you tell me that the hunchback did not lie with you in this chamber?' 'Let us hear no more of the hunchback, my father. Allāh curse him, and his father and his mother, and all his people! You must see that I know all about the trick which you played to avert the evil eye.' Then she told her father all the details of that night, adding: 'Ah, how happy I was, fastened to the lap of my dear one, my dark-eyed lover, my glorious husband, whose manners are a god's and his brows like hunters' bows!'

'Are you mad, my daughter?' asked the wazīr. 'Where is this young man that you call your husband?' 'He has gone to the privy,' answered Sitt al-Husn; so the wazīr in great disquiet ran to the privy and found the hunchback with his feet in the air and his head thrust deep in the hole. 'Is that you, hunchback?' cried the wazīr once and again; but the little man answered nothing, being terrified and thinking that it was the Jinnī who had come . . .

At this point Shahrazād saw the approach of morning and discreetly fell silent.

But when the twenty-second night had come

SHE SAID:

It is related, O auspicious King, that Jafar continued his story to the Khalīfah Hārūn al-Rashīd in these words:

The terrified hunchback, thinking that the Jinnī had come back, would not answer until the angry wazīr threatened to cut him in pieces with his sword. Then words came up through the hole after this manner: 'Pity me, sweet king of all the Jinn and all the Afārīt! I swear that I have not moved once during the night!' 'What are you saying?' cried the wazīr. 'I am no Jinnī, but the father of your bride.' A great sigh of relief came up from the privy and a voice saying: 'If it is you, you can go out from here. I never want to set eyes on you again! Run away, or the soul-shaking Ifrīt will come for you! I do not want to see you; you are the cause of all my troubles; you have married me to a lover of buffaloes, of asses, and of Afārīt. Be you accursed, and your daughter also, and every manner of unrighteous person!' 'You are mad!' said the wazīr. 'Come out, so that I can understand a little of what you say!' But the hunchback answered: 'I may be mad but I am not so mad as to come out without the Ifrīt's permission. He said that I must not leave the hole till sunrise. Go away and leave me in peace. But first tell me if the sun has risen or not.' More and more perplexed the wazīr asked him of what Ifrīt he was talking, and the hunchback told him all about his arrival at the privy, the appearance of the Ifrīt under many forms, a rat, a cat, a dog, an ass, a buffalo, and, lastly, what he had been made to undergo and what he had been forbidden to do.

The wazīr seized the hunchback, who was howling, by the legs and drew him out of the hole. No sooner had the mannikin stood upright, with his face all filthy and yellow and weeping, than he cried out: 'Curses upon you and your daughter who loves buffaloes!' and ran as hard as he could, yelling aloud and not daring to turn his head, until he came to the palace and, throwing himself at the Sultān's feet, sobbed out all the story of the Ifrīt.

But Shams al-Dīn returned to his daughter, and said: 'My child, I feel that I am going mad; help me to see this tale clearly.' 'It is quite simple, father,' answered the girl; 'that charming young man, who was so much honoured at the wedding festivity, lay with me all night and took my virginity. I am certain that I am already with child by him. See, here is proof of what I say: his turban on the chair, his trousers on the couch, his drawers upon my bed; and I remember there is something under the trousers which he hid there.' Going up to the chair, the wazīr took the turban and began to scrutinise it carefully. 'But this is such a turban as a wazīr of Basrah might wear,' he said. First he unrolled the stuff and, finding a pleat sewn in the bonnet, hastened to take the little packet out of it; then he examined the trousers and found beneath them the purse of a thousand dīnārs which the Jew had given to Hāsan. In this purse there was a small piece of paper on which the Jew had written these few words: 'I declare that I so-and-so, merchant of Basrah, have paid over these dīnārs to the lord Hasan Badr al-Dīn, son of the wazīr Nūr al-Dīn, on whom be peace, in exchange for the cargo of the first ship of his which comes to Basrah.' When he had read this receipt, Shams al-Dīn uttered a great cry and almost fainted; but he controlled himself and with shaking fingers opened the packet which he had taken from the turban. At once he recognised the signature of his brother Nūr al-Dīn and began to weep and beat his breast, exclaiming: 'Alas, my poor brother! Alas, my poor brother!'

When he was a little calmer, he said: 'Surely Allāh is Almighty! Daughter, do you know the name of him who lay with you all night? He is my nephew Hasan Badr al-Dīn, the son of Nūr al-Dīn your uncle: these thousand dīnārs are your dowry, and God be praised!' He murmured these lines:

> Of all our mutual landmarks I am fain,
> I recollect our memories with pain;
>   And every prayer that I have ever prayed
> Is that some god would send him back again.

When he had brought this verse to a close, he read over his brother's testament with deep attention and found the story of Nūr al-Dīn and the birth of Badr al-Dīn set out in full. When he had verified and compared the dates given by his brother with those of his own marriage and the birth of his daughter and found that in every respect they tallied, he was so amazed that he went straightway to the Sultān and, showing him the papers, told him the whole affair. The Sultān, in his turn, was so struck by the matter that he told the palace scribe to write out all its circumstances and preserve them with the utmost care in his library.

Shams al-Dīn returned to his daughter and the two sat down to wait for Hasan Badr al-Dīn. At last, when they began to understand that he had disappeared though they might not know why, Shams al-Dīn said: 'As Allāh lives, this is an extraordinary and disquieting adventure. In truth never in all my life . . .'

At this point, Shahrazād saw the approach of morning and discreetly fell silent, rather than tire the Sultān Shahryār, King of the Isles of India and China.

But when the twenty-third night had come

SHE SAID:

It is related, O auspicious King, that Jafar al-Barmaki, wazir of Harūn al-Rashīd, thus continued his tale to the Khalīfah:

When the wazīr Shams al-Dīn saw that his nephew Hasan had disappeared, he said to himself: 'Since the world is full of change and chance it will be well for me to take such precautions that, when my nephew Hasan does come back, he may be able to identify the circumstances of his marriage by detailing to me the exact disposition of all things in the bridal chamber.' So he took pen and paper and wrote down, object by object, every least thing that had been in the room, thus: 'Such a press was in such a place, such a curtain in such a place,' and so on. When he had finished, he read the list to his daughter and then, sealing it, locked it carefully in his chest of documents. Also he put away beyond reach of mischance the turban, the trousers, the robe, and the purse of his nephew.

As Sitt al-Husn had thought, she had indeed become pregnant on her marriage night; and at the end of nine months she gave birth to a son more beautiful than the moon and, if that were possible, as handsome and as perfect as his father. The women washed him and strengthened his eyes with kohl, then cut the cord and gave him to a nurse. Because of his beauty they called him Ajīb, that is to say the Marvellous.

When the admirable little Ajīb was seven years old, the wazīr Shams al-Dīn sent him to a famous school, recommending him especially to the master. Every day Ajīb would walk to school accompanied by Saīd, his grandfather's faithful black eunuch, returning for the midday meal and in the evenings. He remained at school for five years, during which time he made himself quite insupportable to the children, cuffing and kicking them and saying: 'Who are you beside me? I am the son of the wazīr of Egypt!' At last, when Ajīb was twelve, the other boys combined together and complained about him to the master. This good man, seeing that all the warnings he had given to the wazīr's grandson had been in vain and yet not wishing himself to send him away from the school, said to the children: 'Listen, and I will tell you something to say to Ajīb which will prevent him coming among you any more. To-morrow in play time all of you gather round him and one say to the others: "By Allāh, I know a good game; only no one must play unless he first says in a loud voice his own name and the names of his father and mother. Anyone who cannot say the names of his father and mother is a little bastard and cannot play with us." ' So next morning, when Ajīb arrived at school, the other boys clustered round him and one of them cried out: 'Yes, it is a splendid game, only no one can play unless he says his name and the names of his father and mother. Come, let us start.'

One of the children came forward saying: 'I am Nabīh; my mother is Nabīhah, and my father is Izz al-Dīn.' Another said: 'I am Najīb; my mother is Jamīlah, and my father Mustafā.' Others said the like till it came to Ajīb's turn, when Ajīb very proudly cried: 'I am Ajīb; my mother is Sitt al-Husn, and my father is Shams al-Dīn, wazīr of Egypt!' Then all the children cried: 'No, by Allāh, he is not!' And Ajīb answered angrily: 'Allāh confound you, the wazīr *is* my father!' On this the boys giggled and clapped their hands and, turning their backs on Ajīb, cried: 'He does not know the name of his father! Shams al-Dīn is the name of your grandfather, not your father! You cannot play with us.' Then they all ran away shouting with laughter.

As Ajīb sat alone, sobbing as if his heart would break, the master approached him saying: 'Surely, my dear Ajīb, you know that the wazīr is not your father but your grandfather, the father of your mother, Sitt al-Husn. Neither you, nor we, nor anyone knows who your father is. The Sultān married your mother to a hunchback groom but he did not lie with her and has never ceased to tell about the city wonderful tales of having been shut up that night by all manner of Jinn so that they might themselves lie with Sitt al-Husn. The story is embroidered with asses, buffaloes, dogs, and other equally credible things. So, my little Ajīb, no one knows the name of your father, and it is fitting for you to walk very humbly before Allāh, and before your little companions who rightly consider you a bastard. Remember, Ajīb, that you are exactly on an equality with any little slave boy sold in the market; so carry yourself a little more lowly from henceforward.'

Hearing this discourse, little Ajīb ran home straight to his mother, but he was so strangled with tears that he could not say a word to her. She took him up and kissed and comforted him, saying: 'My boy, tell your mother what has happened.' Then said little Ajīb: 'Tell *me*, mother, who my father is?' Sitt al-Husn was astonished and answered: 'The wazīr, who else?' But Ajīb said: 'No, no, he is not my father, he is yours. If you do not tell me the truth I will kill myself with that dagger!' And the boy told his mother all that the master had said.

Remembering her cousin-husband and all the charm and beauty of her first night in the arms of Hasan Badr al-Dīn, Sitt al-Husn wept and sighed these verses:

> He took my heart and carried it
>   I know not where;
> I curse the day I married it
>   To such an one.
>
> I told my tears to stint awhile
>   For I was fair:
> And yet I let them glint awhile
>   Bright in the sun,
>
> In case he should come back and see
>   I had no tear
> Or miss my mourning's lack and see
>   My cheeks undone.

She sobbed and Ajīb sobbed too, so that the wazīr Shams al-Dīn heard them and came in. His heart bled at the tears of his children and he asked them why they wept. So Sitt al-Husn told him of what had happened at the school and the wazīr, who could not prevent himself from calling to mind all the misfortunes which had fallen first on himself, then on his brother Nūr al-Dīn, then on his nephew

Hasan Badr al-Dīn, and finally on little Ajīb, sat down and wept in his turn. Afterwards he went in desperation to the Sultān, and telling him the whole story, assured him that such a state of things could not continue without bringing dishonour on his name and on those of his children. The Sultān therefore gave him leave to journey into the East, to the city of Basrah, to try to find his nephew, and also wrote decrees for him, empowering him to make any researches that he wished in any place whatsoever. The wazīr rejoiced at the bounty of the Sultān, thanking him in many different ways and extolling his goodness and greatness. Finally he bowed down and, kissing the earth between the Sultān's hands, took his leave. Without an hour's delay he made ready for his journey and set out, accompanied by his daughter Sitt al-Husn and by little Ajīb. They travelled for many days towards Damascus, which was the first city on their journey, and in the end arrived there safely. Halting near the gates in the plain of Hasabah, they pitched their tents for two days' repose. All the retinue found Damascus a truly wonderful city, filled both with trees and running water. There is a song which says:

> There's no place like Damascus,
> I had a day and night there;
> There's beauty in Damascus,
> The trees are full of light there.
>
> The flower dew in Damascus
> Is worth its weight in rubies,
> And they who hate Damascus
> Are a saintly sort of boobies.
>
> The white lakes of Damascus
> Are books and the birds read in them;
> And the taverns of Damascus
> Are good to those who feed in them.
>
> The clouds write little stanzas
> On all Damascus waters;
> And I've heard the gentle answers
> Of the slim Damascus daughters.

No one in all the wazīr's caravan failed to visit the city, buying in its markets and even selling there a few things which they had brought from Egypt, bathing in the famous hammāms, and visiting the mosque of the Umayyads, which is in the middle of the city and has not its equal in the world.

While the others were doing these things, Ajīb went up into the city to amuse himself, accompanied by the good eunuch Saīd, who walked a few paces behind him carrying a whip large enough to stun a camel; for he knew the reputation of the people of Damascus and hoped to prevent them with his whip from approaching his beautiful young master. His precautions had not been wasted, for scarcely had they seen the handsome Ajīb than all the men of Damascus began to call each other's attention to his grace and charm, saying that he was sweeter than the northern breeze and more to be desired than water in thirst or health in sickness. Half the people left their houses and shops and ran behind Ajīb all the time, in spite of the great whip, and the other half ran on ahead of him and sat down that they might watch his coming at greater leisure. At last Destiny led Ajīb and the eunuch to the shop of a pastrycook; and, when they were in front of it, they halted because the crowd was increasing at every moment.

Now you must know that this shop was none other than that of Hasan Badr al-Dīn, Ajīb's father; for the old cook had died and Hasan as his adopted son had inherited the place. That day Hasan chanced to be preparing a delicious confection of choicely-sugared pomegranate pulp. Seeing the two strangers stop before his shop Hasan looked up and was not only charmed by Ajīb's unusual beauty but felt himself stirred and drawn towards him in a manner that was both divine and extraordinary. Full of this new love he called: 'My little lord, you who have come to snatch away my heart and reign within my soul, you towards whom my bowels are moved within me, will you not honour my shop by stepping in? I pray you out of compassion for me, deign to taste some of the sweet things that I have made.' Hasan's eyes were filled with tears as he spoke and he wept at all the memories which came back to him at the sight of Ajīb.

The boy, hearing his father's words, felt his heart drawn towards him, so he turned to the eunuch saying: 'Saīd, this pastrycook has touched my heart. I think he must have a son who is like me and who is far away. Let us go in to pleasure him and take what he sets before us. If we are compassionate to him in his grief, surely Allāh will have pity on us and further our search for my father.'

But Saïd the eunuch cried: 'Oh no, no, my master! As Allāh lives, we cannot do that! The son of a wazīr cannot go into a common pastrycook's and eat there publicly. If you are afraid of all these ruffianly men who are following you about, rest assured that I can drive them off with my excellent whip. But as for going into the shop—no, decidedly no!' Hasan the pastrycook heard the eunuch's words, so he turned his weeping eyes and tear-stained cheeks towards him, saying: 'Honourable one, why will you not have compassion on me and come into my shop? Your outside may be as black as a chestnut's but inside I am sure you are as white as she is. O you who have been praised in admirable verses by all our greatest poets, enter and I will reveal to you a future as white without as you are white within!' At this the brave eunuch burst into thunderous laughter, crying: 'Really, really, have they so? Can you now? Well well, in Allāh's name let me hear!' So Hasan Badr al-Dīn made up these lines in praise of eunuchs on the spur of the moment:

> His exquisite manners and tact
> Have made him the trusted of kings;
> And peris would come down on wings
> To help him control every act
> Of the Sultān's divine little things.

These lines were so well turned and so pleasantly recited that the eunuch was greatly flattered; therefore, taking Ajīb's hand, he entered the shop.

Hasan Badr al-Dīn was in the seventh heaven of delight and bustled about to do them suitable honour. He filled the fairest of his porcelain bowls with his conserve of sugared pomegranate, amended with almonds and delicately perfumed. This he presented on a beaten copper tray and watched his guests eat with every sign of satisfaction, saying: 'This is indeed an honour for me! This is my lucky day! May all go down sweetly!'

After the first few mouthfuls, little Ajīb asked the cook to sit down with them, saying: 'Eat with us and it may be that Allāh will help us in our search.' 'What, my child,' said Hasan, 'can you who are so young have already felt the pain of parting?' 'Indeed I have, good fellow,' answered Ajīb, 'my heart is already sorely tried by the loss of one I love, my own father. Even now my grandfather and I have set out to look for him through all the countries of the world.'

So saying Ajīb wept and Badr al-Dīn also could not restrain his tears, while the eunuch looked on and sympathetically shook his head. Yet their grief did not prevent them from doing full justice to the delicately-confected sweetmeat; in fact, so exquisite was it that they ate more than they really needed. The time passed all too swiftly for Hasan, and soon the eunuch took Ajīb away and set out with him for his grandfather's tents.

Badr al-Dīn felt that his soul had left with Ajīb and, not being able to resist the desire to follow him, shut up his shop and, going after them in all haste, caught them up before they had passed through the great gate of Damascus. All this time Hasan had no idea that Ajīb was his son.

When the eunuch saw that the cook was following, he turned and asked him why he was doing so. 'I have a business appointment outside the city,' answered Badr al-Dīn, 'and wished to accompany you two as long as our road lay together. Truly your going away left me very desolate.' 'As Allāh lives,' cried out the eunuch angrily, 'that wretched bowlful is going to cost us dear; for see, the giver of it wishes to turn our stomach by dogging our footsteps from place to place!' But when Ajīb saw the cook he blushed and stammered: 'Let him be, Saīd. God's road is free to all good Mussulmāns. If he follows us to the tents we will know that it is indeed I he is pursuing, and then we can drive him off.' With this he went on his way, hanging his head, and the eunuch followed a few paces behind.

Hasan continued to follow them right to the plain of Hasabah, where the tents of the wazīr were pitched. When the other two turned and saw him just behind them, Ajīb became really angry, fearing that the eunuch might tell his grandfather that he had gone into a cookshop and been followed about by the cook. Terrified at this thought he took up a stone and, supposing, since Hasan stood there motionless and with a strange light in his eyes, that the cook's intentions were dishonourable, threw the stone with all his might, striking his father on the forehead. Ajīb and the eunuch hastened to the tents, while Hasan fell fainting to the earth his face covered with blood. By good fortune he soon came to himself and, staunching the blood, bandaged his forehead with a piece torn from his turban. Then he began to blame himself for what had happened, saying: 'It was all my fault; to shut my shop was ill-considered and to follow that lovely boy until he thought I had dishonourable designs upon him was even more incorrect.' He returned, sighing and murmuring:

'God is good!', opened his shop again and settled down once more to the making and selling of pastries. Yet all the time he found himself thinking of his poor mother at Basrah who had given him his first lessons in the art. He would weep and say over this couplet:

> Destiny will be fair to you and me;
> But when she is, she'll not be Destiny.

Unwitting of all this, the wazīr Shams al-Dīn, uncle of Hasan Badr al-Dīn the pastrycook, broke up his camp at the end of the third day and continued his journey towards Basrah. He fared through Hims, Hammah and Aleppo, Diyār Bakr, Maridīn and Mosul, enquiring all the way, until he reached Basrah.

Without even waiting to rest, he presented himself before the Sultān, who received him cordially and enquired courteously about the reason of his journey. Shams al-Dīn told him that he was the brother of the wazīr Nūr al-Dīn, and at this name the Sultān exclaimed: 'Allāh have mercy on his soul! Indeed, my friend, Nūr al-Dīn was my wazīr and I loved him dearly. He died fifteen years ago leaving a son Hasan Badr al-Dīn who was the apple of my eye. One day the boy disappeared and I have heard nothing of him since. But his mother, your brother's wife, still abides in Basrah, she who was the daughter of my old wazīr, Nūr al-Dīn's predecessor.'

Shams al-Dīn rejoiced at this piece of news and obtained permission to go to visit his sister-in-law at once. He hurried as fast as he could to his dead brother's house, thinking all the way of Nūr al-Dīn and his lonely death in a far country. He wept as he went, and recollected these lines:

> I go back to the house and kiss
> That wall and this:
> Each panel a sweet ecstasy recalls,
> I kiss and yet I do not love the walls.

Entering the great courtyard in front of the house, he found a mighty door which was of granite picked out with multicoloured marble. In its lower part there was a splendid plaque on which the name of Nūr al-Dīn had been cut in letters of gold. Shams al-Dīn bowed down and kissed the name, freshening the gold work with his tears and calling aloud these verses:

> I ask the rising sun for news,
> I ask the evening star for tidings.

Sleep cannot tell me of you
And the wastes of the night cannot report of you.

My heart is a still green fen;
Can you not come back
And make it run again in laughing water?

Men have called me large-hearted;
Yet my heart is not great enough
To hold anything but you.

Leaving the name wet with his tears he entered the house and came at last to the private apartment of his sister-in-law, Hasan's mother.

She had shut herself in this one apartment ever since the disappearance of her son, and passed each day and night there in grief. In the middle of the apartment she had had a tomb built for her child, whom she had long since given up as dead. All day she sat weeping by the tomb and at night slept with her head upon the stone of it. While Shams al-Dīn was still outside the door of this place he heard the voice of his brother's wife, sorrowfully chanting:

Is he wasted, tomb?
Has he all gone down into you, tomb?
    Will I never see him again?
The world is barren with snow and dust,
But you in whom he put his trust,
    You within whom
    He lay down as a young bridegroom,
Are full of stars and flowers
And the bright hours
    Of Spring after the rain.

Shams al-Dīn entered and, saluting his sister-in-law with great respect, told her that he was the brother of her husband Nūr al-Dīn. He made known the whole story to her, how her son Hasan had lain one night with his daughter Sitt al-Husn, how he had disappeared in the morning, and how Sitt al-Husn had given birth to Ajīb. 'Ajīb is here with me,' he added, 'he is your child as much as mine.'

The widow, who had so far sat like a woman beyond the uses of the world, leapt to her feet as soon as she heard that her son had at least been alive after she had seen him last. She threw herself down before Shams al-Dīn, wazīr of Egypt, and recited these lines in his honour:

> I can refuse
> Nothing to him who brings the news.
> Give gold and silver, corn and wine,
> Everything that is mine;
> And add, if so he wishes, to all else
> A trusting heart torn too much by farewells.

The wazīr sent for Ajīb; and when he came his grandmother fell on his neck and wept. Then said Shams al-Dīn: 'Mother, this is not a time for tears; rather must you prepare immediately for your departure with us to Egypt. God grant that we may all yet be united with your son Hasan.' On this Ajīb's grandmother rose quickly and got together all her goods, together with provisions for the way and her own personal servants. Shams al-Dīn went to say farewell to the Sultān of Basrah, who gave him many presents and entrusted him with others for the Sultān of Egypt. Then the wazīr, with Ajīb, the two women, and all his people, set out on his return journey.

When in the course of time they reached Damascus and pitched their tents in the same place as before, the wazīr said: 'I intend to stay here for a whole week in order to purchase fitting presents for the Sultān of Egypt.'

While the wazīr was occupied with the rich merchants of the place, Ajīb said to the eunuch: 'Bābā Saīd, I want to be amused. Let us go up into the city and see what has been happening. I want to hear news of that pastrycook whom we treated so badly; for, when he gave us pleasant things to eat, I knocked him down with a stone.' Saīd answered: 'I hear and I obey!'

The two left the tents, Ajīb being driven forward by the blind force of filial love, and after going through all the markets reached the cookshop just at that time when the Believers were flocking to the mosque of the Banū Umayyah for the evening prayer. It so happened that Hasan Badr al-Dīn was again preparing the same delicious confection, an artistic compost of pomegranate pulp with almond, sugar, and perfumes. Ajīb, looking in, saw that the mark of the stone was still upon the cook's forehead, so his heart was moved and he called to him: 'Peace be with you, O pastrycook! I have come all this way to have news of you: do you not recognise me?' At the first sight of his son Hasan felt his bowels turn over within him, his heart bound frantically, his head bow over of its own weight and his tongue cleave to the palate of his mouth. Very humbly he answered with these lines:

> I ranged my grievances and came
>   To where your golden eyes looked down;
>   I tried, but could not make a frown,
> I tried, but could not hide a flame.
>
> I wrote a commination
>   Of things that proved that you were foul;
>   I stood there like a love-sick owl
> And had forgotten every one.

'Come in, my masters,' he added, 'just out of the kindness of your hearts, come in and taste my wares. As Allāh lives, little lad, my heart was drawn towards you the first time I saw you. I am sorry that I followed you, for that was foolishness.' 'You are a very dangerous friend,' answered Ajīb, 'you imperilled us all because of that little bite you gave us to eat. I will not come in and eat with you to-day unless you swear solemnly not to follow us. If you will not do so I shall never come here again. We are going to be in Damascus a whole week, while my grandfather buys presents for the Sultān.' 'I swear that I will not follow you!' cried Badr al-Dīn; so Ajīb and the eunuch entered the shop and as before Badr al-Dīn filled them a bowl with his pomegranate speciality. 'Come and eat with us,' said Ajīb, 'and it may be that Allāh will help us in our search.' Hasan sat down in front of them with great delight, but he could not help looking fixedly at Ajīb all the time. So persistently did he do so that the boy was disturbed and said: 'As Allāh lives, you are importunately, uncomfortably, even oppressively loving, my good friend! I have already had to speak to you about that. I pray you cease eating all my face with your eyes.' Badr al-Din answered with these rhymes:

> I have a secret ecstasy, my friend,
> Which you could never comprehend
>   Although you put the sun to rout
>   And chased the silver stars in doubt
>   Through all the heavens round about
>   And put the white moon out.

> I have a guiltless love, dear lad,
> Which I should hide although you had
> > Thrown all the sweetness in eclipse
> > Of a thousand China trading ships
> > With the lithe verses of your hips
> > And the sugar of your lips.

To these lines Badr al-Dīn added many others, some addressed to the eunuch, some to Ajīb, until, after having eaten for a full hour, they could not swallow another grain. Then Hasan brought forward a fair copper ewer and poured perfumed water for their hands, afterwards wiping them dry himself with a towel of coloured silk which hung at his belt. He fetched down a silver rose-water spray, which was kept for great occasions on the highest shelf of the shop, and perfumed them deliciously. Nor was this all. Darting out of the shop for an instant, he returned with two great tumblers filled with sherbert scented with musk-rose. Offering a tumbler to each, he said: 'Put the keystone upon my happiness by drinking with me.' Ajīb and the eunuch drank and drank in turn until they felt fuller than they had ever been in their lives. So they thanked the cook and set off as quickly as they were able, wishing to arrive at the caravan before sundown.

As soon as they reached the tents Ajīb hurried in to kiss his mother and his grandmother. As his grandmother was kissing him, she remembered her son Badr al-Dīn and burst into tears. When she was a little recovered she said over these lines:

> If I did not know that God Who breaks in two
> > A many thing, would some day mend it,
> I could not live as calmly as I do.
>
> He gave me life in trust, and I would end it
> > Did I not know He could renew
> And bring back love however far He send it.

Then to Ajīb she said: 'My child, where have you been?' 'Through the markets of Damascus,' he answered. 'Then you must be hungry,' said she, and rising quickly brought him a great china bowl filled with a dish for which she was justly famous, a conserve of sugared pomegranate pulp which she had invented in her youth at Basrah and the art of which she had taught to her child Badr al-Dīn.

She also said to the slave: 'You may sit down and eat with your young master.' So the unfortunate eunuch, trying to smile and saying below his breath: 'As God lives, I cannot!', sat down by Ajīb's side. Ajīb, whose belly was one swelling clutter with all that he had eaten at the pastrycook's, took a mouthful and tasted it, but so full was he that he was quite unable to swallow. He seemed to find too little sugar in it, although this was not the case. With a wry face, he said to his grandmother: 'This is no good, grandma.' Hearing him, grandma choked with rage, crying: 'How, my child, do you dare to pretend that I cannot cook? Is there anyone in the world who knows more about pastries and sweetmeats than I do, except perhaps it be your father Hasan, whom I taught!' But Ajīb answered: 'As Allāh lives, grandma, your conserve is not very delicately finished off; it lacks sugar. Let me tell you, only you must not tell grandpa or my mother, that we have just been offered some of the same by a pastrycook in one of the markets, and my heart opened only at the smell, the way he made it. As for the taste, it would have brought appetite to a man dying of indigestion. Your conserve is not to be mentioned in the same breath, grandma.'

At this slight upon her handiwork, grandma was even more incensed, so turning to the eunuch she said: . . .

At this point Shahrazād saw the approach of morning and discreetly fell silent. Then Dunyazād said to her: 'Your words are sweet and pleasant to the taste.' 'But this is nothing,' Shahrazād answered, 'to that which I would tell you to-morrow night, if I were still alive and the King wished to preserve me.' Then the King said in his soul: 'By Allāh, I will not kill her until I have heard the rest of this truly marvellous tale!' Then they passed the rest of the night in each other's arms. In the morning the King went down to the Hall of Justice and the dīwān was filled with people. The King sat in judgment, giving power and taking it away, guiding the people and making an end of cases that were brought before him until the fall of day. When the dīwān rose he went back to his palace. At nightfall he went in to Shahrazād and did with her as was his wont.

The twenty-fourth night came

AND YOUNG DUNYAZĀD, when she saw that the act was ended, got up from her carpet, saying to Shahrazād:

'Sister, I pray you finish your savoury tale of the beautiful Hasan Badr al-Dīn and his wife, the daughter of Shams al-Dīn. You had

just got to the words: "Grandma turned to the eunuch and said ..."
What in heaven's name was it that she said?'

Shahrazād smiled at her sister, saying: 'I will finish my tale with
all my heart and the best will in the world, but only if this courteous
monarch gives me leave.'

On this the King, who was devoured by curiosity to hear the end
of the tale, said to Shahrazād: 'You may continue!'

AND SHAHRAZĀD SAID:

It is related, O auspicious King, that Ajīb's grandmother threw a
furious glance at the slave, saying: 'Wretch, is it you who have been
corrupting this child? How dared you take him into a pastrycook's
shop?' The eunuch, who was frightened out of his wits, shook his
head saying: 'We did not go into the shop, we only passed by.'
But the foolish little Ajīb cried: 'By Allāh we did go in, and had
something fine to eat! I assure you, grandma, it was very much
better than yours.'

Grandma ran in her rage to the wazīr and told him of what she
called 'the terrible crime of the black eunuch.' She so worked on
Shams al-Dīn, who was naturally choleric and had a supply of spleen
ever ready for his people, that he hurried back to the tent with her
and shouted: 'Saīd, did you or did you not take Ajīb into a pastrycook's?' 'No, my lord,' answered the terrified slave, but Ajīb said
maliciously: 'Yes, we did go in and, listen, grandma, what we ate
was so good that we are full to our throats; and then we drank a
sherbert made with powdered snow. How good it was! The cook
was not stingy with his sugar like grandma.'

The wazīr was now doubly enraged against the eunuch, both for
what he had done and for giving the lie to Ajīb. 'Saīd,' he said, 'I will
only believe you if you sit down and eat every morsel of this excellent conserve which my sister-in-law has prepared. That will prove
to me that you are fasting.'

Saīd determined to do his best. He sat down before the pomegranate conserve and tried to begin, but he was forced to spit out
even the first mouthful. There was no room for it inside him. He
told the wazīr that he had been overcome by an indigestion the
night before while over-eating with the other slaves; but the wazīr
knew that he lied, so he had him thrown to the ground by the other
slaves and beat him mercilessly until the eunuch confessed the truth,
saying: 'Indeed, my lord, indeed we did go into a pastrycook's in
the market; and the dish he set before us was more delicious than

anything I have dreamed of in my life. It is profanity to have tasted this other disgusting mess. You cannot think how bad it is.'

On this the wazīr burst out laughing, but grandma was by no means contented. Wounded in her tenderest spot, she cried: 'Liar! I defy you to bring me a like dish from your pastrycook! It is all your imagination. Take this bowl if you dare, and bring me back some of the conserve. My brother-in-law shall be the judge between it and mine.'

So the eunuch, clutching a half dīnar and a porcelain bowl, hurried back to the shop and said to the pastrycook: 'Look here, my fine fellow, some of the gentlemen of our house have taken on a bet about that dish of yours. Please give me half a dīnar's worth in this bowl that the gentlemen may compare it with a pomegranate conserve that one of them has made. Put all your art in it, for I do not want to eat any more stick because of you. I am still all sore about my back.' Hasan Badr al-Dīn burst out laughing and answered him: 'Do not be afraid. No one in the world can make the dish as I do, except perhaps my mother who is in a far country.'

Badr al-Dīn carefully filled the bowl and ended by adding just a suspicion of musk and rose-water. When the cook was at last satisfied, the eunuch hurried back with the bowl to the caravan. Ajīb's grandmother at once took hold of it and placed some of its contents in her mouth upon the spot. But hardly had it touched her lips than she gave a great cry and fell all in a heap on the ground. She had recognised the hand of her son Hasan.

The wazīr and all who were with him threw water in grandma's face and at the end of an hour she recovered consciousness, saying with her first words: 'As God lives, the man who made this pomegranate conserve was no other than my son Hasan Badr al-Dīn. I taught the art to Hasan and no one else in all the world knew of it.'

The wazīr's joy and impatience were both thus raised to fever point. 'At last God has been good to us!' he cried, and, calling his servants, he reflected for a few moments over a plan that had come into his head, and then issued these instructions: 'Let twenty men go to the cookshop of one known in the markets as Hasan of Basrah, and raze it to the ground, destroying it utterly, and let them bind the pastrycook's hands behind his back with his own turban and bring him to me; but on no account must they hurt him in any way while doing so.'

The wazīr himself took horse and carried the letters which the

Sultān of Egypt had given him to the Cairene lieutenant-governor in Damascus, who kissed them respectfully and carried them to his forehead in veneration. He asked the wazīr whom he wished seized and the other answered that it was only a pastrycook in one of the markets. 'Nothing is more simple,' said the governor and ordered his guards to go to help the wazīr's men at the shop. Shams al-Dīn then took leave of the lieutenant-governor and returned to the caravan.

A host of men armed with sticks, mattocks, and axes appeared before Hasan Badr al-Dīn and began to break his shop into little pieces, smashing all its appointments and casting the pastries and sweetmeats into the road. Then they fastened Hasan's hands behind his back with his turban and hurried him away without saying a word. As he was being haled along, Hasan kept on saying to himself: 'By Allāh, I believe that pomegranate conserve is at the bottom of all this!'

When he had been led into the presence of the wazīr, Hasan burst into tears, crying: 'My lord, what crime have I committed?' 'Was it you who prepared the pomegranate conserve?' asked the wazīr. 'I did, my lord,' answered Hasan. 'Is that a hanging matter?' 'A hanging matter?' replied the wazīr. 'That shall be the least of your punishments. Prepare for much worse!'

You must know that the wazīr had asked the two women to let him carry out the matter in his own way, as he did not wish to tell them the result of his search until they should all be returned to Cairo.

He called one of his camel-boys and bade him bring a great wooden chest, into which the terrified Hasan was thrust. Then the chest was fastened with a heavy wooden cover and mounted on a camel.

Breaking camp the wazīr's party proceeded in the direction of Cairo till nightfall. When they halted for food, Hasan was allowed out of his case for a few moments, given something to eat, and then put back. For some days the journey continued, Hasan being let out from time to time and brought up for a fresh interrogation before the wazīr, who asked on each occasion: 'Was it you who prepared the pomegranate conserve?' The trembling Hasan invariably replied: 'Yes, my lord,' and then the wazīr would say: 'Bind this man and put him back in the chest.'

When they came within sight of Cairo, they halted at the camping ground Zaidānīyah and the wazīr commanded Hasan to be brought to him. When Hasan had come, Shams al-Dīn sent also for a carpenter, to whom he said: 'Take this man's measures and prepare a cross for him; then fasten the cross firmly upright in a buffalo cart.' 'My lord,' cried Hasan, 'what are you going to do to me?' 'I am going to crucify you,' answered the wazīr, 'and have you dragged through the streets as a show for the inhabitants.' 'But for what crime?' moaned the unfortunate Hasan. 'For your pomegranate conserve,' answered Shams al-Dīn, 'there was not enough pepper in it.' On this Badr al-Dīn beat his cheeks and cried: 'By Allāh, is this my crime? Is it for this I had to undergo the long torture of the journey, with food only once a day and a crucifixion at the end of it?' 'That is so,' answered the wazīr very sternly, 'not enough pepper, not enough pepper!' Hasan Badr al-Dīn sank to the earth and remained there a long time in deep and sorrowful reflection. At last the wazīr said: 'What are you thinking of?' 'Nothing very much,' answered Hasan, 'simply that of all the incredibly thick-headed fools on the earth, you are the most incredibly thick-headed. If you were not the supreme ass of all time you would not treat me so for the matter of a little pepper.' 'I see no other way of ensuring that you do not do it again,' answered the wazīr. 'What is the use of talking to such a mud-witted madman?' exclaimed Hasan. 'If anyone has committed a crime, you have: in fact, you have committed several.' 'I am afraid it must be the cross,' answered the wazīr.

All the time that they were talking the carpenter went on working at the cross, casting an eye from time to time at Hasan, as much as to say: 'Ah, you are still there!'

Night fell while they were speaking and Hasan was put back in his box, the wazīr crying after him: 'You will be crucified to-morrow!' Shams al-Dīn waited a few hours until Hasan was fast asleep in the box and then, loading him again on the camel, set out with all his retinue and came to his own house in Cairo.

It was only then that the wazīr was willing to tell his daughter and his sister-in-law of all that had happened. First he went to Sitt al-Husn and said: 'Praise Allāh, my child, who has at last given Hasan Badr al-Dīn back to us. Rise up my daughter and be happy! I wish you carefully to arrange all the carpets and furniture of the house, and especially of your bridal chamber, exactly as they were on the night of your marriage.' Although Sitt al-Husn was trembling with joyful surprise she gave the necessary order to the slaves, and they set to work. The wazīr took the list that he had made and, reading slowly, helped them to arrange the least thing in its proper place. So well were his instructions carried out that the sharpest eye would have believed that it was still the night of the marriage of Sitt al-Husn and the hunchback.

With his own hand the wazīr placed all the clothes of Badr al-Dīn where they had been before: his turban on the chair, his drawers on the disordered bed, his trousers on the couch, and, below the last, the purse which held the thousand dīnārs and the Jew's receipt. Finally he sewed Nūr al-Dīn's memorial back in its place between the bonnet and sash of the turban.

He told his daughter to get into the same undress as on that other night, to go into the bridal chamber, and prepare to receive her husband Hasan back again. 'When he comes,' said Shams al-Dīn, 'tell him he has been long at the privy and ask him if he is unwell.' Also he recommended his daughter, though she did not need such counsel, to entreat her cousin sweetly and make him pass a pleasant night, not forgetting to regale him with pleasant conversation and the beautiful verses of the poets.

Leaving his daughter to make these preparations, he hurried to the chamber where Hasan's box had been placed and took him from it in a heavy sleep. He undressed him, put a fine shirt and nightcap on him, such as he had worn on that other night, and lastly carried him to the doors of the bridal chamber and, opening them, went away on tip-toe.

Soon Hasan awoke and his wits went all astray at finding himself almost naked in a brilliantly lighted corridor, which he seemed to have seen before. 'Is this the deepest of deep dreams?' he asked himself. 'Or am I awake?'

After a few minutes of stupefaction he got up and walked a few steps along the corridor. As he looked through one of the doors, his breathing stopped altogether. To one side was the very hall in which he had been so honoured and the hunchback so much humbled; while on the other side appeared the bridal chamber with his turban on a chair and his trousers on a couch. Sweat broke from his face, and he asked himself first whether he was awake, next whether he was asleep, and lastly whether he was mad. Moving towards the bridal chamber by taking as it were one step forward and one step back, he said to himself: 'As Allāh lives, my boy, this is no dream! And yet I was shut up in a box and that was no dream either.' With this he put his head round the door of the room.

There, below the finest of blue silk quilts, lay Sitt al-Husn in all her vivid nakedness, who gently held up one side of the quilt, saying: 'Dear master, you have been a long time in the privy. Come to me, come!'

Poor Hasan at these words burst into peal after peal of foolish laughter, as if he had eaten hashīsh or smoked opium. 'Ho, ho, ho! What a dream! what a dream!' he hiccoughed, and began to walk forward as if he were treading on snakes, holding up his shirt-tails with one hand, feeling the air with the other, and taking all the infinite precautions of a blind man or a drunkard. Suddenly he sank down on the carpet in the middle of the room and began to consider owlishly, making imbecile gestures with his hands. More than at anything else he stared at the strings of his purse still hanging down under his trousers and at his turban still in the same folds as he had known before.

Sitt al-Husn spoke again from the bed: 'What is it, my love? You seem to be perplexed and to tremble a little, and yet we were only at the beginning. Can it be . . .?' On this Badr al-Dīn began to open and shut his mouth, saying: 'So we were only at the beginning, were we? That is good. What beginning and of what night? My dear, I have been away for years and years.' 'Calm yourself for the love of Allāh,' said his bride. 'I speak of to-night and the fifteen exploits of your ram within my breach. You went to the privy and have been away an hour. You must be ill, my darling. Come and I will warm you, my heart, my eyes, my very dear.' 'Can it be true?' answered Badr al-Dīn. 'Can I have gone to sleep in the privy and dreamt the whole of that horrible dream? I thought I was a pastry-cook in Damascus for ten years and a beautiful boy came to me. . . .' Here he brushed the sweat from his forehead and felt his scar there. 'It cannot be a dream!' he exclaimed. 'The boy made this scar with a stone; and yet it must be a dream. Perhaps you gave me this mark when we were coupling just now. I dreamed that I made a pome-granate conserve and put too little pepper in it, that I was shut up in a box and about to be crucified. By Allāh, that wretched box felt real enough!'

'But why should anyone wish to crucify you?' asked Sitt al-Husn, and he answered: 'Because I had put too little pepper in the pomegranate.' Shams al-Dīn's daughter, being unable to contain herself longer, threw herself upon his neck and, kissing him with all her stored up love, drew him to the bed, where he fell down in a heavy slumber. Sitt al-Husn watched over him all night, and sometimes he muttered: 'It is a dream!' and sometimes: 'No, it is real!'

In the morning Hasan woke with a calm mind to find himself in the arms of Sitt al-Husn and the wazīr Shams al-Dīn standing at the foot of the bed. Said Badr al-Dīn: 'Was it not you who broke up all my shop for the sake of a little pepper?'

To which, since there was no reason any longer for keeping silence, the wazīr answered:

'Listen to the truth, my child. You are my nephew Hasan Badr al-Dīn, son of my dear brother Nūr al-Dīn, wazīr of Basrah. I was forced to submit you to these trials in order to be sure that it was really you who had lain with my daughter on her marriage night. I was hidden behind a curtain and saw you recognise everything. You must excuse me, my boy; there was no other way, as I had never seen you in my life. To think, to think, that all this should have come about through one small misunderstanding between Nūr al-Dīn and myself!'

The wazīr told him all the story of that early quarrel and added: 'Dear son of mine, I have brought your mother from Basrah; you shall see her soon and you shall see your son, Ajīb, child of your bridal night.'

The good old man ran to look for them, and the first to come was little Ajīb, who did not fear his father as he had feared the amorous pastrycook, but threw himself upon his neck in a passion of love. Badr al-Dīn lifted up his eyes, murmuring these lines:

> I swore by the blood of my tears
> That I would never let you go in all the years
> If Allāh should repent,
> But Allāh never sent
> My fair one to his dear that I might mind him
> And I took weary years to find him.
>
> Yet who could praise His name enough
> Who after all has given
> So constant a return of all my constant love
> And made a heaven
> In which two empty hearts can lie down sated
> And perfected and mated?

Then came Badr al-Dīn's mother, almost fainting for joy, and threw herself into his arms.

You can imagine what tears of delight there were, what exchange of stories, what healing of old wounds. They all thanked Allāh who had brought them together safely in the end; and each lived in joyful prosperity and pure delights until the end of their days, which were many. They left behind them a galaxy of children, each one having the combined beauty of the moon and stars.

That, O auspicious King, said Shahrazād, is the incredible tale which Jafar al-Barmaki told in Baghdād to the Khalīfah Hārūn al-Rashīd, Prince of Believers.

Yes, that is the tale of the wazīr Shams al-Dīn, his brother the wazīr Nūr al-Dīn, and of Hasan Badr al-Dīn, Nūr al-Din's son.

You must know that the Khalīfah Hārūn al-Rashīd did not fail to say: 'As Allāh lives, that is not only a marvellous but a very pleasing tale.' So delighted was he, that he not only spared the life of the negro Raihān, but also took under his protection the young man whose wife had been cut in pieces, as is related in the story of the Three Apples. To make up to him for the loss of his wife he selected a very beautiful virgin to be his concubine, made him a sumptuous allowance, and honoured him as an intimate and cup-mate. Lastly he ordered the palace scribes to record Jafar's tale in their most refined calligraphy, and had the whole shut away among the records, that it might serve as a lesson to his children's children.

'But,' continued the nimble and discreet Shahrazād, addressing herself to King Shahryār, Sultān of the Isles of India and China, 'do not believe, O auspicious King, that this story is in any way as admirable as one which I had reserved for your ears if you are not weary.' 'What story is that?' asked King Shahryār. 'It is a much more wonderful tale than any of the others,' said Shahrazād. 'But what is it called?' asked the King.

She replied:

'It is the Tale of the Hunchback, the Tailor, the Jew, the Christian, and the Barber of Baghdād.'

'You may tell it to me,' said King Shahryār.

The Tale of the Hunchback
with the Tailor, the Christian Broker,
the Steward and the Jewish Doctor;
what followed after;
and the Tales which Each of Them Told

THEN SHAHRAZĀD SAID TO KING SHAHRYĀR:

IT is related, O auspicious King, that there was once long ago in a city of China a prosperous and merry-minded tailor. He was fond of pleasure and it was his custom from time to time to go out with his wife for a walk through the streets and gardens to look at the life of the city. One day, when they were returning home in the evening after a long pleasure jaunt, they met a hunchback of such droll appearance that neither grief nor melancholy could live for a moment in his presence, and the saddest man would have laughed aloud on seeing him. The tailor and his wife were so greatly amused by the little fellow's sallies that they asked him to come back home with them and spend the night as their guest. The hunchback accepted and, when they had all arrived at the shop, the tailor hurried out to the market and managed to buy, before it closed, some fried fish, bread, limes, and a great cake of white sesame sweetmeat for dessert. When he had brought these back and set them before the hunchback, all three sat down to eat.

During the gay meal the tailor's wife moulded a great lump of fish in her hands and, popping it in the hunchback's mouth for a joke, placed her hand over his lips so that he could not spit out the morsel. Then she cried: 'By Allāh, you must take it down in a single mouthful or I will not let go!'

With a mighty effort the hunchback swallowed the piece of fish, but as ill-luck would have it there was a large bone concealed inside which stuck in his throat, so that he died upon the spot.

At this point Shahrazād saw the approach of morning and discreetly fell silent, not wishing to take further advantage of the King's permission.

Then Dunyazād said to her: 'Your words are sweet, pure and pleasant to the taste!' 'What would you say then,' Shahrazād answered, 'to the thing which I will tell you to-morrow night, if I am still alive and the gracious King wishes to preserve me?'

The King said in his soul: 'By Allāh, I will not kill her until I have heard the rest of this truly marvellous tale!'

Then he took her in his arms and they lay together lovingly all night. In the morning the King went down to the Hall of Justice and the dīwān was filled with people. He sat in judgment, giving power and taking it away, guiding the people and making an end of cases which they had brought before him, until the fall of day. When the dīwān rose he went back to his apartments and there he found Shahrazād.

And when the twenty-fifth night had come

DUNYAZĀD SAID TO SHAHRAZĀD: 'Sister, I pray you finish your tale of the hunchback with the tailor and his wife.' Shahrazād answered: 'I will finish it with all my heart and the best will in the world, but only if this courteous Monarch gives me leave.' 'You may continue!' said the King hastily.

SO SHAHRAZĀD SAID:

It is related, O auspicious King, that when the tailor saw the hunchback die before his eyes, he cried: 'There is no power nor might save in Allāh! O cursed fate that this poor man should have died thus under our hands!' 'What is the use of lamenting like that?' asked his wife. 'Do you not know these lines:

> The last place where a helper shall be found
>   Is in that quarter whence the danger came;
>   You would not treat a scalded hand with flame,
> Or give a cup of water to the drowned?'

'What must I do then?' asked the tailor. 'Rise up,' she said, 'and help me carry out the body. We will cover it with a silk shawl and take it away this very night. I will walk in front and you must follow me, saying in a loud voice: "This is my child. That is his mother. We are looking for a doctor. Where is the doctor?" '

As soon as he heard his wife's plan the tailor wrapped up the hunchback's body and carried it out of the house. His wife walked in front of him, calling: 'My child, my child! Who will save him? Tell me, little one, where is it hurting now? Ah, this cursed small-pox! Where are the pustules, little one?' Everyone who passed them heard her and, saying: 'This man and woman are carrying their child to the doctor. He has been stricken down by the smallpox,' gave them as wide a berth as possible.

The tailor and his wife walked on in this way, asking on all sides for a doctor, until they were directed to the door of a certain Jewish physician. They knocked and, when a negress came down and opened the door, the wife said to her: 'We want the doctor to examine our poor child. Take this quarter dīnār and give it to your master in advance. Beg him to come down quickly, for the child is very ill.'

When the slave had gone up to inform her master, the tailor's wife darted into the house and, beckoning her husband to follow her, said: 'Leave the body here and let us flee for our lives!' The tailor set up the hunchback's corpse on one of the stairs, propping it against the wall; then the two ran away as fast as their legs could carry them.

As soon as the slave told the doctor who was below and gave him the quarter dīnār he rejoiced and began to run downstairs, forgetting in his haste the lamp with which he was accustomed to light himself. He ran down so quickly that his foot struck against the body and he toppled it over. Terrified at seeing a man tumbling down the stairs, the Jew ran to him. Finding him dead and thinking that he himself had just killed him, he called out: 'Lord, Lord! O jealous God! By the ten Sacred Words, how can I get rid of the body?' At last, still calling on the names of Aaron, Joshua the son of Nun, and the rest, he carried the body into the courtyard of his house and showed it to his wife. When she saw the corpse, the terrified woman exclaimed: 'It cannot stay here; we must get rid of it. If it is still in the house at sunrise we are lost! I know, we will take it out on to our terrace and from there throw it into the house of our neighbour the Mussulmān. He is steward of the Sultān's kitchen and his house is infested by cats and rats and dogs who come down by way of the terrace to eat the butter and the fat, the oil and the corn; they will devour the body and no one will be any the wiser.'

In accordance with this plan, the Jew and his wife took up the body of the hunchback and gently lowered it from their terrace into the steward's house, until it rested against the wall of his kitchen. Then they went back quietly the way they had come.

Now it so happened that the very next minute the steward, who had been away from home, returned and saw, by the light of a candle which he lit as soon as he opened the door, the figure of a man leaning up against the wall of his kitchen. 'By Allāh,' he cried, 'so my robber is a man after all and not an animal! To think that he should have taken all the meat and fat which I have been so careful to lock away from marauding cats and dogs! What was the good of my plan for killing every cat and dog in the neighbourhood, when all the time it was this fellow, slipping down from the terrace and taking everything he could lay hands on?' So saying, the steward took up a mighty club and, knocking the man over with one blow, began to belabour him about the breast. But the figure did not move, and bending over it the steward discovered that the man was dead. In his terror and grief he cried out: 'There is no power or might save in Allāh! Curses on the butter and the fat, on the meat and on this thrice unlucky night! Ruin seize this corpse! Was it not enough for you to be a hunchback? Why had you got to be a thief as well and steal my meat and fat? Merciful God, hide me beneath Thy veil!' Then, seeing that the night was far advanced, the steward took up the hunchback on his shoulders and, leaving the house, walked with him as far as the outskirts of the market. There he placed the body upright in the angle of a shop at the corner of a side-street, and went his way.

Soon after a Christian passed that way, a broker who, being drunk, was going to bathe at the hammām. The wine had given birth to curious fancies in his head, so that he went along murmuring: 'Christ is coming! Christ is just coming!' and zigzagging from one side of the road to the other. When he came opposite the body without noticing it, he stopped and turned round to make water. Seeing the figure close to him against the wall he thought that it must be a robber, perhaps even that one who had stolen his turban earlier in the evening. With these thoughts buzzing in his head, the Christian leapt upon the hunchback and fetched him so heavy a blow across the neck that he fell to the ground. The drunkard then fell upon his adversary, calling loudly for the market-guard, beating the figure below him with his fists and trying to strangle him. When the market-guard ran up and saw a Christian thus assaulting a Mussulmān, he called out: 'Leave go, and get up!'

The Christian got up and the market-guard, bending over the hunchback, discovered that he was dead. 'Whoever saw the like of this!' he cried. 'A Christian daring to kill a Believer!' Thereupon he seized the broker, bound his hands behind his neck, and led him to the house of the walī. All the way the prisoner lamented, saying: 'O

Jesus! O Our Lady! However did I come to kill this man? How came he to die so easily? Drunkenness is over and done, cometh reflection.'

When they came to the walī's house, the Christian and the hunchback were locked up until the walī should wake in the morning. After sunrise the Christian was examined concerning the crime and could not deny the testimony of the market-guard. There was no course open to the walī except to condemn the Christian to death, so he ordered the public executioner first to announce the broker's punishment throughout the city and then to make ready the gallows. While the executioner was making a running noose in the rope and fitting it about the Christian's neck, the Sultān's steward suddenly burst through the crowd and, forcing a path for himself right to the foot of the gallows, cried: 'Stop, stop! It was I who killed the man!' 'Why did you kill him?' asked the walī. 'I will tell you,' answered the other. 'To-night, when I returned to my house, I saw a man who had broken in by way of the terrace to steal my provisions. I beat him on the breast with a club and he died. Then I carried the body on my shoulders and set it upright against a shop in the market, in such and such a place. Ah me unhappy! Not only have I killed a Mussulmān, but I have only just escaped killing a Christian too! I am the one to be hanged!'

When the walī heard the steward's story, he let the Christian go, saying to the executioner: 'Hang this man instead, for he is condemned out of his own mouth.'

The executioner fitted the same rope to the steward's neck and, leading him under the gallows, was about to hang him, when suddenly the Jewish doctor forced his way through the crowd, crying: 'Wait, wait! It was I who killed the man! He came to consult me, and as I was running down the stairs in the dark I tripped him, so that he fell to the bottom and died. It is not the steward whom you ought to hang, but I.'

The walī gave orders for the death of the Jewish doctor, and the executioner, having taken the rope from about the steward's neck, put it round the throat of the doctor and was on the point of hanging him, when the tailor broke through the crowd about the gallows, crying: 'Stop, stop! It was I alone who killed the man. Yesterday I took a holiday and when I was returning to my house in the evening I met the hunchback, who was drunk and very gay, playing a tambourine and singing with all his heart most merry songs. I asked him to come home with me, and when I had bought some fish and other things we sat down to eat. Then my wife, by way of a joke, moulded a lump of fish in a lump of bread and stuffed the handful into the hunchback's mouth. The fish choked the poor little fellow so that he died on the spot. My wife and I took the body and carried it to the house of this Jewish doctor. A negress opened the door to us and I gave her a quarter of a dīnār for her master, asking her to tell him that we had brought a patient to see him. She hurried away, and I set the hunchback upright against the wall of the staircase; then we both made off as fast as we could. The doctor came running down the stairs to see his patient, knocked against the body which fell to the bottom, and then thought that he had killed the man himself. Is that not true?' continued the tailor, turning to the doctor. 'That is the very truth,' answered the Jew. 'Then you must release this man and hang me,' said the tailor to the walī.

At this last turn of the business the walī was more astonished than he had ever been in his life. 'The tale of this hunchback ought to be put in the annals and written in books,' he said. Then he ordered the executioner to release the Jew and hang the tailor on his own confession. The hangman led the tailor under the gallows and put the rope round his neck, saying: 'This is the last time. I will not change my prisoner again.' With this he seized the rope. . . .

Now the hunchback, whom all this bother was about, was the Sultān's jester, and the King could not abide him out of his sight for an hour. The day before the jester had got drunk, left the palace, and stayed out all night. When the Sultān asked for him in the morning, they said: 'My lord, the walī informs us that the hunchback is dead and that his murderer is about to be hanged. In fact the walī had had the murderer placed below the gallows and the executioner was about to hang him, when there came a second person, then a third, and finally a fourth, each saying: "It was I who killed the hunchback!" and each telling the walī the circumstances of the murder.'

The Sultān on hearing this called a chamberlain to him and bade him run with all speed to the walī and order him to bring all those concerned in the death of the hunchback to the palace.

The chamberlain set out at once and arrived just in time to prevent the executioner from hanging the tailor. He told the walī how the matter had come to the Sultān's ears, and the latter at once presented himself before the King, followed by the tailor, the Jewish doctor, the Christian broker, and the steward, and with the body of the hunchback carried behind him.

He kissed the earth between the King's hands and told him the whole story with every detail from beginning to end. But as you have heard it twice already I shall not repeat it. Before the end of it the astonished King burst into a hearty fit of laughter. He ordered the palace historian to write out the tale in letters of liquid gold, and then asked all who were before him: 'Have you ever heard a story equal to this one?'

The Christian broker advanced and kissed the earth between the King's hands, saying: 'Ruler of the ages and of all time, I know a tale much more astonishing than our adventure with this hunchback. If you allow me I will tell it to you, for it is both more marvellous and more pleasant than the tale which you have just heard.'

'Certainly,' said the King, 'let us hear it, that we may judge.'

So the Christian broker told:

The Tale of the Christian Broker

KING of all time, I came to this land on business and as a stranger whom Fate guided to your kingdom. I was born in Cairo, a Copt among the Copts of that place, and was brought up in that city by my father who was a broker before me.

When he died I had already reached man's estate, so I adopted his profession, seeing that I had every qualification for this business, which is a most usual one among us Copts.

One day, as I was sitting outside the gate of the grain-market, I saw a young man coming towards me mounted on an ass with a red saddle. He was as handsome as a man could be and was dressed in clothes of surprising richness. When he caught sight of me he saluted, and I rose and greeted him. He handed me a handkerchief which contained a small sample of sesame, saying: 'How much is an irdabb of this kind worth?' 'A hundred dirhams,' I answered, and he said: 'Pray bring grain measurers with you and come to the Khān al-Jawāli by the Gate of Victory. I shall be waiting for you.' He left the handkerchief containing the sample with me, and rode on his way.

At once I visited the grain merchants and, when I showed them the sample which I had quoted at a hundred dirhams, they bid a hundred and ten for an irdabb, to my great delight. I took four measurers with me and, going to the place he had mentioned, found the young man waiting. He took me to his granary and there my measurers loaded the grain in sacks, estimating the whole at fifty irdabbs. 'You shall have ten dirhams for brokerage on each irdabb sold for a hundred,' said the young man. 'I pray you collect the whole of the money and keep it carefully by you till I come for it. As the whole price will be five thousand dirhams, you will keep five hundred and the other four thousand five hundred will be for me. When I have finished my other business, I will come and take the money.' Kissing his hands, I answered: 'Be it as you desire!' and went my way.

That day I gained a thousand dirhams in brokerage, five hundred from the seller and five hundred from the buyers, making that total profit of twenty in the hundred which is usual with us.

The young man came to me in a month and asked where his money was. I told him that it was ready for him in a bag, and he begged me to keep it a while longer. At the end of another month he returned and asked for his money. I made him the same answer, and added: 'Will you not this time so far honour my house as to come in and eat a little?' But he refused and went away, again begging me to keep the money until his other businesses were completed.

I guarded the money carefully until, at the end of another month, he came to my shop, saying: 'This evening I shall be passing and will take the money.' I got the sum ready for him and waited till late at night, but it was a month before he came again. As I waited I could not help saying to myself: 'How trusting is this youth. Since I have been a broker among the khāns and markets I have never seen a youth so trusting.' At last he came to me again, mounted as ever upon his ass and very richly dressed. He was quite as beautiful as the full moon, his face was always bright and fresh as if he had just come from the bath, and there was a black beauty spot at the corner of his lips as if it had been a drop of dark amber. He was like the boy in the song:

> The boy and girl have set
> Their slender lips and kissed,
> The gold procession of the sun has met
> The silver journey of the moon,
> The silver journey of the moon
> Is lost within a crimson sunset mist.

When I saw him, I kissed his hands and called down on him all the blessings of Allāh. 'I hope, my lord,' I said, 'that you will take your money this time.' 'Be patient a little longer,' he answered. 'When I have concluded all my business, I will come back for the money.' Then he departed.

Feeling sure that he would again be absent for some time, I ventured his money in a twenty in the hundred investment, as is the custom in our country, and cleared my profit with ease. 'By Allāh,' I said to myself, 'when the youth comes back I must certainly entertain him sumptuously, for through him I am in some sort becoming a rich man.'

A year passed away in these visits and delays, and then he came again, dressed more sumptuously than ever and mounted upon his mettlesome white ass.

I begged him to honour my house by becoming its guest, and he laughingly accepted on the understanding that I should spend only his own money on his entertainment. I laughed also and consented. When I had conducted him into the house and seated him upon a seat of honour, I ran to the market and bought all kinds of meat and drink, with everything suitable to a banquet. I set the table and begged him in God's name to fall to. He did so, and all the time to my great surprise ate with his left hand. When we had finished, he washed his left hand without the help of his right, and, after I had served him with a napkin, we began to talk.

At last I plucked up courage to say: 'My lord, I pray you relieve me of a great anxiety. Why did you eat with your left hand? Has your right met, by any chance, with some accident?' The young man answered with these lines:

> If you would ask the tempest rack
> If he is wet,
> Ask if I'm sad. . . .
> If you would ask the blackest jet
> Why he's not black,
> Ask why I'm glad.

So saying, he took his right arm from the folds of his robe and I saw that the hand was cut off at the wrist. Seeing my astonishment, he said: 'You need not be surprised at this, only I beg you not to think that I ate with my left hand with any thought of incivility towards you. As you see, I had to do so. The reason for the cutting off of my right hand was indeed a strange one.' 'What was it?' I asked, and he told me the following tale:

I was born in Baghdād, where my father was one of the principal merchants, and as I grew up I listened to accounts given of the marvels of the land of Egypt by such travellers, pilgrims and merchants as stopped at my father's house. Until the old man died I brooded in secret on what I had heard; but, as soon as I became my own master, I realised all the money that I could and, laying it out in fabrics of Baghdād and Mosul and other merchandise of price, left my home with what I had bought. Allāh had decreed that I should arrive in safety and in health at this fine city of Cairo.

Here the young man burst out weeping and recited these lines:

> The blind man still escapes the ditch
> In which the seeing stumble,
> The poor inhuman mad thing which
> You pity for his mumble
> Escapes the just too clever speech
> That makes the statesman tumble;
> So I, who had a lofty mind,
> Became the meanest of mankind.

When he had mournfully spoken this, he continued his tale.

I entered Cairo and, putting up at the khān of Masrūr, loaded the goods from my camels into a storehouse which I hired. I gave my servant money to buy food and, after sleeping a little, went to recreate myself in the street called Bain al-Kasrain. Then I returned to the khān, where I passed the night.

When I woke in the morning, I opened up my goods and, setting a selection of them on the shoulders of my slaves, went out towards the market to see how business was. I found the principal trading-place to be a lofty building surrounded by doors, all its available space being taken up by either shops or fountains. This is called the Kaisarīyat Jirjis; it is, as you know, the headquarters of the brokers.

I had let the brokers know of my coming, so that they lost no time in dividing up my goods and taking my rare fabrics round to the principal buyers. Soon they returned and told me that the price which they could get would not cover my cost price and the porter-age from Baghdād. I was considering what to do when the chief broker said to me: 'I know how you can obtain a profit on your goods. You have only to adopt the method of all the other merchants who deal here. Sell your goods on credit for a fixed period to the shopkeepers, on a contract drawn up by a notary and duly witnessed. Then, every Thursday and every Monday, you can collect your profit and make two dirhams or even more on each one which you have spent. Also, while you are waiting, you can pleasantly visit about Cairo and admire the Nile.'

'That is an excellent plan,' I said, and at once took the brokers and advertisers back with me to the khān of Masrūr and gave them all my goods to take to the exchange. Then I sold everything I had to the shopkeepers in detail, having contracts drawn up by the notary of the exchange.

After this I returned to the khān and lived idly, stinting myself for nothing. Every day I breakfasted sumptuously, and there was always on my table wine and excellent mutton, and all kinds of sweetmeats and jams. For a month I lived in this pleasant way, until the day came round for me to take my first profit. Thenceforward I went regularly every Monday and Thursday to the shop of one of my retailers and waited there while a broker made a tour of all the other shops and brought me back my money.

Sometimes I would choose one shop, sometimes another. It happened one day (when I had bathed, rested, eaten a chicken, drunk some glasses of wine, washed my hands, and perfumed myself with aromatic essences) that I came to the Kaisarīyat Jirjis and sat down in the shop of a certain silk merchant whose name was Badr al-Dīn al-Bustānī. He received me well, and we started chatting together.

While we were doing so a woman whose head was covered with a blue silk veil came into the shop to buy fabrics, and sat down on a stool by my side. Her light face veil was a little awry, letting delicate wafts of scent escape from it. Her beauty at once began to attack my reason, and the victory was completed when she pushed aside her veil a little and I saw the darkness of her eyes. When she had greeted Badr al-Dīn and he her, he began to show her every kind of expensive stuff, while I sat watching, listening to the sweetness of her voice, and feeling the little hand of love close more and more firmly about my heart.

She looked at several pieces and, not finding anything beautiful enough, asked Badr al-Dīn if he had by any chance a length of white silk embroidered with threads of pure gold, which she needed for the making of a dress. Badr al-Dīn went to the back of the shop and, opening a chest, took from beneath many other rolls of silk just such a piece as she had desired. He opened it out before her and she, finding it exactly suitable, said: 'I have not the money with me. Give it to me now and when I reach home I will send payment.' 'This time, madam, I am not able to do that,' answered the merchant, 'because the stuff does not belong to me, but to this traveller, and I am under a bond to pay him his profit to-day.' Angrily the lady said: 'Wretch, have you forgotten that it is my custom always to buy very expensive goods from you and to give you such a profit as you would never dare to ask for yourself? Do you not know that I never delay a moment in sending you the money?' 'That is true, lady,' he replied, 'but to-day I am obliged to ask for cash down.' At these words she threw the silk back into his arms, saying: 'You are all alike in this market, you cannot discriminate between people!' Then she rose in a passion of anger and departed.

I felt that my heart was going with her, so I rose and, bowing, called after her: 'Dear mistress, have pity! Be good enough to come back and vouchsafe me a word or two!' She turned to me with a little smile and answered: 'I will come back into the shop, but only for your sake.'

When she had sat down facing me, I asked Badr al-Dīn his cost price for the silk. 'Eleven hundred dirhams,' he answered. 'Very well,' I said; 'I will give you a receipt allowing you an extra hundred for profit.' I wrote him the receipt and, lifting up the silk of gold, gave it to the lady, saying: 'Take it and pay me when you will. I am always to be found on Monday and Thursday at one of the shops in the market. Further, if you will do me the honour to accept the silk as a gift, I shall be still more happy.' She answered me jestingly: 'May Allāh overwhelm you with his favours! May you come to possess all I have and be my master! Also Allāh favour this wish of mine!' 'Accept the silk then, Madam!' I exclaimed. 'It will not be the only piece. But grant me as a suppliant to see your face!'

She lifted the light veil, which hid all her face below the eyes, and the single glance which I was able to take threw me into a cauldron of love, tore all the passion which lay about my heart, and robbed me of my power of thought. In an instant she lowered the veil, took the silk, saying: 'Master, let your absence not be long, lest I die!', and departed.

I was left alone with the merchant until nightfall, sitting there as one mad, eaten with the wonderful folly of a sudden passion, and questioning him all the time about the lady. Before I rose to go he had told me that she was very rich, the heiress of a well-known amīr who had recently died.

When I got back to the khān of Masrūr, my servants offered me food, but I could eat nothing. I lay awake all night and, rising at dawn, put on the most beautiful robe I had, drank some wine, ate a little and returned to the shop. Hardly had I sat down in my accustomed place and begun to talk with Badr al-Dīn when the girl came again, this time accompanied by a young slave. She sat down and greeted me, without taking the least notice of the merchant. Then in a voice as sweet as running water, she said: 'Send someone with me for the twelve hundred dirhams.' 'There is no hurry,' I answered. 'How generous you are!' she exclaimed. 'Still, you must not let me be the cause of loss to you.' On this she gave me the price with her own hand, and we talked together until I was emboldened to sigh the greatness of my passion to her. When she understood how eagerly I desired that we might come together, she rose and left the shop with a few words of ordinary leave-taking. Unable to control myself, I also left the shop, my heart beating violently in love for her, and followed at a respectful distance until we came out beyond the market. Suddenly I lost sight of her, but at the same moment a young girl, closely veiled, came up to me and said: 'My lord, I pray you come to my mistress who wishes to speak to you.' As I did not know the girl, I answered: 'I am acquainted with no one in this part.' 'Do you forget so quickly?' she asked. 'Do you not recall the slave who was with a lady in a silk shop half-an-hour ago?' Hearing this, I walked with her until I saw her mistress at the corner of the Street of the Money-Changers. She came quickly to my side and led me into the angle of a wall, saying: 'Dear one, you have filled all my mind and overflowed my heart with love. Since the hour I saw you I have not tasted sleep, I have not eaten, and I have not drunken!' 'All these misfortunes and more have also happened to me,' I said, 'but my present bliss disarms the least complaint.' 'Tell me, sweetheart,' she asked, 'shall it be at my house or at yours?' 'I am a stranger,' I answered, 'I have no lodging but the khān, and that is too populous for our sweet business. If you have sufficient confidence in my love, I pray you accept me as a guest in your own house, for then my happiness will be complete!' 'It shall be so,' she replied, 'but not to-night, for it is Thursday. To-morrow, after the midday prayer, mount an ass and make for the Habbānīyah quarter and there enquire for the house of the syndic Barakah, known as Abū Shāmah. That is where I live. Do not fail me, for I shall be dying of impatience till you come.'

I made my way back joyfully to the khān and passed another sleepless night. At dawn I put on new clothes, scented myself with a selection of the most expensive perfumes and, knotting fifty gold dīnārs in a handkerchief, walked to the Bāb Zawīlah and hired a donkey there. I told the boy to lead me to the Habbānīyah quarter. In a very short time we reached it and paused in a street known as Darb al-Munkarī. I told the boy to find the house of the nakīb Abū Shāmah, and he returned in a few minutes with the address. I got down from the donkey and made the boy go before to show me the house. When we had reached the door, I gave him a golden quarter dīnār and dismissed him, saying: 'Come for me to-morrow morning.' He kissed the coin and made off, promising to return at the appointed hour.

The door was opened to my knocking by two little girls, virgins with breasts as round as small full moons, who said: 'Enter, my lord. Our mistress is impatient for your coming. She has not slept all night because of her desire for you!' I went into the courtyard and saw in front of me a wonderful building with seven doors. The front of it was pierced with windows which looked on to a great garden filled with coloured and tasting fruit trees. These were washed by little silver streams, and the birds sang in them. The house itself was built of white marble, at once so fine that it seemed almost wind-blown and so bright that the visitor might see his face in it. It was decorated with all kinds of inscriptions and pictures, and was filled with cunningly-wrought furniture. The floors were a vast mosaic of coloured marble; in the middle of the central hall was a fountain basin all inlaid with pearls. A heavy carpet lay beside the fountain, and the walls were covered with silks of as many colours as there are flowers in spring. Couches stood about the hall, and hardly had I sat down on one of them . . .

At this point Shahrazād saw the approach of morning and discreetly fell silent.

But when the twenty-sixth night had come

SHE SAID:

It is related, O auspicious King, that the merchant went on with his tale to the Christian broker of Cairo, who, in his turn, reproduced it for the Sultān of that city of China, in the following words:

I saw the sweet girl coming towards me, glittering with pearls, her face shining, her eyes lengthened by kohl. Smiling she pressed me to her breast and, crushing her mouth to mine, sweetly sucked my tongue. I did the same to her, and then, 'Is it really you?' she asked. 'It is your slave,' I answered. 'O joyous day, O delight!' she murmured. 'By Allāh, I am blind with my passion for you! I cannot eat or drink.' 'It is so with me,' I answered, and was thrown into such happy confusion by so sweet a greeting that I hung my head down as we talked together.

A cloth was spread before us with rich roasts, stuffed chickens, and pastries of every kind. We ate until we were more than satisfied, my lady putting little bits of the food into my mouth with her own fingers and urging me on in exciting terms. When we had washed our hands in a copper basin and perfumed ourselves with roses, we sat down again side by side and she said these lines to me:

> I would have knit my eyes up with my heart,
>   A black and purple carpet for your feet,
> And rent the damask of my cheeks apart
>   To spread cool beds of roses and entreat
> Your weary body; but I did not know
> That you would come, or that I loved you so.

Then she told me the secrets of her heart, and I told her mine, until we loved each other all the more dearly. Soon we began playing with each other, adding a thousand caresses to a thousand until nightfall. When the lamps were lit, the slaves again brought us abundant food and drink, and we passed the cup from one to the other until midnight. Then we lay down and moved or were still in each other's arms until morning. There had never been a night like that in all my life.

In the morning I rose and, slipping the handkerchief which held the fifty gold pieces under the pillow of the bed, took leave of my mistress and was about to depart. But she wept and said: 'When shall I look on your dear face again?' 'I will come to-night,' I answered. When I went out, I found the donkey-boy with his ass, and he conducted me to the khān of Masrūr; there I dismounted and gave him a gold half-dīnār, saying: 'Return this evening at sunset.' 'Your word is law,' he answered and made off.

I entered the khān and, after breaking my fast, left it again to collect some of the money which was due to me. Coming back with my profits, I had the cook prepare an exquisite grilled sheep, which I gave, with an abundance of sweet stuffs, to a porter with instructions to carry all to the lady's house. I went on regulating my business affairs until the evening and, when the donkey-boy came for me, set forth, carrying another fifty gold dīnārs in a handkerchief.

I found the house washed and garnished for my reception, with all the kitchen things highly polished, torches and lamps alight upon the walls, and the meat prepared and the wine poured. As soon as she saw me, my mistress threw herself into my arms, caressing me and saying: 'Ah, how I desire you!' We ate to satiety and then, when the cloth was drawn, drank wine and cracked almonds, nuts, and pistachios until midnight. We bedded together until the morning; I rose at dawn and, leaving my packet of dīnārs beneath the pillow, left the house. I found the ass waiting for me with his driver, and soon came to the khān, where I lay down to sleep. In the evening I set about preparations for dinner. I had a dish of rice stewed with butter and garnished with nuts and almonds, a dish of fried artichokes, and many another thing beside. These I sent, with an abundance of fruits and flowers and nuts, to the house of my lady, and soon after mounted the ass and made my own way thither. We ate and drank and coupled until the morning. At sunrise I got up and, leaving a third handkerchief filled with gold below the pillow, returned to my khān.

Things went on like this from day to day until one fine morning I found that I was ruined; I had not a single dirham, much less a dīnār, in all the world. I did not know what to say and, considering that this chance was the direct work of the devil, recited these lines:

> As the sun yellows before setting,
> So man, who sinks to his forgetting,
>   Shines in his dying;
> And as the death-struck bird sings loudest,
> So a man's soul is puffed and proudest
>   Poised for its flying.
>
> Yet better die and be as nothing
> Than with scurfed feet and filthy clothing
> Crawl the hot streets, a thing of loathing
>   To honest men;

Or hear the friend you loved through tears
Greet the recital of your name with jeers
Even before your first white hair appears,
    Even before then.

Not knowing what to do, and all my mind being in a turmoil, I left the khān to walk a little in the streets, and happened at last into the square of Bain al-Kasrain near the Zawīlah gate. It was a fair day and the square was one mass of people, swaying so thick together that I found myself pressed heavily against a horse-soldier. My hand being just on a level with his pocket, I was able to feel that it contained a little hard packet. With a quick movement I thrust my hand into the pocket and drew out its contents, but I had not been dexterous enough to escape my victim's notice. The soldier, feeling his pocket lightened, explored it with his hand and found that he had been robbed. Turning round in fury, he gave me a violent blow on the head with his mace, so that I fell to the ground. At once I was surrounded by a crowd, some of whom prevented the soldier from moving by catching at his horse's bridle. 'Shame,' they cried, 'to strike an unarmed man because he has jostled you!' 'Nothing of the sort,' answered the soldier, 'the man is a thief!' My wits were beginning to clear, so that I heard the people saying: 'He is too excellent and distinguished a youth ever to be a robber!' Then there was a great babble and movement in the crowd, some saying that I had stolen and some saying that I had not. Quarrels, discussions, and explanations were bandied over my head, and I was just on the point of being drawn off and lost in the crowd when, as ill-luck would have it, the walī and his guard passed by on their way from the Zawīlah gate. The walī questioned the soldier as to what had happened, and the man answered: 'By Allāh, O amīr, this fellow is a thief. I had in my pocket a blue purse containing twenty dīnārs of gold; he lifted it when the crowd jostled us together.' 'Did anyone see the deed?' asked the walī and, when the soldier replied that none had, he called to his chief of police: 'Seize that man and search him!' The chief did so, since the protection of Allāh had been removed from me, and stripping off all my clothes came upon the blue purse. The walī took the purse, counted the money and found that it tallied exactly with the soldier's claim.

The amīr called angrily to his people to bring me before him. 'Tell me the truth, young man,' he said, 'do you confess that you stole the purse?' I stood there ashamed with hanging head, and, reflecting that whatever I said it would be a bad business for me, answered that I had stolen it. On this the walī called witnesses and made me repeat my statement. The witnesses stood by Bāb Zawīlah and I confessed.

Straightway the walī ordered me to have my hands cut off; the executioner had cut off the right one and was turning to the other, when the soldier interceded with the walī for me, and he spared me the rest of my punishment. Some of the good folk who stood around gave me wine to drink to compensate for the great quantity of blood which I had lost and my consequent weakness. The soldier did more than this. He put the purse into my hand, saying: 'You are too fine a youth to be a robber, my friend.' I accepted the purse with these words:

> O chief
> Of friends, I am no thief;
> There are
> Who threw me from my car,
> Debate
> Of Destiny and Fate;
> Not I
> Rained arrows from the sky,
> But He
> Transfixed unhappy me.

The soldier left me, after having made me accept the purse, and I, binding my wrist with a handkerchief and hiding it in my sleeve, wandered away pale and sorrowful from that place.

Not knowing anywhere else to go, I walked to my mistress's house and, entering, threw myself on the bed in a state of exhaustion. Seeing the state I was in, my dear one asked me what the matter was and why my usual colour and mien were so changed. 'I have a headache and am not at all well,' I answered. Very sadly she said: 'Master, do not burn my heart in this way. Sit up, I beg you, and tell me what has happened to you to-day. I can read many and terrible things in your face.' 'Spare me the pain of answering,' I replied. On this she began to weep, saying: 'Ah, I see what has happened. I have nothing more to give you now, you are tired of me, you do not love me any longer.' So saying, she wept and sighed until nightfall, pausing every now and then to ask me questions, to which I could give her no answer. At twilight we were served with food as was our custom, but I refused it for shame that I should have to eat with my left hand, and for fear that she should ask me the cause. 'I do not want to eat just now,' I said. 'I can see that, my dear,' she answered, 'tell me what has happened to you to-day and why you are so weak and miserable.' 'I will tell you presently,' I said, 'little by little and slowly.' On this her manner changed to one more sprightly and, stretching out a cup to me, she begged me: 'Drink of that juice which banishes all sorrow, in which all thoughts that are not happy ones must drown. When you have drunk, you will be able to tell me of your sorrow.' 'If you insist,' said I, 'give me to drink with your own hand.' She brought the cup to my lips and tilting it slowly let me drink of it; then filling it anew she held it out again. This time, by an effort of will, I stretched out my left hand and took the cup myself, but even so I could not restrain my tears. I said:

> His fingers can bemuse us with a touch;
> The man who sees too far or hears too much
>   He with a breath subdues.
> He plucks our reason as we pluck a hair
> And then, that erring man may be aware,
>   The silly brain renews.

When I had finished intoning, I sobbed as if my heart would break, and at my tears my dear friend sobbed also, taking my head between her hands and weeping over it. 'For pity's sake, tell me why you weep,' she said, 'you are breaking my heart. And tell me why you took the cup with your left hand.' 'I have an abscess on my right,' I answered. 'Let me see it,' she said, 'I will cut it for you and that will give you relief.' 'It is not ready for that,' I replied. 'Do not insist, for I am quite resolved not to show you my hand.' On this I drank off the cup of wine, and went on emptying it as often as she filled it, until I was quite drunk. I stretched myself out where I was and went fast asleep.

She took advantage of my slumbers to uncover my right arm and saw at once that I had lost my hand; then, searching me, she found the blue purse with the gold in it. When she recognised the full extent of my wretchedness, she fell into a boundless melancholy, a depth of grief such as no one on the earth has felt before.

When I woke in the morning, I saw that she had already prepared food for me, four boiled chickens on a dish, with chicken broth, and wine in abundance. She brought these to me and I broke my fast. After this, I wished to take my leave and go away, but she stopped me and asked my destination. 'I am going to a place,' I answered, 'where I can get relief and distraction from my miseries.' 'Rather stay here,' she said, sitting down and regarding me for a long time. At last she spoke: 'My friend, you were very foolish. Your love for me has taken away your wits, I see that well; you have ruined yourself because of me. Further I do not find it hard to guess that it is on account of me that you have lost your hand. So now I swear, and Allāh is my witness, that never more will I be separated from you or let you out of my sight. You will soon see that I am telling you the truth. I wish us to be married at once with every rite of the law.'

She sent for witnesses and, when they came, she said: 'I wish you to witness my marriage to this young man. Write out my contract with him, and above all bear testimony that I have already received my marriage portion from him.' The witnesses wrote out our marriage contract, and my wife addressed these words to them: 'I bid you attest that all the riches which belong to me, both in that chest which you see and in every other place, belong from this moment to my husband.' The witnesses took note of her declaration and my acceptation, and then went away with their fees.

When we were alone, my bride took me by the hand and, leading me to a press, opened it and disclosed a great chest, the lid of which she threw back, saying: 'See what is within.' I looked inside and saw that it was entirely filled with little packets made from handkerchiefs. 'All these are yours,' said my wife. 'Each time you left a handkerchief with fifty dīnārs inside it, I shut it away in this chest and kept it for you. Now take back what you gave. Allāh wrote in your destiny that all this should be preserved for you; to-day He protects you with the shadow of His hand and has made me the instrument to fulfil His words toward you. But you have lost your right hand because of me, and for that I could not even pay you with my life. Nay, though I gave my soul in exchange for all your love and devotion, yet would you be the loser. Take hold of your inheritance, my love.' To please her I bought a new chest and transferred to it, one by one, all the packets of money. Thus my money was returned to me, my heart was filled with joy once more, and all my grieving vanished like a shadow.

I took her in my arms, and we sat down together, talking and drinking gaily for a long time. With sweet, well-chosen words she excused herself for having given me, as she said, so little when I had given so much. At last, wishing to put a crown on what she had done for me, she rose up and made over to me by deed of gift, written and sealed with her own hand before witnesses, all that she had of precious garments, jewels and properties, buildings and lands.

That night, for all the love we showered on one another, she went to sleep in a depth of sadness, because of the troubles which she deemed had fallen upon me through her fault, and which at last she had made me describe to her in full.

Thenceforward she so plagued herself with lamentation on my account that, by the end of the month, she had fallen ill of a melancholia which, increasing day by day, killed her at the end of the second month, so that she passed to be one of the elect in Paradise.

I placed her in the earth with every circumstance of mourning and every expensive rite which is allowed. When I came back from the burial-ground and entered the house, I carefully went over each article of my inheritance. I found that she had left me great riches, made up of every sort of property, including great barns filled with sesame. It was that sesame which I bade you sell for me, good sir, and for which I wished you to accept so inconsiderable a brokerage.

As for my continued absences which so astonished you, they are explained by the fact that I had to realise on all the other properties which she had left me. It is only to-day that I have received the last of my money.

I beg you not to refuse me the opportunity of doing you a slight favour, friend, who have so well entertained and feasted me in your house. I wish you to accept all the money which you have been keeping for me, the proceeds of the sesame.

Such is my story: the reason why I eat with my left hand.

Then, O powerful King, I said to the young man: 'Indeed you overwhelm me with your favours!' 'That is nothing,' he answered, 'moreover I have another thing to ask. Would you be willing, O broker, to join yourself to me and accompany me to Baghdād in the country of my birth? I have made mighty purchases of Alexandrine and Cairene goods which I hope to sell in Baghdād for a great profit. Will you come to be my companion upon the way, and to share the proceeds of my venture?' 'Such a desire is as an order to me,' said I, and fixed the end of the month for our departure. While waiting I realised all my property without the loss of a single dirham, and with the money purchased a great quantity of merchandise for trade. In brief, the youth and I reached Baghdād and, after taking a magnificent return for all our goods, set out once more and journeyed to this land of yours, O King of all the ages.

Having sold here, the youth did not tarry but set out again for Egypt. I was on the point of starting to rejoin him when, last night, I became mixed up in the affair of the hunchback, owing to my ignorance of the country. For you must know that I am but a stranger travelling on business.

That, O King, is the story which I think more singular than the one concerning the hunchback.

'Not so,' answered the King; 'I do not find it nearly so strange as the other, O broker. I am going to have you all hanged out of hand for the crime which you have committed on the person of my jester, this poor dead hunchback.'

At this point Shahrazād saw the approach of morning and discreetly fell silent.

But when the twenty-seventh night had come

SHE SAID:

It is related, O auspicious King, that when the King of China cried: 'I am going to hang you all out of hand,' the steward came forward and bowed to the ground, saying: 'If you will allow me, I will tell you of an adventure which happened to me quite recently and which is both more marvellous and more astonishing in every way than the story of the hunchback. If you agree with this estimate of the tale when you have heard me, I pray that you will spare us all.' 'Be it so,' answered the King of China. 'Let us hear the thing.' Then said the other:

The Tale of the Steward

K N O W, O King of ages and of time, that I was asked last night to a marriage feast where were gathered many doctors of the law and sages learned in the Sacred Books. When the perlection of the Koran had been accomplished, the cloth was laid and all manner of meats and necessary things were brought. Among other succulencies was a dish with garlic called zīrbājah, which has a great reputation and is exceedingly delicious if the rice, which is the basis of it, be cooked to a turn, and both the garlic and the other aromatic seasonings be apportioned with nicety. We guests began to eat it with great appetite, except one, who resolutely refused to touch this particular dish. When we begged him to have just a mouthful, he would not do so. We redoubled our invitations, but he said: 'I beg you not to press me in this matter. I was quite sufficiently punished the one time I had the misfortune to taste that dish.' Then he recited this stanza:

> If you would give your friend the slip
> Don't hunt about for an excuse,
> Just kick him basis over tip
> And send him to the deuce.

We did not wish to insist further but could not help asking him: 'What reason can there be for refusing to eat this delicious zīrbājah?' 'I have made an oath,' he said, 'never to eat zīrbājah without first washing my hands forty times with soda, forty times with potash, and forty times with soap, a hundred and twenty times in all.' Generously the master of the house ordered his slaves to bring water and the other necessary things; then the guest washed his hands the requisite number of times and sat down again. But it was an unwilling, trembling, hesitating hand that he put out to the common dish of which we were all eating. We were astonished, first by the timid way in which he ate, and secondly and more especially by the appearance of his hand, which lacked a thumb. 'Allāh be good to you,' we said, 'how came you to lose your thumb? Were you born so, or have you met with an accident?' 'Brothers,' he answered, 'you have not seen all. It is two thumbs and not one that I have lost. Also there are only four toes apiece upon my feet. Look for yourselves!' With that he showed us his other hand and both his feet, and we saw that what he said was true. In our astonishment we could not help saying: 'Our curiosity has grown very great and we are most desirous to learn how you came to lose your two thumbs and your two big toes, and the reason why you have washed your hands a hundred and twenty times.' Then he told us this tale:

Know, all of you, that my father was one of the great merchants in the city of Baghdād at the time of the Khalīfah Hārūn al-Rashīd. He was an experienced lover of good wines, of selected pleasure, and of stringed instruments; therefore when he died he left no money at all. Nevertheless, as he was my father, I buried him according to his rank, entertaining my friends at funeral feasts in his honour, and mourning for many days and nights. At length I went to inspect his shop and, opening it, discovered that there was nothing there of any value, but rather that he had died heavily in debt. I interviewed his creditors and prevailed on them to give me time in which to repay them as much as I could. I set to work and, by shrewd buying and selling, managed to pay a small portion of the debts, week by week, with my profits. A time came when I had paid everything and had increased my original small capital.

One day I was sitting in my shop when I beheld a girl, the like of whose beauty these eyes had never seen before. She was dressed with unusual magnificence and rode upon a mule; in front of her walked one black eunuch and behind her another. At the entrance of the market she dismounted from her mule and entered, followed by one of her attendants. This eunuch kept on saying: 'Mistress, for mercy's sake, do not enter the market in this way and show yourself to passers-by. Some terrible thing will come of it. Let us go hence.' But she, paying no attention at all to his words, walked along looking at all the shops one after another. None was fairer or better kept than mine. She came over to me, followed by the eunuch, and, sitting down in my shop, wished me peace. Never in all my life have I heard a voice so sweet or words so finely chosen. She put aside her veil so that I saw her face, and at once I was thrown into a violent confusion of the heart. With my eyes still fastened upon her face I said:

> She is as delicate as a dove's wing,
> I desire death now more than anything.

She answered with these lines:

> I trained my heart for you
>   And now he will not move
>   For any other love
> However true.
>
> A year or two I wasted
>   And then I drank it up,
>   Love which is love, a cup
> You never tasted.

Then she said to me: 'Young merchant, have you any beautiful fabrics to show me?' 'Mistress,' I answered, 'your slave is poor, and has nothing worthy of your eyes. Have the patience to wait for a little, for it is early and the other merchants have not yet opened their shops. Soon I will go to them myself and buy all that you may need of precious stuffs.' While we waited I chatted to her, and was drowned in the sea of her love, lost in the desert of the folly of my desire. When the other merchants opened their shops, I went and bought from them all that she had told me she needed, the price, for which I made myself responsible, coming to five thousand dirhams. I gave my purchases to her slave, and at once she left me and went to where her other follower was holding the mule. She mounted at the market door and disappeared.

She had not asked me for any account, or said a word about the money she owed me and for which I had made myself responsible to the other merchants. She had not mentioned either her name or the place where she lived, and I, for my part, had been ashamed to ask her. There was I engaged to pay five thousand dirhams to the merchants at the end of the week; you can imagine that I had a most lively desire to see the girl again. Drunken with love I returned to my own house; my servants brought me food but I could scarcely eat for thinking on the sweet seduction of my lady, and, when I tried to sleep, I could not.

For a week my existence was of this sort, but at the end of that time the merchants came to demand their money. As I had heard nothing of the sweet lady, I begged them to have patience and allow me another week in which to pay. They consented; and, as the second week was drawing to its close, I saw coming towards me, early one morning, her who was the picture of my thoughts. She was mounted upon her mule and accompanied by two eunuchs and a body servant. She greeted me, saying: 'Master, pray excuse me for having delayed a little in coming to pay you. Here is the money; fetch a money-changer to check the gold pieces, and take over what is owing to you.' A changer came and checked the money which one of the eunuchs gave him; then I put the sum away and went on talking to the young girl until the market opened and the merchants had come down to their shops. Then she said to me: 'I have need of such and such things. Go buy them for me.' I bought all that she wanted on my own credit and gave the goods to her; after this she went away without saying a word of the money which she owed me.

When I saw her disappear, I repented that I had had quite so much faith in her, because the goods I had bought would cost a thousand golden dīnārs. I said to myself: 'I understand nothing of this position or of her friendship towards me. She brings me money to the value of four hundred dīnārs, and then takes away goods to the value of a thousand. If this goes on, not only will my ruin result, but a serious loss will fall upon these others; they will come down heavily on me, besides, when they find that they are out of pocket. I am afraid the girl is only an artful baggage who came on purpose to cozen me with her beauty, an adventuress who first pillages poor unprotected shopkeepers and then laughs behind their backs. To think that I did not even take her address!'

For a whole month I remained a prey to such torturing thoughts, and at the end of that time the other merchants came to claim their money. They insisted so vehemently upon immediate payment that I was obliged to contract to sell all that I had, my shop with its merchandise, my house, and all my goods. I was standing thus, filled with bitter thoughts and on the very edge of ruin, when I saw my lady coming again through the door at the top of the market and making her way towards me. Both my suspicions and my griefs fled at the sight of her, and I forgot how unhappy I had been during her absence. She came up to me and began to talk in that golden jewel of a voice which said the sweetest things man ever heard. 'Bring the scales and weigh the money which I have got for you,' she said at last. And, in truth, she handed over, not only all the money she owed for my purchases on her behalf but a great sum beside. When all was paid, she sat by my side and spoke with such freedom and friendship that I nearly died of joy. 'Are you married?' she asked at last. 'No,' I answered, weeping, 'I have never known a woman.' 'Why do you weep?' she said. 'Because of something that passed through my mind,' I answered.

Leaving her, I drew her eunuch to the back of the shop and, giving him a handful of golden dīnārs, begged him to act as go-between in my love affair. He burst out laughing and said: 'She loves you a great deal more than you love her. She had no need to buy those fabrics, but only did so as an excuse to talk with you and make known her passion to you. Ask what you will of her, and I assure you that she will not deny you or be at all angry.'

She was just getting up to take her leave, when she saw me passing the money to the eunuch. Interpreting the action, she came back and sat down in the shop smiling. Then said I to her: 'Give your slave leave to ask you something, and pardon him beforehand for what he is going to say.' I poured forth from my lips all the passion that was in my soul, and saw that it did not displease her. She answered gently: 'This slave of mine will bring you my reply and tell you all my will. Do exactly as he bids you.' Then she rose and left me.

When I had repaid the merchants all their money and their profit, I had nothing left to do but wait, and esteemed my own profit from the affair not great when time went by without bringing news of her. For days and nights I knew no sleep. But at last the eunuch came again and I received him rapturously, begging for news. He told me that she had been ill for a few days. Then I said: 'But who is she?' and he answered: 'She is the foster child of our mistress Zubaidah, favourite wife of Hārūn al-Rashīd. The queen brought her up herself, loves her as her own child, and can refuse her nothing. The other day she asked our royal lady permission to go out, saying "There is in my soul a desire to go for a walk." Leave was given her, and, since then, not a day has passed without her going into the city and returning to the palace. Soon she became so experienced a buyer that Zubaidah raised her to the position of cateress. It was on one of these expeditions that she saw you and, speaking about you on her return, begged the queen's leave to marry you. Our mistress said: "I cannot give my sanction until I have seen the young man. If I find that he equals you in quality I shall marry him to you myself." I have come to inform you that all our business now is to smuggle you into the palace. If we can manage that without attracting attention you may be certain of your bride, but if you are discovered your head will answer for it. What do you say?' 'Surely I will go with you,' I answered. 'You have but to tell me your plan.' Then said the eunuch: 'When night falls, make your way to the mosque which our lady Zubaidah built on the Tigris. Enter, pray and sleep; the rest will be in our hands.' 'I love, I honour, I obey!' I answered.

When evening came, I walked to the mosque and, after saying my prayers, lay down for the night. At dawn I saw a boat coming towards the mosque, filled with slaves and empty cases. The slaves unloaded the cases and, when they had stored them in the mosque, all save one retired. The one who stayed I recognised as my lady's eunuch, and in a few moments I saw my lady herself, the attendant of Zubaidah, coming up into the mosque from the land side. We embraced each other passionately, and sat talking for just as long as was needed for her to explain her plan. Then she put me into one of the chests and locked it; in less time than it takes to tell I was borne right into the women's quarters of the palace. There I was helped out of the box, and given costly robes and presents to the value of fifty thousand dirhams.

Presently I found myself surrounded by twenty other white slaves, all virgins and all with tantalising breasts, in the middle of whom stood Zubaidah, scarcely able to move because of the great weight of her splendid jewels and robes. When she was near me, the attendants divided into two ranks, so that I walked between and kissed the earth before her. She signed to me to sit down and began to question me about my ancestry and my present life. She was so pleased with my answers that she cried: 'Praise be to Allāh, I have not wasted my time in bringing up this girl since here is a husband worthy of her! Know, friend, that we look upon this lady as a child of our own; she will make you a wife tender and submissive before Allāh.' So I bowed and consented in due form to marry the lady.

The queen invited me to stay at the palace for ten days and, during all that time, I did not see my future bride again; but other damsels brought me food. At the end of the time necessary for preparing the marriage Zubaidah begged the Prince of Believers to give his leave; he did so, and added a gift of ten thousand dīnārs of gold for the lady. Then Zubaidah sent for the kādi and witnesses, and, when my marriage contract had been written out, the festival began. Sweet things of every sort and the customary meats were prepared in abundance; all the harīm ate and drank, and the pieces were distributed throughout the city. It was only after the feasting had continued for ten days that the girl was taken to the hammām to be prepared according to the rite.

While she was there, a wonderful supper was spread before me and before the other guests. Among roast chickens, pastries of every kind, delicious minces, and sweetmeats perfumed with musk and rose water, appeared so exquisitely confected a dish of zīrbajāh that it might have driven the wisest mad and disturbed the poise of the best-balanced soul. As for me, hardly had it been set before me when, as Allāh lives, I threw myself upon it and gorged. When I was full, I wiped my hands, but forgot to wash them. After the meal I rested quiet until full night came. Torches were lighted, singers and musicians performed before us, and all the women decked the bride several times in several robes. At each circle that she made of the hall every guest threw a gold piece into a dish which was borne after her. The whole palace was packed with guests, who stayed until the end of the ceremony. At last I went into the chamber set apart for us; they brought the bride to me, undressed her from all her clothes, and left us. When I saw her naked and knew that we were alone together upon a bed, I took her in my arms and could hardly believe for very joy that she was mine. But just at that moment she smelt the garlic upon the hand with which I had eaten the zīrbājah, and gave a great cry. The women ran in from all sides and found me trembling with emotion, quite ignorant of the reason for this disturbance. 'What is it, sister?' they asked, and she replied: 'For Allāh's sake, rid me of this stupid fellow, whom once I thought to be a man of breeding.' 'How have I been silly?' I asked. 'You are mad!' she replied. 'Why did you eat zīrbājah and not wash your hands? As Allāh lives, I wish nothing more to do with you since you are so silly, so vulgar, and so criminal!' With these words she seized a whip that was beside her, and beat me over the back and buttocks so long and fiercely that I lost consciousness. Then she said to the other women: 'Take him away and lead him to the governor of the city, so that the hand which ate zīrbājah and was not washed may be cut off for a warning.' These words brought me to my feet, crying: 'There is no might nor mercy save in Allāh! Is my hand to be cut off just because I ate zīrbājah and did not wash? Whoever heard of such a thing!' The other women also interceded for me, saying: 'Sister, do not punish him so severely this time. Pardon him, we beg of you!' At last she said: 'Be it so. His hand shall not be cut off this time. Nevertheless, I must cut off something of his ends.' Then she went out and left me alone.

At the end of ten days during which I did not see her, she came back, saying: 'O you whose face is blackened, am I so little in your eyes that you eat zīrbājah and do not wash your hands?' Then she cried to her women: 'Bind his arms and legs!' and, when they had done so, took a very sharp razor and cut off both my thumbs and my big toes. That is why, good friends, you see me as I am.

I fainted away, and she stopped my bleeding with applications of powdered aromatic roots. When I recovered consciousness, I said in a loud voice: 'I will never eat zīrbājah without first washing my hands forty times with potash, forty times with soda, and forty times with soap.' She made me repeat these words in the form of an oath to the effect that I would never eat zīrbājah without doing as you have seen me do.

So, my friends, when you all pressed me to eat the dish at this feast, I changed colour, my cheeks turned sallow, and I said to myself: 'This is that zīrbājah which lost me my thumbs.' Also, when you forced me to eat, I was obliged by my oath to wash as you saw me wash.

So I, O King of the ages, (continued the steward) said to the young merchant of Baghdād, while all the others listened: 'What afterwards happened between you and your wife?' He answered:

When I took that oath, her heart was softened towards me and she pardoned me. I took her and lay with her, and for a long time we lived together in the palace, but at last she said: 'No one in the court knows what has happened between us; no man but you has ever entered the women's quarter of this palace, and it was only thanks to our dearest queen that you accomplished the entry.' Then she gave me fifty thousand dīnārs in gold, saying: 'Take this money and buy some great and beautiful dwelling for us, where we may live together.'

So I went forth and bought a magnificent house, to which I transported all my wife's riches, all the gifts that had been given to her, the jewels, the fair silks, and the costly furniture. She joined me and we lived together in great happiness and contentment.

But at the end of a year Allāh took my wife away, and I did not marry again, preferring rather to see the world. I sold all my belongings and left Baghdād. Since then I have travelled with my money and, as you see, have come even as far as this city.

'That, O King of time,' concluded the steward, 'is the story of the young Baghdād merchant. As for the rest, after the feast was finished we went homewards, and it was then that that happened to me with the hunchback of which you have heard.

'Such is the tale which I believe to be more astonishing than the adventure of the hunchback.

'Peace be with you!'

'You are mistaken,' said the King of China, 'it is not in any way more astonishing than the adventure of the hunchback; on the contrary, the adventure of the hunchback is considerably more marvellous than it. There is nothing for it but to hang every one of you.

But at that moment the Jewish doctor came forward and kissed the earth, saying: 'King of time, I have a tale to tell you which is

without doubt infinitely more extraordinary than the two which you
have just heard or the adventure of the hunchback.'

'Tell us,' said the King of China, 'for I am all impatience.'

And the Jewish doctor said:

The Tale of the Jewish Doctor

M Y tale concerns a most extraordinary thing which happened to
me in my youth. I was studying medicine and other forms of
science in the city of Damascus. When I had learnt my trade, I went
into practice and earned a fair livelihood.

One day a slave from the house of the governor of Damascus
came to me and, bidding me follow, led me to the governor's palace.
There, in the middle of a great hall, I saw a bed of cedar wood plated
with gold, on which the most beautiful young man in all the world
lay sick. Standing at his bedside I wished him a speedy return to
health, but he answered me only with a movement of his eyes, so I
said: 'Give me your hand, my lord.' Then he held out his left hand, a
circumstance which so astonished me that I could not help considering how a youth with such a noble air of breeding could be so
impolite. Nevertheless I felt his pulse and wrote him a prescription.
When I had visited him daily for ten days, he recovered and rose
from his bed; so I prescribed, as a completion of his cure, that he
should take a bath at the hammām and then return to sleep.

As a tribute to my skill, the governor of Damascus clothed me in
a rich robe of honour and appointed me to be both his private
physician and chief doctor of the Damascus hospital. The young
man, who had always given me his left hand throughout his illness,
begged me to accompany him to the bath. When the slaves of the
hammām, which had been specially reserved for us, had undressed
him, taken away his clothes, and set out others ready for him, I was
able to see, during the time of his nakedness, that his right hand was
missing. This sight both surprised and grieved me, and I was the
more perturbed when I also saw the marks of whips all over his
body. Turning to me, he said: 'O doctor of this age, let not my state
cause you any surprise, for I intend to tell you, when we have left the
bath, the reason of all this. It makes a remarkable story.'

Leaving the hammām, we returned to the palace and sat down to
rest before our evening meal. 'Would you not prefer to go into the

upper chamber?' asked the young man. 'Certainly,' I answered. So
he ordered the cooks to spit a sheep and roast it for us, and to have
the meal laid in the upper chamber. Soon the slaves brought us the
roast sheep and every kind of fruit; we sat down to eat, and the
young man used his left hand all the time. 'Now tell me your story,'
said I, and the youth answered: 'Chief physician of these hundred
years, listen and I will tell you.'

I was born in Mosul where my family were considered among the
most important people of the city. On his death, my grandfather left
ten sons of whom my father was the eldest; by the time he died all
ten sons were married, but only to my father had a child been given.
My uncles, being childless themselves, held me in great affection and
were pleased at all times to have me of their company.

One day I went with my father to the great mosque of Mosul to
make the Friday prayer; when the ceremony was over, all the con-
gregation departed except my father and my uncles. These sat down
on a great rug and began to talk of voyages and the marvels of
strange countries and of great cities far away. Especially did they
speak of Egypt and the city of Cairo, reciting the wonderful stories
of travellers who had visited that country and reported it to be the
most beautiful in the world. The poets, they said, had been no more
than right in singing the beauties of that land and of her river the fair
Nile. One has written:

> Ah, Euphrates, ah, Euphrates,
>   Silver river men put first,
> How can an Egyptian sate his
>   Native-born Egyptian thirst
>   Save in the smile
>   Of the mild Nile?

My uncles detailed the marvels of Egypt. One spoke of her golden
dust, her women, her light sweet waters, and her air passing the
scent of aloe wood. Another praised the flowers and islands of the
Nile, and the sun shining like swords on the green-banked Abyssinian Pond. A third delighted to recall the Night of Nile-full and the
Garden at eventide. And all spoke with such warm eloquence that,
when they ceased talking and went their way, I remained dreaming
and in a trance, my soul being unable to detach itself from the fair
images which had been born in my mind. When I reached home, I
could not sleep; for days I lost appetite and refused to eat or drink.

A few days later I heard that my uncles had made preparations for a voyage to Egypt, and I so wrought on my father with supplications and tears that he allowed me to accompany them and even bought merchandise for me to trade with on the journey. He advised my uncles, however, not to take me as far as Egypt, but to leave me at Damascus. When all was ready, I bade farewell to my father, and the caravan set out from Mosul.

First we came to Aleppo, where we tarried for a few days, and then went forward towards Damascus, which we reached safely in the fullness of time.

We found the city of Damascus a place set in the midst of gardens with running waters, trees and birds in excess of all other places. But especially did it abound in every colour and taste of delightful fruits.

We put up in one of the khāns, and my uncles stayed in the city until they had sold all their goods from Mosul and bought Damascus wares to sell in Cairo. After they had traded my goods at a profit of five dirhams on one, to my great delight, they left me alone in Damascus and set out for Egypt. I rented a beautiful house, a thing of marvel such as the tongue of man might not describe, paying two dīnārs a month in gold for it. There I lived in pleasant extravagance, satisfying all my senses, eating and drinking of the best, until I had considerably encroached upon my fortune.

One day, as I sat taking the air at the door of my house, an expensively-dressed girl approached, the like of whose elegance I had never seen in my life before. I sprang to my feet and invited her to honour my house with her presence, an invitation which she accepted in the best of gentle humours. When she was in the house, I shut the door behind us and, taking her joyfully in my arms, carried her into the central hall. There she took off her veil and appeared in all her beauty, so that I fell into a complete madness of love for her.

I ran about and, spreading a cloth, covered it with rich meats, fruits of choice, and all else that is suitable on such an occasion. We ate and sported together, and then drank until we were very pleasantly drunk. I took her, and we passed a night together such as was worthy to be enshrined among the historical love nights of the world. Determined that everything should be in keeping, I offered her ten gold dīnārs in the morning; but she refused them haughtily, saying that she would never accept anything from me. 'Besides, my dear,' she continued, 'in three days' time I will visit you again at twilight. And, as it is I who do the inviting, I insist on bearing the expense. Take this money and with it prepare a feast like yesterday's.' She forced me to accept ten golden dīnārs and then left me, taking my soul along with her.

But in three days she came again, dressed more gloriously than before, and I do not think that human tongue could describe the gold and embroidered fabrics and silks from which her beauty shone. I had prepared all as before, without sparing expense, so that we were able to sit down at once to eat and drink as we had done the last time, and we lay together again until the morning.

She came a third time after the same interval, and all went as before. When I had received her in honour and generosity, she said: 'Dear lover, do you think I am really beautiful?' 'As God lives, you are beautiful!' I cried. 'Good,' she said, 'now I can ask your permission to bring a younger and more beautiful girl with me next time, so that she can joy with us and we can all three laugh and play together. She has begged me to allow her to accompany me and make a third in our mad follies.' I accepted this suggestion with all my heart, and this time my mistress gave me twenty dīnārs so that nothing should be lacking in the reception. At last she parted from me again and went her way.

On the fourth occasion, I made even more splendid preparations in honour of the newcomer. Hardly had the sun set than my dear mistress came, bringing with her another woman who was enveloped in a large veil. When they were seated, I lit the torches and placed myself at their disposal; so they removed their veils and I was able to see the second girl. Allāh, Allāh, she was like the full moon, a fairer thing than any I had set eyes on in the world. I served them with meat and drink and, while they were feasting, kissed the newcomer and, filling her cup, drank with her again and again. This made my mistress very angry, but she concealed her feelings, saying to me: 'By Allāh, is she not delicious? Do you not find her much more beautiful than I am?' Like a fool I answered: 'Indeed I do!' Then said she: 'Take her and lie with her, for that would give me more pleasure than all else.' 'Your word is the law of my head and eyes!' I answered. So my mistress rose and made our bed herself, dragging us both to it with loving gestures. I lay down against my new friend and took my joy of her body until the approach of morning.

When I woke, I found my hand covered with blood, so that I thought I still dreamt and rubbed my eyes. Then I saw that the blood was real. As it was high morning I turned to wake my sleeping companion, but, when I touched her head lightly with my fingers, it fell from her body and rolled upon the ground.

Jealousy had done its work.

Not knowing what to do, I sat for an hour in deep cogitation; then I rose and, stripping myself naked, set about preparing a grave in the very room in which we had slept. I lifted some of the marble slabs from the floor and dug a hole in the earth beneath, large enough to hold the body. Thrusting it in, I filled up the grave and replaced the marble flooring so carefully that all seemed as before.

Then I dressed and, collecting all the money which I had, went to my landlord and paid him another year's rent in advance, saying: 'I am obliged to set out for Egypt where my uncles are waiting for me.'

Arriving at last in Cairo, I found my uncles, who were delighted to see me and questioned me as to my reason for seeking them out. 'I longed to behold you,' I answered, 'also I was afraid that I might spend all my money if I stayed longer in Damascus.' They invited me to live with them and, for a whole year, I bore them company, amusing myself in many ways, drinking, eating, visiting the sights of the city, and taking pleasure in the admirable aspects of the Nile. Unfortunately at the end of a year my uncles, who had completed all their business in the city, decided to return to Mosul. I had no wish to accompany them as I knew that they would pass through Damascus, so I left them and hid myself in the city. They set out alone, thinking, as I knew that place so well, that I had gone forward to Damascus to prepare accommodation for them.

For three years I stayed in Cairo, enjoying my money to the full and sending the rent of my house in Damascus regularly to the landlord. But at the beginning of the fourth year, finding that I had scarcely money enough left for the journey, I set out myself towards Damascus.

My landlord welcomed me joyously on my arrival and, giving me the keys of my house, showed me that the lock was still sealed with my seal. When I entered, I found everything just as I had left it.

The first thing I did was to wash the flooring near the bed, in case any trace remained of the blood of the poor woman who had been murdered by her jealous friend. When this was done, I went towards the bed to lie down and rest after my tiring journey. Happening to move the pillow, I found beneath it a collar of solid gold with three tiers of nobly perfect pearls; this had belonged to the slain woman and she had placed it below the pillow before that tragic night of ours. I wept bitter tears on finding this relic and then thrust it into the bosom of my robe.

After three hours' sleep in my house I walked down to the market, to find employment and to see my old friends there. But Destiny, whom none can gainsay, had ordered that the Evil One should tempt me and that I should fall. An irresistible thought came to me to get rid of the collar by selling it. So I took it from my robe and showed it to the most able broker in the market. He invited me to sit down in his shop and, when the market was at its busiest, took the collar and hawked it round for sale. At the end of an hour he returned, saying: 'At first I thought that the collar was of real gold with genuine pearls, and worth at least a thousand dīnārs; but now I find that it is false, artificial stuff made by the Franks, who can imitate every metal and precious stone. The highest offer I can get for it is a thousand dirhams.' 'You are quite right,' I answered, 'the collar is false. I had it made to play a joke on a woman to whom I had to give a present, but, by a most extraordinary chance, the woman died and left the collar to my wife. We have decided to sell it at any sacrifice. Take it, complete the business quickly, and bring me back the thousand dirhams.'

At this point Shahrazād saw the approach of morning and discreetly fell silent.

But when the twenty-eighth night had come

SHE SAID:

It is related, O auspicious King, that the Jewish doctor thus continued his story:

When the young man said to the broker: 'Bring me back the thousand dirhams,' the latter knew that the youth had no idea of the value of the collar and, supposing that he had either found or stolen it, considered that the matter ought to be looked into. He therefore took the collar to the chief broker of the market, who himself took it to the walī of the city, saying: 'The collar was stolen from me. We have just found the thief, a young man dressed like a merchant's son who is at the moment at such a place in the shop of the broker so-and-so.'

And the young man continued to tell me his story in these words: While I was waiting for the broker to bring me the money I was surrounded and seized by the guards, who forcibly dragged me before the walī. He questioned me about the collar and I told him the same tale as I had told the broker. But the walī burst out laughing and said: 'I myself will teach you the exact price of the collar!' With that he signed to the guards, who stripped off my clothes and beat me with both rods and whips until my body was a mass of blood. 'I will speak the truth!' I cried out in my pain, 'I stole the collar from the chief broker.' I made this false confession, thinking it better to be punished on the lesser count than to tell of the terrible murder which had happened at my house and to be condemned and killed outright to avenge the death of the young woman.

But hardly had I accused myself of the theft, when my arm was seized and my right hand cut off. When the stump was dipped in boiling oil to cicatrise the wound, I fell down in a faint. Someone forced a mixture of drugs between my lips, which brought me to myself; I picked up my severed hand and returned to my house. My landlord, who had heard of the affair, was waiting for me. 'Now that you are known as a thief and lawbreaker,' he said, 'I cannot allow you to occupy my house any longer. You must pack up your goods and find a lodging elsewhere.' 'My lord,' I answered, 'I beg you to allow me two or three days in which to look for another place.' 'I will willingly concede you that,' he answered, and went his way.

When he had gone, I threw myself on the ground, weeping and saying: 'How shall I ever be able to return to Mosul and see my people again? When they see my severed hand, they will not believe that I am innocent, whatever I say. Things have come to such a pass that I see nothing for it but to leave all in the hands of Allāh, for He alone can lead me into a way of safety.'

So sad and ill was I that I could not hunt for another house, and I was still lying upon the bed when, on the third day, I saw the house invaded by a party of soldiers belonging to the governor-general of Damascus. In their midst were my landlord and the chief broker. The former said to me: 'I have to inform you that the walī has told the governor-general about the theft of this collar and it has come out that the precious thing belongs, not to the chief broker, but to the governor-general himself, or rather to one of his daughters who disappeared three years ago. These soldiers have come to arrest you.'

All my limbs became loose and trembled at these words, and I thought 'Now there is no help for it, I go to my death. My one hope is to tell the truth and leave my life in the hands of the governor-general.' A chain was put about my neck and I was dragged before the governor, who, as soon as he saw me, addressed his courtiers and people in these words: 'This young man is no thief and his hand has been cut off unjustly. The chief broker is a liar and has borne false witness. Seize him and throw him into prison.' Then to the chief broker himself, he continued: 'You shall pay this poor young man in full for his severed hand, otherwise I shall hang you and confiscate all your goods, O broker of lies!' To the guards he cried: 'Bring the young man face to face with me, and then let everyone else depart!' My arms were unbound, the iron collar taken from about my neck, and I was left with the governor.

He looked at me with a great pity in his face, saying: 'My child, speak to me frankly and tell me the whole truth. I wish to know how the collar came into your hands.' 'My lord and master, I will tell you the full truth,' I answered, and I informed him of all that had occurred between myself and the first girl, of how she had brought the second girl to me, and finally killed her through jealousy. I told him the whole thing without omitting a single detail.

When he had heard me, the governor-general bent his head on his breast in bitter grief, covered his face with his handkerchief, and wept for a long time. At last he came over to me and said: 'Know, my son, that the first girl was my eldest daughter. She had been perverse from her childhood, and therefore I had trained her with great severity. But, even so, hardly had she reached puberty when I made haste to send her to her uncle in Cairo to be married to my nephew, one of his sons. She was married, but her husband died a short time afterwards, so that we were obliged to receive her home again into my house. Her stay in Egypt, however, had not been for nothing. She had learnt all the vices of the Egyptian women and all the lascivious corruptions which they practise. You have been in Egypt and must know how expert are the women there in every kind of lust. Men do not suffice them: they love and couple with each other, wearing themselves out upon the bodies of their own kind. It was soon after her return to our house that my eldest daughter met you and made her four visits to you. But that was not enough. She had already had time to debauch my second daughter and to make herself passionately loved by her, so that it was not difficult for her to persuade the younger one to make a third with you. My second daughter obtained leave from me to go to the market with her sister. When my eldest child returned alone, I asked her where her sister was. She answered only with tears, but at last managed to say: "I lost her in the market. I do not know at all what has happened to her." This was what she told me, but she opened her heart to her mother and ended by telling her the whole story of her sister's murder in your house. From that time on she did not cease from tears, and we would hear her moaning day and night. "Needs must I weep myself to death!" she would cry. What you have told me, my son, only confirms what I already knew, and proves that you spoke the truth. I am a most unhappy man, therefore do not refuse a request which I have to make of you. I wish you to become one of my own house and marry my third daughter, who is a virgin, wise and pure, ignorant of the vices of her sisters. I ask no marriage settlement from you; rather will I make you a great allowance and you shall live with me in my palace as a son.'

'My lord,' I answered, 'all shall be as you wish. But there is one thing I must tell you: I have just heard that my father is dead and I would return to receive my inheritance.'

The governor sent a quick envoy to Mosul, my native city, who, in my name, collected all that my father had left me, while I stayed here and married the governor's daughter. Since then we have all three lived the happiest of lives together.

You can see for yourself, O doctor, how loved and honoured I am in this palace. Also you will no longer think that it was incivility on my part which caused me, during all my illness, to hold my left hand out to you.

I was thunderstruck by this story (continued the Jewish doctor) and congratulated the young man heartily on the way in which he had escaped from the adventure. He loaded me with presents, kept me three days as his guest at the palace, and sent me away a rich man.

Since then I have travelled about the world, perfecting myself in my art, and in doing so I have come at last to your kingdom, O powerful and generous King. Last night there happened to me an unfortunate adventure with your hunchback. Such is my story.

Then said the King of China: 'Your tale has interested me greatly, but you are mistaken, O doctor, in thinking that it is in any way as wonderful as the adventure of the hunchback. It only remains for me to hang all four of you, and, higher than all the rest, that cursed tailor who was the cause and beginning of your crimes.'

Hearing this, the tailor advanced and faced the King of China, saying: 'Glorious monarch, before you hang us allow me also to have my say. I will tell you a story which in itself contains a thousand aspects of greater marvel than all the tales you have heard put together, and surpasses by many properties the affair of the hunchback.'

'If what you say is true,' answered the King, 'I will pardon you all. But woe betide you if the story lacks interest and is not packed with sublimity! For, as Allāh lives, I will not hesitate to have you all impaled, yes, hollowed right through from the bottom to the top.'

Then the Tailor said:

The Tale of the Tailor

KNOW, O lord of time, that, before my adventure with the hunchback, I was guest at a certain house where a feast was being given to the principal members of our city's guilds: tailors, cobblers, cloth-merchants, barbers, carpenters, and the like.

As soon as morning broke we were all seated in a circle, ready to begin the feast and only waiting for the master of the house. Presently he entered accompanied by a strange young man, handsome and well built, mannered and costumed in the Baghdād fashion. He was as striking a young man as one could wish to see, but quite noticeably lame. He came among us, wishing us peace and being in turn greeted by the company, and was about to take his seat when we saw him change colour, rise again, and make as if to leave the hall. We all strove to detain him, and the master of the feast pressed him heartily to remain, saying: 'We do not understand this matter at all. Tell us at least, I pray, why you wish to leave us.'

'As Allāh lives, my lord,' answered the young man, 'I beg you not to try to keep me. There is one among you whose presence makes it absolutely necessary that I should retire. If you must know, it is that barber sitting there.'

The master of the feast turned to us in surprise, saying: 'How comes it that this youth who has just arrived from Baghdād can be in any way inconvenienced by the presence of a barber in this city?' Many of us who were guests turned to the youth, begging him to tell us the reason of his aversion from the barber. 'Gentlemen,' he answered, 'this tar-faced and pitch-spirited barber was the cause of a very strange adventure which happened to me in my native city of Baghdād. Also he was directly responsible for my lameness. I swore never to live in a city where he dwelt, or to sit down in a place where he was seated. I left Baghdād because of him and journeyed into this far country; yet here I find him also. I will set forth at once, and hope this evening to be far from your amiable city and from the presence of that malevolent dotard over there.'

During this speech the barber's cheeks had become quite yellow; he lowered his eyes and did not say a word. The rest of us so persuaded the young man that at last he told us the following story.

The Tale of the Lame Man with the Barber of Baghdād

(*Told by the Lame Young Man and reported by the Tailor*)

YOU must know, gentlemen, that I was, by the grace of Allāh, the only son of one of the principal merchants in Baghdād. Though my father was a very rich man and held in high repute throughout the city, he yet passed a very quiet life peaceably in his own house and brought me up in the same tradition. When I became a man, my father passed to the mercy of Allāh, paying that debt which we all owe to Him, and left me master of his slaves and of his house. From that time on I lived in serene prodigality, dressing myself sumptuously and eating of the best. But there is one thing which I should tell you. Allāh, in whom is all power and glory, had planted in my heart a horror of women, so that but to see one of them discomfited me and vexed me. I lived without troubling about them at all, happy in other ways and not wishing for any different kind of life. One day, as I was walking in the streets of Baghdād, I saw a crowd of women coming towards me. In order to avoid them I fled up a side-street which ended in a blank wall. Against the wall there was a bench on which I sat down to rest.

I had not been there long when a window opened opposite me, and a young woman appeared holding a little watering pot with which she began to water the flowers standing in vases outside the window.

I must tell you, gentlemen, that, at sight of this girl, there sprang up in my heart an emotion which I had never felt before in my life. I cannot say more than that she was as beautiful as the full moon, that her little arm was white and transparent like crystal, and that she watered the flowers so prettily that any man's soul might have been caught thereby. In that one moment my heart was both burnt up

and reduced to a condition of slavery. Henceforth my mind had no
other thought than her, and my former horror of women was
turned into a great desire for them. When she had watered the
flowers, she looked casually to left and right and, seeing me, gave me
one long glance which snared my soul and drew it up to her. Then
she shut the window, and I waited there till sunset without seeing
her again. I sat there like a sleep-walker or a ghost who has no more
concern with the living world.

While I remained there in this state the kādī of the city, preceded
by negroes and followed by attendants, rode up on his mule and
dismounted at the door of that house where I had seen the young
girl. When he disappeared through the door, I understood that he
was her father.

I returned home in a lamentable state of spirit, full of sadness and
care, and threw myself down on my bed. My women, together with
the slaves and the folk of my house, clustered about me, asking me
unceasingly the reason for my collapse, but I would not answer them.
From day to day my heart grew more afflicted, until I fell seriously
ill and was an object of acute anxiety to my friends and family.

One day I saw an old woman come into the room who, instead of
groaning and weeping over my condition as the others did, sat down
and calmed my spirit with sprightly commonplace. Having regarded
me closely for a long time, she asked all the people who were by me
to leave me alone with her. When they had left, she said to me: 'My
child, I know why you are ill, but it is necessary for you to give
details.' I told her the whole story, and she continued: 'My son, that
girl is the daughter of the kādī of Baghdād, and the house which you
saw is his house. But he does not live on the same storey as his
daughter, having his apartments in the lower part of the building.
Yet, although the young woman lives alone, she is very carefully
guarded and spied upon. I am, however, a friend and constant
visitor of the family, and you will never gain your ends except
through me. Stiffen up, now, and be a man.'

These words gave me both courage and resolution. I rose, and
felt myself to be quite well again and indeed in a state of bodily
perfection. All my family rejoiced, and the old woman left me,
promising to return on the morrow to tell me the result of the interview which she intended with the young daughter of the kādī of
Baghdād.

She kept her promise, but at the first sight of her face I knew that, as is usual in such cases, she had no good news to give me. She said: 'My child, do not ask me what has happened. I am still all of a tremble. Hardly had I whispered the object of my visit to the young lady than she sprang up and talked to me very angrily. She called me an ill-omened old woman, and said that if I did not cease my evil proposals she would have me punished as I deserved. I could not say more, dear boy, but I promise to return to the attack at once. Never have I undertaken a project of this sort without something coming of it, for no one in the world knows more about the business.' With these words she left me.

Because of this disappointment I fell more seriously ill than before and ceased either to eat or drink.

In a few days the old woman came back, as she had promised, and said to me with a smiling and contented face: 'Come, my son, give me the reward of good news.' Instantly I felt the vigour return to my body for very joy, and I said to the old woman: 'Mother, you shall have everything you wish.' Then she told me these good tidings: 'Yesterday I went back to the dear young lady and, when she saw that I wore a humble and defeated air and that my eyes were filled with tears, she said: "Auntie, I see that you are in trouble. What is it?" I replied, weeping all the time: "My daughter, my dear mistress, do you not remember that I came to speak to you about a young man who had fallen passionately in love with you? To-day that young man is lying at the point of death for your sake." On this her heart was softened, and she asked: "But who is this young man of whom you speak?" "He is as an own son to me, as the fruit of my body," I answered. "A few days ago he saw you watering the flowers at your window; just for a moment he saw your face and on the instant, though until then he had refused to look upon the face of woman, he felt himself lost in love for you. When I told him a few days ago of the naughty reception you had accorded me, he fell into a worse state of love-sickness than before. I have just left him stretched upon his bed in act to render his last breath to Allāh. I do not think that there is any chance of saving him!' The girl paled at my words, saying: "And is all that because of me?" "As Allāh lives, it is," I answered. "What are you going to do now? I am your slave and will carry out any orders you care to give me." "Go to him as quickly as you can," she said, "greet him for me and tell him that I have much sorrow for his sorrow. Tell him that I will wait for him here to-morrow after the Friday prayer. Let him come and I will open to him; he shall come up into my apartment and we will spend an hour together. But tell him that he must be sure to go away promptly, before my father returns from the mosque." '

When I heard the delightful words of the old woman, my manhood came back to me and all my sorrows slipped away. I gave her a purse filled with dīnārs which she accepted, saying: 'Lift up your heart and be content!' 'My illness is over,' I answered. And indeed my sickness had quite left me, so that my friends and the people of my house were delighted at my sudden cure.

Impatiently I waited for the morrow; with it came the old woman, asking news of my health. I said that I did wonderfully well, and we talked together for some time. Then I dressed myself in the costliest robes I had and scented myself with essence of roses. I was on the point of setting out for the girl's house, when the old woman said: 'You have plenty of time. Why not go to the hammām while you are waiting, to bathe and be massaged, shaved and depilated? These things will improve your appearance after your illness.' 'An excellent plan!' I answered. 'First I will send for a barber to shave my head here, and then I will go down to the hammām.'

I ordered one of my young slaves to fetch me a barber, adding: 'See to it that he not only has a light hand, but is a man wise and discreet, sparing of words and questions, one who will not split my head with his babble as would most of his kind.' My slave ran to obey me and brought back with him a barber who was none other, gentlemen, than the sinister old man you see before you.

When he entered, he wished me peace, and I did the like by him. Then said he: 'May Allāh move very far away from you all grief, all care, all anxiety, all trouble and all misfortune!' 'May Allāh grant your wishes!' I answered. 'Well, well,' he continued, 'I bring you good news, my master, very good news, or rather not exactly good news, but good wishes for your complete return to health and strength. Yet business is business. What exactly would you wish me to do? To shave you or let blood? You cannot be ignorant that the great ibn Abbās once said: "He who has his hair shortened of a Friday makes himself acceptable to Allāh, Who thereafter averts from him seventy different kinds of calamity." On the other hand, you cannot have forgotten that the same ibn Abbās said on another occasion: "He who has his blood let on a Friday, or submits on that day to an application of the cups, goes in great danger of losing his sight and is apt to attract every kind of malady to himself." '

'Old man,' I answered, 'I would wish you to cease your conversation for a time and shave my head as quickly as you can, for I am still weak from my illness and ought neither to speak nor to listen very much.'

The barber rose and, taking a bundle wrapped in a handkerchief such as the men of his trade use to carry their basin, their razors and their scissors, he opened it and took out, not a razor, but a seven-faced astrolabe. Walking with it into the middle of the courtyard of my house, he lifted his head gravely towards the sun and, after regarding it for a long time and then examining the astrolabe for even longer, he returned to me saying: 'You must know that this day of Friday is the tenth of the month of Safar in the seven hundred and sixty-third year of the Hijrah of our Sacred Prophet, on whom be all the best that there can be of prayers and of peace. Now such knowledge as I have of the science of numbers tells me that this Friday coincides exactly with the moment of conjunction of the two planets Mars and Mercury, the ascension being exactly seven degrees and six minutes, which seems clearly to denote that to-day is not only lawful but auspicious for the action of shaving the head. The same series of calculations tells me that it is your intention to pay a visit to-day to a young lady, of which good may come or possibly evil; I do not say that I actually need my science for the purpose of prophesying exactly what will happen when you and the young lady are together, but that hardly matters, as there are some things about which it is necessary sedulously to keep silence.'

'As Allāh lives,' I cried, 'you suffocate me with your talk; it will kill me in a minute! Besides, you do not seem to be prophesying very pleasant things. I brought you here to shave my head. Do so at once with no more words.' 'Be it exactly as you say,' he answered, 'though I cannot help thinking that if you knew the truth you would ask me for many more details and demonstrations. For you must know that though I am a barber, I am not only a barber. So little so, in fact, that, though I am perhaps the best known barber in Baghdād, I have at my fingers' ends not only the arts of the doctor, the herbalist, and the chemist, but also, to name but a few of my accomplishments, the whole science of the stars, the theory of grammar, the art and rule of poetry, rhetoric, arithmetic, geometry, algebra, philosophy, architecture, history, and the traditional folk-lore of all the peoples of the earth. I only tell you this that you may see that I had a certain amount of right on my side, my lord, when I advised you to follow my instructions exactly in the matter of obeying the little horoscope which I have just had the great pleasure of making for you, thanks to my knowledge of astral calculation. If I were you, I would thank Allāh, my son, that it was I who came to you and not some other, and I should obey the suggestions of one who only speaks in your own interest. You must not think that I do these things for money, or indeed for any reason save from the purest good will. I am ready enough to shave you, nay, even to stay in your service for a whole year, and not ask a penny in wages. Only there is one thing that I think I have a right to ask, and that is that I should be recognised and spoken to as a man of some merit. I think that you will agree that that is only just.'

Here I broke in upon him, crying: 'Would you drive me mad and kill me with impatience at the same time, old murderer?'

At this point Shahrazād saw the approach of morning and discreetly fell silent.

And when the twenty-ninth night had come

SHE SAID:

It is related, O auspicious King, that when the young man broke in impatiently on the barber's speech, the latter answered: 'That is exactly the one point on which you are mistaken, master. Everyone without exception knows me as al-Sāmit, the silent man, because of the scant use that I can make of words. If you consider for a moment you will see how unjust you have been to me in thinking me talkative, especially if you spare an instant to compare me with my six brothers who, I admit, are a little given to babbling. Perhaps you have not heard of them? Well, just that you shall know them when I speak of them again, I will tell you their names. The eldest is called al-Bakbūk, that is to say, he who when he tattles makes a glucking noise like water coming out of a jar. The second is called al-Haddār, that is to say, he who continually lows like a camel. The name of the third is Bakbāk, or the swollen clucker. The fourth, al-Kūz of Uswān, or the unbreakable jug. The fifth is al-Ashar, that is to say, either the gravid she-camel or the great pot. The sixth is Shakkāshik or the cracked guglet. And the seventh is al-Sāmit, the silent man. This silent man is your humble servant.'

At this fresh start of the barber's I felt my gall-bladder on the point of bursting and I cried out to one of my young slaves: 'For

God's sake, give this man a quarter of a dīnār and have him out of this. I am not going to have my head shaved after all.'

Hearing what I said to the slave, the barber continued: 'I should call those harsh words, master; yes, I should think anyone would be entitled to call them harsh words. I do not think you quite realise that I wish to have the honour of attending to you without any thought of money and, if I am willing to shave you without asking anything in return, you can understand that I would be quite incapable of taking money when I had not even been allowed to do you that slight service. No, no, I could not think of such a thing; I should consider myself dishonoured for ever if I took the least little matter from you under those circumstances. I quite see that you have no idea of my value. That does not prevent me from having a very exact idea of your great value. I assure you that I consider you in every way a worthy son of your dear old father, whom may Allāh be now lodging in His compassion. Now there was a gentleman for you! Yes, your dear old father was a gentleman if ever there was one. I owed a lot to your father. For some reason he was always showering benefits upon me. Never was a more generous man, never was a grander man, if I may be allowed to say it, and for some reason he used to value me very highly. I remember one day, just as it might have been to-day, your dear good father sent for me. I found him surrounded by noble visitors, but he left them at once and came up to greet me, saying: "I beg you to let me a little blood, old friend." On that I unwrapped my astrolabe, measured the height of the sun and found out that that particular hour was peculiarly inauspicious for blood-letting. I assure you that it would have been both a difficult and dangerous undertaking. Well, I went and told my fears to your poor dead father—woe is me that such a delightful patron should have passed into Allāh's keeping! He believed me at once and waited patiently, chatting with me more as if he had been my friend than my employer, until the suitable moment came for the operation. When the right hour came, I bled him well—he was always a good patient—and then he thanked me warmly. And he was not the only one; all the guests gathered round and thanked me as well. Now that I come to think of it, though I had quite forgotten when I began to tell you of this, your dear father was so pleased with the way I bled him that he gave me a hundred golden dīnārs on the spot.'

When he had got thus far, I shouted: 'May Allāh have no pity on my dead father if ever he was fool enough to have anything to do with a barber like yourself!'

Laughing and shaking his head, the barber answered: 'There is no other God but Allāh and Muhammad is his prophet! Blessed be the name of Him Who changes some things and does not change others! I thought at first that you were in full possession of your senses, laddie, but now I see that your illness has a little affected your head. Not that I am surprised, mind you; I remember the Sacred Words which Allāh wrote in our Holy and Precious Book; the verse begins I think: "Blessed are they who control their anger and forgive the offender. . . ." I will not hear of you apologising for anything you may have said to me. I forgive it all. And yet, I must confess, that I do not quite understand this impatience and hurry of yours. You ought to know better than anyone else that your dear old father never took any important step without first asking my advice. He at least knew the worth of the proverb which says: "The man who takes good council has provided himself with a shield." I am rather an exceptional man, as a matter of fact. In all my life, though I have searched diligently, I have never found a man who can give better advice than I can. I suppose it is because I have made myself master of all wisdom and have had an excellent business experience. Well, here I am, standing on my two old feet before you, just waiting for you to tell me what I can do for you. One interesting point occurs to me: why is it that I should not be in the least tired of you when you are so manifestly tired of me? And yet I suppose that that is not really difficult to understand. If I show more than ordinary patience in my dealings with you, my boy, it is because of the great regard I shall always feel for your dear old father.'

'By God, this is too much!' I yelled, 'your voice is a slow torture. I sent for you to shave my head. Now I command you to leave the house as quickly as possible!' So saying, I jumped up and made as if to eject him forcibly, although my head was by this time covered with soapy lather.

But, without heeding me at all, the wretched old man went on: 'I am afraid I am irritating you, young man, and yet I am too wise to care about a little thing like that. I can see well that your mind is not quite recovered from its illness. Still you are young and there is plenty of time for that. Dear me, dear me, it seems only the other day that I used to carry you to school, you riding piggy-back on my shoulders and I taking you all the way to the school like that and you kicking me in the sides and not wanting to go. It seems just like the other day.'

'My friend,' I said seriously, 'I must beg you by all that you hold most holy to let me go about my business.' With this I tore my clothes and began shrieking like a madman.

When he saw me behaving in this way the barber hunted about for his razor and, when he found it, began to strop it and passed it up and down the leather so many times that I thought if he did not stop my soul would incontinently leave my body. At last, however, he took my head in one hand and made one little pass with the razor, removing a few hairs. Then he lifted his hand and said: 'Young master, impatience comes by the temptation of the Evil One!' And he recited the following ill-conceived moral stanzas:

> The wise man hatches out a plan
>   By sitting on it like a hen,
> The cautious and inactive man
>   Is blessed above all other men.
>
> The man who would admirèd go
>   Should carefully regard this text:
> Have mercy on a fallen foe,
>   You know not what may happen next.
>
> However strong a tyrant is
>   Allāh is even more than he is:
> He raises up the poor to bliss
>   And brings the tyrant to his knees.

Then said he: 'I know quite well, my master, that you have no regard either for my talents or for my inner worth, yet the hand which is quite ready to shave you if you give the word has caressed the heads of kings, of amīrs, of wazīrs, of governors-general, of governors, of assistant governors, of princes, of men famous in every way. I think it must have been in my honour, or in the honour of someone very like me, that the poet said:

> All trades are jewels in the crown of state,
>   But one round pearl of price the centre harbours,
> Which to themselves each guild would arrogate;
>   While I have always said it was the barber's,
> Who stands with subtle steel and phrases bland,
> Holding the heads of kings beneath his hand.'

To this vomit of words I answered: 'Are you or are you not going to shave me? I am not far from dead because of you.'

Then said the barber: 'An idea has suddenly struck me. I really believe that you are in a hurry.'

'Of course I am, of course I am, of course I am!' I answered.

'Well, well,' he said, 'who would have thought of your being in a hurry! It is my duty to give you counsels of moderation; haste is one of the most obvious snares of the Tempter. I have never known haste to lead to anything except repentance. Our dear Lord, Muhammad, on whom be prayer and peace, used to say: "The most beautiful thing in the world is something quite ripe which has been made slowly." But what you have just said about being in a hurry interests me very much. I should very much like to hear your reasons. I hope your hurry is what one might call a pleasant hurry, a hurry, that is to say, leading to pleasant things. I cannot tell you how desolate I should be if your hurry were a disagreeable hurry. Now I know you will excuse me if I interrupt my operation for a moment, for I think that the time has been slipping away and there remain only a few more hours of suitable sunshine.' With this he put down his razor, took up his astrolabe, and went out into the sun. He stayed an intolerable time in the courtyard, taking the exact height of the sun but keeping an eye on me all the time and satisfying himself that I was there by asking me questions. When he came back, he said: 'If by chance you are in a hurry to be in time for midday prayer, calm yourself, laddie, for you have three good hours to spare. I never make a mistake in matters of time.'

Then said I: 'As Allāh lives, let us have no more prattle; your voice is pulverising my liver.'

At this the barber consented to take up his razor again and began to shave a small part of my head very gently and deliberately; but he went on talking all the time in this fashion: 'I am sorry to see you so impatient. I feel sure that if you were to tell me the reason I would be able to help you. You have no excuse for hiding anything from me, since you now know how much your poor father valued my advice.'

There seemed no possible way of extricating myself from under the hands of this horrible barber, and I said to myself: 'The time for prayer is at hand and I ought very soon to be at the house of the young woman, otherwise it will be too late and I shall hardly get there before prayer ends and folk come out of the mosque. Then all will be lost.' So I said to the barber: 'Make an end now. Try to control your flow of talk and your ill-mannered curiosity. If you really must know, I am in a hurry to get to a feast at the house of one of my friends.'

On the word feast, the barber cried out: 'Well, well, Allāh bless you! Surely this is my lucky day! You have just reminded me that I am giving a feast to-night. Many of my friends have been invited and I have completely forgotten to prepare the necessary entertainment. It is a pity that you could not have reminded me a little sooner. Now it is too late.' 'Do not worry about that,' I said, 'I can get you out of the difficulty. As I have told you, I am going to a feast, so that I shall not be dining at home. I will therefore give you all the meats and drinks which I have in the house, on condition that you waste no more time in shaving my head.' 'Allāh smother you with gifts, my master, and make each generous act of yours come home as a blessing to you. Tell me a little, sweet master, about the things with which you are about to overwhelm me, for I confess that I would like to know.'

'I have five pots for you,' I answered, 'all containing admirable foods: egg-apples and stuffed marrows, filled vine-leaves seasoned with lemon, cakes of bruised corn and minced meat, sliced fillet of mutton cooked in tomatoed rice, a stew of little onions; further I have ten roast fowls and a roast sheep, and two great dishes, one of kunāfah and the other of a pastry made with sweet cheese and honey; fruits of every kind: melons, cucumbers, limes, and fresh dates.' 'Ah, master, master!' cried the barber, 'delight me with the sight of all these wonderful things.'

I ordered the food to be brought in to us, and the barber examined and tasted every dish. Then, turning to me with a happy smile, he said: 'I have known no generosity to equal yours, young man. And did you not say something about drinks?' 'I did,' I answered. 'May I not just look upon them?' said he. So I had six great jars brought in, each filled with a different wine, and the barber well tasted all of them. 'Allāh will requite you for all this!' said my tormentor. 'You are the soul of generosity. All would be most bounteously complete with a little incense, some benzoin, a few scents for burning, a touch of rose-water and orange-water to sprinkle my guests withal.' In desperation I had a little chest brought, containing more than fifty golden dīnārs' worth of ambergris, aloewood, nard, musk, incense and benzoin, and had it packed up for him with aromatic essences and silver water-sprays. Afterwards, as my time had become even less than my patience, I said: 'You may carry away all this as soon as you have finished shaving me; therefore in the Lord's name be quick!' Then said the barber: 'I can never take away so handsome a little box without first seeing what is inside and thanking you for all.' So one of my young slaves opened up the chest again and the barber, setting aside his astrolabe, sat on his heels and began to finger all the perfumes, the incense, the benzoin, the musk, the ambergris, and the aloewood, sniffing one after the other in so slow an ecstasy that I nearly died upon the spot. At long last he rose and, after thanking me elaborately, resumed his razor and went on shaving. Hardly had the blade passed once along my scalp, however, when he stopped again and said: 'As Allāh lives, my child, I hardly know which to thank for this blessed day, you or your poor dead father. The feast which I shall be giving to-night could never have been save for your kind thought and most unexpected gifts. And yet there is one thing which I feel I ought to say, though it is not the sort of thing that a man usually confesses. To tell you the truth, my guests for to-night are hardly such as would usually be considered worthy of such magnificent entertainment. They are just common humble men, like myself, who have to work for their living. Mind you, I am not saying a word against them; they are all excellent fellows, delightful companions, full of interest to the seeing eye. You will understand better if I tell you who they are. First there is the excellent Zantūt, rubber at the baths; then the delightful Sīlat, who sells roast bruised chickpeas; then Salīah, the corn-merchant; Akrashah, the vegetable seller; Humaid, the scavenger; and, last but not least, Abū Makārish, the curdled-milk man.

'As is natural, all these friends of mine are like myself in this, that they are never talkative or curious, yet they are all good drinkers and side-splitting fellows. I love the least of them above all kings. Each has his own song and dance, renowned throughout Baghdād. Lord bless you, I could run all of their songs and dances off for you if it would amuse you.

'Just look here, this is Zantūt, the rubber's little dance this way, that way, and round about like this. His song goes this way:

> My little friend is like a lamb
> All soothe to fondle and to feel;

> Her happiness is where I am,
>   And if to make a jest I steal
> Away from her, she runs instead
> To jump and tumble on my bed.

'Ah, but you should see the dance of my friend Humaid, the scavenger! There is a fellow for you! . . . What do you think of it? Gay and suggestive, is it not? And yet it has a certain technical perfection. His song is a sweet thing:

> My wife who is a stingy bitch,
>   As ugly as the Day of Reckoning,
> Hides all the bread-crusts out of reach,
>   And yet she is for ever beckoning
> My duty to her breach.

> If I must curb my stomach's lust
>   Then she shall starve between her legs,
> For if she'll not provide a crust
>   I'll break my eggs.'

Straightway, before I could interfere, this disgusting old man danced me off the dances and sang me the songs of the rest of his friends. Then said he: 'Now that you know what my jolly companions can do, if you want a good laugh I would advise you to come and make one of us at my feast to-night, and give your friends the go-by for the time being. You will enjoy yourself more, and we will be all the happier. I have a special reason for inviting you in this way. There are traces of fatigue on your face and you have just risen from a bed of sickness; it is just possible, if you went to your grand party, that you might find some talkative individual among the guests who would weary you by clothing his ideas in too many words and asking indiscreet questions. If that were so, you might fall ill again and be worse than before.'

'For to-day, good barber,' I answered, 'I am afraid that it is impossible for me to accept your invitation, but another time I shall be delighted to come.' 'And yet,' said the barber, 'I cannot help repeating that I think it would be to your best advantage to come to my house, with as little delay as possible, to enjoy the polished urbanity of my good friends and to take advantage of all their admirable qualities. You know that the poet says:

> When pleasure offers, dear my friends,
>   Catch hands or feet or breasts of her,
> She is a woman and up-ends
>   The tantalising bests of her
> Perhaps three times a week. The other days
> "How gross a thing is man!" she says.'

Although my soul was flaming with anger, yet I could not help the barriers of my reserve being washed away by this stream of nonsense. So I burst out laughing and said: 'Surely such wonderful friends must be waiting impatiently for so wonderful a host! Finish your work and be gone!' 'And yet,' said the barber, 'I cannot understand why you refuse. I only ask a very small favour of you, to allow me to gladden your soul for the rest of its days by introducing you to all the jolly and discreet old lads of my acquaintance. Once you have met them, you will make constant companions of them and give up all your other friends for ever.' 'God increase you all in your friendship,' I answered, 'I promise that some day I will invite them to my house and give a special feast for them alone.'

'Thank you, thank you,' mumbled the wretched scraper, 'now that I see you really prefer your own friends to the chance of meeting mine, just spare me a moment to run home with all these excellent things that you have given me and set them before my friends, who know me too well to take offence if I leave them alone; then I will return, finish your shaving, and accompany you wherever you may wish to go.'

'There is no power nor might save in Allāh!' I cried. 'Shave me quickly and then hurry to your friends and have a fine old-fashioned evening with them. But let me go my own way by myself. My hosts are expecting me even now.' 'Never, never,' said the barber, 'I should feel dishonoured if I allowed you to go alone.' Keeping tight hold of myself lest I should insult the old scourge, I answered: 'My good man, the place where I am going is one which I must approach quite alone.' 'I was afraid so,' he said, 'I was very much afraid of that. You are going to meet a woman, otherwise you would have taken me with you. You do not seem to realise that I am the best sort of person in the world for such an expedition. I can be of a great deal of use, especially if, as I fear, the woman turns out to be some cozening stranger. It would be very rash to go alone. You would probably be murdered. Those sorts of meetings are hardly advisable in present-day Baghdād; in fact, they are not advisable at all. I gather that it is all the fault of the new governor, who is very hard on irregularities of the kind, owing, it is said, to the fact that he has neither zabb nor eggs, and therefore considers love making a wicked thing.'

It was at these words that I lost my temper for the first time and shouted: 'Will you clear out of here, you traitor, you hangman, you vilest of old busybodies!' So the barber, also for the first time, fell silent and, taking up his razor, finished shaving me; but by this time the hour for midday prayer had come and gone, and the prayer itself must have been drawing towards a close, or so it seemed to me in my impatience.

When the barber had finished shaving me, I said in order to get rid of him: 'Carry all this food and drink to your house. I promise to wait for you so that you can accompany me on my expedition.' 'I see that you want to get rid of me,' he answered, 'and go off by yourself. I must beg you not to be so rash as to stir from your house until I return. Otherwise I cannot be responsible for any calamities which befall you.' 'Very well,' I said, 'only do not be too long.'

I helped the old man load the two platters of pastry on his head and all the other things I had given him on to his shoulders; but no sooner had he left my house than he gave all to two porters to carry to his own home and slunk into a shadowy byway to wait my coming out.

Left alone, I washed in all haste and, dressing myself in my richest robe, left the house. At the moment I did so I heard the voice of the muezzins calling to the sacred Friday midday prayer:

> Allāh! Allāh! Allāh! The Tender-Hearted,
> Whose mercy exceeds all understanding;
> Praise be to the Master, the Clemency,
> Passing the knowledge of men.
> He Who was our help since time began,
> The Same shall judge us on the last day.
> Lead us therefore into the broad path of Thy blessing,
> And let us not go down into the anger of our God.

I ran as fast as I could to the girl's house and, just as I had reached the door which had been left open for me, threw a glance over my shoulder and saw the perfidious chin-slicer stealing after me down a side-street. I sprang into the house and shut the door after me. The old woman, who was impatiently waiting, led me at once to the

upper storey where her mistress lodged. But, even while I was greeting my phantom of delight, we heard a noise of people in the street
and, looking out, perceived the kādī and all his followers returning
from prayer. Also I caught sight of the barber standing across the
street and evidently waiting for me.

My dear lady reassured me by saying that her father seldom
visited her, and that there were plenty of hiding-places for me; but,
as ill-luck would have it, a single circumstance brought about my
ruin. It chanced that one of the kādī's girl slaves had merited the rod,
so that her master immediately on his return began thrashing her as
hard as he could across the buttocks. She made so much noise that
one of the negroes of the house ran in and begged pardon for her.
Turning on him furiously the kādī began to belabour him also, and
he set up a yelling which might have brought the roofs down. The
noise was easily heard in the street, and this ill-omened nose-pincher,
as soon as he heard it, thought that I was being set upon in the
house. At once he let out great cries for help, tearing his garments,
covering his head with dust, and begging all the passers-by to rescue
me. 'They are killing my master in the kādī's house!' he shouted
again and again, and, still yelling, ran with a great crowd at his heels
to my house, where he roused all my servants and slaves. Every
able-bodied man within my house armed himself with a stick and
formed a bodyguard, which raced back with the crowd, under the
leadership of the barber, and began to make a great tumult outside
the kādī's door. Hearing the clamour of the mob, the kādī looked
out of the window and saw a great multitude battering on his door
with sticks. Seeing that, though they were noisy, they were not in a
very bad humour, he went down and opened the door, crying:
'Good friends, what is the matter?' Then all my servants yelled: 'You
have killed our master!' 'Who is this master of yours?' he asked.
'And what fault did he commit that I should kill him?'

At this point Shahrazād saw the approach of morning and discreetly fell silent.

But when the thirtieth night had come

SHE SAID:

It is related, O auspicious King, that when the astonished kādī
cried: 'Who is this master of yours and what fault did he commit that
I should kill him? And above all what is this barber doing in the

midst of you, braying like a wild ass?', the barber answered: 'Wretched old man, you have just laid my master low with a rain of blows. I myself was in the street and heard his cries.' 'But what master?' asked the kādī. 'Whence does he come, whither was he going? How could he be in my house? And why should he have deserved a rain of blows?' 'Treacherous kādī,' answered the barber, 'do not try to deceive me, for I know all: both why my master entered your house and every other detail of the matter. Let all these good people present learn that your daughter is in love with my master and he with her. I accompanied him as far as this place, and hardly had he entered when you surprised him in bed with your daughter and, aided by your vile servants, stunned him with many sticks. Either you must come with me to the Khalīfah who shall be sole judge between us, or you shall give us back our master on the spot, paying him handsomely for the wrongs you have done him, or else I shall have to enter your house by force and rescue him myself. Haste then to give him back to us!'

The kādī was robbed of speech, put to confusion and overcome by shame when these intimate things were shouted out before all the people; but nevertheless he answered the barber: 'If you are not a liar you have but to come in with me. I give you free leave to search the entire house.'

Without loss of time the barber threw himself through the door and across the threshold into the house. When I, who had witnessed the whole scene through the trellis of the window, saw his entry, I wished to flee, but could find no way out which would not take me in sight of the people of the house or else make me meet the barber. At last, in one of the rooms where I was hunting for an exit, I saw a great empty wooden chest; into this I jumped, and then pulled the lid down on top of me and waited, holding my breath. When the barber had ferreted through the whole house, he came into the room where I was and, looking to right and left, saw the chest. Instantly divining what was in it, the indiscreet fool lifted it on his head and ran downstairs with it into the street. I was bumping about in the chest, more dead than alive, when, as ill-luck would have it, the crowd insisted on knowing what was inside the box. The lid was opened in a twinkling. Feeling that I could not bear the shame and jeers that would greet my appearance, I threw myself to the ground, breaking my leg in my fall. That is why I limp to this day. At the moment I had no other thought except flight. So, throwing handfuls of gold to the crowd, I took advantage of the subsequent stooping and struggling of the people to hop away from that street as fast as I could. I had painfully passed through many of the lesser streets of Baghdād, when I suddenly heard the detested voice of the barber behind me, who cried in a loud voice as he ran: 'Good people, good people, thanks be to Allāh that I have found my master again! They wished to strike me to the heart by hurting him, but Allāh would not allow the wicked to triumph. He made me victorious against them and allowed me to deliver my master out of their hands!' Then, running up behind me, he said: 'Master, you can see now how ill-advised you were to practise impatience and ignore my counsels. Had it not been for Allāh, Who raised me up for your deliverance, you would have suffered the worst of deaths and been lost for ever. Pray then to Him, my son, that He may long preserve me to be always with you, as it were a wise old guide, now that you have proved yourself a lad of feeble mind, little better than an idiot. . . . But where are you running to? Wait for me.' Not knowing how else to get rid of him, except possibly by dying, I stopped short and said very solemnly: 'O barber, does it not suffice you to have reduced me to this state? Do you wish my death also?'

As I was speaking I noticed, opposite to me in the market where I had halted, the open shop of a merchant whom I knew. Dragging myself inside this, I begged my friend to prevent my senile pursuer from coming in after me. This he did by shaking an enormous whip and rolling his eyes terribly. But, even so, the barber only departed after cursing the shopkeeper, and the father and the grandfather of the shopkeeper, with every evil wish and foul word that he knew.

My friend was naturally curious, so I told him the whole tale of the barber and begged him to allow me to stay in the shop until my leg was better, as I had no wish to return home where I might at any time be haunted by the hateful barber, whose face was to me by this time more bitter than death itself. When my leg had well set, I gathered together all the money I had, made a will leaving every-thing of which I should die possessed to members of my family, and appointed a man I could trust to look after all my interests at home. Then, sheerly that I should be done for ever with this barber, I left Baghdād, my native city, and set out for this far country, where I thought I could never by any chance come face to face with my intolerable foe. Yet no sooner had I arrived here, gentlemen, than I found him sitting among you an honoured guest at the first feast to which I have been invited.

You may rest assured that I shall know no moment's peace until I have left this country as I left my own. And all my wandering and expense is due to that white-haired fiend, that perverse relic, that murderous barber! May Allāh curse him! May Allāh curse his folk! May Allāh curse each child who ever bears the least taint of his blood!

When the lame young man had told this sorrowful tale (continued the tailor to the King of China), he rose, quite yellow in the face, and, wishing us peace, hurried away from among us.

We others looked searchingly at the barber, who had sat silent all the time with lowered eyes. 'Is the young man's story true?' we asked him. 'And, if so, why did you behave in such a way as to lead the poor youth into all these misfortunes?' 'Lead is it, by God!' cried the barber, raising his head. 'I would have you know that I behaved as I did only after scrupulous thought, and that if it had not been for me he would have fallen more deeply still into the mire of accident, and perished for ever! He should thank Allāh and he should thank me that it was his leg and not his life which paid the penalty. You are all wise men here, my masters, so to prove to you that I am neither talkative nor indiscreet, two qualities with which the good God has seen fit to afflict my six brothers, I will tell you my story and you shall see for yourselves that I am wise, cautious, discreet and, above all, very silent. Judge now!'

We sat, continued the tailor, and listened to the barber's tale.

THE TALE OF THE BARBER OF BAGHDĀD AND THE TALES OF HIS SIX BROTHERS

(Told by the Barber, and reported by the Tailor)

The Tale of the Barber

THE BARBER SAID:

YOU must know, my masters, that I lived in Baghdād during the reign of al-Mustansir Billāh, Prince of Believers. Those were good days for the people, because he loved the poor and the low-born, though he himself was ever companioned by sages and seers and poets.

One day the Khalīfah had a judgment to do upon ten men who lived not far from the city, so he ordered a minor governor to bring them before him. Fate willed that, just as they were being embarked on a boat to cross the Tigris, I was walking on the banks of the river. Seeing so many in a boat together I said to myself: 'This is a pleasure party. They are going out for the day to make merry together with eating and drinking. Though I die for it, I will be their guest and share the sport.'

I went down to the water's edge and, without saying a word, for I am the Silent Man, jumped on board and mingled with the merry companions. But hardly had I done so when the walī's guards came aboard and put iron chains about the necks and wrists of all the ten, and about my neck and wrists also. And yet I never said a word, never whispered a syllable, which proves I think, my masters, that I have both courage and the gift of holding my tongue. I made no protest, the crossing was accomplished, and all of us were led before the Khalīfah al-Mustansir Billāh, Prince of Believers.

Seeing us, the Khalīfah called the executioner and said: 'Cut off the heads of these ten rogues!' The executioner made us kneel in line before the Sultān and, lifting his thin sword, cut off all ten heads, one after the other, each with a single blow. When he came to me, he stopped, since ten heads lay upon the ground already, and told the Khalīfah that the execution was over. But, seeing me still upright, the Sultān cried: 'I ordered you to cut off all ten heads!' 'As true as Allāh is good to you and you are good to us,' the executioner answered, 'I have cut off ten heads.' 'Count them,' said the King. The count was made and there lay ten heads and ten bodies. So the Khalīfah turned to me, saying: 'Who are you and what are you doing among these lovers of bloodshed?' Then and then only, my masters, I decided to break through my habitual rule of silence and said: 'Prince of Believers, I am an old man called al-Sāmit, because of the brevity of my speeches. Wisdom I have in plenty; but of my acute judgment, the weight of such discourse as I use, my excellence in reason, my keen intelligence, and my habit of judicious silence I will say nothing, since these things speak for themselves. I am a barber by trade and one of the seven sons of my father. Now for the adventure which brought me here! This morning I was walking beside the Tigris when I saw these ten poor mortalities embarking in a boat.

Thinking that they were going off for some jaunt on the water, I made myself one of their number. I soon saw that I had fallen among criminals, because your guards came and chained us all by the neck, yet even then, and although I did not know any of my companions, I neither protested nor spoke. I have a habit, you see, of resolution and silence.

'Thus it was that I was led before you, O Prince of Believers. When you ordered the heads of the ten criminals to be cut off and I alone remained beneath the stroke of the executioner, even then I did not say a single word. That, I think, is a proof of considerable courage. And, when I come to think of it, the very fact that I associated myself willingly with these ten unknown men argues a greater heroism than I have heard of elsewhere. Yet you must not be astonished at what I did, Prince of Believers, for all my life I have gone out of my way to oblige strangers.'

When the Khalīfah heard my words and understood that I was a courageous and manly ancient, loving silence and the well-considered thought, detesting all curiosity and indiscretion, whatever that lame young man may have said just now (he whom I saved from so much trouble too!), he said to me: 'Venerable sheikh, high-souled and decorous barber, tell me, are your six brothers also dowered with all knowledge and discretion?' 'Allāh preserve me!' I answered. 'They are so different, Prince of Believers, that you almost insult me by comparing me with them. They are six mad, slack-mouthed fellows, and there is all the difference of the world between us. Because of their insane babblings, their indiscretions, and their unnatural cowardice, each has drawn on himself many calamities and at least one deformity of body. While I am vigorous and healthy of mind and limb, my first brother is lame, my second is one-eyed, my third broken-mouthed, my fourth blind, my fifth ear-cropped and with his nose sliced off, and my sixth lip-gashed.

'But I would not like you to think, Prince of Believers, that I am exaggerating the faults and disqualities of my brothers. You will only understand how different they are from me if I tell you all their stories. The tales about them are full of moral lessons for the circumspect. Without more ado I will tell you:

The Tale of Bakbūk,
the Barber's First Brother

KNOW, O Commander of the Faithful, that the eldest of my brothers, he who became lame, is called Bakbūk because when he tattles he makes a glucking noise like water coming out of a jar. At one time he was a tailor in Baghdād.

He used to do his sewing in a small shop which he rented from a very rich merchant, who himself lived in the top part of the house above the shop. In the basement there was a mill where a miller lived and kept his bullock.

One day, as my brother Bakbūk was sitting sewing in his shop, he chanced to raise his eyes and saw a woman looking out at the passers-by from a skylight let into the terrace floor above him. She was the wife of the owner of the building, and her looking forth was like the rising of the young moon. Bakbūk's heart was fired with passion at the sight of her. He could sew no more, but spent all day with his head fixed, looking up at the skylight as if he were an idiot. Next morning he was in his place by dawn, and every time he took a stitch his eye wandered to the skylight, so that he pricked his fingers more than the cloth. For several days he did the same, neither working nor bringing in any money.

It was not long before the young woman understood my brother's feelings and made up her mind to derive both profit and amusement from them. One day, as Bakbūk was sitting there in his customary adoration, she threw him a laughing glance which pierced his heart. He gave her back a languishing look which was so ridiculous that she had to retire precipitately to laugh at her ease. And the fool Bakbūk was overjoyed that day by the conquest which he thought he had made.

Next morning, therefore, my brother was not astonished to see his landlord entering the shop, carrying a great roll of rich silk under his arm. The merchant said: 'I have brought this piece of stuff so that you can sew some shirts for me.' 'Certainly, certainly, they shall be ready this very evening,' answered Bakbūk, who supposed that the landlord had been sent by his wife to further their intrigue in some way. He set to work so quickly, not allowing himself a moment for food, that twenty beautifully cut and sewn shirts were ready by the evening. The landlord came down to the shop again and asked: 'How much do I owe you?' but just at that moment the young woman appeared secretly at the skylight and signed to Bakbūk with her eyes and brows not to accept any money from her husband. So Bakbūk refused any payment, although he was extremely poor at the time and the smallest coin would have meant much to him. Yet the ass thought himself very lucky to be able to do the husband's work for the love and bright eyes of the wife.

That was only the beginning of my infatuated brother's trials. Next morning the landlord came again and handed a new roll of silk to Bakbūk, saying: 'They tell me at home I must have some new trousers to go with the new shirts, so I have brought you the stuff. Let them be plenty large enough, do not stint the material, and use the finest needlework.' 'I hear and I obey!' answered my brother, and for three whole days he worked fasting, so as to lose no time and also because there was not a single dirham in the house with which to buy food. When he had finished the fine new trousers, he folded them together and carried them joyfully upstairs to the landlord.

It is unnecessary to tell a person of your sagacity, O Commander of the Faithful, that the young woman was in league with her husband to make a laughing-stock of my unfortunate brother and to play him every trick that she could think of. When the landlord had received the trousers, he pretended to want to pay for them, but just at the right moment the pretty head of his wife appeared round the door and signed again to the tailor to refuse. So Bakbūk said that he would take no sort of payment. The husband withdrew for a moment to confer with his wife and then returned, saying: 'As my wife and I feel that we must repay your splendid services in some way, we have determined to marry you to our white slave girl, that you may become in some sort one of the family. She is both beautiful and submissive.' My witless Bakbūk thought that this was a clever ruse of the wife to give him free entry to the house, so he accepted without hesitation and was married straightway to the young slave.

When evening came, Bakbūk wished to approach his bride, but she said: 'No, no, it cannot be to-night,' and he was not able to take even a kiss from her.

Usually Bakbūk slept in the shop, but that night it had been arranged that the couple should sleep in the millroom, as it was larger; so, when the slave refused to let him lie with her and went upstairs again to her mistress, my brother was obliged to sleep in that unpleasant place alone. In the morning he was awakened by the loud voice of the miller saying: 'Devil take the bullock! He has had a great deal of rest lately. Now I must harness him up to grind all the accumulated store of corn. My customers will be wanting their flour to-day.' Then, feigning to take my brother for the bullock, he said: 'Up lazy one! Come and be harnessed!' and with that he fastened the dumbfounded Bakbūk by the middle to the pole of the mill and gave him a great blow with the whip, crying: 'Yā Allāh!' Feeling the whip sting about his loins, my brother began to low like a bullock and started to turn the mill. For a long time the miller thonged him on, and Bakbūk trotted round and round, lowing dismally and snuffling between the blows just as a bullock does.

In course of time the landlord came down to see what was happening. Satisfied that the plan was going well, he returned to his wife, who sent the slave girl down to my brother. By this time the miller had disappeared, so the young girl unfastened Bakbūk from the mill, saying in tones of the deepest concern: 'My mistress begs me to say that she has just heard of the abominable mistake which has been made. She is desolated, and so am I.' The unhappy bridegroom was so exhausted by the blows and the unusual labour that he could not answer a word.

The slave girl left him alone, and soon the clerk who had drawn up the marriage contract appeared and saluted him, saying: 'Allāh grant you a long life and a fortunate marriage! You seem to have passed the happiest of nights, with amusing and intimate embraces I am sure, sweet kisses and fornications from night till day.' 'Allāh confound such lying snakes, O thousandfold traitor!' answered my brother. 'Your contract has caused me to turn a mill all night.' The clerk asked for details of this singular thing and, when he had heard them, said: 'I understand it all. Your star does not agree with the star of the young woman.' 'Wretch,' cried Bakbūk, 'get out of this and play your dirty tricks elsewhere!' Then he went up to his shop and began to work sorrowfully to make a little money, he who had worked so joyfully for love.

While he was sitting sewing the white slave came down to him and said: 'My mistress desires you madly. She bids me say that she is about to mount on the terrace for the pleasure of looking at you through the skylight.' At the same moment Bakbūk saw the face of the lady of his love all bathed in tears appearing at the skylight. She wept, saying: 'My dear, my darling, why will you not look at me? Why will you not smile at me? I swear that I was in no way privy to what happened in the mill. As for this foolish slave, I beg that you will not honour her even with one glance. I and I only shall be yours, my love.' She spoke so sweetly that Bakbūk at last lifted his head and gazed fully at her. Then were all his trials forgotten and his eyes filled with joy through looking on her charms. They spoke a little together, and soon he began to think that his misfortunes had happened to someone else.

Bakbūk continued to work assiduously in his own place, sewing shirts and trousers, undergarments and overgarments, for many hours a day in the hope of seeing his fair tormenter again. One day the slave girl returned, saying: 'My mistress greets you and would have you know that my master will be away all night at a feast given by one of his friends. She will wait you with loving impatience and lie with you all night in delicious love and amusement.' Hearing this, my all too simple brother thought that he was already in Paradise.

Now you must know that the graceless young woman had conceived a plan, with the help of her husband, to get rid of my brother and so avoid all payment for the work he had done for them. The landlord had said to his wife: 'How can we persuade him to visit you, so that I may surprise him and send him up before the walī?' And the wife had answered: 'Leave it to me, and I shall so deceive and compromise him that he shall be shamed throughout all the city.'

To think that they should have been at such pains to do him hurt, and the poor fool guess nothing of it! Alas, alas, he knew little of women!

When evening came, the slave girl led Bakbūk to her mistress, who smiled on him, saying: 'As Allāh lives, my master, I burn to have you near me!' 'And I burn, too,' said Bakbūk. 'Let us be quick, first to kiss and then . . .' He had not time to finish his sentence before the door opened and the husband rushed in with two black slaves, who fell upon my brother, bound him, threw him to the floor and belaboured his back with whips. But that was only the beginning; when he had been well trounced, they took him upon their shoulders and carried him before the walī, who condemned him to the following punishment: after two hundred stripes had been laid on with rods, he was to be hoisted on the back of a camel and led through all the streets of Baghdād, preceded by a public crier who should announce in a loud voice: 'Thus shall adulterers be punished!'

This sentence was carried out, and, during the procession, the camel became unmanageable and began to make great jumps about the street. Bakbūk was thrown to the earth and broke his leg; since then he has always walked with a limp. Further, the walī banished him, and he was forced to drag his broken limb away from the city. But just in the nick of time, Commander of the Faithful, I was told of what had happened, so I ran after him and brought him back secretly to the city. Since then I have cured him at my own charges and kept him in food and raiment.

When the Khalīfah al-Mustansir Billāh heard this story of Bakbūk, my masters, he rolled on his throne in laughter, calling out: 'A capital tale and a capital teller!' 'I hardly deserve such praise as yet,' I answered, 'though you may be able to say somewhat of the same truthfully when you have heard the stories of all my elder brothers. Only I am afraid that you may think me talkative or indiscreet.' 'Far from it,' answered the Khalīfah; 'hasten to tell me all about your other brothers, that each tale may adorn my ears as with gold rings. Also, do not fear to dwell upon all the details, for I am sure that they will be very savoury and delicious.' Then I told him:

The Tale of al-Haddār,
the Barber's Second Brother

KNOW, O Prince of the Faithful, that my second brother is called al-Haddār, because he continually lows like a camel. He is broken-mouthed, and used to do absolutely nothing for his livelihood. Much trouble has he put me to with his scrapes among women. Listen to one out of a thousand of them.

One day, while he was walking aimlessly through the streets of Baghdād, he saw an old woman coming towards him, who said in a low voice: 'Listen, my man, I have an offer to make you which you can accept or refuse as you think fit.' 'Tell me what it is,' said my brother. 'I will not make the proposition,' the old woman continued, 'unless you promise not to tattle or talk too much.' 'You may speak,' said Haddār. Then the old woman whispered: 'What would you say to a fair palace set about with running waters and fruit trees, where wine flowed from goblets ever full, where faces of ravishing beauty surrounded you, cheeks smooth for kisses, small pliant waists for holding, and supreme joys till morning? You shall taste of all these things if you agree to a condition.' 'But,' asked my brother, 'why

should you have come with this offer to me of all the sons of men?
What quality is there in me that I should be preferred before all
others?' 'I have just told you,' she answered, 'neither to talk nor to
tattle nor to be indiscreet. Follow me and ask no questions.'

The old woman led my brother, licking his lips at all the delights
which were promised him, until they came to a magnificent palace.
Entering, my brother found that the inside was even more splendid
than the outside and the furnishing most grand of all. His guide led
him up to the second storey and introduced him to a group of four
young girls, who lay in flowerlike beauty upon carpets, singing such
songs as would have melted rocks.

After greetings, the fairest of them rose and, filling a cup with
wine, drank it off. 'May that be delicious in its going down!' said my
brother Haddār, wishing above all to be polite, and went on his
knees to bear away the cup. But the girl filled it again, handed it to
my brother and bade him drink. While he did so, the girl began to
caress his neck, more with violence than with love, and finished by
giving it a slap with the palm of her hand. Haddār was angry at this
and, forgetting his promise, made as if to leave the place. But the old
woman came near and winked, as much as to say: 'Stay and wait the
end.' My brother controlled himself and suffered with the best
possible grace all the young girl's antics. She pricked him, pinched
him, and slapped his neck as if she hated him, while her three friends
rivalled her in being disagreeable. One pulled his ears, one flicked
him very painfully, and the third did nothing but nip his flesh with
her nails. As the old woman was signing to him all the time to keep
silent, my brother supported these things, and at last as a reward the
first young woman rose up and bade him undress himself quite
naked. This Haddār did and, when all his clothes were off, the girl
sprinkled him with rose-water, saying: 'I find you very much to my
liking, but I cannot abide either beard or moustaches in a man who
kisses me. They prick my tender skin. If you want to possess me,
you must have your face shaved.' 'That would be great shame,' he
answered. 'I cannot love you otherwise, so you must,' said the young
girl. My brother allowed himself to be conducted into a neighbouring room by the old woman, who there shaved off his beard,
moustaches, and eyebrows. Afterwards she made up his face with
red and white, and brought him back to the young women, who were
so struck by his appearance that they fell over on their bottoms and
rolled laughing on the floor.

The first and fairest of them said: 'Master, now have all these many charms conquered my soul. I have but one more favour to ask of you, dance elegantly before us in all the beauty of your nakedness.' Haddār held back at first, but when she begged him on her life to do it and promised him that he might have her afterwards, he wrapped a little bit of silk round his middle and danced before them all to a rhythm played by the old woman.

The girls laughed at him as if their sides would burst and pelted him with everything that came to hand, cushions, fruit, wine, and even wine jars.

Only when they were tired was the last part of the entertainment allowed to begin. The first girl stood up and began to take off her clothes one by one, posing all the time and giving my brother passionate sidelong glances. When nothing remained but her fine chemise and baggy silk drawers, Haddār stopped his dance, crying: 'Allāh, Allāh!'

The old woman came up to him and said: 'Now you must run after the dear young lady and catch her. It is her custom, when heated by dance and wine, to undress naked and not to give herself to her lover until she has been able to examine his bare limbs, his rampant zabb, and the agility of his running. You must follow her from room to room, with your zabb in the ascendant, until you catch her. That is the only way she will be mounted.'

My brother cast aside his silk loin-cloth and made ready for the race. The girl threw off her chemise and drawers, appearing like a young palm tree which moves a little under the west wind. Then speechless with laughter she began to run, and Haddār chased her twice round the hall, with his zabb well up and out.

At this point Shahrazād saw the approach of morning and discreetly fell silent.

But when the thirty-first night had come

SHE SAID:

It is related, O auspicious King, that the tailor told the King of China the rest of the tale which the barber of Baghdād had related to the guests about his second brother, Haddār, and which had been in the first place told to the Khalīfah al-Mustansir Billāh in these words:

Haddār, with his zabb well up and out, ran round and round after the light and laughing girl. The other three and the old woman, seeing his face painted and quite hairless and his madly straining zabb, laughed as if their sides would break, clapping their hands and stamping on the floor.

The girl fled through a long gallery and in and out of many rooms, always followed by my panting brother and his pursuing zabb. She tripped easily along, laughing with all her teeth and swaying her haunches provocatively.

At length she slipped through a certain door, and my brother found himself in a dark chamber where he could no longer see her. He ran on, and suddenly the floor gave way beneath him; in another moment he found himself falling headlong into the street of the leather-sellers of Baghdād. When these good fellows saw Haddār appear among them, shaven, naked, and with his face all ruddled like a harlot's, they hooted at him and began thrashing him with their skins, until he fell down in a faint. Laughing robustly, they set him on an ass and made a procession with him round all the markets. Finally they carried him to the walī, who asked: 'Who is this?' 'He fell among us,' they answered, 'through a trap in the house of the grand wazīr. He was like this when he did so.' The walī then ordered Haddār to receive a hundred lashes on the soles of his feet and to be driven from the city.

I followed him in his exile, Commander of the Faithful, and, bringing him back secretly, hid him in a safe place. Since then he has lived at my expense, and you can judge for yourself my qualities of courage and generosity in paying out good money for such a fool. The story of my third brother is very different, as you shall hear.

The Tale of Bakbāk, the Barber's Third Brother

BAKBĀK, or the Swollen Clucker, is my third brother. He is blind and is counted among the chief of the brotherhood of beggars in Baghdād. One day Allāh led him to beg at the door of a great house, on which he beat with his stick demanding alms in the usual fashion and calling out: 'Giver! Generous one!' Now I must tell you, O Commander of the Faithful, that my brother Bakbāk, who was the cleverest of all the beggars, had a way when he knocked at a door of not answering any voice which cried: 'Who is there?' He used to keep quite quiet until someone came to open the door, knowing that if he said: 'It is a beggar come for alms,' the people would not open the door, but would cry: 'Allāh have pity on you!' and let him go about his business.

So on that day, when someone cried: 'Who is there?' my brother did not answer. After a short time the door was opened by a man with such a cast of countenance that, if my brother had been able to see it, assuredly he would not have begged from him. But every man carries his destiny fastened about his neck.

The man asked: 'What do you want?' and Bakbāk answered: 'Some little thing, in the name of Allāh Almighty.' 'Are you blind?' questioned the man. 'Master, I am blind and very poor,' answered my brother. Then said the man: 'Give me your hand and I will lead you.' My brother stretched out his hand, and the man led him up many stairs until they came out on to a high terrace. Bakbāk, who was all out of breath, thought: 'Surely he is going to give me the remnants of a great feast.'

'What do you wish, blind man?' asked the owner of the house at length. 'Alms for the love of Allāh!' answered my brother in surprise. 'Allāh open another door for you,' jeered the householder. 'O thing,' said Bakbāk, 'could you not have given me that answer when we were below?' 'O lower than my arse,' questioned the man, 'why could you not answer when I called out to know who was there? Unless you want to be thrown down like a ball, get out of here, you sticky mass of misery!' My poor brother, blind as he was, had to go down alone. When he was twenty steps from the bottom, his foot slipped and he fell down all the rest of the stairs, striking his head a terrible blow on the last step. He made his way down the street, complaining bitterly. Soon some of his companion beggars came round and asked the reason for his woe. He told them and added: 'Now, my friends, I must go home and take a little money to buy food for this ill-omened day. I shall have to encroach on our savings, which, as you know, are very great and have been put under my care.'

Now all this time the man who had treated him so scurvily had been following my brother, unseen either by Bakbāk or the two blind companions who had agreed to accompany him. He walked quietly behind them until they came to my brother's dwelling and, when the three had entered, slipped in after them before they had a chance to shut the door. When all were inside, Bakbāk said to the other two: 'First search the place well, in case a stranger is hidden anywhere.' Hearing this suggestion, the man, who was a professional thief held in high reputation among his brotherhood, seized a cord which was hanging from the ceiling and, climbing up it noiselessly, seated himself comfortably upon a beam. After the two blind men had thoroughly searched the chamber with their sticks, my brother uncovered the hidden store of money and the three sat down to count it. When they found that it came to ten thousand dirhams, one of them took two or three of the coins and, while the others carefully hid the sacks again, hurried out and returned in a few minutes with three loaves, three onions, and some dates.

While they were eating the thief slid noiselessly down the cord, squatted beside them and began to eat also. My brother, whose hearing was very acute, became aware of a fourth pair of jaws working near him. So crying: 'There is a stranger here!' he stretched out his hand and caught the robber's arm. All three threw themselves upon the thief and, blind as they were, belaboured him with their sticks, calling out all the time: 'Thief! thief! Help, Mussulmāns, help!' Many neighbours ran in and found the three blind men holding the struggling robber. When the latter saw that help had come, he shut his eyes and, pretending to be blind, cried out: 'By Allāh, friends, I am a blind beggar, an associate of these three. They are trying to kill me that they may keep my share of the ten thousand dirhams we have saved. I swear it by Allāh, by the Sultān, by the Amīr! Lead me, O lead me to the walī!'

At this moment the walī's guards came up and dragged all four before the minister. 'What are these men?' asked the walī. The thief cried out: 'Just and far-seeing walī, listen to me and you shall hear the truth! And yet, and yet, how can I dare to hope that you will believe me until I have been put to the torture? Beat me first, and then these others, and we will tell the truth.' 'Throw that man down and beat him,' said the walī, 'as he is so anxious for it.' On this the guard seized the pretended blind man and, while some held him spread, others rained great blows upon him with their whips. After the first ten strokes the man began to yell and opened one eye. After a few more he very deliberately opened the other.

Seeing this, the angry walī cried: 'What shame is this, O wicked trickster?' 'Let me up and I will tell you all!' yelled the robber. So the walī bade the blows cease, and the victim got to his feet, saying:

'We are four men who pretend to be blind that we may extract alms and get into houses to look at women when they are undressed. Then we corrupt them and mount them and ride them, and afterwards we steal from them and make plans of the houses for burglars. We have been doing this for a long time, so that now we have amassed as much as ten thousand dirhams between us. To-day I asked for my share, but these other three refused to give it to me and were on the point of beating me to death when your guards came up and saved me. That is the whole truth, O walī, as my companions will confess, when they have been well and truly beaten. Only do not spare their punishment, for they are hardy rogues and will keep their eyes shut for a long time.'

Deceived by the wicked thief, the walī ordered my brother to be thrown down and beaten. In vain did he protest that he had been born blind, they showered blows upon him till he fainted. When he came to himself, he received three hundred strokes because he would not open his eyes and after that a further three hundred. The same treatment was given to the other two, who also did not open their eyes in spite of the blows and the loud exhortations of him who claimed to be their companion.

At last the walī sent the thief under guard to fetch all the money from Bakbāk's house. He gave a quarter, that is to say two thousand five hundred dirhams, to the robber and kept the rest himself.

Then he addressed my brother and his two companions in this fashion: 'Miserable impostors, you eat bread which is the gift of Allāh and feign in His name that you are blind. Depart hence, and be never more seen in all Baghdād.'

When I heard of what had happened, O Commander of the Faithful, I left the city to look for my brother Bakbāk and, when I found him, brought him back secretly to Baghdād, where he now lives my eternal pensioner, dependent on me for lodging, food and raiment.

That is the tale of my third brother, Bakbāk the blind man.

The Khalīfah al-Mustansir Billāh laughed heartily at my recital and said: 'Give this barber some money and let him depart!' But I answered: 'As Allāh lives, Commander of the Faithful, I could never accept aught at your hands until you have heard the stories of my other three brothers, well and concisely told, so that you may know that I am no babbler.' 'Be it so,' said the Khalīfah, 'I do not mind having my ears split by your harsh imbecilities if it gives you any pleasure.' So I told him:

The Tale of al-Kūz,
the Barber's Fourth Brother

MY fourth brother, the one-eyed al-Kūz of Uswān, the Unbreakable Jug, was a butcher in Baghdād. He was a famous meat seller and a successful breeder of fat-tailed sheep. He knew exactly for whom to reserve the best meat and on whom to palm off the worst, so that the largest buyers and richest merchants in the city dealt at no other shop, but bought his mutton exclusively, and it was not long before he became the rich owner of many flocks.

His prosperity lasted until a certain day when, as he was sitting in his shop, a tall white-bearded old man brought certain silver coins to him and asked for some of his best meat. My brother cut of his best, took the silver and thanked the old man, who promptly departed.

Al-Kūz, examining the money which he had received from the stranger, noticed that all the coins were new and of a silver freshness, so he put them aside in a special coffer, saying: 'These coins will bring me good luck.'

Every day for five months the white-bearded old man bought excellent meat from my brother in exchange for more and more of these bright new pieces, and every time al-Kūz put them aside. One day, wishing to buy some fine sheep and certain rams which might be trained as fighters (a most popular sport in Baghdād), he began to count his money. But no sooner had he opened the chest in which he had stored the old man's coins than he found it filled only with little rounds of white paper. He beat himself about the face and head, weeping and wailing, and soon was the centre of a large crowd to whom he told the whole story. No one could suggest an explanation, but while my brother was gesticulating and shouting: 'Would that the wicked old man might come for me to tear his beard out and pull his turban off!' the stranger himself appeared and, clearing a path through the crowd, advanced towards my brother as if he would buy from him as usual. Al-Kūz fell upon him and gripped him tightly, crying: 'Come quickly, O Mussulmāns, here is the shameless thief!' The old man lost nothing of his great calm and, without attempting to escape, whispered: 'Be silent or I will put you to public shame on a more terrible charge than you wish to bring against me.' 'What shame could you bring upon me, you black-souled old reprobate?' cried my brother. 'I could prove,' answered the old man, 'that you sell people human flesh instead of mutton.' 'That is not true, son of a thousand lies!' yelled al-Kūz. 'What more wicked liar can there be,' said the old man, 'than one who at this moment has a corpse hung up on the hooks of his butcher's shop instead of a sheep?' 'Dog and son of a dog,' protested my brother, 'if you can prove this thing against me, my goods and my life are yours.' Accepting the challenge, the old man turned to the crowd, crying at the top of his voice: 'My friends, look at this butcher! He has deceived us all until this very day, and has sullied all the principles of the Sacred Book. Week in, week out, he has slain his brother men and sold their flesh to us as mutton. You have but to come inside his shop to see the truth of what I say.'

The crowd rushed into my brother's shop with a yell, and, lo, it seemed to all that the corpse of a man was hanging from one of the hooks, flayed and prepared, trimmed and gutted, while on the sheep's-head shelf three human heads lay skinned and trimmed and ready to be sold. The truth is that the old man with the long white beard was a sorcerer, who by his enchantments was able to make men see what he wished them to see.

Thinking that they had really beheld this horrible sight, the crowd, crying out: 'Sacrilege! impious cheat!' threw themselves on my brother with sticks and whips, his oldest clients and best friends delivering the hardest blows. The old man contented himself with striking al-Kūz violently in the left eye with his fist, so that the sight went from it for ever. Lifting down the supposed corpse to carry with them, they bound my brother and haled him before the amīr. The old man made himself spokesman, saying: 'My lord, we bring a terrible criminal to your justice, one who for many months has murdered his fellow-men and sold their bodies as mutton. You have but to pronounce sentence and let the justice of God proceed, for here are all the witnesses.'

My brother tried to defend himself, but the judge, refusing to hear a word, sentenced him to receive five hundred blows of the stick on his back and buttocks. He confiscated all his goods and outlawed him. Indeed, if he had not been so rich he could in no wise have escaped death.

Blind of one eye and nearly dead from the sticks, my brother left the city and journeyed straight ahead until he came to a far off and unknown town, where he set up as a cobbler in a very small way of business.

He made his shop in the angle of a wall at the corner of two streets, and worked there for a living. One day, while he was sewing a piece into an old slipper, he heard the neighing of horses and the noise of many riders. Asking the reason for this and being told that the King and all his court were going hunting, my brother left his hammer and awl for a moment and rose to see the procession pass. While he stood there pensive and dreaming of his past and present, how from a famous butcher he had fallen to be the least of cobblers, the King passed at the head of a handsome troop and, happening to glance round, let his eye fall on the blind eye of al-Kūz. The King changed colour, crying: 'Allāh preserve me from the evil eye and this unhappy day!' With that he turned his horse about and led all his followers back by the way they had come, not forgetting to order my brother to be seized and punished. Slaves fell upon al-Kūz and, beating him, left him for dead in the road. When they had gone, my brother crawled painfully back to the shelter of the little awning with which he had roofed his corner and lay there, all broken with blows and nearer death than life. When one of the King's followers passed his retreat, he begged him to stop and, explaining the circumstance to him, asked the reason of his treatment. The man burst into fits of laughter, saying: 'Brother, our King cannot bear the sight of a one-eyed man, especially should the blind eye be the left one. He says that it brings him ill-luck, and always has the man killed. I cannot understand how you have escaped.'

My brother delayed not a moment on hearing these words but, collecting the few poor tools of his trade, dragged himself forth from that city and stumbled on until he came to another, a long way off, where there was neither king nor tyrant.

He stayed for a long time in his new place, taking care never to show himself out-of-doors; but one day, being sadder than ordinary, he went forth to taste the air and rejoice his sight with the bustle of his fellow-men. Suddenly he heard behind him the neighing of horses and, remembering the misfortunes which that sound had heralded before, fled away, searching in vain for a place to hide. At last he saw a great door in front of him, which opened at his touch. He leapt across the threshold and found himself in a long dark corridor, where he stood trembling. Hardly had he entered, however, when two men hurled themselves upon him and cast chains about him, saying: 'Allāh be praised that we have caught you at last, O enemy of God and man! Three days and three nights we have lain in wait for you, eschewing sleep and tasting thereby the bitterness of death.' 'But, good people,' said my brother, 'what thing is this that He has brought upon me?' 'You are going about to kill the master of this house and us his servants. Was it not enough for you to make all his friends miserable and to ruin him, that you should now wish to kill him? Where is the knife with which you chased us yesterday?' With that they searched al-Kūz and found his soling knife in his belt. They were about to strangle him, when he cried out: 'Listen, good people, I am neither a thief nor a murderer. I will tell you my story if you let me up.' But, instead of listening, they searched him from head to foot, beat him, and, tearing away his clothes, saw the old marks of stick and whip upon his naked back. 'Wretched criminal,' they cried, 'here are the marks of your old punishment, witness of other crimes!' Without more ado they haled my poor brother before the walī, and, as he went, al-Kūz said bitterly to himself: 'However great my sins may have been, surely they are now expiated! I have done nothing wrong, and there is no help save in Allāh.'

The walī looked angrily on my brother, saying: 'Shameless ill-doer, it is quite clear from these marks upon your back that you have practised every sort of crime and malversation.' He had my brother given a hundred strokes with canes and hoisted on the back of a camel, in front of which criers went throughout all the city, calling: 'Thus shall all be punished who enter other people's houses with criminal intent!'

The news of this series of calamities came to my ears, so I set out to search for my brother and found him just at the moment when they were lifting him down in a swoon from the camel's back. I thought it my duty, Commander of the Faithful, to heal his hurts and bring him back in secret to Baghdād, where he has lived ever since, eating and drinking in comfort at my expense.

That is the story of the unfortunate al-Kūz. The tale of my fifth brother is an extraordinary one and will prove to you, Commander of the Faithful, how much wiser and more prudent I am than any of my relations.

The Tale of al-Ashār,
the Barber's Fifth Brother

PRINCE of Believers, this tells of my brother who had his ears and nose split up. He was called al-Ashār, either because he was very fat with a swagging belly like a gravid camel, or else because he was like a big pot. Whatever the reason, he was an exceedingly lazy man, making his little monies by doubtful enterprises in the night and lying up in the daytime. When our father died, we each inherited a hundred dirhams in silver. Al-Ashār took his with the rest, but did not know what to do with it. At last, after turning over a thousand ideas, he decided to buy glass-ware and sell it retail, because such a trade does not require going to and fro.

So al-Ashār became a glass merchant; he bought a great basket to hold his wares and installed himself at the corner of a much-frequented street. With his basket in front of him and his back propped up against the wall of a house, he would sometimes cry to the passers-by:

> Glasses, glasses,
> Blown drops of the sunrise,
> Breasts of alabaster little girls,
> Frozen breath of virgins under desire,
> Eye-coloured of the fairest,
> Glasses, glasses!

But more often he would sit spinning visions in silence. On a certain Friday at about the hour of prayer he was day-dreaming to himself in this wise:

I have put all my capital into these glasses; they cost me a hundred dirhams and I shall certainly sell them for two hundred. With the two hundred I shall buy more glasses and sell for four hundred. I shall go on buying and selling till I have a large capital. Then I shall buy other kind of goods, unguents and attars which should yield me enormous interest. On these profits I shall be able to afford myself a great palace with slaves and horses and saddles embroidered in gold. I will eat and drink, and there shall not be one singer in the city whom I do not bring into my palace to sing to me. I shall get into communication with the subtlest marriage-women of Baghdād and send them on my quests among the daughters of kings and of wazīrs. But perhaps, if I can stoop so low, I will marry the daughter of the grand wazīr, for I hear that she is as beautiful as dawn and excellently cultivated. I will give her a marriage portion of a thousand golden dīnārs, and if her father does not agree at once to the match I will carry her off from underneath his nose and ravish her to my palace. I will buy ten little eunuchs for my own service, and dress myself more royally than any king. The most skilful jeweller I can find shall make me a golden saddle encrusted with diamonds and pearls, and I shall set this on a marvellous horse bought from the Badāwī of the desert. Then I shall ride through the city, with hundreds of slaves about me, behind me and before me, and so come to the grand wazīr's palace. He will rise up at my coming and give me his own seat, standing below me in humility because I have honoured him by marrying his daughter. Two of my little slaves shall carry great purses with a thousand dīnārs in each; one I shall hand to my father-in-law as the marriage portion and the other I shall give him as a simple present to show my generosity, my high-mindedness and my little care for money. Gravely I shall return to my own house and, when my bride-to-be sends some woman to me with her greetings, I shall overwhelm the visitor with gold and a gift of the richest robes and fabrics. If the wazīr sends me a marriage gift I will not accept it; I will return it to him, however valuable it may be, just that he may know I have a lofty soul and am incapable of meanness. I will fix the marriage day and all the details of the ceremony myself, and give orders that no expense shall be spared. I will choose the number and quality of the musicians, of the male and female singers, and of the dancers. My palace shall be spread with carpets, and its floors strewn with flowers from the door to the feast-hall. All the marble shall be washed with rose-water and essences of delight.

On the night itself I shall dress in my most sumptuous clothes and show myself to the people seated upon a throne set on a dais, hung with silk stuffs, bearing pictures of flowers and coloured lines subtly placed. During all the time of the ceremony and of my wife's walking the hall, shining in beauty like the full moon of Ramadān, I shall stay motionless with impassive face, neither looking at her nor turning my head to right nor left. So shall men know that I am wise and grave. My wife will be brought before me in the freshness of her beauty and the charm of mingled perfumes, but I will not move. Gravely indifferent, I will sit there until all the women come round me, crying: 'Master and crown of our heads, here is your wife, your slave, standing respectfully before you, waiting for you to delight her with a look. She is tired with standing and has no other hope but that you will order her to sit.' I shall answer never a word until all the women and all the guests have thrown themselves down, kissing the ground before my greatness. Then only will I lower my eyes and look upon my wife just once; after a single glance I will raise my head again and resume my air of magnificent unconcern. The slaves will take my wife away for the second robing and, in the meanwhile, I will come down from my place and change my garments for richer ones. They will bring my wife before me a second time, dressed in other robes and other tires, lost beneath a mass of gold-set jewels and perfumed with other and sweeter scents. I will wait till they beg me to look at her and, just when she thinks I am about to do so, will raise my eyes to the ceiling. This I will do till all the ceremonies are over.

At this point Shahrazād saw the approach of morning and discreetly fell silent.

But when the thirty-second night had come

SHE CONTINUED HER TALE TO KING SHAHRYĀR IN THESE WORDS:

It is related, O auspicious King, that the barber told the rest of the story of his fifth brother, al-Ashār, in these words:

.... until all the ceremonies are over. Then I shall order some of my little slaves to take a purse containing five hundred dīnārs' worth of small money and scatter handfuls of it about the hall, among the musicians and singers and all my wife's attendants. Then the slaves will lead the bride to the marriage-chamber and thither will I go myself, after I have made them wait a long time for me. When I enter, I shall walk, without looking at my wife, between the two poised lines of women and, seating myself on the couch, call for a cup of perfumed and scented water. This I will drink calmly, giving thanks to God.

I will take no notice of my wife stretched on the bed ready to receive me. To humble her and let her know how little I think of her, I will not say one word. This will teach her how I intend to use her in future, for if you would have women sweet and docile it is as well to begin as you mean to end. Soon the bride's mother will come in, kissing my head and hands, and saying: 'Master, deign to regard your slave, my daughter, who ardently desires the alms of a single speech.' In spite of these respectful words I will not answer the woman, nor will she dare to call me son-in-law for fear of seeming familiar. She will continue to supplicate and at last, throwing herself down, will kiss my feet and the hems of my robe, saying: 'Master, I swear by Allâh that this child of mine is beautiful and a virgin. I swear by Him that no man has ever seen her face or known the colour of her eyes. Cease, then, from humbling her like this. Behold she is submissive and sweet; she waits only a sign to satisfy you in all things.'

My wife's mother will rise and, filling a cup with rare old wine, give it to her daughter, who will offer it to me with a trembling hand. Leaning carelessly upon my elbow among the gold-sewn velvet cushions of the bed, I will let her offer it to me and, without looking at her, I shall take much pleasure in thinking that she, the daughter of the grand wazîr, stands before the glass merchant who used to cry his wares at the street corners:

> Glasses, glasses,
> Blown drops of the sunrise,
> Breasts of alabaster little girls,
> Frozen breath of virgins under desire,
> Eye-coloured of the fairest;
> Navels of small sweethearts,
> Hardened spun honey;
> Glasses, glasses!

Standing before so much nobility and grandeur, she cannot but take me for the son of some illustrious sultân whose glory filled the world. Weeping she will say: 'Have mercy, my lord, do not refuse this cup or put away the hands of your servant. I am even as the lowest of your slaves.' I will not answer her and when, becoming a little bold in the face of my silence, she comes nearer with the wine cup and puts it sweetly to my lips, I will become furious at so much familiarity. I will look at her terribly and, giving her a great slap on the face, will kick her violently in the belly like this. . . .

So saying my brother launched a violent kick at the wife of his dreams, which took the fragile basket of glasses full in the centre and sent all the contents crashing in pieces to the ground. If I had been there at the moment, Commander of the Faithful, I would have beaten that mad brother of mine for the false grandeur and excessive vanity which had lost him his little fortune! Al-Ashâr began to give his face great blows and tear his garments, weeping and wailing as the folk went by to midday prayer. Some stopped and pitied him; others went by, bursting with laughter when they had heard from bystanders the extravagant details of the accident.

While my brother sat moaning the loss of his capital and all the fine interest of which he had dreamed, a well-born lady passed on her way to the mosque for Friday prayer. She outdid the fairest with her loveliness, a lively odour of the rarest musk floated about her and she rode on a mule whose harness was of velvet and gold brocade. She was accompanied by many servants and slaves, one of whom, in her tenderness of heart, she sent to enquire the reason of my brother's despair. When she heard that the poor man had upset his basket in which all his wealth was represented by brittle glass, she told one of her servants to give al-Ashār all the money which he carried. The servant took a great purse from about his neck and gave it to my brother, who found inside five hundred golden dīnārs. He nearly died for joy and gratitude, and called down all the blessings and mercies of Allāh on his helper until she was out of sight.

Having thus become rich in the twinkling of an eye, my brother hurried to his house, his breast swelling with pleasure, to hide away his fortune. He was on the point of setting out again to find some mansion in which he might live at ease, when he heard a gentle knocking at the door. He rose and, opening, found an old woman on the threshold whom he had never seen before. 'My son,' she said, 'the time for prayer on this holy Friday is almost past and I have not yet been able to make the ablutions necessary before praying. I beg you to let me come in for a moment and make the requisite washings out of reach of prying eyes.' 'Certainly you may do so,' answered my brother and, leading the old woman in, conducted her to the kitchen, where he left her alone.

A few minutes later the old woman appeared before my brother in his room and, taking up her position on a threadbare piece of matting which served him as a carpet, made a few hasty genuflexions, and finished her prayer by calling down the best blessing from on high upon her entertainer in excellent heartfelt phrases. My brother, who was bursting with happiness, thanked her for her prayers and, taking two gold dīnārs from his belt, offered them to her. The old woman pushed them back with dignity, crying: 'My child, Allāh be thanked that He has made you so generous. It does not surprise me that you can so quickly inspire sympathy in other people, even when, like myself, they have only seen you once. But put this money back in your belt, for you seem a poor man who needs it more than I do. If you are determined to get rid of it, why not return it to the noble lady who gave it to you when she saw that you had broken all your glasses?' 'What, do you know that woman, good mother?' asked al-Ashār. 'In that case, I beg you of your kindness to tell me how I may see her again.' 'My son,' said the old trot, 'that very beautiful young woman only gave you the money to express a liking which she had taken to your youth and vigorous good looks. Her husband is wellnigh impotent, slow indeed when he is in bed with her, being afflicted with a pair of the coldest eggs in the world. Rise up now, my boy, put all your gold in your belt, lest it should be stolen from this unprotected house, and follow me. I have been in the young lady's service for a long time and carry out all her secret commissions. My advice is that, when you are once in her presence, you should go to it roundly with gentle words but with your lustiest deeds. The more pressing you are, the better will she love you. She will stint you of no pleasure, but put all her beauty and wealth at your disposition.'

My brother rose and followed the old woman until they came to a great doorway, on which the latter knocked in a peculiar fashion, while al-Ashār stood beside her in an ecstasy of impatience. The door was opened by a young and pretty Greek slave, who welcomed my brother with a charming smile. He followed the old woman into the house, and the little Greek introduced him into a great and splendidly-furnished hall, hung with silk curtains finely sewn in gold, and very richly carpeted. Finding himself alone, he sat down on a couch and, taking off his turban and holding it on his knees, wiped his forehead and waited. Almost immediately the curtains parted and a girl, incomparable in the dazzled sight of all men and dressed to confound the imagination of poets, entered the apartment.

Al-Ashār rose, as the girl smiled at him with her eyes and shut the door which had been left open. Coming to my brother, she took his hand and led him to a couch of golden velvet. It would be impossible to tell you all they did for the next hour, what with embraces, couplings, kisses, bitings, huggings, twistings, great strokes of the zabb, variations, first, second, and third positions, and the rest. After these games the young woman rose and, saying to my brother: 'Eye of my heart, do not move till I return,' quickly left the chamber.

Suddenly the door was burst open violently and there rushed in a horrible negro with eyes of fire, holding a sword which shot forth blinding lightnings. 'Woe on you, wretch!' he cried to the terrified al-Ashār. 'How have you dared to sneak into this house, son of a whore, child of adultery, mingled spawn from the rotting eggs of a host of criminals?' Hearing these violent words my brother did not know what to answer. His tongue sickened in his mouth, his muscles died within him, and he turned yellow. The negro gripped him and, stripping him naked, thrashed him twenty-four times about the body with the flat of the sword to prolong his punishment; then he stabbed him in several places so that he fell to the earth and the negro thought him dead. The black man called out in a terrible voice, and immediately a negress ran in with a plate of salt. Laying the plate on the ground, she filled all my brother's wounds with salt, but he bore the terrible agony lest they should kill him if he cried out. When all al-Ashār's body had been treated with salt, the negro gave a second horrible cry and the old woman appeared, who helped him to search my brother's belt and clothes and took away his gold. Then she gripped him by the feet and dragged him through the rooms to a courtyard, where there was an opening in the stone floor. Below this was a dark cellar into which it was her habit to throw the corpses of all those solid riders whom she enticed to her mistress. They would be stripped and robbed and their bodies covered with salt so that they should not set up a stinking. Into this terrible place she threw my brother.

The cellar was very high and full of shadows; bodies lay piled there one on top of the other as they had fallen. For two days al-Ashār remained among the dead, being unable to move because of his wounds and his fall; but Allāh (praise the glory to Him) saw to it that the salt pickling which he had undergone was the means of saving his life, for it prevented his wounds from suppurating and stanched the flow of blood. When his hurts were fairly healed and his strength had come back to him a little, he managed to climb over the bodies and make his way along the cellar, guided by a feeble light which showed at the end of it. Groping his way forward, he found a little skylight high in the wall of the cellar. With infinite pain he hoisted himself through this, and stood once more in the light of day.

He hastened as fast as he could to his own house, and there I found him. I cured him completely with certain remedies which I know how to extract from plants and vegetable saps; soon he was able to plan a punishment for the old woman and the others. First he hunted for the old woman and, getting on her track, made himself acquainted with the haunts to which she proceeded every day for the purpose of finding young men to satisfy her mistress and endure the after fate. When he was sure of his ground, he disguised himself as a Persian. Filling the pouch of his belt with fragments of glass, as if it were bursting with gold, and hiding a great sword under his long Persian robe, he waited until the old woman came and then, approaching her, said in an imitation of the barbarous accent with which a Persian speaks Arabic: 'Good mother, I am a stranger in this city. Can you tell me where I may find a pair of scales to weigh these nine hundred golden dīnārs which I have in my belt? It is the sum which I have just obtained for the goods which I brought from my own country.' 'You have come to the right person, my young friend,' answered the wicked old woman. 'My son, who is just such another handsome young man as yourself, is a money-changer by profession and would gladly lend you his scales. Come, I will lead you to his house.' After thanking her, my brother followed her until he was led again to the ill-omened dwelling. The same young Greek opened the door with a charming smile, and the old woman whispered to her: 'I bring solid muscle and fat meat to-day.' The slave took al-Ashār by the hand and led him into the silken hall. There she left him and went to fetch her mistress, who came in a few moments and did with my brother all that she had done on the first occasion. It is useless to repeat it here. Then she retired as before and suddenly the terrible negro, appearing with the naked sword in his hand, abused him more foully than the first time and bade him follow. When my brother was behind the negro, he whipped his own sword from beneath his robe and with a single stroke cut off the black man's head. The negress with the salt ran in at the sound of the fall and was killed instantly in the same way; then the Greek slave rushed in and her head fell beside the rest. Lastly, the old woman hurried up, ready to lay her hands on the booty, but, seeing my brother with bloody arms and sword in hand, fell to the ground in terror. Al-Ashār seized her by the hair, crying: 'Old whore, daughter of a whore, corrupt misfortune, do you recognise me?' 'I do not, my master,' interrupted the old woman. 'Know, old zabb-swallower,' shouted my brother, 'that I am the man to whose house you came to do your washings, and whom you led to this place before, old ape's bottom. Yes, I am he whom you dragged by the legs and threw into the cellar.' So saying, he cut the old woman into two pieces and, leaving her, set out to find the young woman who had twice coupled with him.

Soon he found her, tittivating and scenting herself in a far chamber. She threw herself at his feet with a terrified cry, begging my brother to spare her life. Remembering the pleasures which she had given him, he pardoned her and asked: 'What are you doing in this house, in the power of that terrible negro whom I have just killed with my own hand? Surely the life you have led with him has been full of horrors?' 'Master,' she answered, 'before I was shut up in this wicked house I was in the family of a rich merchant of the city. The old woman often used to come to see us and singled me out especially as a favourite. One day she came to me, saying: "I have been invited to a marriage feast the like of which the world has never seen. I come to take you with me." Accepting with pleasure, I put on the most beautiful dresses that I had and, taking with me a purse of a hundred dīnārs, went out with the old woman. She led me to this house and, once here, I fell beneath the hands and power of the negro. After ravishing me, he kept me by force and made me a party to his crimes on the bodies of rich young men whom the old woman brought to him. For three years I have been a tool and slave to that wicked hag.' 'Unfortunate woman,' said my brother, 'surely, in all this time, you must have found out where these criminals stored their great wealth?' 'Indeed I have,' she answered, 'and there is so much that not ten men could carry it away. Come and see for yourself.' With that she showed my brother great chests filled with the money of all lands and purses of every fashion. As he stood dumb before such vast wealth, she said to him: 'There is no way in which we can carry off all this gold. Go out and return with many porters. In the meanwhile I will make the gold up into bundles.'

My brother went forth in haste and returned, after a certain time, with ten strong men, each carrying an empty case.

But, on arriving at the house, he found the door wide open and both the girl and the great chests of money gone. He understood how she had tricked him, in order to keep the greater part of the money to herself, but even so he was well enough pleased with all the beautiful things which remained in the house. There were valuables shut away in presses and furnishings which alone would make him rich for the rest of his days. Telling himself that he would remove all these things on the morrow, my brother, who was broken by the fatigue of his adventure, lay down on the rich bed and slept.

Waking in the morning, he was terrified to find himself surrounded by twenty of the walī's guards, who said: 'Rise up and come with us to our master, for he requires you.' They shut and sealed the doors, and led al-Ashar to the walī, who regarded him sternly, saying: 'I have heard all the story of the murders you have committed and the theft you meditated.' 'Walī,' cried my brother, 'give me the sign of mercy and I will tell you all the truth!' The walī handed him the little kerchief of pardon, and my brother told him all his adventures from beginning to end, adding: 'Now if you wish it, O just and resourceful walī, we shall share what remains in the house on equal terms.' 'Do you dare to speak of sharing?' cried the walī. 'By Allāh, I will have it all and you shall have nothing. You may think yourself lucky to escape with your life. As it is, you must leave the city and never return, unless you wish to pay the last penalty.' Thus the walī, fearing that the khalīfah might hear of his appropriation of the money, exiled my brother, and he was obliged to leave the city on the instant. That his destiny might be fulfilled he had hardly got beyond the gates when he was set upon by brigands who, finding that he had neither valuables nor money, took his clothes, beat him severely and, to pay themselves for their disappointment, cropped his ears and split his nose.

When I heard of the misfortunes of poor al-Ashar, O Commander of the Faithful, I went forth and rested not until I found him. I took him into my house, cared for him and cured him; finally I made him an allowance of food and drink for the rest of his days.

That is the tale of al-Ashar.

The story of my sixth and last brother so merits attention that I will tell it at once, without pausing for breath.

The Tale of Shakkāshik, the Barber's Sixth Brother

HE was called Shakkāshik, the broken pot, O Commander of the Faithful; he was that one of my brothers who had his lips cut off and his zabb shorn away as the result of certain extraordinary adventures.

He was the poorest of us all; he was always poor. I say nothing of the hundred dirhams which he, like us, inherited from my father; for Shakkāshik, never having seen so much money in his life, rioted it away in a single night with the terrible roisterers of the left quarter of Baghdād.

He possessed none of the vain riches of this perishable world and lived on the alms of people who received him at their houses for the sake of his jokes and witty sayings.

One day Shakkāshik went out to search for some food with which to sustain his starving body, and found himself at length in front of a magnificent house which had a great portico raised upon many steps. On these steps came and went a crowd of servants and young slaves, officers and porters. My brother approached one of these and asked him who was the owner of so fair a dwelling. 'It belongs to one of the royal family of the Barmaki,' answered the man. Hearing this, my brother went up the steps and solicited alms in the name of Allāh from certain porters who sat on a great bench in the entrance. 'Where can you come from,' one of them said to him, 'not to know that you have but to go into our master and be loaded with gifts?' So Shakkāshik went through the great door, and crossed the spacious courtyard and a garden which was full of singing birds and fair trees. The courtyard was paved with alternate squares of black and white marble, and the garden was more beautifully kept than any other which eye of man had seen. Round the two there rose a day-gallery paved with marble and shaded with silk curtains which kept it cool from the heat of noon. My brother went on and entered the principal hall which was built of porcelain tiles coloured blue, green and gold, with laced leaves and flowers, and had in its centre a fair alabaster basin from which cool water fell with a sweet lisping. A marvellously-coloured mat carpetted the higher part of the floor, and upon it, among cushions of gold silk, reposed a handsome old man with a long white beard and a benevolent smile. Shakkāshik advanced towards the full-bearded ancient, saying: 'Peace be with you!' The old man rose and answered: 'Peace be with you, together with the clemency and blessing of Allāh! What do you wish, my friend?' 'I only ask an alms, master; I am dying of hunger,' said my brother.

Hearing thus of my brother's misfortune, the old man expressed great compassion and an excessive grief, tearing his robe and crying: 'By Allāh, is it possible that I should be in a city and there should be also in it a man so hungry as you are? This is a thing that I cannot well bear!' Raising his hands to heaven, my brother cried: 'Allāh bless your goodness and your posterity for ever!' Then said the old man: 'There is nothing for it but that you stay here and share my meal with me, eating the salt of my cloth.' 'I thank you, master,' answered my brother, 'for I can fast no more.' The old man clapped his hands and said to a slave who came at this summons: 'Make haste! Bring the silver ewer and basin that we may wash our hands!' Then to Shakkāshik: 'Come here and wash your hands, my guest.'

So saying, the old man rose and, although the boy had not returned, made a movement as if he were pouring the water upon his hands from an invisible ewer, and then of drying them as if they had been really wet. Shakkāshik did not know what to think of this, but, as the old man insisted, he supposed it must be some sort of joke; therefore, being himself renowned for humour, he went through all the movements of handwashing as the old man had done. When he had finished, his host called out: 'Come you others, spread the cloth quickly and let us eat, for this poor man is hungry.' Numerous servants hurried in and made a great running to and fro, as if they were spreading a cloth and covering it with many meats and groaning dishes. Although Shakkāshik was at the extreme of hunger, he said to himself that the poor have to enter into the caprices of the rich and schooled himself not to show the least sign of impatience. So, when the old man said: 'Seat yourself by my side, dear guest, and hasten to do honour to my entertainment,' my brother sat down by him at the edge of the imaginary cloth. The old man moved his hands about as if he were touching dishes and taking samples from them, also he moved his jaws and lips as if chewing. Soon he said to my brother: 'O guest, my house is your house and my cloth your cloth. Fall to, then, and eat your fill without shame! Just look at this bread, it is not excellently white and baked to a turn? I should like your opinion of this bread.' 'It is the whitest bread I have ever seen,' said Shakkāshik, 'and I have never tasted the like in all my life.' 'I can well believe it,' said his host. 'The negress who baked it is the cleverest of her kind. I had to pay five hundred gold dīnārs for her. Now try a little of this dish; see how golden it lies there, this excellent pasty of buttered harīsah! Believe me, my cook has spared neither good red mince, nor bruised corn, nor cardamoms, nor pepper. Eat, my poor starved friend, and tell me what you think of the taste, the smell, the soul of it?' 'This harīsah melts against my lips,' replied my brother, 'its perfume fills my breast. I will be bold to say that never has such a harīsah been cooked even in kings' palaces.' To give effect to his words, Shakkāshik began to move his jaws, to chew and swallow, and shake his cheeks as if he were eating. 'What you say pleases me very much, dear guest,' continued the old man, 'yet I do not think that what you have tasted so far of my cooking deserves so high a eulogy. What will you have over to say about these dishes on your left, those heavenly roast chickens, stuffed with pistachio and almonds, rice and raisins, pepper, cinnamon and paste of lamb? Their aroma, my friend, their aroma!' 'Allāh be good to us,' cried my brother, 'never was such an aroma! The birds are the soul of all savoury, and their stuffing a poem.' Said the old man: 'You display a well-bred indulgence to my kitchen, very gratifying to me. Now, if I may, I will give you a mouthful of this other dish with my own fingers.' With that he made as if to roll a mouthful from an invisible dish, and popped the imperceptible dainty into my brother's mouth, saying: 'Eat that, dear guest, and give me your opinion on such stuffed egg-apples and their titillating sauce.' My brother reached forward his lips, opened his mouth, and took a great swallow. Then, with closed eyes, he said: 'As Allāh lives, it is perfection! I say, without fear of contradiction, that never elsewhere have I tasted such egg-apples. In the stuffing I detect the hand of an artist; the shredded lamb, the chick-peas, the pine kernels, the cardamom seeds, the nutmeg, the cloves, the ginger, the pepper, and the various aromatic herbs, I taste them as a whole and I taste them separately, so exquisite is the blending.' 'My dear friend,' replied the old man, 'that being the case, I shall be infinitely obliged if you will eat all the forty-four stuffed egg-apples on this plate.' 'Nothing is easier,' replied my brother, 'for they are sweeter than the nipples of my nurse and tickle my palate like the fingers of little girls.' Then Shakkāshik made as if he lifted and swallowed each of the forty-four in turn, nodding his head and clicking his tongue with delight. All the time the poor fellow's mind dwelt on this food as it was mentioned and he became so ravenous that he would willingly have died for a dried beancake or lump of maize bread. At the same time he was careful not to betray his feelings.

Soon the old man said: 'Your language is that of a well-bred man accustomed to eat with kings. Eat then, my friend, with good appetite and easy digestion.' 'Do you know,' answered my brother, 'I have really eaten enough of the meat courses.' When he heard this, the old man clapped his hands, calling: 'Remove the cloth and bring on dessert. Let us have all the pastries, the conserves, and the choicest fruits!' The little slaves ran in and bustled about as before, making quick gestures with their hands and lifting angled arms above their heads as if they were indeed changing one cloth for another. At last, on a sign from the old man, they retired. 'Now, dear guest,' said my brother's host, 'at last the time has come to give ourselves up to sweetness. Let us begin with the pastries. What say you to these almond pastes with sugar and pomegranate? Taste one or two to try. Is it not a royal confection? The syrup is just thick enough, the top-sprinkling of cinnamon done with a fairy lightness. One could eat fifty on end; but we must keep room for that sublime katāif on the carved copper plate. There you have my pastrycook at his best; see into what suggestive shapes he has rolled the beards of the vermicelli. Be quick, be quick, and rejoice your senses before all the juice drip out and the so delicate paste itself crumble away. Ah, here is something worth looking at, a mahlabīyah of rose-water, powdered with snow of almonds. And here are little porcelain bowls of whipped creams, sharpened with orange-water and spices. Eat, my friend, eat, and stay not your hand.' With that the old man set an example by lifting his hand greedily to his mouth and swallowing, as if the farce were life itself. Shakkāshik did the same, but in his case there was real moisture upon the lips.

'Now for the conserves and fruit!' said the old man presently. 'In the matter of conserves, dear guest, there is an embarrassment of choice; there, before you, are dry conserves and yonder are those with rich juices. I advise you to confine yourself to the dry, which I prefer myself, although the others are dear enough to my heart. See this shining, translucent, dry conserve of apricots, cut in long thin slices, melting, caressing, friendly; this preserve of crystallised citrons, perfumed with amber. Or these other flushed cakes of rose petals and orange flowers. And this, oh, this! it will be the death of me one of these days. Leave the others for a moment and bathe your soul a little in this moist jam of dates stuffed with almonds and cloves. It comes to me from Cairo; they cannot make it in Baghdād. One of my Egyptian friends sends me a hundred pots of it every year. But do not eat too much of it, although the eagerness of your appetite does me honour. I wish you to pay particular attention to this dry conserve of sugared carrots, diversified with nuts, scented with virgin musk.' Said Shakkāshik: 'This passes all my dreams, my palate kneels before its excellence. And yet, dare I say that I find that there is a shade too much musk . . .?' 'No, no,' answered the old man, 'I cannot agree with you; musk and amber are the mainstays of my soul. My cooks and confectioners have orders to put plenty of each into all they make for me.'

'But,' he continued, 'we must not forget the fruit. I hope you have a little space left for the fruit. Here are limes, bananas, figs, fresh dates, apples, quinces and grapes. There are fresh almonds, hazel nuts, fresh walnuts, and many more. Eat, my guest, for Allāh is good!'

But my brother, who by this time could hardly move his jaws from the exercise of chewing on nothing, and whose stomach was in a state of excitation, excused himself, saying: 'My lord, I must confess that I am full, and that even my throat will not take another mouthful.' 'It is extraordinary that you are so easily satisfied,' said the old man. 'Come, let us drink; we have not had a single glass so far.'

With that he clapped his hands and young boys ran in, with carefully-bared arms and lifted robes, who gestured as if they were clearing away and were setting two cups on the cloth, with flasks, wine jars, and heavy pots of precious metals. Then the old man pretended to pour wine in the cups and to hand one of them to my brother, who carried the shadow to his lips and drank, saying: 'Allāh, Lord Allāh, what a wine!', and rubbed his stomach with pleasure. After this the old man went through the movements of lifting a heavy jar of old wine, and of pouring slowly and delicately for my brother. They acted in this way until Shakkāshik pretended to be overcome by the fumes of all these drinks, and began to nod his head and speak in a more sprightly fashion. All the time he was thinking to himself that the moment had come for paying out the old man in his own coin.

So my brother jumped up suddenly, as if he were quite drunk, lifted his arm so high that the pit was seen, and brought his hand down so violently on the old man's neck that the whole hall echoed with the slap. Raising his arm again, he struck more violently than before. At this the old man grew very angry and cried: 'What are you doing, O vilest of earth's creatures?' To which my brother made answer: 'Master and crown of my head, I am your obedient slave whom you have weighed to the dust with gifts, whom you have received in your house, whom you have nourished at your cloth with the choicest meats such as kings have never tasted, whose soul you have sweetened with your conserves, your composts and your suavest pastries, and whose burning thirst you have quenched with old and precious wines. What would you, my lord? He has taken so much of the wines of your hospitality that he is drunk and has raised his hand against his saviour. Pity your slave then, since your soul is higher than his soul, and forgive the madness wrought in him by wine!'

At these excuses the old man burst out laughing, and, when he could speak, cried out to Shakkāshik: 'Long have I searched the world, and among the most reputed wits and jokers, for a man as humorous and patient as you. None has so fooled with me in my own bent, none has so entered into the spirit of my humour and my taste, to bear so long a joke so well. I freely pardon you the round turn you gave to my jest, and ask you to sit down with me this minute to eat in very truth all the meats and sweets and fruits about which we have jested. And I shall see to it that we are not parted as long as I live.'

So saying the old man ordered his slaves to serve the whole meal and spare nothing.

This was done, and, after both had eaten of all the meats and indulged themselves with the pastries, conserves, and fruits, his host invited my brother to pass with him into a chamber specially reserved for the drinking of wine. On going in, they were received with lute-playing and singing by white slaves as fair as a flock of summer moons. They sang while my brother and the old man drank the oldest wines, and charmed them with the most pleasing melodies. Then certain of them danced like birds with quick and perfumed wings. The day ended with kisses and games more precious than those which come to a man in dreams.

From that time the old man bound my brother to himself with every tie of kindness, making him an intimate and inseparable friend, loving him with all his heart, and daily giving him novel and expensive presents. They ate and drank and lived in sweet luxury for twenty years.

But what Destiny has written comes surely to pass. The old man died, and the walī seized all his goods for himself, as there were no heirs and my brother was not a relation by blood. Shakkāshik was obliged to flee from the wicked persecution of the walī and leave our city of Baghdād behind him.

He set out upon a journey across the desert to Mecca, that he might return holy. But one day the troop of pilgrims to which he had attached himself was attacked by a band of roving Arabs, cut-throats of the road, evil Mussulmāns, not having before their eyes the law of our Prophet (on whom be the prayer and peace of Allāh). All were robbed and taken as slaves, my brother falling to the lot of the most bloodthirsty of all the Badāwī, who took him to his far-away tribe and kept him there as a menial. He beat and tortured him every day, saying: 'You seem to have been a very rich man in your own country. Send for a ransom or I will torture you more and more, and in the end kill you by my own hand.' Then would my brother weep and say: 'As Allāh lives, O chief of the Arabs, I have nothing. I have never known the road which leads to fortune; I am your slave, do to me as you wish.'

Now the Badāwī had among his tents a marvel of women, a wife with black brows and eyes like night, hotly insatiable in the matter of coupling. Each time that her husband was away from his tent she would come and be gracious to my brother, offering him all the sweets of her body, that fine flower of the Arabian desert. But, unlike the rest of us, my brother Shakkāshik was by no means a famous rider and tumbler, so he always refused the woman for fear that his sin should be seen by Almighty Allāh. Nevertheless a day came when the girl, who was red-hot, succeeded in troubling my brother's chastity by moving round and round him with a rhythmic invitation of her hips, her breasts, and her belly. Shakkāshik took her, made all the preliminary movements, and ended by placing her across his thighs. While they were in this position, on the very point of fornication, the terrible Arab rushed in and saw all. With a furious movement he drew a large scimitar from his belt, such a blade as might have halved a camel's jugular with one stroke, and, seizing my brother, cut off his adulterous lips and stuffed them in his mouth. Then, crying: 'Foul traitor, you have soiled my wife!' he grasped my brother's still warm zabb and cut it off at the root, eggs and all. Lastly, he dragged Shakkāshik out and, throwing his body over the back of a camel, hurried with him to the top of a mountain, where he threw him down to die.

This mountain lay on the road to Mecca, so that certain pilgrims from Baghdād found my brother and, recognising him as Shakkāshik, the Broken Pot, who had so often pleased them with his jests, gave him food and drink, and hurried to tell me what had happened.

I ran to find him, O Commander of the Faithful, and bore him back on my shoulders to Baghdād. I healed his wounds and made him a life-allowance at my table.

Such as I am, I stand before you, O Commander of the Faithful, having been at some pains to tell you the tales of my six brothers in the fewest possible words. I could have elaborated them, but I preferred, instead of taking advantage of your patience, to prove that I am a taciturn man, not only the brother of my brothers, but in some sort their father. In fine to show you that they are nothing compared with myself, al-Sāmit, the Silent Man.

Hearing my last tale (went on the barber to the guests) the Khalī-fah al-Mustansir Billāh burst out laughing and said to me: 'It is very true, O Sāmit, that you are a man of few words, incapable of indis-cretion, curiosity, or ill-breeding, yet I have particular reasons for wishing you to leave Baghdād this very hour and take yourself elsewhere. Hasten to do so!' So, you see, the Khalīfah exiled me unjustly and for no possible fault of mine.

From that time, my masters, I travelled through all lands and in the varying heat and cold of the world, until I heard that al-Mustansir Billāh was dead and that the Khalīfah al-Mustasim had succeeded him. Then I returned to Baghdād and found that all my brothers were dead also. It was after my return that the young man who has so rudely left us sent for me to shave his head. I assure you, gentlemen, that, notwithstanding all he has told you, I was of the very greatest service to him. If it had not been for me he would surely have died by the hand of his mistress's father, the kādī. All that he has said of me is lies, all that he has spoken of my curiosity, my indiscretion, my slack tongue, my gross character, my lack of all tact and taste, is absolutely false. This, gentlemen, I assure you most solemnly.

Such, O auspicious King, continued Shahrazād, is the sevenfold tale which the Chinese tailor told his sovereign. When the stories were done he proceeded thus:

When the barber al-Sāmit had finished his tale, the rest of us guests needed no further proof that he was the most astonishingly garrulous and indiscreet of all barbers upon earth. From what we had heard we had no doubt at all that the lame young man of Baghdād had been the victim of insupportable importunity. So, although the barber's tales had amused us very much, we decided to punish him. After a short deliberation we seized hold of him, in spite of his expostulation, and shut him in a dark room filled with rats. The rest of us continued our feast, eating, drinking, and making merry until the time of evening prayer. Then we separated, and I returned home to give my wife something to eat.

But, when I reached my house, my wife angrily turned her back on me, saying: 'Is it thus that you leave me all day moping and miserable at home, while you enjoy yourself? If you do not take me out at once and give me a pleasant jaunt for the rest of the evening, I shall go to the kādī and demand a divorce.'

I have always hated temper and domestic brawls: therefore, tired as I was, I went out with my wife, and we wandered among the streets and gardens until sunset. As we were returning home, we met your little hunchback quite by chance, O clement King. He was very drunk and very gay, saying deliciously clever things to every-one he met, and bawling these lines continually:

> Between this purple cup and wine of mine
> . I cannot make my drunken senses up,
> Because the cup resembles so the wine
> And the mauve wine resembles so the cup.

Every now and then he would break off to play some joke upon the passers-by or to dance to the accompaniment of his little drum. My wife and I, thinking that he would be an agreeable table com-panion, asked him to share our evening meal. We all ate together, because my wife, who would never have sat down in the presence of a strange man, did not consider your hunchback to be wholly such.

What happened afterwards you know; as a jest my wife thrust a great handful of fish into the hunchback's mouth and choked him. We took the body and left it in the house of the Jewish doctor, he threw it into the house of the steward, and the steward left it in the way of the Christian broker.

Such, O generous King, is the whole tale of the barber and his brothers, which I deem to be not only more extraordinary than the other tales which you have heard to-day, but even surpassing in marvel and pleasantry the story of the hunchback.

When the tailor had finished speaking, the King of China said: 'I must admit, O tailor, that your story has points of great interest and is even perhaps more suggestive than the adventure which befell my unfortunate hunchback. But where is this prodigious barber of whom you speak? I must see and hear him before I make up my mind as to the fate of the four of you. After that we must bury our hunchback, for he has been dead since yesterday. We will build a fair tomb above him because he greatly amused us in his life and, even in his death, caused us to hear the story of the lame young man and of the barber's six brothers and the three other tales.'

So saying, the King ordered his chamberlains to go with the tailor and bring back the barber. An hour later they returned, having set the barber free and bringing him with them.

The King looked at the barber and saw that he was an old man, ninety years of age, with a very dark face and a very white beard, with white brows, ears pierced and hanging, an astonishingly long nose, and a proud conceited cast of countenance. Having well looked him over, the King broke into a roar of laughter and said: 'O Silent Man, I hear that you can tell excellent tales. Come, give me a sample of your quality.' 'O King of time,' answered the barber, 'you have not been misinformed, but before all else I would myself know why this Christian, this Mussulmān, this Jew, and this dead hunchback are combined here in so strange a juxtaposition.' The King of China laughed heartily at this, saying: 'Why are you so interested in these people who are strangers to you?' 'I only asked,' replied the barber, 'in order to prove to my King that I am discreet, incurious in all save my own concerns, and innocent of those calumnies which some people have put about to the effect that I am given to tattling. I am worthy of the name "Silent Man," which has been given to me. A poet has said:

> If any man has earned a name
> I deem him worthy of the same.'

'I like this barber,' said the King, 'I will tell him the story of the hunchback, then the Christian's tale, the Jew's, the steward's, and the tailor's.' And straightway he did so without omitting a single detail, but it would be useless for me to repeat them here.

When the barber had heard all the stories and learnt the cause of the hunchback's death, he shook his head gravely, saying: 'By Allāh, this is a most extraordinary thing! Lift the veil from the hunchback's body, some of you, that I may see him.' As soon as the corpse was uncovered, the barber went up to it and, sitting down, took the head upon his knees. After he had attentively examined the face for a long time, he went off into shouts of laughter, toppling over on his backside in his amusement. 'Truly there is a cause for every death,' he spluttered at length, 'but the cause of this death is, I dare swear, unique. Yes, the cause of this death should be written in posterity.'

Amazed by the barber's words, the King insisted that he should explain them. Then said the Silent Man: 'I swear by your sacred head, O king, that there is life in your hunchback yet. I will show you.' So saying, he took from his belt an unguent in a phial with which he anointed the hunchback's neck, covering it afterwards with linen until the flesh sweated. Then he introduced a pair of iron forceps into his patient's throat and drew out the lump of fish with its bone. Immediately the hunchback sneezed violently, opened his eyes, felt his face with his hand, and jumped to his feet, crying: 'There is no God save Allāh, Muhammad is His prophet, on whom be the Master's prayer and peace!'

All who stood round were amazed at this sight and filled with great admiration for the barber. When they had recovered a little from their astonishment, the King and all who were with him could not help laughing at the jester's expression. 'By Allāh,' said the King, 'this is a prodigy if you will! I have never seen anything like it in my life! Have any of you good Mussulmāns ever seen a dead man brought to life like this? Only to think, if Allāh had not sent us this barber, this venerable al-Sāmit, our hunchback would have been buried to-day! We owe his life to the knowledge and excellence of this worthy old man.' 'It is a prodigy of prodigies,' said all the rest, 'it is a miracle of miracles!'

Joyfully the King of China ordered all the tales centring round the hunchback, and all those concerned with the barber, to be written out fairly in letters of gold and preserved in the royal library. While this was being done, he gave magnificent robes of honour to each of the accused, to the Jewish doctor, the Christian broker, the steward, and the tailor, and created them all positions about his palace. Also, he reconciled them with the hunchback. To his restored jester he gave rich presents, appointing him to various high offices, and naming him his own perpetual cupman. For the barber he could not do enough; he clothed him in a sumptuous robe, and had made for him a golden astrolabe and golden scissors and razors encrusted with pearls and diamonds. Also he appointed him royal barber and called him friend.

All with whom these tales have been concerned lived thereafter in pleasure and prosperity, until their joys were cut short by the Thief of time, the Breaker of friendships.

'But,' said Shahrazād to King Shahryār, ruler of the Isles of Hind and China, 'do not believe this story is in any way more astonishing than the tale of the beautiful Sweet-Friend.' 'What Sweet-Friend is that?' cried King Shahryār.

Then Shahrazād said:

The Tale of Sweet-Friend and Alī-Nūr

IT is related, O auspicious King, that there was once, on the throne of Basrah, a sultān, tributary to the Khalīfah Hārūn al-Rashīd, whose name was Muhammad ibn Sulaimān al-Zainī. He loved the poor and lowly, raised the fallen, and parted with his gold to all Believers in the Prophet, on whom be the prayer and peace of Allāh. He was in every way worthy of that ode which a poet wrote in his honour. It begins:

> His ink was blood and his good lance at rest
> A ready pen
> For fair calligraphy;
> It wrote red songs in praise of victory
> Upon the white papyrus of the breast
> Of other men.

This king had two wazīrs, the one al-Muīn son of Sāwi, and the other al-Fadl son of Kahkān. Now you must know that al-Fadl ibn Kahkān was the most generous man of all his time, admirable in virtue and manner, urbane in character, loved by all and esteemed by all for his wisdom and knowledge. Men came to him in their difficulties; in all the kingdoms there was no one who did not pray long life and prosperity for him, knowing him to be above evil and beyond injustice. The second wazīr, the son of Sāwi, was the exact opposite of this good man in every way. He hated men and abominated goodness, his daily practice was evil. A certain poet has said of him:

> I rose and walked away when he was nigh,
> I lifted up my robe as he went by;
> I leapt upon my horse and rode all day
> To find some place beneath a cleaner sky.

The difference between these two wazīrs has been well summed up by another poet, who said:

> Scan Noble's lineage and you will find
> Age after age a Noble of that kind:
> Vile's line is just as long, for, all the while,
> Vile's father's father's father's name was Vile.

It is to be remembered that men hated the wazīr al-Muīn just as deeply as they loved the wazīr al-Fadl, also that al-Muīn, while pretending a great friendship for al-Fadl, lost no opportunity of prejudicing him in the eyes of the King.

One day Muhammad ibn Sulaimān heard that there was newly arrived in Basrah a fresh batch of young slaves from all countries, so, sitting on his throne among his amīrs and the chief nobles of his court, he said to his wazīr al-Fadl: 'I wish you to find me a young slave without equal in the whole world. She must have perfect beauty, superior attributes, and an admirably sweet character.'

Wishing to cross the King because of this sign of confidence shown to his rival, the wazīr Sāwi cried: 'But, even supposing such a woman could be found, she would cost ten thousand golden dīnārs.' The King, made all the more eager by this obstacle, immediately caused his treasurer to deliver ten thousand golden pieces at the palace of al-Fadl and ordered the favoured wazīr to execute his commission at once.

Al-Fadl lost no time in going to the slave market, but he could find no woman fulfilling the conditions of the King. He called together all the brokers concerned in the selling of black and white slaves, and bade them search for what he required, commanding that any woman offered for over a thousand dīnārs should be shown to him before a sale was made. After this not a day passed without two or three brokers bringing some chosen slave to the wazīr, so that by the end of a month more than a thousand girls had passed before his eyes (a troop able to bring back fire to the limbs of a thousand ancients) without his having been able to decide on one.

One morning, as al-Fadl had mounted his horse and was about to ride to the palace to beg an extension of time, a certain broker of his acquaintance ran up and, holding his stirrup, honourably greeted him with these lines:

> O grand wazīr
> Whose hand holds up the glory of this reign
> Making the old times come again,
> O grand wazīr
> Whose sword was never turned aside,
>
> Whose breath brings back the life when life has died,
> O grand wazīr
> Whose every action God approves,
> Whose every thought His Prophet loves,
> O grand wazīr!

Concluding these verses, the broker said: 'Noble al-Fadl, great son of Kahkān, I come to announce that such a slave as you have honoured me by requiring has been found and is ready for you.' 'Bring her quickly to my palace that I may see her,' said the wazīr, dismounting from his horse and returning to his apartments. An hour later the broker returned, holding a young girl by the hand. She was tall and slim, with marvellous outpointing breasts, brown lids over night-coloured eyes, smooth full cheeks, a laughing chin just shaded with a dimple, hips in firm curves, a bee's waist, and a heavy swelling croup. She stood before him dressed in rare stuffs. Her mouth was a flower, the wet of it sweeter than sherbert; her lips were redder than flowering nutmeg, and all her body wavered like the tender shoot of a willow. Her voice had more music than the song of a light wind, sweeter than a light wind which has passed over gardens of flowers. A poet has sung this of her:

> Her body is silk like water,
> With the curves of water,
> Pure and restful as water.
>
> To be with her in the night!
> Her hair, the wings of night,
> And her hands the pale stars of night.
>
> God said: Let there be eyes,
> And lo! the dew of her eyes,
> The dark wine of her eyes.

This girl, ripe and young like a flower, was called Anīs al-Jalīs, Sweet-Friend.

When the wazīr saw her, he marvelled and asked the broker her price. 'Her owner asked me ten thousand dīnārs,' answered the other, 'and I agreed to that price because I thought it not excessive. He claims that he will lose on the transaction for various reasons which I would prefer you to hear from his own lips.' 'Bring him to me at once,' said the wazīr.

The broker fetched the owner of the slave with all speed, and the wazīr saw that he was an old and very feeble Persian. Such was the poet when he wrote:

> Time has undone
>   My body's quickness
>   Ruthlessly;
> Once I was straight and walked towards the sun,
>   But now I keep the house with my friend, Sickness,
>   And my last mistress, Immobility.

The old man wished the wazīr peace, and the other said: 'It is agreed, then, that you sell me this slave for ten thousand golden dīnārs? She is not for me, but for the King.' 'As she is for the King,' answered the old man, 'I would willingly offer her for nothing; but, since you insist, most generous of wazīrs, I will accept ten thousand dīnārs. At the same time, I must tell you that sum would hardly pay for the white chicken-meat she has eaten, much less for her clothes and her education. She has had numberless masters; she has learnt the most excellent calligraphy, together with both Arabic and Persian grammar and syntax; she knows the commentaries of the Book, moral law, jurisprudence, philosophy and ethics, geometry, medicine, cadastral survey, and the like; but her chief excellence is in poetry, music of all kinds, singing and dancing. She has read all the books of the poets and the historians, but her knowledge is only the sweetening to a noble character and great good humour. That is why I have named her Sweet-Friend.'

'I do not doubt that you are right,' said the wazīr, 'but I can only pay you ten thousand dīnārs. I pray you, therefore, count the sum.' Al-Fadl paid the old Persian his money, but before he left the slave merchant said: 'If I may give you a word of advice, I would suggest that you do not take Sweet-Friend at once to our sovereign Muhammad ibn Sulaimān, for only to-day she has finished a long journey and is a little worn by the change of climate and of water. It would be better both for you and her if you were to keep her ten days in your own palace where, resting and bathing and changing her garments, she can recover the fine flower of her beauty. Then you can present her to the Sultān, and he will honour you all the more for your precaution.' The old man's advice seemed good to al-Fadl, so he received Sweet-Friend in his own home and prepared a private room where she might rest.

Now the wazīr al-Fadl ibn Kahkān had a son so handsome that people beholding him thought that the moon was rising. His skin was marvellously white, but roses blushed below the silky down of his cheeks, and on one of them lay a beauty spot like a sprinkle of ambergris. He was like the boy in the song:

> Roses sweeter than red dates and grapes,
> But my hand falters
> In putting forth to touch his cheek
> And my eyes close sleepily
> After their feasting.
>
> If his heart were as tender
> As the peeled wand of his body
> He would not so coldly have sinned against me.
>
> You cannot accuse me, for I am mad,
> Nor my darling, for he is more than royal.
> Arrest my heart,
> But you will find no room for punishment,
> No room for chains.

This young man, whose name was Alī-Nūr, knew nothing of the purchase of Sweet-Friend. But the wazīr his father had most strictly recommended this precept to the girl: 'Know, dear child, that I have bought you for our master, Muhammad ibn Sulaimān; therefore guard yourself well and avoid any occasion on which you, and consequently I, might be compromised. I have a son who is a very handsome fellow but somewhat of a rascal; there is not a girl in all the quarter who has not freely given herself to him, whose flower he has not plucked. Avoid any meeting with him, let him not hear your voice or see your face; otherwise you will be lost.' 'I hear and I obey,' answered Sweet-Friend, and the wazīr left her to go about his business.

Allāh had written that things should turn out very differently from the intentions of the good wazīr. A few days later Sweet-

Friend went to the bath in the wazīr's palace, and all the little slaves set themselves to give her such a bath as they had never achieved in their lives before. After washing her hair and all her limbs, they rubbed and kneaded her, depilated her carefully with paste of caramel, sprinkled her hair with a sweet wash prepared from musk, tinted her finger-nails and her toe-nails with henna, burnt male incense and ambergris at her feet, and rubbed light perfumes into all her skin. Then they threw a large towel, scented with orange-flowers and roses, over her body and, wrapping all her hair in a warm cloth, led her to her own apartment, where the wazīr's wife waited to wish her the customary wishes of the bath. Sweet-Friend advanced on seeing Alī-Nūr's mother and kissed her hand. The wazīr's wife embraced her on both cheeks, saying: 'Health and delight to you from this bath, Sweet-Friend! How fair and bright and scented you are, my child! You light our house, and we have no need of torches.' Sweet-Friend, moved by this kind speech, lifted her hand to her heart, her lips and her brow, and answered with an inclination of the head: 'Mistress and mother, I thank you heartily. May Allāh give you all joy on earth and in Paradise! My bath was delicious and I only wish you could have shared it with me.' Alā-Nūr's mother had sherberts and pastries brought for Sweet-Friend, and wished her health and a good digestion.

The old lady herself wished to take a bath, but, before leaving for this purpose, she commanded two of the little slaves to guard the door of Sweet-Friend's apartment, and to allow no one in on any pretext whatever, since, as she said, Sweet-Friend was quite naked and might catch cold. The little ones answered: 'We hear and we obey!' and the wazīr's wife went with all her women to the bath, after kissing Sweet-Friend a last time and being wished by her a pleasant visit to the hammām.

Hardly had she left when young Alī-Nūr entered the house and sought his mother that he might kiss her hand as was his daily custom. He hunted through the rooms until he came at last to the one reserved for Sweet-Friend. Astonished to find the door guarded by the two little slaves, who smiled at him because they secretly loved him, he asked if his mother was within. They answered, trying to push him back with their little hands: 'Oh no, oh no, our mistress is not here, she is not here! She is at the hammām, at the hammām. She is at the hammām, Alī-Nūr.' 'Then what are you doing here, my lambs? Come away from the door that I may go in and rest,' said Alī-Nūr. But the little ones answered: 'You cannot come in, Alī-Nūr, you cannot come in! Our young mistress, Ṣweet-Friend, is inside.' 'What Sweet-Friend is that?' asked Alī-Nūr. They answered: 'It is the lovely Sweet-Friend whom your father, our master, the wazīr al-Faḍl, bought with ten thousand dīnārs for the Sultān al-Zainī. She has just come from the bath and is quite naked. She only has on a big towel. You cannot come in, Alī-Nūr. She will take cold and our mistress will beat us. You cannot come in, Alī-Nūr!'

All this time Sweet-Friend, who had heard what was being said outside her room, was thinking: 'This must be young Alī-Nūr, whose exploits his father told me. Can it really be that handsome youth who has not left one girl a virgin or one woman unloved in all the quarter? By my life, I would like to see him!' Unable to contain herself, she rose to her feet, all scented from the bath, her happy body bare to the joy of life, and, slightly opening the door, looked out. She saw Alī-Nūr as if the stars were just beyond her door; from that one look she reaped a thousand joys and sorrows. And Alī-Nūr also took one glance through that little space, and the sight remained with him for ever.

Alī-Nūr, carried away by passion, shouted at and pushed the two little slaves so violently that they fled weeping away. They stopped, however, in the adjoining room and, looking from far off through the door which the young man had forgotten to shut, saw all that passed between him and Sweet-Friend.

Alī-Nūr entered and found Sweet-Friend trembling and submissive upon the couch, stretched out naked with wide eyes; he bowed to her with his hand on his heart, saying tenderly: 'Sweet-Friend, was it you whom my father bought for ten thousand dīnārs of gold? Did they then weigh you in the other scale? Sweet-Friend, you are more beautiful than molten gold, your hair falls fuller than the mane of a desert lion, your naked breast is sweeter and cooler than the foam of streams.' 'Alī-Nūr,' she answered, 'to my frightened eyes you are more terrible than the desert lion, to my desirous body you are stronger than a leopard, to my pale lips you are more deadly than a tempered sword. Alī-Nūr, you are my king. You shall take me. Come, oh come!'

Alī-Nūr threw himself on the couch by Sweet-Friend's side, drunken for very joy, and they gripped each other. The little slaves were astonished, for what they saw was strange to them and they did not understand it. After kisses given and taken, Alī-Nūr slipped towards the foot of the couch and, bending Sweet-Friend's legs about his waist, plunged into her. Sweet-Friend wound her arms about him until they were one body, and, as they lay there sucking each other's tongues, nothing was to be heard for a long time but kisses, or seen save many movements. In their terror the little slaves fled weeping to the hammām, from which Alī-Nūr's mother was just emerging, all sweaty with her bath. 'Why do you weep and run, my little ones?' she asked. 'O mistress, O mistress!' they stammered. 'What harm has fallen, little wretches?' she asked sharply. Then, crying all the more, they said: 'O mistress, our young master Alī-Nūr beat us and chased us away. Then he went in to Sweet-Friend, our mistress, and they sucked each other's tongues. What he did afterwards we do not know, for he was on top of her and she was sighing. We are very frightened.' Although the wife of the wazīr was an old woman and wore at the time high wooden bath-clogs, she ran as hard as she could when she heard what had happened, and came to Sweet-Friend's room with all her women just as Alī-Nūr, having ravished the young girl, had slipped away.

The wazīr's wife, all yellow in the face, went up to Sweet-Friend and asked her what had happened. The girl answered in terms which that rascal Alī-Nūr had prepared for hèr: 'Mistress, as I was resting on the couch after my bath, a young man came in whom I had never seen before. He was very handsome, my mistress, and about the eyes and lashes he much resembled you. He said: "You are that Sweet-Friend whom my father bought for me with ten thousand dīnārs." "I am Sweet-Friend," I answered, "and was indeed bought with ten thousand dīnārs, but it was for our King, Muhammad ibn Sulaimān." "Not at all, Sweet-Friend," he answered laughing, "I know my father meant you for the King at first, but now he has changed his mind and given you to me as a present." Mistress, I am but a slave whose lot is to obey, and I think I did well. I would rather be Alī-Nūr's slave than the legal queen of all Baghdād.' 'Alas, alas, my child, what a misfortune!' cried the wazīr's wife. 'It is Alī-Nūr, my scapegrace son, who has betrayed you. Tell me what he did.' 'I gave myself to him,' said Sweet-Friend, 'he took me and hugged me close.' 'But did he take you altogether?' asked the old woman. 'Indeed he did, and that three times, dear mother,' answered Sweet-Friend. Then Alī-Nūr's mother, crying out: 'Woe, woe, the rascal has destroyed you utterly!' began to weep and beat her face with her hands. Her women imitated her, for they all now went in deadly fear of the wazīr, who, though ordinarily a mild and generous man, would never tolerate an escapade which called his own and the King's honour in question. He was quite capable, in his anger, of killing Alī-Nūr with his own hand. Therefore his wife and all her women wept as if the youth were dead already, and lo! as they did so the wazīr al-Fadl entered the room and asked them the cause of their sorrow.

His wife wiped her eyes and blew her nose, saying: 'Father of my son, first swear by the Prophet (on whom be the prayer and peace of Allāh) that you will deal with this thing exactly as I tell you, otherwise I would rather die than speak.' The wazīr swore, and then his wife told him of Alī-Nūr's pretended trick and of the irrevocable harm which had come to Sweet-Friend's virginity.

His father and mother had put up with a multitude of Alī-Nūr's riots, but at this last one al-Fadl was stricken down. He tore his clothes, hit himself in the face, bit his hands, pulled out his beard and threw his turban far from him. Wishing to console him, his wife said: 'Do not distress yourself. I will pay you back the ten thousand dīnārs out of my own money, for I have lately sold some jewels.' 'What are you saying, woman?' cried al-Fadl. 'Do you think that I weep for the money? It is for the loss of my honour that I weep, and for the death which will surely come upon me.' 'But, my dear, nothing is lost,' said his wife. 'The King does not know of the existence of Sweet-Friend, therefore the loss of her virginity can mean nothing to him. I will give you ten thousand dīnārs and you can buy another beautiful slave for the King. Then we can keep Sweet-friend for Alī-Nūr, who already loves her and recognises the treasure we have found in her.' 'But, mother of my son,' objected the wazīr, 'have you forgotten that there is an enemy always lying in wait for us, Sāwi, the second wazīr, who will one day hear this tale? And, when he does, he will go to the Sultān and say . . .'

At this point Shahrazād saw the approach of morning and discreetly fell silent.

But when the thirty-third night had come

SHE SAID:

It is related, O auspicious King, that the wazīr al-Fadl told his wife that their enemy, the wazīr Sāwi, would go to the Sultān and say: 'O King, you gave that wazīr, whom you always claimed to be so faithful to you, ten thousand dīnārs, with which to buy you a slave. He bought you one without her equal in the whole world and, finding her beauty beyond parallel, said to that corrupt youth, his son: "Take her, my boy, you are more worthy of her than the old King who has a hundred concubines and cannot manage the virginity of one." Then that Alī-Nūr, whose special trick is the destruction of maidenheads, laid hold of the slave and slit her through and through. He still enjoys her now among the women of his father's house, the good-for-nothing stallion.'

'When my enemy Sāwi says this,' continued al-Fadl, 'the Sultān, who believes in me, will tell him that he lies. Then Sāwi will ask leave to come down upon my house with a troop and bring Sweet-Friend to the King. The Sultān will give leave, and, when he questions Sweet-Friend, she will not be able to deny the fact. Sāwi will say in triumph: "Master, you see that I am a good counsellor, and yet that traitor al-Fadl is ever preferred before me." The heart of the Sultān will be changed, and I shall be punished and made a laughing-stock before all who love and reverence me. Also I will lose my life.'

'My dear,' answered his wife, 'tell no one what has happened and no one will know. Trust in Allāh, for only what He wishes can come to pass.' The wazīr became calmer at his wife's words and began to feel more confident about the future, but his anger towards Alī-Nūr remained.

Alī-Nūr himself, when he had slipped from Sweet-Friend's room on hearing the cries of the little slaves, wandered about all day, and returning only late at night, hid himself from his father's anger with his mother in the women's apartments. She pardoned him with a kiss and secreted him carefully, helped by her women, who were all a little jealous that Sweet-Friend should have had so mighty a stag within her arms. With their assistance Alī-Nūr kept from his father's sight for a whole month, slipping into his mother's room late at night to find Sweet-Friend.

One day Alī-Nūr's mother, seeing her husband less sad than usual, said to him: 'How long is your anger going to last against our son? We have lost a slave, do we wish to lose our boy also? If this goes on he will leave us altogether and we shall bitterly mourn the only child of our bodies.' 'But what is to be done?' asked the wazīr. 'Stay with me to-night,' answered his wife, 'and, when Alī-Nūr comes in, I will make peace between you. At first you can pretend to chastise him, even to kill him; then, softening by degrees, you can marry him to Sweet-Friend. She is in every way admirable, and they love each other. I myself, as I have said, will give you the money which you have paid for her.'

The wazīr, falling in with his wife's plan, leapt upon Alī-Nūr that night as soon as he came to his mother's apartment and, throwing him on his back, brandished a knife above him. 'What would you do?' cried the mother, throwing herself between them. 'I will kill him!' cried the wazīr. 'But he repents!' wept his wife, and Alī-Nūr said: 'Father, would you kill your son?' 'Unhappy boy,' answered the wazīr, weeping, 'how could you bring yourself so to jeopardise my honour and my life?' 'Listen, father,' said Alī-Nūr, 'to these words of the poet:

> Ah, kill me not!
> The more my sins,
> The greater is your pardoning.
> In my heart's plot
> The spider spins,
> Weeds grow, the ground is hardening;
> A barren lot,
> Until begins
> My clement father's gardening.'

The wazīr, hearing these lines, allowed his son to rise to his knees; compassion entered his heart and he pardoned him. Alī-Nūr rose and, kissing his father's hands, stood submissively before him. 'My son,' asked al-Fadl, 'why did you not tell me that you truly loved Sweet-Friend and that it was not a passing fancy? If I had known that you were ready to deal faithfully by her, I would have given her to you.' 'I am ready to deal very faithfully by her,' answered Alī-Nūr. 'Then my dear child,' said the wazīr, 'I have only one recommendation to make to you, which I charge you never to forget, if you would not forfeit my blessing. Promise me that you will never take other wife than Sweet-Friend, that you will never ill-treat her, and never sell her.' 'All this I swear,' said Alī-Nūr solemnly, 'on the life of our Prophet and upon the Sacred Book.'

All the house was filled with joy at this agreement, and Alī-Nūr became freely possessed of Sweet-Friend. He lived with her in perfect accord for a whole year and, during that time, Allāh took from the King all memory of having given ten thousand dīnārs to al-Fadl for the purchase of a slave. The wicked wazīr Sāwi soon came to hear of the matter, but he dared say nothing to the King because of the high opinion in which his rival was held both by the Sultān and by all the people of Basrah.

It happened that one day the wazīr al-Fadl, hasting away from the hammām before his sweat was dry, took cold from a change in the weather and had to keep his bed. He speedily grew worse, being unable to sleep night or day, and at last a consumption gripped him so that he became but a shadow of his former self. He dared no longer put off the last duties of his life; he sent for his son and, when he came weeping, said to him: 'My child, joy has an end, good has a limit; each bill falls due, each draught has bitter dregs. To-day I drink the sharp cup of eternity.' Then he murmured these lines:

> Once he will miss, twice he will miss,
> He only chooses one of many hours;
> For him nor deep nor hill there is,
> But all's one level plain he hunts for flowers.

'Now, my son,' he went on, 'I can but tell you to put your trust in Allāh, to keep your eyes fixed on the end of man, and to take care of Sweet-Friend.' 'Father, O father, you are leaving us,' cried Alī-Nūr, 'and who will be left like you in all the earth? None knows your name save to bless it, the preachers in the mosque on Friday speak of you in their discourses and pray for you.' 'My child, I hope that Allāh will receive me and will not cast me out,' said al-Fadl. Then he pronounced the two acts of faith in a firm voice: 'I witness that there is no God but Allāh! I witness that Muhammad is His Prophet!' and, rendering his last sigh, became for ever written among the blessed.

The palace was filled with grief, news was borne to the King, and all the city of Basrah learnt of the death of the wazīr al-Fadl, son of Kahkān. Then the people, and even the little children in the schools, wept for him. Alī-Nūr spared neither trouble nor expense to make the funeral worthy of his father's memory. In the procession walked all the amīrs, wazīrs and grandees of the kingdom; the people followed after, and the wicked Sāwi was obliged to be one of the eight who carried the coffin. When the house of death was left behind, the principal sheikh who was solemnising the burial said these, among many other stanzas, in honour of the dead:

I said to the obsequious ministers of death:
  You waste your breath
In wailing him whom many mournful angels weep
  In heaven's deep.
Spread if you must the lustral water on his thighs,
  From glory's eyes
Purer aspersion sprinkles. If your fingers must
  Preserve his dust
With dark sweet gums, forget not the far sweeter balms
  Of his rich alms.
Fear not but that the shoulders of the mourners can hold well
  The shallow shell
Of him whose kindly mercies every head bowed down
  In all the town.

For long after his father's death Alī-Nūr shut himself in with his grief and refused to see anyone, but one day, as he sat sadly thinking of his father, a knock came at the door and a young man of his own age, the son of one of his father's friends, craved his admittance. When Alī-Nūr had let him in, he kissed the mourner's hand, saying: 'My friend, no man dies. He lives again in his posterity. One must not grieve for ever; your father lives again in you. The master of us all, Muhammad, the Prophet of Allāh, upon whom be prayer and peace, said: "Lift up your hearts and cease to mourn." '

Alī-Nūr did not know well what to answer. Yet he determined to renounce his grief; he had his guest-hall filled with all that was necessary for the reception of his friends and, from that time, kept open house for old and young. More especially he cultivated the companionship of ten young men, sons of the chief merchants of Basrah, and with them passed all his days in joy and feasting. He gave presents to every man and no stranger was introduced to him without having a feast given in his honour. So prodigally did he live, in spite of the sage warnings of Sweet-Friend, that one day his steward came to him, saying: 'My master, do you not know that too much generosity destroys the giver, that too many presents waste the house, and that he who gives without account deals penury to himself? The poet was right when he said:

  My silver hoard
  Is all my sword,
  Then shall I give my enemy my sword?

> My gold's a spear
> And those I fear
> Would gladly plunge it in my back, I fear.
> I will keep my golden spear,
> I will keep my silver sword,
> So shall my foes be friends and hear
> My lightest whispered word,
> And run to me and sweetly swear
> I am their lord,
> Fawning below my golden spear,
> Kissing my silver sword.'

Alī-Nūr looked curiously at his steward when he said these lines, and answered: 'Your words cannot touch me. I have but one thing to say to you, I say it once and for all: as long as you find I have enough to buy me breakfast, take no thought for my dinner. I also know the poets. One of them said:

> If I were cleared of all my minted joys,
> My golden jolly-boys,
>   I would not take it ill.
> I would forget my old expensive sweets,
> My gaily coloured treats,
>   By sitting still.
>
> There's no excess in a poor lad
> Who stays content, when things are bad,
> After the ripe expense of all he had;
>   And such am I, Sir.
>
> For whatsoever fate befall
> I'd rather die a prodigal,
> One who had lived beyond them all,
>   Than be a miser.'

After this there was nothing left for the steward to do but to bow respectfully to his master and retire.

From that day forth Alī-Nūr put no bounds to his generosity and to a certain natural kindliness which made him give all he had to friends and strangers. A guest had but to say: 'How beautiful that is!' for him to answer: 'It is yours!' A friend had but to remark: 'My lord, what a delightful house you have in such and such a place!' for Alī-Nūr to take pen and paper and, after he had written and sealed a deed of gift, hand it to the friend, saying: 'Now it belongs to you.' He behaved in this way for a whole year, giving a daily feast at morning and at night to all his friends; and at these the most reputed singers and dancers were always in attendance.

Sweet-Friend was not listened to in those days and was even a little neglected, but, instead of complaining, she consoled herself with her poetry and other books. One day, when Alī-Nūr was with her in her own apartment, she said: 'O Nūr, light of my eyes, listen to this poem:

> Surely it is a pleasant thing
>   To fill the mouths of friends with golden gifts.
>   (Only beware the shifts
> Of fortune's wing.)
>
> The drowsy nights are sent to steep
>   The over-laboured senses of the day.
>   (But of what uses are they,
> If she'll not sleep?)'

As she was saying these lines, there came a knock on the door. Alī-Nūr went to it and, finding the steward, led him to a little room next to the guest-hall, where many of his friends were feasting at the time. When they were alone together, Alī-Nūr asked the other why he had so long a face, and the steward answered: 'Master, that which I feared has come to pass; my occupation has gone, since there is nothing left for me to look after. Of each and every thing you had, not a penny remains. Here are my accounts; the two books balance exactly.' On this Alī-Nūr bowed his head, saying: 'There is no power or might save in Allāh.'

Now one of his friends in the hall had heard all this, and immediately told the others that Alī-Nūr was penniless; also the face of their host, when he returned to his guests, confirmed the news.

So one of them rose and said to Alī-Nūr: 'My lord, may I have leave to retire? My wife is lying in to-night, and I must not stay any longer away from her.' Alī-Nūr gave him leave to depart, and soon a second rose, saying: 'My brother celebrates the circumcision of his little boy to-day; I must really be present at the ceremony.' Thus, one by one, all the guests made excuse and left Alī-Nūr alone in the middle of his hall. Calling Sweet-Friend, he said: 'My dear, you do not know the misfortune that has happened to me.' With that he told her of his ruin, and she said: 'Dear Alī-Nūr, for a long time I have feared that this would happen. You would never listen to me. One day, even, you answered my remonstrances with these lines:

> If painted Fortune pass your door,
>   Seize her and bear her in and tumble her;
> She has the soul of any whore,
>   Do what you will you cannot humble her;
> Throw all your gold about and she will stay,
> Try to economise and she's away.

Not wishing for any more answers like this, I have since kept silence.'

'Sweet-Friend,' said Alī-Nūr, 'you know that I have spent all my goods on my friends, stinting them nothing. Now you will find that they will not abandon me in my misfortune.' 'By Allāh, but I am sure they will!' answered Sweet-Friend. 'We shall see,' said Alī-Nūr, 'I will go this minute and obtain some money from each of them. Then I can set up in business and leave all this pleasuring for ever.' So he went out and soon came to that street, the most beautiful in all Basrah, in which his ten friends lived. Knocking at the first door and being asked his name by a negress, he answered: 'Tell your master that Alī-Nūr is at the door, ready to kiss his hand and beg his generosity.' The negress reported this to her master, and, being told to say he was from home, returned to Alī-Nūr with that message. 'The bastard hides from me,' thought the young man, 'but the others will not treat me so scurvily.' Yet, at the second door he tried, he received the same answer and could not help murmuring these lines:

> No sooner had I come to visit these,
>   Than all the house, wife, husband, son and daughter,
> Ran out behind and hid among the trees
>   For fear I'd ask them for a cup of water.

'Surely one of them will help me, though the others are so niggard,' said Alī-Nūr, but he found not one of the ten who would give him so much as a crust of bread. So, intoning these lines:

> Man is a tree of golden oranges
>   Which all his friends delight to cluster under,
> But, as the fruit falls to them by degrees,
>   Their flight's like lightning and their scorn is thunder;
> Nor can I call this a disease in nature
> Since it applies to every living creature,

he returned downcast to Sweet-Friend and told her what had befallen. 'Did I not say it would be so, my master?' she answered. 'My advice to you now is to sell all the furniture and costly ornaments which we have in the house. We could live on them for a long time.' Alī-Nūr did as she suggested, but soon there was nothing left in the house for him to sell. When they were again penniless, Sweet-Friend threw her arms about the neck of Alī-Nūr, who was weeping, and said: 'Master, why do you weep? There still remains that same Sweet-Friend whom you called the fairest of all Arab women. Take me down to the market and sell me. You cannot have forgotten that your father paid ten thousand dīnārs for me. If God is good to us, I may fetch even more now. As for our separation, if Allāh wills that we come together again, we shall come together.' 'Sweet-Friend,' answered Alī-Nūr, 'I could not abide to lose you even for an hour.' 'I do not wish it either, dear,' she said, 'but necessity is a very powerful law. A poet has said:

> Know that the attempted thing is worth
>   Your soul's full stretch, what e'er it be;
> For though you own no king on earth,
>   Remains our lord, Necessity.'

Alī-Nūr here took Sweet-Friend in his arms and kissed her hair and the tears on her cheeks, reciting this song:

> One look from your dark eyes
> Viaticum supplies,
> I take from my last kiss
> Wine for all drynesses,
> And from one smile
> Food for a hundred mile.

Sweet-Friend then spoke with such gentle persuasion to Alī-Nūr that she won him to her plan, showing him that there was only one way by which he, the son of al-Fahl ibn Kahkān, might escape shameful poverty. Therefore he took her down to the slave-market and said to the cleverest broker there: 'I would have you know the value of her you are going to sell. I do not wish there to be any mistake about it.' 'O Alī-Nūr, my master, I am your servant and will do the best by you that I am able,' answered the broker, leading them both into a room in a nearby khān. Here Sweet-Friend lifted the veil from her face, and the broker cried: 'By Allāh, this is the slave Sweet-Friend whom I myself sold to the late wazīr two years ago for ten thousand dīnārs!' 'It is the same,' answered Alī-Nūr. Then said the broker: 'My master, each carries round his neck a destiny and may in no wise escape from it, but I swear that I will use all my cunning to sell your slave and get you the highest price in the whole market.'

Immediately the broker ran to the usual meeting place of the merchants, and waited for them there. At that time they were scattered all over the market, but very soon they assembled at the point which the broker had chosen, where Turkish, Greek, Circassian, Georgian and Abyssinian women were collected for sale. When all the buyers were assembled, the broker climbed on to a great stone, crying: 'Merchants, rich gentlemen all! Not every round thing is a nut, not every long thing a banana, all is not meat that is red, or fat that is white, all that is rosy is not wine, nor every brown thing dates! O famous traders of Basrah and Baghdād, to-day I put up for your consideration so rare a pearl of price that all your money put together would not equal her worth. See her for yourselves, gentlemen! Now what price shall we say for her?' He let them all take a good look at Sweet-Friend, and the bidding began at four thousand dīnārs. 'Four thousand dīnārs I am bid, gentlemen, for this pearl among white slaves!' cried the broker, and immediately a merchant called out: 'Four thousand five hundred!'

Just at that moment the wazīr Sāwi passed on horseback through the slave-market and, seeing Alī-Nūr standing by the broker, said to himself: 'This wastrel is probably selling the last of his slaves, after having got rid of all his furniture.' Then, hearing the price which was being asked for the white slave, he continued: 'He has not a penny, he must be selling that young woman we have heard so much about. If that is so, what joy, what joy is mine!'

Straightway he hailed the broker who, recognising him, ran up and kissed the earth between his hands. 'I myself will buy the slave,' said the wazīr. 'Bring her quickly to me that I may inspect her.' The broker, who dared not disobey, brought forward Sweet-Friend and unveiled her before the old man's eyes. Seeing the woman's unparalleled face and form, the wazīr marvelled and asked what price had already been bid. When he was told that the second bid was four thousand five hundred dīnārs, he cried: 'I will buy her at that price!' At the same time he looked so fixedly at the other buyers that they dared not raise his price for fear of his notorious vengeance. 'Well, broker, why are you standing still?' added the wazīr. 'I take the slave for four thousand dīnārs, and you may have the five hundred for your brokerage.'

The broker answered not a word but went with hanging head to Alī-Nūr and said to him: 'Master, we have not been fortunate! The slave has gone for a ridiculous price. Your father's enemy, the wicked wazīr Sāwi, must have guessed that she is your property. He insists on taking her at the second bidder's price, and none of the merchants dare to bid against him. If he were likely to pay, we might thank Allāh for a small mercy, but this abandoned wazīr is the worst payer in the whole world. I have known all his shifts and evasions for longer than I care to remember. This is what he will do: he will write you a cheque on one of his agents and send word to him not to pay you. Each time you go there the agent will say: "Tomorrow!" but that to-morrow will never come. When you are tired out with his delays, you will let him take the cheque in his hands and he will at once tear it up. Thus you will not get a penny for your slave.'

Alī-Nūr was furiously angry at this and asked the broker what could be done. 'I have a plan which I think will get you out of your difficulties,' answered the broker. 'I will walk with Sweet-Friend towards the middle of the market; you must run after us and, snatching her away from me, say to her something of this sort: "Where are you going, wretched woman? You know that I am only doing as I swore to do, pretending to have you sold at the slave-market to humble you out of your evil behaviour." Then you can give her a slap or so, and take her away; the wazīr and everyone else will believe that you simply brought her here in fulfilment of an oath.' 'That is an excellent plan,' agreed Alī-Nūr.

The broker then took the slave by the hand and led her to the wazīr, saying: 'My lord, her owner is that young man just behind us. See, he is coming this way.' As he spoke, Alī-Nūr approached the group and gave Sweet-Friend a blow with his fist, crying:

'Where are you going, wretched woman? You know I am only doing as I swore to do, pretending to have you sold at the slave-market to humble you out of your evil behaviour. Go home and try to be less disobedient in future. Do you think I need the money you would fetch? Even if I were in want, I would rather sell the least thing I have than put you up to auction.'

The wazīr Sāwi cried out, on hearing these words of Alī-Nūr: 'You young fool, you speak as if you had a least last thing remaining. All of us know that you are penniless.' With that he made as if to seize the girl by force, but all the brokers and merchants looked enquiringly at Alī-Nūr, whom they knew and loved for his good father's sake. Alī-Nūr said to them: 'I call you all to witness that you have heard this man's insolent words!' But the wazīr said: 'Good friends, it is only on your account that I do not kill this knavish fellow with a single blow.' The merchants, hearing both sides, consulted each other with their eyes and, deciding to back Alī-Nūr, cried: 'This is none of our business. Arrange it as best you can.' On this Alī-Nūr, who was naturally both courageous and splenetic, leapt for the wazīr's bridle and threw his enemy to the earth. He knelt on him and rained blows upon his head and belly; then, spitting in his face, he cried: 'Dog, son of a dog, Bastard! Curses upon your father, and your father's father, and your mother's father! O swine, O filth!' Lastly he gave the wazīr one smashing blow in the mouth which knocked out several teeth, so that his beard was dyed with blood where it was not black with mud.

The ten slaves who were with the wazīr drew their swords and were about to cut Alī-Nūr in pieces when the crowd prevented them, saying: 'Do not mix yourselves in this affair! Your master is a wazīr, but his foe is the son of a wazīr. When they are reconciled, it will be bad for you.' So the slaves prudently abstained from interfering.

When Alī-Nūr was tired of beating the old man, he took Sweet-Friend by the hand and went up to his own house, followed by the plaudits of the crowd.

The wazīr got to his feet covered, to the great delight of the people, with mud and blood and dust, and made his way to the Sultān's palace. Pausing at the lower end of the hall of King Muhammad ibn Sulaimān, he cried: 'Oppression! Oppression!' The Sultān recognised his wazīr and asked who had dared so to maltreat him. Sāwi wept and answered:

'Shall I be torn by savage hounds
And you not think
Or heed?
Shall I go thirst, while others drink,
O sacred cloud from off whose bounds
Falls rain at need?

Master, such things are committed against all you love and allow
to serve you.' 'But who has done it?' asked the King. Sāwi answered:
'My lord, I went this morning to the slave-market to buy a cook-
maid in place of the one who habitually burns my meals, and there
I beheld a young slave more beautiful than anything I have seen in
my life. I asked a broker who she was and he told me that she belonged to young Ali-Nūr, son of your late wazīr al-Fadl. Perhaps,
my lord, you remember giving the son of Kahkān ten thousand
dīnārs to buy you some perfection among slaves? It appears that this
was the slave he bought. But he found her in every way admirable
and therefore gave her to his son Ali-Nūr, a lad who, since his
father's death, has wasted every penny of his inheritance in riotous
living, and thus had been forced to put his mistress up for sale.
When I found that four thousand dīnārs had been bid for her, I
thought to buy her myself for my King, who had provided her
original price; but, when I bid four thousand dīnārs, Ali-Nūr ran
up to me, crying: "Death's-head! Calamitous and unjust old man! I
would rather sell her to a Jew or a Christian, even if you filled her veil
with solid gold." "Young man," I answered, "I do not buy for myself
but for our master, our benefactor, the King." At that he became
more angry still and, throwing me off my horse, began to beat and
maltreat me in every way, in spite of my great age and the respect due
to my white beard, until I became even as you see me now. It would
never have happened if I had not wished to please my King and buy
him a slave who was already rightly his, one worthy of his bed.'

On finishing his recital the wazīr threw himself at the King's feet
and wept for justice. Sweat stood out upon the Sultān's forehead
between his eyes; he made a single sign to those who were around
him, and on the instant forty armed guards, with great and naked
swords, stood before him. The King said to them: 'Go to the house
of al-Fadl, who was my wazīr, and destroy it utterly. Bind Ali-Nūr
and his slave, and drag them here by ropes.' The forty guards bowed
and set out upon their mission.

Now one of the young chamberlains about the palace, a youth called Sanjar, had been a mameluk of al-Fadl and brought up with Alī-Nūr, whom he had learnt to love. Chancing to be in the King's presence when Sāwi entered and the Sultān gave his orders, he slipped out and ran through side-streets until he came to the youth's house. Alī-Nūr, hearing a violent knocking, opened the door himself and would have embraced his friend, but the young man put him aside, saying: 'Dear master, this is no time for friendly words and greetings. Hear rather what a poet has said:

> Pull up the roots of your soul and flee away,
>   Torn and in exile she is better
>   Than held in fetter
> On her native clay.
>
> God spreads the vast of His carpet for your feet
>   Woven of rainy hills and valleys,
>   Gardens and alleys
> Lilied and complete.'

'What are you telling me, Sanjar?' asked Alī-Nūr, and Sanjar said: 'Rise up and flee with your sweet slave. The wazīr Sāwi spreads a net for your feet and, if you fall therein, will kill you. The Sultān has sent forty of his guards with naked swords against you two. Flee at once lest worse befall!' Then, handing a fistful of gold to Alī-Nūr, he continued: 'Here are forty dīnārs, master; pardon me that it is no more. But you lose time. Escape, in God's name.'

Alī-Nūr hastened to warn Sweet-Friend, and, when she had wrapped herself in her veils, the two left the house and came, by Allāh's help, undetected to the sea side. There they found a ship ready to set sail. The captain stood amidships, crying: 'If any have goodbyes to make, or food to buy, or a forgotten thing to fetch, let him do it now, for we are off!' All the passengers answered that they were ready, and the captain was just crying: 'Drop your moorings!' when Alī-Nūr approached and asked him whither he went. 'To the home of peace, to Baghdād,' answered the captain.

At this point Shahrazād saw the approach of morning and discreetly fell silent.

And when the thirty-fourth night had come

SHE SAID:

It is related, O auspicious King, that when the captain answered that he was going to Baghdād, the home of peace, Alī-Nūr and Sweet-Friend went aboard. At once the ship spread all her sails and left the harbour. A poet has written:

> Behold the ship!
> She races the wind
> And is victorious,
> A bird with white wings
> Lighting and balancing on the sea.

We will leave Alī-Nūr and Sweet-Friend on board her, wafted by favourable winds, and return to Basrah.

The forty guards invested the whole of Alī-Nūr's house, searching every inch of it for the fugitives. Finding no one, they destroyed the house piecemeal and returned to report to the Sultān, who thereupon gave them orders to search the city. Then he called Sāwi to him and gave him a magnificent robe of honour, saying: 'None but I shall avenge you, I swear it.' Later, after the wazīr had wished him a long and peaceful life, he ordered criers to go throughout the city and proclaim: 'If any light upon Alī-Nūr, son of the dead son of Kahkān, and hale him before the King, he shall receive a fair robe of honour and a thousand dīnārs. If any hide him, his head shall answer for it.' But, in spite of these steps, none could find out where Alī-Nūr had gone.

The ship which carried the two lovers arrived safely at Baghdād, and the captain said to them: 'This is the famous city of Baghdād, the home of sweetness! She lies beyond the assaults of winter, sleeping in the shade of her roses in an eternal Spring, with flowers and gardens and the murmur of many streams.' Alī-Nūr thanked the captain for all his kindness and, giving him five dīnārs for their passages, led Sweet-Friend towards the city.

It was decreed that Alī-Nūr, instead of taking the ordinary road, should chance on that one which leads into the middle of the gardens which surround Baghdād. Soon the two stopped at the gate of a garden surrounded by a high wall, outside which all was well swept and watered and furnished with benches. The shut door was of exceeding beauty, hung about the top with coloured lamps and having a fountain of bright water beside it. The approach of this door lay between two lines of posts which held brocaded flags.

'This is a fair spot,' said Alī-Nūr, and Sweet-Friend answered: 'Let us rest on one of these benches for an hour.' So they climbed to the top of one of the high seats, after having washed their faces and hands in the refreshing waters of the fountain. As they sat delighting in the tender breeze, sleep came to them; they covered their faces and slept.

Now the garden at whose door they slept was named the Garden of Delight, and in its midst was a palace called the Palace of Marvels. Both belonged to Hārūn al-Rashīd and, when the Khalīfah was sad, it was his wont to come to the garden and the palace to forget his cares. The palace consisted of but one great hall, pierced with forty-five windows, in each of which was hung a brilliant lamp. In the middle of the hall was a great lustre of solid gold. The place was never opened, save on the coming of the Khalīfah; on his arrival the lustre and all the lamps were lighted, the windows thrown open and the great couch spread with silk and golden velvet. Seated upon this, the Khalīfah would listen to his singers and musicians until the delight of their artistry, the calm of the night, and the cool suavity of the flower-laden breeze would widen his chest again and bring him joy. But more especially did he delight in the voice of his favourite singer, the illustrious Ishāk, whose songs are known over all the world.

The Khalīfah had appointed a good old man as guardian of the palace and gardens, one Ibrāhīm, who kept careful watch to prevent indiscreet promenaders, and especially women and children, from entering the garden to spoil or steal the flowers and fruit. That evening he was making his usual slow round of the garden when, chancing to open the great gate, he saw two people asleep on one of the benches, their faces covered with the same covering. In great indignation he cried: 'What, can these audacious people dare thus to flout my lord's commands? They little know that the Khalīfah has authorised old Ibrāhīm to punish most severely any who approach this palace. To think that they should make use of a bench reserved for the Sultān's own people!'

With that the old man cut a pliant branch and, going up to the sleepers, made it whistle in the air above their heads. He was about to give them a good thrashing when suddenly he thought: 'Ibrāhīm, Ibrāhīm, what are you doing? Would you whip people of whom you know nothing, who may be strangers, or beggars upon the road of Allāh whom He has guided to your presence? First I must see their faces.' He lifted their covering and started back in delight at the sight of two faces, fair with sleep, more lovely than all the flowers of his garden. 'What shall I do?' he asked himself. 'Yes, what shall you do, O blind old Ibrāhīm? You ought to be whipped yourself for your unjust anger.'

After a few moments of consideration, the old man covered the faces of the sleepers and, sitting on the ground before them, began to massage the feet of Alī-Nūr, for whom he had taken a sudden liking. Alī-Nūr woke up suddenly on feeling his hands and, seeing that he who treated him so bountifully was an old man, withdrew his feet in shame. Then he leapt from the bench, and taking the old man's hand, carried it to his lips and then to his brow. 'My son, whence do you two come?' asked Ibrāhīm. Tears started to Alī-Nūr's eyes as he replied: 'My lord, we are strangers.' 'My child,' said the old man, 'I am not one of those who forget the commands of the Prophet, on whom be the prayer and peace of Allāh. He has written in many places in his Book that we should be hospitable to strangers and receive them with a cordial heart. Come then, my children, and I will show you my garden and my palace, so that you may forget your troubles.' 'Whose is the garden, my lord?' asked Alī-Nūr, and the sheikh Ibrāhīm, so as not to frighten him and perhaps also from a little vainglory, replied: 'The garden and the palace are mine. I received them as part of an inheritance.' The two young people followed him, and he led them into the garden.

Alī-Nūr had seen very splendid gardens in Basrah, but he had never dreamed that there could be one like this. Away from the great door led arches of carved wood, covered with climbing vines from which hung heavy masses of grapes, some red as rubies, others black as ebony. The alley in which they walked was shaded by trees bending under the weight of ripe fruit. In their branches birds piped their airy music; the nightingale drew out her sweet complaint, the turtle-doves sang love songs, the blackbird whistled like a boy, the ringdove murmured as if drunk with wine. Each fruit-tree was represented by the richest of her kinds. There were sweet-almond and bitter-almond apricots, together with apricots of Khurāsān; the fruit of the plum trees fell crimson like the lips of girls; the mirabelles were sweet as sugar; there were red figs, white figs, and green figs all together.

The flowers were pearl and coral; there were roses fairer than the cheeks of a first love; violets looked like sulphur burning in the night; white flowers of the myrtle shone there with stocks and gilli-flowers, anemones and lavender. Their heads shone in the dew; the camomile laughed to the narcissus with all her lips; the narcissus looked at the rose with deep dark eyes. Citrons hung down like splendid cups, lemons were lamps of gold. Everywhere lay the coloured carpets of a thousand flowers, for Spring reigned in the garden; nourishing streams moved through the grass like silver snakes, waterfalls tinkled, birds sang to each other and then fell silent waiting for a reply. The South wind murmured like a flute and the West wind answered with a sound of piping.

Thus was the garden as Alī-Nūr and Sweet-Friend saw it with the sheikh Ibrāhīm. Soon the old man, who did not wish to do things by halves, led them into the Palace of Marvels itself.

They stopped on the threshold, their eyes dazzled by the splen-dour of what they saw, for indeed there was never such a hall in all the world, such riches or such taste in the arrangement of them. For a long time they examined the place, and then looked out of one of the windows to rest their eyes from such bright splendour. As Alī-Nūr leant there, the moon shining over the garden reminded him of his past honours, and he said to Sweet-Friend: 'Indeed, my love, this place is very pleasant to me; it recalls only pleasant things. Peace has fallen upon my soul, and the fire which burned about my heart has sunk to a spark only.'

The sheikh Ibrāhīm brought them things to eat, and they feasted abundantly. Then, after washing their hands, they returned to the window and stood looking out. Soon Alī-Nūr turned to his host, saying: 'O Ibrāhīm, have you no drink to give us? Surely it is usual to drink after eating.' Ibrāhīm brought them a porcelain cup filled with fresh water, but Alī-Nūr said: 'That is not quite the kind of drink I wanted.' 'Is it wine you wish for?' asked the old man. 'Certainly it is,' said Alī-Nūr. 'Allāh protect me from its snare!' cried Ibrāhīm. 'For thirteen years I have not touched the wicked stuff, for the Prophet (on whom the peace and prayer of Allāh), has cursed them who taste fermented drink, with him who makes it and him who sells it.' 'I can resolve your difficulties in two words,' said Alī-Nūr. 'If I can show you a way of complying with my request without either drinking or making or buying wine, will you be accursed?' 'I think not,' answered the other, so Alī-Nūr continued:

'Take these two dīnārs and these two dirhams, mount your ass and ride to the market. Stop before the shop of a rose-water seller, for such folk always keep wine at the back of their shops, and call on the first passer-by to purchase two dīnārs' worth of wine and keep the two dirhams for himself. He will load the wine upon the ass and we shall drink it without your suffering the least stain in the sight of God.' The old man laughed aloud at this suggestion, saying: 'By Allāh, I have never met a more charming or witty fellow.' 'Then,' said Alī-Nūr, 'in God's name do as we require.'

On this old Ibrāhīm, who had not wished his guests to know before that there was great stock of fermented liquor in the palace, said to Alī-Nūr: 'My friend, here are the keys to the cellar. It is always kept filled in case the Prince of Believers should visit his palace. Enter and help yourself to all you need.'

Alī-Nūr entered the cellar and stood thunderstruck. Along all the walls and in great racks were ranged row on row of golden flagons, silver jars, and crystal bottles crusted with every kind of gem. The young man chose the rarest wines and set out the bottles on the carpet by Sweet-Friend's side. Then, after pouring wine into gold-circled cups, he sat down. While they drank together and regarded all the splendour round them, Ibrāhīm brought them perfumed flowers to crown their cups and then, as there was a woman present, sat down far from them. Soon wine brightened the cheeks of the lovers, their eyes wantoned like those of gazelles, and Sweet-Friend let down all her hair. It was not long before old Ibrāhīm became jealous of their happiness, saying to himself: 'Why should I sit far off when I may never find another chance in all my days to feast with two such beautiful young people?' He therefore got up and moved nearer to them, and then, on Alī-Nūr's invitation, sat frankly down beside them. The young man filled a cup of wine and offered it to Ibrāhīm, saying: 'Drink this generous wine, old man, for joy is at the bottom of the goblet.' 'Allāh save me from its snare, young man,' answered Ibrāhīm. 'I have not tasted it for thirteen years, and in that time I have twice made the sacred pilgrimage to Mecca.'

Alī-Nūr, who very much wished to make him drunk, took two or three cups himself and fell over as if asleep. Sweet-Friend then looked sorrowfully at the old man and said: 'See, Ibrāhīm, how he behaves towards me. It is always the same. He drinks and drinks and then sleeps, so that I am left without a companion in my cups. How can I enjoy the wine when I have no one to drink with me, or sing when there is none to hear?' Softened by her burning glances and her sighing voice, old Ibrāhīm replied: 'I must confess it does not seem a very gay way to drink.' Sweet-Friend filled a cup and, handing it to him with a languorous glance, said: 'Drink it to please me. I will be so grateful.' Ibrāhīm drank one cup and then a second, but, when Sweet-Friend poured him out a third, he answered that he had already had enough. Nevertheless she gently insisted and leant over him, saying: 'As Allāh lives, you must.' So he took the cup and was carrying it to his lips when Alī-Nūr burst out laughing and sat up.

At this point Shahrazād saw the approach of morning and discreetly left the rest of her tale for the morrow.

But when the thirty-fifth night had come

SHE SAID:

It is related, O auspicious King, that Alī-Nūr burst out laughing, and said to Ibrāhīm: 'What are you doing? Did I not beg you to drink just now and did you not refuse, telling me some great tale about a thirteen years' abstention?' The old man was ashamed and hastened to explain that Sweet-Friend had made him drink. The two young people laughed afresh, and Sweet-Friend whispered to Alī-Nūr: 'Leave me alone, and do not mock him. We shall have a good laugh presently.' So saying, she poured a cup for herself and one for Alī-Nūr, and the two went on drinking round after round without paying any attention to the old man. At last Ibrāhīm could contain himself no longer and called out: 'This is a strange way to invite people to drink! Have I got to look on all the time?' At this the hilarity of the other two knew no bounds, and the three drank together in great amity until a third of the night had passed.

At length Sweet-Friend asked Ibrāhīm's permission to light one of the candles in the lustre. 'One only, one only,' answered the old man, who was already half drunk, but Sweet-Friend lit all the eighty candles before returning to her seat. Then Alī-Nūr asked leave to light one of the lamps, and proceeded to light the whole eighty, including the forty-five in the windows, without Ibrāhīm taking the least notice. Thus the whole palace and garden were one blaze of light, and Ibrāhīm, who was now quite reckless with his drink, rose, saying: 'You are two pretty scamps!' and himself threw open all the windows. Afterwards he sat down with the two lovers and drank again, making the hall ring with laughter and song.

Now Destiny, which lies between the hands of God, the Hearer, the Maker, had decreed that the Khalīfah Hārūn al-Rashīd should be looking out, just at that time, from a window of his palace on the Tigris, enjoying the moonlight and the cool of the dark. Chancing to look across the water, he saw a great glare in the sky and, not knowing what to make of it, called for his wazīr Jafar al-Barmaki. When Jafar came, the King cried: 'Dog of a wazīr, is this how you inform yourself of what passes in my city? Baghdād might be taken by assault and you not know it. Do you not see, wretch, that my Palace of Marvels is all lighted up, that someone has had the impudence to light all the lights and throw open all the windows? How can I be Khalīfah of Baghdād and such a thing come to pass?' 'My lord,' asked Jafar, 'even if it were so, who can have told you of it?' 'Look for yourself,' said the Khalīfah. So Jafar looked from the window and lo! the Palace of Marvels shone like a fire across the river and dimmed the lustre of the moon.

The kind-hearted Jafar, imagining that this was some imprudence committed by old Ibrāhīm to make a little money, said to the Khalīfah: 'Prince of Believers, old Ibrāhīm came to me last week and, saying that he was most anxious to perform the rites of circumcision for his son during your lifetime and mine, begged leave to have the rites performed in the Palace of Marvels. I told him to go forward with his preparations and that I would ask your leave, but somehow the whole affair slipped from my mind.' 'That is not one fault but two,' replied the Khalīfah. 'Not only did you forget to tell me, Jafar, but you did not fulfil poor old Ibrāhīm's desire. His request only meant that he would like some money for the necessary expenses, but you gave him none yourself and deprived me of the chance of doing so.' 'O Prince of Believers, I forgot,' repeated the wazīr.

'You are pardoned,' said the Khalīfah, 'but now, by the virtue of my fathers, I swear that I will spend the rest of the night with old Ibrāhīm. He is a good man, a religious man; the elders love him. I have heard that he feeds the poor, I am sure that at this moment he sits within the hall surrounded by holy men. If we visit him, some one of them may make a prayer for us which will be of benefit in the hereafter. At any rate Ibrāhīm will be delighted by the honour of our presence.' 'But the night is far spent, my lord,' objected Jafar, 'his guests will be on the point of departure.' 'Nevertheless I shall go,' said the King, and with that Jafar had to be content, though he mightily feared the upshot of the expedition.

Without more ado the Khalīfah set out towards the Garden of Delights, followed by Jafar and Masrūr, all three being carefully disguised as merchants.

The Khalīfah, who went first, found the great gate of the garden open and turned to Jafar, saying: 'He has left the gate open; that is not like old Ibrāhīm.' When they had crossed the garden and come to the outside of the palace, the Khalīfah turned to Jafar again, saying: 'First I must see, without being seen by all the holy guests of this faithful old man, I wish to take stock of who is there and what rich presents Ibrāhīm has given to each. But it seems that they must be deeply absorbed in their ceremonies, for I hear no sound of praying.' So saying, the Khalīfah climbed, with Jafar's assistance, into a high nut tree and raised himself branch by branch until he could look through one of the windows.

He saw a youth and a girl more beautiful than twin moons (glory be to Him who made them) and old Ibrāhīm, the keeper of his garden, sitting between them with a wine cup in his hand. The old man was saying: 'Queen of all beauties, one does not taste the full savour of the wine without a song. To start that marvellous voice of yours, I will myself sing you a trifle. Listen:

> O night, O eyes of love!
>
> Never drink without a song,
> Grooms who take a horse to water
> Whistle it along.
>
> O night, O eyes of love!
>
> Never, never drink at all
> Save with girls to make your passion
> Great as they are small.
>
> O night, O eyes of love!'

The Khalīfah, seeing and hearing old Ibrāhīm busied about a song which sorted ill with his white hairs, felt the vein of anger swell between his eyes. He hurried down from the tree and fixed Jafar with a piercing glance, saying: 'Never have I been so edified as by this group of holy men piously performing the ceremonies of circumcision. The night is full of salvation; climb up and take some share of the blessing for yourself.' Jafar did not know what to make of this, but he climbed into the tree as he had been told.

When he saw the three drinkers, Ibrāhīm singing and waving his cup, Alī-Nūr and Sweet-Friend looking, listening and laughing, he felt that at last his time had come. He climbed out of the tree and threw himself down before the Prince of Believers. 'Praise God, Jafar,' said the Khalīfah, 'who has made us of those who ardently follow the way of salvation and has removed the unrighteous from about our path, as we may see to-night. You are silent, Jafar, you know not what to answer? Jesting apart, I desire to know what has brought these two young strangers here, for I have never seen such beauty, such bodies, such gestures or such charm. I pardon you, Jafar, I pardon you. Let us both climb into the tree and see what more they do.' With that they both ascended to the branch opposite the window and again looked in.

Ibrāhīm was saying: 'My queen, this wine of the South slopes has destroyed my unbecoming gravity for good and all, but I shall not be truly happy until I hear you pluck the cords of harmony.' 'How can I pluck the cords of harmony, my friend, without a lute?' asked the girl, and straightway Ibrāhīm rose and left the hall. 'What is the old rascal about now?' whispered the Khalīfah to Jafar, but Jafar answered: 'I know no more than Your Majesty.'

Ibrāhīm returned in a few moments carrying a lute which the Sultān recognised as belonging to the glorious Ishāk, his favourite singer. 'This is too much!' he cried, 'I will hear her sing and if she sings badly I will crucify the lot of you, O Jafar. If she sings well I will spare the others and kill only you.' 'Allāh grant she know not how to sing!' cried Jafar. 'Why is that?' asked the astonished King. 'Because bad company is better than none, even in crucifixions,' answered the wazīr, and the Khalīfah laughed silently.

The young girl took the lute and tuned it skilfully; then, after she had played a low sweet melody which would have set the soul to dancing in a dead man and melted the heart of rocks, she sang:

> O night!

> When they saw my thirst appeased
> Where the fountain of love bubbled,
> Lo, they said, the spring is troubled.

> O eyes of love!
>
> Therefore is my love displeased;
> Let him go, I shall not scold him,
> Wanton memories shall hold him.
>
> O night!

Sweet-Friend went on playing the lute after she had finished her song, and it was all the delighted Khalīfah could do not to cry out: 'Bravo!' or 'O night!' Turning to Jafar, he said: 'Never have I heard so beautiful or so thrilling a voice!' 'Then I trust,' said Jafar, 'that my lord's anger has departed.' 'It has departed,' answered the Khalīfah. The two climbed down from the tree, and the Sultān said: 'I am determined to enter the hall and hear the young slave sing again.' 'But, my lord,' objected Jafar, 'if you go in as you are, the two young people will be confused and the old man die of fright.' 'If that be so,' said the King, 'you must think out some plan by which I can discover the whole matter without being recognised.'

While the Jafar was racking his brains, the Khalīfah walked towards a sheet of water which lay in the middle of the garden. This water communicated with the Tigris and held a multitude of fishes which came up to enjoy the food which was thrown to them. Once the Khalīfah had seen many fishermen collected about this water while he was looking out from the Palace of Marvels; therefore he had commanded old Ibrāhīm to allow no fishermen into the garden and to punish any who disobeyed the order.

That night a certain fisherman called Karīm, who was well known up and down the Tigris, had seen the garden door open and had said to himself: 'Now is my chance for a little good fishing.' As the Khalīfah approached, he was standing by the lake watching his net and singing:

> O you who go with heavy bales
> Beneath a press of sounding sails,
>   Pity the fisher by his nets at sea:
> Under a night of stars
> Weary and worn he wars,
>   That you may eat your fish in luxury.
>
> Night-long he sees the heaving breasts
> Of his nets on the water crests
>   And never any other breast sees he;

> While you wake with the day
> Beside a sleeping may
>   Whose breasts are like the sun upon the sea.
>
> Yet my laborious nights and days
> Are consecrated to His praise
>   Who gives each man a station carefully;
> By Whose eternal wish
> There're some to eat the fish
>   And some to catch them in the nets at sea.

As Karīm finished his song, the Khalīfah came up behind him and, recognising him, cried out: 'Karīm!' The fisherman turned and saw the Sultān standing there in the moonlight. Quaking with terror he said: 'As Allāh lives, O Prince of the Faithful, I have not done this through disobedience but because of poverty and a great family.' 'That is well, Karīm,' said the Khalīfah. 'I have seen nothing. Now cast your net in the water that I may have notice of my luck.' Joyfully the fisherman threw his net, calling upon the name of Allāh, and waited for it to sink. When he drew it to shore, it was bursting with a multitude of fishes of all kinds. 'Good!' said the Sultān. 'Now undress yourself.' Karīm hastened to do so; he drew off his deep-sleeved robe, patched with a miscellany of rags and jumping alive with every kind of bug and enough fleas to cover the whole earth; next he took off his turban which had not been unwound for three years. As the months went by he had sewn chance rags and tags of stuff to it, and now it was full to bursting with great and little lice, black and white lice, lice of all colours and all sizes. When he stood naked before the Khalīfah, the latter also undressed, removing his first robe of Iskandar silk, his second robe of Baalbakk silk, his velvet mantle, and his embroidered waistcoat, and put on the fisherman's robe and turban. Wrapping the head-veil about his chin, he said: 'Put on my clothes and go your way.' Thereupon Karīm improvised this stanza:

> My thanks shall swell in lasting tones
>   Because your gift is choice;
>   While I'm alive I'll praise you with my voice
> And when I'm dead by rattling of my bones.

Hardly had Karīm finished speaking than the Khalīfah felt all the skin of his body violently attacked by the bugs and lice which lived in the rags. He started throwing them from him with both hands, casting them by multitudes from his neck and breast with expressions of horror. 'Miserable Karīm!' he cried to the fisherman. 'How have you collected all these deadly beasts?' Then said Karīm: 'My lord, in a week's time you will not even feel them.' 'How, must I wear this terrible garment for a week?' asked the Sultān. 'My lord,' answered Karīm, 'I have a thing to say, and yet dare not.' 'Speak,' said the Khalīfah. 'An idea has struck me, Commander of the Faithful,' said Karīm. 'I believe that you wish to learn how to get your living as a fisherman. If that is so, you could not have better clothes than mine.'

The Khalīfah laughed again and, dismissing the fisherman, covered all the fish in their palm-leaf basket with fresh grass, and went to rejoin Jafar and Masrūr. When Jafar saw him coming, he said: 'What are you doing here, Karīm? I advise you to go away at once, as the Sultān is in the garden to-night.' At this Hārūn al-Rashīd laughed so much that he fell over on his backside, at which Jafar cried out: 'By Allāh, it is the King!' 'It is, good Jafar,' answered the Sultān, 'and you, who live ever about me, do not recognise me. How then will Ibrāhīm recognise me when he is drunk? Wait for me here.'

The Khalīfah knocked at the palace door, and old Ibrāhīm rose, crying: 'Who is there?' 'It is I, Karīm the fisherman,' answered the Khalīfah. 'I heard that you had guests, so I have brought you some fine live fish.'

Both Alī-Nūr and Sweet-Friend were very fond of fish, so, when they heard this talk of fresh and living fishes, they called delightedly to Ibrāhīm to open the door. He did so, and the disguised Khalīfah entered with many respectful greetings. Ibrāhīm, seeing who it was, laughed and called out: 'Welcome, robber! Welcome, thief! Welcome, poacher! Let us have a look at these wonderful fish.' The Khalīfah lifted the grass and showed the wriggling, leaping catch. 'They are excellent! Would that they were fried!' cried Sweet-Friend. 'You are right,' said Ibrāhīm. 'Why did you not bring them here fried, O fisherman? Take them, cook them, and bring them back.' 'I hear and I obey!' said the Khalīfah, and, as he went out, all three called after him: 'Fry them, fry them, and bring them back!'

The Khalīfah found Jafar and told him what had passed. 'I will fry them myself, Prince of Believers,' said the wazīr. 'By the tomb of my fathers, I will fry them,' insisted the Khalīfah. With that he went to the little hut of reeds where Ibrāhīm lived and hunted about until he found frying-pans, butter, salt, thyme, laurel, and all else that he needed. He went to the fire, saying: 'Remember, O Hārūn, how you were ever about the kitchen as a boy, delighting to help the women. Now is the time to show your skill.' He put butter in the pan and, while waiting for it to boil, cleaned, washed and salted the fish, and covered them lightly with flour. When the butter was piping hot, and not before, he placed the fish in it. After one side was done, he turned each piece with infinite art. When the other sides were coloured a crisp brown, he spread all the fillets on fresh green banana-leaves. Lastly, he took lemons from the garden and, garnishing the leaves with slices of them, carried all to the three in the palace.

Alī-Nūr, Sweet-Friend and old Ibrāhīm ate all the fish, and, when they had washed their hands, Alī-Nūr said: 'It is a good deed that you have done to-night, O fisherman.' Then he drew out three of the gold dīnārs which the faithful Sanjar had given him at Basrah and, handing them to the fisherman, continued: 'Excuse, in Allāh's name, the poverty of my thanks. Before some things which came to pass had come to pass, I would have freed you from the bitterness of thrift for ever. As it is, I can only give you these.' The Khalīfah kissed the coins and then pressed them to his forehead, in sign that he thanked both God and the giver.

All this time the Sultān's desire to hear the young slave sing again had been increasing, so, slipping the money into his pocket, he said to Alī-Nūr: 'I will never forget your generosity, young master. But dare I ask a further thing, that which I most desire in all the world? I long to hear this young girl play upon the lute and sing a song; lute-playing and singing are more than life itself to me.'

Alī-Nūr turned to Sweet-Friend, saying: 'If my life is dear to you, sing something for this fisherman.' So Sweet-Friend took the lute and, playing a brilliant prelude on the strings, sang this:

> Wind-blown like a reed
> Playing and singing
> She stood before us,
> The deaf took heed,
> And, as the notes came ringing,
> The dumb made chorus.

She went on playing so melodiously when her song was finished that those who heard her nearly wept. Then she smiled and broke into a second song:

> Your eyes chased all the shadows from our house,
>> Your boyish foot trod on our sill,
>> It is singing and shining still.
> Would I not scatter over all our house
>> Rare gum and musk-rose and rare gum again
>> If that could make you come again?

Sweet-Friend sang this song so pleasantly that the heart of the Khalīfah was moved within him, and he cried: 'Good, by Allāh! Good, by Allāh! Good, by Allāh!' 'You like her singing and her playing, then?' asked Alī-Nūr. 'Indeed I do!' replied the Khalīfah. So the young man who, as we have seen, was accustomed to give his guests anything that pleased them, said: 'Since you find her to your liking, O fisherman, she is yours. I am not one of those who give and then take back. She is yours as a free gift.' He rose and, throwing his cloak about his shoulders, was about to leave the hall without saying a word of farewell to Sweet-Friend, in order that the fisherman might take immediate possession of her, when she looked at him with her eyes full of tears, saying: 'Alī-Nūr, would you cast me aside and leave me thus without a word of farewell? Stay but for a moment; speak to me; listen to me:

> Blood of my heart,
> Who lie between my breast-bone and my womb,
> Would you depart?

> God of pity,
> Let death be the enchanted lover whom
> You send to me.'

Alī-Nūr drew near her and answered:

> 'Her tears are falling as I go away,
> And how will I do far from her, she asks.
> To answer that is one of the sweet tasks
> Of him who stays behind with her, I say.'

The Khalīfah was both grieved at being the cause of the separation of these two young people and surprised at the ease with which

Alī-Nūr could part with her. 'Tell me, young man,' he said, 'for I am old enough to be your father, are you afraid of being arrested and punished for having stolen this slave from someone?' 'The damsel and I have gone through stranger adventures than that,' answered Alī-Nūr. 'If our sorrows were written with needles on the corners of an eye, yet they would be a lesson to the circumspect.' 'Let me hear all,' said the Khalīfah, 'for you never know when succour may be at hand, and the consolation of Allāh is never far away.' 'How would you like to hear my story, fisherman,' asked the young man, 'in verse or prose?' 'Prose is embroidery on silk,' answered the Khalīfah, 'but verses are a thread of pearls.' 'Let it be pearls, then,' said Alī-Nūr- and, shutting his eyes, he improvised these lines:

> I am far from the bed of my mirth
> And the land of my birth,
> My father who walked the earth
> (Whose soul may Allāh save!)
> With silvered virtues such as the saints have
> Lies long in the cold grave.
> But before he died
> He gave me a slave to bride
> For whom I sighed.
> I lived in sweet expense
> With a plentiful lack of sense,
> And I date my ruin thence.
> There was much gentle strife
> Between us; to save my life
> I consented to sell my wife.
> But an old goat tried to buy her,
> Without letting the folk bid higher,
> So I rose up in my ire
> And beat him about the face.
> He was a man of place
> And plotted my disgrace.
> A friend I had at the King's
> Hinted at terrible things,
> So I took the sea's white wings.
> I am beggared in your city
> Save for this sweet-voiced, witty,
> Young and scented and pretty

Girl of the rose's hue.
If I give her to you,
I am giving my heart's blood too.

'So much for this fair series of pearls, my master,' said the Khalī-fah, 'now let us have a little of the silk embroidery of your tale.' So Alī-Nūr told him all his story with full details, still thinking that he spoke to Karīm the fisherman.

When the Khalīfah understood the whole tale, he asked Alī-Nūr what he intended to do. 'The roads of Allāh are wide roads,' answered the other. 'Listen to me, young man,' said the Khalīfah. 'I am only a lowly fisherman, yet I can sit down now and write you a letter to take to the Sultān of Basrah which will have very happy consequences for you.'

At this point Shahrazād saw the approach of morning and discreetly fell silent.

And when the thirty-sixth night had come

SHAHRAZĀD SAID:

It is related, O auspicious King, that Alī-Nūr answered the Khalīfah in these words: 'Who has ever heard of a fisherman writing to kings?' 'I will explain all the mystery,' said Hārūn al-Rashīd. 'When I was a child, I learned to read and write in the same school and under the same master as Muhammad ibn Sulaimān al-Zainī. I learned more quickly than he did to say the Koran by heart and to write beautifully; but we remained great friends, though he has become a king and I am a simple fisherman. He has never been proud or ceased to correspond with me. I have but to ask a thing for him to do it.' 'Write then, in God's name,' said Alī-Nūr, 'that I may see if it advantage me.'

The Khalīfah sat down cross-legged upon the floor and, spreading a sheet of paper over his left palm, wrote the following letter:

IN THE NAME OF ALLĀH, THE MERCIFUL,
THE COMPASSIONATE!
And after!

This letter is sent by me, Hārūn al-Rashīd, son of Mahdī of the race of Abbās, to my tributary Muhammad ibn Sulaimān al-Zainī, who is wrapped with my grace and a king over one of my kingdoms through my kindness!

The bearer of this is Alī-Nūr, son of al-Fadl ibn Kahkān, lately your wazīr, now dwelling in the clemency of Allāh.

When you have read this, come down from your throne and anoint Alī-Nūr king in your place. The authority I gave to you, I now invest in him.

Let there be no delay.

Peace be with you.

The Khalīfah sealed this letter and handed it to Alī-Nūr without telling him what was in it. The young man folded it in his turban, after having kissed and carried it to his forehead, and set out immediately for Basrah, leaving Sweet-Friend to weep her heart out in a corner.

Old Ibrāhīm, who had said nothing all this while, now turned to the Khalīfah, crying: 'Most evil of all fishermen, you have brought us two or three wretched fish worth twenty copper pieces and now, not content with receiving three golden dīnārs, you want to add this young girl to your price. But I know a trick worth two of that. You shall halve the money and share the girl with me, and, what is more, I will have first turn at her.'

The Khalīfah threw a terrible glance at old Ibrāhīm and, going to one of the windows, clapped his hands. His two companions rushed in; Masrūr threw himself upon Ibrāhīm, and Jafar handed a magnificent robe, which he had sent for in haste, to the Khalīfah, who straightway threw aside his rags and dressed himself in silk and gold.

Ibrāhīm recognised the Sultān and, though doubting he was awake, began to bite his finger-ends for shame. 'What a state is this?' asked the Khalīfah in his ordinary tones. Then the old man came out of his drunkenness and threw himself face downward on the floor, crying through his dusty beard:

> Let clemency begin
> Before your heart can harden,
> You have the power to pardon,
> I, but the power to sin.

'I pardon you,' answered the Khalīfah, and then turned to Sweet-Friend, saying: 'My dear, now that you know who I am, let me lead you to the palace.' So all of them left the Garden of Delights.

At the palace the Khalīfah gave Sweet-Friend a chamber to herself, and appointed servants and slaves to attend her. When she was settled in her new quarters, he said to her: 'Sweet-Friend, for the time being you belong to me, because I desire you and because Alī-Nūr has given you to me. I have recompensed him with the kingship of Basrah and very soon, if Allāh wills, shall send him a costly robe of honour. You will bear it to him and reign by his side as queen.'

He then took Sweet-Friend in his arms and they lay lovingly together all night.

When Alī-Nūr arrived, by the grace of Allāh, at Basrah, he went directly to the palace of the Sultān and cried a great cry. The Sultān, hearing the cry, commanded the messenger to be brought to him and, when he recognised the writing of the Khalīfah in the letter, stood up and carried the paper three times to his lips and to his brow. He read the lines attentively and said: 'I hear and I obey. The voice of the Khalīfah is the voice of God.' He called the four kādīs of the city and the amīrs, and was about to resign his throne in their presence when the wazīr Sāwi came into the hall. The Sultān showed him the letter and bade him read it. Sāwi did so and then with a quick movement of his hand tore off the bottom of the paper which bore the Khalīfah's black seal, chewed it in his mouth, and spat it to the ground. 'Miserable Sāwi,' exclaimed the Sultān in flaming anger, 'what devil possessed you to do that?' 'My King, this rascal has never seen the Khalīfah or his wazīr,' answered Sāwi. 'He is a gaol-bird, a vicious trickster. He must have found an odd scrap of the royal writing and forged this letter. If the Khalīfah had sent him, he would have provided him with a true King's letter, written out fairly by the palace scribe, and with some chamberlain or wazīr to bear him company.' 'What shall I do then?' asked the Sultān, and Sāwi answered: 'Trust the young man to me and I will learn the truth. I shall send a chamberlain with him to Baghdād; if what he says is true, he can bring us back an official letter; if not, I will find a way to make him pay in full for his misdeeds.'

Sāwi went on talking to the Sultān in this strain until the latter grew to believe that Alī-Nūr was really guilty of forgery. He flew into a violent rage and called to his guards to seize the young man and beat him. They threw him to the earth and rained blows upon him till he fainted. Then, at the Sultān's orders, they chained him hand and foot, and fetched the chief gaoler into the royal presence.

In the King's name the wazīr ordered the gaoler Kutait to throw Alī-Nūr into the deepest dungeon and to torture him night and day. Answering that he would do so, Kutait led the young man to gaol.

But, when they were in the cell, Kutait shut the door, swept the ground and, cleaning a bench near the door, covered it with a thick carpet. Then, approaching Alī-Nūr, he took off his chains and bade him repose himself on the bench, saying: 'Master, I have not forgotten the generosity of your father. Fear nothing!' Thereafter, for forty days, he treated Alī-Nūr with every consideration and at the same time sent a daily bulletin to the wazīr describing the terrible tortures and beatings which the young man was supposed to be suffering.

On the forty-first day a magnificent present came to the King of Basrah from the Khalīfah. As ibn Sulaimān was not able to understand the exceeding richness of it or why it was sent, he called his amīrs and asked their advice. Some suggested that the gift was meant for the young man who had claimed to be the new Sultān, and this reminded the King of Alī-Nūr's existence. Then said the wazīr Sāwi: 'My lord, did you not decide that it would be better to get rid of this fellow?' 'By Allāh, so I did!' answered the Sultān. 'Send for him immediately and cut off his head.' Sāwi then asked leave to have the following announcement cried through the public streets: 'Let all those who wish to see the execution of Alī-Nūr, son of al-Fadl, son of Kahkān, assemble straightway outside the palace.' The Sultān gave him permission, and he departed with his heart refreshed by gratified hatred.

When the announcement was made in the city, all the people wept, the merchants in their shops, the little children in the school. Some ran to the palace to see the sad spectacle of the death itself, and others hurried in a crowd to the gates of the prison to make a procession when Alī-Nūr should be led forth.

The wazīr Sāwi took ten of his guards and, hastening to the prison, demanded admittance. But Kutait pretended not to know why he had come and asked what he wanted. 'Bring me that young villain whom I entrusted to you forty days ago,' said Sāwi, and the gaoler answered: 'He is far gone with all the blows and tortures, but I obey.' He made his way to Alī-Nūr's cell and found him murmuring these lines:

> Walls rise about my guilt,
> My life is done,
> My blood is spilt,
> The measure of my heart is nearly run.

> There is none to save
> The remnant of my breath,
> I pant for the sweet grave
> And thirst after the sleepy cup of death.

> Guide to the feet of saints,
> Master above,
> My spirit faints,
> I sink within your love.

Kutait explained what had happened and, helping Alī-Nūr off with his own clothes, dressed him in a prisoner's rags and led him out to the wazīr. Alī-Nūr saw his foe trembling with rage and understood how lasting was his hatred. Nevertheless he spoke up boldly, saying: 'Here I am, O Sāwi. Do you think that Destiny will be always on your side? It has been written:

> They sat on a high seat
>   And snipped the robe of Justice by the hem;
> But now they lie with folded feet
>   And the worms out-argue them.

Allāh alone disposes; remember that, O my enemy!' 'Do you think, O Alī, that you can put me out of countenance with all your quotations?' answered the wazīr. 'I would have you know that I am going to cut off your head in spite of all the dogs in Basrah. As you would say, I am going to follow the advice of a certain poet:

> Let time do what it will,
> I shall do ill.

Another poet has beautifully written:

> Who sees his foe lie dead, the same
> Scores one point in the game.'

With that he ordered his guards to throw Alī-Nūr on to the back of a mule; yet they hesitated because the crowd called out to Alī-Nūr as soon as he appeared: 'Say but the word and we will stone this man. We will tear him to pieces if we die for it!' But Alī-Nūr called back: 'Do not do so, my friends. Remember rather what the poet has said:

> Fate has determined on a minute
> And I die in it.'

The guards hoisted Alī-Nūr on the back of a mule and led him through all the city, crying: 'Thus forgers die!' until they came to the Sultān's palace. Here Alī-Nūr was stationed on the place of blood, and the executioner, with a drawn sword in his hand, approached him, saying: 'I am your slave. If there is anything I can do for you, tell me now and I will do it, for your life lasts only until the Sultān puts his head out of the window.' Alī-Nūr looked to right and left, and cried aloud these lines:

> Is there none
> To strike a stroke with the sword
> Against this horde?
> He can be my lord.
> Is there none?
>
> Is there none,
> Is there none of you all
> With a hand to stay the fall
> Of life's down-tottering wall,
> Is there none?
>
> Is there none
> To fill cold water up
> In a simple cup
> For my dying lips to sup?
> Is there none?
> Is there none?

The crowd began to weep, and the executioner himself handed a glass of water to Alī-Nūr. But the wazīr Sāwi jumped from his place and broke the cup, crying in a furious voice: 'What are you waiting for?' So the executioner bandaged the young man's eyes, and all the crowd rose, as it were a sea of indignation, and their threats and curses against the wazīr were like the sudden rising of a storm. Alī-Nūr's last moment seemed to have come, but suddenly the noise of an approaching troop was heard and a great cloud of dust was seen to be sweeping towards the palace.

At this moment the Sultān put his head out of the window and, seeing the dust, told those about him to go and find out what it meant. 'Let us cut off this head first!' cried Sāwi, but the Sultān said: 'Be silent!'

Now that dust was raised by the feet of the horses of the

wazīr Jafar and his companions. The reason of their coming was this:

The Khalīfah, after one night of love passed in Sweet-Friend's arms, remained for thirty days without thinking of her once, or remembering anything of the tale of Alī-Nūr. There was no one to remind him. But on a certain night, as he was passing Sweet-Friend's apartment, he heard the sound of tears and a voice singing very low:

> Delight,
> Your shadow leaves me not
> By day or night.
> I still have got
> This semblance of a lover:
> Your shadow and your name Delight,
> Delight, Delight,
> Said and said over.

As the sound of the weeping was redoubled after the song had finished, the Khalīfah opened the door and entered the room. When Sweet-Friend saw him, she threw herself at his feet and kissed them three times. Then she said:

> Do not forget, O tree of trees
> Bowed down by generosities,
> You have not kept your promise yet;
> O golden branch, do not forget.

But still the Khalīfah did not recall her and asked who she was. 'I am the gift of Alī-Nūr, son of Kahkān,' answered Sweet-Friend. 'May I beg my King to fulfil the promise which he made of sending me back honourably to Alī-Nūr? I have been here for thirty days without tasting the nourishment of sleep.' At these words the Khalīfah sent in haste for Jafar and said: 'It is thirty days since I have heard any news of Alī-Nūr. I think it possible that the Sultān of Basrah has put him to death. But I swear, by my head and by the tomb of my fathers, that I shall kill anyone who has harmed the young man, even though he were my greatest friend. I wish you to set out instantly for Basrah and bring me news of how Muhammad ibn Sulaimān has treated Alī-Nūr.'

Jafar set out and arrived at Basrah as has been related. Hearing the cries and lamentations of the excited crowd, he asked the reason of these things, and a thousand voices told him what had happened to Alī-Nūr. Jafar hastened into the palace and wished the Sultān peace, saying: 'If any harm has come to Alī-Nūr, I am ordered to kill his oppressor and to take full vengeance on you also, O Sultān. Tell me now, how is it with the young man?'

The Sultān sent for Alī-Nūr from the place of execution and no sooner had he entered the palace than Jafar ordered the guards to arrest the Sultān and his wazīr Sāwi. He named Alī-Nūr King of Basrah and set him on the throne instead of Muhammad al-Zainī.

Jafar abode for three days of ceremony with the new King of Basrah, but, on the morning of the fourth day, Alī-Nūr told him that he greatly desired to set eyes again upon the Prince of Believers. Jafar approved his wish, and, after the saying of the morning prayer, they both set out for Baghdād, accompanied by a numerous retinue and haling Muhammad ibn Sulaimān and Sāwi along with them. Through all the long journey the wicked wazīr had plenty of time to reflect and to bite the fists of repentance.

Alī-Nūr rode joyfully beside Jafar until the company reached Baghdād, the home of peace. As soon as they arrived, Jafar told the whole story to the Khalīfah, who bade Alī-Nūr approach and said to him: 'Take this sword and cut off the head of your enemy, the most miserable Sāwi.' So Alī-Nūr took the sword and went up to the false wazīr. The latter looked at him, saying: 'O Alī-Nūr, I have behaved towards you according to my character. Do you now behave towards me according to yours.' So Alī-Nūr threw down the sword, and saying to the Khalīfah: 'Prince of Believers, he has disarmed me,' bitterly quoted this couplet:

> I saw my foe was noble, so I found a way of beating him
> By acting very nobly and by generously treating him.

The Khalīfah cried out to Masrūr, who approached the wazīr Sāwi and cut off his head with a single blow. Then Hārūn al-Rashīd told Alī-Nūr to ask for whatever recompense he wished, and the young man answered: 'Master, I desire no kingdom, nor would I willingly have anything to do with the throne of Basrah. I shall consider that I have attained the greatest happiness of my life if I may remain near Your Majesty for the rest of my days.' 'That is well spoken, and sits close to my heart,' answered the Khalīfah. He sent for Sweet-Friend and returned her to Alī-Nūr, also he showered riches upon both of them, gave them one of the fairest palaces in all

Baghdād, and appointed them a magnificent pension from the treasury. He made an intimate friend of Alī-Nūr and pardoned the Sultān Muhammad al-Zainī, re-establishing him upon his throne and warning him to be more careful in future whom he chose as wazīr. They all lived in joy and prosperity until their deaths.

'But,' continued the wily Shahrazād, 'do not believe, O King, that this story of Alī-Nūr and Sweet-Friend, pleasant though it be, is as marvellous as the tale of Ghānim ibn Ayyūb and his sister Fitnah!' 'I do not know that tale,' answered King Shahryār.

The Tale of Ghānim ibn Ayyūb and his Sister Fitnah

AND SHAHRAZĀD SAID:

It is related, O auspicious King, that there was once long ago a rich merchant called Ayyāb who had two children. The son's name was Ghānim son of Ayyūb, known afterwards as the Slave of Love. He was as beautiful as a moonlit night and combined great eloquence with a most musical voice. His sister was called Fitnah, that is to say Seduction, because she was so fair.

When Ayyūb died, he left great riches to his children . . .

At this point Shahrazād saw the approach of morning and discreetly fell silent.

But when the thirty-seventh night had come

SHE SAID:

When Ayyūb died, he left great riches to his children. There were, among other things, a hundred loads of silks, brocades and precious fabrics, and a hundred vessels of pure musk pods. These were wrapped up and plainly directed: TO BAGHDĀD, for Ayyūb had meant to take them to be sold in that city.

Young Ghānim decided, on his father's death, to go to Baghdād himself, so he said goodbye to his mother, his sister, and all his relations, and left for that city with a caravan of merchants, taking his bales with him, loaded upon hired camels.

He arrived by Allāh's good grace at the City of Peace, and hired a beautiful house, which he furnished with fine carpets, with cushions, curtains and couches. He saw to the unloading of his merchandise and then rested in his house until the traders and notables of Baghdād came to pay him visits of welcome.

Later he went down to the market, bearing a package of ten fair silk embroideries, each marked with its price, and was honourably received and entertained by the merchants. The chief of the market, after one glance at his goods, bought them for a sum in cash which gave Ghānim a profit of two dīnārs for one. This delighted him and he continued for a whole year to make daily sale of fabrics and musk pods at the same advantageous rate.

One day, at the beginning of the second year, he went down to the market as usual, but found all the shops shut and the great gates closed. As it was no feast day, he asked the reason for this, and was told that, one of the principal merchants having died, the others had all gone to take part in his funeral. Being advised by a bystander to acquire merit by attending the obsequies himself, Ghānim made the necessary ablution in a nearby mosque and hurried after the procession. He accompanied the mourners to the great mosque, where the usual prayers were said, and then walked with them out of the city to the place of tombs.

The relations of the dead man had spread a great tent over his tomb and hung it with torches and candles, so that the mourners might collect under shelter. They deposited the body in the tomb and covered it again. Then the imāms and readers of the Koran recited the usual chapters of the Book, while the crowd sat round in reverent silence. Ghānim stayed to listen with the others, although he was in a considerable hurry to return home.

The ceremonies ended only at nightfall, and, after they were finished, slaves brought abundance of meats and pastries to the mourners who ate and drank until they could hold no more. Lastly they washed their hands and sat round the tomb in silence.

As no one seemed likely to make a move until morning, Ghānim, who was very much afraid lest his house—that of a stranger and one reputed rich—should be pillaged by robbers while he was away, excused himself on the plea of urgent business and left the assembly. He managed to make his way back to the city gates in the dark, but, as it was already midnight, he found them closed. No sound was to be heard save the barking of dogs, the far-away yelping of jackals, and the howling of wolves, so Ghānim became afraid and said to himself: 'There is no power or might save in Allāh! I feared for my goods, but now I fear for my life.' With that he went back on his road to hunt for some shelter for the night, and came at last to a tomb surrounded by four walls, in the midst of which grew a palm-tree. The granite door was open, so Ghānim entered and lay down to sleep. But he could not close his eyes for fear of thus being among the dead, so he rose and looked out of the door. He saw a light coming towards him from the city, which seemed to be making for the tomb; he therefore shut and locked the door and climbed up into the top of the palm-tree. The light came nearer, and soon he could make out three negroes, two carrying a great chest, and the third bearing a lantern and a spade.

The man holding the lantern stopped with a gesture of surprise when he was quite near the tomb, and one of the others said: 'What is the matter, Sawwāb?' 'O Kāfūr,' answered Sawwāb, 'do you not see that the door which we left open this evening is now shut and locked?' The third negro, whose name was Bukhait, broke in saying: 'What a fool you are! Do you not know that the owners of these fields, when they come to visit them in the day, lock themselves in the tombs at night for fear lest wicked black men should roast and eat them?' 'That is absurd, Bukhait,' said the other two, but Bukhait answered: 'You will not believe till we have gone into the tomb and found someone there. I will tell you a further thing; if anyone is there now, he has seen our light and climbed up into the palm-tree. We will find him in the palm-tree.'

'Allāh confound all Sūdān negroes!' said Ghānim to himself. 'There is no power or might save in Allāh! How am I going to get out of this fix?'

The two negroes tried to persuade Sawwāb to climb over the wall and unlock the door, promising to cook specially for him the fattest person they found inside, without letting a drop of grease escape, but Sawwāb refused, saying: 'I may be a fool, but it seems to me much better to throw the chest over the wall, since we have been ordered to get rid of it inside the tomb.' 'But it will break,' objected the other two. 'Possibly,' answered Sawwāb, 'but if we go inside ourselves we may find a band of brigands hidden there. They often frequent tombs to share their booty.' 'You are an idiot to think of such things,' said the other two. Setting down their burden, they climbed over the wall and opened the door, while Sawwāb held the light. They dragged the chest inside the tomb, reclosed the granite door, and sat down to rest. 'We have had a long journey,' said one of them, 'and are tired enough with all this scaling of walls and opening and shutting of heavy doors. Also, it is midnight. Let us rest awhile before digging the grave and hiding the unknown contents of this box. I suggest that, as we are three black eunuchs met together, each of us should tell the story of his castration. Thus the night will pass pleasantly.'

At this point Shahrazād saw the approach of morning, and discreetly fell silent.

But when the thirty-eighth night had come

SHE SAID:

It is related, O auspicious King, that the three Sūdān negroes agreed to tell the tales of their castration and that Sawwāb was the first to speak:

The Tale of the Negro Sawwāb, the First Sudanese Eunuch

WHEN I was five years old, my brothers, I was brought to Baghdād and sold to one of the men-at-arms about the palace. He had a little girl of three, with whom I was brought up. All the people of the house were delighted that I was never tired of amusing the child with comic dances and all the songs I knew. Everyone loved the little negro.

We grew up together, without being separated, until I was twelve and she was ten.

One day I found her in a retired spot and went up to play with her as was my wont. She had just come from the hammām and was scented deliciously, her face shone like the moon upon its fourteenth night. She ran up to me and we began to play a thousand games together; she bit me and I scratched her; we pinched each other so wantonly that very soon my little zabb rose up and swelled, sticking out under my garment like a great key. The little one laughed and, throwing me to the ground, straddled across my belly. She began to rub herself along me and very soon succeeded in uncovering my zabb. Seeing it rise up so straight, she took it in her hand and began to tickle it with the small lips of her part through the fabric of her drawers. This game moved me so passionately that I hugged the little girl with all my force. She replied by grappling with me. All of a sudden, my zabb, which had become as hard as iron, pierced her drawers, penetrated between the lips and took her virginity with one stroke.

The little girl was soon laughing and kissing me again, but I was terrified at having ravished her and ran away as hard as I could.

While I sought refuge with a negro of my acquaintance, the little girl re-entered the house. As soon as her mother saw her disarranged clothes and her torn drawers, she cried out and made a close examination. When she found what she found, she fainted from grief and rage, but when she came to herself she took every precaution to hide the irrevocable accident from her husband and from everybody else. For two months she waited quietly, trying to lure me back to the house with little gifts, and when at last I returned she continued to hide the matter closely, for she loved me and did not want me killed.

It was not long before the mother managed to affiance her daughter to the young barber who waited on her husband. She paid the dowry and the wardrobe out of her own pocket, and soon the marriage-day arrived. Then came the young barber with his instruments, and people held me down while he cut my eggs from their purses and made me a eunuch. After the marriage ceremony I was given to my young mistress as a slave, to accompany her wherever she went, and all the time the mother had managed things so craftily that no one guessed the secret of what had gone before. That the guests might believe in her daughter's virginity, she stained the bride's chemise with pigeon's blood and had it carried among all the women guests, who wept with emotion.

After that, I lived with my mistress in the barber's house and was able to enjoy the perfection of her body in complete safety, since my eggs had gone from me but my zabb remained. I continuously made love to my little mistress until the time of her death. Then, when her husband, her father, and her mother had all entered into the peace of Allāh, I became the property of the treasury and was numbered among the eunuchs of the palace. That is how I am able to be with you to-night, my brothers.

Such is the story of my castration, and may peace be with you.

Sawwāb fell silent and Kāfūr, the second negro, told the following tale:

The Tale of the Negro Kāfūr,
the Second Sudanese Eunuch

BROTHERS, when my story begins I was only eight years old, but already an accomplished liar. I never told more than one lie a year, but it was always of such comprehensive brilliance that my owner, who was a slave merchant, used to drop down flat on his backside when he heard it. At last he could stand me no longer, so he had cried through the market: 'Who will buy a little negro with one fault?' A certain merchant asked what my fault might be and, when he was told that I lied once every year, bought me, fault included, for six hundred dirhams and twenty brokerage.

My new master dressed me in fitting clothes which became me very well, and I lived with him for the rest of that year. When the new year came, it was seen that she was full of fruitful promise for field and orchard, so the merchants gave feasts to each other in the gardens outside the city. When my master's turn came, he had abundant food and drink carried to his suburban garden and royally entertained his friends from morning till night. But it so happened that he had left something at his house, so he commanded me to mount my mule and ride back to the city. I was told to ask my mistress for the forgotten thing and then to return with all speed.

As soon as I drew near the house, I began to cry aloud and to shed great tears, so that the people of that quarter flocked about me; women put their heads from the windows, and my mistress rushed to open the door to me, followed by her daughters. All of them asked me the cause of my grief and I answered through my weeping: 'My master was with his guests in the garden, he went to do something against the wall, and the wall fell on him and destroyed him. I leapt upon my mule and came to tell you.' Hearing this news, my mistress and her daughters wailed and tore their robes and beat their faces, until the neighbours ran round to comfort them. Then my master's wife, to show her grief at the sudden death of the lord of the house, began, as is usual in such cases, to set the building in confusion, to break the shelves and the furniture, to throw all that might not be broken out of the windows, and to tear down the doors. She smeared all the walls with mud and indigo, crying out to me to help her in the business of grief. I did not need to be invited twice, but set to with a will to destroy the presses, the heavier furniture and all the china. I burnt all the beds, the carpets, the curtains and the cushions, and then took hold of the house itself, wrenching and hacking away at the ceilings and the walls until the whole was a ruin. And all the time I did not cease to weep and cry: 'My master, oh, my master!'

My mistress and her daughters next tore away their veils and ran out into the street with uncovered faces and dishevelled hair. They commanded me to lead them to the place where their lord was buried under the ruin of the wall, as they wished to coffin him and give him a noble funeral. I went before them, crying: 'My master, oh, my master!' and soon a huge crowd joined themselves to us, the men mourning and the women weeping with uncovered faces and disordered hair. I took great pleasure in leading them through every street in the city, so that more and more men and women, children, maidens and old grannies joined themselves to our band, crying, when they heard of the disaster: 'There is no power or might save in Allāh!'

Soon certain of our followers advised my mistress to tell her grief to the walī; therefore they all turned aside to seek him while I went forward alone towards the garden.

At this point Shahrazād saw the approach of morning and discreetly fell silent.

But when the thirty-ninth night had come

SHE SAID:

It is related, O auspicious King, that the eunuch Kāfūr continued his story in these words:

While I ran towards the garden, the women told the walī of their grief, so he mounted on horseback and, commanding workmen to follow him with spades and sacks and baskets, joined the mourning crowd which was hastening along the road I had pointed out to them.

I threw earth on my hair, beat my face, and approached the garden, crying: 'My poor mistress, my poor little mistresses, my poor young masters!' I rushed into the middle of the guests with an extravagant show of grief, yelling: 'Ah, who will help me? What woman will ever be so good as my poor mistress?' Naturally my master changed colour when he heard me and asked what had happened. 'Master,' I answered, 'I came to the house and found that it had fallen in ruins about my mistress and your children.' 'But my wife was saved?' he cried. 'Alas, she was not!' I answered. 'No one escaped. Your eldest daughter was the first to go.' 'But my youngest daughter?' he questioned. 'Dead, dead!' I replied. 'But my mule?' he cried next. 'No, master, no,' I said, 'the walls of the house and the walls of the stable fell upon all you owned with life in it, even upon the sheep, the geese, and the hens. There is nothing beneath the ruins but a mass of dead flesh. Nothing is left alive.' 'But my eldest son?' he cried. Then said I: 'No one is left alive. You have neither house nor family, nor the least remaining trace of either. As for the sheep, the geese, and the hens, the cats and dogs are gorging upon them at this moment.'

Light changed to darkness before my master's eyes, his back relaxed and he wavered upon his limbs. He tore his clothes, pulled out his beard by handfuls, threw his turban far from him, and beat his face until the blood came, crying: 'My children, my wife! My grief, my extravagant misfortune!' and all his guests flocked round him, weeping and wailing and tearing their garments.

Staggering like a drunken man and still beating himself about the face, my master hurried from the garden followed by all the merchants, but the first thing he saw was a great cloud of dust from which proceeded lamentable cries. Presently from out the dust appeared the walī and a great crowd of folk who wept and hurried forward.

The first person whom my master met, as he ran to join these people, was his own wife. When he saw that she was followed by all his children, he laughed like a madman. His family threw themselves upon his neck, crying: 'Husband!' 'Father!' 'Thank God that you are safe!' 'Are you all well, my dears?' he shouted. 'What happened to you in the house?' 'Thank God that I look upon your face again!' cried his wife. 'How did you save yourself from the ruins of the wall? We are all safe and well, nothing has happened save the terrible piece of news announced by Kāfūr.' 'What news is that?' asked my master, and his wife answered: 'Kāfūr came to the house in a miserable state of grief, telling us that you had gone aside to do something against the wall, and that the wall had fallen upon you and crushed you.'

'But, as God lives,' broke in my master, 'Kāfūr came to me just now and told me that the house had fallen on you all and killed you!' So saying he turned and saw me pouring earth upon my head, weeping, tearing my garments, and throwing my turban afar off, first to one side and then to the other. He ran up to me, crying: 'Miserable slave, ill-omened blackamore, son of a whore and a thousand dogs, cursed child of a cursed race! Why have you plunged us all into such terrible grief? As Allāh lives, I will tear your skin from your flesh and your flesh from your bones!' Fearlessly I answered: 'I defy you to do me the least harm. You bought me with my fault before witnesses. You were particularly told that my fault was the telling of one lie a year, and, let me assure you, this is only half a lie; I shall hold the other half in reserve and complete my lie in some other manner.' 'Vilest of all blacks!' cried my master, 'do you call that only half a lie? Son of a dog, I free you, you are no more man of mine!' 'You free me, do you?' I answered. 'Well, I shall not free you until my year is up and I have achieved the other half of my lie. Then, if you like, you can sell me again, with fault; but as for freeing me, you cannot do that because I know no trade. Such is the law.'

While we were speaking the crowd formed round us, the walī and all the merchants joining in. My master explained what had happened, adding: 'That, I beg you to observe, is only half a lie.' His hearers, thinking that the matter was too serious to be called half a lie, loaded me with curses, but I stood there laughing and said to them all: 'I was bought with my fault. How can you blame me?'

When we came at last to the street in which my master lived, he saw a heap of ruins where his house should have been and, being told by his wife with some exaggeration that I had done all the damage, he waxed even more furious than before. 'Bastard son of a bitch!' he cried. 'If this was a half lie, what would one of your whole lies be like? I should imagine a couple of cities would be destroyed by one of your really good whole lies.' With that he haled me before the walī and I tasted an artistic meal of stick, till I fell in a faint.

During my unconsciousness a barber was sent for, who castrated me completely and cauterised the wound with red-hot irons. I woke to find myself a eunuch for good and all, and to hear my master saying: 'You destroyed things which were very dear to me: I have destroyed things which were very dear to you.' Later he took me to the market and sold me for a much greater price than I had fetched before, because I was a eunuch.

Since that time I have sown as much discord and trouble as I could in all the houses where I have been employed as eunuch, therefore I have been constantly moved on from one master to another, one amīr to another, one notable to another, until at last I am in the service of the Prince of Believers himself. But I am very much reduced now, my old strength has failed me since I lost my eggs.

That, brothers, is the story of my castration. I have finished. Peace be with you!

When the two other negroes heard his story, they mocked him, saying: 'Rascal, son of a rascal, that was a splendid lie!'

Then Bukhait, the third negro, turned to his two friends and said:

The Tale of the Negro Bukhait, The Third Sudanese Eunuch

K NOW, O cousins of mine, that the two stories we have heard are useless and ridiculous. I will tell you about the destruction of my eggs, and you shall see that I deserved an infinitely worse fate. I outraged my mistress and fornicated with her little son.

But the details of this fornication are so extraordinary, so rich in savoury incident, that the tale is too long to tell you here. Morning approaches and we may get into very serious trouble if the light surprises us before we have dug a hole and buried this chest. Let us do the work for which we were sent, and afterwards, when we are safely home again, I will tell you all the details of my fornication and castration.

The negroes then rose from their rest and dug, by the light of the lantern, a hole large enough to contain the chest. Kāfūr and Bukhait dug, while Sawwāb carried the earth out in a basket and threw it beyond the tomb. When the hole was sufficiently deep, they buried the chest, smoothed the earth above it, and hurried away with their tools and lantern.

Although Ghānim was alone at last and very anxious to know what the chest might contain, he waited till dawn to climb down from the palm-tree. When light had fully come, he dug in the soft earth with his hands and lifted the chest out of the hole. Then, picking up a stone, he broke the locks and threw back the lid. Inside was a sleeping girl, drugged seemingly with banj, whose bosom rose and fell in regular breathing.

You have never seen a girl so beautiful, with such surprising delicacy of colour. She was decked from head to foot with gold and jewels; about her neck was a collar of solid gold, half hidden by bright stones; a single splendid gem hung from each ear, and there were diamond bracelets about her ankles and about her wrists. She was worth a sultān's ransom as she lay there.

When Ghānim saw that this girl had received no violence from the lecherous negroes who had buried her alive, he took her in his arms and laid her down in the open air. The life-giving breeze entered her nostrils, her colour deepened, and she sighed. Then she coughed and sneezed, and there flew from her mouth a lump of banj, enough to send an elephant to sleep for twenty-four hours. She opened her eyes—ah, God, what eyes they were!—and turned their adorable glances upon Ghānim. She was still under the influence of the drug and very sweetly murmured: 'Where are you, little Breeze? I am thirsty, give me something to drink. Where are you, Garden Flower, and you, Dawn? Where are you all, my ladies, Light on the Road, Night Star, Morning Star, Sweetness of Gardens? Why do you not answer?' As none spoke, the girl opened her eyes fully and looked about her. She cried in terror: 'Ah me unhappy! I am alone among the tombs! Who has taken me from among the beautiful curtains of my palace and thrown me upon the stones of the dead? That such wickedness can be! O You from Whom no secrets are hid, O Avenger, I pray You bear this crime in mind upon the day of judgment!'

Ghānim, who had been standing silent all this time, now stepped forward and said: 'Queen of beauty, whose name is doubtless sweeter than date juice, whose body is certainly more pliant than a palm frond, I am Ghānim ibn Ayyūb. There are no curtains here, it is true, but neither is there anything to fear. Our omnipresent Lord has sent your slave to make an end of all your misfortunes and lead you back into the way of happiness. Think a little kindly of me, O desirable.' With that he fell silent.

The young woman perceived that he was real and not the creature of a dream, so she said: 'I witness that there is no God but Allāh! I witness that Muhammad is His Prophet.' Then, turning her bright eyes on Ghānim, she placed her hand upon her heart and continued in a voice sweeter than water: 'O thrice welcome youth, I have woken up in a strange place; can you tell me who brought me here?' Ghānim told her the whole story of the three negroes and begged her in return to make him acquainted with the circumstances which had led up to the crime. But she answered: 'I praise God, who has raised me up a helper such as you. I beg you first to help me back into the chest and then to go out as quickly as you can and hire a mule. I can travel in the chest as far as your house without being seen, and, when I get there, I will not only tell you all my story, but will bring you more happiness and fortune than you can dream possible.'

Ghānim joyfully left the tomb and, as it was now full day, found no difficulty in hiring a man with a mule and returning with him. He helped the man to load the chest upon the animal, and, while they journeyed towards his house, his mind was filled with pleasant thoughts. He knew that he loved the girl and rejoiced to think that she would belong to him, seeing that she was worth a good ten thousand dīnārs in herself, and had jewels and robes worth untold gold. When they arrived at the house, he helped the muleteer to carry the chest indoors.

At this point Shahrazād saw the approach of morning and discreetly fell silent.

But when the fortieth night had come

SHE SAID:

It is related, O auspicious King, that Ghānim helped the girl out of the chest, and she began to examine the dwelling in which she found herself. Seeing a well-built house, carpeted with joyous colours and hung with silks of a thousand pleasant tints, seeing rich furniture, fabrics of price, bales of merchandise and vessels of musk pods, she realised that Ghānim was a great merchant, so she lifted the little veil from off her face and looked fixedly at the young man. She found him handsome and taking in his ways, therefore she loved him and said: 'See, Ghānim, I have uncovered my face before you! But I am very hungry, I beg you bring me something to eat.'

Ghānim hurried to the market and bought an exquisitely-roasted lamb, a plate of the best pastries made by Hajj Sulaimān, a plate of halwā, almonds, pistachios, fruits, jars of old wine, and flowers in varied abundance. Returning, he arranged the fruits in great porcelain dishes, the flowers in vases of price, and placed all he had bought before the young girl. She smiled and pressed herself close to him, throwing her arms about his neck and saying a thousand sweet things. Ghānim, who felt love growing in his heart by leaps and bounds, sat down with her, and the two continued to eat and drink until nightfall. During that time they became accustomed to each other and fell more and more in love, since they were of the same age and both beautiful. At nightfall Ghānim lit candles and lamps all about the place, and the hall shone with a double splendour, because their faces were lighted with the flame of love. He brought stringed instruments and more wine, and the time passed upon young wings, with song and verse and laughter, and a thousand pretty games. As the hours slipped away their passion grew. Glory be to Him who joins the hearts of men and women, and brings young lovers together in the night!

They joyed together until the dawn, and then slept in each other's arms without more than sleep befalling. As soon as he woke Ghānim bought more entertainment of all kinds from the market, wishing to give his lover of the best. After they had eaten, they drank long and deep until their cheeks became red and their eyes shone black and bright. At length Ghānim, who ardently desired to kiss the girl and lie with her, asked leave to quench the fire in his entrails by touching her mouth with his lips. But she said: 'Wait, my dear, till I am drunk and do not know what is happening. Then you may kiss me and I will not feel your lips suck mine.'

Later, when the wine had overcome her modesty, she took off all her clothes, save her drawers and a fine chemise and the little veil of white silk pounced with gold which confined her hair. Seeing her so, Ghānim called out in his desire: 'My love, may I not kiss you now?' 'O Ghānim that I love,' answered the girl, 'that is one thing which I cannot allow you, for there is a sinister word written upon the string of my drawers. Nor may I show it to you yet.' As Ghānim could not do what he wished his passion knew no bounds, so he seized his lute and sang:

> I begged a kiss from her red mouth,
> A little kiss to cool my drouth,
> One kiss to set my heart at rest;
> But she said: 'Talking is the best.
>   No, no, no, no; no, no, no, no;
>   Well-bred young men do not do so.'
>
> I must confess I urged: 'Yes, yes!'
> So she said: 'If by force you press

Your lips to mine, know, there's no bliss
In an unwilling or rude kiss.
    No, no, no, no; no, no, no, no;
    Well-bred young men do not do so.'

I said: 'A kiss against the will,
That has a touch of pleasure still,
It has a tang of mild delight.'
But she: 'Such kisses are not right.
    No, no, no, no; no, no, no, no;
    Well-bred young men do not do so.'

Fire blazed in Ghānim's body when he had made an end of this song, for the girl allowed him nothing, though she appeared to return his love. He pressed and she denied till nightfall, when Ghānim rose and lit all the lights about the hall. Then he threw himself down before the girl and pressed his lips to her intoxicating feet, and they melted under his kisses like fresh cream. He thrust his head between them and pushed on up the legs and thighs, pasturing his lips on warm flesh of rose and musk and jasmine. She trembled like a bird with all its plumes, and Ghānim cried, the tears of passion filling the corners of his eyes: 'Pity the slave of love, my mistress, the captive of your body. I was at peace before you came.' 'Light of my eyes,' answered the girl, 'I swear that I love you madly and that all my body cries for you. Yet you must never do this thing, for a reason which I will tell you to-night.' She sank into his arms, kissing and promising a thousand follies, until the morning came without her having told her secret.

Day and night, with increasing passion, this frustrated love continued for a whole month, till, on a certain night when they lay side by side drunken with wine and unfulfilled desire, Ghānim slipped his hand below the girl's chemise and, stroking her belly down until he reached her navel, began to play with the petals of the flesh he found there. As his finger wantoned within this crystal cup, the girl achieved a moment of sobriety and, carrying her hand to her drawers, felt that they were still fastened by their gold-tasselled cord. Reassured, she fell again into a half slumber, and Ghānim took hold of the cord that he might loosen it and enter into the garden of delight. The young woman, feeling him do this, sat bolt-upright and asked him what he was about. When he answered that he wished to possess her completely, she said: 'Listen, dear Ghānim, and I will tell you why I have never let your manhood sweetly pierce me. I do not wish you to judge me too hardly. See the writing that is woven on this cord.' Ghānim looked at the broad of the cord of her drawers and there saw written in gold embroidery: I AM YOURS AND YOU ARE MINE, CHILD OF THE PROPHET'S UNCLE.

Ghānim withdrew his hand from the cord as if it had been a snake, and the young girl said:

'I am the favourite of the Khalīfah Hārūn al-Rashīd, even as it is written upon the cord. For him I keep the savour of my lips and the mystery of my body. I am called Kūt al-Kulūb, the Food of Hearts. I grew up from babyhood in the Khalīfah's palace and became so beautiful that he was enamoured of the handiwork of God as shown in me, gave me an apartment to myself, and allotted ten delightful slaves to be my companions. He made me presents of all those costly things which you found upon me when I was buried, and preferred me even to his favourite wife Zubaidah, so that she hated me.

'One day, when the Khalīfah was absent making war against a tributary who had rebelled against him, Zubaidah corrupted one of my slaves, who had previously been in her own service, gave her a piece of banj, and commanded her first to drug my drink with it and then, when I was asleep, to place it in my mouth. The girl, delighted by promises of liberty and gold, did as she had been commanded; I fell down in convulsions, my feet were drawn up to my head, and I thought that I was dying. The slave sent for Zubaidah when she saw that I was fast asleep, and the queen bribed three eunuchs and the door-keepers; I was carried out at night and buried in the tomb from which you delivered me. Now I abide a thrall to your generous hospitality.

'Only two things trouble me: the first, that I do not know what the Khalīfah will think when he comes back and does not find me; the second, that I am bound by the cord of my drawers never to feel you moving in the depths of me, O Ghānim, O beloved!

'Such is my story. I pray you keep it secret.'

Ghānim retired to the bottom of the hall out of respect for the Khalīfah, when he heard that Kūt al-Kulūb belonged to him. As if she had become a sacred thing, he dared not look upon her, but sat alone in a corner bewailing his criminal intentions, his presumption in having touched the girl's royal flesh, and the calamitous love which had come upon him. Nevertheless he said: 'Glory to Allāh, who lets grief work within noble hearts, while the wicked heart is merry!' Then he intoned these lines:

> Hearts held within the small hot hand of love
>   Burn, turn, and yearn,
> The wits of him who shrines a girl above
>   Turn, yearn, and burn,
> One kiss or two comes; if that's not enough,
>   Yearn, burn, and turn.

The girl went down to Ghánim and, throwing herself upon his breast, strove to console him, but he did not dare to answer her tenderness because she was the favourite of the Prince of Believers. He let her do what she would, but did not return her kisses. She had not expected so sudden a change on the part of her lover, so she redoubled her caresses and with a fluttering hand tried to make him answer that passion which his coldness had notably increased in her own heart.

But Ghánim repulsed her and, when morning had come, hastened to the market and was absent for a whole hour, laying in even more costly provisions than he had provided when he did not know the rank of his guest. He bought all the flowers in the market, the finest of roast sheep, the freshest of pastries, those sweetmeats which were fullest of fruit juice, the most delicious creams, the ripest dessert, the biggest and most golden rolls.

Scarcely had he entered the house again when the girl ran to him, rubbed herself against him languorously and, with a smile, turned upon him eyes black with passion and swimming with desire. 'By Allāh, my darling, my heart,' she cried, 'you have been away a year! I can hold myself back no longer! My passion has become more than I can bear. Take me, Ghánim, take me or I die!' 'Allāh save me from doing so, my dear mistress,' answered Ghánim, pushing her gently away from him. 'Can a dog go up into the place of a lion, or a slave take that which belongs to the master?'

Sadly he sat himself in his corner, but she took him by the hand and led him to where the cloth was spread. They ate and drank together, and she saw to it that he became drunk. When he lay back, overcome with wine, she threw herself upon him and pressed against him. Allāh alone knows what she did with him. At last she took her lute and sang:

My dear
Is timid as a deer,
And yet a flying deer sometimes looks back.
My heart
Is given to a hart
Which snuffs the taint of love upon its track.
My hair
Is loosened for a hare,
A flying leaf, which lets me die of lack.

Ghānim wept for a little at these lines and the girl wept with him, then they drank and made verses together until the day's decline.

That night Ghānim made two beds far apart upon the floor instead of one, and answered Kūt al-Kulūb's reproaches by saying: 'That which is the master's cannot belong to the slave.' But she cried out: 'Away with this obsolete morality, dear my lord! Let us ensnare the flying lust to-night! To-morrow she may be gone. What will be, will be, O my heart's desire.' But Ghānim would not. She burned the more and cried: 'As God lives, we will lie together to-night!' But Ghānim would not. 'Come, my beloved,' she entreated, 'all my flesh lies open to you. My desire is crying and calling towards you. Ghānim of my life, take these blossoming lips, this body ripened by passion!' But Ghānim would not. 'My skin is moist with my desire, I am naked to your kisses, Ghānim,' she whispered. 'My skin breathes like an orchard of jasmine, touch and smell and be drunken, O my heart!' But Ghānim would not. So the girl wept and took her lute and sang:

I am slim,
I have a white limb,
Pleasing to all but him;
But he,
He does not care for me.

I never sleep.
My purple eyelids keep
Watch on a weary deep;
But he,
He does not care for me.

I am a tall
Flower branch; each and all

Would wish to make me fall;
But he,
He does not care for me.

My love is a flying
Hind; the world is sighing
To be in at the dying;
But he,
He does not care for me.

I am a flower
In the garden: at the hour
Of my scented fall in a shower
Of coloured petals, kings shall lower
And throw down their power;
But he, but he,
He does not care for me.

Yet Ghānim would not, though he was dying of desire. For
another month he dwelt with Kūt al-Kulūb, darling of the Khalīfah,
without once doing to her that for which they both longed.

While the Khalīfah was away at the war, Zubaidah could not fail
to be troubled as to what would happen when he returned and asked
news of Kūt al-Kulūb. At last she sent for a cunning old woman,
whom she had known from her infancy, and, telling her the secret,
asked what she should do.

'I understand, my mistress,' answered the old woman. 'Time
presses and the Khalīfah will soon return. I could show you many
ways out of your difficulty. The simplest and quickest is this: get a
carpenter to make a wooden dummy and ceremoniously bury that
within the palace. Have torches and wax candles lighted all about the
tomb, clothe your slaves and those of Kūt al-Kulūb in mourning
garments and spread the corridors of the palace with black. When
the Khalīfah asks the reason for this, tell him that Kūt al-Kulūb is
dead and that you have given her a funeral worthy both of him and
her. The Khalīfah will weep bitterly and call readers to watch over
the tomb and intone the Book above the dead. If by any chance he
suspects you and has the tomb opened, you need not be alarmed,
for he will find the dummy, covered with jewelry and precious stuffs,
in a rich coffin. And, if he wishes to touch her, all who are by can
tell him that it is unlawful to look upon a naked woman who is dead.

He will believe that his favourite has really departed to the peace of Allāh. He will have the tomb closed again, and you will be quit of the whole business. I promise, should Allāh show Himself propitious, that this method will be successful.'

Zubaidah gave the old woman a fair robe of honour and much gold for her excellent advice, and bade her carry out the project in her own way. A wooden dummy was made by the royal carpenter and the two women dressed it in the sumptuous robes of Kūt-al-Kulūb and fastened it in an expensive coffin. The fullest rites of funeral were undertaken, lustres, candles, and torches were lighted, and a costly dome was built above the tomb. Carpets were spread for those who prayed, the palace was strewn with black cloths, and all the slaves wore mourning; thus the news of Kūt al-Kulūb's death spread through the palace and everyone, even Masrūr, believed it.

It was not long before the Khalīfah returned from his war and, entering the palace, hastened first to the apartments of Kūt al-Kulūb, for she filled his heart. Seeing the slaves clothed in black, he started to tremble, and, when Zubaidah came to him, dressed also in black from head to foot, and told him that his favourite was dead, he fell down in a swoon. He came to himself at length and asked for the tomb of his love, that he might visit it. 'Prince of the Faithful,' answered Zubaidah, 'for the love I bore her I buried her in my own palace.' The Khalīfah went, just as he was in his travel-stained garments, and visited the tomb. Seeing the candles and the torches and the carpets, he thanked his queen for her goodness and returned to his own apartments.

Nevertheless, as he was suspicious by nature, the Khalīfah soon began to be tortured by doubts and dark considerations. The tomb was opened at his orders, but, thanks to the stratagem which the old woman had taught to Zubaidah, his suspicions were lulled and he became convinced that it was his beloved who lay within the coffin. He had the tomb closed again and called a great army of religious teachers and readers to intone the Koran above the dead, while he himself sat with them on a carpet and wept day after day until he fell into a decline.

For a whole month these ceremonies went on, and the Khalīfah ceased not to mourn over the tomb of his favourite.

At this point Shahrazād saw the approach of morning and discreetly fell silent.

But when the forty-first night had come

SHE SAID:

It is related, O auspicious King, that on the last day of the month the prayers and readings lasted from dawn till dawn. Only then might each depart to his own place. The Khalīfah, who was worn out by tears and watching, entered his palace without caring to see either Zubaidah or his wazīr Jafar, and fell into a heavy sleep watched over by two women slaves. One sat at his head and one at his feet, so that an hour later, when he woke, he was able to hear them talking together. Said one: 'This is a sorry business, Subhīyah.' 'What is a sorry business, Nuzhah?' asked Subhīyah, and Nuzhah said: 'That our dear master should pass his days and nights weeping over a tomb with nothing but a wooden dummy in it.' 'Where is Kūt al-Kulūb, then?' questioned Subhīyah, and Nuzhah continued: 'I have heard from our mistress's favourite slave that Zubaidah had Kūt al-Kulūb drugged with banj and buried among the tombs by the three eunuchs Sawwāb, Kāfūr, and Bukhai.' 'Did she die that terrible death?' asked Subhīyah weeping. 'Allāh forbid,' said Nuzhah, 'I heard Zubaidah tell Zahrah that the girl had escaped and had been living for four months with a certain young merchant of Damascus, called Ghānim ibn Ayyūb, the Slave of Love. Thus is our master deceived and weeps over an empty tomb.'

The Khalīfah listened to all they had to say, then jumped to his feet with a terrible cry which sent them fleeing, and yelled in his rage for his wazīr Jafar al-Barmaki. When Jafar came, the King said: 'Take your guards with you instantly and surround the house of one Ghānim ibn Ayyūb, rescue my favourite Kūt al-Kulūb and bring the young man to me that I may have him tortured.' Jafar hastened to do as he was bid. He summoned his guards and the walī of the city, and, having found out where the house was situated, proceeded to surround it.

At that same hour, Ghānim had set a beautifully roasted sheep, stuffed with spiced meats, before Kūt al-Kulūb, and both were eating it with joyful fingers. Suddenly the girl looked from the window and saw a troop of guards, sworders and mamelūks, led by Jafar and the walī, surrounding the house as closely as the white of the eye surrounds the black. She knew then that the Khalīfah had heard the whole story and was like to be bitterly jealous of Ghānim. Her cheeks grew yellow with dismay, and she cried: 'Save yourself, save yourself, my love!' 'Light of my eyes, how can I escape when the house is surrounded?' asked Ghānim. 'I will manage it,' she said, and, tearing off his clothes, dressed him in rags and set on his head an earthen pot filled with scraps of bread and meat. 'You can go out like this,' she said, 'they will take you for a slave and do you no harm. Have no fear for me. I know how to manage the Khalīfah.'

Without even waiting to say goodbye, Ghānim left the house with the kitchen-stuff upon his head, and Allāh took him safely through the ranks of the besiegers.

Soon Jafar lighted from his horse and, going into the house, saw the fair Kūt al-Kulūb sitting alone among rich merchandise. She had taken the precaution to put on her rarest robes and jewels, and to pack the rest in a great box. She rose as Jafar entered and kissed the earth between his hands, saying: 'This meeting was written by the pen of God. I give myself up to you.' 'Dear mistress,' answered Jafar, 'my orders were only to seize a certain Ghānim ibn Ayyūb. Can you tell me where he is?' 'Certainly,' answered the young woman, 'some days ago he packed up the greater part of his merchandise and left for his native city of Damascus, to see his mother and sister. I can tell you no more than that. As for this box of mine, it contains all my costliest belongings, so I pray you have it borne carefully to the palace.' Jafar ordered some of his men to carry the box, and himself, with every sign of deference and honour, requested the young woman to accompany him to the Khalīfah. The rest of his men he left behind to sack and destroy the house, as Hārūn al-Rashīd had commanded.

Jafar hastened to tell the Khalīfah of Ghānim's departure for Damascus, and the Sultān, believing the young man had done with Kūt al-Kulūb all that can be done to a beautiful young woman belonging to another, flew into a terrible rage and ordered Masrūr to imprison his favourite in a dark room, under the charge of an old woman who was officially concerned with such affairs.

To deal with Ghānim was not such an easy matter. The Khalīfah sent out horsemen to seek him, and also, taking pen and paper, wrote the following letter in his own hand:

HĀRŪN AL-RASHĪD, PRINCE OF BELIEVERS, FIFTH KHALĪFAH IN THE GLORIOUS LINE OF ABBĀS, TO SULTĀN MUHAMMAD IBN SULAIMĀN AL-ZAINI, HIS TRIBUTARY IN DAMASCUS.

IN THE NAME OF ALLĀH, THE MERCIFUL, THE COMPASSIONATE.

News is asked of your health, for you are dear to us, and prayer made to Allāh for your joy and your long life.

And after!

Dear tributary, a young man of your city, named Ghānim ibn Ayyūb, came to Baghdād and violated one of my slaves, doing to her what he did. Now he has returned to Damascus and lies hid from my revenge with his mother and sister.

He is to receive five hundred lashes and be carried on a camel through the streets of your city. This proclamation shall be made before him: 'Thus is a slave punished who lays hands on his master's goods.' Then send him to me and I will do in the way of torture what need be done.

You will sack his house and lay it waste, so that none may know where it stood. You will strip the mother and the sister of the young man naked, expose them for three days to the eyes of the curious, and then cast them from your city.

You will execute this order with great zeal.

Peace be with you.

A courier set out straightway for Damascus with this letter, and reached it in eight days, instead of the usual twenty.

Sultān Muhammad kissed the Khalīfah's letter and carried it to his forehead, then he set about obeying the commands which it contained. He caused criers to cry in the streets: 'Let those who would plunder repair straight to the house of Ghānim ibn Ayyūb and plunder as they will!'

Taking his guards with him, he went himself to the house and knocked at the door. Fitnah opened to him and, seeing a man, covered her face and ran to tell her mother.

The elder woman was sitting by a tomb which she had built in memory of her son Ghānim, whom she supposed to be dead since she had not heard tell of him for a whole year. She was used to sit there weeping, and took neither food nor drink. She bade Fitnah show in the Sultān and, when he came up to the tomb saying that his purpose was to seize Ghānim and to send him to the Khalīfah, she answered: 'Unhappy that we are! Ghānim, child of my bowels, left us more than a year ago and we do not know what has happened to him.' Then Muhammad saw no course open to him, though he was a kind-hearted man, but to sack the house, raze it to the ground, and bear the stones of it beyond the city. Much against his will, he stripped the mother and sister of Ghānim naked (though he allowed them each a sleeveless shift) and, after exposing them to the eyes of the curious for three days, cast them from the city. Thus they became wanderers even as Ghānim.

To return to the Slave of Love. He walked away from Baghdād, weeping as if his heart were broken, and journeyed all day without eating or drinking until he came to a certain village. He entered the mosque and threw himself down on a mat in the courtyard, his back leaning against the wall. He was more dead than alive from grief and want, his heart was beating wildly, and he had not the strength to ask for succour. He remained on the mat all night, and, in the morning, the people of the village, when they came up to the mosque to pray, found him stretched out without movement. Seeing that he was ill and destitute, some of them brought him a pot of honey and two loaves, and gave him an old tattered sleeveless lousy robe. Ghānim opened his eyes when they asked him whence he came, but he could not answer; so they stayed by him for a while and then went about their business.

Ghānim fell very ill and lay for a whole month upon the old mat, feeble, pale, and devoured by fleas and lice. His appearance became so deathly that at last the Faithful of the mosque decided to send him to the hospital at Baghdād. Some of them found a camel driver and said to him: 'If you take this poor young man on your camel and leave him at the door of the Baghdād hospital, where he may be cured by medical attention and the change of air, we will pay you well on your return.' The camel driver consented to do so and, with the help of these good people, lifted Ghānim upon the back of his animal, mat and all, and fastened him there.

Just as the camel driver was setting out and Ghānim was weeping from weakness and despair, two poorly-clad women in the crowd said to each other: 'That unfortunate young invalid is very like Ghānim, but it cannot be he in such a sorry state.' These women were covered with dust and had just entered the village; they were none other than Ghānim's mother and his sister Fitnah, who were making their slow way from Damascus to Baghdād.

The camel driver mounted his ass and, taking the camel by the halter, made the best of his way to Baghdād. Arriving at the hospital, he lifted Ghānim down and laid him on the steps, as the place was not yet open for the day. Then he returned to the village.

The people of that part of Baghdād soon began to come out of their houses and, when they saw Ghānim lying like the shadow of a man outside the hospital, they clustered round him with a thousand suppositions. While each was telling the other what he thought, the principal sheikh of one of the markets approached and said to himself: 'By Allāh, if that young man is to be taken into the hospital, he is as good as dead already. I will have him carried to my house, and Allāh may perhaps recompense me for it when I come to the Garden of Delights.' He made his slaves bear the youth to his own home, and prepared a clean bed for him with good mattresses and new soft pillows. He called his wife and said: 'Allāh has sent us a guest, my dear. See that he is well looked after.' 'Be it upon my head,' she answered, and, with that, tucked up her sleeves, heated water in a great cauldron, and washed the young man all over. Then he dressed him in clean clothes belonging to her husband, made him drink a glass of delicious sherbert, and sprinkled his face with rosewater. Ghānim began to breathe more freely, his strength came back little by little and with it returned the memory of his past and of Kūt al-Kulūb, his beloved.

Now, when the Khalīfah was so incensed against Kūt al-Kulūb . . .

At this point Shahrazād saw the approach of morning and discreetly fell silent.

But when the forty-second night had come

SHE SAID:

It is related, O auspicious King, that when the Khalīfah was so incensed against Kut al-Kulūb, she abode in the dark chamber for twenty-four days, watched over by the old woman and holding no communication with anyone else in the palace. The Khalīfah had quite forgotten about her when, happening one day to pass the room in which she was confined, he heard a sad voice saying over certain verses of the poets and then the same voice speaking clearly in this wise: 'O Ghānim ibn Ayyūb, fair-souled, generous and chaste, how lofty do you appear in face of him who has persecuted you! You respected the woman of him who has shamed yours, you have guarded his woman from shame and he has dishonoured the women of your house. But a day will come when you and the Khalīfah shall stand up before the Sole Just Judge, the angels themselves will witness on your behalf and Allāh Himself confound your oppressor.'

The Khalīfah then understood for the first time that he had acted unjustly towards Ghānim; therefore he sent for Kūt al-Kulūb into his presence and, when she came weeping and with bent head, he said, 'My love, I heard you accuse me of injustice and oppression, saying that I had acted ill against one who had acted well by me. Who is this man who has protected my woman while I dishonoured his, and respected my woman while I put to shame those of his house?' 'It is Ghānim ibn Ayyūb, the Slave of Love,' answered the girl. 'I swear to you, O Khalīfah, by the kindness that once you showed me, that Ghānim ever held himself towards me as an honourable man, being by nature incapable of all brutal abominations.' 'I have made a sad mistake!' cried the Khalīfah. 'Indeed there is neither power nor wisdom save in Allāh. Ask what you will, Kūt al-Kulūb, and you shall receive it.' 'Prince of Believers, I ask for Ghānim ibn Ayyūb,' answered the girl, and the Khalīfah, in spite of the love which he still felt for her, answered: 'He is yours, the gift of a generous giver who never takes back. Furthermore, I will raise him to honour.' Then said Kūt al-Kulūb: 'My lord, I would wish to be married to Ghānim when he returns to us.' 'So you shall,' answered the Khalīfah. 'Prince of Believers,' said the girl, 'none knows where to find this Ghānim. The Sultān of Damascus himself has told you that he knows not what has become of him. Allow me myself to make the necessary search, for I feel that Allāh will give him back to me.' 'You have my leave to do what you think fit,' answered the Khalīfah.

Kūt al-Kulūb was overjoyed at this permission and hastened to leave the palace, carrying with her a purse of a thousand gold dīnārs.

On the first day she travelled throughout the city of Baghdād, making enquiries which led to nothing.

On the second day, she visited all the shops in several markets and, telling her story to the principal sheikh of each, gave him a large sum of money to distribute among the stranger poor.

On the third day, she visited the market of the goldsmiths and jewellers, and, when she had told her story to the principal sheikh of that guild, giving him gold at the same time for all needy wanderers, he said to her: 'Curiously enough, my mistress, I have just taken a strange young man, who is very ill, into my own house. I know neither his name nor his condition. (Indeed the young man was Ghānim ibn Ayyūb, but the sheikh did not know this.) I imagine him to be the son of noble parents, for, though he is worn to a shadow, he is still beautiful and has exquisite manners. Probably he was reduced to his present state by running into debt, or by some unhappy love affair.' Kūt al-Kulūb felt her heart beat wildly at these words and said: 'Old man, I know that you may not leave the market at this hour, therefore I pray you lend me someone who can lead me to your house.' The sheikh of the goldsmiths called a small child who knew his house, and said: 'Fulful, lead this lady to my house at once.' So little Fulful walked in front of Kūt al-Kulūb and led her to the sheikh's house where the stranger was lying ill.

As soon as they reached the house, the young woman saluted the sheikh's wife, who recognised her, and bowed to the earth before her. 'Good mother,' said Kut al-Kulūb, after the necessary cere-monials, 'tell me where I may find the young stranger who is lying ill here.' The older woman began to weep and, leading her into another chamber, said: 'There he lies upon the bed. If we may go by appearances, he is surely of a noble race.' Kūt al-Kulūb leant over the bed and scrutinised the stranger with eager attention, but she could not recognise her Ghānim in this feeble ghost of a man. Nevertheless, her heart was moved to pity and she wept, saying: 'Hard is the lot of strangers, even if they are princes in their own country.' She gave what was left of her money to the sheikh's wife and recommended her to spare no expense in curing the young man; she herself prepared the draughts which had been prescribed for the invalid and gave them him to drink; then, after sitting for an hour by the head of his bed, she said farewell to the sheikh's wife and returned to the palace.

Every day she visited different markets and spent her time in continual research. Once, as she was hunting hopelessly, the sheikh of the goldsmiths met her and said: 'Mistress Kūt al-Kulūb, you commanded me to bring you any stranger that I should find passing through Baghdād. I have here for your benevolence two women of high rank, a mother and a daughter whom I found wandering in goat-skin garments, with wallets about their necks as if they were beggars. They were weeping and weary, therefore I have brought them to you, O queen of goodness, knowing that you would pity and sustain them without asking indiscreet questions. As we are good to them, I trust that Allāh may reward us in his paradise.' 'I would much like to see them,' answered Kūt al-Kulūb.

So the sheikh brought them to her and, when she saw their beauty, their nobility and their rags, she wept, saying: 'As Allāh lives, they are of noble birth and little accustomed to hardship. Their faces were born for honour and repose.' 'You say truly, my mistress,' answered the old man, 'surely tyranny has been at work upon their house and upon their goods. Let us help them, since Allāh has promised rewards to them who love the poor.' All three women wept at this, for each remembered Ghānim ibn Ayyūb, the Slave of Love, though they could not read each other's thoughts. At last they dried their eyes, and the older woman said: 'Generous lady, pray to Allāh that we may find whom we seek. We are looking for the child of my bowels, my son Ghānim ibn Ayyūb.' At this name the girl understood that these were the mother and the sister of Ghānim; she uttered a loud cry and fell fainting on the floor. When she came to, she threw herself into the arms of the other women, saying: 'Trust in Allāh, my sisters, and trust also a little in me, for this day shall be the last of your misfortunes, the first of your happiness. Be comforted!'

At this point Shahrazād saw the approach of morning and discreetly fell silent.

But when the forty-third night had come

SHE SAID:

It is related, O auspicious King, that when Kūt al-Kulūb had said: 'Be comforted!' to Ghānim's mother and sister, she turned to the sheikh of the goldsmiths and gave him a thousand dīnārs, saying: 'Conduct them to your house, and tell your wife to take them to the bath and give them fair new robes. I wish her to spare neither expense nor trouble in looking after them.'

Next morning Kūt al-Kulūb went to the sheikh's house to see for herself that her instructions had been carried out, and scarcely had she entered when the sheikh's wife, with many expressions of thanks, introduced Ghānim's mother and sister to her, shining and transformed from the bath. Nobility and beauty shone from their faces, and the Khalīfah's favourite was pleased to sit and talk with them for an hour. Then she asked after the invalid and was told that he was much the same. So she took the other women with her, who had not previously seen the young man, and went to visit him. All looked at his unconscious form with pitiful tenderness and sat down to talk beside his bed. In the course of their conversation the name of Kūt al-Kulūb was mentioned, and immediately the young man's colour came back to him, he rose on his elbow in a little strength, and opened his eyes, crying: 'Where are you, Kūt al-Kulūb?'

The young woman recognised his voice and leant over him, saying: 'O my dear, my dear, you are indeed Ghānim!' 'Yes, I am Ghānim,' said he, and straightway Kūt al-Kulūb fell fainting to one side of the bed, and Ghānim's mother and sister to the other.

When they came to, they cast themselves upon Ghānim, and you can imagine that there was no lack of kisses and of tears and of cries of joy.

Soon Kūt al-Kulūb became calmer and said: 'Praise and thanks be to Allāh, Who has brought us all together again at the last.' She told Ghānim the whole story, as far as she knew it, and added: 'The Khalīfah believes me, he has taken you into favour and wishes to see you. Also he consents to our marriage.' Ghānim, who had so lately been near dying of sorrow, now was not far off dying of joy. He went on kissing the hands of his mistress, until at last she said: 'Wait here for me, I will return in a little while.'

She hurried to the palace and, providing herself with great store of dīnārs, gave them to her friend the sheikh, saying: 'For the two women and for Ghānim buy four complete costumes of the most beautiful material you can find, with twenty handkerchiefs each, ten belts, and ten changes of each garment.' Then she returned to the house and led all three to the baths. When they were bathed and soothed, she prepared chickens, meat broth, and purified wine, with which she fed them for three days, until they all became as strong, as beautiful, and as happy as they had ever been. On the fourth day, she took them again to the hammām, had them change their clothes there, and sent them back to the sheikh's house, while she herself went to interview the Khalīfah.

She bowed to the earth before him and told him of the happy reunion of Ghānim and his mother and sister, taking care to lay stress upon the beauty and virginity of young Fitnah. 'Fetch Jafar!' cried the Khalīfah to a slave, and, when Jafar approached, he said to him: 'Fetch Ghānim ibn Ayyūb!'

In the meanwhile Kūt al-Kulūb had hurried to the sheikh's house and told Ghānim that he was about to be taken into the presence of the Khalīfah. 'Dear lover,' she said, 'now is the time for you to display all your eloquence and resolution.' She dressed him in the most sumptuous of his new robes and gave him a purse of gold, saying: 'Throw money about in handfuls when you reach the palace and as you journey up the hall.'

In a minute or so Jafar arrived on his mule, and Ghānim hastened to kiss the earth between his hands and give him fitting welcome. He was now the handsome Ghānim of old time, whose face was a glory and a snare.

When they came to the palace, Ghānim saw the Prince of Believers surrounded by his wazīrs, his chamberlains, his tributaries, the chief persons of his kingdom and the commanders of his guards and of his armies. Being an eloquent and resolute man, an agreeable talker, a pleasing poet, an excellent improviser, he took his stand before the Khalīfah, looked at the ground for a moment in reflection, and then, raising his head, improvised these lines:

> You are the rain upon the earth of prime,
> We spring up green and abundant in your time,
>   O King.
>
> The Sultans trail their white beards in the dust,
> They offer up their crowns because they must,
>   O King.
>
> Your armies fill the earth and fright the stars,
> Heaven is kept busy to record your wars,
>   O King.
>
> The moon with every glittering satellite
> Comes down to hang among your lamps at night,
>   O King.

The Khalīfah was charmed by the beauty of these verses, by the variety of their rhythm, and by the sweet eloquence of their author.

At this point Shahrazād saw the approach of morning and discreetly fell silent.

And when the forty-fourth night had come

SHE SAID:

It is related, O auspicious King, that when Ghānim so charmed the Khalīfah, Hārūn al-Rashīd bade him approach, saying: 'Tell me your story and hide none of the truth from me.' Ghānim recounted the whole tale to him, but it would be a weary business to repeat it here. The Khalīfah was completely persuaded of Ghānim's innocence and of the purity of his intentions, especially in respect to the words embroidered upon his favourite's drawers. 'I pray you pardon my injustice,' he said, and Ghānim answered: 'O Prince of Believers, I freely pardon it. All that belongs to the slave belongs also to the master.'

The Khalīfah was so delighted with this answer that he gave the youth a great position in the kingdom, a royal income, a retinue of men and women slaves, and a palace to which Ghānim immediately transferred his mother, his sister Fitnah, and his beloved. Not long afterwards the Khalīfah, perceiving that Ghānim's sister was Fitnah indeed, asked her in marriage. When Ghānim consented, the Sultān thanked him and gave him a hundred thousand dīnārs in gold. He called the kādi and his witnesses, and had two marriage contracts written out together. On the same hour of the same night the Khalīfah lay with Fitnah, and Ghānim ibn Ayyūb, the Slave of Love, with Kūt al-Kulūb.

The Khalīfah was so pleased, when he woke in the morning, at the memory of the night he had passed in Fitnah's virgin arms, that he had the palace scribes write out the whole history of Ghānim from beginning to end in their most elaborate calligraphy, and caused the story to be added to his library, that it might serve as a lesson to future generations and, by delighting the minds of wise readers, lead them to an admiration of the works of God.

'But do not believe, O King of the ages,' continued Shahrazād, 'that this extraordinary story which I have just told you is either as pleasant or as wonderful as the warlike and heroic tale of Umar al-Numān and his sons, Sharkān and Dū al-Makūn.' 'You may tell me that warlike story, for I do not know it,' answered King Shahryār.

The Tale of King Umar al-Numān and his Two Remarkable Sons, Sharkān and Dū al-Makān

THEN SHAHRAZĀD SAID TO KING SHAHRYĀR:

IT is related, O auspicious King, that there was once in the city of Baghdād, after the reign of many khalīfahs and before the reign of many others, a king called Umar al-Numān. He was formidable in war, had conquered all the Khusraus, and brought the Cæsars under his dominion. None might warm themselves at his fire; none might stand against him in feats of arms; and sparks of fire jetted from his nostrils when he was angry. He had conquered all the lands there are; the cities of the world were subject to him. With God's help, he had subdued all the human race and sent victorious armies into the ends of the earth. The East and the West acknowledged him as King, with Hind, Sind and China, Yemen, Al-Hijāz and Abyssinia, Sūdān, Syria and Greece, the provinces of Diyār Bakr, together with all the isles of the sea and the territories watered by Saihūn and Jaihūn, the Nile and the Euphrates. He had sent messengers into the confines of the world to find out the true news of his empire, and they had returned to tell him that the rulers of the world acknowledged his supremacy. He had spread the garment of his generosity over all his tributaries, had drowned them in the waters of his benevolence and, out of the greatness of his soul, had spread safety and sweet concord among them all.

All manner of gifts and the unending tributes of the earth flowed continually towards his throne, because he was loved as well as feared.

Umar al-Numān had one son who was called Sharkān, that is to say An Evil Has Arisen, because he showed himself the prodigy of that time, surpassed in boldness the greatest heroes of tournay, and wielded the lance, the sword and the bow with a skill that was more than human. His father loved him with an abiding love and had named him as the successor to his throne: for at the age of twenty, by Allāh's help, Sharkān had bowed the heads of all before the illumination of his brave renown. He had already taken strongholds by assault, reduced whole countries, and spread his fame among the peoples. As the months went by he grew in pride and power.

The King had no other child but Sharkān, though he possessed, as the Book allowed him, four wives. Besides these four, three of whom had remained barren, he had three hundred and sixty concubines, each of a different race, as many as there are days in the Coptic year. For each of these he had built a separate apartment in the body of the palace, and these apartments were divided into twelve groups, one group for each month and each group containing thirty concubines. To every concubine he allotted one night of the year on which he slept with her, and then for a whole twelve months he did not see her again. This was a rule to which he adhered during all his lifetime, so that he became renowned as much for his admirable wisdom as for the strength of his manhood.

One day He who divinely orders all things allowed one of King Umar's concubines to conceive. When the news became known in the palace and reached the King, he rejoiced exceedingly, crying: 'God grant that all my posterity be males!' He had the date of the conception inscribed upon a register, and heaped both presents and attentions on the woman.

Sharkān, the King's son. . . .

At this point Shahrazād saw the approach of morning and discreetly fell silent.

But when the forty-fifth night had come

SHE SAID:

Sharkān, the King's son, also heard of the conception and became very sorrowful for fear that there might be a newcomer to dispute his succession to the throne. This preyed on his mind so much that he resolved to kill the child if it should be a male.

The concubine was a young Greek slave called Saffiah, who had been sent by the Greeks of Cesarea with other rich presents. She was by far the most beautiful of all the palace slaves; her face and form were fairer, her thighs and shoulders stronger than those of any of them, and she had, moreover, an excellent intelligence. She had known how to speak sweet words to the King when he lay with her, words that stayed in his mind and disposed him towards her. When her pains had come, she sat on the child stool and prayed to Allāh, Who heard her prayer.

Both King Umar and Sharkān had posted a eunuch to tell him immediately the sex of the child; so, as soon as Saffiah bore a child and the midwives announced that it was a girl whose face shone like a slip of the moon, each eunuch ran and informed his master; and Sharkān at least rejoiced. No sooner had the eunuchs departed than Saffiah said to the midwives: 'Wait, O wait! There is something yet inside me.' Again she uttered the 'Oh's!' and 'Ah's!' of labour, and brought forth a second child. The midwives eagerly bent over it and lo! it shone like the full moon: a boy, with a brow of brilliant white and cheeks which were flowering roses. The slaves, the servants, and the guests rejoiced, filling the palace with the shrillest joy, so that the other concubines heard and understood and withered where they were from envy.

Umar al-Numān joyfully thanked Allāh when he heard the news

and ran to the apartment of Saffïah. Taking her head in his hands he
kissed her and then bent over the newborn child; while he kissed his
son the slaves beat musically upon drums, the lute players and singers
discoursed fitting melodies.

Then the King named his son Dū al-Makān and his daughter
Nuzhat al-Zamān; that is to say, Light of the Place and Delight of
the Age. Those who were present bowed to signify that the names
were fitting, and the King chose nurses, slaves, and servants for his
two offspring, giving to every person in the palace an abundance of
wines and perfumes, with other pleasant matters of celebration too
numerous to mention.

The people of Baghdād were highly delighted when they heard
of the double birth; they decorated and illuminated the city, and
sent the amīrs, wazīrs, and chief notables to present humble congratulations to the King. Umar thanked them, and bestowed riches
and robes of honour on high and low alike. For four years he did not
let a day pass without sending for news of Saffïah and his children,
and from time to time bestowed upon the mother prodigious gifts
of jewelry and goldsmith's work, robes and silks, gold and silver,
and dear-bought marvels of all kinds. The education and safeguard-
ing of the children he confided to the wisest and most trusted of his
people.

Sharkān, who was far from the city fighting and raiding, taking
towns and adding to the glory of his wars, knew nothing of the
birth of his brother al-Makān.

One day as Umar al-Numān sat upon his throne, certain of the
chamberlains entered and kissed the earth between his hands, saying:
'O king, envoys wait without from Afrīdūn, Sultān of Rome and
Constantinople. If it be your wish, we will bring them in; or if it be
your wish, we will send them away.'

Umar had the envoys brought before him and greeted them
kindly, asking after their health and the reason of their coming. One
of them kissed the earth between his hands and said:

GREAT AND VENERABLE KING, we are sent by King Afrīdūn,
master of Greece and Ionia, commander of the armies of all Christian
peoples, whose throne is in Constantinople. He has commanded us
to tell you that he is about to undertake a most bloody war against
the fierce tyrant Hardūb, King of Cesarea.

The cause of it is this: some time ago an Arab chief found, in
some newly-conquered territory, a treasure of the time of Alexander

the Great, a hoard of incalculable richness, containing, among a thousand other things, three round jewels as big as ostrich-eggs, white and flawless, surpassing in beauty and value all other gems of land and sea. Each is pierced for a neck-cord and has mysterious inscriptions engraved upon it in Ionian character. One of the least of the virtues of these stones is that all who wear them, and especially newborn children, are protected from all diseases and especially from fevers and constipation.

The Arab chief learnt something of the strange powers of these jewels and thought that an occasion had arisen for obtaining the good graces of our King; so he prepared two ships, loading one with the three gems and a great part of the rest of the treasure as a gift for King Afrīdūn, and the other with guards to protect the valuables; though he did not think that any would dare directly to lay hands on goods intended for the powerful Afrīdūn, especially as the way of the ships lay over the sea on which Constantinople stands.

Nevertheless, soon after the ships had sailed, when they were putting into a bay not far from our country, a band of Greek soldiers belonging to King Hardūb of Cesarea, our vassal, attacked them; they bore off all the treasure including the three magic jewels, put both the crews to the sword, and carried away the ships.

When our King heard of this, he sent an army against Hardūb, who destroyed it, then a second, which was put to flight in its turn; now our master has sworn a great and angry oath that he will put himself at the head of his massed armies and not turn back until he has destroyed Cesarea, laid waste all the kingdom of Hardūb, and razed those towns to the earth which are tributary to him.

Glorious Sultān, we come to claim your assistance, and solicit the power and glory of an alliance with you. You cannot fail to add to the lustre of your fame by helping us, and our King has sent great gifts of every kind as a sign of the reliance which he places in your generosity. He begs you to accept them and to look favourably upon his request.

The envoys fell silent and bowed to the ground, kissing the earth between the King's hands.

Now these are the presents which Afrīdūn, lord of Constantinople . . .

At this point Shahrazād saw the approach of morning and discreetly fell silent.

But when the forty-sixth night had come

SHE SAID:

Now these are the presents which Afrīdūn, lord of Constantinople, sent to Umar al-Numān: fifty of the fairest virgins in all Greece, and fifty of the most glorious boys from Rome, dressed in gold-embroidered silken full-sleeved robes, with coloured pictures in needlework upon them, and silver damascened gold belts holding up double skirts of brocaded velvet which fell in unequal lengths, gold rings in their ears from which depended single round white pearls each worth a thousand pound weight in gold. The girls, too, were sumptuously decked.

These were the two principal presents, but the rest did not fall short of them in value. So King Umar accepted them with pleasure and ordered the envoys to be honourably entertained. Then he assembled his wazīrs, that they might advise him as to what answer he should return to King Afrīdūn. The grand wazīr Dandān, a venerable old man who was respected and loved by all, rose in his place and said:

Sultān of Glory, it is true that King Afrīdūn of Constantinople is a Christian, infidel to the law of Allāh and His Prophet (on whom be prayer and peace), and that his people are unbelievers; it is also true that the man against whom he asked our help is equally an unbeliever; therefore their affairs concern them only and do not touch the policy of Believers. Yet I advise you to ally yourself with King Afrīdūn and to send him a great army with your son Sharkān at its head. I counsel this for two reasons: first, that the King has sent you presents which you have accepted; second, that, in helping him against the little king of Cesarea, whose resistance to you will be negligible, you will achieve another victory whose fame, spreading about the west, will cause the kings of the west to seek your friendship with numerous presents and extraordinary gifts.

Umar al-Numān approved this speech and gave Dandān a robe of honour, saying: 'Truly you are an inspired counsellor of kings; I shall place you at the head of the army, and Sharkān, my son, can command the rearguard.'

The King sent for his son, who had just returned from his glorious expedition, and, telling him of Dandān's advice, bade him make ready for war, distributing largesse among the soldiers and choosing from them all ten thousand well-equipped cavaliers, accustomed to privation and fatigue. After listening respectfully to his father's words, Sharkān gave presents of gold and selected his troop, allowing to each man three days for repose and refreshment. The ten thousand kissed the earth between his hands and went out to spend the money which they had received on equipment for the expedition.

Sharkān himself chose, from the treasuries and armouries of the palace, weapons inlaid with gold, having lucky inscriptions on ivory and ebony, until he was accoutred from head to foot. Then he went to the stables and inspected the stud of noble horses, each of which had his pedigree fastened about his neck in a leather amulet worked with silk and embossed with turquoises. He selected a bay horse with shining coat and wide-starting eyes, large-hoofed and proudly-tailed, with ears as sensitive as those of a gazelle. This animal had been given to Umar al-Numān by the sheikh of a powerful tribe, and was such a horse as has been seldom seen upon the earth.

After the three days of preparation, the army assembled outside the city, and Umar al-Numān went out to say farewell to his son and his grand wazīr. He gave seven chests of treasure to Sharkān and advised him to be guided by the wise Dandān. Sharkān promised, and the King recommended him and all the army to Dandān, who kissed the earth between his hands and accepted the charge. Then Sharkān mounted his horse and reviewed his troops in front of the King and the wazīr. Finally the two generals galloped off at the head of the army with a throbbing of war-drums, a shrilling of fifes, and a blaring of clarions, and the standards and banners lying out in the wind above their heads. They went forward for twenty days under the guidance of the envoys and came at length, on the twenty-first night, to a large, well-wooded and well-watered valley. Here Sharkān ordered the tents to be pitched and proclaimed a rest of three days. The cavaliers made their camp and disappeared among the woods; the wazīr Dandān rested in his tent in the middle of the valley with the envoys of King Afrīdūn camped about him.

Sharkān dismissed his guards and ordered them to attend the wazīr; then he gave rein to his charger and set out to explore the valley, since they were now near enemy country and his father had advised him to see all for himself. He explored the whole neighbourhood until a quarter of the night had passed; then sleep weighed upon his eyes and, as he was accustomed to sleep on horseback, he left the courser to find its own way and fell into a deep slumber.

He was wakened at midnight by his horse pawing the ground

violently and halting in the middle of a wooded solitude, brightly lighted by the moon. Sharkān was startled to find himself in so lonely a place, but he said aloud the word which never fails: 'There is no power or might save in Allāh!' and felt no further fear of the savage creatures of the wood. The moon poured magic silver down into the glade, as if it had been one of the glades of Paradise, and Sharkān heard near at hand sweet words in a perfect voice and laughter that might have been the moonlight itself. Any man would have been lost in a delicate lechery to drink that laughter from the mouth which made it, and to die.

Sharkān leapt from his horse and proceeded through the wood toward the voices until he came to a white river of happy water, running and singing; its song was answered by the chanting of birds, the plaining of gazelles, and a unison of all the beasts of the field, so that it was not many songs but one song, deep and delicious. The bank was embroidered and jewelled with flowers and grasses. A poet has said:

> How sad-coloured the earth would seem,
> How grey each water stream,
> If flowers were dead.
> God said:
> Let there be flowers,
> Let streams be filled with showers;
> And then decreed my lazy hours
> Should pass in water-meadows filled with flowers.

Sharkān saw, rising in the moonlight on the other bank of the stream, a monastery built of white stone and dominated by a tall tower. This building refreshed its feet in the living waters of the river, and beside it stretched a green sward, upon which ten young women were seated about one. The ten were virgin and marvellous, carved from moonlight, lightly robed in soft and flowing draperies. A poet has thus spoken of them:

> The moon shines and the grasses shine
> With candid girls and argentine,
> The grasses sigh and shine.
>
> Those slimly dancing bodies wave
> With the same sway that green reeds have,
> Or as the grasses wave.

> Ah, vine-borne clusters of new grapes,
> So the hair falls down on their napes
> Like yellow grapes and purple grapes.

> As long brown arrows dipped in gold
> Their eye-glances; the shots are told
> And my heart is the gold.

The woman about whom these ten sat might have been supposed the moon herself had not that round been shining down upon the lawn. Her brows were black bows lying in the dawn-light of her forehead, long lashes of curved silk fringed her eyelids and the little clusters of her hair curled sweetly about her temples. She was such a one as the poet had in his mind when he sang:

> With black glances
> And haughty poses
> Of her white slimness
> (Bow down, lances
> Famed for straightness!)
> She proposes
> Now to flout me
> For my lateness
> And advances—
> Starlit-dimness
> Of wet roses
> Grows about me.

> When as now
> Her tumbled hair
> Falls adorning
> A clear brow,
> (Who has seen the phœnix nesting
> On an aromatic bosom
> Woven of the sweet and rare
> Branches of his fabled gum-tree?)
> Lo, the night's black wing is resting
> On the blossom
> Of the plum-tree
> Of the morning.

It was her voice which Sharkān had heard, and now she was laughing and speaking in Arabic to the young slaves who were with her: 'By the Messiah, little shameless ones, that is not a pretty thing that you are doing! If one of you starts again I will tie her up with her belt and slap her bottom. Come, my dears, let us see if one of you can beat me at wrestling; step forward before the moon sets.'

One of the young girls came forward and was soon thrown to the ground. Then a second and a third. Before long all ten were trussed up and punished as the young woman had promised. Suddenly an old woman came out of the forest and approached the band of young wrestlers, saying to the victorious one: 'What are you doing with these young girls, O perverse maiden? Do you think that there is any glory in conquering weak children such as these? If you want to wrestle, try a turn with me. I am old but I can master you.' Although the young woman was angry at this interruption, she smiled and said: 'By the Messiah, old Mother-of-Calamity, is this a joke, or do you really wish to wrestle with me?' 'This is no joke,' answered the old woman.

At this point Shahrazād saw the approach of morning and discreetly fell silent.

But when the forty-seventh night had come

SHE SAID:

It is related, O auspicious King, that the young woman cried out: 'Come on, then, if you are strong enough, O Mother-of-Calamity!' and leapt towards the old woman who stood strangled by anger, with all the hairs of her body pricked like a hedgehog's spines. 'By the Messiah,' exclaimed the old woman, 'we must wrestle quite naked.' And with that the nasty old creature undressed completely even to her drawers, leaving only a handkerchief which fell below her navel. She stood for a moment in all the horror of her ugliness, most like a black and white striped snake, and then said to the young woman: 'Why do you not do as I do?'

Slowly and delicately the girl undid her garments one by one and, when all were put aside, took off her drawers of immaculate silk. Then appeared thighs moulded of marble in their glory and above them a soft hill of milk and crystal, shining and round and tended, a scented belly with rosy dimples faintly breathing of musk and coloured like a garden of anemones, and a breast laden with twin pomegranates, swollen to ripeness and crowned with buds of the same.

As the two wrestlers leant forward and closed, Sharkān nearly died of laughing at the appearance of the old woman, and then, seeing the perfect harmony of the young one's body, lifted his head to the sky and prayed fervently to Allāh for the victory of the fair one.

In the first exchange, the young wrestler slipped free, seized the old woman by the neck with her left hand and, passing her right hand between the other's thighs, lifted her in the air and threw her heavily to the ground. She lay twisting about, with her legs waving in the air, so that she showed all the laughable horrors of her wrinkled and hairy flesh. Twice she terribly broke wind; at the first discharge a cloud of dust sprang up, and the second shot went fuming towards the moon.

Sharkān fell over with silent laughter but, when he got up again, he said: 'Well is she called Mother-of-Calamity, for she is a Christian just as these others are Christians.' Little by little he drew nearer the lawn, and saw the young girl throw a silk veil over the nakedness of the old woman. She helped her into her clothes, saying: 'Mistress, I only wrestled with you because you asked me; what happened afterwards is not my fault, for you slipped from between my hands. The Lord be praised that you are not hurt.' The old woman made no answer, but fled rapidly in her confusion and disappeared within the monastery. On the lawn were only the ten young girls lying about their mistress.

Sharkān said to himself: 'Destiny ever has some end in view. It was written that I should sleep on my horse and wake in this place. I have every hope that this desirable wrestler and her ten intoxicating companions may serve to pasture the fire of my longing.' With that he mounted his horse and galloped, sword in hand, towards the lawn. His horse went like an arrow shot by a lusty arm, and soon Sharkān was upon the lawn, crying: 'Only Allāh is great!'

The young woman jumped lightly to her feet when she saw him and, running towards the river, which was more than six arms wide at that place, leapt lithely to the opposite bank and stood there. Then she cried with a loud musical voice: 'Who are you who dare to trouble our solitude with a drawn sword, as if you were a soldier coming among soldiers? Tell me whence you come and whither you are going; speak the truth, for a lie will only harm you and this is a place from which you will not easily get away. I have but to give a signal cry and four thousand Christian warriors will run to our assistance. Tell me what you want. If you are lost in the forest, we will put you upon your road again.'

'I am a stranger, a Mussulmān,' answered Sharkān, 'I am not lost, but am hunting for some booty of young flesh which can pasture the fire of my longing to-night under the moon. These ten would seem to suit me well enough. If they are willing I will take them with me to my friends.' 'Insolent soldier,' answered the young woman, 'this pasture of which you speak is not for you and, further, you lie as to the purpose of your coming.' Sharkān replied: 'O lady, happy is he who can be content with Allāh and has no desire which is not centred in Him.' 'By the Messiah,' said the young woman, 'I would call the warriors to me and have you seized were I not naturally pitiful towards strangers, especially when they are young and hand-some. I consent to this pasturing of your desires, on condition that you light off your horse and engage in single combat with me, swearing not to make use of your weapons. If you can put me upon my back, all these girls will belong to you and you can carry me away upon your horse. But if I conquer you, you will be my slave.'

Thinking to himself that the girl knew nothing of his strength and that the combat would be easy, Sharkān said: 'I promise to leave my weapons behind and to wrestle with you in the way you wish. If I am thrown, I have enough money on me to pay my ransom; if I win, I shall secure booty fit for a king. I swear by the goodness of the Prophet, upon whom be the prayer and peace of Allāh.' 'Swear rather by Him, Who has inspired souls into the bodies of men and has given a law unto His people,' said the young woman, and Sharkān so swore.

The young girl leapt across the river again on to the lawn and laughed, saying to Sharkān: 'I grieve to see you go, noble stranger, and yet it were better for you to go at once. For morning is at hand and how could you stand against my warriors when the least and littlest of my women can overthrow you?' With that she made off towards the monastery without having said a word of the proposed wrestling match.

Sharkān called after her in his astonishment: 'Spurn, if you will, a contest with me, my sweet mistress, but do not depart and leave a stranger so alone.' She halted smiling and asked: 'What do you wish, young stranger? Speak and it shall be accomplished.' Sharkān answered: 'Now that I have touched the ground which your feet have trodden and felt my heart sweetened with your courtesy, how can I go away before I have tasted of your hospitality? I am only a slave among your slaves.' 'What you say is right,' she answered, and her smile became more winning. 'It is a hard heart which will not entertain a guest. Remount your horse and ride opposite to me along the bank of the river. From henceforth you are my guest.'

Joyfully Sharkān did as he was told, and rode opposite the young woman and her followers until he came to a drawbridge of poplar wood, which was lowered across the river from the monastery gate by means of chains and pulleys. He dismounted, and the young woman confided his horse to one of her slaves, bidding her see that it lacked for nothing. 'My queen of fairness,' said Sharkān to his hostess, 'now have you become a thing doubly sacred to me because of your beauty and your hospitality. Why not turn back here and accompany me to my city of Baghdād, in the land of the Mussulmāns, where you will see many marvels and true warriors? Also when we have reached there you will learn who I am. Come, dear Christian, come with me to Baghdād.' 'By the Messiah, I thought that you were a youth of sense,' said she. 'So you wish to carry me off to that city, where I would fall into the hands of the terrible Umar al-Numān, who has three hundred and sixty concubines for his bed, housed in a dozen palaces according to the days and months of the year? For one night I would serve those rough desires which are allowable to a Mussulmān and then lie by neglected. Do not speak of this again and never hope to persuade me. Even if you were Sharkān himself, the son of Umar al-Numān, whose armies, as I know, have marched into our territory, I would never listen to you. Ten thousand horsemen of Baghdād, led by Sharkān and the wazīr Dandān, have crossed our frontiers to join their arms with those of Afrīdūn, King of Constantinople. If I wished, I could go myself into the middle of their camp and kill Sharkān and Dandān with my own hand. They are the enemies of my people. Now come with me, young stranger.'

At this point Shahrazād saw the approach of morning and discreetly fell silent.

But when the forty-eighth night had come

SHE SAID:

It is related, O auspicious King, that Sharkān was mortified to learn the hatred in which he and Dandān and all the army were held by this young woman. If he had not listened to his evil genius he would have told her who he was and been rid of her. As it was, the rights of hospitality and the witchcraft of her beauty prevented him from doing this. Instead he recited these lines:

> A thousand sins you go about
> And then the sum begins again,
> Because your beauty sins again
> And blots the thousand out.

She crossed the drawbridge slowly and made towards the monastery with Sharkān walking behind her. Thus he was able to see her sumptuous buttocks rising and falling like the waves of the sea. He regretted that the wazīr Dandān was not there to wonder at their splendour with him, and there crossed his mind these words of the poet:

> Before my eyes were preparate
> Her bottom slipped from out its wrapping:
> Behold! two silver moons half separate,
> Half overlapping.

They came to a great door arched with transparent marble and by it entered a long gallery, running below a colonnade of alabaster, from the arches of which hung lamps of rock-crystal like mimic suns. A troop of young slaves, carrying sweet-scented candles, came to meet their mistress, with their heads cinctured by silk bands worked with coloured jewels. They fell in on either side and conducted the two young people into the principal hall of the monastery. Sharkān saw sumptuous cushions arranged in order along the wall and curtains hanging over the doors, each surmounted by a crown of gold. All the floor was inlaid with little chips of many-tinted marbles, and a fountain basin rose in the middle of the hall, musically discoursing silver water through four and twenty golden mouths. A bed was spread with silk at the bottom of the hall and was of such a kind as is only found in kings' palaces.

'Lay yourself upon this bed and be at ease,' said the young woman and, when Sharkān had done so, left him alone with the young slaves.

As she did not return, Sharkān asked the girls what had become of her, and was told that she was sleeping. While he sat there not knowing what to think of this, the slaves brought him every kind of appetising food on dishes of rare goldsmiths' work. He ate all he could and then poured rose-water and orange-water upon his hands from a golden ewer, holding them over a golden bowl with silver pictures in relief upon it. Soon his mind began to be troubled for his soldiers, left alone in the valley; he upbraided himself for having forgotten the counsels of his father. His anxiety increased when he considered that he knew nothing about his young hostess and was ignorant of the place in which he found himself.

He said over this song to himself:

> I am a soldier led aside from duty
>   By many things.
> I was an eagle, but the hand of beauty
>   Captured my wings.
>
> I am a soldier whom you must not censure,
>   Seeing that she
> Bound me and threw me, left me to adventure
>   In love's dark sea,

and fell asleep. He woke in the morning to find the hall filled with a troop of twenty virgin slaves surrounding their mistress, as clear stars surround the moon. His hostess was dressed royally in figured silk. Her waist lay small and her haunches swelled wonderfully beneath a filigrine gold belt brightened with pearls, so that her body might have been thought to be a silver branch let into a wave of diaphanous crystal. Also, because of the belt, her breasts came forward more proudly. Her hair was confined in a little chaplet of pearls, and she came towards him among her women, lifting the skirts of her robe and balancing in her beauty.

Sharkān forgot his soldiers, his wazīr, and the counsels of his father. He rose up and proclaimed these lines:

> I have those eyes of magic fire
> That pierce through silk
> To find desire:
>   Balancing hips
>   Like sailing ships,
> Dimpled and dancing and white as milk;
>   Wavering breasts
>   With crimson crests,
> Like golden birds that shake their nests.

When the young woman was quite near, she looked at him long and long and said suddenly: 'You are Sharkān, son of Umar al-Numān, the magnanimous, the light and honour of our dwelling. Speak to me and pretend no more. Leave lies to the liar, for a crooked word befits not one who is a King among kings.'

Sharkān understood that nothing would be gained by denying his identity, so he answered: 'O you who are very dear to me, I am indeed Sharkān, son of Umar al-Numān, whom Destiny has thrown bound and defenceless at your feet. Do as you will with me, O unknown black-eyed girl!' The woman reflected a moment with her eyes lowered, and then glanced up at Sharkān, saying: 'Calm your fears and look not so sternly. Have you forgotten that you are my guest, that there is bread and salt between us, and much friendly conversation? You are under my protection and my loyalty shall advantage you. Fear not, for although all the world should come against you, by the Messiah, I would die before they touched you.' She sat down gently at his side with a very sweet smile and spoke to one of her slaves in the Greek tongue. The slave departed and fetched in a troop of servants carrying every sort of food on great plates, with jars and flasks of excellent wine. But Sharkān hesitated to touch these things, so the young girl said: 'You fear that there is betrayal in the food and wine. Do you not know that I could have killed you any time since yesterday if I had wanted to?' With that she took a mouthful from each plate, and Sharkān was shamed out of his suspicions. They both ate their fill and then, after they had washed their hands, flower-crowned drinks were poured for them in bowls of gold, silver, and crystals of all colours. The young woman drank first and then filled again for Sharkān; as he drained the cup, she said: 'Life is a pleasant and an easy thing, O Mussulmān.'

At this point Shahrazād saw the approach of morning and discreetly fell silent.

But when the forty-ninth night had come

SHE SAID:

It is related, O auspicious King, that the two went on drinking till wine lifted their hearts and love seeded deep in the soul of Sharkān. One of the young woman's slaves, named Coral-Pearl, retired and brought back with her four girls, one with a Damascus lute, one with a Persian harp, one with a Tartar cithern, and one with an

Egyptian guitar. Sharkān's light-of-love took the lute and, to the accompaniment of the three girls, played and sang in a voice purer than the breeze or water gushing from a rock:

> Know you the surliest
> Heart hid away from you,
> Parted away from you,
> Lies broken-hearted?
> And mine with the earliest?
>
> Know you how many
> Slaughters your eyes have made,
> Daughters your eyes have made
> Waver as waters?
> And I before any?

She fell silent, and one of the young girls sang a song in the Greek tongue which Sharkān did not understand. Then the mistress sang other songs of the same kind, one after the other, in such exquisite accord with the instruments that her voice might have proceeded from the hollow bodies of the mandores themselves. At length she asked Sharkān if he had understood the songs, and he answered: 'I did not understand the words, but the moist smiling lips and the lightness of the fingers on the instruments I understood well enough. Also the sound and harmony of the words moved me more than a hundred songs with which I am familiar.' She smiled and asked him what the effect of an Arab song would be upon him, and he answered that the remainder of his wits would not survive it. Then she changed the key of her lute and sang this song of the poet:

> Though there is myrrh in the cup of parting,
> Aloes in the bowl of setting forth,
> And cassia in the wine of separation,
> I could drain all three
> Were they not offered by a hand I love.

Hearing this song and also because he had drunken a great deal, Sharkān fell back insensible and when he woke the young woman was no longer beside him. 'She has gone to her room to sleep,' the slaves told him, and 'Allāh have her in His protection!' answered Sharkān.

Next morning Coral-Pearl came to Sharkān as soon as he was

awake and conducted him to her mistress's apartment. He was received with the sound of instruments and welcoming songs, as soon as he entered by the massive ivory door incrusted with pearls and jewels of a hundred dyes. He saw a great hall carpeted with silk rugs of Khurāsān and lighted by high windows giving upon leafy gardens and pleasant streams. Against the walls were ranged figures, dressed as if they were alive, which moved their arms and legs astonishingly and spoke and sang by some concealed device.

His hostess rose when she saw Sharkān and, taking him by the hand, made him sit down beside her. She asked him how he had passed the night and made other complimentary enquiries. At length she asked him if he knew any words of the poets concerning lovers and the slaves of love, and, hearing that he did, requested him to recite them. Said Sharkān: 'This is a song that the eloquent Kuthair made for the fair Izzah whom he loved:

> I may not sing
> The beauties that lie hid by Izzah's dress
> Beneath her coloured clothes,
> Because my oaths
> Have undertaken not to tell this thing.
>
> If you could guess. . . .
>
> If you could guess,
> Ascetics in the dust of chastity,
> You would bow down in bands
> Between her hands
> And worship her in mystical excess.
>
> If you could see. . . .'

'Indeed, eloquence was his second nature,' said the young woman. 'I remember he also wrote:

> I dreamed that Izzah and the sun stood still
> Before His chair whom beauty cannot blind,
> He weighed their splendour with a patient skill
> And Izzah was the brighter to His mind.
>
> Yet women dare to say she has a flaw. . . .
> May He who judged her perfect and complete
> Break them in pieces utterly, and straw
> Their cheeks as yellow roses for her feet.'

The hostess said again: 'How she was loved! Do you remember anything that Jamīl wrote about her?' Said Sharkān: 'I only recall this one stanza:

> I cannot call you cold,
>   For you desire
> To melt my heart like gold
>   In a red fire.

This I remember because I am that Jamīl and you are Izzah who wish my death.' The young woman smiled silently at these words, and the two continued to drink together until morning came. With the first light she rose and disappeared, so that Sharkān had to sleep alone upon his couch.

On the third morning slaves conducted him as before, with the sound of music and beating upon little drums, until they brought him to a second apartment more marvellous than the first, filled with images and paintings of animals and birds. Sharkān was charmed with all he saw and sang these lines as he advanced:

> She rises with the burnished fruit
> Of the Seven-pointed Archer,
> A drop of gold among the steel of the stars,
> A pearl announcing silver dawns,
> Water flowing over silver,
> A topaz with a gilded face,
> The reincarnate ghost of all white roses.
>
> There is blue kohl about her mauve eyes.

The young woman took him by the hand and seated him beside her, saying: 'Prince Sharkān, no doubt you can play chess?' 'I know how to play, my lady,' he answered, 'but I fear the fate of the poet who wrote:

> For very love I cannot speak;
> She sends for chess, her dreaming cheek
>   Shines rose above the pieces.
> I lose my head, I lose my queen,
> I lose my heart: was never seen
>   So quaint a game as this is.
>
> I only take through skirmishing
> A knight and rook, while my poor king
>   At every point she teases;

> Yet I'd have triumphed after all
> If we had but agreed to call
> Knights nights and castles kisses.'

The young woman went smiling up to the chess board, and the game began. Sharkān, looking in her face, made every possible mistake, moving the knight for the elephant and the elephant for the knight, so that she won and laughed at him for his lack of skill. He excused himself because it was only the first game, and they ranged the pieces again; but she beat him five times and he could only find this to say: 'My queen, to be beaten by you is in itself a victory.' After this they ate and drank, and she sang sweetly to the harp, which was her favourite instrument, this song of long chords and dying cadences:

> Though fate is dark and time is strong,
>> They are not near so dark or strong as wine is;
>> So drink, my love,
>> And think, my love,
> Though there are beauties in your song,
>> No beauty is so freely yours as mine is.

She stopped and only the harp went on singing beneath her crystal fingers. Sharkān felt himself lost in infinite desire and prevailed upon her to sing again. This was her song:

> The moon is palest when she sets;
> Only pretended love forgets.

Hardly was this song finished when cries and a great tumult were heard without; a host of Christian warriors with naked swords rushed into the apartment, crying: 'Sharkān has fallen into our hands! Death to Sharkān!' The young man at once thought that his hostess had betrayed him but, as he turned to reproach her, he saw her grow very pale and heard her ask the armed knights what they wanted. So Sharkān retired behind a pillar. He who was chief among the knights advanced and said: 'Lady Ibrīzah, glorious queen, pearl among the pearls of the waters, did you not know that this man was in the monastery?' 'Of whom do you speak?' asked Queen Ibrīzah, and the knight answered: 'I speak of Sharkān, son of Umar al-Numān, master of heroes, destroyer of cities, he who has never left a tower standing or a fortress unsubdued. Your father and our master, King Hardūb, learnt in Cesarea from her who is called Mother-of-Calamity that Sharkān himself was here and that she herself had seen him arrive at the monastery. To have caught such a lion in your toils is a notable deed, O queen, for with one stroke it shall destroy the Mussulmān army.'

Queen Ibrīzah, daughter of Hardūb, King of Cesarea, looked angrily at the leading warrior and asked him his name. 'I am the knight Masūrah, son of Mausūrah, son of Kāshirdah,' he answered. 'Insolent Masūrah,' she cried, 'how did you dare to enter my monastery without warning and before soliciting an audience?' 'My queen,' he replied, 'none of your porters barred my way, but rather they fell in beside me and brought me to your presence. Now I wait for you to give up Sharkān to me as your father has ordered.'

Then cried Queen Ibrīzah: 'What is it that you are saying? Do you not know that old Mother-of-Calamity is the worst of liars? It is true that there is a man here, but he is far from being the Sharkān of whom you speak. He is a wandering stranger whom I am entertaining. But if he were Sharkān, the laws of hospitality would oblige me to protect him against the whole earth. It shall never be said that Ibrīzah betrayed a guest, when there was bread and salt between them. There is nothing left for you to do, Sir Knight, save to return to my father, the King, and tell him that Mother-of-Calamity has deceived him.'

'Lady,' answered Masūrah, 'I cannot return to King Hardūb except with the man he commanded me to take.' 'You mix in affairs which do not concern you,' cried the lady angrily. 'You are paid to fight: therefore fight when you are ordered to do so, but leave loftier concerns to others more noble than yourself. If this stranger were Sharkān and you attacked him you would pay for your rashness with your life and the lives of all your followers. Wait, and I will bring him before you armed with sword and shield.' Said the knight: 'Unfortunately I have to choose between your anger and that of the King: therefore, if Sharkān presents himself before me, I will have him bound by my men and led in mean captivity to Cesarea.' 'You speak a great deal for a soldier, Masūrah,' exclaimed Ibrīzah, 'and yet you have not learnt to avoid pretension and insolence. You are a hundred to one; if this recent knighthood of yours has not extinguished all your courage, you will fight him man to man. Should you be slain, another may take your place and then another, until

Sharkān is overthrown. This will be a means of deciding if there are many heroes among so knightly-seeming a band.'

At this point Shahrazād saw the approach of morning and discreetly fell silent.

But when the fiftieth night had come

SHE SAID:

It is related, O auspicious King, that the knight Masūrah made answer: 'You counsel well, and I shall be the first to go up against him.' 'Wait till I tell him and hear his answer,' replied the queen. 'If he accepts, the fight shall be as I say; if he refuses, he is still my honoured and protected guest.'

Ibrīzah went behind the pillar where Sharkān stood concealed and told him of the test she had proposed. Sharkān was thrown into consternation, both because he had doubted the young woman and because he had so foolishly ventured into the enemy's country. After a little thought, he said: 'Lady, it is not my custom to fight against a single warrior, but against ten at a time.' With these words he rushed towards the Christian warriors, with his sword on high and his shield well forward.

The knight Masūrah bore down like a bolt upon Sharkān, but the Moslem stood firm against his onslaught and, leaping like a lion, gave him so terrible a shoulder-stroke that the bright blade whipped through the belly and intestines, and came out by the thigh.

The young queen saw this and placed Sharkān upon a higher throne within her heart, saying: 'This is the man with whom I would have wrestled in the forest!' Then she cried to the rest of the knights: 'Is there none to avenge your leader?' Masūrah's brother, who was a giant of a man with a bold face and mighty muscles, strode towards Sharkān; but Sharkān did not give him time to strike a blow, his terrible sword cleft the second as the first and came out shining from his hip. One by one the other knights attacked him, but the lightning of his sword killed fifty of them. The remaining fifty threw themselves upon him in a mass but Sharkān received them with a breast harder than stone, a heart more finely tempered than his sword, and scattered them like chaff upon the threshing-floor, so that their lives fled shrieking.

Queen Ibrīzah cried to her servants to know if there were any men left in the monastery and, hearing that none remained but her

own porters, she went to Sharkān and taking him in her arms kissed
him, all bloody as he was. Then she counted the dead and found
that there were eighty of them; for the other twenty had fled with
their wounds upon them. When he heard the count, Sharkān wiped
his bloody sword and, taking Ibrīzah by the hand, led her into the
great hall, chanting these lines:

> The knights came to me,
> They bade me defiance;
>   Ungird me now.

> They wished to take me,
> They looked for compliance;
>   Ungird me now.

> I fed them all
> To my brothers, the lions;
>   Ungird me now.

Ibrīzah kissed Sharkān's hand and, lifting her robe, showed him
that she wore below it a coat of close mail and had girded about her
a sword of finely tempered Indian steel. In answer to his surprise,
she said: 'I hastened to arm myself that I might come to your aid,
but there was little need.'

After this she called the monastery porters to her and said: 'Why
did you let the King's men in without my permission?' 'It is not
usual,' they answered, 'to deny entry to the King's men or to the
chief of all his knights.' 'You wished to shame me and to kill my
guest,' said Ibrīzah, and begged Sharkān to cut off their heads. The
young man did so, and the queen said to her other slaves: 'They
merited a worse fate.' When they were left alone together again, she
turned to Sharkān, saying: 'Now I will reveal all that I have so far
kept hidden from you.' She started her tale in these words:

'I am Ibrīzah, the only daughter of Hardūb, the Greek king of
Cesarea. The old woman, Mother-of-Calamity, who was my father's
nurse and is still greatly considered in his palace, is my deadly
enemy for a reason which I will not tell you now, as there are certain
young girls mixed up in the affair about whom you are bound to
hear at some future time. It is certain that Mother-of-Calamity will
redouble her efforts for my destruction when she hears of the death
of all these knights and will tell my father that I have embraced the
Mussulmān faith. My only hope of safety is to leave my native land;

I ask you to help me to do so, and to deal with me as I have dealt with you, seeing that you are in some sort the cause of what has happened.'

Sharkān felt his breast expand with joy and all his soul ready to take flight when she threw herself thus upon his protection. 'By Allāh,' he cried, 'who will dare come near you while I live? But, my very dear, can you bear the separation from your father and your people?' 'I can,' she answered, 'and my heart has ceased to be troubled. But I have one condition to impose upon you.' 'What is that?' he asked, and she answered: 'That you return to Baghdād with all your soldiers.' 'Dear mistress,' replied Sharkān, 'my father, Umar al-Numān, sent me into your country for the sole purpose of conquering your father, against whom King Afrīdūn of Constantinople had asked our help. The cause of the war is that your father seized a ship loaded with treasures and young slaves and, above all, with three most valuable jewels of magic virtue.' 'Be at ease on that account,' answered Ibrīzah, 'and listen to the true story of our enmity with King Afrīdūn.' She said:

'We Christian Greeks have an annual festival at this monastery; it lasts for seven days, and all the Christian kings are present at it, together with the nobles and great merchants, their wives and daughters. One year the daughter of King Afrīdūn was present at this festival; her name was Saffīah, and she is now the concubine of your father, Umar al-Numān, and the mother of a child by him.

'When the ceremonies were over, Saffīah refused to return to Constantinople by land; so a ship was prepared for her and she set sail with all her companions and belongings. A contrary wind drove the vessel across the way of a mighty barque, in which five hundred Franks were journeying from the Isle of Kāfūr. These were all armed to the teeth and did not let the occasion slip for making a profitable booty. They boarded the smaller boat and, putting her in irons, towed her behind them as a prize. A tempest rose, and both vessels were wrecked upon this coast; the men of these parts killed such pirates as remained, and captured all their treasure, including sixty young girls, among whom was Saffīah. They gave the girls to my father as a present and kept the treasure for themselves. The King of Cesarea chose out the ten most beautiful of the maidens and parted the rest among his followers. Then, of the ten, he chose the five fairest, and sent them as a gift to King Umar al-Numān. Though none of the people of this country knew who she was, Saffīah, the

daughter of Afrīdūn, was one of the five sent to your father, with a
present of rare silks and Greek embroideries.

'At the beginning of this year, the King my father received a letter
from Afrīdūn containing many insults which I cannot repeat, and
these lines among the rest:

'Two years ago you captured sixty maidens from certain
pirates, and did not let me know, O King Hardūb, that among
them was my daughter, Saffīah. That was a great wrong and a great
shame. If you do not wish to become my enemy, send back my
daughter, unsoiled and unharmed, as soon as you receive this
letter. If you delay I will treat you as you deserve, and my anger
shall exact a terrible vengeance.

'This letter placed my father in a considerable difficulty, since he
had sent Saffīah to Umar al-Numān, who had had a child by her. It
was therefore impossible to send her back in the state which her
father demanded.

'My father realised that a great calamity had fallen upon him.
He could do nothing but write a letter to Afrīdūn, telling him all the
truth and excusing himself, with a thousand vows as to his ignorance
of the identity of the girls whom he had sent. When the King of
Constantinople received this letter, his rage knew no bounds; he
rose, he sat down again, he trembled and foamed at the mouth,
saying: "By the true Christ, is it possible that my daughter, whom
every Christian king has sought in marriage, has become the slave of
a Mussulmān, a plaything for his desires, a chattel of his bed!
Verily I will take a vengeance on this unbeliever that shall astound
the East and the West for many years to come."

'Then it was, my dear Sharkān, that Afrīdūn conceived a snare
for Umar al-Numān and sent ambassadors with rich gifts to make
your father believe that he was at war with us and to ask for assistance. In reality he planned to lead you and your ten thousand into
a trap and destroy you all.

'The three miraculous gems of which you speak actually exist.
They belonged to Saffīah, were taken by the pirates, and came at
length into the hands of my father, who gave them to me. I have
them still and will some time show them to you. But, for the moment,
it is most urgent that you return to your soldiers and lead them back
to Baghdād before they fall into the nets of the King of Constantinople.'

Sharkān kissed Ibrīzah's hand, saying: 'Praise be to Allāh who placed you upon my way that you might save my people. Delicate and helpful queen, I cannot leave you, after what has passed, to stay here alone, threatened by unknown dangers. Come with me, Ibrīzah, come to Baghdād.'

But Ibrīzah had had time to reflect, so she said: 'Set out immediately and seize the envoys whom you have with you; make them confess, and you will know that what I have said is true. In three days I will rejoin you and we will go together to Baghdād.'

She rose weeping, and took his head between her hands to kiss him. Sharkān wept also when he saw her tears, and murmured these lines:

> My tears are bitter on the lips that kiss me,
>   Though they are honey-sweet in their goodbye;
> For though they mourn for me and say they miss me,
>   Only not all lips lie.

Sharkān left Ibrīzah and, mounting his war-horse, which two girls were holding, galloped off. He crossed the drawbridge and rode by forest paths until he came to the clearing. Hardly had he entered this than he saw three riders check their horses at sight of him. He had drawn his sword lest their intentions should be hostile, when he recognised them as the wazīr Dandān and his two principal amīrs. They lighted off their horses and greeted the prince respectfully, telling him with what foreboding his absence had filled the army. Sharkān related his story and informed them of the treachery which King Afrīdūn had plotted through his envoys, saying: 'It is likely that they have taken advantage of your absence to escape from the army and warn their King of our arrival in his territory. His people may have destroyed our soldiers already. Let us return as quickly as possible.'

They galloped with all speed until they came to the valley, where they found that their army was safe, but that the envoys had disappeared. The camp was struck in haste and the whole army retreated until they came without mishap into the outskirts of their own country. The people gave them food and fodder for their horses, and the troop rested there for some time. Then Sharkān sent the wazīr Dandān forward with all the army save a hundred picked knights, whom he chose to act as rearguard with him and with whom he set out a day after the rest.

Two parasangs from where they started, they came to a narrow defile between two rocky hills, from the other end of which they saw a thick cloud of dust advancing. It came on rapidly and cleared as it approached, showing a hundred knights clad in coats of mail and vizors of steel, who cried: 'Dismount and give up your arms, O Mussulmāns, or by Mary and John we will slay you all!'

The air about Sharkān darkened with his anger, his eyes blazed and his cheeks suffused. 'Christian dogs,' he cried, 'do you dare to threaten us, after having had the impudence to cross our frontier? Do you think to speak these saucy words to us and return safe to your own country? Come, charge the dogs, you Faithful!' With this he set heels to his horse and rode forward, followed by his hundred. The two troops met with a great clang of battle, spear fell on spear and sword on sword, body upon body and horse on horse, so that nothing was heard but the din of arms till nightfall. When they could no longer see to fight, the two troops separated; Sharkān discovered that not one of his men had received any serious hurt, so he addressed them as follows:

'Comrades, you know that all my life I have swum in a sea of battles, beaten by the waves of many swords, and have fought with heroes not a few, but I have never found such valorous and knightly foes as we have fought with this day.'

His men answered: 'What you say is true, Prince Sharkān, especially of the chief of these Christians, who is the bravest and most courteous. Each time one of us was at his mercy he turned aside and let him escape.'

Sharkān was perplexed at this, and said: 'We are a hundred against a hundred, therefore to-morrow we will attack them in full line of battle and pray to Allāh for the victory.' Then the Mussulmān troop lay down and slept.

In the meanwhile the Christians had surrounded their chief, saying: 'We have not been victorious to-day.' And their leader answered: 'To-morrow we will attack them and overthrow them one by one.' With that the knights also slept.

When morning had come—and the sun rose fair upon the warlike and the unwarlike, praising the Prophet for the beauties of this world—Prince Sharkān mounted his horse and rode forward between two ranks of his warriors, saying to them: 'Our foes are drawn up for battle. Let one of you go forward and challenge one of them to single combat, so that each in his turn may bear the assault of Destiny.'

Immediately one of Sharkān's cavaliers rode from the ranks towards the enemy, crying in a loud voice: 'Oh, is there any will fight with me?' Hardly had he spoken when one of the Christian knights, covered in shining arms from head to foot, gleaming with silk and gold, mounted on a grey horse and showing a ruddy hairless face below his helmet, pricked forward and hurled his horse upon the champion. With one trick of the lance, he unseated the Mussulmān and led him back captive to the Christian rank. The brother of the captive next rode out; a knight engaged him and, taking advantage of a false thrust, dashed him to the ground with the heel of his lance and took him prisoner. By nightfall twenty of Sharkān's men had thus been captured in single combat.

Sharkān was angry at so many victories, and said to the remnant of his followers: 'This is a strange thing which has happened to us. To-morrow I myself will fight the leader of these men and learn his reason for thus violating our territory. If he refuses to explain, we will kill him; but if he be amenable, we will make peace.'

Next morning Sharkān advanced alone towards the enemy and a knight came forward to meet him on horseback, surrounded by fifty warriors on foot, wearing a blue silk cloak over his close-woven coat of mail, and waving a sword of Indian steel above his head. He rode a black horse with a white mark like a silver coin on its forehead, and had himself the rosy beardless cheeks of a very youth, together with a moonlike beauty that was more than mortal.

This young knight addressed Sharkān in the purest Arabic, saying: 'Sharkān, son of Umar al-Numān, leaguer of towns and cities, destroyer of towers, prepare for battle. We are both leaders, so let the army of him who conquers hold the field.' Sharkān charged like an angry lion, and the heroes met as if two mountains were in combat, or two great seas were warring with each other. They fought till night was black and then each returned to his own people.

On his return, Sharkān said: 'I have never met with such an adversary! Each time that his opponent uncovers a vital part, he touches it lightly with the heel of his lance instead of sending the steel home. I do not understand what he would be at; but I could wish that we had men like him in our army.'

On the morrow this mighty duel raged all day and neither warrior gained the advantage; but, on the third day, the young Christian reined in his horse at full gallop, so that it fell and he was thrown to earth as if by accident. Sharkān leapt from his courser and was about to pass his sword through the body of his assailant when the fallen Christian cried: 'Is this the way of heroes? Is this how a gallant warrior treats a woman?' Sharkān looked closely at the speaker and recognised Queen Ibrīzah.

He threw away his sword and knelt before the young girl, saying: 'What is the meaning of this, O fairest of all queens?' 'I wished to try your valour,' answered Ibrīzah. 'My hundred warriors are all maidens of my train. If my horse had not stumbled it might not have gone so well with you, dear Sharkān.' The youth smiled as he said: 'Praise be to Allāh for reuniting us!' Ibrīzah gave up her twenty prisoners to Sharkān and, when all his men had kissed the earth between her hands, the prince turned to the virgin warrior and said: 'There is no king who would not think himself fortunate to have such heroes to fight for him.'

Without further delay the two hundred set out together, and in six days they saw far off the shining towers of the City of Peace.

At this point Shahrazād saw the approach of morning and discreetly fell silent.

But when the fifty-first night had come

SHE SAID:

Sharkān begged Ibrīzah and her followers to put off their warlike dress and habit themselves again as Grecian women. They did so, and the prince sent certain of his cavaliers forward to announce their coming to Umar al-Numān. They camped where they were that night, and at dawn, as they were taking their way towards the city, Dandān rode forth to greet them with a thousand horsemen; kissing the earth between the hands of the two young people, he led them into the city.

Umar al-Numān rose when he saw his son and, kissing him, asked his news. Sharkān told him the whole story of his adventures with Ibrīzah, the daughter of Hardūb, King of Cesarea, and informed him of the Sultān of Constantinople's treachery and the reason for it. Then he dwelt on the hospitality, good sense, and warlike qualities of Ibrīzah, until the King grew most anxious to see her. Deep down in his heart he savoured the idea of feeling that virgin and doughty body in his bed, nor did he disdain the thought of her hundred followers, fresh girls encased in warlike steel; he was a very muscular old man, able to rise triumphant from between the arms of women so ardent that they would have put a younger man to shame.

Sharkān, who could not see into his father's mind, led young Ibrīzah into the King's presence. Umar dismissed all save his eunuchs and, when Ibrīzah kissed the earth between his hands and spoke to him in pure and elegant Arabic, marvelled and thanked her heartily for all the favour she had shown his son. He bade her seat herself, and, when she had done so and removed her veil, his reason fled before the fairness of her face. Not until he had given orders for the most sumptuous apartments in the palace to be assigned to her and to her followers, did he broach the subject of the three miraculous jewels.

'Those three white stones never leave me; I will show them to you,' said Ibrīzah. She sent for a chest from among her baggage and drew from it a box; from the box she took a golden jewel case, and from the jewel case three great round shining gems. She kissed them and gave them to Umar al-Numān as a guest-present; then she retired.

Umar al-Numān felt his heart go with her; he sent for Sharkān and gave him one of the stones. The young man asked what was to become of the other two, and the King answered: 'I shall give one to your little sister Nuzhat, and the other to your little brother Dū al-Makān.'

Sharkān was much disturbed on hearing for the first time of the existence of Dū al-Makān, and said: 'Father, have you another son beside myself?' 'Indeed I have,' answered Umar, 'he is at present six years old, for he was born at one birth with Nuzhat. His mother is Saffīah, daughter of the King of Constantinople.' Sharkān could not help shaking the dust from his garments at this unwelcome news, but he controlled himself, and said: 'May Allāh bless them both!' Nevertheless the King saw that his son's mind was troubled, and asked him: 'My child, why are you so disturbed? You know well that the throne is destined for you, and also that I gave you the most beautiful of the three jewels.' Sharkān could not answer; therefore, not wishing to displease his father, he bowed his head and left the hall where they had been talking. He made his way into Ibrīzah's apartment, where he was gently received and bidden to sit down. When the princess asked why his brow was clouded with care, he told her of Dū al-Makān, and added: 'But that is not the chief cause of my worry, dear Ibrīzah. I am sure that I have seen signs in my father of a strong desire towards your most dear self. What do you say to that?' 'You can set yourself quite at ease on that score,' she answered. 'Your father will never possess me in my lifetime. He has three hundred and sixty women to satisfy him, and my virginity was not destined for a man so fully occupied. Do not take any further thought on my account.' After this they ate and drank together, and Sharkān returned to his own place to sleep, a prey to gloomy thoughts.

As soon as Sharkān left him, King Umar al-Numān took up the two jewels and went to visit his concubine, Saffiah. Saffiah rose as he entered, and the two children, Nuzhat and Dū al-Makān, ran to greet their father. He delighted them by hanging the two jewels round their necks on light gold chains, and then turned to their mother, saying: 'Why did you never tell me, dear Saffiah, that you are the daughter of King Afrīdūn of Constantinople? If I had known I could have given you hospitality more in accord with your noble birth.' 'Generous King,' answered Saffiah, 'what could you give me that I have not got? You have heaped benefits upon me, and made me the mother of these two fair little ones.' King Umar was delighted by the delicacy and tact of this answer, and immediately assigned to Saffiah a more beautiful palace and augmented both her income and her retinue. Then he returned to his dīwān to judge the people according to his custom.

But from that day his heart was tortured with thoughts of young Ibrīzah; he spent all his evenings conversing with her and dropping hints of his desire. But the queen would ever answer him that she had no wish for men, and this reply so teased and excited him that he fell ill. At last he had recourse to his wazīr Dandān, and asked him how he might come to possess the woman of his choice.

Dandān considered for awhile and then said: 'O King, when you go to visit Ibrīzah to-night take with you a morsel of banj, and slip it into her drink; then when she has reached her bed, you can master her and calm the fever in your blood.' 'That is an excellent plan, and as far as I can see the only one,' answered the King.

He chose out a little piece of banj, the smell of which would have sent an elephant to sleep from one year's end to the other, and carried it in his pocket when he went to visit the young queen. As they were talking together he expressed a desire for wine, and the wine-set was brought with fruits and nuts of all sorts and gold and crystal cups. When the drinking had a little risen to Ibrīzah's head, Umar poured out a cup and drank the half of it himself. Into the other half he secretly slipped the drug and handed it to the queen, saying: 'Drink this for my sake, royal girl.' Ibrīzah laughingly drained the cup, but scarcely had she done so when the apartment reeled before her eyes and she had just the strength to drag herself to her bed. She fell back on it with stretched arms and parted thighs and lay there in the light of two great torches.

Umar al-Numān came near and untied the silk cord of her ample drawers. These he drew down gently until the queen was covered only by a light chemise. He lifted this last veil and that which appeared between her thighs, minutely detailed in the strong light of the torches, ravished his soul. Nevertheless he found patience to undress and put himself at ease, before throwing himself upon the young body before him and covering it. Who knows what passed that night! . . . Thus Queen Ibrīzah lost her virginity.

The King rose and found Coral-Pearl in the adjoining room. 'Run quickly to your mistress; for she has need of you,' he said. Ibrīzah's favourite slave ran to her mistress and found her lying on her back with her chemise pulled up and her thighs stained with blood. Coral-Pearl understood from the pale face of the queen that instant cares were needed; she wiped the dishonour of her mistress with a kerchief and cleaned her belly and thighs with a second. After that she sprinkled her face, her hands, and her feet with rose-water, and washed her lips and mouth with orange-water.

Ibrīzah sneezed and opened her eyes, saying to Coral-Pearl: 'Ah, tell me what has happened, for I feel ill.' The slave could but tell her mistress in what a state she had found her, so that Ibrīzah understood that Umar al-Numān had satisfied his desires to her irreparable loss. She fell into a black grief and ordered Coral-Pearl to refuse all entrance to her apartment and to tell King Umar that she was ill.

When the King received this message, he sent slaves daily to Ibrīzah with meats and wines of every sort, cups full of fruits and jams, and porcelain bowls frothing with sweet creams; but for many weeks she stayed shut up in her apartment, until she perceived that her belly was waxing and that she was certainly with child. The world lay in ruins before her eyes and she would in no wise listen to the consolations of Coral-Pearl. At length she said to her slave: 'I alone am responsible for what has happened, for I sinned against myself in leaving my own kingdom. Life means no more to me, my courage has gone from me, and my strength has failed. I who was Ibrīzah, a thing of fame and prowess, have lost my might with my virginity. I could not stand up against a child or hold the reins of my horse. What shall I do, what shall I do? If I am brought to bed here, these pagan women will laugh at me when they have learnt the manner of my ravishing; yet if I return to my father's house, how will I dare to look him in the face? Indeed the poet knew the truth of things when he wrote:

> No native land, no family,
> No home, awaits adversity.'

'Dear mistress, I am your slave, my life is yours; command me in all things and I will obey,' said Coral-Pearl. 'Then listen carefully,' answered Ibrīzah, 'I have no course open to me except to leave this palace secretly and return to my father and mother; for when a body stinks, its family must look to it, and I am no better than a lifeless body.' 'That is the best thing that you can do,' said Coral-Pearl, and forthwith she began to make secret preparations for departure. It was necessary, however, for Ibrīzah to wait for a suitable occasion, when the King should be hunting and Sharkān inspecting the strongholds on the frontier. These two things did not happen at one and the same time until Ibrīzah was near her term. At last the moment came when she said to Coral-Pearl: 'We must leave this very night, for I shall bear a child in three or four days, and I would rather die than do so in this palace. You must find some man to accompany us, for my arm has lost its power.' 'I know of one man who would defend us very well,' answered Coral-Pearl, 'one of the King's porters, a gigantic negro called Sullen, who was once a highwayman, and to whom I have accorded many favours. I will give him gold, and promise that when we arrive in our own country he shall wed the fairest girl in Cesarea.' 'Rather bring him to me, my child,' said the queen, 'and I will arrange matters with him.'

Coral-Pearl found the negro and led him to her mistress, saying as they went: 'Your fortune is made, O Sullen, if you do all that my mistress tells you.' When the queen saw the blackamore, a violent repulsion swelled in her heart, but, as necessity knows no law, she smiled on him and said: 'Do you think, O Sullen, that you could help us in our difficulties and, at the same time, keep a secret? I wish you to prepare two mules for our baggage and two horses for ourselves; you must help us to escape to-night and, when we have reached my country, I will marry you to the fairest of the Greeks and give you more gold than you can dream. If you wish to return to your own land, you will be able to do so as a rich man.'

The negro Sullen, who had felt all his desires passionately excited by his first glimpse of Ibrīzah, answered: 'All shall be as you say, my mistress; I consecrate my life to your service. I go to make my preparation.' With that he departed, thinking to himself: 'What a booty and what a chance of securing it! I shall enjoy myself in the flesh of these two moons, and if either of them resist, I will kill them and make off with their treasure.'

That night all three set off under cover of darkness, but on the fourth day of their journey the queen felt her pains come on her and was obliged to call a halt. 'It is the end,' she said, and called to the negro to lift her down and to Coral-Pearl to stay by her and help her in her labour.

When all three had dismounted, Sullen, who now had an opportunity of seeing all the charms of the queen, was so moved that his zabb swelled terribly and lifted his garment in front of him. Being unable to contain himself, he pulled it forth and went up to the young woman, who was like to faint from horror and indignation, saying: 'Pity me, mistress, and let me have you.'

At this point Shahrazād saw the approach of morning and discreetly fell silent.

But when the fifty-second night had come

SHE SAID:

It is related, O auspicious King, that Queen Ibrīzah answered: 'Black man, son of a black man, son of a slave, do you dare thus to expose yourself before me? How great is my shame that I lie defenceless in the hands of the lowest slave that ever crawled. If God should help me and cure these womanish parts which make me weak, I will punish you with my own hand. I would rather kill myself and be quit once and for all of the sufferings and sorrows of my life than be touched by one of your fingers!' Then she extemporised these lines:

> Though I have suffered much,
>   I will not suffer you;
> God will ward off the greasy smutch
>   Of your black touch.

> Though I am cut to earth,
>   I will not suffer you;
> The clean child of a noble birth,
> My blood has worth.
>
> You lust with your beast's eyes,
>   I will not suffer you;
> Thing of obscene black thighs
> And filthy destinies,
>   I will not suffer you.

When Sullen heard these lines, his face swelled with rage, his nostrils dilated, his fat lips gave back from his teeth, and he cried these lines:

> Your angry voice
> Might drive aback raw boys
>   When they aspire,
> My lust's too high,
> There's lighted in my eye
>   Too fierce a fire;
> Lash me with words
> Or ring your bed with swords,
>   I'll come to my desire.

Ibrīzah wept with rage at these lines, and cried out: 'Do you think that all women are alike, indecent slave, black child of shame, that you dare to speak to me in this way?' Then Sullen, seeing that the queen would have nothing to do with him, flung himself upon her in a fury and, seizing her by the hair, passed his sword through her body. Thus died Queen Ibrīzah at the hands of a negro slave.

Sullen seized the mules which carried Ibrīzah's treasure and, driving them before him, fled into the mountains, while the queen, as she breathed her last sigh, gave birth to a son between the hands of Coral-Pearl. The faithful slave covered her head with dust, tore her garments and beat herself about the face until the blood came, crying: 'Alas, alas, for my mistress! The warrior, the valorous girl!'

Hardly had the young slave ceased to mourn, when she saw a cloud of dust filling the sky and coming rapidly towards her; as it approached she could see that it was raised by mounted soldiers dressed in the fashion of Cesarea. Indeed, the oncoming troop was none other than the army of King Hardūb, which he was leading against Baghdād on the news that his daughter had fled from her monastery.

Hardūb came at length to the place where his daughter lay dead and, when he saw her blood-stained body, he fell in a dead faint from his horse; therefore Coral-Pearl wept and lamented the more bitterly. When the King came to himself, she told him what had happened, adding: 'The murderer was one of the negroes of Umar al-Numān, the licentious King who outraged my dear mistress.' Hardūb saw the world turn black before his eyes when he heard this and resolved to take terrible vengeance for his daughter, but first he had Ibrīzah's body borne back to Cesarea in a litter for honourable burial.

As soon as he reached his palace he called for Mother-of-Calamity, his nurse, and said: 'See what the Mussulmāns have done to my daughter! The King has ravished her, a slave has killed her, and that which Coral-Pearl is holding is her base-born child. I swear by the Messiah that I will avenge my daughter and my shame, or die by my own hand.' With that he wept hot tears, and Mother-of-Calamity said to him: 'Take no thought for this vengeance, my King, for I concern myself about it. I will kill this unbeliever and his children in such a way that tales shall be told of my vengeance for years to come and over the whole earth. Only you must listen carefully to what I say and help me in this manner: choose out the five most beautiful and high-breasted virgins in Cesarea and, at the same time, call before you the most learned and expert Mussulmān teachers in your kingdom. It will be the business of the teachers to instruct the virgins in the unbelievers' law, in Arab history, the annals of the Khalīfahs, the acts of the heathen kings, etiquette, conversation and polite drinking, poetry and elocution, verse-writing and the art of song. Their education must be complete even if it takes ten years; for the Arabs have a saying: "Revenge is still new after forty years" and my revenge depends upon the thorough instruction of these girls. To ease your mind in the meanwhile, I tell you that this heathen King has a passion for coupling with his slaves; he owns three hundred and sixty concubines as well as the hundred maidens left by Ibrīzah and women sent to him as tribute from all lands. It is by this weakness that I shall destroy him.'

Hardūb rejoiced greatly and, kissing his nurse's head, sent straightway for the Mussulmān teachers and the high-breasted virgins.

At this point Shahrazād saw the approach of morning and discreetly fell silent.

But when the fifty-third night had come

SHE SAID:

It is related, O auspicious King, that Hardūb lavishly gave both instruction and gifts to the teachers, and confided the chosen girls to them. Thereafter the learned men took special pains to give their young charges the finest Mussulmān education.

When Umar al-Numān returned from hunting and learned that Ibrīzah had disappeared, he cried out in his grief and anger: 'How could a woman pass from my palace and no one know it? If my kingdom is as well guarded, I am like to lose my throne. Another time I shall know how to have the gates well sentinelled.' As he was speaking, Sharkān also returned and learnt the news about Ibrīzah from his father. From that time the young prince could hardly support life at his father's court, especially as he saw that his small brother and sister occupied all the attention of the King. Day by day he became sadder, until at last Umar al-Numān noticed it and asked the reason for his sorrow. 'My father,' answered Sharkān, 'there are many reasons why it is intolerable for me to remain in the palace. As a last favour, I would ask you to make me governor of one of your outlying strongholds, that I may end my days far off from Baghdād. A poet has said:

> Were I to stay
> I'd see the places where her absence is
> And hear her silences,
> Let me away.'

King Umar understood his son's sorrow, and consoled him, saying: 'My child, it shall be as you wish. The city of Damascus is the most important outpost of my kingdom. I appoint you its governor.' He sent for his nobles and the palace scribes and appointed Sharkān governor of Damascus, both by speech and in writing. The prince said goodbye to his father and mother, gave last instructions to the wazīr Dandān, and set out at the head of a cavalcade amid the good wishes and protestations of the amīrs. When he arrived at Damascus, the people ornamented and illuminated the city in honour of his coming, and a great procession went out to meet him to the sound of fifes, cymbals, trumpets and clarions, those to whom it was due walking upon the right hand, and the rest upon the left.

Soon after the departure of his son, King Umar was approached by those who were in charge of the education of Nuzhat and Dū al-Makān with the information that the children had completed their studies and had nothing more to learn, either of book-knowledge or of deportment. The King was delighted to hear this and sent the teachers away with magnificent presents. He soon saw for himself that Dū al-Makān, who was now fourteen, had become a graceful, handsome and accomplished cavalier, yet one much given to piety and consorting by preference with learned men, poets, and experts in the Law and the Koran. The men and women of Baghdād loved him and blessed him.

One day certain pilgrims passed through Baghdād on their way from Irāk to Mecca for the annual pilgrimage and a visit to the tomb of the Prophet in Madinah. (The prayer and peace of Allāh be upon him!) When Dū al-Makān saw the saintly procession, his piety flamed up and he ran to his father, saying: 'Can I have your permission to go on pilgrimage?' Umar al-Numān tried to dissuade him, saying: 'You are too young, my son, but next year, if Allāh wills, I will go on pilgrimage myself and take you with me.'

Dū al-Makān found this too long to wait, so he ran to his twin sister Nuzhat, and found her at prayer. When she had made an end of praying, he said: 'Dear sister, I am consumed by a desire to go on pilgrimage and to see the tomb of the Prophet (upon whom be prayer and peace!). But our father will not give me leave. So I am determined to take a little money with me and to set out secretly without telling him anything about it.' Nuzhat was seized with the same ardour, and cried: 'I conjure you by Allāh to take me with you and not to deprive me of the chance of seeing the tomb of the Prophet, on whom be prayer and peace!' 'Be it so,' said her brother. 'Come to look for me at dusk to-night, and take care not to tell anybody.'

That night Nuzhat dressed herself as a man in certain clothes of her brother's, who was much of a size with her, and, providing herself with some money, went out of the palace gate. There she found Dū al-Makān with two camels; on these they set off, and arrived under cover of darkness in the middle of the band of pilgrims. Next morning the caravan from Irāk left Baghdād and proceeded towards Mecca where, by the mercy of Allāh, all arrived in safety.

Dū al-Makān and Nuzhat rejoiced exceedingly when they came to mount Arafāt and accomplished the sacred rites upon its summit. After that they visited the tomb of the Prophet (upon whom be prayer and peace!) and, when the pilgrims returned to their own country, preferred to extend their journey and see the sacred city of Abraham, the Friend of God, which Jews and Christians call Jerusalem. They joined a small caravan which was going in that direction and made the journey with a certain amount of difficulty, for both were stricken with fever on the way. The girl recovered after a few days, but the boy became worse and was very ill when they reached Jerusalem. His sister settled him in a small room in one of the khāns, but he became delirious and Nuzhat nursed him in grief and anxiety, feeling that she was a stranger and had no one to whom to turn.

As Dū al-Makān's illness continued, Nuzhat spent the last of their money and sold her garments one by one through the porter of the khān, until she had nothing but the robe she wore and the ragged rug which served them for a bed. On the evening that they came to the end of their resources, and while Nuzhat sat weeping in the little room, Dū al-Makān recovered consciousness by Allāh's grace, and said to his sister: 'I feel my strength returning to me; I could very well eat a grill of skewered mutton.' 'But how shall I buy it for you?' answered Nuzhat. 'I cannot make up my mind to beg in the public streets. To-morrow, though, I will hire myself as a servant to some rich notable and make a little money. I do not mind doing that, except that I shall have to be away from you all day. There is neither power nor might save in Allāh, and He alone can send us safe back to Baghdād.'

With that she wept again; but next morning, though she had no notion of where to look for work, she set out cheerfully from the khān, after having lovingly embraced her brother and veiled her face with a remnant of camel's hair cloth which a neighbour had given her. Dū al-Makān waited all that day and night and then all the next day and the next night, but his sister did not return. He grew very troubled and, though he had not eaten for two days, dragged himself to the door and begged the porter of the khān to help him to the market. The porter lifted the boy on his shoulders, carried him to the market and, setting him down against the closed door of a ruined shop, wished him well and went his way.

The merchants and passers-by clustered about Dū al-Makān and mourned over his pitiable state. When he made signs to them that he would eat, they made a collection for him among the merchants on a copper plate, and bought him food. As thirty dirhams remained they consulted how best to use it, and an old man belonging to the market said: 'The best thing that we can do is to hire a camel and send the poor young man to the hospital which has been opened in Damascus by the kindness of the Khalīfah. If he stays here he will surely die.' All determined to adopt this advice; but, as it was late, they put off doing so until the morrow and returned to their homes, leaving water and food by the side of Dū al-Makān and lamenting his fate out of the kindness of their hearts. The young man was too feeble to eat or drink, and passed a sleepless night. In the morning the good folk of the market hired a camel and told its owner to carry the youth to the Damascus hospital. The man answered: 'I shall certainly do so, my lords,' but in his own mind the rascal thought: 'To think that I should carry a dying man from Jerusalem to Damascus!' He set off among the blessings of the bystanders, but, after passing through a few streets, stopped at the door of the hammām and laid Dū al-Makān down in a dead swoon on a pile of wood which was used to heat the baths. Then he hurried off as fast as his beast would take him.

The fireman of the hammām came to his work at dawn and, seeing the body, said to himself: 'Who has thrown this dead man here?' He was on the point of dragging Dū al-Makān further off, when the young man made a movement. 'He is not dead then!' cried the fireman. 'But surely he has eaten hashīsh and fallen upon my wood without knowing it. Hullo, drunkard! Hashīsh-man!' he bellowed, and in so doing brought his face close to that of the youth. When he saw that he was but a beardless boy and both beautiful and noble, in spite of the ravages of fever, the fireman felt his heart filled with pity. 'There is no power or might save in Allāh!' he said to himself. 'Here am I rashly judging a poor invalid stranger, when our Prophet (on whom be the prayer and peace of Allāh!) told us to guard against hasty judgments and to be kind to the stranger and distressed.' Without further consideration, he lifted the young man on his shoulders and, returning to his own house, confided him to the care of his wife. She bedded him softly with rug and clean pillow, heated water in the kitchen, and washed his hands and feet and face. In the meanwhile the fireman brought rose-water and sugar, sprinkled the face of his guest with the former, and gave him a sherbert to drink made of both articles. Also he took a clean shirt, perfumed with jasmine, from his great chest and dressed Dū al-Makān in it.

The boy felt a sweet coolness enter his body under these cares and revived as if a delicious west wind blew upon him. . . .

At this point Shahrazād saw the approach of morning and discreetly fell silent.

But when the fifty-fourth night had come

SHE SAID:

It is related, O auspicious King, that Dū al-Makān could now lift his head a little on the pillows. When the fireman saw him do so, he cried out joyfully: 'Praise be to Allāh, for He has restored this young man's health! Oh, may He grant, in His infinite mercy, that I can cure him altogether!' For three more days he made prayer for his guest's recovery and dosed him with refreshing decoctions of rose-water, attending to him in every way. Strength came back little by little to Dū al-Makān's body and, at length, he was able to open his eyes and breathe freely. At the very moment when his fever lifted, the fireman entered and, finding him seated, cheerful and without pain, asked: 'How are you feeling, my son?' 'I feel both strong and well,' answered the boy, so the fireman again thanked Allāh and ran to the market, where he bought ten of the plumpest chickens. He returned with them to his wife, saying: 'Prepare two every day for our guest, one in the morning and one in the evening.'

The woman straightway killed a chicken and boiled it, making the young man eat the flesh and drink the broth. Then she gave him water for his hands and covered him warmly, so that he fell into a peaceful sleep which lasted till midday. When he woke, she boiled and carefully carved a second chicken, saying: 'Eat, my child, and restore your strength.' As Dū al-Makān was eating the fireman came in and sat down by the bed, saying: 'How is it with you, my boy?' 'Thanks to Allāh, I am well and even vigorous,' answered the youth. 'I pray fervently that He will shower His benefits upon you.' Delighted with this answer, the good man hurried again to the market and returned with rose-water and syrup of violets, which he gave his invalid to drink.

Now the fireman only earned five dirhams a day. For a whole month he set aside two of these five for chickens, sugar, rose-water and syrup of violets, and these things completely restored Dū al-Makān and removed every trace of illness from his face. When the fireman and his wife saw that he was thoroughly recovered, the former suggested that the boy should take a bath for his health's sake, and himself hired a donkey on which he carefully led his guest to the hammām. While Dū al-Makān was undressing, the fireman bought all that was necessary for the bath and then, invoking the name of Allāh, began to rub the boy's body from the feet up. Soon the rubber of the baths came in and, being thrown into confusion by the sight of the fireman usurping his functions, excused himself for coming so late. 'Good friend,' answered the fireman, 'I am delighted both to take a little work off your shoulders and to wait on this young guest of mine.' Dū al-Makān was shaved, depilated and washed, then dressed in a fine shirt, one of his host's best robes and a tasteful turban, then girt with a belt of many-coloured linen, and lastly carried back to the house on the ass.

The fireman's wife had prepared the whole dwelling for his reception; the place had been washed, and the rugs and cushions cleaned and refreshed. The fireman put his guest to bed and gave him first a rose sherbert and then one of the chickens carved by his own hands. When the youth had eaten and drunk his fill, he thanked Allāh for his safety and said to his host: 'How much do I not owe you for all that you have done for me?' 'Do not speak of that, my son,' answered the good man. 'There is one thing which I want to ask you, for you seem by your face and manner to be well-born: where do you come from and what is your name?' 'Tell me first, I pray you, where and how you found me,' replied Dū al-Makān, 'and then I will tell you my story.'

'I found you on a pile of wood by the hammām, when I went to work one morning. I do not know who left you there. I brought you to my house, and that is all,' said the fireman, and the boy cried: 'Praise be to Him who makes dead bones to live again! My father and my friend, you have not succoured an ingrate; some day I hope to prove this to you. Tell me in what country I am.' 'You are in the sacred city of Jerusalem,' answered his host. Thereupon the young man reflected bitterly on his far exile and his separation from his sister, till the tears came and he sorrowfully told his story to the fireman, without however revealing the nobility of his birth. Then he recited these lines:

> My burden is more grave than I can bear;
> For, when I asked in parting from my fair:

'Can you not wait awhile, delightful creature?'
She said: 'Oh, waiting is not in my nature!'

'Do not weep, my child, but rather thank Allāh for your safe
delivery,' said the fireman, and then, when Dū al-Makān asked him
how far it was to Damascus, answered that the journey would take
six days. 'Ah, how I wish to go there!' said the boy. 'Young master,'
answered his host, 'I cannot let so young a boy go to Damascus; it
would not be safe. If you insist on going, I shall accompany you and
perhaps my wife also, for they say that it is a fair city, rich in water-
courses and fruit trees.' With that he turned to his wife, saying:
'Child of my uncle, will you come with us to the delightful city of
Damascus, or would you rather wait here for my return? You will
see that I, at least, must go with him, both because I cannot bear to
be separated from him and because the people of Damascus have a
reputation for corruption and excess.' 'I will accompany you with
all my heart,' answered his wife, and the fireman cried out joyfully:
'Praise be to Allāh who has made us agree upon this point!' Without
further delay, he got together all his household goods, his rugs, his
cushions, his cooking-pots, his cauldrons and mortars, his tables and
mattresses, and sold them for fifty dirhams. With part of this money
he hired an ass for the journey. . . .

At this point Shahrazād saw the approach of morning and discreetly fell silent.

But when the fifty-fifth night had come

SHE SAID:

It is related, O auspicious King, that the fireman made Dū
al-Makān ride upon the ass while he and his wife walked behind,
until they came at last to the city of Damascus on a certain evening;
there the woman and the boy put up at a khān while the fireman went
to buy food and drink for the three of them.

They stayed at the khān for five days, and there the fireman's
wife, who was worn out by the journey, took a fever from which she
passed into the infinite mercy of Allāh.

Dū al-Makān, who had become fond of his faithful nurse, took
her death very much to heart. He tried to comfort the poor fireman
in his grief, saying: 'Do not be sad too much, my father, for we all
travel that road and go in by that door at last.' The elder man turned

to him, and said: 'May Allāh reward you for your compassion, my child, and also one day change our sorrows into perfect joy. As you say, the same end is written for all of us; therefore let us not grieve too long. Rather, as I wish you to be happy and at ease after your own affliction, let us go out and explore this city which we have not yet had time to see.'

The young man consented; and they wandered hand in hand through the streets and markets of Damascus, until they came to the vast stables of the walī of that city and saw a host of horses, mules and kneeling camels being loaded with cushions, bales, chests, and every kind of rich merchandise, while a crowd of slaves and overseers worked and wrangled together in a tumult of noise. 'To whom can all these things belong?' asked Dū al-Makān, and one of the slaves answered: 'It is a gift of the walī to King Umar al-Numān and goes with the annual tribute to the city.' On receiving this answer the boy felt his eyes fill with tears and recited these lines:

> If the men I loved aforetime
> Turn from me in pique,
> If my friends resent my silence
> Yet I cannot speak,
> Cannot trust the voice of sorrow
> For the soul is weak.

Then he fell silent for a moment, and these words sang in his memory:

> I sat in the sunlight at the tent door,
> I sat at the tent door in the morning;
> The slim brown back that I adore
> Receded in the golden sands' adorning.
> Till he was gone, to ward off the approaches
> Of blinding tears,
> I started to prepare the sweet reproaches
> I shall not need for years.

Dū al-Makān wept, and the good fireman said to him: 'Be reasonable, dear lad; we have only just managed to bring you back to health and all these tears will make you ill again. I, who am strong, have cause to weep and may weep; but I pray you not to do so.' Nevertheless the youth continued to lament his father and his sister, reciting this admirable poem:

The earth remains beneath all pondering,
  There's hardly time enough to taste its mirth;
Pluck all the flowers of this short wandering
  And be the blithe man-errant of the earth.

The fireman listened to these lines with rapture and tried to learn them by saying them over and over again, while Dū al-Makān stood apart and brooded upon his lot. At last the elder man said: 'Young master, it seems to me that you are always thinking of your native land and your people.' 'That is so, my father,' answered the younger. 'I do not think that I can stay an hour longer in this country. I must say farewell now, and join this caravan to go by easy stages to Baghdād.' 'And I will go with you,' answered the fireman. 'I have undertaken the work of looking after you and do not wish to turn back before it is finished.' Dū al-Makān called down all the blessings of Allāh upon his faithful friend and rejoiced that he should have company upon the road.

The fireman made him mount upon the ass, saying: 'Ride as much as you wish and, whenever you are tired of doing so, you can get down and walk.' The young man thanked him warmly, saying: 'Indeed, no brother has ever done for a brother what you have done for me.' They waited for sunset and departed in the cool of the evening with the caravan for Baghdād.

We must now return to Dū al-Makān's twin sister, the exquisite young Nuzhat. She left the khān, as you remember, to find a place as servant with some notable and earn enough money to buy her brother the grill of skewered mutton which he desired. She walked the streets at haphazard, her face covered with a rag of camlet and her heart preoccupied with her brother and the long distance which they both were from their own land. She lifted her thoughts to the pitiful mercy of Allāh and said these lines:

Tell him, O night,
How your black sword has killed my golden days
And your black brush obscured the smooth delight
About my eyes' dim ways.

The breasts of my distress
Are pressed against the thorns of appetite,
Desire my food and my drink sleeplessness;
  Tell him, O night.

As young Nuzhat wandered thus in thought about the streets, she met a Badawī chief walking with five others, who looked long upon her and violently desired her; for her beauty shone out the more because of her rags. He waited until she had come into a narrow and solitary lane and then stopped before her, asking whether she was slave or free. Nuzhat stopped also, saying: 'I beg you not to ask me questions which remind me of my grief.' 'If I question you, my child,' answered the Badawī, 'it is because I, who had six daughters, have now one only and she pines for a companion. If you are free I beg you to become a member of my house and help my child to forget her sorrow.'

The princess answered in confusion: 'O sheikh, I am a stranger and have a sick brother. I accept your offer if I may return every evening to my brother.' 'You shall only bear my daughter company during the day,' said the Badawī, 'or, if you like, I will adopt your brother also and you need never leave him.' These words decided the girl to accompany the Badawī, though, in fact, he was a base rascal who had neither children nor house. Presently he and Nuzhat, with the others, came out beyond the city to a place where the camels were already loaded and the waterskins filled. The Badawī mounted his camel and, with a quick movement, lifted Nuzhat up beside him; then the troop rode off at full speed.

Poor Nuzhat understood that she had been deceived and carried off, but the tears which she wept for herself and her brother had no effect on the Badawī. He rode on until dawn, and did not halt before he had reached a place of desolate safety in the desert. Then he said to Nuzhat: 'Vile rabbit-hearted city filth, will you stop crying or shall I beat you to death?' The girl's heart revolted at these brutal words and, without caring whether she died for it, she cried: 'Robber chief, ill-omened brand of hell, how have you dared to deceive me? What will you do with me?' The traitor raised his whip and bellowed angrily: 'I see that you love a whip about your behind, O city filth. Now I swear by my bonnet that if you weep again or are impudent again I will cut out your tongue and thrust it up between your legs.' At this horrible menace Nuzhat, who was not used to such language, trembled and was silent, hiding her face in her veil. Nevertheless, she could not prevent herself from sighing this mournful poem:

> Carry my tears to the place of their begetting,
>   Carry them home.

> Ah, for the petting
> I had there once!
> Yet I would roam;
> I was mad there once!
> Carry my tears to the place of their begetting,
> Carry them home.

At the sweet rhythm of these lines, the Badawī, who instinctively loved the sound of words, pitied the fair unfortunate, wiped her tears, and gave her a barley cake to eat, saying: 'Another time, do not try to answer me when I am angry. I cannot stand it! You ask me what I am going to do with you? I do not want you either as concubine or as slave, so I shall sell you to some rich merchant, who will treat you gently and make you happy as I have done.' 'Be it so,' answered Nuzhat. The Badawī put her on the camel again and rode off towards Damascus, while she ate a little of her barley cake for very hunger.

At this point Shahrazād saw the approach of morning and discreetly fell silent.

But when the fifty-sixth night had come

SHE SAID:

It is related, O auspicious King, that they arrived at Damascus and lodged at the Sultān's khān near Bāb al-Malik. As Nuzhat was sad and pale and ever wept, the Badawī said: 'If you do not stop crying you will lose your beauty and I will sell you to some hideous old Jew. Think of that, city filth!' He shut her into one of the rooms of the khān and, hastening to the slave market, offered her for sale to the merchants, saying: 'I have brought a young slave from Jerusalem. I was obliged to leave her sick brother to be tended by my family, so that, if any of you wish to see her, let him remember to say that he himself is having her brother looked after at Jerusalem. That will calm her and, if you do this thing, I will sell her cheap.' One of the merchants asked how old this slave might be, and the Badawī answered: 'She is a virgin just marriageable, full of intelligence, beauty and manners. Unfortunately since her brother's illness she has become a little worn and thin, but that can soon be remedied by her purchaser.' Said the merchant: 'I will go and see this slave on condition that, if I do not like her, there is no sale. If she answers your description, I will only pay you the price on which we agree after I have resold her. I intend her for King Umar al-Numān, lord of Baghdād, whose son, Prince Sharkān, is governor of our city. I will show her to Prince Sharkān and ask for a letter of introduction to his father, whose taste for virgin slaves is excellently known. Then I will pay you the price.'

The Badawī accepted these conditions, and the two went together to the Sultān's khān, where the Badawī called out: 'Najiyah, Najiyah!' for this was the name which he had given to Nuzhat. The poor girl wept when she heard him and did not answer. Then said the Badawī to the merchant: 'Go in yourself and examine her, but treat her gently because I have accustomed her to such indulgence.' The merchant passed into the room and approached Nuzhat, saying: 'Peace be with you, my child.' She answered in a voice as sweet as sugar and with an exquisite pronunciation of Arabic: 'The peace and blessings of Allāh be upon you!' The merchant was charmed by her reply and looked at her as closely as he might under her great veil, saying to himself: 'What grace and purity of language!' Nuzhat, in her turn, looked at the merchant, and thought: 'Here is a kind and venerable old man. Allāh grant that I become his slave and leave the repulsive and ferocious Badawī. I must answer him with intelligence and show him my best manners and my sweetest eloquence.' So, when the merchant asked her how she did, she looked modestly upon the ground, and answered with a charming intonation: 'Venerable old man, you ask me how I am. I might answer that I am as you would not wish your greatest enemy to be; but each of us carries his destiny about his neck, said our Prophet, on whom the prayer and peace of Allāh!'

The merchant both marvelled and rejoiced at these words, saying to himself: 'Now, though I have not seen her face, I am sure that she is very beautiful, and that I may have what I wish for her from Umar al-Numān.' Turning to the Badawī, he asked: 'What is the price of this admirable slave?' Furiously the Badawī answered: 'She is the vilest of creatures! How dare you call her admirable? When she has heard you say that, how will you be able to control her? Depart, depart! I do not wish to sell her!' The merchant understood that the Badawī was a fool of all fools, so he tried to turn the difficulty by saying: 'I will buy this vilest of creatures with all her faults.' 'How much will you give for her?' asked the other, and the merchant answered: 'There is a proverb which says that it is for a father to name his own son. Ask what you consider a fair price.' But the Badawī would not make a price and the merchant said to himself: 'This man is a maggot-head! How can I name a price for so eloquent and charming a damsel? He knows nothing of her worth; she has been blessed by Allāh, and I doubt not but that she can read and write.' He turned to the Badawī, saying: 'I offer you two hundred dīnārs, free of tax.' 'Depart, good man,' said the Badawī, 'I would not sell the old piece of camlet which she has about her head for two hundred dīnārs. I have decided not to sell her. I shall take her back to the desert with me to herd my camels and grind corn. Get up, corruption! We are about to start. As for you, sir, I advise you to be gone, otherwise I swear by my bonnet that you shall hear things not to your liking.'

'This Badawī, who swears by his bonnet, is quite mad,' thought the merchant. 'She is worth her weight in jewels. I will buy her out of hand.' Then taking the Badawī persuasively by the mantle, he said: 'Have patience, my friend. I can see that you are not used to buying and selling. Both patience and knowledge are required. We shall not disagree about the price; but I must first see her face, for that is the custom.' 'I do not mind if you do,' answered the Badawī. 'Look at her as much as you like; strip her naked and feel her all over.' The merchant raised his hands to heaven, crying: 'Allāh protect me from such a misdeed! I only wish to look upon her face.'

At this point Shahrazād saw the approach of morning and discreetly fell silent.

But when the fifty-seventh night had come

SHE SAID:

It is related, O auspicious King, that the merchant advanced towards Nuzhat, excusing himself for the liberty, and sat down by her side in confusion, asking her name in a solicitous voice. She sighed and said: 'Do you want to know my present name or the name I used to bear? Once I was called Delight of the Age, but now I call myself Despite of the Age.' The merchant's eyes filled with tears at this answer, so that the girl wept also and plaintively recited these lines:

> I who grow the rose of sorrow
>   By the pool of tears,
> Do not know to what far country

When the dawn appears
You will shape your vagabonding,
Pilgrim of the years.

The Badawī found that this conversation was taking too long, so he ran to Nuzhat with raised whip, crying: 'Enough chattering! Lift your veil and let him see you.' Then Nuzhat looked pitifully at the merchant, sighing: 'For God's sake deliver me from the hands of this robber, old man, otherwise I will kill myself to-night.' So the merchant turned to the Badawī, saying: 'O chief, this young girl is only an embarrassment for you. Name a price for her, and I will buy her.' 'I repeat,' replied the barbarian, 'that you must name a price for her, or I will take her back to herd my camels and gather their dung.' 'I offer you fifty thousand dīnārs,' said the merchant. 'God help us, is that a joke?' asked the Badawī. 'Seventy thousand dīnārs,' said the merchant. 'God help us, I have spent more than ninety thousand on barley cakes for her.' 'My friend,' answered the merchant, 'all your family and all your tribe have never eaten a hundred dīnārs' worth of barley. A hundred thousand is my last word, and, if you do not accept it, I will report your treatment of this slave, whom you have most certainly stolen, to Prince Sharkān, the walī of Damascus.' 'Very well,' answered the Badawī, 'I will take a hundred thousand for her, as I have to buy some salt.' The merchant laughed and took them both to his own house, where he had the price weighed out carefully, piece by piece, by the public accountant. The Badawī remounted his camel and set off towards Jerusalem, saying to himself: 'If the sister has fetched a hundred thousand dīnārs, her brother will be worth more. I will look for him.' When he reached Jerusalem, he hunted in all the khāns for Dū al-Makān, but, as the boy had already departed with the fireman, his greed went unsatisfied.

At this point Shahrazād saw the approach of morning and discreetly fell silent.

But when the fifty-eighth night had come

SHE SAID:

The good merchant took Nuzhat to his house, where he dressed her in the richest and finest garments, and then led her to the market of the goldsmiths and jewellers and bought a great quantity of such jewels as pleased him. These he carried back to his house in a satin scarf, and gave them to Nuzhat, saying: 'I only ask you for one thing in return: that you do not forget to tell the viceroy the price I paid for you, and to urge him to mention it in the letter of introduction which I hope that he will write for me to King Umar al-Numān in Baghdād. Also I wish him to give me a safe conduct and a patent freeing my goods from taxation on their entry into Baghdād.'

Nuzhat sighed and her eyes filled with tears, so that the merchant asked her: 'Why, my child, do you sigh and weep at every mention of Baghdād? Does someone dear to you abide there, one of your family, one of the merchants? Speak without fear, for I know all the merchants in Baghdād.' 'As Allāh lives,' answered the girl, 'I know no one there save King Umar al-Numān himself.'

When the merchant heard her answer, he gave a sigh of content-ment, as much as to say: 'At last my goal is reached.' He asked the young girl whether she had already been offered to the king, and she answered: 'No, but I was brought up with his daughter in the palace. He used to love me, and anything I ask he will do; if you wish a favour from him you have but to give me pen and paper and I will write a letter to Umar al-Numān. You will take it to him and say that it comes from his humble slave Nuzhat, who has suffered many mis-fortunes by day and night and has passed through the hands of many masters. You can add that she stays at present with his viceroy at Baghdād and sends humble greeting.' The merchant's respect and affection for Nuzhat increased, and he asked her whether she had not been taught to read the Koran in the palace. 'Venerable old man,' she answered: 'I know the Koran and the Rules of Wisdom, I know medical science and the book of the Introduction to the Mysteries, I know the commentaries on the works of Hippocrates and have my-self annotated the books of Galen, the physician; I have read philo-sophy and logic, I have studied the Simples of Ibn-Baitār and have disputed with sages concerning the canon of Ibn-Sīnā, I have studied the unriddling of allegories and can draw all the figures of geometry, I have discoursed with knowledge about architecture, I have learnt anatomy and the Shāfi books, I have a thorough understanding of syntax and grammar and the history of language, and have attended the society of the most learned in every branch of knowledge; also I am myself the author of many books on eloquence, rhetoric, arithmetic, pure syllogism and spiritual science. And what is more, I have remembered all I ever knew. Give me pen and paper, and I will write a letter in rhythmical verses, so that you can read it again and again, easing your heart in the solitude of the journey from Damascus to Baghdād, and dispense with carrying any books.'

The poor merchant was a little overcome at this recital; therefore he exclaimed: 'Allāh, Allāh! Happy the house that shelters her and he who stays with her!' and very respectfully brought out the necessaries for writing. Nuzhat took the reed pen, dipped it in the inky oakum and, trying it first on her nail, wrote this letter:

> This is the letter
> Of one in time's fetter,
> Spoiled by love's tetter;
> The lights forget her,
> The stars are the sole begetter
> Of this letter.
>
> This is the verse
> Of one whose bad has turned to worse,
> Who never had joy to nurse,
> Whose prayer came home a curse;
> Sorrowful words and terse,
> This is my verse.
>
> This is the verse
> Of my letter.

Nuzhat al-Zamān

She sanded and folded this carefully, and then handed it to the merchant, who took it respectfully and, after carrying it to his lips and brow, fastened it in an envelope of satin, saying: 'Glory be to Him who moulded you as you are, O marvel of His creatures!'

At this point Shahrazād saw the approach of morning and discreetly fell silent.

But when the fifty-ninth night had come

SHE SAID:

It is related, O auspicious King, that the merchant did not know how to pay enough honour to his guest. He showed her every mark of respect, and ventured to suggest that she might need a bath. She consented gladly, and he walked before her ceremoniously to the hammām, carrying all that was necessary to dress her wrapped in a piece of velvet. He confided her to the most skilled rubber and, while she was being bathed by this woman, bought many sorts of fruits and sherbets, which he placed beside the couch where she would come to dress.

When the bath was finished, the rubber wrapped Nuzhat in perfumed linen and set her on the couch; they both ate and drank what had been set there and gave the remnants to the old woman who looked after the hammām.

Soon the good merchant arrived with a sandalwood box, which he opened, crying on the name of Allāh. Then he and the rubber began to adorn the young girl for her visit to Prince Sharkān.

First a fine white silk chemise was put on her, and a fillet of cloth of gold worth a thousand dīnārs was wound loosely about her hair. Then she was given a Turkish robe, stitched with gold thread, and red leather boots, perfumed with musk and ornamented with gold tassels and little flowers of pearl and coloured jewels. Pearls worth a thousand dīnārs each were hung at her ears, a collar of engraved gold passed about her neck, jewelled nets fastened over her breasts, and a belt slung below her navel consisting of ten rows of alternate amber balls and golden crescents. Each amber ball carried a great ruby, and each crescent nine pearls and ten diamonds. Thus was Nuzhat dressed at the cost of more than a hundred thousand dīnārs.

The merchant, when he judged her perfect, walked from the hammām with her, leading the way with a respectful air and parting those whom they met to right and left. Those who saw the young girl were at first stricken dumb by her beauty, and then cried: 'Allāh, Allāh! Glory be to Allāh for the work of His hands! Happy the man to whom she shall belong!'

When the merchant came into the presence of King Sharkān, he kissed the earth between his hands, saying: 'I have brought you the most marvellous present of all time, a girl who unites in her sole person those charms and gifts and qualities which have made famous women famous.' 'Let me see,' said Sharkān, and the merchant led in Nuzhat by the hand and set her before him. Sharkān, who had never seen his little sister, did not of course recognise her. He was ravished by the beauty of her body and was more pleased still when the merchant said: 'Beauty is her natural gift, but she has learnt besides all religious and civil knowledge, all political and mathematical science. She will answer any questions which the wisest in the empire put to her.'

Prince Sharkān did not take a moment to make up his mind, but said to the merchant: 'Tell my treasurer to pay you, and depart in peace.' The merchant plucked up courage and said: 'Prince of all valour, I had meant this girl for King Umar al-Numān and only brought her to you to see, that you might write me a letter of introduction to that august monarch. However, as she pleases you she is yours. May I beg in return a patent which will free all my goods from any tax for ever?' 'I grant it,' said Sharkān. 'Also, tell me what you paid for the girl and I will refund the price.' 'She cost me a hundred thousand dīnārs, and her trappings a hundred thousand more,' answered the other. So Sharkān called his treasurer and said: 'Pay this venerable old man two hundred thousand dīnārs, and twenty thousand for profit. Also give him a fair robe of honour from my presses and write him a patent protecting him in my name from all taxation.' After this Sharkān sent for the four kādīs of Damascus, and said to them. . . .

At this point Shahrazād saw the approach of morning and discreetly fell silent.

But when the sixtieth night had come

SHE SAID:

Sharkān said to the kādīs: 'I call you all to witness that I free this slave, whom I have bought, and take her to be my wife.' The kādīs wrote with all speed a bill of franchisement and a marriage contract, sealing both with their seals. Sharkān threw handfuls of gold among those present and dismissed all save the kādīs and the merchant. To the kādīs he said: 'I wish you to listen to the discourse which I am going to ask this maiden to give us, in proof of her eloquence and this old merchant's claims.' He had a great curtain let down in the middle of the hall and placed the young girl behind it, that she might not be confused in her eloquence by having strange men look upon her.

As soon as the curtain was lowered, all the women of the palace clustered about their new mistress, helping her off with the weightier of her clothes, and kissing her feet and hands in joy and admiration. Also when the wives of the amīrs and wazīrs heard the news, they obtained leave from their husbands and came to greet Nuzhat and hear the address that she was about to make to Prince Sharkān and the kādīs of Damascus.

Nuzhat rose on the entrance of these great ladies and, kissing them cordially, bade them be seated beside her. She smiled so sweetly upon them and acknowledged their good wishes with so much gentle tact, that they marvelled at her politeness and intelligence, saying among themselves: 'They told us that she was a freed slave, but she has more the appearance of being a queen by birth.' Then to Nuzhat they said: 'Mistress, you have lighted our city with your presence and honoured our land by journeying into it. This kingdom is your kingdom and this palace is your palace, and we are your slaves.'

She was thanking them in agreeably chosen words, when Sharkān called from the other side of the curtain: 'Dear girl, sweet jewel of this age, we are ready to listen to your delightful words, for we have heard that no learning is hidden from you, not even the difficult syntax of our language.' Nuzhat answered in a voice sweeter than sugar: 'Your desire is as a commandment to me. I will proclaim for your satisfaction, my master, those excellent sayings which are upon the *Three Doors of Life*.'

The Sayings on the Three Doors

NUZHAT said from behind the curtain:
I speak of the *First Door*, of the *Art of Conduct*.

The true end of life is the development of enthusiasm, and the chief enthusiasm is the beautiful passion of faith. None can reach enthusiasm who does not live a burning and passionate life, which is equally possible in the four great ways of mankind: Government, Commerce, Husbandry, and Craftsmanship.

To deal first with Government: those rare beings who are called the rulers of this world must have political knowledge, perfect tact, and a natural gift for what they do. Especially must they never be led aside by their own inclinations, but keep steadfastly in view a policy which has its end in God. If they so rule themselves to this aim, justice shall reign with them and discord shall not share their throne. If, as very often happens, they are led aside by what they wish themselves, they are apt to fall into errors which can never be repaired. For a ruler must be impartial and a foe to all oppression if he would not be considered by Allāh to have neither use nor excuse.

Great Ardashīr, third King of the Persians, one of the Sassanids, said: 'Government and faith are twin sisters; faith is a treasure, and government the guardian of the treasure.'

Our Prophet, upon whom be prayer and peace, said: 'Two things are powerful in this world. When they are pure, the world goes well; when they are corrupt, the world is corrupt also. These things are Government and Knowledge.'

A wise man said: 'A king should guard the rights of God and the rights of his people. More especially should he keep peace between the men of the pen and the men of the sword; for when the pen is oppressed the throne falls.'

King Ardashīr, who was a conqueror of many lands, divided his empire into four districts and wore four seal-rings upon his hand, one for each district, so that there might be order among all. This plan was followed until the era of Islām.

The great Kasrā, King of the Persians, wrote to his son, who was in charge of one of his armies. . . .

At this point Shahrazād saw the approach of morning and discreetly fell silent.

But when the sixty-first night had come

SHE SAID:

He wrote to his son: 'My child, beware of pity for it weakens government, and beware of a lack of pity for this stirs revolt.'

An Arab came to the Khalīfah Abu Jafar Abdallāh al-Mansūr and said: 'Starve your dog if you wish it to follow you.' The Khalīfah was wroth and the Arab continued: 'But take care that some passer-by does not hold out a piece of bread to your dog.' Al-Mansūr understood and profited by this advice, when he had sent the Arab away with a gift.

The Khalīfah Abd al-Malik ibn Marwān wrote to his brother Abd al-Azīz, who was in charge of his army in Egypt: 'Your counsellors can teach you nothing, but your enemy can teach you how strong your army is.'

The excellent Khalīfah, Umar ibn al-Khattāb, took none into his service until he swore never to ride on a beast of burden, never to take loot from the enemy, never to wear rich clothes, and never to be late for prayer. He loved to say: 'Intelligence is wealth, quickness of intellect a talisman, and study a glory.'

The same Umar, whom Allāh keep, said: 'There are three kinds of women: the good Mussulmān who thinks only of her husband and has eyes only for him, the good Mussulmān who looks to obtain only children from marriage, and the harlot who lies as a collar about the neck of the whole world. There are three kinds of men: the wise man who reflects and acts only after reflection, the wiser man who reflects and then takes the advice of others, and the fool who neither reflects nor takes advice.'

The sublime Alī ibn Abī Tālib, whom Allāh keep, said: 'Be on your guard against the tricks of women and never take their advice; but do not oppress them, for that will only make them worse. The road away from the house of moderation leads to the town of foolishness. Be just, especially towards slaves.'

Nuzhat was continuing with this chapter of her discourse, when she heard the kādīs saying behind the curtain: 'By Allāh, we have never heard such eloquence, but we would like to hear something of the other two doors.' So Nuzhat said, with a clever transition:

On some other day I will speak of enthusiasm in the three other ways of mankind, for it is time to turn to the *Second Door*, of *Good Manners* and *The Intellect*.

This door might also be called the door of perfections, and, though it is the largest of all, none may enter by it unless he was born with a blessing on his head. I will cite only certain chosen examples.

At this point Shahrazād saw the approach of morning and discreetly fell silent.

But when the sixty-second night had come

SHE SAID:

One day the Khalīfah Muāwiyah asked the witty club-foot Abu-Bahr ibn Kais, who had begged for an audience, if he had any advice to give him. The club-foot answered: 'Prince of Believers, I advise you to keep your head shaved and your moustaches trimmed, to look after your nails, to depilate your armpits, to shave your groin, to clean your teeth, and take care of your gums; but never on a Friday, for that were sacrilege.' 'Have you any advice to give yourself?' asked the Khalifah, and he answered: 'My advice to myself is to put one foot forward after another and to keep an eye on both.' 'How do you behave towards your superiors?' asked the Sultān. 'I greet them without exaggeration and wait for them to answer my greeting,' replied the club-foot. 'And how do you behave towards your wife?' was the next question, but Abu-Bahr exclaimed: 'Excuse me from answering that question, O Prince of Believers!' 'But I insist,' said the Khalīfah, and the club-foot replied: 'My wife, like all other women, was created from the last rib, that is to say from something both weak and crooked.' 'And what do you do when you wish to lie with her?' asked Muāwiyah. 'First, I talk pleasantly to her to put her in good humour,' said Abu-Bahr, 'then I kiss her warmly all over to excite her, and, when she has reached that stage which you doubtless know, I lay her on her back and charge her. When the drop of nacre is well incrusted, I cry, "Grant, O Lord, that this seed be covered with your blessing and modelled in beauty." After that I rise and, taking water in both hands, make my ablutions. At the very last, I thank Allāh for the pleasure he has given me.' 'I am charmed with your answer,' said the Khalīfah. 'Ask what you will, and I shall grant it.' 'Rule justly, that is all I ask,' said the club-foot as he went away. And the Khalīfah said: 'If he were the only wise man in Irāk, yet would it be enough.'

At this point Shahrazād saw the approach of morning and discreetly fell silent.

But when the sixty-third night had come

SHE SAID:

It is related, O auspicious King, that Nuzhat continued:

In the reign of the Khalīfah Umar ibn al-Khattāb, the venerable Muaikib was treasurer. One day Umar's little son went with his nurse to visit the old man and Muaikib gave the child a new silver dirham. Some time afterwards the Khalīfah called his treasurer and said: 'O peculator, what is this I hear?' 'What have I done, Prince of Believers?' exclaimed the honest old man, and Umar answered: 'To give a silver dirham to my son was a theft on the whole Mussulmān race.' Muaikib never ceased to exclaim throughout the rest of his life: 'Where is there a man so honest as Umar?'

The Khalīfah Umar was walking one night with Aslam Abū Zaid when he noticed a fire afar off. He approached it and saw that a poor woman had lighted it beneath a pot. Umar, seeing that two feeble infants were wailing by the side of the woman, asked her what she was doing, and she replied: 'My lord, I am warming a little water to give my children who are dying of cold and hunger. Yet one day Allāh will ask the Khalīfah Umar concerning our misery.' 'But, my good woman, do you imagine that if Umar knew of your misery that he would not help you?' asked Umar of the woman. 'Why should

he be Khalīfah,' she answered, 'if he does not know of the misery of
each of his people?' Umar took Aslam Abū Zaid with him and returned with all speed to his palace from which he procured a sack of
flour and a jar of mutton fat; then he said to Abū Zaid: 'Help me to
get them on my back,' But Abū Zaid cried: 'I will carry them, O
Prince of Believers.' 'And will you also carry my sins on the Day of
Judgment?' asked the Khalīfah. With that he bore the flour and fat
himself to the poor woman and, mixing some of each in the pot,
began to cook, blowing the fire himself, so that the wood smoke
wavered up through the hairs of his great beard. When the dish was
ready, he fed the woman and her children until they could eat no more,
blowing each morsel himself until it was cool enough to eat. He left
the remainder of the flour and the fat with the woman, and, as he was
going away, said to Abū Zaid: 'I saw a fire and it enlightened me.'

At this point Shahrazād saw the approach of morning and discreetly fell silent.

But when the sixty-fourth night had come

SHE SAID:

It is related, O auspicious King, that Nuzhat continued:

The same Umar one day passed a slave who was tending his
master's flock and stopped to buy a goat from him. But the shepherd
answered: 'She does not belong to me.' So the Khalīfah said: 'Excellent fellow, then I will buy you and free you, for one does not meet
an honest man every day.'

One day Hafsah, a kinswoman of Umar, came to him and said:
'Prince of Believers, I have heard that your last expedition brought
you in a great deal of money, so I have come to claim a little of it
through the rights of our kinship.' Umar answered: 'Allāh has made
me a guardian over the goods of the Mussulmāns, O Hafsah. All this
money belongs to them. I cannot touch any of it to give you pleasure
or because I am related to your father, any more than I can touch it
for myself.'

Nuzhat heard satisfied exclamations from behind the curtain;
therefore she ceased speaking for a moment, and then continued:

Now I will speak of the *Third Door*, which is the *Door of Virtues*.
I will quote certain examples from the lives of the Companions of the
Prophet (upon whom be prayer and peace) and of just men among
the Mussulmāns.

Hasan al-Basrī said: 'Everyone when he lies dying regrets three things: lost opportunity, unfulfilled hopes, and unrealised ambition.'

They asked Sufyān one day whether a rich man could be virtuous. 'Yes,' he answered, 'he can be virtuous on two occasions, when he has lost his money, and when he says to a man who is thanking him for a gift: "In receiving my gift you have accomplished a perfumed deed towards Allāh."'

When Abdāllāh ibn Shaddād felt the approach of death, he sent for his son Muhammad and said to him: 'Here are my last instructions: be pious, be truthful, and thank Allāh always, because thanks are apt to bring renewed gifts. Also know, my son, that there is no pleasure in riches but only in piety; you cannot share your riches with Allāh, but you can give him all your piety.'

When the pious Abd al-Azīz became the eighth Khalīfah of the Umayyads, he called all his rich family about him and made them transfer all their belongings to the public treasure. They went and complained of this to Fātimah, daughter of Marwān, who was Umar's aunt and for whom he had a great respect. Fātimah entered the presence of the Khalīfah one night and sat in silence on the carpet. 'Speak, my aunt,' said the Khalīfah, but Fātimah answered: 'Prince of Believers, you are the master, it is for you to speak first. Also nothing is hidden from you, so that you know even the reason of my coming here.' The Khalīfah Umar answered: 'Allāh sent His Prophet (on whom be prayer and peace) to be balm to His people and a consolation for mankind. The Prophet (upon whom be prayer and peace) gathered and took only what he considered necessary, leaving the rest as a river to allay the thirst of his people until the end of the world. It is my business to see that this river is never deflected, never dried up in the desert.'

At this point Shahrazād saw the approach of morning and discreetly fell silent.

But when the sixty-fifth night had come

SHE SAID:

It is related, O auspicious King, that young Nuzhat, from behind the curtain, continued thus to Prince Sharkān, the four kādīs, and the merchant:

Fātimah said: 'I have understood your words and mine have become useless.' Then she returned to the rest of the Umayyads and said: 'You do not know how great your fortune is to have Umar ibn Abd al-Azīz for your Khalīfah.'

When that same upright Umar came to die, he called his children to him and said: 'The smell of poverty is sweet unto the Lord.' Maslamah ibn Abd al-Malik, who was present, replied: 'Prince of Believers, is it right to leave your sons to poverty when you could make them rich? Would that not be better than leaving all to your successor?' The Khalīfah was both angry and surprised upon his deathbed, and answered: 'O Maslamah, do you think that I, who have been just in life, will give an example of injustice when I am dying? Once I was at the funeral of one of my predecessors, a son of Marwān, and my eyes both saw and understood, so that I swore an oath never to behave as he had behaved, if I came to be Khalīfah.'

The same Maslamah al-Malik has said: 'One day, when I went to sleep after coming back from the funeral of an old ascetic, there appeared to me the man whom we had just buried, dressed in garments whiter than jasmine, walking in a place of delights watered by foaming streams and refreshed by a breeze drunken with its delay among the lemon trees. He said to me: "O Maslamah, what would one not do in life for such a reward?"'

He also tells this story: a certain young man during the reign of Umar ibn Abd al-Azīz visited a friend who was a shepherd and saw, in the middle of the flock, what he took to be two great and savage dogs. He asked his friend why he kept them there, and the shepherd answered: 'Those are not dogs, they are tame wolves. I am the master of this flock and they do no harm, for when the head is sound the body is sound.'

One day the Khalīfah Umar ibn Abd al-Azīz preached to the people from a pulpit of mud, saying: 'Abd al-Malik is dead and his fathers are dead, and his posterity is not yet born. Also I shall die myself.' Maslamah said to him: 'Prince of Believers, this pulpit is not worthy of a Khalīfah. Let me at least put a cushion for you to lean on.' 'Would you like to see Umar rise on the last day with a cushion chained about his neck?' asked the Khalīfah.

At this point Shahrazād saw the approach of morning and discreetly fell silent.

But when the sixty-sixth night had come

SHE SAID:

It is related, O auspicious King, that Nuzhat continued:

The same Khalīfah said one day: 'I hope that Allāh will not make me immortal, for death is His greatest gift to any true Believer.'

Khālid ibn Safwān came one day to the Khalīfah Hishām, when he was surrounded by writers and servants in his tent, and said: 'Allāh prosper you, Prince of Believers, and mingle no drop of bitter in your cup. I will tell you a story which has the merit of being old. There was once a king of ancient time who said to those about him: "Has anyone of you seen a king to equal me either in prosperity or generosity?" Then a man who was sanctified by pilgrimage and true learning replied: "O King, you have asked us a weighty question. Before I answer, will you tell me whether this prosperity of yours is of eternal or of passing things?" "Of passing things," answered the King, and the other continued: "How then can you ask us a weighty question about a thing so light?" "There is sense in what you say, O man. What then must I do?" asked the Khalīfah and the man answered: "Sanctify yourself." So the King put by his crown and, dressing himself in rags, departed upon pilgrimage to the Sacred City. And as for you, O Prince of Allāh, what will you do?' Hishām was much moved, and wept till all his beard was wet. Then he re-entered his palace and shut himself in to meditate.

At this moment the kādīs and the merchant cried from behind the curtain: 'By Allāh, she is supremely excellent.'

Then Nuzhat said: 'This door has many and many an example more, and more sublime than these, which it is impossible for me to tell you in a single discourse, my masters. But Allāh will grant us many days and I will be able to teach you everything.'

Then Nuzhat fell silent.

At this point Shahrazād saw the approach of morning and discreetly fell silent.

But when the sixty-seventh night had come

SHE SAID:

It is related, O auspicious King, that the four kādīs cried: 'Prince of time, this young girl is the marvel of our age and of all ages. We have neither seen for ourselves one like to her nor have we heard tell

of her equal.' With these words they kissed the earth between Sharkān's hands and went their way.

Sharkān called all his servants, and, at his order, they hastened to
make preparations for the marriage and to cook meats and sweets for
the festival, while the prince himself graciously retained the wives of
the amīrs and wazīrs who had come to listen to Nuzhat as guests for
the ceremony. As soon as evening fell, cloths were laid and served
with all that might satisfy the senses and rejoice the eyes. The guests
ate and drank till they were satisfied, while far-famed singers sang,
and all the slave girls of the palace rejoiced. The hall rang with
happiness and the palace was illuminated from the centre to the outskirts, with all the alleys upon its right and the garden upon its left.
Also the amīrs and the wazīrs came and presented homage and
congratulations to Sharkān, as soon as he came out from the
hammām.

When the prince was seated upon the bridegroom's dais the
women entered slowly in two ranks, leading the bride, who leant
upon the arms of her sponsors. After the seven-fold ceremony of
clothing, they led Nuzhat to the marriage-chamber, where they
undressed her and would have gone on to the preparation of her
body. But they soon saw that preparation was unnecessary to this
immaculate mirror, this incensed flesh. So the sponsors told Nuzhat
those things which are customary and, putting a thin chemise upon
her, left her alone with many good wishes.

When Sharkān came to the couch, he was as ignorant that this
beautiful girl was his sister as she was unwitting that she had to do
with her brother. He entered into possession of her and their delights
were great, so that she conceived straightway and told Sharkān that
this was so.

The prince therefore rejoiced in the morning and ordered the
physicians to inscribe the happy day of that conception on their
rolls. Then he ascended his throne to receive the congratulations of
his amīrs, his wazīrs and the chiefs of his kingdom.

Lastly he called his private secretary and dictated a letter to his
father, King Umar al-Numān, saying that he had married a beautiful
and learned girl, whom he had bought from a merchant and afterwards freed, that she had conceived by him on the first night, and
that it was his intention presently to send her to Baghdād, in order
that she might see her father-in-law the King, and her sister-in-law
and brother-in-law, Nuzhat and Dū al-Makān. Sharkān sent this

letter by rapid courier to Baghdād, and in eight days the man returned with an answer from the King.

At this point Shahrazād saw the approach of morning and discreetly fell silent.

But when the sixty-eighth night had come

SHE SAID:

After the Invocation to Allāh, King Umar al-Numān's letter read as follows:

'This is from the desolate Umar al-Numān, grief-stricken, robbed of his heart and of his children, to the well-loved Sharkān, his son.

'Learn, my child, that living indoors irked me during my grief at your departure, so I went to hunt in the fresh air and lessened my sorrow in this way for a whole month. When I returned to my palace, I heard that your brother Dū al-Makān and your sister Nuzhat had set out with the pilgrims for sacred Mecca, though I had forbidden Dū al-Makān to go because of his age and had promised to take him myself next year. It seems that they could not wait and so set out secretly, hardly taking sufficient provision for the journey. I have heard no news of them since; the pilgrims returned without them and not one could tell me what had happened to them. I wear mourning and am drowned in tears.

'Do not delay in sending me your news, my son. I send all my wishes for peace on you and yours.'

Some months after receiving this letter, Sharkān, who had previously left his wife in ignorance of its contents because of her pregnancy, resolved to tell her of his father's grief. She had given birth to a girl in the meanwhile; therefore, when he went to visit her, he first embraced his little daughter. Nuzhat said to him: 'The child is seven days old. You must name her to-day!' Sharkān took the baby in his arms and saw that there hung by a golden chain from her neck one of the three talismanic jewels which had belonged to Ibrīzah, the ill-starred princess of Cesarea.

In his surprise, Sharkān cried out: 'Where did you get that jewel, slave?' and Nuzhat, strangled with indignation at the word slave, cried: 'I am your mistress and the mistress of all who live in this palace! How dare you call me a slave when I am a queen? I shall keep my secret no longer: I am a King's daughter, I am Nuzhat al-Zamān, daughter of Umar al-Numān!'

At this point Shahrazād saw the approach of morning and discreetly fell silent.

But when the sixty-ninth night had come

SHE SAID:

As soon as Sharkān understood what she had said he trembled throughout all his body, his head fell to one side in consternation, the colour drained from his face little by little, and he dropped forward in a swoon. When he recovered, he could not believe that he had heard aright, so he said: 'Mistress, are you the daughter of Umar al-Numān?' 'I am his daughter,' she answered. Then said he: 'That jewel is sign that you speak the truth, but I pray you vouchsafe me other signs.' So Nuzhat told her brother all the story of her adventures, which it would be useless to repeat in this place.

Sharkān was convinced and said to himself: 'What have I done? How can I have married my own sister? There is only one way of salvation: I must find her another husband, I must marry her to one of my chamberlains, so that if the thing becomes known I can say that I divorced her before I lay with her.' Then to Nuzhat he said: 'O Nuzhat, know that you are my sister, for I am Sharkān, son of Umar al-Numān. Allāh pardon us!'

Nuzhat uttered a great cry and fell down fainting. She came to herself, weeping and lamenting, and beat her cheeks, crying: 'We have fallen into great sin! What shall we do? What shall I answer when my father and mother ask me where I got my baby?' Sharkān replied: 'The best way to arrange the matter is for you to marry my chamberlain, then our child can be brought up in his house as if it were his own. I will call the good man at once, before our secret gets noised abroad.' With that he began to console his sister, kissing her gently, and she said: 'That will be the best way. But in the meanwhile, my brother, how do you wish our little one to be named?' 'I will call her Kudīya fa-Kāma, Power-of-Destiny,' answered Sharkān.

The prince lost no time in marrying Nuzhat to his chamberlain, in heaping riches upon him after the ceremony and in sending the bride and her child to abide in his house at once. The chamberlain received them, and treated his wife with bountiful and loving respect, and provided nurses and attendants for the little girl.

All this happened while Dū al-Makān and the good fireman were getting ready to set out for Baghdād with the Damascus caravan.

Soon a second courier arrived from Umar al-Numān, carrying another letter for Prince Sharkān. This letter, after the Invocation, went on as follows:

'This is to tell you, my dear son, that I am still a prey to bitter grief on account of my two children.

'As soon as you receive my letter, send the annual tribute of your province and, with the caravan which carries it, send also your young wife, because I am anxious to see her and to test her knowledge and intelligence. For you must know that there have come to my palace from Constantinople a venerable old woman and five great-breasted virgins. These girls know as much of human learning as any man, and no tongue could describe their perfection or the wisdom of their ancient instructress. I have become very fond of them and wish to keep them by me in the palace, for no king on earth has a similar ornament for his throne. I asked their price and the old woman told me that I might have them in exchange for the annual tribute of your province. And, as God lives, I do not consider that expensive. Indeed, any one of the five is worth more than that. I have agreed to buy, and the girls abide with me until the tribute comes. Hasten to send it, my child, for the old woman is in a hurry to return to her own country.

'Above all, do not forget to send me your wife, because her learning will be useful to me in making trial of the girls. I promise you that, if she overcomes them in knowledge and quickness of intellect, I will send you the five girls for yourself and make you a present of the annual tribute of Baghdād.

'Peace be on you and yours, my son.'

At this point Shahrazād saw the approach of morning and discreetly fell silent.

But when the seventieth night had come

SHE SAID:

As soon as he had read his father's letter, Sharkān sent for his brother-in-law, the chamberlain, and said to him: 'Bring me that young slave whom I gave you in marriage,' and, when Nuzhat appeared before him, he gave her the letter and asked her opinion of it. After reading carefully his sister replied: 'Your thought is always well thought and your plan the better plan; but, as you ask me, my greatest desire is to see my father and mother in their own country.

Therefore I beg you to let me depart with my husband and tell my story to our father: how the Badawī took me and sold me to the merchant, how the merchant sold me to you, and how you divorced me before lying with me, and married me to your chamberlain.' 'Be it as you wish,' said Sharkān.

The chamberlain, who had no idea that the prince was his brother-in-law, was commanded to set out for Baghdād at the head of the caravan which carried the tribute, and to take his young wife with him. Sharkān had two great camel-litters prepared for him, one for himself and one for his wife, and intrusted a letter to him for Umar al-Numān. He said goodbye to the pair, and saw them depart. Then he himself took his little daughter, Power-of-Destiny, back to the palace and placed her in the charge of nurses and servants, commanding them to see that she kept ever about her neck that magic jewel which had belonged to the unhappy Ibrīzah. Nuzhat, who was quite contented with these cares for her child, mounted, with her husband, upon two costly racing dromedaries and took her place with him at the head of the caravan.

It was on that same night that the fireman and Dū al-Makān had seen in the course of their walk the camels, mules and torch-bearers moving about the stable of the governor of Damascus, and had asked to whom these might belong. When a man answered that this was the tribute of the city of Damascus to King Umar al-Numān, Dū al-Makān wished to know who was at the head of the caravan. The man replied: 'The chamberlain, the husband of that young slave who is so learned and well-educated.' Dū al-Makān wept at this, remembering his sister and his native country. 'Let us leave with this caravan, my brother,' said he to the good fireman. 'Surely, surely,' answered his friend. 'I will not let you go alone to Baghdād after bearing you company from Jerusalem to Damascus.' 'I love and respect you for this, my brother,' said Dū al-Makān. The fireman saddled the ass and put a bag of food upon it; then he tightened his belt over the skirts of his robe and lifted Dū al-Makān into the saddle. 'Mount behind me,' said the youth, but the fireman answered: 'Master, I wish to keep myself entirely at your service.' 'Still,' said Dū al-Makān, 'you might get up behind me for an hour to rest yourself.' 'I will if I get tired,' answered the other, and Dū al-Makān exclaimed: 'Brother, I am left with nothing to say to you at this hour, but, when we come to my father and mother, I hope that you will see that I am not forgetful.'

The caravan set out in the cool of the evening; the fireman going on foot, Dū al-Makān on the ass, and the chamberlain and his wife riding at the head of the procession on blood-dromedaries.

They journeyed forward till dawn and halted, when the heat grew too intense, in the shade of a clump of palm-trees. They rested there and watered their beasts, and then set out again, travelling during the cool of five nights until they came to a certain city where they rested for three days. In this way they went on and on, until they came so near Baghdād that men might recognise the breeze which blows from her alone.

At this point Shahrazād saw the approach of morning and discreetly fell silent.

But when the seventy-first night had come

SHE SAID:
When Dū al-Makān felt the well-remembered breeze of his country, he drew in with it a memory of his sister Nuzhat, and of his father and mother. Thinking of the grief which these last would experience when he returned alone, he wept and recited these lines:

> As this our parting looks to be endlong,
>   We'll be alert to catch the broken minute;
> The breathing space between a song and song
>   Shall have enough sweet suppliancy in it
> To throw our hearts together with the threat:
> Take me, but do not tell me to forget.

'My child, you have wept enough,' said the fireman. 'Besides, remember that we are near the tent of the chamberlain and his wife.' 'Friend, let me weep and recite poems to soothe the agony about my heart,' answered Dū al-Makān, and with that he turned his face again towards Baghdād, which shone in the moonlight. Nuzhat, who lay in the tent unable to sleep, with tears in her eyes, dreaming sad waking dreams of the absent, heard a voice near her passionately chanting these lines:

> The star of joy shone gold above,
>   But he has fallen and night lies the thicker;
> The cup is broken, and my love
>   Thirsts all the more for having tried that liquor.

At the conclusion of his song Dū al-Makān fell down in a dead faint.

When Nuzhat, wife of the chamberlain, heard this song ringing through the night, she rose and called the eunuch who slept at the door of the tent. He came to her, and she said: 'Run out quickly to find the man who was singing and bring him to me.' 'I heard nothing,' said the eunuch. 'The night is dark, and I can find no one without waking up all our people.' 'Nevertheless it must be done,' said Nuzhat. 'If you find anyone awake, you may be sure it was he who sang.'

At this point Shahrazād saw the approach of morning and discreetly fell silent.

But when the seventy-second night had come

SHE SAID:

The eunuch dared not make any further objection, so he went out and, looking all about him, found that the only man who seemed to be awake was the fireman, since Dū al-Makān still lay in a swoon. The fireman, seeing by the light of the moon that the eunuch was in a very bad temper, feared that the singing had disturbed the chamberlain's wife; therefore, when the eunuch asked him if he had been singing, he answered: 'No, no, certainly not.' Then said the eunuch: 'But who was it? Show him to me, for you were awake and must have seen him.' More terrified than ever for Dū al-Makān's sake, the fireman insisted that he had seen and heard nothing. 'You lie!' said the eunuch. 'Never will I believe that you heard nothing.' 'But it is true!' cried the fireman. 'It was some desert wanderer on a camel who sang; it was his ill-omened voice which wakened me, Allāh curse the same!' The eunuch shook an unbelieving head and returned grumbling to report to his mistress that the song had been sung by a wanderer who was now far away on his camel. Nuzhat looked at the eunuch in her disappointment and said nothing.

Soon after this, Dū al-Makān came to himself and saw the moon shining in the clear bowl of the sky above his head. The magic zephyr of memory lifted in his soul, and there sang in his heart innumerable birds and the modulation of invisible flutes. The desire came irresistibly upon him to deliver his sorrows in song, and he said to the fireman: 'Listen, and I will recite certain beautiful verses to calm my heart.' Then said the fireman: 'Do you not know what has happened? Do you not know that I only saved you from the eunuch by the ingratiation of my manners?' 'What eunuch?' asked Dū al-Makān. 'Master,' returned the fireman, 'the eunuch of the chamberlain's wife came here, scowling and brandishing a great stick of almond wood. He examined all the sleepers and, finding that only I was awake, asked me, rudely enough, whether I had been singing. I answered that it was some wanderer passing by on the road, and, although the eunuch did not seem to believe me, he went away, commanding me to seize anyone I heard singing so that he might take the culprit to his mistress. You can see, dear master, that I had considerable difficulty in allaying the suspicions of this black fellow.'

Dū al-Makān cried: 'What man dare stop me singing the songs which please me? I shall sing all the verses that I love, let what will come of it. What have I to fear now that I am so near my own country, where nothing can touch me?' 'You want to destroy us all!' cried the poor fireman. 'I am sorry, my friend, but I must sing,' replied Dū al-Makān firmly. 'Then you will drive me away,' said the fireman, 'for I would rather leave you than see you come to harm. Have you forgotten, my child, that we have been together for a year and a half and you have never had to reproach me? You must understand that everyone is very tired and wishes to sleep. I know that your verses are beautiful, but do not keep us all awake with them.' Nevertheless Dū al-Makān was quite unable to restrain himself and, as a little breeze ruffled the tufts of the palms above him, he sang at the top of his voice:

> Time, where are the old hours in whose gold mirth
> I lay with love upon adored earth?
>
> Time has put by the coloured days of laughter
> And all the smiling nights which followed after.
>
> Time has gnawed thin the pillow of my rest.
> Who evilly worked where I had loved the best?
> Time!

With the last word of this, he uttered three great cries and fell into a swoon again, so that the fireman rose and covered him with his mantle.

Nuzhat this time recognised the voice of her brother beyond any doubt, and called to the eunuch through her sobs: 'Unhappy wretch!

the same man has sung a second time quite near my tent. As Allāh lives, if you do not bring him to me at once, my husband will give you a good beating and dismiss you from his service. Take these hundred dīnārs and give them to the singer, politely inviting him to come to me. If he refuses, give him this purse of a thousand dīnārs. If he refuses again, do not insist further, but find out where he lodges, what he is doing, and from what country he has come. Above all, make haste!'

At this point Shahrazād saw the approach of morning and discreetly fell silent.

But when the seventy-third night had come

SHE SAID:

The eunuch went out on his search, stumbling among the legs of the sleeping and looking into the faces of each, but could find no one awake. So he went up to the fireman, who was sitting without his mantle and with his head uncovered, and seized him by the arm, crying: 'It was you who sang!' 'As Allāh lives, it was not I, O chief of the eunuchs!' answered the terrified man. 'Very well,' said the eunuch, 'I will not leave go of you until you point out who it was, for I dare not go back to my mistress without him.' The unfortunate fireman began to cry out in his fear for Dū al-Makān and said to the eunuch: 'I swear by God that it was someone passing along the road and singing. If you harm me you will have to answer for it at Allāh's judgment. I am only a poor man, but I come from the city of Abraham, who was the Friend of God.' 'That may be so,' said the eunuch, 'but you had better come and tell your story to my mistress, for she will never believe me.' Then said the fireman: 'Sublime and admirable servant, it were better for you to go back to the tent. If the voice is heard again, you can hold me personally responsible and treat me as the guilty party.' Then to calm the eunuch and persuade him to his advice, he overwhelmed him with sweet compliments and kissed him upon the forehead.

At last the eunuch pretended to be convinced, but, instead of returning to his mistress whom he dared not face, he walked round the tents and, coming back silently, hid himself in the shadow not far from the fireman.

As soon as Dū al-Makān woke from his swoon, the fireman said: 'Rise up and listen to what has happened because of your singing.'

And he told the youth the whole story; but Dū al-Makān answered:
'I do not wish to understand anything. I can in no wise hold my
sensations within me, now that we are so near my native land.'
Then said the fireman in horror: 'My child, do not listen to these
suggestions from the Evil One! How can you be so bold, when I
have enough fear for both of us? I conjure you by Allāh not to sing
again until we have actually reached your native land. Really, my
son, I did not know that you were as mad as all this. The chamberlain's wife wants to have you beaten because you have robbed
her of her rest. She has already sent her eunuch to look for you
twice.'

Dū al-Makān paid no attention to the fireman's words, but lifted
his voice a third time and sang with all his soul:

> Enough, I cannot live without my sleep,
>   Destroy my heart outright, or you will rue it.
> Friends said: 'Ah, love has got you in his deep.'
>   I answered: 'Do you think that love could do it?'

Hardly had he finished his song when the eunuch appeared before
him. This terrified the fireman to such an extent that he ran away
and stopped far off to see what might happen.

The eunuch advanced very respectfully towards Dū al-Makān,
saying: 'Peace be with you!'

At this point Shahrazād saw the approach of morning and discreetly fell silent.

But when the seventy-fourth night had come

SHE SAID:

It is related, O auspicious King, that Dū al-Makān answered:
'And with you the peace, the mercy, and the blessing of Allāh!'
'Master,' said the slave, 'this is the third time that my mistress has
sent me to say that she wishes to see you.' 'Your mistress!' cried Dū
al-Makān. 'What bitch is that who dares to send for me? A curse of
Allāh be upon her and upon her husband!' Not content with this
beginning, he cursed the eunuch for a whole minute, and the other
dared not answer because of his mistress's instructions. Rather he
tried with sweet and oily words to win the youth over, saying among
the rest: 'My boy, this invitation was not meant to offend or disturb
you, but simply that you should bend your generous steps towards

the ardent desires of a lady who knows very well how to repay complacency.'

At last Dū al-Makān allowed himself to be persuaded to accompany the eunuch to the tent. When the fireman saw this, he trembled for the youth and followed afar off, thinking: 'That he should die so young! Surely he will be hung at dawn.' Then another thought came to him, and he said: 'Suppose he puts the blame on me and says that I was singing! That would be very wicked of him.'

Dū al-Makān and the eunuch moved with difficulty among sleeping men and animals, and came at last to the door of Nuzhat's tent. Here the eunuch begged Dū al-Makān to wait for him and entered alone, saying to his mistress: 'I have brought the man. He is both young and handsome, and seems to be of noble birth.' Nuzhat felt her heart beat violently at these tidings and said to the eunuch: 'Make him sit down near the tent and beg him to sing something more that I may hear it near at hand. Afterwards ask his name and country of him.' The eunuch went out and said to Dū al-Makān: 'My mistress begs you to sing again and wishes to know your name and country.' 'With willing heart and as in duty bound,' answered Dū al-Makān, 'but my name has been blotted out from among men, just as my heart has been blackened. My tale is worthy to be written with needles in the corner of an eye, for I am as one who has become drunken with long sitting at the wine, a sleep-walker, a drowned man floating on a sea of folly.'

Nuzhat heard what he said from inside the tent and commanded the eunuch with tears to ask the youth whether he had lost someone dear to him: a mother or a father or a brother. The eunuch did so, and Dū al-Makān answered: 'Alas, I have lost all these, and also a sister who loved me. I know not where she is, for Fate has separated us.' The eunuch bore back this answer, and Nuzhat said: 'God grant that he find consolation in his grief and a reunion with those he loves.'

At this point Shahrazād saw the approach of morning and discreetly fell silent.

But when the seventy-fifth night had come

SHE SAID:

It is related, O auspicious King, that Nuzhat said to the eunuch: 'Go to him and beg him to sing some verses concerning the bitterness of separation.' The eunuch carried this petition to Dū al-Makān, who was sitting near the tent, resting his cheek upon his hand. In the strong moonlight which bathed the sleeping encampment, Dū al-Makān's voice mingled sweetly with the silence:

> My song
> Of coloured music
> Overlaid with gold
> Has chanted and extolled
> The power of bitterness
> A thought too long.

> My themes are these,
> If so you please:

Dark-glancing deer that tread a garden of roses,
Where bees bring honey and the dawn weeps her dew
To fashion breasts like summer-dreaming pears.
The wind stirs in the branches of the women
Pure as unthreaded pearls;
I smell the flower-essences upon them
To sunset flutes
And wine drunk out on the narcissus lawns.
Water of red lips to be drunk
Beside garden streams:

> These are my themes.

> My song
> Of coloured music
> Overlaid with gold
> Has chanted and extolled
> The power of bitterness
> A thought too long.

Nuzhat listened to this excellent poem in ravished silence. But, when it was finished, she feverishly lifted the door of the tent and, leaning out, looked at the singer in the light of the moon. Then indeed with a great cry she recognised her brother and leapt towards him, stretching out her arms and calling: 'Dū al-Makān, Dū al-Makān!'

Dū al-Makān recognised his sister; they cast themselves into each other's arms and both sank down fainting.

Speechless and astonished, the eunuch hastened to fetch a great
coverlet from the tent and to stretch it respectfully above them so
that they might be hidden from any who chanced to pass. Then he
waited, as in a dream, until they should come to themselves.

Soon Nuzhat recovered and, a moment or so afterwards, Dū
al-Makān did the same. The young girl forgot all her past misfortunes in her present joy, and recited these lines:

> In spite of my deserts
> Fate would have quite undone us,
> But I tricked Destiny.
> My lover is with me
> And fate tucks up his skirts
> To wait upon us.

Hearing her words, Dū al-Makān clasped his sister to his breast
and said, with tears of joy flowing from his eyes:

> My eyes have caught the trick, I fear,
> Of using tears for all they wish to say;
> They wept with bitter sorrow for a year
> And weep with joy to-day.

Nuzhat asked her brother to come into the tent and to tell her his
whole story before she should tell him hers, but Dū al-Makān said:
'Tell me yours first, dear sister.' So Nuzhat told her brother all that
had happened to her, with details which it would be useless to repeat
here, adding: 'I will presently make you known to my husband, the
chamberlain. I am sure you will be friends, for he is an excellent man
in every way. Now tell me all that has happened to you since the day
I left you sick in the khān at Jerusalem.' Dū al-Makān then told the
whole of his story and finished by saying: 'Above everything, dear
sister, I shall never find words to tell you of all that excellent fireman
of the hammām did for me: he spent his money on making me well,
he served me night and day with more zeal than a brother might
show a brother, or a lover a lover, went hungry that I might eat, and
walked while I rode upon his ass. If I am alive now, it is due to him.'
Then said Nuzhat: 'If Allāh wills, we will find a fitting recompense
for him when the days of our power come again.'

Nuzhat called the eunuch, who ran in and kissed Dū al-Makān's
hands, standing respectfully before him. 'Servant whose face is of
good augury,' said the young girl, 'keep the purse with a thousand

dīnārs in it, for you were the first to bring me the news. Now hasten to inform your master that I wish to see him.' The eunuch ran rejoicing to fetch the chamberlain, who came quickly, and was thunderstruck to find a strange young man in his wife's tent at midnight. Nuzhat reassured him by telling him the whole story, and added: 'So you see, O venerable chamberlain, that, instead of a slave-girl, you have married the daughter of King Umar al-Numān. This is my brother, Dū al-Makān.'

When the chamberlain heard the story, the truth of which he could not doubt, he rejoiced exceedingly to know that he had become the son-in-law of King Umar, and said to himself: 'Surely I shall be made the governor of some great province.' He tendered many respectful congratulations to Dū al-Makān on his delivery from tribulation and his meeting with his sister. He was about to order his slaves to pitch a second tent for the new arrival, when Nuzhat said: 'That is not necessary since we are so near Baghdād. My brother and I will be only too pleased to live in the same tent, as we have not looked upon each other for so long.' 'Be it as you wish,' answered the chamberlain, and he left them alone together, taking care to send them torches, syrups, fruits, sweetmeats and jams, from a store which he had brought from Damascus to distribute to those who should come out from Baghdād to welcome him. He provided Dū al-Makān with three sumptuous changes of raiment and a blood-dromedary with coloured trappings. When he could think of no more to give the young man, he walked up and down outside his tent, puffing his breast with complacency and thinking of his good fortune, his present importance, and his future greatness.

When morning had well come, he hastened to the tent and saluted his brother-in-law. Nuzhat said to him: 'We must not forget the fireman. I pray you tell the eunuch to saddle a fine horse for him and serve him two good meals a day. Let him by no means go far from us.'

The chamberlain gave these orders to the eunuch, who took some of the men of his master's following and set out with them to look for the fireman. They found him at last at the tail of the caravan, saddling his ass with trembling hands, that he might escape from that place which had been so fatal to his young friend. Seeing the eunuch and the slaves suddenly all about him, he was like to die. His cheeks turned yellow and his knees knocked together, for he did not doubt that Dū al-Makān had informed on him to the chamberlain's wife to get himself out of a difficulty.

At this point Shahrazād saw the approach of morning and discreetly fell silent.

But when the seventy-sixth night had come

SHE SAID:

It is related, O auspicious King, that the eunuch cried to the terrified fireman: 'O liar, why did you say that you did not know who had sung? We have learnt that the singer was your close companion. I shall not leave you for a single moment till we reach Baghdād, where you shall meet the same fate as your friend.' The fireman wept, thinking that his worst fears were realised. While he did not know very well what was happening because of his tears, the slaves took away his ass and mounted him on a magnificent horse belonging to the chamberlain. Then the eunuch said to them: 'Serve as guards to this fireman throughout all our journey; your heads shall answer for his safety. Attend to his least wants and hold yourselves respectfully towards him.'

The fireman, who never doubted that he should die when he saw himself guarded so closely, said to the eunuch: 'O generous captain, I swear that that young man is neither my brother nor any relation of mine. I am alone in the world, a simple hammām fireman. I found the youth stretched dying upon some wood outside the door of the bath, and picked him up for Allāh's sake. I have done nothing to merit punishment.' As the caravan went on, he wept and indulged in a thousand gloomy thoughts, each more terrifying than the last. And the eunuch who walked beside him amused himself by saying from time to time: 'You both troubled my mistress's sleep with your execrable songs.' Although at each stopping place he ate from the same dish and drank from the same cup as the fireman, the latter ceased not weeping and was sore perplexed as to what had happened to his young friend.

The caravan journeyed on until only a single day's march separated it from Baghdād. On the last morning of the journey, as they were getting ready to move forward, they saw a thick cloud of dust rise up in front of them, obscuring the heavens until it seemed that night had come again. The chamberlain, telling his people not to move, went forward with fifty mamlūks in the direction of the dust-cloud. They had not gone far before they saw a formidable army, with banners and flags, marching in battle-order to the sound of drums. From this army a group of warriors detached themselves and galloped towards the chamberlain, so that in a minute he and each of his mamlūks was ringed by five horsemen.

The chamberlain cried out in consternation: 'What is the meaning of this?' In their turn the horsemen questioned him, calling out: 'Who are you? Whence do you come and whither do you go?' The chamberlain answered in a firm voice: 'I am the chamberlain of the amīr of Damascus, Prince Sharkān, son of King Umar al-Numān, master of Baghdād. I am sent by him to his father with the annual tribute.'

The horsemen covered their heads and wept at these words, so that the chamberlain was astonished.

At last, after weeping, the chief of them said to the chamberlain: 'Alas, where is Umar al-Numān of whom you speak? Umar al-Numān is dead. He died of poison. Oh, heavy day! . . . Come with us, O venerable chamberlain, and we will lead you to the wazīr Dandān in the middle of the army, that he may give you all the details of this sorry business.'

The chamberlain himself wept, crying: 'O inauspicious journey!' Then he allowed himself to be led to the wazīr Dandān, who immediately granted his demand for an audience. When he had been invited below the tent and bidden to sit down, he told Dandān of the mission with which he was intrusted and detailed the presents he bore to Umar al-Numān.

Dandān shed many tears at the mention of this beloved name and then said to the chamberlain: 'It is sufficient for the moment to tell you that Umar al-Numān was poisoned: the details I will reserve for another time. The present situation calls for immediate attention.

'When the King passed to the mercy and limitless kindness of Allāh, the people rose up to know who should be elected in his stead, and would have come to blows had it not been for the intervention of the nobles and the highest in the kingdom. At last it was agreed to abide by the decision of the four great kādīs of Baghdād. These consulted together and named Prince Sharkān, governor of Damascus, King in his father's place. When I was told of this, I put myself at the head of the army to carry the news to Prince Sharkān at Damascus.

'But I must tell you, venerable chamberlain, that there is also a party in Baghdād which favours the election of young Dū al-Makān.

Only no one knows what has become of him or his sister for this long while, seeing that it is five years since they departed on pilgrimage and passed beyond the knowledge of men.'

Hearing these words of the wazīr Dandān, the chamberlain, though he was naturally grieved at the death of King Umar, rejoiced exceedingly to think what an excellent chance Dū al-Makān had of becoming King of Baghdād.

At this point Shahrazād saw the approach of morning and discreetly fell silent.

But when the seventy-seventh night had come

SHE SAID:

It is related, O auspicious King, that the chamberlain turned towards Dandān, saying: 'It is a strange tale that you tell me; but, confidence for confidence, I think that I have a stranger one which will rejoice your heart and put your worries away from you. Allāh has made our road easy for us by giving us back the prince Dū al-Makān and his sister Nuzhat.'

Dandān's joy knew no bounds when he heard this news, and he cried: 'Hasten to tell me the details of this happy chance, O venerable chamberlain.' Nuzhat's husband told him the whole story of the brother and sister, and by no means omitted the fact that he himself had become the brother-in-law of the young prince.

At this last intelligence, Dandān bowed before the chamberlain and presented him with such homage as is due towards an equal. Then he called together all the amīrs and captains of the army and chiefs of the kingdom, as many as there were with him, and made the new situation known to them. At once they kissed the earth between the chamberlain's hands and rejoiced at the new order, giving praise to the God of Destiny for the diversity of his marvels.

Later in the day the chamberlain and the wazīr Dandān sat each on a raised chair and took council with the amīrs and the wazīrs. After an hour's discussion it was unanimously decided to elect Dū al-Makān to the throne of King Umar, instead of going on to Damascus to bring back Prince Sharkān. At this decision, Dandān rose from his seat as a sign of respect to the chamberlain, who had now become the most important person present. And both he and the wazīrs and the amīrs gave the old man magnificent presents, that he might look upon them favourably. Dandān said to him in the name of all: 'O venerable chamberlain, we hope that, through your magnanimity, each may keep, under the new King, the place which he now holds. Now we will hasten to Baghdād to make suitable preparation for our young King, while you yourself return and inform him of his election.' The chamberlain promised his protection and that all should keep their present employments, and then left them to return to the tents of Dū al-Makān, while Dandān and the army set off towards Baghdād. Before he left, however, he took care to receive from Dandān both men and camels and sumptuous tents and every kind of royal ornament and robe.

As he returned to the brother and sister, the chamberlain felt himself even better disposed towards Nuzhat than he had been before. He said to himself: 'A blessed and a prosperous journey!' and when he arrived would not go into his wife's tent without first soliciting an audience, which was immediately granted.

He entered ceremoniously and told all that he had heard of the death of King Umar and the election of Dū al-Makān, adding: 'It now only remains for you, O generous King, to accept the throne without hesitation, for, if you refuse, harm may come to you from the one elected in your place.'

Though he and his sister were both in tears at the death of their father, Dū al-Makān answered: 'I accept the decree of Destiny, since no one can escape his fate; your words are full of counsel and good sense. Tell me, venerable brother-in-law, how shall I conduct myself towards my brother Sharkān?' 'The only just solution of the difficulty,' answered the chamberlain, 'is that you should divide the empire between you, you becoming Sultān of Baghdād, and your brother Sultān of Damascus. If you determine on this and follow your determination closely, peace will result.' And this advice seemed good to Dū al-Makān.

After he had finished speaking, the chamberlain put upon Dū al-Makān the royal robe which he had received from Dandān and, giving him the great gold sword of kingship, withdrew. Once outside the royal presence, he chose a piece of rising ground on which he had the royal tent pitched and prepared, with a high cupola and a double inside veil of coloured silks wrought with pictures of trees and flowers. He ordered the carpet-bearers to spread great carpets upon the earth, after it had been well beaten and watered; and then hastened to beg the King to pass that night within the tent.

The King did so, and hardly had dawn appeared when a far noise of war-drums and clarions made itself heard from out a column of dust raised by the army of Baghdād, at the head of which the wazīr Dandān was marching to receive his King, after having made all necessary preparations in the city.

At this point Shahrazād saw the approach of morning and discreetly fell silent.

But when the seventy-eighth night had come

SHE SAID:

King Dū al-Makān, dressed in his royal robes, mounted a tall throne raised in the middle of the tent. He held the great sword of rule resting on his knees between his two hands, and sat motionless while the mamlūks of Damascus and the guards of the chamberlain ringed him with naked swords.

Then, under direction of the chamberlain, a procession of homage began. By a corridor of silk, the chiefs of the army were led into the royal presence ten by ten, beginning at the lowest grade in the manner of old time, and ten by ten swore fealty to the King and kissed the earth between his hands in silence. At last there remained only the four kādīs and the wazīr Dandān. The kādīs entered as the others had done and, taking their oath, passed out in silence; but, when Dandān entered, Dū al-Makān rose from the throne to do him honour and went to meet him, saying: 'Welcome, dear father of us all, welcome, worthy wazīr, whose every act is perfumed with a great wisdom, whose every plan is confected by cunning and secret hands.' So Dandān took the oath upon the Book and the Faith, and kissed the earth between the King's hands.

While the chamberlain was giving orders for a feast, for the choicest meats and a pleasing service of songs, the King said to his wazīr: 'We must give great largess to the soldiers and all their officers, to mark my coming to the throne; therefore I decree that the whole of the tribute which we carry from the town of Damascus shall be divided among them. Also they must eat and drink until they can eat and drink no more. When these things have been attended to, I desire you to tell me the cause and coming of my father's death in fullest detail.' Dandān carried out the King's orders and, further, gave three days' leave to the soldiers and informed the notables that, for the same period, they were excused attendance on the King.

Leaving the whole army crying down good fortune on Dū al-Makān's reign, Dandān returned towards the royal tent. While his wazīr was away, Dū al-Makān had said to his sister: 'My dear, you have heard of the death of our father, but not the manner of it. Stay with me and you shall hear what report the wazīr Dandān makes of it.' With that he installed Nuzhat under the dome of the tent and had a great silk curtain lowered between her and the throne.

When Dandān entered, he said to him: 'O wazīr, tell me now all that you know concerning the death of that most sublime among kings,' and the wazīr Dandān said:

The Tale of the Death of King Umar al-Numān and the Admirable Discourses Which Went Before It

ONE day, when King Umar al-Numān felt himself oppressed by sorrow at your disappearance and had called all of us round him that we might attempt to distract him with our conversation, we saw a venerable old woman enter the presence, bearing all the marks of a saintly life upon her countenance. With her were five young virgin girls, round-breasted and as beautiful as moonlight, shining with such natural perfection that no tongue may do justice to their charms. Each had, in excess of her miraculous beauty, an astonishing knowledge of the Koran, the books of science, and the words of all Mussulmān sages. The holy old lady kissed the earth between the King's hands, saying: 'I bring five jewels to you such as the court of no other king upon the earth has seen. I pray you to look upon their beauty and put them to the proof, for beauty is never apparent save to the search of love.'

King Umar was charmed by the old woman's words and conceived a great respect for her appearance. Moreover the five young girls pleased him infinitely, and he said to them. . . .

At this point Shahrazād saw the approach of morning and discreetly fell silent.

But when the seventy-ninth night had come

SHE SAID:

It is related, O auspicious King, that King Umar said to the young girls: 'Pleasant children, if it be true that you are so filled with the knowledge of the delicious deeds of history, let each one of you come forward in turn and make some little discourse to sweeten my ears.'

Then the first girl advanced with an air of charming modesty and kissed the earth between the King's hands, saying:

The Discourse of the First Girl

O KING of time, life lives only by the will to live, planted in man that he may become master of himself and, with Allāh's help, draw nearer to Allāh. Life was given to man that he should increase in beauty and tread all error under his feet. Kings, who are the first of men, should be also the first in virtue and disinterestedness. A wise and cultivated man should act gently and judge suavely in all things, especially those connected with his friends. He should guard himself carefully from his enemies, but choose his friends with greater care; and once they are chosen, he should never allow another to come between himself and them, but rather decide all matters between them with forbearance. For if he has chosen his friends among those who care not for the things of this world, he should listen to their judgment; and if from among those who are attached to the things of this world, he should be the more careful not to harm their interests, gainsay their habits, or contradict their words. For contradiction may alienate even the love of a father or a mother; yet it is a thing of no worth, while a friend has a value which is above price. A friend is not like a wife, who can be divorced and replaced; a wound between friends is never healed. A poet has said:

> You must be careful of a comrade's heart,
> Alas, alas,
> It breaks more easily
> Than the fine glass
> Which drinkers set apart
> To crown their ecstasy.

Let me recall certain words of the sages. A kādī who would judge justly should look upon both sides of a fact and make no difference between rich and poor. His duty is to reconcile the two parties if possible, so that peace may reign among the Faithful. When there is a doubt, he should make long reflection and come up to the affair from many sides; then, if the doubt remains, he should reserve judgment. Justice is the first duty of man. It is better for a man who has been unjust to turn towards justice, even than for a just man to remain in that way. Let it be remembered that God has placed judges upon the earth to judge appearances; but He Himself will judge the hidden thing. A judge should never try to extract a confession by torture or starvation, for that is unworthy of the Faithful. Al Zāhiri said: 'Three things make a judge useless: respect of place, love of praise, and fear of losing his appointment.' A judge one day asked the Khalīfah Umar why he had deprived him of his situation, and the King answered: 'Because your words exceed your deeds.' Alexander the Great one day brought together his judge, his cook, and his chief scribe. To the judge he said: 'I have confided to you the highest and heaviest of my kingly duties. See that your soul be kingly.' To his cook he said: 'My body is in your care; let your art be without violence.' To his scribe he said: 'The children of my mind are in your care, O brother of the pen; see then that they suffer no defacement throughout the ages.'

When the girl had finished speaking, she covered her face again with her veil and rejoined her companions.

At this point Shahrazād saw the approach of morning and discreetly fell silent.

But when the eightieth night had come

SHE SAID:

The wazīr Dandān continued in this fashion:

The second girl, who had bold glancing eyes and a laughing chin, kissed the earth seven times between the hands of your late father, and said:

The Discourse of the Second Girl

AUSPICIOUS King, Lukmān the Wise said to his sons: 'There are three things which are possible only under three conditions: you may not know if a man be really good until you have seen him in his anger; you may not know if a man be brave until you have seen him in battle; and you may not know if a man be a friend until you have come to him in necessity.' A tyrant will pay for his injustice, in spite of the flattering words of his courtiers; and the oppressed will escape perdition, in spite of all injustice. Deal with people according to their deeds and not according to their words. Yet deeds are not worth the intentions which inspire them; therefore each man shall be judged according to his intentions and not according to his deeds. The heart is the noblest member of the body. A wise man said that the worst of men is he who allows an evil desire to take root in his heart, for he shall lose his manhood. A poet said:

> The wise will keep
> His treasure hid apart;
> True gold is hidden in the heart,
> A miner never had to dig so deep.

Our Prophet (upon whom be prayer and peace) said: 'The true wisdom is to prefer immortal things.' It is related that the ascetic Thābit wept so much that his eyes became weak. A doctor, who was called, said: 'I can only cure you on one condition.' 'What condition is that?' asked Thābit. 'That you cease to weep,' answered the doctor. 'But of what use would my eyes be, if I did not weep with them?' said Thābit.

A disinterested action is the most beautiful thing in the world. There were two brothers in Israel; one asked the other: 'What is the most terrible thing that you have ever done?' His brother answered: 'One day as I was passing a poultry run, I seized a fowl, wrung its neck, and threw it back again. That is the most terrible thing that I have ever done. And you?' The first replied: 'I once prayed to God *for* something.'

At this point Shahrazād saw the approach of morning and discreetly fell silent.

But when the eighty-first night had come

SHE SAID:

It is related, O auspicious King, that the second girl continued thus:

A poet has excellently well said:

> There are two beings you may not offend:
> God and a friend.

With these words the second girl retired. A third, who united in herself the perfections of the other two, took her stand before Umar al-Numān, and said:

The Discourse of the Third Girl

AUSPICIOUS King, I will only speak briefly to-day, because I am a little unwell and because the sages have recommended brevity.

Sufyān said: 'If the soul had her habitation in the heart of man, man would be winged and might fly lightly to Paradise.'

Sufyān said again: 'To look upon the face of one who has been afflicted with ugliness is a supreme crime against the spirit.'

After these two admirable phrases the girl retired, and a fourth advanced with the balancing of sublime hips, and said:

The Discourse of the Fourth Girl

AUSPICIOUS King, I shall relate certain incidents from the lives of just men. Bishr the Barefoot said: 'Beware of the abominable thing.' Those who were about him asked what that might be, and he answered: 'To make long prayers; for that is the ostentation of piety.' Then one who was with him besought him to teach the hidden truth and the mysteries of existence. The Barefoot answered: 'My son, these things are not for the herd, therefore we may not give them to the herd. Were there a hundred just men yet only five of those would be as pure as refined silver.'

The sheikh Ibrāhīm tells this tale: 'I chanced one day upon a poor man who had lost a little copper coin, so I offered him a silver dirham. He refused me, saying: "What would I do with all this silver, whose expectations are centred upon a felicity which shall endure for ever?" '

At this point Shahrazād saw the approach of morning and discreetly fell silent.

But when the eighty-second night had come

SHE SAID:

Bishr the Barefoot's sister came one day to the Imām Ahmad ibn Hanbal, and said: 'Make a thing plain to me, O holy Imām of the Faith. It is my custom to sit upon our terrace at night and spin thread by the light of the torches which pass in the street, for we have no lamp in our house. Tell me if it is lawful so to use light which does not belong to me.' 'Who are you, O woman?' questioned the Imām, and she replied: 'I am the sister of Bishr the Barefoot.' Then the Imām rose and kissed the earth between the girl's hands, saying: 'Most sweetly perfumed soul and sister of the saints, might I but respire the purity of your heart all my life long!'

A certain sage said: 'When Allāh wishes well to one of His creatures, He opens for him the door of inspiration.'

It is related that when Mālik ibn Dīnār used to see anything which he liked as he wandered through the markets, he would reprove himself, saying: 'It is no good, my soul! I shall not listen to you.' He loved to repeat this phrase: 'The one way by which you can save your soul is by not obeying her; if you would lose her, listen to her.'

Mansūr ibn Umar tells the following tale: 'I once passed through the city of Kufah on a dark night, while I was making pilgrimage to Mecca. Near me in the bosom of the darkness I heard a loud voice saying this prayer: "Great Master and Lord, I am not of those who revolt against your laws and are ignorant of your kindness. Though I have sinned greatly, I ask for pardon and remission, seeing that my intentions did not sin but only my acts." As soon as this prayer was finished, I heard a heavy fall. As I could make nothing of the voice or the sound which followed it, I called out: "I am Mansūr ibn Umar, a pilgrim bound for Mecca. Is there need of help?' No one answered me, so I went my way. Next morning I saw a funeral procession passing, among whom walked an old and sorrowful woman. I asked her who the dead might be, and she replied: "Yesterday my son, after saying his prayers, recited that verse from the Book which begins with the words: O you who believe in the word, lift up your hearts. No sooner had my son read this verse than a man who was passing broke his heart and fell dead. That is all that I can tell you of this death." '

The fourth girl here retired, and the fifth, who was as it were a crown about the heads of the other four, advanced and said:

The Discourse of the Fifth Girl

O AUSPICIOUS King, I will speak to you a little of the things of the spirit as revealed in history.

Maslamah ibn Dīnār said: 'Each pleasure that does not forward the soul a little nearer God is not so much a pleasure as a calamity.'

It is related that while Moses (peace be with him!) sat by the rivers of Midian, two maidens drew near to water the flock of their father Shuaib. Moses (peace be with him!) drew water for the sisters to drink, and poured also for their flock into the hollow palm-tree trough. When the girls returned to their father's house and told him of this, he bade one of them return and bring the stranger to him. She went back to the well and, covering her face, said to Moses: 'My father begs you to accompany me to his house to share our repast, in return for the kindness you did us.' Moses at first did not wish to go with her on account of such a trifling matter, but at last he was persuaded and set out behind her.

At this point Shahrazād saw the approach of morning and discreetly fell silent.

But when the eighty-third night had come

SHE SAID:

It is related, O auspicious King, that the fifth girl continued thus:

Now this girl had a very big bottom; sometimes the wind moulded her light robe to it, sometimes it lifted the robe altogether and showed the naked prominence. Each time it appeared Moses shut his eyes, and at last, fearing that the temptation to open them would become too great, insisted on walking in front of the girl. When Shuaib saw Moses enter, he rose and said to him: 'Dinner is ready, Moses. Be very welcome for the kindness which you did to my daughters.' 'My father,' replied Moses, 'I do not sell my good deeds upon this earth for gold, silver, or food. I store them up towards the Day of Judgment.' Then said Shuaib: 'Young man, you are my guest and we have a tradition of hospitality; therefore sit down and eat with us.' Moses did so, and at the end of the meal Shuaib said to him: 'If you wish, you may stay with us and feed our flocks. At the end of eight years I will marry you to my daughter who went back to the well to fetch you.' Moses joyfully accepted this offer, saying to himself: 'Now that the matter has been put upon a lawful footing, I can think upon that bountiful bottom without sin.'

A man met a friend who asked him why he had not seen him for a long time, and he answered: 'I have been spending the time with my friend So-and-So. Do you know him?' 'Indeed, I know him,' answered the other, 'he has been my neighbour for over thirty years and I have never spoken a word to him.' 'My poor friend,' said the man, 'do you not know that he who does not love his neighbour is not loved by God? Do you not know that a neighbour owes as much to a neighbour as to a brother?'

One day ibn Ad-ham said to a friend, who was returning with him from Mecca: 'How do you live?' 'When I have something to eat, I eat; when I have nothing, I wait in patience,' his friend answered. Then ibn Ad-ham said: 'The dogs of Balkh do very much the same. When Allāh gives me bread, I glorify Him; and when He denies me, I thank Him.' The other cried out: 'O my master!' and said no more.

Muhammad ibn Umar one day asked a man of austere life his view on our grounds of faith in Allāh. The man answered: 'I repose my trust in Him for two reasons: I have found by experience that the bread I eat is not eaten by another, and I know that I could not have been born into this world if Someone had not willed it.'

The fifth girl rejoined her companions, and the saintly old woman advanced with slow and holy steps. She kissed the earth nine times between the hands of your late father, King Umar al-Numān, and said:

The Discourse of the Old Woman

O KING, you have heard from my five charges edifying discourse concerning the despite of mundane things. I will speak to you about certain acts of the greatest in times past.

The Imām al-Shāfīi (whom Allāh keep!) divided the night into three parts: the first for study, the second for sleep, and the third for prayer. Towards the end of his life, he waked all night and kept none of it for sleep.

The same Imām al-Shāfiī said: 'During ten years of my life, I have never eaten as much barley bread as I wanted. To eat too much hurts everything. It thickens the brain, hardens the heart, destroys the intellect, brings on sleep and laziness, and sucks away all energy.'

Young ibn Fuād tells the following story: 'One day in Baghdād I sought the bank of the river to perform my ablutions. While I was stooping down, a man, followed by a silent crowd, passed behind me and said: "Be diligent in your ablutions, young man, and Allāh will be diligent about you." I turned and, seeing a man with a great beard whose face was stamped with benediction, hastened to finish my ablutions and to follow him. When he saw me, he turned and said: "Do you wish to ask me anything?" "Venerable father," I answered, "teach me, I pray, how one may take certain hold on Allāh." This was his answer: "Learn to know yourself; when you know yourself, do anything and everything you wish, so that it does not interfere with other people." With that he continued his road, and I turned to one of his followers, asking whom he might be. "He is the Imām Muhammad ibn Idrīs al-Shāfiī!" the man answered.'

At this point Shahrazād saw the approach of morning and discreetly fell silent.

But when the eighty-fourth night had come

SHE SAID:

It is related, O auspicious King, that the holy old woman continued thus:

The Khalīfah Abū Jafar al-Mansūr wished to make Abū Hanīfah a judge and to allow him ten thousand dirhams a year. When Abū Hanīfah learnt of this intention, he made his morning prayer and wrapped himself in the silence of his white robe. He made no answer to the herald sent by the Khalīfah to pay him the ten thousand dirhams in advance, and to announce his nomination; at last the herald said: 'Be very sure, dear master, that this money I bring you is a lawful thing, allowed by the Book.' Then said Abū Hanīfah: 'In truth money is lawful, but Abū Hanīfah can never serve a tyrant.'

After these instances, the old woman added: 'I would willingly adduce further examples from the wise lives of old time, but night approaches and Allāh allows us many days.' With that, she wrapped her great veil about her shoulders and withdrew with her five pupils.

Here the wazīr Dandān ceased speaking for a moment to Dū al-Makān and to his sister Nuzhat who was behind the curtain; but after a few seconds he continued:

When the late King, your father, heard these edifying discourses he understood that these five women were as learned as they were beautiful, the supreme marvels of their time. He did not know how to show his great desire for them and his respect for the sainted old woman who accompanied them. To begin with, he gave them those apartments which had before belonged to Queen Ibrīzah of Cesarea, and every day for ten days he himself came for news of them and to see that they lacked nothing. On each occasion he found the old woman in prayer, and heard that she had passed the day in fasting and the night in meditation; at length he said to me: 'O wazīr, what a blessing it is to have so holy a woman staying in my palace. My respect for her is as great as my love for her young charges. Now that the ten days due to hospitality are passed and we may talk of business, come with me and we will ask her to fix a price for these sweet-breasted virgins.' We did so, and the old woman answered: 'O King, the condition of the sale of these girls is other than the condition of the markets, their price cannot be weighed in gold or silver or precious stones.'

Your father was astonished and asked of what such a price might consist. Then the old woman said to him: 'I can only sell them on condition that you fast for a whole month, passing your days in meditation and your nights in washing and prayer. At the end of that time, when your body has become purified and worthy of communion with them, you may enjoy their bodies for nothing.'

The King was extremely edified at this condition. His respect for the old woman knew no bounds and he hastened to accept. Then said the old woman: 'I will myself help you with my prayers to endure the fast. Now fetch me a copper pitcher.' When this was brought, she filled it with pure water and murmured unknown words over it for the space of an hour; then she covered the mouth with a piece of light fabric, which she sealed with her own seal, and gave it to your father, saying: 'At the end of the first ten days of your fast, you must unseal this and drink of its holy water, which will strengthen you and wash away the impurities of your life. Meanwhile I will depart to find my brothers, who are the Unseen Folk, since I have not communed with them for a long time. On the morning of the eleventh day I will come again.'

The old woman then wished the King peace and departed.

Your father took the pitcher and placed it as sole furnishing in an isolated cell which was in the palace. Then he locked himself in, to fast and meditate and become worthy of the bodies of the girls. He put the key in the depth of his robe and began his fast.

At this point Shahrazād saw the approach of morning and discreetly fell silent.

But when the eighty-fifth night had come

SHE SAID:

On the morning of the eleventh day the King unsealed the pitcher and drained it at a single draught. At once he felt a pleasant well-being throughout his body and a feeling of comfort in his bowels. Soon after he had drunk there was a knocking at the door of the cell and, when the King unlocked it, the old woman entered carrying a packet covered with fresh banana leaves.

To the welcome which your father accorded her the old woman answered: 'O King, the Unseen Folk are delighted that we are friends; they send through me their greetings and this packet of delicious jams, wrought by the black-eyed virgins of Paradise. On the morning of the twenty-first day of your fast, you must unfasten these banana leaves, and appease your hunger with the holy jams.' Umar al-Numān joyfully answered: 'Praise be to Allāh who has given me brothers among the Unseen Folk!' Then he kissed the hands of the old woman in thanks and escorted her, with many compliments, to the door of the cell.

On the morning of the twenty-first day, as soon as your father had obeyed his instructions, the old woman returned, saying: 'O King, I have told my brothers of the Unseen that I am making you a gift of the five young girls. They are delighted to hear this, as they feel friendly disposed towards you. They have commanded me to take the girls to them before they come into your hands, so that they may breathe over them such scents as shall intoxicate you; then they will send them back, bearing as a gift from the Unseen a treasure long hoarded up within the breast of earth.'

'This is almost too much,' said the King. 'I fear that in taking the treasure I might wrong someone.' But the old woman reassured him, so that at last he asked: 'When will you return them to me?' 'On the morning of the thirtieth day,' she answered, 'when you have finished your fast and sanctified your body, I shall bring them in a sweet purity as of jasmine, and you shall lie with them, though each is worth more than your kingdom. . . . Have you not some other woman whom you love, whom I may take with my charges to receive the perfumed purification of my immortal brothers?' 'Thanks, thanks,' rejoined your father. 'I have a Greek woman in my palace, Saffïah, daughter of King Afrïdun of Constantinople; she bore me two children who have been lost to me, alas, these many years. Take her with you, O venerable saint, that the Unseen Folk may assoil her and give her back her children.' 'Certainly I will do so,' said the holy creature. 'Bring her to me.'

At this point Shahrazad saw the approach of morning and discreetly fell silent.

But when the eighty-sixth night had come

SHE SAID:

The King sent at once for Saffïah and intrusted her to the old woman. The latter went for an instant into her own apartment and returned with a cup covered and sealed, which she gave to Umar al-Numan, saying: 'On the thirtieth morning when your fast is over, rise and bathe at the hammam; then return to your cell, and drink this cup which will complete your purification. Peace be with you now, my son, and the mercy of Allah and all His blessing.'

When the old woman had left the palace with the five girls and your mother, Queen Saffïah, the King continued his fast until the thirtieth day. In the morning he rose and went to the hammam, and after bathing returned to his cell. He forbade anyone to disturb him, locked the door again, unsealed the cup and, drinking its contents, lay down to rest.

We knew that this was the last day of the fast, so we waited until evening, and then through the night, and lastly until the middle of the next day. We said to ourselves that the King slept long because of his many watchings. But at last, when he would not open to us and did not answer our cries, we burst down the door and entered the cell.

The King was not there, but on his couch there were shreds of flesh mingled with black and crumbling bones.

Each of us swooned away; but when we recovered we examined the cup and found inside the cover of it a paper, on which was the following writing:

'Let there be no tears for an evil man! Who reads this shall know what punishment waits for one who seduces and corrupts the daughters of kings. This man sent his son Sharkān to abduct Ibrīzah, the unhappy daughter of our King. When she was brought to him, he took her, virgin as she was, and did to her that which he did. Then he gave her to a black slave, who meted out to her indignity and death. King Umar al-Numān did this thing and lo! he is not. I killed him, I the brave, the avenger, the Mother-of-Calamity. Also I have taken Saffīah, daughter of King Afrīdūn of Constantinople, back to her father. We will return in arms to slaughter you all upon the ruins of your houses. Over the whole earth there shall remain none but Christians who adore the Cross!'

When we had read this, we understood the full horror of our calamity. We wept, though weeping was useless, and beat our faces, though no beatings can bring back the dead.

At last, after a month of discord among the people as to who should succeed Umar al-Numān, it was decided to elect Prince Sharkān of Damascus. But Allāh in His mercy threw us across your path, though we had not heard of you for many years.

Such, O King, was the death of your father, Umar al-Numān.

When the wazīr Dandān had finished his story of the death of King Umar al-Numān, he covered his face and wept, as did also Dū al-Makān and Nuzhat behind her curtain, and the chamberlain.

The chamberlain was the first to recover himself; he said to Dū al-Makān: 'O King, tears cannot bring your father back again; therefore harden your heart with courage to watch over the interests of your kingdom. As all fathers live again in worthy sons, so shall your father live again in you.' Therefore Dū al-Makān ceased to weep and prepared to hold the first council of his reign.

He sat on his throne under the dome, with the chamberlain upright at his side, the wazīr Dandān before him, the soldiers behind his throne, and the amīrs and notables grouped sedulously about him according to their rank.

His first care was to enquire into the state of his father's treasury and, when Dandān had furnished him with a complete list of all the treasure and jewels which Umar al-Numān had left, said to the old man: 'O wazīr of my father, you shall be my wazīr.' Dandān kissed the earth between his hands and wished him a long life. Then the King said to the chamberlain: 'Let all the riches which we brought with us from Damascus be distributed among the army.'

At this point Shahrazād saw the approach of morning and discreetly fell silent.

But when the eighty-seventh night had come

SHE SAID:

The chamberlain opened the cases and parted every sumptuous item of their contents among the soldiery, reserving the best for the officers, but keeping nothing for himself. The officers kissed the earth between his hands and called down blessings on the King, saying: 'Never have we beheld such an act of generosity!'

Only after this division had been made did Dū al-Makān strike his tents and lead the army towards Baghdād. He entered a city of which every stone was decorated, and passed to his palace between terraced masses of his people, deafened by the shrill joy of women.

His first act was to call his chief scribe and to dictate a letter to his brother Sharkān, containing a detailed account of all that had passed, and concluding with these words:

'We beg our brother to make immediate preparation of his army and to unite his forces with ours, that we may join in sacred war against the threatening Infidels and avenge the death of our father.'

When he had folded and sealed this letter, he intrusted it to Dandān, saying: 'My friend, only you are capable of carrying through this delicate negotiation. You must speak sweet words to him, and add from me that I am very ready to give up the throne of Baghdād and take his place as governor of Damascus.' Dandān made his preparations in haste, and departed that very morning for Damascus.

While he was away, two important things came to pass in the palace of Dū al-Makān. The first was this: the King called his friend, the old fireman of the hammām, loaded him with honours and distinctions, and gave him a palace for himself, spread with the rarest carpets of Persia and Kurāsān. There will be much more to say of this excellent fellow as the tale goes on. The second was this: ten young white slaves were sent in tribute to the King, and one of them appeared so indescribably beautiful to him that he lay with her, and she conceived. Our story will also have more to tell concerning this woman.

In the course of time, Dandān returned and reported to the King that his brother Sharkān had listened favourably to his request and was even then on his way at the head of the army. 'We should go out to meet him,' said the wazīr, and the King answered: 'Certainly, O wazīr.' He immediately left Baghdād with all his forces, and, hardly had he pitched his camp after the first day's march, when the scouts of Prince Sharkān's army appeared in sight.

Dū al-Makān, taking the initiative, went forward to meet his brother and would have lighted off his horse to greet him, but Sharkān from far off saw what he would be at and called to him not to dismount. Then he himself jumped to the ground and ran and threw himself into his brother's arms. The two embraced each other with many tears and words of mutual mourning for their father.

As soon as both armies had returned to Baghdād, word was sent to all parts of the empire with promises of booty and promotion; therefore, for a whole month, a constant stream of warriors flowed into the city. While they were waiting, Sharkān told Dū al-Makān all his story, and Dū al-Makān told Sharkān his, insisting especially on the services of the fireman. Sharkān asked him if he had already rewarded that faithful friend for his devotion, and the King answered that he meant to complete the work of recognition when he returned from the war.

At this point Shahrazād saw the approach of morning and discreetly fell silent.

But when the eighty-eighth night had come

SHE SAID:

Sharkān was now able to test the truth of the story which had been told him by his sister Nuzhat, who had borne him the girl Power-of-Destiny, and he thought to ask news of her. He begged the chamberlain to carry his greetings to her, and the chamberlain returned with Nuzhat's salutation and enquiries about the child. Sharkān was able to set her mind at rest, as little Power-of-Destiny stayed in perfect health at Damascus.

When all the troops were assembled and Arabs from every tribe had brought a great force to the city, the two brothers put themselves at the head of the massed army (Dū al-Makān had said tender farewells to his pregnant slave-girl and provided her with a fitting service in all things) and set out from Baghdād questing for the lands of the Infidel.

The vanguard was formed by Turkish warriors under a chief named Bahrmān, the rearguard of Persian soldiers commanded by Rustam; the centre was under Dū al-Makān, the right wing was commanded by Prince Sharkān, and the left by the chamberlain. Dandān was second-in-command of all the forces.

They moved forward for a month, resting three days at the end of each week, until they came into the country of their enemies; thereupon the inhabitants fled to Constantinople and informed King Afrīdūn of the Mussulmān invasion.

King Afrīdūn called for old Mother-of-Calamity (for you must know that she had come to him to return his daughter Saffīah, and had persuaded her nursling, King Hardūb of Cesarea, to accompany her, bringing with him all the army to join with that of Afrīdūn. This he had done willingly as he was not content with the death of Umar al-Numān, but wished further vengenace for his daughter) and asked her advice as to what should be done.

Mother-of-Calamity answered: 'Great King, lieutenant of Christ upon this earth, I will show you what to do, and Satan himself with all his arts shall never unwind the threads which I am weaving for the feet of our enemies.'

At this point Shahrazād saw the approach of morning and discreetly fell silent.

But when the eighty-ninth night had come

SHE SAID:

Mother-of-Calamity outlined her plan as follows:

'Send fifty thousand warriors by boat to the Mountain of Smoke, at whose foot our enemies are encamped, and all the rest of your army round by the land way, so that our foul oppressors may be taken on both sides and not one escape.'

To this Afrīdūn replied: 'Truly that is an excellent idea, queen of old women, inspiration of the wise.' Straightway he put her plan into execution; his ships landed the warriors at the Mountain of Smoke, where they hid without any noise behind the high rocks, and the rest of the army went round by land until they were opposite the enemy.

At this time the opposing forces had these numbers: the Mussulmān army from Baghdād consisted of twenty thousand horsemen led by Prince Sharkān; the two bands of the impious Christians amounted to a thousand thousand on one side, and six hundred thousand on the other, so that, when night fell on the mountains and the deserts, the earth seemed like one brazier with all the camp fires of the unbelievers.

The kings Afrīdūn and Hardūb called their amīrs and their captains to a solemn council, in which they were on the point of deciding to attack next morning from both sides, when Mother-of-Calamity frowned and thus addressed the company:

'Brave warriors, to fight with the body when the soul is not sanctified is to ensure defeat. Therefore, O Christian men, I counsel you to draw near to Christ before the battle and to purify yourselves with the supreme incense of the patriarchal excrements.' The two Kings and all the captains shouted: 'Your words are wise, venerable mother!'

To tell you something of the supreme incense of the patriarchal excrements:

When the High Patriarch of the Christians in Constantinople made a motion, the priests would diligently collect it in squares of silk and dry it in the sun. Then they would mix it with musk, amber and benzoin, and, when it was quite dry, powder it and put it up in little gold boxes. These boxes were sent to all Christian kings and churches, and the powder was used as the holiest incense for the sanctification of Christians on all solemn occasions, to bless the bride, to fumigate the newly born, and to purify a priest on ordination. As the genuine excrements of the High Patriarch could hardly suffice for ten provinces, much less for all Christian lands, the priests used to forge the powder by mixing less holy matters with it, that is to say, the excrements of lesser patriarchs and even of the priests themselves. This imposture was not easy to detect. These Greek swine valued the powder for other virtues; they used it as a salve for sore eyes and as a medicine for the stomach and bowels. But only kings and queens and the very rich could obtain these cures, since, owing to the limited quantity of raw material, a dirham-weight of the powder used to be sold for a thousand dīnārs in gold. So much for it.

At this point Shahrazād saw the approach of morning and discreetly fell silent.

But when the ninetieth night had come

SHE SAID:

In the morning King Afrīdūn assembled the captains and lieutenants of his army and, making them kiss a great cross of wood, fumigated them with the incense described above. On this occasion there could be no doubt as to the genuineness of the powder as it smelt terribly and would have killed any elephant in the Mussulmān armies. The Greek pigs were accustomed to it.

After this ceremony, Mother-of-Calamity rose and said: 'O King, before we fight with these Unbelievers, it were better to assure our victory by getting rid of Prince Sharkān, who is Satan in person. He not only commands the whole army but is the heart of its courage; when he is dead, his men will fall an easy prey to us. Let the boldest of our warriors challenge him to single combat and slay him.'

Acting on this advice, King Afrīdūn sent for the most valorous of his knights, whose name was Lūkā ibn Shamlūt, and with his own hand not only fumigated him with the excremental incense but spat upon some of the powder, to make it into a paste, and daubed the gums, nostrils, cheeks, eyebrows and moustaches of his champion with it.

This hateful Lūkā was certainly the most terrible fighter among the Christians; none could so hurl the javelin, direct the sword, or wield the terrible lance. His valour was only equalled by his ugliness. At first sight you would take his face for that of a mongrel ass; looking more closely, you would find much of the ape in it; when you had, as it were, learnt it by heart, you would recognise in it a cross between a toad and one of the most loathsome serpents. To come near him was less supportable than to be separated from a friend; he had stolen his colouring from night and his breath from old latrines. For these reasons he was known as the Sword of Christ.

When Lūkā had been well fumigated, he kissed the feet of Afrīdūn, and the latter said to him: 'Go out, my son, challenge the wretched Sharkān to single combat, and rid us of our woes.' Lūkā kissed the cross and then mounted a magnificent chestnut horse, with a jewelled saddle and red housings. As he was armed with a three-pointed javelin, he appeared, when the heralds led him towards the camp of the Believers, like Satan in person.

One of the heralds cried out in Arabic, as the troop came near the tents: 'O Mussulmāns, behold Lūkā ibn Shamlūt, a champion who has put to flight Turks, Kurds, and Persians with his single sword! Let Sharkān of Damascus come out against our giant if he dare!'

Hardly had the challenge ended when galloping hoofs shook the earth, troubled the air, and terrified the heart of the wicked knight. Sharkān himself, in appearance like a lion and mounted upon a horse lighter than a young gazelle, charged with couched lance towards the Christian, shouting these verses:

> My horse might borrow from the winter cloud
>   Its swift grey stuff;
> My lance is but a war-song cried aloud;
>   It is enough.

The barbarian Lūkā, born in a brutish land, understood no Arabic, so he could not appreciate the rhythmical beauty of these lines; he contented himself with touching the tattooed semblance of a cross upon his forehead and then carrying his hand to his lips. Suddenly, looking as hideous as a hog in the saddle, he urged his horse towards Sharkān, reined it in quickly, and hurled his javelin so high in the air that it disappeared from sight. At length it fell, but, before it could touch the earth, the vile fellow caught it in his hand, as if he had been a sorcerer, and with the same motion hurled it at Sharkān with all his strength. The three-pronged weapon hummed through the air like a thunderbolt, but, just at the moment when it would taste the life of Sharkān, the prince stretched forth his hand and caught it. Glorious Sharkān! He also hurled the javelin in the air so that no man's eye might follow it and, as it fell, with a single movement both caught it and flung it back to the Christian, crying: 'A lesson for you, in the name of Him who made the seven stages of the sky!'

The gigantic Lūkā attempted to imitate Sharkān's feat, but, as he stretched forth his hand and thus uncovered himself, the prince launched his own javelin, which struck the Christian full in his tattooed cross. His unbelieving soul fled through his backside and went to mingle with the fires of hell.

At this point Shahrazād saw the approach of morning and discreetly fell silent.

But when the ninety-first night had come

SHE SAID:

When the Christian soldiers heard from the heralds of the death of their champion, they first beat their faces in grief and then sprang to arms, crying for death and vengeance.

The two Kings gave a signal, and their men rushed upon the Mussulmāns. Warrior engaged with warrior, cry answered cry, blood bathed all the harvest of the fields, bodies were crushed beneath the feet of the horses, and men got drunk with blood as if it had been wine. The dead fell upon the dead, and the wounded upon the wounded, until merciful night separated the opposing forces.

Dū al-Makān congratulated his brother on his immortal exploit, and then addressed Dandān and the chamberlain in these words: 'Take twenty thousand warriors and march them seven parasangs towards the sea, then wait in the valley of the Mountain of Smoke, until I call you to decisive battle by hoisting a green standard. The rest of us will pretend to flee, but, when the Infidels pursue us, we will turn upon them; thus they shall be caught between two ranks and destroyed before we can cry victory.'

Dandān and the chamberlain did as they were ordered; under cover of night they took up their position in the valley at the foot of the Mountain of Smoke. It will be seen that they would have all been destroyed if Mother-of-Calamity's better and earlier plan had been adhered to. But that part of the Christian army which had hidden among the rocks there, had already joined the main band. In the morning the warriors stood to arms on both sides, standards and crosses shone above the tents, and prayers were made for victory. The Believers listened to a perfection of the Chapter of the Cow, which is the first in the Koran, while the Christians called upon the Son of Mary and fumigated themselves with a doubtless inferior brand—for they were many—of fecal incense. It did not save them from destruction.

The battle re-engaged more terribly than before; heads flew through the air like balls, arms and legs lay thick as grass upon the ground, and rivers of blood reached the breasts of the horses. Suddenly the Mussulmāns, who had fought like heroes, seemed stricken by panic, for they turned and fled to a man. Afrīdūn, seeing this, sent a runner to Hardūb, whose troops had not yet taken part in the battle, saying: 'The Mussulmāns are fleeing because we are invincible; this is owing to the supreme incense of the patriarchal excrements with which we have fumigated ourselves and rubbed our beards. Pursue them, so that you may put a crown upon our victory and avenge the death of our champion, Lūkā.'

At this point Shahrazād saw the approach of morning and discreetly fell silent.

But when the ninety-second night had come

SHE SAID:

King Hardūb, burning to avenge the death of his admirable daughter Ibrīzah, and not knowing that the retreat was but a ruse of the brave Sharkān and Dū al-Makān, cried to his warriors: 'The Mussulmāns flee like women!' and set out in hot pursuit. But, hardly were they within striking distance, when the retreating army turned and threw themselves upon their pursuers. Sharkān cried out: 'Allāh akbar! Allāh akbar!' and Dū al-Makān cried: 'This is the day of religion, O Faithful, this is the day for gaining Paradise in the shadow of the sword!' The Faithful charged like lions, and truly it was not a day on which any Christian grew old. Few of them lived to bewail the coming of white hairs.

It would be impossible to describe the deeds of warlike daring done by Sharkān upon that day. While he was hewing in pieces all who came before him, Dū al-Makān hoisted the green signal and would have precipitated himself into the fray. Sharkān saw this from far off and galloped up to his brother, saying: 'Do not expose yourself to the chances of the battle, for you are necessary to the government of our people. If you needs must fight, stay by my side and I will protect you.'

Dandān and the chamberlain saw the signal and at once advanced in a half circle, so that the Christians were cut off from their boats. In these circumstances the issue was never in doubt. The Christians were terribly destroyed by Kurds, Persians, Turks and Arabs; a hundred and twenty thousand swine lay dead upon the field of battle, while a pitiful handful escaped in the direction of Constantinople. The people of Afrīdūn, who had retired to the heights with their King, sure that Hardūb and his Greeks would carry the day, watched in impotent agony the destruction and flight of their allies.

On that day the Believers gained enormous booty; they captured all the ships, with the exception of twenty which managed to reach

Constantinople with news of the disaster, and all the riches which
were in the ships, and they took a thousand delicately-harnessed
horses, with tents, weapons, and provisions beyond counting.
For this they thanked Allāh.

The stragglers dragged themselves into Constantinople, their
souls winged by the ravens of disaster, and the whole city was
plunged in gloom. Houses and churches were draped in black, the
people collected in disaffected groups crying sedition and, when
only twenty vessels of the fleet and twenty thousand men of the
army returned, accused their Kings of treason.

At this point Shahrazād saw the approach of morning and discreetly fell silent.

But when the ninety-third night had come

SHE SAID:

The trouble and terror of King Afrīdūn were so great that his
nose was bowed to his feet, his stomach turned inside out, and his
bowels loosed so that they slid forth from him. He called Mother-of-
Calamity to advise him, and she came.

You must know that old Mother-of-Calamity, who was the real
cause of all these misfortunes, was indeed a horror among old women.
She was libertine, faithless, and rotten with curses; her mouth was a
cess-pool, her red eyelids had no lashes, her cheeks were dirty and
lacked lustre, her face was as black as night, her eyes were blear and
her body covered with scabs, her hair was filthy, her back was bent,
and her skin was a mass of wrinkles. She was a festering sore among
festering sores, and a viper among vipers. The horrible old thing
passed most of her time in the palace of King Hardūb in Cesarea,
because of the great quantity of young men and women slaves which
she found there. She used to compel the young male slaves to mount
her, and she herself loved to mount the young female slaves. Above
all things she loved to tickle and rub herself against these virgin
bodies; she was terribly expert in the titillant art, and could suck the
delicate parts of a girl voraciously while rubbing her nipples in an
agreeable manner. To bring on the last spasm, she would anoint
their womanhood with saffron, and they would throw themselves
into her arms in a dying ecstasy. She had taught these practices to
all the slaves in the palace and, in times past, to the young followers
of Ibrīzah; but she could never win over the slim Coral-Pearl to her

447

desires. Ibrīzah herself held her in detestation for many reasons: her foul breath, the smell of fermented piss which rose from her armpits and her groin, the putrid aura, like that of rotten garlic, which remained from the many times that she had broken wind, her hairiness which was more than that of a hedgehog, and the palm-fibre-like texture of her skin. Excellently applicable to her are the words of a certain poet:

> All her perfumers with their scented arts
> Could not disguise the fetor of her farts.

It must be admitted, however, that Mother-of-Calamity could be very generous to all those who submitted to her desires; it was only because she had been refused that she had so much hated Ibrīzah.

Both Kings rose when she entered, and she said to Afrīdūn, who had requested her advice: 'O King, the time is come to set on one side all patriarchal blessings and excremental incenses, and to act by the light of reason. The Mussulmāns are marching upon our city; it is therefore necessary to send out heralds to command all the people and the soldiers in far garrisons to take refuge within the walls of Constantinople. As for myself, if you give me a free hand, the world will soon be ringing with my deadly inventions against the Mussulmān. I depart at once. May Christ, the Son of Mary, have you in His keeping.' She left the city, and King Afrīdūn hastened to give effect to her advice.

Now let us consider the plan which that old libertine had devised.

She took with her from the city fifty chosen warriors who could speak Arabic, disguised as Mussulmān merchants from Damascus, and a hundred mules laden with silks of Antioch and Damascus, satins having a metal sheen, and royal brocades. She had also taken care to provide herself with a safe conduct from Afrīdūn in the form of this letter:

'These are Mussulmān merchants from Damascus, strangers to our country and our faith; but they have traded with us. As in trade resides the prosperity of kingdoms and as these men are not in any sense warriors, we give them this safe conduct that none may hinder them where they wish to go, or levy tithe and tax upon their goods.'

The guileful old woman disguised herself as a Mussulmān ascetic, putting on a white linen robe and rubbing a magic unguent of her own invention into the skin of her face until it shone with peerless sanctity. She drew cords tight about her feet until they bled and indelible marks were left upon them. Then she addressed her companions in these words:

First you must beat me with whips until my body bleeds and bears lasting scars: spare me not, for necessity knows no law. Then place me in a chest like the other chests of our merchandise and load me upon a mule. After that, march straight forward until you come to the camp of the Mussulmāns under Sharkān. When they wish to prevent your going further, show this letter, in which you are described as Damascus merchants, and demand to see Prince Sharkān. You will be led into his presence and he will question you concerning your trade among the Christians. You must say to him:

'Auspicious King, the best and most meritorious profit of our trading journey among these unbelieving Christians was the freeing of a certain holy ascetic whom we were able to remove from between the hands of his persecutors. For fifteen long years they had tortured him to make him abjure the blessed faith of Muhammad, upon whom be prayer and peace! The thing happened in this way:

'We had been some time buying and selling in Constantinople and were seated in our lodging one night, calculating the gains of the day, when suddenly we saw a very great shadow appear on the wall of the room, in the likeness of a man with weeping eyes and a venerable white beard. The sad lips of this apparition spoke slowly to us thus: "If there are any among you who fear Allāh and follow letter by letter the precepts of our Prophet (upon whom be prayer and peace!) let them depart from this land of Unbelievers and journey towards the army of Prince Sharkān, of whom it is written that he will surely some day hold within his hands the city of Constantinople. At the end of three days' march you shall come to a certain monastery. Within this building, at such and such a place, you will find an underground cell in which a holy ascetic from Mecca, who is called Abdallah and whose virtues are pleasant to God, has been shut up by Christian monks for fifteen years and tortured horribly for the sake of his religion. To free this saint will be a beautiful action in the sight of Allāh, and may have other advantage beside. I say no more; peace be with you."

'With that the appearance of the sad old man faded from before our eyes.'

At this point Shahrazād saw the approach of morning and discreetly fell silent.

But when the ninety-fourth night had come

SHE SAID:

'Without a moment's delay we packed up all the merchandise which yet remained to us and all which we had bought in the city, and left Constantinople the same night. After three days we found the monastery. It stood near a little village. In order not to excite suspicion, we exposed a part of our goods in the market-place and bought and sold until nightfall. Then, under cover of the darkness, we stole towards the monastery, stunned the monk at the gate, and made our way to the underground chamber. There, as the apparition had told us, we found the holy ascetic Abdallah, whom we have brought to you in one of our cases.'

When you have obeyed me in all these things, my children, I will do the rest myself and exterminate these Mussulmāns.

The fifty soldiers, after listening to this speech, made obeisance to the old woman, beat her till the blood flowed copiously, and then placed her in a chest on the back of one of their mules. After this they set off to fulfil the rest of her strategy.

The victorious army of the Believers divided the booty which they had taken and glorified Allāh for their victory. Dū al-Makān and Sharkān took each other's hands and embraced, while Sharkān said to his brother: 'I pray that Allāh may grant your pregnant slave a son, whom I can marry to my daughter Power-of-Destiny.' They ceased not to rejoice and congratulate each other until the wazīr Dandān said: 'O Kings, it would be wise and fitting if you pursued your defeated foe without loss of time, so that the last one of them may be destroyed from off the face of this earth. A poet has said:

> It is great ease
> To feel your enemies
> Trod down by the wild horse between your knees.
>
> It is greater ease
> To read love's messages
> When she is following close after these.

It is greatest ease
When by forced urgencies
She comes to you before her messages.

But it is great ease
To feel your enemies
Trod down by the wild horse between your knees.'

Dandān made an end of this recitation, and the two Kings immediately led their army towards Constantinople.

They continued for six days without rest across burnt plains, where only grew a little yellow grass in solitudes else inhabited by God. At the end of this harassing march over waterless wastes, they came to a region which had been blessed by Allāh. Fresh meadows stretched before them, diversified by noisy waterfalls above which grew fruit trees. Birds sang there, gazelles leapt there, so that the place seemed some new Paradise, its great trees drunken with the dew upon their branches, and its flowers smiling to a vagabond south wind. A poet has said:

First look:
The garden moss stretches an emerald cloak
Shadowed by the kisses of the sleeping flowers.
Then shut your eyes:
Streams are singing about the feet of rose-trees.

Now look again:
Water glitters in the sunlight
Like tears upon a cheek in willow shade,
And flings up drops
To hang for silver bells
In the bright-hued pavilion of the flowers.

O flowers, crown my belovèd.

The two brothers breathed in the delights of this place and thought of resting there for some time. Dū al-Makān said to Sharkān: 'Brother, I do not think that you have ever seen gardens in Damascus as beautiful as this. Let us remain here for two or three days, so that our soldiers may be refreshed by the good air and sweet water, and fight the better against the Unbelievers.' Sharkān found this plan to his taste, and it was carried out.

They had rested in that pleasant place for two days and were on the point of departure, when they heard voices upon the outskirts of their host and were told that a caravan of Damascus merchants, returning to their own country after trading with the Infidels, had been stopped by the soldiery, who wished to punish them for holding communication with the enemies of Allāh. Soon the merchants were haled before the two Kings, and threw themselves upon the ground, protesting and saying to Dū al-Makān: 'We have been in the land of the Infidel and they have let no man harm us; but now that we have fallen among our own people, among Believers, we encounter oppression for the first time.'

They gave their letter of safe-conduct, written by the King of Constantinople, to Dū al-Makān, who read it and passed it to Sharkān. When Sharkān had also glanced at the contents, he said: 'What has been taken from you will be restored. But tell me why you traded with the enemies of our Faith?' The merchants answered: 'O master, Allāh led us among the Christians that we might win a victory greater than all the victories of your army.' 'How was that?' asked Sharkān, smiling, and they answered: 'We can only speak of it in some retired spot, where none may overhear us. If the thing became noised abroad, never might Mussulmān again set foot in a Christian land, even in times of peace.'

Dū al-Makān and Sharkān conducted the merchants to an isolated tent.

At this point Shahrazād saw the approach of morning and discreetly fell silent.

But when the ninety-fifth night had come

SHE SAID:

It is related, O auspicious King, that the merchants told the two Kings the tale in which they had been coached by Mother-of-Calamity. The brothers were much moved when they heard of the sufferings of the holy ascetic and his deliverance from the dungeon. They asked the merchants where he might be now, and received this answer: 'When we killed the monk who was guarding the monastery, we shut the saint in a chest that his departure might not be perceived, and brought him to you. But, before we left the monastery, we had time to see that it contained great weights of gold and silver, gems and jewellery, of which the holy man will be able to tell you more than we can.'

So saying, the merchants hastened to unload the mule and, opening the great chest, led the ascetic into the presence of the two Kings. He was so thin and wrinkled that he looked like a black cassia-pod, and there were the marks of whips and chains upon his flesh.

Seeing him (but you must remember that it was really old Mother-of-Calamity!) the brothers were convinced that they were in the presence of one of the holiest of men, the more so since that mysterious ointment made the old schemer's face to shine like the sun with holiness. Weeping and sobbing at his sufferings, they kissed his hands and feet and asked his blessing. The saint signed to them to rise, saying: 'Weep not, but listen to me:

'I have willingly submitted to the will of my Master, knowing that each scourge He sends me is but a test of patience and humility. Glorify Him, glorify Him! A man who cannot abide His chastening shall never enter into the delights of Paradise. If I rejoice at all at being freed, it is not because my sufferings have come to an end, but because it has led me to you, to a place where I may die under the feet of the horses in a Holy War. He who is killed in a Holy War does not die, but inherits eternal life.'

The two brothers kissed the saint's hands again, and tried to persuade him to eat, but he refused, saying: 'I have fasted in Allāh's name by day for fifteen years. It would be impious to break that fast now that He has delivered me out of affliction. Perhaps I will eat a little to-night when the sun has gone down.' They insisted no further at that time, but in the evening they prepared meats and presented them with their own hands. Then said the treacherous old dame: 'Now is not the time to eat but to pray!' All that night and the next and the next, she stayed without sleeping in the prayer-niche, so that the brothers venerated their ascetic progressively more and more and gave him a large tent, with special slaves and cooks. As he still would not eat at the end of three days, the Kings themselves brought him food such as the eye and the soul might dream of, yet he would only eat a little dry bread with salt. Said Sharkān to Dū al-Makān: 'Here is a man who has given up every joy of earth. If my business were not war, I would consecrate myself to his service, following him all my life that he might bless me. But now, as we have to march on Constantinople, let us beg him to say somewhat to us that we may profit by it.' Then said the wazīr Dandān: 'I also would see this saint, and beg him to pray for me in case I lose my life in the coming battle and go to present myself before the Master. I think that I have had enough of this life.'

All three entered the tent of sly old Mother-of-Calamity, and found their saint in an ecstatic trance of prayer. They sat down to wait until he should have finished praying, but as three hours passed without his paying the least attention to them, in spite of the tears and sobs of admiration with which they tried to attract his notice, they advanced at length and kissed the ground in front of him. Then, and only then, he rose and wished them welcome, saying: 'Why do you come to see me at this hour?' 'O holy dreamer,' they answered, 'we have been here several hours already. Did you not hear our tears?' The saint replied: 'He who is in the presence of God knows nothing of what passes on the earth beneath.' 'Holy one,' they said, 'we came to ask a blessing before the battle and to hear the story of your captivity among those whom by God's grace we shall slay to-morrow.' 'As Allāh lives,' answered the wily old baggage, 'if you were not the princes of the Believers I would not tell you, because he who hears my story may draw therefrom considerable worldly advantage. Listen then:

The Tale of the Monastery

FOR a long time I lived in Sacred Places with pious men, and, as Allāh had given me humility, I never set myself against them. I had thought to pass the rest of my life in peace, accomplishing the uneventful duties of piety, but I reckoned without my destiny.

A night came when I wandered towards the sea, which I had never seen before, and the resolution suddenly formed within me to walk upon the water. I set myself to do this and was astonished to find myself moving easily upon the surface of the waves without wetting the soles of my feet. After walking great distances, I returned towards the shore, marvelling all the time at my new gift, so that my heart became uplifted with pride and I thought: 'Who can walk upon the water as I can?' Hardly had I formed this thought when Allāh punished me by planting in my mind a love of travel. I left the Sacred Places, and since then I have been a wanderer upon the face of the earth. One day in those travels, during which I fulfilled all the duties of religion, I came to a Christian monastery on the top of a high mountain. The monk who was in charge of this, a certain Matrūhanā whom I had known before, ran out to greet me and invited me to enter and rest myself. In reality he was plotting my destruction. Hardly had I accepted his invitation when he led me along a gallery and, pushing me into darkness through a door at the end, locked me into an unlighted chamber. There I was left for forty days without food or drink, to die of hunger and thirst, as a witness to our religion.

While I was thus confined, the chief general of all the monks came on a special visit to the monastery. As is the custom of these gentry, he had with him ten pretty young monks and a girl fairer than them all, dressed in a monk's robe which showed off her breasts and hips to lascivious perfection. Allāh alone knows what the monk-general used to do with this girl, who was called Tamāthīl, and with the young monks.

Matrūhanā told his superior of my imprisonment and starvation, and the latter, whose name was Kaiyanūs, ordered them to open the door of my dungeon and cast away my bones, saying: 'This Mussulmān must be by now so bare a thing that even the birds of prey will not molest him.' Matrūhanā and the young monks opened the door and found me kneeling in an attitude of prayer. Calling out: 'Sorcerer, sorcerer, break him to pieces!' they fell upon me with sticks and whips, until I thought that I was lost. Then I understood that Allāh was punishing me for pride, seeing that I had taken to myself the glory of walking upon the water, while I was all the time but an instrument between His hands. When Matrūhanā and the other sons of dogs had well-nigh killed me, they chained me and threw me back into the dungeon. I would surely have died of hunger, had not the Lord touched the heart of Tamāthīl and caused her to provide me daily, in secret, with a barley loaf and a pitcher of water. The monk-general stayed a long time at that monastery because it pleased him; he decided to make it his permanent abiding place and, when he had to leave it to continue his inspections, put Tamāthīl under the charge of the monk Matrūhanā.

I remained in the dungeon for five years, while the girl grew up into the most beautiful damsel of her time. I affirm to you, O Kings, that neither in our country nor among the Christians is her equal to be found. Nor is she the only jewel shut up in that monastery. The place is stored with inordinate gold and silver, and with jewels whose worth defies arithmetic. My advice to you if you would get possession of Tamāthīl and the other treasures is to take that monastery by assault without an hour's delay. I myself will act as your guide, because I can open the secret doors and point out the hiding places where Kaiyanūs has stored his holy vessels of carved gold. Also I will be able to win the girl over to you. Besides her beauty she has the gift of song and knows all the Arabic compositions, whether city songs or Bedawī. Your days shall be full of light and your nights of sugar and benediction.

You have already heard of my escape, from those excellent merchants who risked their lives to save me. Allāh curse all Christians from now to the Day of Judgment!

The two brothers heard this tale with great delight, for they dreamed of acquisitions and especially of young Tamāthīl, who was reported to be most expert in pleasure in spite of her few years. But Dandān had heard the story with considerable misgivings, and had only prevented himself from rising and leaving the tent because of the respect which was due to the two Kings. The words of the strange ascetic neither convinced nor satisfied him, but he said nothing of his feelings, fearing lest they had led him astray.

Dū al-Makān wished to march upon the monastery at the head of all his army, but Mother-of-Calamity dissuaded him, saying: 'I fear that when Kaiyanūs sees the army he will carry off Tamāthīl and all his treasure.' So Dū al-Makān called the chamberlain and the amīrs Rustam and Bahrmān, and said to them: 'To-morrow morning you must march on Constantinople; I will rejoin you there in a little while. The chamberlain shall take my place of general commander, Rustam will act for my brother Sharkān, and Bahrmān for the wazīr Dandān. Take good care that the army does not learn of our absence, for we shall only be away three days.' Then the King, Sharkān, and the wazīr Dandān chose a hundred of the bravest warriors, and also a hundred of the strongest mules which they loaded with empty chests to hold the treasure of the monastery. They took with them old Mother-of-Calamity whom they thought to be an ascetic loved of Allāh, and set out under her guidance for the monastery.

The chamberlain and the rest of the Mussulmān army folded their tents at dawn of the next day and, obeying the command of the King, set out towards Constantinople.

At this point Shahrazād saw the approach of morning and discreetly fell silent.

But when the ninety-sixth night had come

SHE SAID:

Old Mother-of-Calamity had not been idle. No sooner had the troops which escorted her left the camp than she took, from one of the chests which were on her mule, two trained pigeons; to the necks of these she attached a letter written to King Afrīdūn of Constantinople. She told him of all that had happened, and ended with these words:

'Also, O King, you must send ten thousand of your finest warriors to the monastery immediately. When they come to the foot of the mountain, they must wait there for me; I will deliver the two Kings, the wazīr, and a hundred warriors into their hand. My plan cannot come to fruition without the death of the monk Matrūhanā who guards the monastery. I sacrifice him for the general good, as the life of a monk is nothing to the safety of our religion.

'Praise be to Christ, our Lord, now and for ever more!'

The pigeons winged safely to their high tower in Constantinople, and the attendant hastened with the letter to King Afrīdūn. As soon as he had read it, the King assembled ten thousand knights, each with a racing camel and a mule to carry the spoil, and sent them off hot-foot towards the monastery, as Mother-of-Calamity advised.

When the two Kings and Dandān came with their following to the base of the mountain, they had to climb it alone, for Mother-of-Calamity, who was tired out by the journey, remained below, saying: 'I will come after you, when you have captured the place, and show you the hidden treasures of it.'

One by one the warriors reached the monastery and, climbing the walls, leapt into the garden. The monk Matrūhanā ran out at the noise, but this was the last thing that he did. Sharkān cried out: 'Down with the dog!' and immediately the monk was pierced with a hundred swords and exhaled his soul from his backside to mingle with the fires of hell. Then was the monastery well pillaged. A great treasure of jewels and vessels was taken from the walls of the place of sacrifice and loaded upon the mules and camels, but nothing was seen of young Tamāthīl or the ten boys who were her equal in beauty, or of Kaiyanūs the licentious monk-general. When two days had been spent in exploring every place, and yet no trace had been found of any of these, Sharkān said: 'As God lives, my brother, I am anxious concerning the army of Islām which we sent towards Constantinople.' 'I think,' answered Dū al-Makān, 'that we should renounce our hopes in respect to Tamāthīl and, contenting ourselves with what Allāh has given us in the way of treasure, rejoin our troops and lay waste the capital of the Infidels.'

They climbed down into the valley, to fetch the ascetic and then to rejoin their army, but no sooner had they reached the lower ground than a great host of Christian soldiers appeared on all the encircling heights and with a loud cry began to charge down upon their band. 'Who can have warned these Christians of our presence?' cried Dū al-Makān, but Sharkān interrupted him, saying: 'This is no time for conjecture, my brother. Let us stand firm against these dogs and make such a killing that none shall escape to light the fire upon his hearth again.' Said Dū al-Makān: 'If we had been warned, we could have had a greater force and made a better fight.' But Dandān exclaimed: 'Even if we had ten thousand they would be of little use in this narrow pass. But I believe that Allāh will save us, for, through fighting here with the dead King Umar al-Numān, I learnt all the outlets of this valley and the situation of the springs of icy water. Follow me, before all these outlets are occupied by Unbelievers!'

As the band was about to follow him into safety, the holy ascetic appeared, crying: 'Whither are you running, O Believers? Do you flee before the face of the enemy? You are in the hands of Allāh. He will take your lives or spare them according to His will. Have you forgotten that I myself, shut up in a dungeon without food, was yet preserved by the Lord? If death should come, Paradise follows after!'

Courage came back to them at these words, and they halted in face of the enemy, who charged them hotly. They were only a hundred and three men, but a Believer is worth a thousand Christians. Hardly had the Infidels come within reach of their arms than severed heads flew backwards like a flight of birds from the terrible sword play of the Mussulmāns. Dū al-Makān and Sharkān severed each five heads with a single blow of their swords; ten men would rush upon the brothers and ten heads would fly in air. The hundred warriors made a memorable carnage of these dogs, until night brought succour to the larger force.

The Believers retired with their three chiefs into a cavern at the foot of a mountain. They found that the ascetic was missing, and that only forty-five men remained of their own band. 'God grant that the holy man has not perished in the struggle!' said Dū al-Makān, but Dandān answered: 'I saw your ascetic during the battle! He seemed to me like some black Ifrīt, exciting the unbelievers to fight on.' Even as he said this, the ascetic appeared at the entrance of the cave, holding the severed head of the leader of the Christians. The eyes of this terrible warrior were convulsed in death.

The two brothers leapt to their feet, crying: 'Thanks be to Allāh that He has sent you back to us, O holy father!' 'My dear sons,' answered the reprobate and disguised old woman, 'willingly would I have perished and many times did I throw myself among the swords, but even these unbelievers reverenced me and spared me. So freely did they allow me to move about, that I sought out their leader and cut off his head with one stroke of my sword. I bring the spoil to you, that it may encourage you to fight more fiercely against a leaderless army.'

At this point Shahrazād saw the approach of morning and discreetly fell silent.

But when the ninety-seventh night had come

SHE SAID:

Mother-of-Calamity continued: 'Now I shall run as fast as I can to your army below the walls of Constantinople and get them to send help. Be of good cheer and a stout heart until they come. Pasture your blades in this impure blood and thus rejoice the Master of all armies.' The two brothers kissed the speaker's hand in thanks, and said: 'O saint, how can you leave the valley while it is entirely ringed by Christians who will rain rocks down upon you when they see you?' 'Allāh will guard me,' said the old woman. 'He will blind the Infidels before He destroys them.' 'You speak truth, most holy father,' answered Sharkān. 'I myself saw you as a lion among them and not one of the dogs dared to approach you. You will save us, never fear. Night has fallen; the sooner you set out the better. May Allāh guide you through the darkness.'

The false ascetic attempted to take Dū al-Makān with her, that she might deliver him to his enemies; but Dandān, who a little distrusted the strange manners of the equivocal saint, persuaded the King to remain. Therefore Mother-of-Calamity set out alone, with a parting sidelong glance at the wazīr.

You must know that the old woman had lied when she said that she had cut off the head of the chief of the Christians, that is to say she had lied as to the manner of it, for she had cut his head from his dead body. A most warlike youth among the Mussulmāns had killed the opposing general and paid for the exploit with his life. All the Christians, seeing their leader remit his soul to hell, had thrown themselves upon the Mussulmān and cut him in pieces. His soul was already in Paradise between the hands of Allāh.

The band in the cave woke at dawn, refreshed and ready for the fray. They prayed, after the necessary ablution, and, when Dū al-Makān gave the word, hurled themselves upon the enemy as lions attack a herd of swine. That day they satisfied all their foes with carnage. Sword fell on sword, lance upon lance, and javelin upon breastplate. The Believers threw themselves again and again into the fight like blood-maddened wolves, while Sharkān and Dū al-Makān shed such waves of blood that the river of the valley overflowed and the gorge itself was hidden by accumulations of the slain.

At this point Shahrazād saw the approach of morning and discreetly fell silent.

But when the ninety-eighth night had come

SHE SAID:

At nightfall the combatants separated. The Mussulmāns returned to their cave, leaving thirty-five men upon the battlefield. They were reduced to ten warriors, two Kings, and a wazīr; therefore they had the more need to trust in Allāh and the excellence of their swords. Sharkān was grieved at their losses. 'What shall we do now?' he asked with a sigh, and the remnant of his people answered: 'We can do nothing, save with Allāh.'

Sharkān passed the night without sleeping and roused his companions at daybreak, saying: 'My friends, as there are only thirteen of us left, I consider that it would be fatal to go out against the enemy. Even if we fought prodigiously as we have done before, not one of us would come back alive. I decree, therefore, that we hold this cave with our swords and provoke our enemies to attempt the assault. We can easily cut to pieces any who dare to enter the cave, for we have the advantage in a confined space. We shall be able to decimate our foes while waiting for the reinforcements which our holy companion has gone to fetch.'

On this five of the warriors ventured outside the cave and provoked the enemy with cries, until a band of knights advanced towards them. Then they retreated into the cave's mouth, stationing themselves on each side of it.

It came to pass as Sharkān had predicted: each time the Christians stormed the cave they were seized and cut in two, so that not one of them returned to warn their comrades of the danger. More Christians were killed upon that day than on those which had gone before, because Allāh blinded the eyes of the Unbelievers with darkness and put strength into the heart of His servants.

Next morning the Christians took counsel together, saying: 'This war will never cease until both sides are exterminated; therefore, instead of trying to storm the cave, let us surround it with our men and light dry wood against the entrance so that all the enemy may be burnt alive. If, instead of being roasted, they prefer to surrender, we will lead them captive back to King Afrīdūn in Constantinople. If they will not yield, let them become burning coals to feed the fires of hell. Christ smoke and curse them and their seed after them! Christ weave their souls as a carpet for the feet of His children!'

They hastened to carry out what they had determined; they piled great loads of wood about the mouth of the cave, and set fire to it.

At this point Shahrazād saw the approach of morning and discreetly fell silent.

But when the ninety-ninth night had come

SHE SAID:

The Mussulmāns were driven out by the great heat; they massed themselves into one close rank and leapt through the flames. Alas, blinded by smoke and fire, they fell an easy prey to the Christians outside the cave, and would have been put to death had not the leader of their enemies said: 'Let us take them alive to Constantinople, where they may rejoice the King with their captivity and death. Put chains about their necks and drag them behind your horses to the city.'

The devoted few were bound with cords and put in charge of guards, while the whole Christian army sat down to celebrate their capture by eating and drinking. They drank so much that by midnight they fell to the earth in an impotence as of death.

Sharkān saw their bodies stretched all about him and said to his brother: 'Is there no way of escape?' 'Alas,' answered Dū al-Makān, 'I cannot see one, for we are caged up like birds.' Sharkān sighed so deeply at this answer that he broke the cords about his breast, and they fell to the ground. He leapt to his feet and cut the bonds of Dandān and Dū al-Makān. Then, taking from the chief guard the keys of the manacles which confined his ten soldiers, he set them free. Without loss of time the thirteen armed themselves with the weapons of the drunken Christians and fled noiselessly, thanking Allāh in their hearts for their deliverance.

They soon reached the top of the mountain, where Sharkān halted them with these words: 'Allāh has blessed me with an idea. Let us separate and, scattering ourselves about these various peaks, cry with all our might: "To Allāh the victory!" The rocks of the mountains and the valleys will multiply the sound, these drunken Infidels will think that our whole army is upon them, and will put each other to the sword in the panic of darkness.'

At once his men followed Sharkān's advice. Their voices fell sheer from the mountain tops, reverberating a thousand times from rock to rock in the darkness, so that the Christians sprang hastily and clumsily to arms, crying: 'As Christ lives, the whole Mussulmān army has come upon us!' Each man fought with his fellow until morning stopped the carnage, but by that time the little band of Believers was far on its way to Constantinople.

Towards the full light of morning, Sharkān's band saw a great cloud of dust advancing towards them, out of which voices cried: 'To Allāh the victory!'

At this point Shahrazād saw the approach of morning and discreetly fell silent.

But when the hundredth night had come

SHE SAID:

Soon they saw clearly a Mussulmān army with flying standards coming to meet them. The amīrs Rustam and Bahrmān were on horseback at its head, and, among great waves of warriors, were borne banners on which appeared: '*There is no God but Allah! And Muhammad is His Prophet!*' Rustam and Bahrmān threw themselves from their horses at the sight of the King and his companions, and came forward to present their homage. Dū al-Makān asked them how all went with the army before the walls of Constantinople, and they answered: 'The army is well and in good spirits. The chamberlain sent us with twenty thousand men to come to your assistance.' Dū al-Makān questioned them, saying: 'How did you know of our danger?' and they replied: 'The saintly ascetic ran all day and night to inform us and to bid us haste. He is now in safety with the chamberlain, and encourages the Believers in their siege by many a holy discourse.'

The two brothers rejoiced and gave thanks to Allāh for the safety of their spiritual guide. They told the two amīrs all that had happened at the monastery, adding: 'The unbelievers, who have been killing each other during the night, should now be in a tumult of fear at their mistake. Let us not lose an instant; let us fall upon them from the mountains, slay them, and recover our booty.'

Dū al-Makān and Sharkān put themselves at the head of their new army and fell like thunderbolts upon the camp of the Christians, making play with sword and lance. At the end of that day there remained not one Infidel to return with the disastrous news to Constantinople.

When all were dead, the Mussulmāns divided the spoil and passed the night in rest and prayer and mutual congratulation.

At dawn Dū al-Makān determined to depart, and said to the leaders of his army: 'We must reach Constantinople as quickly as possible, because the chamberlain will have been left with very few men; if the besieged find this out before we arrive, they may venture on a sortie, and it will be an evil day for the chamberlain.'

Camp was struck and the whole troop set off towards Constantinople, while Dū al-Makān, who rode at their head, chanted this psalm, which he made up to the rhythm of his horse's feet:

> God is praise and glory;
> Therefore glory and praise be unto Him
> Who led me by the hand in stony places,
> Who gave me a treasure of gold and a throne of gold
> And set a sword of victory in my hand!
>
> He covered the earth with the shadow of my kingdom,
> And fed me when I was a stranger
> Among strange peoples;
> When I was lowly He accounted me
> And He has bound my brow about with triumph.

His enemies fled before my face like cattle;
The Lord breathed upon them and they were not!
Not with the ferment of a generous wine,
But with death's evil grape
He has sent them drunken into the darkness.

We died, we died, in the battle,
But He has set us upon happy grass
Beside an eternal river of scented honey.

As Dū al-Makān made an end of this glorification, a black cloud
which he perceived in front of him parted, and old Mother-of-
Calamity appeared before him, still in the likeness of the holy ascetic.

At this point Shahrazād saw the approach of morning and discreetly fell silent.

But when the hundred-and-first night had come

SHE SAID:
All clustered round to kiss her hands while she exclaimed in a
tearful voice:

'I bring evil news, O people of the Prophet! Hasten, hasten!
Your brothers outside the walls of Constantinople have been
attacked in their tents by those they were besieging, and now flee in
disorder. If you do not hasten to their assistance, the chamberlain
and all his men will leave no trace that they have ever been.'

Dū al-Makān and Sharkān felt themselves grow dizzy with the
beatings of their hearts; in the extremity of their sorrow they knelt
and kissed the feet of the messenger, while all their soldiers cried
aloud in grief.

But the wazīr Dandān did not do so. He kissed neither hand nor
foot, but stayed on his horse and cried with a loud voice: 'As Allāh
lives, O soldiers, my heart experiences a profound aversion from
your saint. If it be a saint at all, it is a saint of hell! Take my advice
and stay far off from such a sorcerer, pay no attention to his words.
Believe an old companion of the dead King and march without loss
of time.'

Sharkān replied to the wazīr Dandān: 'Put these unworthy
suspicions behind you, my friend; they prove that you did not see,
as I did, our holy father standing fearless amid the swords and
lances of the enemy to give us sacred encouragement. To blame a

saint is to become unsaintly; and that he is a true saint, witness the love which Allāh manifested in sustaining him amid the tortures of the dungeon.'

To emphasise his words, Sharkān gave a vigorous and richly-harnessed mule to the ascetic, saying: 'Mount this animal, O father, and walk no more upon your sacred feet.' The treacherous old woman cried: 'How can I rest while Believers lie dead without burial outside the walls of Constantinople?' She refused to mount the mule, but mingled with the foot-soldiers, marching with them and looking upon them as a fox which scents its prey. She recited verses from the Koran in a loud voice and made continuous prayers to the Merciful One, until the broken remnants of the chamberlain's army appeared in sight.

Dū al-Makān called the chamberlain to him, asking for details of the disaster, and the latter, his face undone by grief, told him what had happened.

Now the Mussulmān defeat had been brought about by Mother-of-Calamity. When the amīrs Rustam and Bahrmān, commanding the Turks and Kurds, had gone to the help of the two Kings, the army which remained outside Constantinople found itself so weakened that the chamberlain dared not speak of his numbers to a single one of his men for fear that one should be a traitor. But the old woman, knowing that the moment had come for which she had planned and plotted with so much care and fortitude, hailed one of the officers upon the walls and bade him drop down a cord to her. When this was done, she attached the following letter to it:

'*This from the subtle, the inventive, the terrible Mother-of-Calamity, acknowledged the supreme scourge of East and West, to Afrīdūn, the King whom Christ defend!*

'And after!

'Tranquillity shall soon light again upon your heart, for I have laid a snare which shall destroy the last of the Mussulmāns. Dū al-Makān, his brother Sharkān, the wazīr Dandān, and the remnant of the troop with which they pillaged the monastery of Matrūhanā, are captive and in chains, and I have contrived to weaken the army before your walls by persuading the chamberlain to send two great bands to help their chief in the valley. When they reach that place, these bands will be destroyed by the victorious soldiers of Christ.

'It remains only for you to make a sortie with all your men against the besiegers, to burn their tents and hack the last man of them in pieces. Christ our Lord and his Virgin Mother will help you to do this, and will also one day reward me for all that I have accomplished in Their service.'

Afrīdūn read this letter with joy, and sent at once for King Hardūb, who had taken refuge in Constantinople with his Cesarean troops.

At this point Shahrazād saw the approach of morning and discreetly fell silent.

But when the hundred-and-second night had come

SHE SAID:

Hardūb read this letter with proud satisfaction, crying: 'O King, be astonished at the excellent ruses of my old nurse! She has been more useful to us than all our armies, our foes have but to see her and they are more terrified than they will be by all the devils in hell on the Day of Judgment.' Afrīdūn answered: 'May Christ never remove this invaluable woman from among us. May He make fruitful all her crooked plans within her.'

Afrīdūn gave the order, and his whole army belched through the gate of Constantinople, brandishing swords, invoking the cross, cursing, blaspheming and madly bellowing. When he saw them, the chamberlain understood his danger. He called his men to arms, crying: 'Trust in your faith, O Mussulmāns. If you retreat you are lost, if you stand firm you will win the day. Courage is but patience enduring for a moment, and there is no path which Allāh cannot make large enough for His servants. I call upon the Highest to bless you!'

At this the courage of the Believers knew no bounds; against the invocations of Christ they hurled invocations of Allāh, and the two armies came terribly to grips. Good angels fought on our side, bad angels on the other; blood sprang out in streams and heads encumbered the ground; heroes and cowards proved themselves; the horses walked up to their heads between the piles of the slain. But what could heroism do against numbers? By nightfall the Mussulmāns were in retreat, their tents had been sacked, and their camp was in the hands of the enemy.

In plain flight they met the victorious army of Dū al-Makān returning from the defeat of the Christians in the valley. Sharkān congratulated the chamberlain in a loud voice before all his officers on the heroic stand which he had made, the wisdom of his retreat, and his patience under adversity. The arms of Islām, reunited once more and thirsting for vengeance, made haste towards Constantinople. When the Christians saw them coming, bearing banners on which were inscribed the Words of the Faith, they turned to the colour of saffron, tearfully invoked Christ, Mary, Anna, and the Cross, and prayed their patriarchs and infamous priests to intercede on their behalf with the saints of glory.

The Mussulmān army came under the walls of the city and would have prepared for battle, but Sharkān found out his brother and said: 'King of time, it is certain that the Christians will not refuse battle and we, we long for it. I give you this advice, seeing that method is the essence of order. Place me in the centre in front of the enemy, Dandān on the right centre, the amīr Turkāsh on the left centre, Rustam on the right wing, and Bahrmān on the left wing. I would suggest that you, my King, stay under the protection of the great standard and keep an eye upon all sections, since you are our only support save Allāh. Thus the whole army will serve you as a shield.' Dū al-Makān thanked his brother for this advice and set out the line of battle as he had suggested.

Hardly was each man in his place before a rapid rider spurred from the Christian army and approached that of the Mussulmāns. He was a handsome and venerable old man with a white beard, wearing a white linen mantle and mounted upon a fast mule with a white silk saddle covered by a fair carpet. He came near to Dū al-Makān and cried: 'I carry a message and, being an intermediary, claim safety and a hearing.' 'Speak without fear,' said Sharkān. The messenger dismounted and, taking a cross from about his neck, gave it to Sharkān, saying: 'I come on the part of King Afrīdūn, who has listened to my counsels and agreed that this disastrous war should cease before all God's creatures are destroyed in it. I come to propose a single combat between King Afrīdūn and Prince Sharkān.'

'Return, old man, to your King,' answered the prince, 'and tell him that Sharkān is ready for the test. To-morrow morning, when we have rested from our long march, I will fight with him, and if I am conquered my people will retire as best they may.'

At this answer, which the old man brought back to him, Afrīdūn was in the seventh heaven of joy, for he felt certain of killing Sharkān and had made all his preparations to that end. He passed the night in eating, drinking and praying, and, when morning dawned, rode out into the middle of the plain, dressed in a coat of gold mail at whose centre shone a jewelled mirror, and mounted upon a tall war-horse. He held a long curved sabre in his hand, and there hung from his shoulders a bow fashioned after the complicated manner of the West. When he came near the ranks of his enemies, he lifted up his voice, crying: 'Behold me! He who knows me, knows me and trembles. He who knows me not, shall soon know me. I am King Afrīdun and there are blessings upon my head!'

Scarcely had he spoken when Prince Sharkān thundered towards him on an Arab horse worth more than a thousand pieces of red gold. His saddle was brocaded with pearls and diamonds, and his sword, which was of Indian steel chased with gold, could have cut through all common blades and split the hardest things which God has made. He charged Afrīdūn, crying: 'On guard, you dog! Do you think that I am a youth with a girl's skin, rising from a harlot's bed to do you battle? This is my sign, O Infidel!' With that he cut terribly with his sword, so that Afrīdūn only saved himself by pulling his horse aside. The foemen met like two mountains or two seas coming to battle, they retired and advanced and circled, and advanced and retired, they gave blows and parried blows under the eyes of the two armies, and the two armies cried aloud for their champions until the sun set upon a bloodless field.

At the moment when its red edge was sinking from sight, Afrīdūn cried out suddenly to Sharkān: 'Look behind you, in Christ's name, O champion of defeat, O hero of retreat. They are bringing you a fresh horse while mine is wearied. This is the practice of slaves, not of warriors.'

Sharkān raged at this, and turned to see what horse the Christian meant, but there was nothing there. It was a trick. The Christian hurled his javelin full at Sharkān's back. The prince cried a terrible cry and fell back on his saddle, and Afrīdūn galloped to his own people, leaving his gallant foe for dead.

When the Mussulmāns saw their prince fall with his face against his saddle, they ran out to his help.

At this point Shahrazād saw the approach of morning and discreetly fell silent.

But when the hundred-and-third night had come

SHE SAID:

First to come to him were Dandān, Rustam and Bahrmān. They lifted him in their arms and carried him to the tent of his brother, King Dū al-Makān, who raged and grieved. Physicians were called, and these attended upon Sharkān, while the people wept and stood all night about the hero's couch.

Towards morning the holy ascetic came near the bed of the wounded man and, after reading certain verses of the Koran over him, laid on his hands. Sharkān gave a long sigh and opened his eyes. His first words were of thanks to the Merciful for his life, then to Dū al-Makān he said: 'I was wounded by a trick, but the hurt is not mortal. Where is my ascetic?' 'Here by your bed,' said Dū al-Makān, and Sharkān kissed the hands of the old dissembler, while she prayed for his recovery, saying: 'My son, be patient under your pain, and Allāh will reward you.'

Dū al-Makān, who had been absent for a little time, returned to the tent and kissed his brother, and the hands of the ascetic, saying: 'Dear brother, may Allāh have you in His keeping. I go forth now to avenge you by crushing this dog, this son of a dog, this Afrīdūn.' Sharkān tried to stay him, and the wazīr Dandān, the two amīrs and the chamberlain all offered to go themselves to destroy the Infidel, but Dū al-Makān was already in the saddle. 'By the wells of Zamzam, the vengeance is mine!' he cried, and spurred into the middle of the plain. If you had seen him you would have thought that he was Antar upon his black horse, which was quicker than the wind, quicker than the light of the sun.

Afrīdūn rode out to meet him, and the two champions met with a great noise in this last and mortal fight. With a strength which was increased a hundredfold by his lust for vengeance, Dū al-Makān, after certain feints, crashed his blade against the neck of Afrīdūn, severing the helmet, the flesh and the spine, so that the head itself bounded upon the ground.

As if this had been a signal, the Mussulmāns charged with a noise as of thunder upon the Christians, and killed fifty thousand of them before the shades of night allowed the remnant to flee back into Constantinople. The gates were closed against the victors, to whom Allāh had given such a splendid recompense.

The hosts of the Believers returned to their tents laden with spoil, and the officers congratulated Dū al-Makān, who gave up thanks to the Highest for his victory. When he informed Sharkān of all that had taken place, the prince felt his heart beat healthily once more and his body enter into the way of healing. To Dū al-Makān he said: 'The victory is surely due to the prayers of this holy ascetic, who has not ceased to invoke the blessing of Heaven upon our arms.'

The wicked old woman could not help changing colour when she heard of the death of Afrīdūn, from yellow she became green and tears stifled her. Nevertheless she had enough control to make her tears appear tears of joy. In her dark heart she plotted a burning grief for Dū al-Makān. As had been her custom on the other days, she applied on that day also pastes and balms to the wound of Sharkān and, when she had dressed it carefully, commanded everyone to leave the tent that he might sleep. Soon Sharkān was left alone with his evil nurse.

At this point Shahrazād saw the approach of morning and discreetly fell silent.

But when the hundred-and-fourth night had come

SHE SAID:

When Sharkān slept, the vile old woman, who had been watching him like a wolf or a mad viper, glided terribly towards him, drawing a poisoned knife from beneath her clothing. The bane upon its blade was of such terrible combination that a drop would have split a granite boulder. The old woman stretched forth her calamitous hand and cut off Sharkān's head. Thus died, by the force of Destiny and the machinations of Iblīs gowned in the body of an old woman, Sharkān, son of Umar al-Numān, a champion of the Faith, a hero who shall not be forgotten.

The old woman, whose vengeance was now satisfied, left the following letter near the severed head:

'This from the noble Al-Dawāhī, known because of her exploits as Mother-of-Calamity, to those Mussulmāns at present in Christian territory.

'It was I who had the satisfaction of killing Umar al-Numān in the midst of his palace; it was I who caused your rout and extermination in the valley below the monastery; and it is I who have with my own hand cut off the head of Sharkān as a fitting end to all my strategies. Some day I hope with Christ's aid to cut off the heads of King Dū al-Makān and his wazīr Dandān.

'It is for the rest of you to reflect whether you will do better to stay in our land or return to your own. You will never gain the end you have in view, and I warn you that if you stay before Constantinople my arm and the labyrinths of my wit shall compass your destruction.'

Leaving this letter, the old woman slipped from the tent and re-entered the city, to inform the Christians of her fatal acts. Afterwards she went to church and prayed, weeping for the death of King Afrīdūn, and thanking her master, the Devil, because the proud spirit of Sharkān had passed away.

At the same hour on which the murder was committed, the wazīr Dandān felt himself oppressed by sleeplessness and a foreboding. It seemed to him that the whole weight of the earth lay upon his chest, and he therefore decided to leave his couch. He quitted his tent and, as he walked up and down refreshing himself with the night air, saw the ascetic hurry from the camp. He therefore said to himself: 'Prince Sharkān will be alone. I will go and watch by him, or talk to him if he be awake.'

When he reached Sharkān's tent, the first thing he saw was a pool of blood upon the ground, and the second and third were the head and body of Sharkān lying separate upon the bed.

Dandān gave so great and terrible a cry that all the sleepers woke and jumped to their feet. The army was thrown into an uproar, and Dū al-Makān ran to the tent. He saw his wazīr Dandān weeping by the lifeless body of his brother. He cried: 'O terror, terror!' and fell along the ground in a deep swoon.

At this point Shahrazād saw the approach of morning and discreetly fell silent.

But when the hundred-and-fifth night had come

SHE SAID:

The wazīr and the amīrs clustered round him and fanned him with their robes, until at length he came to himself, crying: 'Sharkān, brother, hero! What devil has made this foul defeat upon your life?' Nothing was heard for a space except the weeping and sobbing of

Dū al-Makān, Dandān, Rustam, Bahrmān and the chamberlain. But at last the wazīr saw the letter lying by the head and read it aloud to Dū al-Makān. 'Now, O King,' he said as he made an end of the letter, 'you may know why that ascetic so displeased me!' Dū al-Makān cried through his tears: 'As Allāh lives, I will take that old woman with my own hands, I will pour boiling lead into the funnel of her sex, I will thrust a spiked stake up her behind, I will hang her by the hair, I will nail her living to the gate of Constantinople.'

The King decreed a splendid funeral for Sharkān, and himself went weeping after the body, until it had been buried at the foot of a hill under a great dome of alabaster and gold.

For long days he let fall his tears, until he was but a shadow; therefore the wazīr Dandān, curbing his own grief, came to him, saying: 'O King, dry your eyes, if that be possible, and place a balm of fortitude upon your grief. Your brother now lives between the hands of Peace, tasting Reward. He has gone through that door which was written for him, and your grieving may not bring him back. Rise up and take your arms again. Let the siege go on, for that way lies revenge.'

While Dandān was encouraging the King in this sort, a courier arrived from Baghdād, bearing this letter from Nuzhat to Dū al-Makān:

'Good news, my brother!

'Your young slave has safely borne you a man-child, who shines like the moon in Ramadān. I have thought well to call him Kāna mā kāna, He Was What He Was.

'Astronomers predict memorable deeds for the child, because his birth was accompanied by prodigies and marvels. I have had prayer and intercession made in all the mosques for you, and for your child, and for your victory.

'We are all well here, especially your friend the fireman. He luxuriates in peace and pleasure, but ardently desires news of you, as do we all.

'There have been abundant rains this year and the harvests should be excellent.

'Peace and safety be with you and about you.'

Dū al-Makān gave a deep breath when he read this letter, and cried: 'O wazīr, now that Allāh has blessed me with a son, a small Kāna mā kāna, my grief is lessened and my heart begins to live again.

Let us worthily celebrate the end of mourning for my dead brother.'
'I think that you are right,' answered the wazīr. Great tents were
pitched about the tomb of Sharkān for the imāms and readers of the
Koran, a quantity of sheep and camels were slain and divided among
the army, and all the night was passed in prayer.

Next morning Dū al-Makān walked slowly towards the tomb,
which was all covered with precious stuffs from Persia and
Kashmir. . . .

At this point Shahrazād saw the approach of morning and discreetly fell silent.

But when the hundred-and-sixth night had come

SHE SAID:
He walked slowly towards the tomb, which was all covered with
precious stuffs from Persia and Kashmir, and, weeping in the presence of the whole army, improvised these verses:

> The lines of tears upon my cheeks rehearse,
>   Weeping for Sharkān,
> A sorrow more significant than verse,
>   Sharkān, my brother.
>
> Louder than Moses' voice breaking the rocks,
>   Breaking for Sharkān
> Your soldiers' cries are, and the echo mocks;
>   Sharkān, my brother.
>
> Deep have we dug the grave for you, dear sleeper,
>   Dug it for Sharkān;
> But our hearts' graves are emptier and deeper,
>   Sharkān, my brother.
>
> I had not thought to see my spirit married,
>   Married to Sharkān,
> Death-wed and lifted up and shoulder-carried,
>   Sharkān, my brother.
>
> Where is the fiery star of Sharkān now,
>   The star of Sharkān?
> Weary, empty, and black the storm-clouds bow,
>   Sharkān, my brother.

> Dark of the tomb is lighted with the rare
> Topaz of Sharkān;
> Earth hides him in her bosom and is fair,
> Sharkān, my brother.

> The winding silk shall start to crimson wings,
> Bearing up Sharkān,
> And carry to the herb-garden of kings
> Sharkān, my brother.

When Dū al-Makān had made an end, he wept again and all the army sighed. Then came the wazīr Dandān to throw himself upon Sharkān's tomb. He kissed the stone and, in a voice strangled by tears, intoned this song of the poet:

> Wise to have gone so early to reward,
> Child of the sword;
> Wise with a single new-bathed eagle's flight
> To have touched the white
> Wild roses spread for feet in paradise.
> Ah, my son, wise
> Soon to have drained the new and bitter cup
> Which, once drunk up,
> Leads onward to an old immortal wine
> Pressed from God's vine.

Such was the end of the mourning for Sharkān.

Nevertheless Dū al-Makān continued to be sad, especially as the siege of Constantinople threatened to drag on into many months. One day he opened his heart to his wazīr Dandān, saying: 'What can I do to forget my griefs, and drive away the weariness which weighs upon my soul?'

'O King,' answered the wazīr, 'I know of but one remedy, and that is that I should tell you a story of time past and famous emperors. I will find no difficulty in doing this, as my chief occupation under the reign of your dead father, Umar al-Numān, was to distract his nights with delicious story, with the songs of the Arab poets, and my own improvisations. To-night, when all the camp is asleep, I will tell you a tale which will make you marvel, which will ease your breast with delight. You will find the siege go quickly. I shall only tell you the title of my story now. It is: *The Tale of Two Lovers, Azīz and Azīzah.*'

Dū al-Makān felt his heart beating with impatience. He had no other desire than to see the evening come when he might hear the promised tale, for the simple title of it made him tremble with pleasure.

Hardly had night begun to fall when Dū al-Makān had all the torches lighted in his tent and all the lanterns lighted in the silken corridor. He caused a service to be laid of food and drink, with braziers of incense, amber, and other aromatics. He assembled the amīrs Bahrmān, Rustam and Turkāsh, together with Nuzhat's husband. When they were seated, he called upon the wazīr Dandān and said to him: 'O wazīr, night spreads over our heads her dark majestic robe and her black hair. We wait for your promised story that we may rejoice.'

At this point Shahrazād saw the approach of morning and discreetly fell silent.

But when the hundred-and-seventh night had come

SHE SAID:

The wazīr Dandān answered: 'With all my heart and as in duty bound, for you must know, O auspicious King, that the tale which I am going to tell you of those things which came to Azīz and Azīzah is specially designed to drive away all grief and to console a sorrow greater than Jacob's.'

The Tale of Azīz and Azīzah, and of Prince Tāj al-Mulūk, Crown of Kings

THERE was once, in the antiquity of time and the passage of the age and of the moment, a city called Green City, behind the mountains of Isfahān in Persia. Its King, Sulaimān Shāh, was dowered with the gifts of justice and generosity, prudence and learning; travellers journeyed from all countries towards his city, and his good fame so spread abroad that merchants with their caravans put trust in his equity.

For many years he governed prosperously, surrounded by the love of all his people, but one thing he lacked, the joy of wife and children.

One day his loneliness weighed upon him more than ever, so he called to him his wazīr, who followed in his master's way of goodness and generosity, and said to him: 'My breast narrows, my patience flows away, my strength diminishes; a little longer and I shall be nothing but skin and bone. I see that to live alone is not an estate of nature for any man, and least of all for a King who has a throne to leave. Also our Prophet (upon whom be prayer and peace!) has said: "Couple and multiply, for your numbers will be my pride in the Resurrection." Advise me, O wazīr.'

Then said the wazīr: 'It is a difficult and delicate question. I shall attempt to satisfy you without transgressing the path of propriety. It would be a great grief to me to see some unknown slave married to my King; we could know nothing of her ancestry and the blood-stream of the King's fathers might be polluted. A child born from such a union always turns out vicious, lying and cruel, one already marked out by Allāh's displeasure from his birth. Such a foundation for a line of Kings is like a plant growing in marshy ground, feeding on stagnant and brackish water, which rots as it grows. Therefore I pray you do not command your wazīr to buy you a slave-girl, even though she were the fairest in the world, for he could not bear the weight of such a sin. If you will listen to the advice of my beard, you will choose a King's daughter of known pedigree, whose beauty shall be an example and exasperation to all the women of the kingdom.'

Sulaimān Shāh answered: 'I am more than ready, if you can find me such a woman, to marry her and bring down on my posterity the blessings of Allāh.' Then said the wazīr: 'Thanks be to Him, she is already found.' 'How is that?' cried the King, and the wazīr replied: 'My wife has told me that Zahr Shāh, King of White City, has a daughter so beautiful that my tongue would become hairy before I could give you the least idea of her charms.' 'Yā Allāh!' cried the King, and the wazīr continued: 'I could never speak worthily of her eyes with their lids of tender brown, of her hair, of her waist so thin that one may scarcely see it, of her heavy hips, of those things which bear these up and of those which increase in curved loveliness about them. As Allāh lives, none may come near her without being suddenly stricken into immobility, and none may regard her without dying. A poet has written of her:

> Her belly's concord can make slaves,
> Her waist might take for its device

The thin green flags the willow waves
    Or "As the poplars grow in paradise."

There is wild honey on her lips,
    She drinks and sweetens all the wine;
Two stars have gone to their eclipse
    When her bold eyes leap wanton into mine.'

At the repetition of this song the King started for joy and cried:
'Yā Allāh!' with his full throat. The wazīr continued: 'My advice is
that you should at once send to Zahr Shāh one chosen from among
your amīrs for confidential tact, a man whose experience is already
known, one who savours the exact meaning of his words before he
utters them. He will persuade the King to give you his daughter in
marriage, and thus you will be able to live in accordance with the
words of the Prophet (on whom be prayer and peace!): "Let the
chaste be driven forth from Islām, for they corrupt the people. Let
there be no abstention from women among the priests of Islām."
Besides, the girl is worthy of you, being the fairest gem upon this
earth or below it.'

Sulaimān Shāh felt his heart swell with pleasure at these last
words; he sighed for joy and said to his wazīr: 'What man better
than you could I choose for so delicate an undertaking? Rise up now,
say your goodbyes and complete your businesses, for you must
leave at once. My heart will be in a ferment until you return.'

The wazīr finished all at his house which needed finishing and
embraced all whom it was fitting for him to embrace. Then he
charged mules and camels with cases containing gifts such as are meet
for kings: jewels and the work of goldsmiths, silk carpets, embroidered fabrics, perfumes, pure essence of roses, and all light
things whose price is heavy; swords damascened with gold having
hilts of rubied jade, arms of light steel and gilded coats of mail; the
thousand nothings which melt pleasantly in the mouths of girls,
rose jam, slivers of apricot, perfumed conserves, and almond paste
aromatic with benzoin from the warm islands. Finally he chose ten
horses of pure Arab stock, and collected a hundred young mamlūks,
a hundred negro youths, and a hundred maidens to be attendant on
the returning bride. As the caravan was setting off, Sulaimān Shāh
stopped him for a moment, saying: 'I warn you not to return without
the girl, and I charge you to make haste. I shall be burning night and
day because of my bride.' The wazīr reassured him and left the city

with his caravan. He journeyed night and day, up hill and down valley, across streams and rivers, by desert and sown, until he came within a day's journey of White City. While he rested with his people beside a pleasant water-course, he sent forward a rapid rider to announce his arrival to Zahr Shāh.

The King was taking the air in one of his gardens near the city gate, and saw the courier as he rode up to the sentinels. Recognising him as a stranger, he sent for him and asked him who he was. The messenger answered: 'I am sent by the wazīr of King Sulaimān Shāh, master of Green City and the mountains of Isfahān. The wazīr is camped even now beside a river which is near your capital.'

Zahr Shāh was delighted at this news and, after giving all refreshment to the courier, sent one of his amīrs to meet the representatives of a king whom he so much respected.

The wazīr of Sulaimān Shāh rested by the river until midnight. Then he set out towards the city, coming to its gates at sunrise.

He had just finished pissing and had given the ewer to one of his slaves after washing himself, when he saw the wazīr, chamberlains and amīrs of Zahr Shāh coming towards him. So, remounting his horse, he spurred forward and, after the most polite salutations on either side, entered White City with his hosts.

When he was led into the main hall of the palace, he saw a tall throne of white diaphanous marble encrusted with diamonds and borne up upon four legs so great that each might have protected an elephant from its enemies. On this throne was a huge cushion of green watered wilk with tassels, fringes, and balls of red gold. Above the throne was a canopy, flaming with gold and bright with ivory, and upon the throne sat Zahr Shāh, in the midst of still guards expectant for his orders.

At this point Shahrazād saw the approach of morning and discreetly fell silent.

But when the hundred-and-eighth night had come

SHE SAID:

When the wazīr of King Sulaimān Shāh saw the glory of these things, he felt inspiration descend upon his soul and eloquence inciting his tongue to polished discourse. With an agreeable gesture, he turned to the King and improvised these stanzas in his honour:

My heart leaps from my breast to you,
I sacrifice my rest to you,
  Nor will my pride be satisfied
Until my lips are pressed to you.

When first my eyes confessed to you
The homage they addressed to you,
  My longing gaze and weeping ways
Seemed little more than jest to you.

Or if my death seems best to you,
Or if my life gives zest to you,
  I'll die indeed or try indeed
To be a loving guest to you.

The wazīr fell silent, and Zahr Shāh, smiling benevolently upon
him, made him sit down beside him and greeted him as a friend. A
meal was served in honour of the wazīr. When all had eaten and
drunken until they were satisfied, the King dismissed his court, only
retaining his chamberlains and his own wazīr.

The envoy of King Sulaimān Shāh rose to his feet and bowed,
saying: 'King of munificence, my errand will result in blessing and
happiness to all concerned. I ask your modest and delightful
daughter in marriage for my master, Sulaimān Shāh, the glorious
King of Green City and the mountains of Isfahān. I bear rich gifts to
prove the impatience of my lord, and would hear your own mouth
speak of the affair.'

Zahr Shāh rose and bowed to the earth, to the astonishment of
his chamberlains, who saw their King showing such honour to a
simple wazīr. Still standing, the Sultān said: 'Tactful, learned and
eloquent wazīr, listen to what I say. I hold myself to be nothing
more than a subject of Sulaimān Shāh, though now honoured above
all other subjects by alliance with him. My daughter is but one of his
slaves. From this hour she belongs to him in absolute possession.
That is my answer to our master, Lord of Green City and the
mountains of Isfahān.'

He sent for the kādīs and for witnesses. When these had drawn up
the marriage contract between his daughter and King Sulaimān Shāh,
the Sultān kissed the document, and received the congratulations of
the kādīs. He bestowed gifts on all the witnesses and gave feasts and
entertainments in honour of the wazīr. Therefore his people rejoiced,

and the more so when food and money were distributed to rich and poor alike.

He chose out slaves for his daughter, Greeks and Turks, black and white, and had a palanquin constructed for her of solid gold set with pearls, which should be carried by ten chosen mules. The convoy set out in the light of morning, the palanquin shining like a palace of fairies, and the veiled girl within it seeming like a hūrī sent from Paradise.

The King himself accompanied the procession for three parasangs and then, saying farewell to his daughter and to the wazīr, returned to White City, filled with great joy and confidence for the future.

At this point Shahrazād saw the approach of morning and discreetly fell silent.

But when the hundred-and-ninth night had come

SHE SAID:

When the wazīr's party had come safely to within three days' march of Green City, he sent a mounted messenger forward to tell his King the news.

Sulaimān Shāh trembled with pleasure when he heard that his bride was so near, and gave the courier a costly robe of honour. Then, at the head of all his army, he set out with flying banners to meet the maiden. And all the city went with him, so that neither woman nor child nor impotent beldame remained behind. When the two parties met, it was decided that the entry into the city should take place ceremoniously at nightfall.

As soon as the sun began to set, the nobles of the city had all the road which led to the King's palace illuminated at their own expense. The city stood in two ranks along the way and the soldiers made a hedge on either hand. Coloured lights broke and flashed in the calm air, great drums boomed, the trumpets cried, flags lapped lazily above the heads of the procession, perfumes were burned in braziers at the street corners, and in all open spaces picked warriors fenced with lance and javelin. With negroes and mamlūks in front of her, with slaves and attendant women behind her, the bride, hidden by the costly gifts of her father, came to the palace of her husband.

The young slaves unharnessed the mule and carried the palanquin on their shoulders to the secret door, cheered loudly by the people and the soldiery. There women met the bride and led her into the marriage-chamber, where it appeared as if the lights were doubled, or that a moon was there with attendant stars, or that a single pearl lay in a plate of gold. When they had couched her on a bed of ivory, they left her and formed a path of living stars between which the King came to his own, prepared, perfect and scented upon the bed. At that hour Allāh lit a great love in the heart of Sulaimān Shāh and also gave him the dear devotion of his bride. He took her virginity with happiness, and forgot between her legs and in her arms all his impatience and the pain of love.

The queen conceived upon that first night, and for a whole month the King lived with her in her apartment, because they loved each other.

At the end of that time, Sulaimān Shāh mounted his throne and attended to the justice of his kingdom and the good of his people, but when evening came he went to visit his wife, and failed not to do so every night until the ninth month.

On the last night of that month the queen was overtaken by her pains and sat upon the chair of bearing. At dawn Allāh eased her birth, so that she brought a son into the world carrying all the signs of luck and fortune.

The King was happier than ever in his life before, when he heard the news of this birth; he gave rich gifts to the one who told him and then, running to the queen, took the infant in his arms and kissed him between the eyes. Then it was that he saw how applicable were these verses of the poet to his first-born:

> God sent a small but complete star
> Into the darkness where we are:
>   Nurses with splendid delicate teats,
>   Accustom not his forces
>   To your slim backs, whose future seats
>   Are lions and wild horses.
>   Nurses with milk too white and sweet
>   Wean him as soon as may be,
>   Red blood of kings shall be the meat
>   To feed this lusty baby:
> Into the darkness where we are
> God sent a small but complete star.

Nurses took care of the newly born, and midwives cut his cord and lengthened his eyes with black kohl. Such was the birth of a son to a King among kings and a Queen among queens, and he shone so fair that they called him Tāj al-Mulūk.

At this point Shahrazād saw the approach of morning and discreetly fell silent.

But when the hundred-and-tenth night had come

SHE SAID:

He was brought up amid kisses and the fairest breasts, while the years passed by. When he was seven, his father called together the wisest professors of calligraphy, literature, deportment, syntax, and civil law, who stayed with the child and taught him these things until he was fourteen. After he had learnt all that his father wished, he was given a master among riding-masters, who taught him horsemanship, lance play, the conduct of the javelin, and the art of hawking for deer. It was not long before Prince Tāj al-Mulūk became the most accomplished cavalier of his time and he was already so beautiful that, whether he went out on foot or on horseback, those who saw him were damned for their thoughts.

By the time he was fifteen, his charms were the main theme for the most loving verses of the poets, while the chastest of philosophers felt their hearts and livers confounded by the seduction of his presence. An amorous poet wrote this about him:

> Musk kisses,
> To faint under musk,
> To feel his body bend like a wet branch
> That has eaten of the west wind and drunk dew.
>
> Musk kisses,
> To madden without wine;
> Should I not know, who get drunk each sunset
> With the musk, musk, musk wine of his mouth?
>
> Musk kisses,
> Beauty looked into his mirror at morning
> And turned from her own shadow
> To love the musk, musk, musk of his nakedness.

This when he was only fifteen! When he was eighteen, it was the same thing, but increased a thousandfold. A young down shadowed his cheeks' flesh of roses, and black amber had sketched a beauty

spot on the whiteness of his chin. He ravished both sight and reason,
even as a poet had said of him:

> Boast, if you will, the magic chance
>> Which took you safely through the fire;
>> A greater wonder I require
> If you would parallel that glance
>>> Of jet,
>>> Which has not harmed me yet.
>
> You tell me other cheeks can show
>> Soft down as they approach a man's;
>> Not so the cheeks of my romance,
> For that which I see overgrow
>>> Their milk
>>> Is ghost of gilded silk.
>
> When we converse of magic streams
>> Replete with youth-returning springs,
>> You tell me there are no such things
> And I am credulous it seems;
>>> Yet I
>>> Would venture this reply:
>
> The spring of youth's delightful joy
>> Myself have tasted where it slips
>> For ever from the dark red lips
> Of a slim-waisted deer-swift boy. . . .
>>> My tongue
>>> Remembers and is young.

This when he was only eighteen! When he was a man, his name
was used as a symbol for beauty wherever Allāh is worshipped. He
had a multitude of friends and intimates who longed to see him some
day reign over the kingdom as he already reigned in their hearts.

In this period of his young manhood, Prince Tāj al-Mulūk was
passionately fond of hunting and roving through the forests, though
his continuous absences were a source of anxiety to his father and
mother. On a certain occasion, after ordering his slaves to prepare
provisions for ten days, he set out with his hunters and came at the
end of the fourth day to a heavily-wooded district rich in game,
filled with all sorts of savage beasts, and watered by a multitude of
streams.

The prince gave the signal for a hunt, and a great net was spread round an area covered with small trees. The beaters worked inwards towards the centre, driving the frightened animals before them. Then panthers, dogs and hawks were set free to chase the swifter prey, and a multitude of gazelles and other light game were taken. In truth, there was a feast for the panthers, dogs and hawks. When the hunt was over, Tāj al-Mulūk sat down to rest beside a river, while the game was divided and the finest of it kept for King Sulaimān Shāh. He slept by the river that night till dawn.

As soon as the prince's hunters woke, they saw that a large caravan had arrived in the night and camped near them. Black slaves and many merchants were seen leaving the tents and coming down to make their ablutions in the river. Tāj al-Mulūk sent one of his men to ask the merchants who they were. The huntsman returned with this answer: 'We are merchants who have camped here, attracted by the greenery and fair water of the place. We knew that we had nothing to fear, since we are now in the secure lands of Sulaimān Shāh, whose reputation for wise government is a balm to the natural fears of travellers! We feel all the safer since we carry rich and numerous presents to that admirable young man, Prince Tāj al-Mulūk.'

Hearing this, the handsome prince exclaimed: 'By Allāh, if these merchants have some present for me, why should we not go down and take delivery of it ourselves? That would be an amusing way of passing the morning.' Without delay the young man called his huntsmen together and went to visit the caravan.

The merchants saw the King's son coming and recognised him, so they ran to meet him and invited him to honour their encampment. With great celerity they pitched a red satin tent of honour, pictured with birds and animals in many colours, and set a magnificent cushion within it on a silken carpet whose borders were fringed with flawless emeralds. The prince sat upon the carpet and leaned against the cushion, asking the traders to undo their merchandise before him. They did so, and he bought all the things which pleased him, obliging them to accept a full price although they many times refused.

He sent his purchases away to his own camp by slaves, and was about to remount his horse when his eye singled out from the merchants a young man of exceeding beauty and attractive pallor, dressed richly and in taste.

At this point Shahrazād saw the approach of morning and discreetly fell silent.

But when the hundred-and-eleventh night had come

SHE SAID:

This youth's face, though it was pale and beautiful, carried the imprint of great sadness, as if he had lost a father, a mother or a dear friend.

Prince Tāj al-Mulūk did not wish to depart until he had made his acquaintance, for he felt his heart drawn to him. Instead of riding away, therefore, he approached and, wishing the young man peace, asked him who he was and why he was so sad. The boy's eyes filled with tears and, saying for sole answer: 'I am Azīz,' he burst into such a storm of sobs that a swoon came upon him and he fell to the ground.

As soon as he came to himself, Prince Tāj al-Mulūk said: 'I am your friend, Azīz. Tell me the reason of your great grief.' For only answer young Azīz leaned upon his elbow and sang:

> There's a black Magus in her eyes
>   And, if you miss his spell,
>   There's a gold bowman there as well—
> An arrow flies.
>
> There's wine of fire within her voice,
>   And you, who will not hear,
>   May still be taken unaware
> By two red toys.
>
> Between neck-gold and ankle-gold
>   So fair is to be seen
>   That half the valleys in between
> May not be told.
>
> There are perfumes on her silken gown,
>   But if their power were spent
>   You could not miss the roses' scent
> Which is her own.

Prince Tāj al-Mulūk was so affected by this song that he did not wish to insist any further, but changed the mark of his conversation, saying: 'Tell me, Azīz, why you did not exhibit your merchandise

485

like the other traders?' 'My lord,' answered the youth, 'my scrip has nothing in it worthy of a King's son.' 'Nevertheless I would see what you have,' said the prince, and Azīz was obliged to sit by him on the carpet and show piece by piece the goods which he had with him. Tāj al-Mulūk did not examine the fabrics, but straightway bought them all, saying: 'Now tell me why you are sad, Azīz. If any oppresses you, I know how to punish him. If any holds you in debt, I shall cheerfully pay him, because I feel my bowels moved towards you.'

Young Azīz could only sob in reply to these words, and passionately sing:

> Black eyes with blue kohl length,
>   White breasts with red coal tips,
> Wine-coloured lips with honey strength,
>   A happiness of hips,
>   Black night where grope
>   The lips of hope
>   Towards a white eclipse.

The prince's emotion was so great on hearing this song that, to hide it, he began to examine the silks and fabrics one by one. Suddenly a doubled square of embroidered silk fell from between his hands. Young Azīz pounced on this and, folding it with shaking hands, hid it below his knees. Then he cried:

> Easier to clasp the Pleiades,
>   Azīzah,
> Or further stars than these
>   Than clasp Azīzah.

> Hard to roll earth up heaven's hill,
>   Azīzah,
> But it is harder still
>   To leave Azīzah.

When the prince saw the quick movement of Azīz and heard his song, he was extremely astonished, and cried. . . .

At this point in her tale Shahrazād saw the approach of morning and discreetly fell silent. Then her sister Dunyazād said: 'Sister, your words are sweet and gentle and pleasant to the taste.' And Shahrazād answered: 'Indeed they are nothing to that which I would tell both of you to-morrow night, if I were still alive and the King thought good to spare me.' On this the King said to himself: 'By Allāh, I will not kill her until I have heard the rest of her truly astonishing tale.'

Then the King and Shahrazād passed the remainder of the night in each other's arms, until the former departed to sit in judgment. When he saw the wazīr approach, carrying under his arm the winding-sheet destined for his daughter Shahrazād, whom he believed already dead, the King said nothing to him, but continued to administer justice, raising some to office and debasing others, until the fall of day. So the wazīr was plunged into perplexity and the extreme of astonishment.

When night came, King Shahryār went to Shahrazād in her apartment and did his ordinary with her.

It was the hundred-and-twelfth night

LITTLE DUNYAZĀD rose from her carpet when the affair was over, and said to Shahrazād: 'Sister, I pray you continue your charming tale of the handsome prince and of Azīz and Azīzah, the tale which Dandān told to King Dū al-Makān under the walls of Constantinople.'

To this Shahrazād answered smiling: 'With all my heart and as my duty is, if our excellent and well-bred King permits.' Then King Shahryār, who could not sleep for anxiety to know the rest of the tale, said: 'You may speak.'

AND SHAHRAZĀD SAID:

It is related, O auspicious King, that Prince Tāj al-Mulūk cried: 'What are you hiding there, Azīz?' Azīz replied: 'My lord, it was because of this thing that I did not wish you to see my merchandise. What shall I do now?' He heaved a heavy sigh; but the prince pressed him so gently, that at last he said:

'My master, the story of my life, which is bound about this double square, is a very strange one and full of sweet memories for me. The charms of those who gave me the two pieces will never fade before my eyes. One side was given to me by Azīzah, and the other by one whose name would be bitter on my lips, for she made me what I am. Now that I have begun to tell you of these things, you shall hear all; for the tale should be pleasant and edifying to one who hears it in the right spirit.'

Azīz took the stuff from beneath his knees and unfolded it on the carpet, so that the prince could examine the two separate squares. On one of them, embroidered in silk with red-gold threads and rainbow-coloured threads, was a gazelle. On the other square was a second gazelle, worked in silver threads and carrying about its neck a red collar from which depended three Eastern chrysolites.

Seeing the excellent work of these gazelles, the prince cried: 'Glory be to Him Who has given such art to His creatures! O Azīz, in pity hasten to tell me the tale of Azīzah and the woman of the second gazelle.'

Azīz therefore said to the prince:

The Tale of Azīz and Azīzah

(*Told by Azīz in the tale of Azīz and Azīzah, and of Prince Tāj al-Mulūk*)

KNOW, my dear lord, that I was the only son of a great merchant, brought up in my father's house with an orphan cousin, whose father, before his death, had made my parents promise that we should be married when we were old enough.

They let us always be together so that we became inseparable. We slept together in the same bed with no suspicion of the results which might arise from such a course. Yet, on looking back, I think that my cousin knew and surmised more about these things than I did, when I remember the way she would clasp me in her arms and press her thighs to mine.

When we reached the required age, my father said to my mother: 'This year we must marry Azīz and Azīzah.' My mother agreed on a day with him, and he invited all his relations and friends, saying: 'On Friday, after the prayer, the marriage contract will be written for Azīz and Azīzah.' My mother informed all her friends and those near to her, and then set to work with the help of her servants to give a thorough wash to the reception hall and make its marbles shine again. She stretched carpets upon the floor and ornamented the walls with golden worked silks, which were taken for the occasion from the great chest. My father undertook the provision of pastries and sweetmeats, and prepared large trays of drinks with expert care. Before the guests were expected, my mother sent me to bathe at the hammām, charging a slave to carry a beautiful new robe behind me that I might put it on after the bath. I went to the hammām and, putting on the robe after my bath, found it so delightfully scented that people stopped in the street to smell the air as I went home.

I was just turning into the mosque to make the necessary Friday prayer when I remembered a friend whom I had forgotten to invite. I began to walk very quickly to his house, as I did not want to be late, and soon found myself in a side-street which was unknown to me. As I was dripping with sweat after my bath and because of my heavy new robe, I took advantage of the cool shadow of the lane to sit down on a bench beside the wall, first spreading my gold-embroidered handkerchief to protect my garments from the bench. The sweat still fell in drops from my forehead, and, as I could not use my handkerchief to wipe it away, I was about to have recourse to the skirt of my new robe when a white silk handkerchief fell on the ground in front of me as lightly as a subsiding breeze. It seemed so cool and its perfume so miraculous that I hastened to pick it up. Then I raised my eyes to see who had so opportunely come to my aid and caught a glimpse for the first time of that lady who was to give me one of the gazelles embroidered on silk.

At this point Shahrazād saw the approach of morning and discreetly fell silent.

But when the hundred-and-thirteenth night had come

SHE SAID:

She leaned smiling from the copper window of an upper storey; I shall not try to paint her beauty for you. When she saw my long regard, she made these signs: she passed her index finger between her lips and, lowering her middle finger so that it pressed against the index of the left hand, carried the two between her breasts. Then she withdrew her head and shut the window.

I sat there, perplexed and burning with desire, fastening my eyes to the window in the hope that she might come again; but, though I remained till sunset unmindful of my marriage and my bride, the casement remained obstinately closed.

At last I desolately left the bench and began walking towards my father's house. As I went I took the handkerchief, whose odour I hope to meet again in Paradise, and, unfolding it, saw these verses embroidered on one of the corners in a beautiful and complicated writing:

Here I my secret heart have stripped
In slight elaborated script;
If you object: 'It is indeed
Too tortured and too fine to read,'
I answer: 'Nothing is too fine
To symbolise this love of mine,
And lines of complicated art
Are no more tortured than my heart.'

On the opposite corner of the handkerchief, this poem was sewn
in bold regular characters:

Pearls seen through amber
Or hint of apples in the green
Interlacing leaves which clamber
The red fruit hardly seen:
So through the down
His young cheeks dimly shown.

If you crave death and nothing less,
His heavy eyes will satisfy;
But if you wish for drunkenness
Leave the singing and the drinking,
For both wine and song are winking
In his cheeks' vermilion dye.

Smell a myrtle after rain,
You will meet my love again;
Bend a slim wet bough to you,
Feel it quiver, feel it strain,
Holding back through all its length;
You'd smile in weeping if you knew
The cool sweetness of his strength.

I was quite insane for love of the unknown, when I reached the
house at nightfall and found my cousin sitting in tears. On seeing
me she dried her eyes and, while she helped me to unrobe, gently
questioned me concerning my lateness and informed me that all the
guests, the amīrs, the great merchants and the kādī with his witnesses, had sat down to meat after waiting for me a long time, and
had gone away having eaten and drunken their fill. She added:
'Your father is very angry and has sworn that we shall not be

married until next year. Tell me, my cousin, why you behaved in this way?'

I told her the whole story and showed the handkerchief; she read the verses upon it and then burst into tears. 'Did she not speak to you?' she asked, and I replied: 'Only by signs which I did not understand. I beg you tell me what they mean.' I imitated my lady's play with her fingers, and my cousin said: 'Dear, dear Azīz, even if you asked my eyes of me I would not hesitate to give them! Console yourself, for I am ready to serve you with all my heart and make easy a meeting between you and this woman who surely loves you and whom you love. Her signs—for women understand these things instinctively—show that she desires you with passion and promises you a meeting in two days: the number is shown by two fingers between two breasts and passion by the finger in the lips. My love for you is a love of service, therefore I take the two of you under the wing of my protection.' I thanked her for her devotion and the hope which she had given me, and remained indoors for two days, eagerly waiting for the hour of meeting. In my grief I lay with my head across my cousin's knees, and she encouraged me. Moreover, when the hour came, she helped me to dress and perfumed me with her own hands.

At this point Shahrazād saw the approach of morning and discreetly fell silent.

But when the hundred-and-fourteenth night had come

SHE SAID:

Azīz thus continued his tale to young Tāj al-Mulūk:

She burnt benzoin below my robe and embraced me tenderly, saying: 'Dearest cousin, behold the hour of your calm. Be courageous and return to me satisfied. I wish you peace, and will have no happiness save in your happiness. Yet do not delay too long to come back and tell me your adventure, for there are fair days and fairer nights to come for us.' Trying to still the beating of my heart, I took leave of my cousin and set forth. When I came to the shady by-street, I sat down on the bench in a state of uncontrollable excitement. In a few minutes the window opened and I thought that I should faint; nevertheless I controlled myself and, looking up, saw all the sweet face of the girl. I lay back trembling while she looked at me with lighted eyes, holding a mirror and a red handkerchief in her hand. Without saying a word she pulled back her sleeves so that I might see her arms to the elbows and then touched her breasts with five extended fingers; next, she waved the red handkerchief up and down three times, twisting and folding it; and lastly, after a long and loving glance, shut the window and disappeared. I was left in indescribable perplexity, not knowing whether to go or stay. To be on the safe side I waited till midnight and then, sick with doubt, returned to my father's house. I found my poor cousin sitting up for me, red-eyed from weeping, with a resigned sadness upon her face. I fell to the floor in a state of pitiable exhaustion, and my cousin, running to me, took me in her arms and kissed my eyes, wiping the tears from them with her sleeve. She made me drink a glass of syrup, lightly scented with water of flowers, and tenderly questioned me as to what had happened.

Although I was broken with fatigue, I told her all, imitating the gestures of the delightful stranger, and my cousin Azīzah said: 'O Azīz of my heart, these signs, especially the five fingers and the mirror, were meant to show that the girl will leave a message for you in five days at the dyer's on the corner of the by-street.' 'Sweet sister, God grant that your interpretation be the right one!' I cried. 'There is, in fact, the shop of a Jewish dyer at one corner of the little road.' At this point I was unable to fight any longer against my memories, so I sobbed on Azīzah's bosom and she comforted me with her caresses. At last she said: 'Lovers often have to suffer and endure through years and years of waiting, and yet they arm themselves with fortitude and do so. You have hardly had to wait a week. Be strong, my dear; eat some of this meat and drink a little of this wine.'

But I could not swallow a mouthful or a sip; I lost my sleep and the colour from my cheeks, for this was the first time that I had known the heat of passion and tasted the bitter excellence of love.

I waited for five days, growing thin the while, and my cousin did not leave me for a moment. Day and night she sat at my bedside, watching over me or telling me tales of lovers to distract me. Sometimes I caught her wiping away furtive tears. When the five days had passed, she heated water for me and sent me to the hammām of the house. Afterwards she helped to dress me, saying: 'Hurry to the appointed place, and may Allāh lead you to your desires and cure your soul with the balm of realisation!'

I hurried to the shop of the Jewish dyer, but it was Saturday and the place was shut. Nevertheless I sat before the door until the time of evening prayer, and then so far into the night that I became afraid of the darkness and decided to leave my post. It was as a drunken man, not knowing what he does or says, that I reached the house and found poor Azīzah standing with her face turned towards the wall and murmuring verses of unhappy love.

As soon as she saw me, she dried her eyes with her sleeve and ran to me, trying to smile. 'Dear cousin, may God extend your happiness for ever!' she said, and then asked me why I had risked a return through the deserted streets, instead of staying the night with my mistress. I flew into a passion, thinking that she laughed at me, and pushed her away from me so violently that she fell across the couch, cutting her brow severely on one of its corners. Instead of railing against my brutality, she rose without a word and, dressing her wound with a little amadou, bound up her forehead with her handkerchief. Lastly, she washed the blood from the marble floor and came to me with a tranquil smile as if nothing had happened.

At this point Shahrazād saw the approach of morning and discreetly fell silent.

But when the hundred-and-fifteenth night had come

SHE SAID:

'Dear cousin,' she said to me very tenderly, 'I am more sorry than I can say if I grieved you with my inapt greeting. Forgive me, and tell me what has happened that I may see if I can help you.' I told her of my failure, and she exclaimed: 'Azīz of my eyes, I can tell you for certain that you will be successful; this is but a proof which the girl has required of your patience and constancy. To-morrow you must sit on the bench outside her window again, and I am sure that you will have some news of her.'

Azīzah brought me a dish covered with various meats in porcelain bowls, but I pushed them roughly away so that the whole fell upon the carpet. My cousin carefully and silently picked up the fallen meats and wiped the carpets. Then she sat down at the foot of the mattress on which I lay and fanned me all night with a fan and soothed me with words of infinite caress. 'Oh what a fool is he who falls in love!' I said to myself.

In the morning I hastened to the bench under my lady's window and, even as I sat down, her delightful head appeared smiling from the casement. For a moment she drew back, and then reappeared holding a bag, a mirror, a lantern, and a vase of flowers. First she put the mirror in the bag, tied the bag, and threw it behind her into the room; then, with an adorable gesture, she loosened her hair which fell heavily all about her face; next she placed the lantern among the flowers; and lastly, disappeared, withdrawing her face and my heart behind the limit of my sight. She shut the window, and thereby shut the window of my soul.

Knowing by experience that nothing was to be gained by waiting, I returned home more dead than alive and found my cousin sitting in tears, with her head wrapped in a double bandage; one fold was passed round her wounded forehead and one across her eyes, weakened by weeping. She did not see me because her head was bent and leaning on her hand. She was sweetly singing to herself:

> Azīz,
> Ah, sweet unfond
> And golden vagabond!
>   Azīz,
> When other hospitality is spent,
> Remember that a warm and crimson tent,
>   Azīz,
> Waits in my heart.
> Let my lips smart,
>   Azīz,
> With salted drink,
> If at the peach-tree pink
> Sources of passion's daughters
> You taste fresh waters,
>   Azīz,
> Ah, sweet unfond
> And golden vagabond,
>   Azīz!

She looked round on finishing her song and saw me; she hid her grief and, after standing silently before me for a few moments, said: 'Sit down, dear Azīz, and tell me what happened.' I informed her of each least movement of my mysterious lover, and she said: 'Cousin, rejoice, for your desires are granted! The mirror placed in the bag means the set of sun, a meeting for to-morrow night; the loosened black hair veiling the white face is but a confirmation of the same thing; the flowers mean that you must go into the garden; the lantern among them, that you will find a lantern there which will lead you to your love.' 'Unhappy Azīz!' I cried in disappointment. 'O sister, how many times have you not raised false hope by false interpretation!' Azīzah was pleasanter to me than ever and sat beside me, though she did not dare to fetch me food and drink because she feared more anger.

Towards the evening of the next day I determined to try my fortune, being encouraged to do so by Azīzah, who had given up all hope for herself although she wept in secret. I bathed and dressed myself in my fairest robes. Before I went Azīzah looked long upon me and said in a woeful voice: 'Take this grain of pure musk and perfume your lips with it. I want you to promise me one thing: when you have met your lover and been satisfied, recite these lines to her.' So saying, she wound her arms about my neck and sobbed. I promised to do as she wished, and she recited this verse:

> Tell me, lovers, tell me truly,
> Shall not love remain unruly
>   In the heart that says him nay?
> Fight upon the red terrain there,
> Fight till all but he is slain there,
> Seem to fall, but rise again there
>   Ever and a day?

I said these lines over and got them by heart, though I was far from knowing either their intention or what they would one day mean to me. When I came to the garden of my beloved's house, I found the gate open and a lantern shining in the depth of the trees. I went towards it through the darkness and found, with a thrill of surprise, a magnificent hall, having an arched dome bearing a cupola of ivory and ebony. Gold torches and large crystal lamps hung from the ceiling by precious chains and lighted a many-tinted fountain, the noise of whose falling waters refreshed more than a draught from a commoner source. Beside the fountain a stool of nacre held a silver tray covered with a piece of silk, and by it on the carpet was a great pitcher of glazed earthenware, the long neck of which was stoppered with a gold and crystal cup.

I lifted the silk from the silver tray, and those delicacies which I found beneath I see even yet in my more happy dreams.

At this point Shahrazād saw the approach of morning and discreetly fell silent.

But when the hundred-and-sixteenth night had come

SHE SAID:

The wazīr Dandān continued to repeat to King Dū al-Makān the tale which Azīz told Prince Tāj al-Mulūk:

There were four roast chicken, golden-brown and odorous, seasoned with fine spices. And there were four deep porcelain bowls: the first contained halwā, perfumed with orange juice, sprinkled with cinnamon and powder of nuts; the second held crushed raisins discreetly sublimated with rose; the third, ah! the third was filled with bakkalāwah, each of whose thousand leaves was the work of an artist and had lozenge shaped divisions of an infinite suggestion; and in the fourth were almond cakes ready to burst because of their generous provision of heavy syrup. The other half of the dish was bright with all my favourite fruits, figs wrinkled with ripeness, knowing themselves desirable, grape-fruit and limes, grapes and bananas; these were divided by intervals of coloured flowers; roses, jasmine and tulips, lilies and jonquils.

When I had considered these delights, I bade my cares be gone, and yet I was troubled to see no creature of God, neither slave, nor servant, nor mistress to serve me with these good things. I waited patiently for three hours and then began to be tortured with hunger, as I had not eaten for a long time because of my passion. Allāh sent me appetite, and I hardly thought of poor Azīzah and her prediction of this garden.

To fill the chasm of my appetite, I threw myself upon my favourite almond cakes and ate I know not how many of them; they seemed drugged with a spiritual perfume from the transparent fingers of girls in Paradise. Next I attacked the brittle squares of the juicy bakkalāwah and, when none of that was left, emptied the white halwā into my mouth and soothed my heart with that. The dish of chicken next attracted me. I ate one, or two, or three, or four; they had been stuffed so learnedly throughout all their hollows and were so aptly seasoned with tart pomegranate seeds that I cannot remember the exact number. Finally I sweetened and caressed my throat by a slow swallowing of fruit, and ended my meal with sweet pomegranate jam. Giving thanks to Allāh, I drank deep of the wine-jar, putting aside the useless cup.

A lassitude of sleep soon overcame my muscles; I had hardly the strength to wash my hands before I fell in heavy slumber on to the cushions of the carpet.

I cannot say what happened during the night; I only know that the sun's rays woke me in the morning, stretched on the naked marble, with a pinch of salt and a handful of powdered charcoal balanced upon the flesh of my belly. I jumped up and shook myself, looking to left and right, but I could see no one. I was furious with myself for my weakness and gluttony, and repented bitterly upon my homeward journey. I entered my father's house sadly and found Azīzah softly lamenting with these verses:

> I know by his scent
> Before he reaches my hair
> That the breeze has risen and dances upon the meadow.
>
> If one could take love as one takes a lover
> And rest his head between the breasts
> And know peace!
>
> These green and gold and blue toys
> Which Allāh calls his world,
> How can I play with them without Azīz?

Azīzah jumped up on seeing me and greeted me with smiles. She helped me to take off my clothes and, as she did so, sniffed each garment many times. Then she said to me: 'As Allāh lives, dear Azīz, these are not such scents as a loving woman leaves upon a man's robe! Tell me what has happened.' She became pale when she heard my story and exclaimed in a frightened voice: 'I am distressed for you, my cousin; I fear this unknown woman intends a bitter future for you. The salt signifies that she finds your body lacking in savour, which can sleep so easily in a watch of love; the charcoal means that your face is black with shame in her eyes. Dear Azīz, this woman, instead of treating you kindly and waking you gently when she came, has shown that she thinks you good for nothing except food and drink and sleep. Therefore God deliver you from such a love!' I beat my breast at the words of Azīzah, crying: 'The girl was right! As Allāh lives, the fault was mine. Lovers do not sleep. In pity's name, tell me what I must do now, Azīzah.'

At this point Shahrazād saw the approach of morning and discreetly fell silent.

But when the hundred-and-seventeenth night had come

SHE SAID TO KING SHAHRYĀR:

It is related, O auspicious King, that the wazīr Dandān continued the tale which Azīz told to Prince Tāj al-Mulūk in this manner.

My poor cousin loved me so much that she grieved for me, and said: 'O Azīz, I will help you; but it would be easier for me if custom allowed me to come and go at my pleasure. As I am supposed to be preparing for marriage I have to keep the house; yet I think that I can watch your interests from afar, though I cannot interfere in person between you and this girl. Return to the same place tonight, my cousin, and fight against your temptation to sleep. This will be easy, if you do not touch the food and drink. Allāh have you in His protection, for I believe that you will see your love towards the end of the first quarter of the night.'

I could hardly wait till sunset and was on the point of setting out when Azīzah stopped me for a moment with these words: 'Above all, when your mistress has given satisfaction to your desires, do not forget to say to her the poem which I taught you.' 'I will not forget,' I answered, and left the house.

On reaching the garden I found the hall lighted and ornamented as before; also the same tempting meats and pastries, fruits and flowers, were set forth on the same service. The combined scent of savour and sweetness soon sapped the resolution of my soul. I ate my fill of everything and drank from the glazed jar until my belly could not hold another drop. Very soon my eyelids fell, and I could not even keep them open with my fingers. 'I am not going to sleep,' I said, 'but just for a moment I will lay my head upon the cushions. I shall rest a little, but most certainly I shall not sleep.' I leaned my head against one of the cushions and woke when the morning was far advanced, not in the bright hall, but in a dirty place among the stables. On my belly was the bone of a sheep's foot, a round ball, some date-stones, some locust-beans, two dirhams, and a knife. I shook these things from me in confusion and, keeping only the

knife, hurried homewards with greater self-reproaches than before.
I found Azīzah singing this song:

> Though I say his beauty lessens
> Horror of my deliquescence,
> Tears have rotted all my heart,
> Soaking soul and self apart;
> And unknowing Azīz stands
> To dig deep gulfs of pain with both his hands.

I attracted her attention with a few oaths, but her sweet patience
would not be moved. Drying her eyes, she threw her arms about my
neck and, leaning upon my breast though I tried to push her away,
said to me: 'Poor, poor Azīz! I see that you have slept again.' At
these words I fell back upon the carpet in a catalepsy of anger,
throwing the knife away. Azīzah took a fan and, sitting beside me,
fanned me, saying the while that all would come right. When at her
request I described the things which I had found upon my belly, she
said: 'O cousin, did I not warn you against sleep and the temptation
of the food?' 'Ah, but tell me what they mean!' I cried.

At this point Shahrazād saw the approach of morning and discreetly fell silent.

But when the hundred-and-eighteenth night had come

SHE SAID:

Azīzah answered: 'The round ball was meant to tell you that,
though you were in the actual house of your mistress, your heart
went idle in the air and was not passionate; the date-stones, that you
have lost your savour, since passion is the fruit of the heart and you
have none of it; the locust-beans, from the tree of Job, father of
patience, were meant to remind you that his virtue is necessary for
lovers; the bone of the sheep's foot I dare not explain.' 'But,
Azīzah,' I cried, 'you have forgotten the knife and the two coins.'
Azīzah trembled at this, saying: 'Dear cousin, I am very frightened
for you. The two silver coins symbolise her eyes and mean to say
that she swears upon her eyes to cut your throat with a knife if you
return to her hall again and sleep. How frightened I am, O Azīz!
Yet I keep my fear to myself. I weep in silence in the empty house,
and have only my tears to console me!' My heart pitied her, and I
said: 'But, dear cousin, what is the remedy of all this? In Allāh's

name, show me a way out of this misfortune.' 'I will do so,' she answered, 'but you must listen carefully to what I say and obey me implicitly, otherwise I shall not succeed.' 'I swear by my father's head that I will obey you in all things,' I said.

Azīzah, delighted with my compliance, kissed me happily, saying: 'You must sleep here all day, so that you will have no temptation to sleep to-night, and when you wake I will give you food and drink, so that you will have nothing to fear at all.' She made me lie down and rubbed me wisely and gently until I fell asleep. I woke towards evening and found her still sitting at my side, fanning me cheerfully: but there were traces of tears upon her garments so that I knew that she had wept. When she saw that I was awake, she brought me food and put it piece by piece into my mouth; therefore I had nothing to do but to swallow and was soon satisfied. Then she gave me a concoction of jujubes with sugared rose-water, and my thirst passed from me. She washed my hands, wiped them with a musk-scented napkin, and sprinkled me all over with flower-waters. She brought me a marvellous new robe and helped me on with it, saying: 'If Allāh wills, to-night you shall come to your desire. Do not forget my advice.' I turned at the door, saying: 'What advice?' and she answered: 'The lines I taught you, O Azīz.'

I came to the garden, entered the vaulted hall, and sat down on the sumptuous carpets. As I was already satisfied, I looked indifferently upon the savoury dishes which were spread for me and waited without difficulty until the middle of the night. I saw no one, I heard no sound, the night seemed long as a year; but I waited patiently.

When three-quarters of the night were already passed and the cocks were beginning to crow for the false dawn, I began to feel hungry. Soon my desire for the exquisite dishes became so great that I could not contain myself. I lifted the cloths, ate till I was satisfied, and drank first one, then two, and finally ten glasses of the wine. My head became heavy, but I jerked it from side to side to fight off sleep. Just as I was about to be overcome, I heard a light sound as of laughter and silks; I had hardly time to leap to my feet and wash my hands and mouth, before the great curtain at the back of the hall was pulled aside. She came, smiling among ten young slaves. They were as bright as ten stars, but she as a moon. She wore a green silk robe, half covered with red gold. I can hardly give you a hint of her loveliness, dear lord, by repeating these words of the poet:

Tall and proud and half undressed,
The white swell of either breast
Breaking from her sea-green vest,
She boasts: 'Like the blue sky I mock
Every echo, like a rock
I stand against the earthquake shock.'
Yet I think my fingers Moses,
Who can make a rock disclose his
Hidden stream of wine and roses
Underneath her frock.

In fact, young sir, I said these lines over to her, and she smiled at me, saying: 'That is excellent. But how is it that I do not find you sleeping?' 'The breeze of your coming fanned my soul awake,' I answered.

She winked at her slaves, and they left us alone in the hall; she sat down beside me, stretching out her breasts to me, and threw her arms about my neck. I pressed my mouth to hers, sucking her upper lip while she sucked my lower one; then I took her by the waist, bending it, and we rolled together upon the carpets. I slipped into the delicate division of her limbs and took all her robes away from her. We began assaults, mingled with kisses and strokings, pinchings and bites, thigh liftings and exposures, and games of hide-and-seek which took us all about the hall. At last she fell passive in my arms, dead from desire. That was a night sweet to my heart, a holiday of the senses. A poet has said:

On this preferred and easy night
    The cup was never empty of its red;
I said to sleep: 'We know you not,' and said:
    'I know you,' to her thighs of silver white.

When morning came, I wished to take my leave, but she stopped me, saying. . . .

At this point Shahrazād saw the approach of morning and discreetly fell silent.

But when the hundred-and-nineteenth night had come

SHE SAID:

Azīz thus continued his tale:

She stopped me, saying: 'I have something to show you and a

piece of advice to give you.' I sat down again a little surprised. Then she unfolded to my sight one of those silk squares embroidered with a gazelle, which you see before you, my lord. She gave it to me, saying: 'Guard it carefully; it is the work of one of my girl friends, the princess of the Isles of Camphor and Crystal. At some time in your life it will be of great importance to you, and, besides, it will always remind you of myself.' I thanked her in equal astonishment and confusion, and took my leave, quite forgetting to recite the lines which Azīzah had taught me.

When I came to my father's house, I found my poor cousin lying on her bed, with every sign of imminent illness in her face; yet when she saw me she tried to rise to her feet and, being unable to do so, dragged herself weeping across the floor to me. She kissed my breast and held me for a long time against her heart. Then she asked me if I had recited her lines. I answered that I had forgotten because of my surprise at receiving the gazelle embroidered upon the square of silk. I showed it to her and Azīzah burst into sobs and murmured between her tears:

> If the red beating heart could speak,
>   You'd hear it undertaking
> That love is weak and very weak
>   And the end of love is breaking.

'Dear cousin,' she added, 'as you hope for mercy, do not forget to recite my lines the next time.' 'Repeat them again, for I have a little forgotten them,' I answered. She did so, and I then remembered them perfectly. At last, when evening came again, she said: 'It is time for you to go. Allāh lead you to your happiness in safety!'

When I got to the garden, I found my mistress impatiently waiting for me. She kissed me and I lay upon her lap. Then, when we had eaten and drunken, we possessed each and every part of the other during the fullness of the night. This time I did not forget to repeat to my lady the lines of Azīzah:

> Tell me, lovers, tell me truly,
> Shall not love remain unruly
>   In the heart that says him nay?
> Fight upon the red terrain there,
> Fight till all but he is slain there,
> Seem to fall, but rise again there
>   Ever and a day?

I cannot hope to tell you the effect which these verses had upon my lady; her heart which she ever spoke of as hard melted within her breast; she wept and improvised these answering lines:

> Just as a lover can be bold,
>   A rival can be true,
> Alas, alas,
>   Guessing at all there was,
> She suffered; and she knew
>   But never told.

I carefully kept this in my mind that I might repeat it to Azīzah. I found her stretched upon a mattress, and my mother seated at her side caring for her. Azīzah was very pale and displayed all the weakness of a swoon. She lifted her eyes unhappily to mine without being able to make any other movement. My mother looked sternly at me, shaking her head and saying: 'Azīz, are you not ashamed to leave your betrothed in this way?' But Azīzah took my mother's hand and kissed it, saying in a low voice: 'Dear cousin, did you forget my advice?' 'Rest assured, dear Azīzah,' I answered, 'I said your lines over to her. She wept exceedingly and answered with these.' I thereupon repeated the poem which my mistress had made. Azīzah wept silently as she listened, and afterwards whispered these verses:

> Though in all indiscretion there is death,
> Too much discretion can cut short the breath.
> Renunciation was the life I led,
> A long corrosive suffering,
> A silent giving up of everything
> With either hand.
> And yet, when I am dead,
> Greet with my greeting radiant and heart-whole
> The other woman, who destroyed my soul,
> For she will understand.

Then she said: 'Son of my uncle, I pray you when you see your love again, say this poem over to her, and may your life be easy and sweet, O Azīz!'

When night fell, I returned to the garden and found my mistress waiting in the hall. We ate and drank and played many pretty games sitting side by side, and then slept in each other's arms until the day. Before leaving I remembered my promise to Azīzah and recited the other verses which my poor cousin had made.

My mistress uttered a great cry on hearing them and retreated in terror. 'As Allāh lives,' she cried, 'she who said that poem to you is now dead! I trust that she was no relation of yours, neither a sister nor a cousin, for I reaffirm that now she lies among the dead.' 'She is my betrothed, the daughter of my uncle,' I answered, and my mistress cried: 'What do you say? Why do you lie? It is not true! If she had been your betrothed you would have loved her.' 'Nevertheless she is my betrothed, my cousin Azīzah,' I answered. 'Why did you not tell me?' cried my love. 'As Allāh lives, I would never have taken her man away from her if I had known of that tie between you. Tell me, did she know of our amorous meetings?' 'Indeed she did,' I answered. 'It was she who explained the signs which you made me at first; without her I would never have won through to you. I achieved my object only through her good advice and willing counsel.' 'Then you have caused her death!' she cried. 'I pray to Allāh that he does not overwhelm your youth as you have overwhelmed the youth of this poor child. Go quickly, and find out what has happened.' Filled with foreboding, I hurried towards my father's house. At the corner of the little street in which it was situated I heard the cries of women coming from the building. Neighbours were hurrying in and out, and one of them said to me: 'They found Azīzah stretched out dead before the door of her chamber.' I rushed into the house and the first person I met was my mother, who said to me: 'You are responsible before Allāh for her death! The weight of her blood is about your neck! My son, my son, you have been but a sorry bridegroom!'

At this point Shahrazād saw the approach of morning and discreetly fell silent.

But when the hundred-and-twentieth night had come

SHE SAID:

She overwhelmed me with reproaches until my father entered the room, and then she fell silent. My father made preparations for the funeral. When all our friends and kinsmen were gathered together, we celebrated the rites of full burial, remaining three days under the tents of her tomb for a reading of the Sacred Book.

I returned to the house with my mother, feeling my heart oppressed with pity for the untimely dead. After we had entered, my mother said to me: 'My son, I wish you to tell me in what way you broke poor Azīzah's heart. I often asked her the cause of her illness, but she would never tell me and never breathed a bitter word against you. Until the end, she never spoke your name without blessings. Tell me then, in Allāh's name, how you brought about her death.' 'I did not do so,' I answered, but my mother insisted, saying: 'I sat by her bedside at about the time of her last breath; she turned towards me, opening her eyes, and said to me: "Wife of my uncle, I pray to the one God that He will ask the price of my blood from no one but rather pardon those who have so tortured my heart. I leave a perishable world for one immortal." "Do not speak of death, my child," I said. "Allāh will make you well again soon." But she smiled sadly at me, saying: "Wife of my uncle, I beg you to give your son Azīz my last advice and supplicate him not to forget it. It is this: when he goes to the place to which he goes, let him say before he comes away:

> Better, sweeter to die
> Than deal in treachery.

He will make me happy if he does this, and I will watch over him after my death as I have done in my lifetime." With that she lifted her pillow and took from under it something which she charged me, under oath, not to give you until you returned to better ways of thought and began sincerely to weep her death. I keep this thing, my son, until I see you fulfil the condition.'

'So be it,' I said to my mother, 'but you might at least show me the thing.' This she vehemently refused to do, and left me.

You can understand, my lord, that at that time I was almost mad with my effort not to listen to the voice of my heart. But soon, instead of weeping for poor Azīzah and carrying my heart in black because of her, I gave myself up to pleasure and distraction. Nothing was sweeter for me than the resumption of my nightly visits to the garden. Hardly had evening come when I hastened to my mistress and found her as impatient for my coming as if she stood upon a gridiron. She ran to me and, hanging from my neck, asked news of my cousin; when I gave her the details of the death and the funeral, she said in a compassionate voice: 'If only I had known of her good services to you and her wonderful abnegation before she died! Indeed, indeed I would have thanked her and found some way of repaying her.'

Then said I: 'Even in death she had counsel for me; she advised me through my mother to say these words to you, the last she ever uttered:

> Better, sweeter to die
> Than deal in treachery.'

When the girl heard these words, she cried: 'Allāh take her to His mercy! Even after her death she has been of great service to you! By these few words she has saved you from the deadly snare which I had prepared for you and the pits into which I had thought to see you fall.'

I was indeed astonished at these strange words, and cried out: 'What are you saying? What talk is this of snares and pits when we are bound together by perfect love?'

'Innocent child,' she said, 'I can see that you know nothing of all the treachery of which we women are capable. I do not wish to undeceive you, but only that you should know that you owe your safety to your cousin. Yet I spare you only on condition that you never give look or word to any woman, young or old, except myself. Woe betide you, oh, woe betide you! For now there is none to deliver you out of my hands, since she who fortified you with her counsels is dead. Take care, therefore, not to forget my condition. . . . Now I have a request to make of you.'

At this point Shahrazād saw the approach of morning and discreetly fell silent.

But when the hundred-and-twenty-first night had come

SHE SAID:

'What is that?' I asked, and she answered: 'That you take me to visit the tomb of poor Azīzah, for I wish to place some words of grief upon it.' 'If Allāh wills, I will do so to-morrow,' I promised, and lay down to pass the night with her. But all the time she asked me questions about Azīzah, saying: 'Ah, why did you not tell me that she was your cousin?' In my turn I said: 'By the way, I forgot to ask you the meaning of the words concerning death and treachery.' But on this point she would tell me nothing.

At the first hour of the next morning she rose and took a large purse filled with dīnārs, saying to me: 'Rise up and lead me to the tomb. I wish to build a dome over it.' I left the garden, walking in front of her, and she followed me through the streets, distributing dīnārs to every poor person, and saying to each: 'These alms are for the repose of the soul of Azīzah.' When we came to the tomb, she threw herself down on the marble and washed it with her tears. Presently she took from a silk bag a steel graver and a gold mallet, and carved upon the polished marble these verses in an elegant script:

> I passed a tomb among green shades
> Where seven anemones with down-dropped heads
> Wept tears of dew upon the stone beneath.
> I questioned underneath my breath
> Who the poor dead might be
> And a voice answered me. . . .
>
> So now I pray that Allāh may be moved
> To drop sleep on her eyes because she loved.
> She will not care though lovers do not come
> To wipe the dust from off a lover's tomb,
> She will not care for anything. But I please
> To plant some more dew-wet anemones
> That they may weep.

When she had finished, she cast a glance of farewell on the tomb and walked back to her palace with me. She had become very tender of a sudden, and said to me again and again: 'Never leave me.' I hastened to reassure her, and went to visit her regularly every night. She always greeted me with warmth and expansion, and spared herself no pains to give me pleasure. Such was my existence: to eat and drink, to kiss and couple, daily to be dressed in robes and shirts finer than the day before, until I became very fat and jubilant, entirely forgetting poor Azīzah.

This lasted for a whole year. On a certain day at the beginning of the second I went to the hammām and dressed myself in my most costly garments. Leaving the bath, I drank a cup of sherbert, inhaling with delight the splendid smells which rose from my robe, feeling more happy than I had ever done, and seeing all things about me coloured in white. Life was exceedingly pleasant to me, and I went walking and running like a man light with wine, in pleased anticipation of seeing my love again.

I was passing by a little street called the Blind Alley of the Flute, quite near my mistress's house, when I saw an old woman coming towards me, holding a lantern to make plain her path and carrying a letter in its wrapping. I stopped, and she wished me peace.

At this point Shahrazād saw the approach of morning and discreetly fell silent.

But when the hundred-and-twenty-second night had come

SHE SAID:

She wished me peace, saying: 'My child, do you know how to read?' 'I know how to read, good aunt,' I answered. Then she said: 'I pray you take this letter and read it to me.' I did so willingly; the writer stated that he was in good health and sent every friendly wish to his sister and his kinsmen. The old woman raised her arms to the sky when I had read, and called down blessing upon me for the good news I had announced. 'Allāh soothe all your griefs as you have soothed mine,' she said and, taking the letter, continued on her way. I had an urgent need to make water, so I squatted against the wall and did so. I rose, shook myself well and, rearranging my robe, was about to depart when I saw the old woman coming back. She took my hand and raised it to her lips, saying: 'Excuse me, my lord, but I have a further favour to ask you. If you grant it, you will make me the happiest of women and will yourself be recompensed by the Master of Reward. I beg you to come with me to the door of our house, which is quite near here, and read this letter again to the women of the household. They would not be content with my version of it. Above all, my daughter will be most delighted to hear the whole of the letter, as she loves her brother very much and this is the first time we have heard of him for ten years. He has been away with a trading caravan, and we have wept him for dead. Do not refuse me, my lord. You will not even have the trouble of coming into the house; you can read the letter from outside. You know the words of the Prophet (on whom be prayer and peace!) concerning those who console their neighbours: "He who lifts any of the griefs of this world from the head of a Believer, Allāh will take count of it and lift seventy-two griefs from his head in the world to come." ' I hastened to comply with her request, saying: 'Walk before me, to light me and show me the road.' The old woman set out in front of me and, after a few steps, we came to the door of a palace.

508

This door was of the largest size, plated with worked bronze and red copper. I stood close to it, and the old woman called out in the Persian tongue. Her cry was answered by the opening of the door, and there in front of me, on the other side of the threshold, appeared a light and dimpled girl, smiling, with naked feet upon the washed marble, holding the fullness of her drawers half way up her thighs for fear of wetting them. Her sleeves were rolled up to her shoulders so that her armpits appeared dark against the whiteness of her robe. I did not know which to admire the more, the alabaster which had been moulded to the shape of her thighs or the crystal which had been worked into arms for her. Her slim ankles were circled by gold rings crusted with colours of jewels, her small wrists bore heavy bracelets of multiple fire, single pearls of marvellous water hung at her ears, and, from her neck, a triple chain of selected emeralds. Her hair was caught up in a light chaplet of diamonds. When I saw that her chemise hung out disordered from her drawers and that the strings of these were all untied, I guessed that she had been indulging in some very pleasant pastime before she opened the door. Her general beauty and the particular beauty of her thighs threw me into a pleasant reflection, and in spite of myself I called to mind these words of the poet:

> Lift your robe quite up, God bless me,
>   Lift your robe quite up!
> I can feel your eyes undress me,
> Lift your robe and I'll confess me
>   Drunken with one scarlet cup.

When the girl saw me, she seemed entirely surprised. With a candid glance of her great eyes and in the sweetest voice I have ever heard in my life, she said: 'Mother, is this the man who is going to read our letter?' The old woman answered that I was, and the exquisite child stretched out her hand to give me the letter which she had already taken from her mother. I leaned forward to receive it when suddenly, just as I was two feet from the door, I felt the old woman push me violently in the back with her head and was hurled forward into the vestibule. Quick as lightning she followed me in and shut the street door upon me. Thus I found myself a prisoner between the two women, without having the least idea what they wished of me. I had not long to wait, however.

At this point Shahrazād saw the approach of morning and discreetly fell silent.

But when the hundred-and-twenty-third night had come

SHE SAID:

While I was still staggering in the vestibule, the young girl tripped me neatly, threw me to the ground and lay all along on top of me, pressing me in her arms as if she would stifle me. I thought that I was to be killed, but my fate was far otherwise! After certain movements, the girl half lifted herself and, sitting upon my belly, began rubbing me with her hands so furiously and so strangely that I began to lose my senses and to shut my eyes like a man stricken with madness. The child helped me to my feet and, taking me by the hand, led me, followed by her mother, through seven corridors and seven galleries to her own apartment. I followed like a drunken man, and indeed I was drunken with the effect of her terribly expert fingers. She made me sit down and bade me open my eyes. I did so, and found that I was in a great hall lighted by four glazed arcades. It was so spacious that warriors might have tilted upon its floor; its pavement was all of marble, its walls were covered with decorations of bright colours mingled together in exquisite design. All the furnishings were of agreeable shape, upholstered in brocade and velvet, and at the bottom of it was a deep alcove, holding a golden bed so covered with pearls that it would have been fit for a King such as yourself, my lord.

Somewhat to my consternation, the girl called me by my own name, saying: 'O Azīz, do you prefer life or death?' 'Life,' I answered. 'If that be so, you have but to marry me,' she said. On that I cried: 'Not so, as Allāh lives, for I would rather die than marry a cunning and licentious woman!' 'Believe me, Azīz,' returned my captor, 'you will be rid once and for all of the Daughter of Wily Delilah.' 'I do not know anyone of that name,' I answered. She burst out laughing, and cried: 'What! You do not know the Daughter of Wily Delilah, when she has been your mistress for a year and four months? Beware, poor Azīz, beware the treacheries of this God-detested harlot. There is not a corrupter soul on earth than hers; she has slain a hundred with her own hands; she has committed a thousand dark treacheries upon her lovers; it is astonishing to me that you should be still alive.'

'Dear mistress,' I answered in confusion, 'will you tell me how you know the person of whom you speak and all those details which are unknown even to me?' To this she replied: 'I know her as well as Destiny knows the designs of Destiny; but before I explain her to you I wish to hear your love adventure from your own mouth. For, as I have said, I am surprised that you should still be alive.'

I told the girl the whole story of my lover and her garden, with the death of poor Azizah. At my cousin's name she wept and beat her hands together in sign of deep despair, saying: 'Allah comfort you, O Aziz! I see clearly that you owe your safety with the Daughter of Wily Delilah to poor Azizah. Now that you have lost her, look well to yourself. . . . But I must not tell you more. Indeed there are no women left to-day as admirable as your dead cousin.' 'You must know,' I said, 'that, before she died, she advised me to say to my mistress these simple words:

> Better, sweeter to die
> Than deal in treachery.'

The girl cried out on these words: 'Those lines have saved you from death, Aziz. Azizah watches over you in death as in life. But let us leave thinking of the dead, for they are in the peace of Allah. The present is for the living. Know then, dear Aziz, that it has long been my desire to have you with me night and day, and only now have I been able to succeed in laying hands on you.' 'That is so,' I answered, and she continued: 'You are young, dear friend, and have no idea of all the tricks which an old woman like my mother can compass.' 'That is so,' I said, and she continued: 'Resign yourself to fate. You have only to allow yourself to be made a husband. I will have nothing at all to do with you except after legitimate contract before Allah and His Prophet (on whom be prayer and peace!). All your wishes shall be fulfilled: you can have treasures, fair stuffs for your robes, light clean turbans, and all for nothing. I will never allow you to loosen the strings of your purse, for in my house the bread is ever fresh and the cup filled. In return for these things, dear Aziz, I require but one thing.' 'What is that?' I asked, and she answered: 'That you do with me as a cock does.' 'And what does a cock do?' I asked in my astonishment.

The young girl laughed so heartily that she fell over on her backside and lay there wriggling and clapping her hands for joy. At last she managed to ask: 'Do you not know what a cock's business is?'

'As Allāh lives, I did not know that it had any business,' I answered. Then said she: 'A cock's business, dear Azīz, is to eat, drink, and couple.'

I was confused to hear her speak in this way, and said: 'I have never heard of that being a business.' 'It is the best business in life, my dear,' she answered. 'Be a man, rise up, tighten your belt, fortify your loins, and go to it: hard, dry and long.' With this she cried out to her mother, who entered with four official witnesses carrying lighted torches. They came forward with ceremonious bowings and sat down in a circle.

The girl lowered the veil over her face and wrapped herself in the izār, the great veil. The witnesses wrote out our contract, in which my new mistress generously acknowledged that she had received from me a dowry of ten thousand dīnārs against all indebtedness past or future. She gave the customary fee to the witnesses, who left by the way they had come with renewed compliments. The mother also seemed to fade from view.

At this point Shahrazād saw the approach of morning and discreetly fell silent.

But when the hundred-and-twenty-fourth night had come

SHE SAID:

We were alone in the great hall with the four glazed arcades.

The girl undressed herself and came to me with a thin chemise floating on her body. Ah, the things pictured in silk on that chemise! Also she had on limpid drawers, but these she let slip to her ankles and kicked away. She led me by the hand to the alcove and threw herself with me on the golden bed, panting and saying: 'Now we may do it! Now it is lawful!' She stretched herself yielding upon the silks and drew me all against her. She groaned, she shivered, she giggled, and then she lifted her chemise right up above her belly.

I sucked her lips while she half fainted, half pulled herself back, and fluttered her eyelids. Then I pierced her through and through. Thus I was able to check the charming exactness of the poet who said:

> She was a child, lifting her robe in the garden,
> There was no sin a lover of love could not pardon;
> It was as narrow as virtue, as easy as flying,
> Yet I was half-way in when her petulant sighing

Stopped me. I asked: 'Why, why?' And she said with a laugh: 'Moon of my eyes, I sigh for the other half.'

When it was once done, she said: 'Go as you wish, I am your slave. Go! Come! Take it! Give it! Right in! Back! My life, my life! Let me put it in myself!' She sighed and groaned among kisses and jumpings; I groaned and sighed with movements and multiple couplings, until the noise of us filled the house and put all the street into an amaze. After that we slept together till morning.

As I was about to depart, she came to me with a wicked smile, saying: 'Where are you going? Do you think that the door of freedom is as large as the door of entrance? Undeceive yourself, dear silly Azīz. Do you take me for the Daughter of Wily Delilah? Have you forgotten that we are well and truly married, and our contract confirmed by the Sunnah? If you are drunk, my Azīz, become sober. The door of this house opens only one day in the year. Rise up and see if I am not speaking the truth.' I jumped up in a fright and ran to the great door. It was locked, barred, nailed up, and heavily chained. I returned to the girl and told her what I had seen. She smiled happily, saying: 'We have a great abundance of flour here, with grains, fruits fresh and dried, preserved pomegranates, butter, sugar, jam, sheep, fowls, and the like; enough to last us for many years. Now I am as sure of your staying with me for a year as I am sure of life itself. So resign yourself and do not look so gloomy.' I sighed, saying: 'There is no power or help save in Allāh!' 'But what have you to complain of, dear fool? Why should you sigh when you have given me such abundant proof that you understand the business of a cock?' With that she laughed, and soon I was laughing too, for I could not help myself.

I stayed in that house, conducting the business of a cock, that is to say, eating, drinking, and making love, hard, dry, and long, for a whole year. By the end of the twelve months, she gave birth to a child, and, at about the same time, I heard again the noise of the door groaning upon its hinges. Then in my heart I uttered a profound: 'Yā Allāh!' of thankfulness.

As soon as the door was open, I saw a number of slaves and porters running to and fro with fresh provisions for a further year: great loads of pastries, flour, sugar, and other necessaries of the kind. I jumped to my feet and was making off as fast as I could towards liberty and the street when my wife took hold of my garments, saying: 'Ungrateful Azīz! At least wait for the evening and the exact hour at which you came to me a year ago!' I constrained myself to be patient; but, as soon as evening came, I went towards the door. My wife came with me to the threshold and would not let me go till I had sworn to return before the door should be shut next morning. Therefore I swore upon the Sword of the Prophet (upon whom be prayer and peace!) and upon his Book, and upon his institution of Divorce.

I left the house and hastened towards the abode of my parents. The way lay past the garden of my mistress, whom my wife had called the Daughter of Wily Delilah. I saw to my astonishment that the garden was open as of old and that the lantern shone in the shrubs.

At this point Shahrazād saw the approach of morning and discreetly fell silent.

But when the hundred-and-twenty-fifth night had come

SHE SAID:

I was uncomfortably affected, and then driven to anger by what I saw. 'I have been away a year,' I said to myself, 'I come back unexpectedly to find everything as it was before. Even before seeing my mother, who must have wept me for dead, I will find out what has happened to my mistress.' With that I walked through the garden and came to the hall with the vaulted roof and the dome of ebony and ivory. I entered abruptly and found my mistress seated, bent over upon herself, her head near her knees and one of her cheeks supported on her hand. She was very pale, her eyes were moist with tears. I have never seen a face so sad. Suddenly she saw me, half started, tried to rise, and then fell back upon her cushions. When she could speak, she cried in a loud voice: 'Praise be to Allāh that you have come back, Azīz!'

I was thrown into confusion by this joy which took no account of my infidelities, and bowed my head. Then I went up to my mistress and kissed her, saying: 'How did you know that I would come to-night?' 'I did not know,' she answered, 'I have been waiting for a year, sitting thus every night in lonely tears. See how my vigils have wasted me. Azīz, I have waited ever since that day when I gave you the new silk robe and you promised to return after you had bathed. Tell me, my dear, what has kept you so long away from me?'

Then, my prince, I foolishly told her every circumstance of my adventure and of my marriage with the girl of the pre-eminent thighs. 'Further,' I added, 'I must warn you that I have but one night to pass with you; I must return to my wife before to-morrow morning, for I have sworn to do so by the three sacred things.'

The young woman turned pale as if stricken into stone by indignation. At last she cried: 'Miserable wretch! I was your first love, and you give me less than one night! You give your mother nothing. Do you think that I am as patient as Azīzah (whom Allāh keep!)? Do you think that I am going to pine away and die because of your infidelities? Detestable Azīz, nothing shall save you now! I have no reason for sparing you, since you are married, and married men are horrible to me. You can serve me no longer, but I do not care that you should serve another!'

She said these words in a voice which turned my blood to ice, while her eyes pierced me as if they had been made fire. Before I had time to think, ten young women slaves, stronger than negroes, hurled themselves upon me and threw me to the earth. My mistress rose and took a terrifying knife, saying to me: 'We will cut your throat as they do to bucks which are too much on heat. With one stroke I will avenge myself and the poor Azīzah whose heart you broke. Say your prayer, Azīz, for your time has come to die!' So saying she leaned her knee on my forehead, while the slaves stopped my breath.

At this point Shahrazād saw the approach of morning and discreetly fell silent.

But when the hundred-and-twenty-sixth night had come

SHE SAID:

I gave myself up for lost when I saw what the slaves were doing. Two sat on my belly, two held my feet, two sat across my knees, while my mistress with the help of two others beat me with a stick across the soles of the feet until I fainted from pain. As they rested, I came to myself, crying: 'Rather death a thousand times than these tortures!'

As if to oblige me, the young woman took up the knife again and, sharpening it on her slipper, called to her slaves: 'Stretch out his neck!'

Just at this fatal moment Allāh made me remember the last words of Azīzah, and I called out:

Better, sweeter to die
Than deal in treachery.

My mistress gave a cry of fear, and then said: 'Allāh have pity on your soul, Azīzah! You have saved your cousin from a terrible death.'

She looked at me and continued: 'As for you, whom Azīzah has saved again with her couplet, do not think that you will get off scot-free. I must avenge myself on you and on the wicked wanton who has stolen you. There is but one way.' Then to the slaves she cried: 'Help me! Tie his feet and do not let him move an inch!'

The slaves did as they were bid, while their mistress put a red copper pot upon the fire, containing oil and soft cheese. When the cheese was well mixed into the boiling oil she came back to me and pulled down my drawers; alternate waves of terror and shame shook me, and I knew what was to happen. Having bared my belly, she took hold of my eggs and bound them at the root with the noose of a waxed cord; the ends of this cord she gave to two of her slaves, who bore strongly upon it, while she herself took up a razor and, with a single stroke, cut off my manhood.

I fainted with pain and despair, my lord. I only know that, when I came to myself, I saw that my front was like a woman's and that the slaves were even then applying the boiled oil and cheese to the wound. My blood soon stopped flowing, and my mistress came to me and gave me a cup of syrup for my thirst, saying scornfully: 'Return whence you came! You are no use to me. I keep all that was ever valuable in you.' She pushed me away with her foot and had me thrown out of the house, crying after me: 'Think yourself lucky that your head is still upon your shoulders!'

Sadly and painfully I dragged myself to my young wife's house; I found the door open and entered silently. As soon as I had thrown myself heavily upon the cushions of the great hall, my wife ran to me and, finding me very pale, made me tell my story and show her my mutilation. I looked at my loss a second time, could not abide it, and fell into a swoon again.

When I came to myself, I found myself in the street outside the great door; my wife also had no further use for me now that I was no more than a woman.

I climbed wretchedly to my feet and tottered towards my father's house. Reaching it at length, I threw myself into the arms of my mother, who had long wept me as dead or lost irrevocably.

At this point Shahrazād saw the approach of morning and discreetly fell silent.

But when the hundred-and-twenty-seventh night had come

SHE SAID:

My mother received me with sobs and, seeing my mortal pallor and great weakness, began to weep afresh. A memory suddenly came over me of my sweet Azizah, the poor girl who had died of heartbreak without one word of reproach. For the first time I truly regretted her and wept tears of despair and repentance on her account. When I was a little calmer, my mother said to me: 'Poor child, this is a house of misfortune; your father is dead.' Sobs rose in my throat at this intelligence. I sat still for a moment and then fell face forward to the ground in a fit which lasted all night.

In the morning my mother made me rise up, and herself sat down by my side; but I stayed without speaking, looking ever at the corner where poor Azizah used to sit. Seeing the tears coursing down my face, my mother said: 'Dear son, for ten days I have been alone in this house, empty of its master; ten days ago your father passed into the infinite mercy of Allāh.' 'Leave speaking of that till another time, my mother,' I answered. 'Just now all my soul is occupied with Azizah. I cannot consecrate my grief to any other end than her. Sweet cousin that I so neglected, you who loved me truly, pardon the wretch who tortured you! He has been punished and more than punished for his sins!'

My mother saw that my grief was true and deep; but she kept silence, contenting herself with healing my wound and building up my strength. When she had done all she could, she watched over me tenderly, saying: 'Allāh is good, my son, for He has spared your life.'

In the course of time my body became completely well, though my soul remained still in a state of fever. One day my mother sat down beside me, saying: 'I think that the time has come, my son, when I may rightly give you the keepsake with which Azizah trusted me. Before she died, she made me swear not to hand it over to you until your grief was sincere and you were finally quit of the evil entanglement which kept you from her.' So saying she opened a coffer and took a packet from it; she undid the packet and handed me this second square of precious silk, embroidered with the other gazelle. As you may see, these verses are interlaced all round the edge:

> You taught my heart to burn while yours was resting,
>   You taught my eyes to watch while your eyes slept;
> Your careless head between my breast lay nesting
>   And dreamed another woman while I wept.
> Dig my grave deep and set this verse above:
> 'She fears not death because she has known love.'

On reading those lines for the first time, I shed abundant tears and beat my cheeks in grief. As I unrolled the stuff, a piece of paper fell out on which I saw lines traced in the hand of the dead Azīzah.

At this point Shahrazād saw the approach of morning and discreetly fell silent.

But when the hundred-and-twenty-eighth night had come

SHE SAID:

These were the lines traced in the hand of the dead Azīzah.

'O dearest cousin, you are more precious to me than my life; after my death I will continue to pray to Allāh that you may prosper and succeed in all you undertake. I know well the misfortunes which await you at the hands of the Daughter of Wily Delilah. Let them be a lesson to you and root from your heart your evil love for treacherous and wanton women. I give thanks to Allāh that he has taken me away so that I need not see your suffering and despair.

'I pray you to keep this parting gift, this silk worked with a gazelle. It has kept me company during the long times you have been away. It was sent to me by the daughter of a king, the lady Dunya, princess of the Isles of Camphor and Crystal.

'When misfortunes fall thick about you, depart in search of princess Dunya, whom you shall find in her father's kingdom, among the Isles of Camphor and Crystal. Only be quite certain, dear Azīz, that the unequalled beauty and delight of this princess are not for your enjoying. Do not fall in love with her, for it is not as a lover that she shall help you, but as a saviour from affliction.

'The peace of Allāh be with you, O Azīz.'

My heart became all the more tender when I had read this letter, and I wept with my mother until nightfall. Thereafter, for a whole year, I kept the house in sluggish grief.

At the beginning of the second year, I began to make plans for going in search of princess Dunya to the Isles of Camphor and Crystal. In this my mother encouraged me, saying: 'The long journey will distract you, my son, and drive away your grief. There is a caravan of merchants just ready to leave our city. I advise you to buy merchandise and join yourself to them. At the end of three years you will come back with the same caravan, quite cured of the grief which now oppresses you. And all my happiness will be to see you smile again.'

I did as my mother suggested. I bought valuable merchandise, joined the caravan, and set out with them; but I never had the courage to expose my merchandise for sale as my companions did. I used to sit apart each day and, spreading these double squares in front of me, weep over them. After a year we came to the frontiers of the kingdom reigned over by the father of Princess Dunya, that is to say the Seven Isles of Camphor and Crystal.

The King of this territory was called Shahrimān, and he was the father of that mistress Dunya who knew so well how to make presents of gazelles embroidered upon silk.

When I reached his kingdom, I thought to myself: 'Poor weak Azīz! What good can you be now to princesses or even the commonest of girls? O poor flat-fronted Azīz!'

At this point Shahrazād saw the approach of morning and discreetly fell silent.

But when the hundred-and-twenty-ninth night had come

SHE SAID:

Nevertheless, as I remembered Azīzah's words, I began to make those enquiries and plans necessary for meeting with the King's daughter.

My efforts were in vain; no one could help me, no one could show me the way. As I was beginning to despair, a day came on which I walked among the gardens which surrounded the city, trying to forget my anxieties in the sight of the green there. Suddenly I came upon a garden gate showing such wonderful trees that my heart leapt upwards. On the bench at the entrance was seated an old gardener with a pleasant face. I walked towards him and, after the usual greetings, asked him to whom the garden might belong. He answered me: 'It belongs to the lady Dunya, daughter of our King.

You may if you wish walk about inside for a little while, my beautiful youth, to breathe the odour of the flowers and herbs.' 'I cannot thank you enough,' I answered. 'Would it be possible, O venerable old man, for me to hide behind one of the great clusters of flowers and wait the coming of the princess? I merely wish to rejoice my eyes with a single glance at her.' 'That cannot be,' he said. I sighed loudly at this answer, so that he looked upon me with tenderness and, taking me by the hand, led me into the garden.

We walked up and down together, and at last he led me into a charming alley shaded by wet leaves. He plucked the ripest and most delicate fruit for me, saying: 'These will be good for you. Only Princess Dunya has tasted the like. Now sit down, and I will return.' He left me for a moment and came back with a roast lamb, of which he carved the tenderest parts for me in extreme benevolence. I was confused by his goodness and did not know how to thank him. As we sat eating and talking in great friendliness, we heard the creak of the garden gate. The old man said quickly: 'Hide yourself among those flowers and do not move!'

I had scarcely obeyed him when the head of a black eunuch appeared through the open gate, calling in a loud voice: 'Old gardener, is there anyone here? Princess Dunya is coming.' 'Chief of the palace, there is no one in the garden,' answered my old friend, as he hastened to open the gate to its full extent.

Then, dear lord, I saw the lady Dunya come through the gate as if the moon herself were entering the garden. Such was her beauty that I remained where I was as if I had been dead. I followed her with my looks without being able to breathe, although I ardently desired to speak to her. During the whole time of her walk I stayed as a stone statue among the flowers, nay, as one who has gone thirsting through the desert for many days and falls at last upon the borders of a lake without being able to drag himself to the cool water.

I understood then, as never before, that neither Princess Dunya nor any other woman would ever again run any danger from the pitiful thing I had become.

I waited till the princess left the garden; then I took leave of the old gardener and hastened to rejoin my caravan, saying to myself: 'Ah, what have you become, O Azīz? A belly so smooth that it shall never tame a single girl. Go back to your mother, Azīz, and die in peace at the masterless house of your father. Life can mean no more to you.' In spite of all the troubles and fatigues which I had under-gone to reach the kingdom of Shahrimān, my despair prevented me from following the advice of Azīzah and ever attempting again to approach the lady Dunya, who should, it was supposed, have brought me happiness.

I left with the caravan to return to my own country, and thus arrived in these lands which are ruled over by your excellent father, King Sulaimān Shāh.

Such is my story.

When Tāj al-Mulūk heard this admirable tale. . . .

At this point Shahrazād saw the approach of morning and dis-creetly fell silent.

But when the hundred-and-thirtieth night had come

SHE SAID:

It is related, O auspicious King, that the wazīr Dandān, who told all this tale to King Dū al-Makān during the siege of Constantinople, began, when he had finished the adventure of young Azīz, to tell the following story, in which Azīz is also intimately bound up with all the marvels you are going to hear:

The Tale of Princess Dunya and Prince Tāj al-Mulūk

WHEN Prince Tāj al-Mulūk heard this admirable tale and had learnt how desirable the mysterious Princess Dunya was said to be, how beautiful and how expert in the art of silk embroidery, he fell into a passion for her which worked greatly in his heart. He resolved to adventure all in an attempt to meet her.

He wished never to be separated again from young Azīz and there-fore took him as a companion when he journeyed back to the city of his father, Sulaimān Shāh, King of Green City and the mountains of Isfahān.

His first action was to place a beautiful and fully-appointed house at the disposal of his friend Azīz. When he was sure that Azīz was provided with all he could possibly need, he returned to his father's palace and shut himself in his own room, refusing to see anyone. In that confinement he wept passionately, for things heard sometimes make a greater impression than things seen.

When Sulaimān Shāh understood from the change in his son's complexion that care sat upon his heart, he asked him the reason of it. Prince Tāj al-Mulūk told him that he was in love with the lady Dunya, passionately desirous of one whom he had never seen, the slave of a word-picture by Azīz, of a gracious walk, dark eyes, and fingers skilled in the needlework of flowers and animals.

Sulaimān Shāh was exceedingly perplexed and said to his son: 'The Isles of Camphor and Crystal are very far from us, and, though the lady Dunya be a marvellous princess, our own city and your mother's palace have fine girls in plenty and fair slaves from all over the earth. Take a walk through the women's apartments and choose any of the five hundred unparalleled beauties you will find there. If none of the women please you, I will find you a wife among the daughters of my neighbouring kings; I promise you that she shall be more beautiful and cleverer than the lady Dunya.' 'My father,' answered Tāj al-Mulūk, 'I only wish to marry Princess Dunya. She is so skilful in portraying gazelles upon brocade. If I cannot marry her, I will flee from my country and kill myself because of her.'

His father saw that it would be harmful to deny him, so he said: 'Have patience and I will send a deputation to the King of the Isles of Camphor and Crystal to ask his daughter's hand in regular fashion, such as I used in begging the hand of your mother for myself. If he refuses, I will powder the earth of his kingdoms and bring his cities about his head in ruin; I will sack them with an army whose vanguard shall have reached the Isles of Camphor while the rearguard is still this side of the mountains of Isfahān.' The King also sent for the young merchant Azīz, his son's friend, and learned by questioning him that he knew the way to the Isles of Camphor and Crystal. Then he said: 'I should be indeed grateful if you would accompany my wazīr, whom I am sending to the King of those places.' 'I hear and I obey,' answered Azīz.

Sulaimān Shāh called his wazīr to him, saying: 'Arrange this affair for my son as you think best. I wish you to set out as soon as possible for the Isles of Camphor and Crystal to ask for the King's daughter in marriage for Tāj al-Mulūk.' The wazīr answered that he would do so; but Tāj al-Mulūk, who was in a fever of impatience, retired to his own apartment, reciting these verses of the poet upon the pains of love:

> Mournful numbers played on my heart-strings,
>> Played by grief:
>> Night, the thief,
> Night will tell you of these things.
>
> Sleepless shepherds counting every star
>> Are my eyes:
>> Night, the wise,
> Night will tell you that they are.
>
> I am as lonely as an aching woman
>> Whom no man seed answers to:
> Night, eternal and inhuman,
>> Night will tell you this is true.

He stayed dreaming all night, refusing nourishment and sleep. When day dawned, his father hastened to find him and, seeing him paler and more out of countenance than the day before, hastened the preparations for the departure of Azīz and the wazīr, swiftly charging them with rich presents for the King of the Isles of Camphor and Crystal and for all his court.

Without an hour's delay the two set forth and, after a journey of many days, reached the Isles of Camphor and Crystal. They pitched their tents on the bank of a river and sent forward a messenger to announce their arrival to the King; the day had not ended before chamberlains and amīrs came out to meet them, who welcomed them to the King's palace.

Azīz and the wazīr entered and gave their rich presents from Sulaimān Shāh into the hands of the King. He thanked them, saying: 'Upon my head and in my eyes! I accept these with a friendly heart.' Then, according to custom, Azīz and the wazīr retired and rested for five days in the palace from the fatigues of their journey.

On the morning of the sixth day, the wazīr dressed himself in his robe of honour and went alone to present himself before the King. He submitted the request of his master and stood in silent respect to wait the answer. When he heard the wazīr's words, the King became very anxious all of a sudden and hung his head; for a long time he remained in dreamy perplexity, not knowing what answer to give to the envoy of the powerful King of Green City and the Mountains of Isfahān. For he was well aware that his daughter held marriage in horror and would indignantly refuse this new offer, as she had already refused all those from the princes of neighbouring kingdoms.

At last the King lifted his head and signed to his chief of eunuchs to approach him, saying: 'Go at once to your mistress, the lady Dunya, present the homage of this wazīr to her and the presents which he has brought us, and repeat to her exactly the request which you have heard him make.'

The eunuch kissed the earth between the King's hands and disappeared, but at the end of an hour he returned with his nose hanging over his feet and said: 'O King of the centuries and of time, I obtained an audience with my mistress, the lady Dunya, but hardly had I hinted at the request of our lord the wazīr when her eyes blazed with anger. She jumped from her seat and, seizing a mace, ran at me to break my head. I fled as quickly as I could, but she pursued me through the door with these cries: "If my father insists on my marrying after all that has happened let him be assured that my husband shall never look upon my face unveiled. I will kill him with my own hand and myself afterwards."'

But when the hundred-and-thirty-first night had come

SHE SAID:

It is related, O auspicious King, that, when all had heard the words of the chief eunuch, the princess's father said to the wazīr: 'You have heard with your own ears. I beg you to take my respectful salutations to King Sulaimān Shāh and report the matter to him, explaining how horrified my daughter is at the thought of marriage. Allāh bring you to your journey's end in all security!'

Azīz and the wazīr hastened to return to Green City and report to Sulaimān Shāh what they had heard. The King flew into a great passion of anger and wished to give immediate orders to his amīrs and lieutenants to mass their troops and hurl them against the Isles of Camphor and Crystal.

But the wazīr asked leave to speak, and said: 'My King, this should not be done, for it is the daughter's fault and not the father's. The unsuccess of our enterprise was due to her alone. Her father is as angry as you are. Besides, I have told you of the terrible threat which she sent us by the frightened chief eunuch.'

Sulaimān Shāh admitted the right of this, and suddenly began to fear lest the vengeance of the princess should fall upon his son. He said to himself: 'If I sack their land and take the girl captive, that would not advantage us, since she has sworn to kill herself.'

He called Prince Tāj al-Mulūk to him and, in a voice sad with the sorrow which he knew he was about to inflict, told him what had happened. But the prince was far from despairing. He said in a firm tone to his father: 'My lord, do not think I will leave things as they are. I swear by Allāh that the lady Dunya shall be my wife. I will come by her in my own way, even at the risk of my life.' 'How is that?' asked the King. 'I will go and seek her in the guise of a merchant,' answered Tāj al-Mulūk.

'In that case,' said the King after consideration, 'take the wazīr and Azīz with you.' He bought a hundred thousand dīnārs' worth of rich merchandise and gave them to his son, at the same time emptying into the saddlebags many treasures from his own presses. He presented him besides with a hundred thousand dīnārs in gold, with horses, camels, and mules, and sumptuous tents lined with many-coloured silks.

Tāj al-Mulūk kissed his father's hands, dressed himself for his journey, and went to find his mother; she gave him a hundred thousand dīnārs and wept much, calling down upon him the blessing of Allāh for the satisfaction of his soul and his safe return. The five hundred women of the palace also wept noisily about the prince's mother and then stood silent, regarding her with tender respect.

Leaving his mother, Tāj al-Mulūk sent for Azīz and the old wazīr, and gave the order for departure. Seeing that Azīz wept at this, he asked him the reason of his tears, and the youth replied: 'Brother, I feel that I can never be separated from you and yet it is a long time since I left my poor mother. When the caravan with which I departed reaches my country, what will she do?' 'Take no thought of that,' said the prince. 'You shall return home as soon as Allāh wills, after we have successfully concluded our adventure.'

The three set out and voyaged for many days. The wise wazīr distracted the two young men with excellent tales, and Azīz both recited and improvised charming verses on lovers and the pains of love. This was one of a thousand:

> You're going to laugh, my friends,
> To hear how loving ends
>   In second babyhood:
> Stretched on a golden rack,
> I cannot sleep for lack
>   Of white breasts and their food.

At the end of a month they arrived at the capital of the Isles of Camphor and Crystal. As they entered the great market, Tāj al-Mulūk felt the weight of his cares lighten within him and his heart beat joyously. On the advice of Azīz they dismounted at the great khān and hired for themselves all the shops on the ground floor and all the rooms above, until such time as the wazīr should obtain a house for them in the city. In the shops they disposed their bales of merchandise and, after resting for four days in the khān, went to visit the merchants of the chief silk market.

As they walked there, the wazīr said to the other two: 'Before we can attain our object there is one thing which we must do.' 'Tell us what that is,' they answered, 'for old men are fruitful in inspiration, especially when, like you, they have been trained in policy.' 'My idea is,' said the wazīr, 'that, instead of leaving all our goods shut up in the khān where no one can see them, we ought to open a large shop for you, my prince, in the silk market itself. You will stay at the entrance to show and sell your goods, while Azīz remains at the back of the shop to pass you the fabrics and unroll them. As you are exceedingly beautiful and Azīz is not less so, in a very short time your shop will be the most popular in the market.' 'That is an excellent idea,' said Tāj al-Mulūk and, dressed just as he was in his beautiful robe, he made his way to the silk market followed by Azīz, the wazīr, and all their slaves.

When the merchants saw Tāj al-Mulūk passing, they were stricken into inactivity by his beauty and ceased to attend to their customers. Those who were cutting silk stopped with their scissors in the air, those who were buying forgot their parcels. Some asked themselves: 'Has not the porter Ridwān, who holds the keys of the gardens of Paradise, forgotten to shut the gates? Has not this youth escaped that way?' Others exclaimed: 'Yā Allāh! we did not know that angels were so beautiful!'

The friends enquired where the chief merchant might be found, and went straight to his shop. Those who were sitting there rose in their honour, thinking: 'This venerable old man is the father of these beautiful youths.' The wazīr asked for the chief merchant and, on his being pointed out, saw a tall old man with a white beard, a dignified expression, and a smiling mouth. This personage hastened to do the honours of his shop with many cordial expressions of welcome; he bade them sit upon the carpet at his side, and said: 'I am ready to help you in any way I can.'

Then said the wazīr: 'Urbane chief merchant, for some years I have been travelling with these two boys through many cities and far countries, to teach them the diversity of peoples, to complete their education, and instruct them in the arts of buying, selling, and taking advantage of the various customs among which they find themselves. We have come to spend some time in this place, so that my children may rejoice in the beauty of your city and learn politeness from its inhabitants. We beg you, therefore, to let us some spacious and well-situated shop, where we may traffic in the goods of our own far country.'

'It will be a great pleasure to do this for you,' answered the chief merchant, and, so saying, he turned towards the two young men to see what they were like. A single glance at their beauty threw him into a measureless sea of confusion, for he openly and madly adored young men, preferring boys to girls and regaling himself with the sharp taste of immaturity.

Thinking to himself: 'Glory and praise to Him who created and moulded these exquisite creatures from lifeless dust!' he rose and, treating them as if he had been their slave, put himself entirely at their disposition. He showed them many shops and ended by choosing one for them right in the middle of the market. It was the fairest and best lighted of all; it had greater accommodation and was more advantageously situated than any; it was built in a gay and handsome style, with fronts of carved wood, and alternate shelves of ivory, ebony and crystal. The street outside was well swept and watered; the door was the one chosen by preference at night for the market guard to lean against. After payment had been made, the chief merchant gave the keys to the wazīr, saying: 'Allāh bless and prosper your shop from this white day! May the young men do well!'

The wazīr had all the merchandise, the silks and the brocades, and the inestimable treasures from the presses of Sulaimān Shāh, carried to the shop and carefully arranged there. When this work was over, he took the two young men with him to bathe in the hammām which stood near the great gate of the market. It was well known for its cleanliness, its shining marble, and the five steps which led up to it, on which the wooden clogs were ranged in order.

As the two friends took their bath quickly and were in great haste to reach their shop, they did not wait for the wazīr to finish his, but joyously left the building. The first person they met was the chief merchant, who was passionately waiting on the steps for them to come out.

At this point Shahrazād saw the approach of morning and discreetly fell silent.

But when the hundred-and-thirty-second night had come

SHE SAID:

The bath had given the last touch of perfection to their beauty and fresh colouring; the old man compared them in his soul with two fawns. He saw that the roses had come to full bloom in their cheeks, that midnight had returned upon their eyes, that they were like two slender branches covered with their fruit or two moons milky and sweet. He recalled these lines of the poet:

> Seeing that a simple pressure of the hand
> Can make the symbol of my senses stand,
> What if I saw your body, where unite
> The lure of water and the gold of light?

He went up to them and said: 'My children, I hope that you enjoyed your bath. May Allāh never take its benefit from you, but renew it eternally.' Tāj al-Mulūk answered in his most charming way: 'Would that we might have shared that pleasure with you.' The two young men pressed in respectfully about the old man and walked before him because of his age and rank, opening up a path and leading him towards their shop.

As they were going in front of him, he was able to see the beauty of their walking and the movement of their haunches below their robes. With shining eyes, unable to repress his transport, he sighed and snuffled and recited these doubtful lines:

> If I see their bottoms tremble
> Though of fine and solid flesh,
> The hot moons which they resemble
> Tremble in the night's blue mesh.

Though they heard these words the two youths were far from understanding the lechery of the chief merchant; rather they thought that he was but treating them with civility, and, being touched by the honour, they attempted to persuade him, as a mark of friendship, to accompany them to the bath again. The old man refused a little, for form's sake, and then accepted with his heart on fire.

When they entered, the wazīr, who was drying himself in one of the private apartments, saw them and came out to them as far as the central basin where they had paused. He warmly invited the chief merchant to enter his own apartment, but the old man excused himself, saying that this was too much honour. Then Tāj al-Mulūk and Azīz took him, each by a hand, and led him to their own apartment, while the wazīr retired to his.

As soon as they were alone, Azīz and Tāj al-Mulūk undressed the old man, after taking off their own clothes, and began to rub him energetically, while he cast furtive burning glances. Tāj al-Mulūk swore that to him should fall the honour of soaping and Azīz requested that for him should be reserved the honour of pouring water from the little copper basin. Between the two of them, the chief merchant thought that he had reached Paradise already.

They went on rubbing, soaping, and pouring water until the wazīr arrived, to the great dissatisfaction of the old man. They sponged him with warm napkins, then dried him with cool perfumed ones, and lastly, when they had dressed him, set him upon the dais and offered him musked sherberts with rose-water.

The old man pretended to take an interest in what the wazīr was saying, but in reality he had only eyes for the two youths, coming and going gracefully to serve him. When the wazīr made him those salutations which are usual after the bath, he answered: 'Your entry into our city is a blessing upon us, a blessing and a great pleasure!' and he recited this poem:

> They came. Our hills put on their green
> And the yellow flower of the sun did bloom again.
> 'Ah, goodbye pain,
> For frost is dead
> And the first violet seen,'
> We said.

The three thanked him for his urbanity, and he replied: 'May Allāh grant you the life you desire and preserve your beautiful children from the evil eye, O illustrious merchant!' 'And may, by Allāh's grace,' replied the merchant, 'your bath give you a double portion of health and strength. Is not water the true beatitude of life upon this earth? Is not the hammām the house of joy?' 'By Allāh, that is so!' returned the chief merchant. 'The bath has inspired some of our greatest poets to admirable lengths. Do you not know some of their compositions?'

Tāj al-Mulūk was the first to cry: 'Listen to this:

> Hammām of delicious bathing,
> Admirable, sense-defying;
> Silver vapour, scented plaything,
> Half to die and after dying
> Half to live in sleepy swathing,
> Hammām of delicious bathing.'

Then Azīz cried: 'I also know a poem about the hammām.' 'Rejoice our ears with it,' said the chief merchant, and Azīz rhythmically recited:

> Take from the lichened rocks their broideries
> And set them round delightful heat,
> With golden breasts and silver feet,
> That is the hammām bath complete;
> And of all sweet
> God's paradise devoider is.

As he made an end of his recitation, Azīz sat down beside Tāj al-Mulūk. The chief merchant marvelled at their talent and cried: 'As Allāh lives, you know how to combine beauty with eloquence. Let me, in my turn, say certain lines to you, or rather sing them; for the rhythms of our songs are made manifest in music.' He leaned his head on his hand, half shut his eyes, wagged his head a little, and sang:

> As the hammām fire renews
> Ageing heart and tired thews,
> I lie and love the kissing air,
> The brightness of the basins there,
> Falling water, falling light
> On the marble hard and white,
> Rooms of shadow filled with blue
> Wreaths of incense, driven through
> By a breeze which carries too
> All the sweet the furnace sends
> From the bodies of my friends.

> Eternal shade, eternal heat,
> There's analogy complete,
> Hammām, dark for all your fires,
> Of my soul and my desires.

Then the old man looked at the youths, allowed his soul to wander for a moment in the garden of their beauty and, thus inspired, recited these two stanzas:

> They welcomed me with silent smiling,
> They warmed me at their fire,
> I found their manners most beguiling
> At the hammām.
>
> Though none of them are my relations,
> They give all I require,
> Good company, sweet conversations,
> At the hammām.

After this song and recitation, they could not but be charmed at the old man's art; they thanked him with effusion and, as night was falling, accompanied him to the door of the hammām. He tried hard to persuade them to sup with him at his house, but they excused themselves and took their leave, while the old man stood still and looked after them.

They entered their rooms in the khān and, after eating and drinking, slept all night in perfect happiness. In the morning they rose and made ablution and prayer. Then, as soon as the market was open, they hastened to their shop and entered it for the first time.

The slaves had arranged the place with considerable taste, stretching out the silks to their best advantage and setting in convenient places two royal carpets worth a thousand dīnārs and two gold cushions worth a hundred. On the ivory, ebony, and crystal shelves the merchandise and kingly treasures were skilfully displayed.

Tāj al-Mulūk sat on one of the carpets, Azīz on the other, and the wazīr placed himself between the two in the exact centre of the shop; the slaves stood round, rivalling each other in the speed with which they fulfilled the least command of their masters.

Soon the people of the city heard of this admirable shop, and customers hurried to it from all parts, eager to receive their purchases from the hand of the young man Tāj al-Mulūk, the fame of whose beauty had turned every head. The wazīr saw that all was going very well, so he recommended great discretion to the two young men and went to repose himself at the khān.

Things went on in this way until Tāj al-Mulūk, seeing and hearing nothing of Princess Dunya, began to get impatient, and finally despaired so utterly that he lost all his sleep.

At this point Shahrazād saw the approach of morning and discreetly fell silent.

But when the hundred-and-thirty-third night had come

SHE SAID:

One day, however, as he was talking over his griefs with Azīz in the frcnt of the shop, an old woman passed through the market, most respectably dressed in a large black satin veil. Her attention was speedily attracted by the wonderful shop and the beauty of the young merchant who kept it; her emotion was so great that she straightway wetted her drawers. Looking earnestly at the young man, she said to herself: 'That is no mortal but an angel or some king of the countries of dream!' She came up to the shop and saluted Tāj al-Mulūk, who returned her greeting and, on a sign from Azīz, rose in her honour and smiled upon her most agreeably. He invited her to sit upon the carpet and, taking his place by her side, fanned her until she was well rested from the fatigue of her walk.

Then the old woman said to Tāj al-Mulūk: 'My child, my graceful and altogether perfect young man, do you belong to this country?' In his most winning voice, the prince answered: 'As Allāh lives, my mistress, I have never set foot in this place before. I have come on a visit of pleasure and only keep this shop as a way of passing the time.' 'Welcome to our city!' said the old woman. 'What fair merchandise have you brought with you? Let me see the most beautiful, for beauty can draw beauty.' Touched by her words, Tāj al-Mulūk smiled his thanks, saying: 'I have nothing in the shop save things which ought to please you, for they are worthy of kings' daughters and ladies such as yourself.' 'I wish to buy some very exquisite piece of stuff to make a robe for Princess Dunya, daughter of Shahrimān our King,' said the old woman.

Hearing the name of her he loved, Tāj al-Mulūk called to Azīz in a trembling voice: 'Bring me the fairest thing we have!' Azīz opened a cupboard constructed in the wall and took from it a single packet.

But what a packet! The outside wrapping was of damask velvet fringed with heavy nuts of gold, and lightly painted with designs of flowers and birds which had in their midst an elephant dancing abandonedly. The whole gave forth a soul-satisfying perfume. Azīz brought it to Tāj al-Mulūk, who unrolled it and took from it a length of material which had been woven with the intention that it should make a single-piece garment for some princess of fable or girl of Paradise. Only poets in their cadent verses could describe it to you; without its covering it was worth at least a hundred thousand dīnārs. Tāj al-Mulūk unrolled it slowly before the gaze of the old woman, who hardly knew whether to look at it or at the black eyes of him who offered it. The youthful charms of the merchant warmed her old flesh and compressed her thighs with fever, so that she would willingly have scratched between them there and then. When she could speak, she looked at Tāj al-Mulūk through eyes moist with passion, and said: 'It will do. How much do I owe you?' 'I am paid in meeting you,' he answered bowing, and she cried: 'Adorable boy, happy indeed will be the woman who lies in your lap and holds your body in her arms! But what woman could be worthy of you? I know but one. Tell me, young fawn, what name you are known by?' 'I am called Tāj al-Mulūk,' he replied, and the old woman exclaimed: 'But that is a name given only to the sons of kings!'

Azīz, who had so far said no word, now answered for his embarrassed friend: 'He is the only son of very loving parents, who wished to give him such a name as kings bear.' 'Indeed,' replied the old woman, 'if beauty herself were to choose a king, I think that his name would be Tāj al-Mulūk. This poor old woman is your slave for ever more, and Allāh is a witness of her devotion. I hope that you will soon find some way by which I can repay you. In the meanwhile Allāh protect you!' With that she took the precious packet and went her way.

The old woman, who had nursed the lady Dunya as a baby and stood to her in the place of a mother, came in to her, still excited by her recent encounter, and stood, holding the packet beneath her arm. When Dunya asked what it was, she unrolled the stuff suddenly, saying: 'Look!' Then the princess cried, with joyful eyes: 'How beautiful, how beautiful, good Dādāh! Surely it was never woven in this country?' 'It is, as you say, beautiful,' answered the old woman. 'I would like to hear what you would say if you saw the beauty of the young merchant who gives it to you. The Porter

Ridwān has forgotten to shut the gates of Eden, and one of the immortals has escaped to rejoice the liver of God's creatures. How I long to see that radiant young man asleep upon your breasts!' 'Enough, good nurse!' interrupted Dunya. 'What smoke has obscured your mind that you dare to speak to me of man? Be quiet, and give me the robe.' She took the stuff, caressed it with her fingers and draped it about her form, posturing before the nurse, who said to her: 'It makes you look very beautiful. But two is beauty, one is not. O Tāj al-Mulūk. . . !' 'You are bewitched, naughty Dādāh!' cried Dunya. 'Say no more, but go to the merchant and ask him to make some request, so that the King my father may recompense him for this robe.' The old woman burst out laughing and winked, saying: 'A request? I believe you! Which of us has not a request?' With that she rose up and ran to Tāj al-Mulūk's shop.

The Prince Tāj al-Mulūk saw her coming and his heart turned over in his breast for joy; he seated her by his side, and waited upon her with sherbert and jams. At last the old woman said: 'I bring you good news. My mistress salutes you with these words: "You have honoured our city in your coming and have illuminated it. If you have any request, make it." '

Tāj al-Mulūk rejoiced, taking great draughts of air into his breast, thinking that his object was already won. He said to the old woman: 'I have but one request: that you will take a letter to the lady Dunya and bring me back an answer.' Azīz brought Tāj al-Mulūk a copper writing set, and the prince wrote this letter in cadenced verse:

> I void my heart on this white page,
>   Things coloured of my heart,
> A golden thought of fires that rage,
>   A green thought hid apart,
> A crimson thought of villenage,
>   A purple thought of art,
> To weave a rainbow wish that says:
> 'Oh, let us meet! I count the hours as days!'

As a signature he wrote:

> Signed
> By the pined
> Love-dwined
> And grief-refined
>   Tāj al-Mulūk.

534

He read this letter over, sanded it, sealed it, and slipped it into the old woman's hand with a purse of a thousand dīnārs. The nurse hurried to her mistress, who said: 'Tell me, good Dādāh, what the young merchant wants and I will go to my father and beg it for him.' 'Indeed, I do not know what he wants,' answered Dādāh. 'He has sent a letter, but I am ignorant of what is in it.'

When Princess Dunya had read the letter, she cried: 'How does this audacious merchant lift his eyes so high? He should be hung at the gate of his own shop!' She beat her cheeks with her hands, and the old woman asked innocently: 'Does he ask too high a price?' 'Price?' said Dunya. 'He speaks of nothing but love and passion!' 'That is certainly very audacious of him,' said Dādāh. 'You ought to send him some sharp answer.' 'But will not that encourage him?' asked the princess. 'No, it will bring him to his senses,' returned Dādāh. Therefore the lady Dunya wrote these verses:

> You who have fought not, have not taken scars,
> Would feed your appetite,
> As if it were a thing of every night
> To reach the stars,
> To reach the silver maidens of the sky
> Whose shy virginity God made for ever.
> Try but once more to come at me,
> I swear to crucify
> The heart of that endeavour
> Upon an unblessed tree.

The old woman ran with this letter to Tāj al-Mulūk, who read it with a lengthening face, and said sadly to her: 'She threatens me with death; but I do not fear death when she makes life intolerable. I will answer her, even though I lose all.' 'By your dear life,' replied the dame, 'I will help you with all my might and share the risk with you. Write your letter and give it to me.' So Tāj al-Mulūk, calling to Azīz: 'Give our good mother a thousand dīnārs, and trust in God!' sat down and wrote the following lines:

> She lacks in skill who threatens death
> When longing ceases with the breath,
> She lacks in wisdom who debars
> A heart adventuring to the stars.

> Rather than let her triumph, we
> Will choose the dark for sanctuary,
> Rather than let her say: 'On earth
> Stays one who dared and was not worth,'
> We will set undesirous feet
> To tread down death with laughter,
> Since to that rash and dark retreat
> She cannot follow after.

He handed his letter to the old woman, saying: 'Do not run any unnecessary risk for yourself; I fear that nothing but death is left for me.' 'Banish such mournful thoughts and false presentiments,' answered Dādāh. 'Are you not like the sun? Is she not like the moon? Very well then. Do you think that I, who have spent all my life among love intrigues, am going to fail to unite such constellations? Be of good cheer; I will soon come back with joyful news.'

At this point Shahrazād saw the approach of morning and discreetly fell silent.

But when the hundred-and-thirty-fourth night had come

SHE SAID:

Dādāh hid the letter in her hair and, entering Dunya's apartment, kissed her hand in silence and sat down. In a few minutes she said: 'Dear child, my hair is all in disorder, and I am too tired to arrange it. I pray you send for one of your slaves that she may comb it for me.' 'Good Dādāh,' answered the princess, 'I will comb your hair myself, for you have often combed mine.' With that she took down the white tresses of her nurse and was spreading them for the comb when the letter fell out on the carpet.

Dunya wished to pick it up, but her nurse cried: 'Give me back that paper, my child. It must have fallen among my hair while I was in the young merchant's shop. I will return it to him.' But Dunya opened the paper and read its contents; her eyebrows rose, and she cried: 'This is one of your tricks, you wicked Dādāh! Who has sent this calamitous merchant to vex me? From what ill-omened country does he come? How can I ever look at a man whose country is not mine, who is of another blood from our people? Did I not tell you that my answer would embolden him?' 'Indeed,' answered the cunning nurse, 'he is a very Satan; his audacity comes straight from

Hell. And yet, my child, I would suggest that you write him a final letter. I myself will guarantee that he becomes submissive. If he does not, let him perish, and let me perish with him.' Princess Dunya took her pen and marshalled these words rhythmically:

> There are hidden streams whose courses
>   No one forces,
> Places hidden in the snows
>   No one knows,
> Pastured stars whose silver beaches
>   No one reaches,
> Hūrīs for the dead to tumble
>   None may fumble;
> And the black crows make a tomb,
>   Fifty flying graves of gloom,
>   To engulf no matter whom.

She gave this letter to old Dādāh, who ran with it to Tāj al-Mulūk on the following morning.

Tāj al-Mulūk read the hard words of the letter and understood that hope had no further excuse for staying lighted in his heart. Turning to Azīz, he said: 'Tell me what to do now, my brother, for I have no inspiration left with which to send her a final answer.' 'Let me write in your name,' said Azīz. 'Do so, and be as trenchant as you can,' returned Tāj al-Mulūk. So Azīz took a paper and composed these lines:

> I am safer with Allāh,
> For though he regards me not,
> The black-eyed disdainful one
> He also regards not.
> Foolish girl,
> Would you set yourself against God?
> I left my home for you,
> But there is One who can deny you a home for ever.
> Look to it, therefore.

Tāj al-Mulūk read over these verses when Azīz had written them and, finding them excellent, gave them to the old woman, who forthwith departed.

The anger of the princess burned hot against her nurse when she had read this last letter. 'Wicked nurse!' she cried. 'Calamitous

Dādāh! It is you who have brought all these humiliations upon me. I never wish to see your ill-omened face again! If you do not depart at once, my slaves shall cut your body into strips with their lashes and I will break your bones under my heels!' The old nurse ran out precipitately and hastened to confide her news and herself to the two friends.

Tāj al-Mulūk was overcome with grief; he touched the old woman gently upon the chin, saying: 'As Allāh lives, my mother, my sorrows are doubled that you should have come into this pass because of me.' 'Do not be anxious, my son,' she replied, 'I have by no means given up hope. It shall never be said that I could not bring two lovers together when I set my mind to it. The greater the difficulty, the more my cunning; we shall win through yet.' 'Can you tell me,' asked Tāj al-Mulūk, 'what caused the lady Dunya's horror of men?' 'It was a dream she had,' answered the old woman. 'Only a dream!' cried Tāj al-Mulūk. 'Only a dream,' said Dādāh. 'Now listen:

'One night, as Princess Dunya slept, she saw a fowler spreading his nets in a clearing of the woods. When he had sprinkled grains of corn about them on the earth, he hid himself and waited.

'Soon birds flew from every quarter of the forest and alighted among the nets. With them were two pigeons, a male and a female, who pecked the corn. As the male fed, he moved in circles about the female without taking any care to avoid the toils; at last one of his feet was taken in a mesh, which tangled about it and imprisoned all his body. The rest of the birds, frightened by the beating of his wings, flew away.

'But the female had no other thought than to deliver her lover. With head and beak she worked so quickly and so well that she cut through the net and freed the foolish male before the fowler had time to come forward and take it. They flew away together and, after circling the air for some time, lit again among the nets to eat the corn.

'As before the male began to wheel round the female, so that she was compelled to back away from his advances; in doing so she also got taken in the nets. The male flew away without a thought for his mistress, and the fowler came and cut her throat.

'Princess Dunya woke in tears from this dream and told it to me in a trembling voice. She said in conclusion: "All males are alike, and men are worse than animals. A woman need hope nothing from their eternal selfishness. I swear before Allāh that I will never submit to the abomination of their approach!" '

'But, my mother,' said the prince to the old nurse, 'did you not tell her that all men are not like that traitorous pigeon, and that many women are quite unlike his virtuous mate?' 'Nothing would alter her opinion,' answered Dādāh. 'She lives alone, adoring her own beauty.' 'You must help me to see her just once, even if I die for it,' answered Tāj al-Mulūk. 'Do that for me out of the abundance of your cleverness, and I will bless your name for ever.'

'Light of my eyes,' said Dādāh, 'there is a garden at the back of the palace where the princess lives. It is reserved for her, and she goes there once a month by a little secret door. In a week from to-day the time will have come for her to walk there. I myself will guide you to the place and bring you into her presence. I am certain that, once she has seen you, none of her prejudices will be able to stand out against your beauty: for love is a gift from Allāh and comes when it pleases Him.'

Tāj al-Mulūk breathed a little more easily at this intelligence. He thanked the old woman and begged her to accept their hospitality. Then he shut the shop, and all three returned to the lodgings in the khān. As they walked, Tāj al-Mulūk said to Azīz: 'My brother, I will have no more leisure to go down to the shop. Therefore I give it up to you. Do as you will with it.'

They came to the khān and hastened to tell the wazīr all that had happened, informing him of the princess's dream and of their plan for meeting her in the garden.

The wazīr reflected for some time and then said: 'I have found the solution. Let us go to this garden and learn our way about it.' Leaving the old woman in the khān, he walked with Tāj al-Mulūk and Azīz towards the princess's garden. When they came near, they saw the old gardener sitting by the door. He greeted them, and the wazīr slipped a hundred dīnārs into his hand, saying: 'Good uncle, we wish to refresh ourselves in this beautiful garden, and eat a little by the flowers and water. We are strangers who are always on the look out for beautiful places in which to enjoy ourselves.' The old man took the money, saying: 'Enter, dear guests, and take your ease, while I run to buy some food from the market.' He led them into the garden and then left them, returning in a very short time with a roast sheep and a quantity of pastries. They all sat down in a circle beside a little stream and ate their fill. Then said the wazīr to the gardener: 'Old man, that palace in front of us seems very dilapidated. Why do you not have it repaired?' 'By Allāh,' answered

the gardener, 'it belongs to Princess Dunya. She would let it tumble
to pieces rather than occupy it. She lives too far retired to pay attention to such details.' 'That is a pity, good uncle,' said the wazīr, 'the
ground floor, at least, ought to be whitened up a little, if only for
your sake. If you like I will pay the cost of the repairs myself.' 'May
Allāh hear you!' said the delighted gardener. The wazīr continued:
'Take these further hundred dīnārs for your trouble and fetch us
some masons and a skilled painter with an eye for colour.'

It was not long before the gardener brought the masons and the
painter who, under the direction of the wazīr, repaired and whitened
the great hall of the ground floor. Then the painter set to work and
devised a forest scene: there was a glade in the centre having bird-
nets in which a pigeon fluttered and could not escape. When this was
finished, the wazīr said: 'Now paint the same thing on the other side,
but show also a male pigeon delivering his mate and captured at
the same time by the fowler. Let him fall a victim to his devotion.'
The painter executed this second picture and departed with a large
reward.

The wazīr, the two young men and the gardener sat down to
judge the effect and tone of the pictures. But Tāj al-Mulūk was still
sad. He examined the scenes in a dreamy fashion, and then said to
Azīz: 'My brother, recite me some more verses to divert the bitterness of my thoughts.' Straightway Azīz said:

> Ibn Sīnā in his book of cure
> Says: 'Children, know that this is sure:
> Love can be cured by constant song
> And wine the garden side along.'
> I took the doctor's sure advice
> And came no nearer paradise;
> Therefore I set myself to try
> A leaf from my own pharmacy,
> And in a hundred sleepless nights
> Assuaged as many appetites.
> Sīnā was wrong, for I can prove
> Love is the only cure for love.

'Perhaps the poet was right,' said Tāj al-Mulūk, 'but it is a difficult
matter when the will for such a cure is lacking.' After this the three
said goodbye to the gardener and returned to their lodgings to speak
with the old nurse.

When the week had passed, the lady Dunya wished to take her usual walk in the garden, but she felt the lack of her old nurse and began to think that she had been inhuman to one who stood to her in the place of a mother. She sent a slave to the market and another slave to all the acquaintances of Dādāh to find her and bring her back. Now the nurse, after telling Tāj al-Mulūk where to meet her in the garden, had started to walk towards the palace; therefore one of the slaves met her and respectfully begged her to return to her mistress. After a little feigned reluctance, Dādāh ran to Dunya, who kissed her upon the cheeks. Then both of them, followed by a group of slaves, went through the small secret door into the garden.

After Dādāh had left them, the wazīr and Azīz dressed Tāj al-Mulūk in a robe of royal magnificence, worth five thousand dīnārs, and fastened his waist with a belt of wrought gold clasped with an emerald clasp. They put a turban of white silk upon his head, with gold pictures on it and a diamond spray. Then they called down the blessings of Allāh upon him and led him to within sight of the garden, themselves returning so that he might enter the more easily.

Tāj al-Mulūk found the good old gardener at the door and greeted him cordially. The gardener answered his salute with great respect and, as he did not know that the princess had entered the garden by the secret door, said to the young man: 'The garden is yours and I am your slave.' He opened the door, let the prince pass through, and shut it again. Afterwards he sat down in his accustomed place, thanking Allāh for the diversity of His creatures.

Tāj al-Mulūk hid himself behind a certain cluster of flowers which the old woman had described to him, and set himself to wait until she should pass.

As they walked, the old woman said to Dunya: 'Mistress, I have something to tell you which will heighten your delight in these fair trees, sweet fruits, and shining flowers.' 'I am ready to listen to you, my good Dādāh,' answered Dunya, and the old woman continued: 'First you should send back all these slaves to the palace; they are only in the way and prevent your full enjoyment of their pleasant air.' 'What you say is true, dear nurse,' replied Dunya, and forthwith dismissed her slaves. Thus she was alone with the old woman as she advanced towards the cluster of flowers behind which Tāj al-Mulūk hid.

So Tāj al-Mulūk saw Princess Dunya and learned to know her beauty, and fainted away in the place where he sat concealed. Dunya walked on and drew near the hall where the wazīr had had the pictures of the fowler painted. At Dādāh's suggestion, she entered it for the first time: never before had she been curious to visit a place reserved for her servants.

The double picture perplexed her a great deal, and she cried: 'Look, Dādāh! There is my dream in opposite! As Allāh lives, it has a strange effect upon me!' Holding her heart with her hand, she sank down upon a carpet and continued: 'Was I mistaken? Was the Evil One laughing at my faith in dreams?' 'My poor child,' answered her nurse, 'I told you of your error long ago. But let us return to the garden and walk again; the sun is setting and the sweetest air of all the day is abroad.' So they went forth.

Now Tāj al-Mulūk had come out of his swoon and was walking slowly in the garden, as Dādāh had advised him, seemingly absorbed in the beauty of the flowers. At the corner of an alley the lady Dunyā saw him and cried: 'O nurse, do you see that young man? Is he not beautiful? How wonderful are his figure and the way he walks. Tell me, do you know him?' 'I do not know him,' answered Dādāh, 'but I should judge from his appearance that he is the son of some king. Ah, ah, my mistress, he is indeed marvellous! Marvellous, upon my soul!' 'His beauty is perfect!' murmured the princess. 'Happy his lover!' ventured Dādāh, and at the same time signed to Tāj al-Mulūk to leave the garden. The prince understood her and walked on towards the gate, while Dunyā followed with her eyes, saying: 'Dādāh, do you feel at all the strange feeling which I feel? Is it possible that I can be troubled by the sight of a man? O nurse, I know that I am taken and, after all these years, shall need a cast of your office!' 'Allāh confound the wicked tempter!' said the nurse. 'Yes, you are taken in the nets, my mistress, but the pigeon who shall free you is handsome enough.' Then said Dunyā: 'Dādāh, my good Dādāh, you must bring this young man to me. I would not wish him at any other hands than yours, my dearest nurse. Run quickly and look for him; you shall have a thousand dīnārs and a robe worth a thousand. If you refuse, I die.' 'Return to the palace, my child,' said the nurse, 'and let me go about this thing in my own way. I promise that the charming union shall take place.'

She left the princess and went to where Tāj al-Mulūk had waited for her; when she told him all that had passed he greeted her joyfully and gave her a thousand dīnārs. Hearing of Dunyā's emotion and what she had said, he eagerly asked when they might come together, and Dādāh replied: 'To-morrow without fail.' The prince then gave her a robe and other presents worth a thousand dīnārs in all, which she joyfully accepted, saying: 'I will come to fetch you myself to-morrow at whatever hour seems favourable to me.'

The old woman hurried off and told her expectant mistress that she had been able to discover the young man and even speak to him. 'To-morrow I will lead him by the hand to you,' she said. The princess was overjoyed and gave her nurse a thousand dīnārs and presents worth a further thousand. That night the three people concerned in this adventure slept a sleep calmed with contentment and hope.

With the first light of morning the old woman came to Tāj al-Mulūk's lodging and there undid a packet containing a woman's clothes. She dressed the prince as a young girl and then wrapped him completely in a great izār, covering his face with a thick veil. 'You must walk as women walk, with little steps and swaying your hips from left to right,' she said. 'Let me answer any questions that may be addressed to us, and do not speak whatever happens.'

The two set out together and came to the gate of the palace, which was guarded by the chief eunuch in person. Seeing a stranger, he said to the old woman: 'Who is this unknown creature? Bring her here, and I will examine her. The rules are strict and I have every right to feel and even to undress anyone I do not know. Let me feel her with my hand and see her with my eyes.'

At this point Shahrazād saw the approach of morning and discreetly fell silent.

But when the hundred-and-thirty-fifth night had come

SHE SAID:

The old woman cried out: 'What are you saying? Do you not know that our mistress Dunya has herself sent for this excellent needlewoman? Do you not know that she is an expert in the art of designing upon silk?' Nevertheless the eunuch scowled, saying: 'I know nothing of designs on silk. I must feel this stranger and examine her all over.'

The old nurse seemed to fly into a great passion at these words: she stood stoutly before the eunuch, saying: 'To think that I ever took you for a model of politeness! What has happened to you all of a sudden? Do you want me to get you dismissed from the palace?'

Then, turning to Tāj al-Mulūk, she continued: 'Excuse our chief eunuch, my child; he is only joking. Pass without fear.'

Tāj al-Mulūk went through the door, moving his hips and sending through his veil a smile which turned the chief eunuch to desirous stone. The old woman led him through a corridor, through a gallery, then through other corridors and other galleries, until they came, at the end of the seventh gallery, to a hall which gave upon a large court by six curtained doors. 'Count the doors one after the other and enter by the seventh,' said the old woman. 'There you will find something surpassing all the treasures of the earth, the virgin flower, the sweet young body which is called Dunya.'

Tāj al-Mulūk counted the doors and entered by the seventh; he let the curtain fall behind him and lowered the veil which hid his face. The lady Dunya was sleeping upon the couch, dressed only in the transparent jasmine of her flesh. Silent calls for unguessed kisses emanated from the whole length of her. In one movement Tāj al-Mulūk slipped off his clothes and, leaping lithe as a deer upon the couch, took the sleeping princess in his arms. Her startled cry was smothered by his lips. Thus came together for the first time the fair Prince Tāj al-Mulūk and the lovely lady Dunya in a confusion of thighs and trembling limbs. For a whole month they did not leave their burning kisses or that laughter which is the gift of Him who has made all things beautiful.

The wazīr and Azīz waited all that night for the return of Tāj al-Mulūk, and when he did not come began to be seriously disquieted. Morning brought no news of their friend, so that they gave him up for lost and were thrown into a turmoil of perplexity and grief. Said Azīz in a tearful voice: 'The palace gates will never again open for our master. What must we do now?' 'We must stay here,' answered the wazīr. So they stayed a whole month, filling the place of food and sleep with lamentation. When the month was over without a sign of Tāj al-Mulūk, the wazīr said: 'My child, we are in a very sad and difficult position. I think that our best plan will be to return to our own country and tell the King of this misfortune. If we do not do so, he may blame us for keeping him in ignorance.' Without further delay they made their preparations and left for Green City.

As soon as they arrived, they hastened to the palace of King Sulaimān Shāh and told him of the lamentable ending to their adventure. Then they stood before him, sobbing silently.

The King felt the earth cracking beneath his feet; he gave a loud cry and fell unconscious to the floor. But of what use are swoons and tears and lamentations? The King controlled the grief which fed upon his marrow and blackened his soul, and swore to take such vengeance for his son as had not been seen upon the earth before. He called to him, by public crier, each man in his kingdom who could hold lance or sword; he brought forth his engines of war, his tents and his elephants; followed by the mighty army of those who loved him for his generosity and justice, he set out for the Isles of Camphor and Crystal.

Meanwhile Dunya's apartment in the palace was lighted by the happiness of the two lovers; for six months they only rose from the carpets of the couch to eat and drink and sing. One day, when love had ravished his soul beyond the ordinary, Tāj al-Mulūk said to Dunya: 'Saviour of my heart, there is one thing lacking to the perfection of our love.' 'Light of my eyes, what further thing could you wish?' she asked in astonishment. 'Are not my lips and my breasts and my thighs all yours, my arms which hold you and my soul which adores you? Are there yet some practices of love which I do not know? Tell me, then, and you shall see that I can do them well enough.' 'My lamb,' replied Tāj al-Mulūk, 'it has nothing to do with the manner of our loving. Let me tell you who I am. Dear princess, I am myself a king's son and not a merchant. My father's name is Sulaimān Shāh, monarch of Green City and the Mountains of Isfahān. It was he who sent his wazīr not long ago to ask your hand in marriage for me. Do you remember that you refused and menaced the chief eunuch with a mace? Now that what you decided against has come to pass, let us both journey to verdant Isfahān together.'

Dunya threw her arms gladly about her lover's neck, giving many signs of her readiness to go with him. For ten months the white of morning had surprised them at their kisses, but that night they slept.

They were still sleeping when the sun was high and the rest of the palace awake. King Shahrimān, seated among the cushions of his throne, surrounded by the amīrs and notables of his kingdom, was receiving the homage of the corporation of jewellers. The chief jeweller offered the King an incredible box, holding more than a hundred thousand dīnārs' worth of diamonds, rubies and emeralds. The King was satisfied with the gift and called his chief eunuch, saying: 'O Kāfūr, take this box to your mistress and return to tell us if the gift pleases her.' So Kāfūr made his way to the private pavilion of the princess.

He found the nurse Dādāh stretched on a carpet before the door of her mistress's room, while the entrances of the pavilion were shut and the curtains lowered. He thought to himself: 'How is it they sleep so late? It is not their custom.' Not wishing to return to the King without an answer, he stepped over the body of the old woman and, pushing open the door, entered the apartment. His eyes started from his head when he saw the lady Dunya lying naked in the arms of a young man, and both bodies showing urgent signs of more than ordinary fornication.

Kāfūr remembered his rough treatment at the hands of Dunya, and said in his eunuch's soul: 'Is this how she hates men? I think that my time has come for vengeance.' He left the place softly, closing the door behind him, and returned to King Shahrimān, who asked him what his mistress had said. 'Here is the box,' answered the eunuch, and the astonished King cried: 'Does not my daughter care any more for jewels than for husbands?' 'My lord, excuse me from answering before all these people,' answered the eunuch, so the King emptied his throne room of all save his wazīr and commanded the eunuch to explain. Said Kāfūr: 'I found my lady in such and such a position. But of a truth the young man is very beautiful.' The King beat his hands together and opened wide his eyes, crying: 'The thing is incredible! You say you saw them, Kāfūr?' 'With this eye and with this eye,' answered the eunuch. 'It is altogether monstrous!' cried the King, and bade the negro bring the guilty pair into his presence.

When the two lovers stood before him, he cried: 'It is true!' in a suffocated voice and, seizing his great sword, would have thrown himself upon Tāj al-Mulūk. But Dunya protected the prince with her arms and, pressing her lips to his, cried to her father: 'Kill both of us!' The King therefore returned to his throne and ordered the eunuch to take the princess back to her own palace. When this had been done, he questioned Tāj al-Mulūk in these words: 'Corrupt miscreant, who are you? Who is your father? How did you reach my daughter's palace?' 'O King,' returned Tāj al-Mulūk, 'if you desire my death, I warn you that your own will follow soon after and that your kingdom will be utterly destroyed.' 'How is that?' cried Shahrimān, beside himself with rage, and the other answered: 'I am the son of King Sulaimān Shāh. I have seized what was refused me, as it was written that I should. Take thought, therefore, O King, before you harm me.'

The King was perplexed when he heard this and did not know how to act, so he consulted his wazīr, who said: 'Do not believe the lies of this impostor. Death is the only punishment for such a son of a bitch. Allāh curse him!' Therefore the King said to his executioner: 'Cut off this man's head!'

At this point Shahrazād saw the approach of morning and discreetly fell silent.

But when the hundred-and-thirty-sixth night had come

SHE SAID:

It would have been all over with Tāj al-Mulūk if, at that very moment, two envoys had not been announced from King Sulaimān Shāh. These were none other than Azīz and the wazīr, who had come ahead of the King and his army. When they recognised their prince, they well-nigh fainted for joy and threw themselves at his feet. Tāj al-Mulūk made them rise and kissed them, telling them in a few words the danger in which he stood. They told him of the coming of the army, in full force and with Sulaimān Shāh at its head, and announced the same to King Shahrimān.

King Shahrimān understood the danger which he had run in nearly causing the death of young Tāj al-Mulūk; he lifted his arms and thanked Allāh for having stayed the hand of the executioner. Then to Tāj al-Mulūk he said: 'My son, excuse an old man who does not always know how to act for the best. It was all the fault of this ill-omened wazīr. I will have him impaled at once.' Tāj al-Mulūk kissed his hand, saying: 'You are a second father to me, O King. Therefore I beg you to pardon me the emotion which I caused you.' 'It is all the fault of this miserable eunuch,' said the King. 'I will have him crucified at once, on a rotten plank not worth two dirhams.' 'I think you are right about the eunuch,' said Tāj al-Mulūk, 'but I pray you pardon the wazīr till his next offence.' Following the prince's lead, Azīz and the wazīr of Sulaimān Shāh interceded and obtained pardon for the eunuch Kāfūr, who stood pissing his garments with terror. Then said Tāj al-Mulūk; 'The first thing that we have to do is to allay the fear of your daughter, who is my whole soul to me.' 'I will go to her myself,' said the King. First he ordered his amīrs, his wazīrs and his chamberlains to escort Prince Tāj al-Mulūk to the hammām and to bathe with him; then he ran to Dunya's pavilion, where he found his daughter about to fall upon a sword, the hilt of which she had rested on the ground. 'He is safe!' cried the King. 'Have pity on your poor old father, my child.' Hearing this Dunya threw the sword far from her and kissed her father's hands, while he told her what had happened. Then she said: 'I will not be at ease until I have seen my dear love.' By this time Tāj al-Mulūk had returned from the bath. The King hastened to bring him to Dunya, who threw herself upon his neck. While they were kissing, the King discreetly shut the door upon them and returned to his palace to give the necessary orders for the reception of King Sulaimān Shāh. He sent Azīz and the wazīr in haste to tell the happy tidings to the advancing King, and at the same time took care to despatch this present: a hundred each of splendid horses, racing dromedaries, boys, young girls, negroes and negresses.

Then King Shahrimān himself went out to meet Sulaimān Shāh, taking Prince Tāj al-Mulūk with him. When the monarch of Green City saw them approaching with a vast retinue, he cried: 'Glory be to Allāh who has brought my son to his desire!' The two Kings embraced, and then Tāj al-Mulūk threw himself upon his father's neck, weeping for joy. The three sat down to eat and drink and talk in the most perfect accord, while the kādīs and their witnesses were sent for and a marriage contract written upon the spot for Tāj al-Mulūk and the lady Dunya. Money presents were given to the soldiers and the people, and for forty days and nights the city was decorated and lighted with coloured lights. Amid the joy and the feasting, Tāj al-Mulūk and Dunya could at last openly indulge their love to the height of their imaginations.

Tāj al-Mulūk did not forget the good services of his friend Azīz. He sent him with a convoy to fetch his mother, who had long been mourning for him. After the death of Sulaimān Shāh, when the prince had himself become King of Green City and the Mountains of Isfahān, he made Azīz his wazīr. He also made the old gardener intendant general of the kingdom, and the chief merchant the supreme general of all the corporations. Those concerned in this tale lived in great happiness until death took them. Death is the one ill for which there is no antidote.

When the wazīr Dandān had finished this tale of Azīz and Azīzah, of Tāj al-Mulūk and Dunya, he asked Dū al-Makān's leave to drink a glass of syrup of roses. 'O wazīr,' cried the King, 'there is no one on earth as worthy as you are to hold company with kings and princes! Your tale has been delightfully told and has pleased me very much.' With that he gave Dandān the most beautiful robe of honour which he had at hand.

The siege of Constantinople. . . .

At this point Shahrazād saw the approach of morning and discreetly fell silent.

But when the hundred-and-thirty-seventh night had come

SHE SAID:

The siege of Constantinople had already dragged on for four years without a decisive result; the soldiers and their officers were suffering very greatly from their exile, and rebellion seemed imminent.

King Dū al-Makān acted with decision; he called the three chiefs, Bahrmān, Rustam and Turkāsh, and said to them in the presence of Dandān: 'You have yourselves seen how we are situated, the fatigue which weighs upon us all because of this unfortunate siege, and the terrible scourges which old Mother-of-Calamity has inflicted upon us, beginning with the death of my brother Sharkān. Take time to consider and then tell me what ought to be done.' The three bowed their heads and thought for a long while before they said: 'O King, the wazīr Dandān has more experience than us all; he has grown old in wisdom.' So Dū al-Makān turned towards Dandān and said: 'We wait upon your words.'

Dandān advanced before the King, saying: 'Monarch of all time, nothing but harm can come from our continuing beneath the walls of Constantinople. You are yourself desirous of seeing your young son Kāna mā kāna, and your niece Power-of-Destiny who is with the women in the palace at Damascus, and all of us are grieving for our country and our own houses. My advice is that we return to Baghdād and come back on some future occasion to raze this wicked city to the ground and leave it for the crows and vultures.' 'You have answered as I would have answered myself,' said the King, and immediately had criers announce throughout the camp that the army would return home in three days.

On the third day the whole force left their camping ground, with trumpets sounding and flags waving, and took the backward road towards Baghdād. After many days and nights they reached the City

of Peace and were welcomed with transports of joy by the inhabitants.

The first thing which Dū al-Makān did was to visit and kiss Kāna
mā kāna who was now seven years of age, and his second thought
was to send for his old friend the fireman of the hammām. When
he saw him, he left his throne and embraced him, causing him to sit
by his side and making much of him before his amīrs and all the
court. After this long time the fireman was hard to recognise, for,
by eating, drinking, and living in happy repose, he had become as
fat as it is possible to be. His neck was like the neck of an elephant,
his belly like the belly of a whale, and his face shone like a round loaf
as it comes from the oven.

At first he objected to sitting by the King and said: 'My master,
may Allāh preserve me from such a liberty! The days have long since
passed when it was permissible for me to sit down in your presence.'
'Those days have begun again, my father, my saviour,' answered
the King, and pulled the fireman down upon the great bed of the
throne.

Then said Dū al-Makān: 'I wish you to ask some favour of me,
for I am ready to grant it, even to the half of my kingdom. Speak and
Allāh will hear you.' 'There is something which I would like to ask,
but I fear it would be indiscreet,' answered the old fireman. The King
became sorrowful and said: 'I command you to speak.' So the fireman ventured: 'Since I must, I wish very much that you would give
me a patent making me general president of all the firemen in all the
hammāms of Jerusalem.' At these words the King and the court
laughed immoderately, and the poor fireman thought that he had
asked too much and became very sad. 'As Allāh lives, ask me something else!' cried the King, and the wazīr Dandān also quietly
approached the fireman, pinching his leg and winking at him as much
as to say: 'Ask something else!' Then said the fireman: 'O King of
time, I am very anxious to be named sheikh of the corporation of
scavengers in Jerusalem.' This time the King and all who were with
him laughed till their legs flew up in the air. At last the King said:
'Come, my brother, I want you to ask me something which is worth
while, something on a level with your deserts.' 'But I am afraid you
could not grant it,' murmured the fireman, and the King exclaimed:
'Nothing is impossible to Allāh!' 'Well then,' cried the fireman,
astonished at his own daring, 'make me Sultān of Damascus in the
place of Prince Sharkān.' 'Be it so,' answered the King, and straight-

way wrote out the patent of the fireman, giving him in his new position the name of Zibl Kān al-Mujāhid. He bade the wazīr Dandān accompany the new King to Damascus with a magnificent following and then to return, bringing with him Power-of-Destiny, his dead brother's little daughter. He took leave of the fireman with a kiss, recommending him to deal justly by his new subjects; then to all who were present he said: 'Let those who would win my regard express their love for Sultān Zibl Kān by means of gifts.' Presents were showered upon the new King and Dū al-Makān himself dressed him in the royal robe and decreed for him, as a special guard by the way, five thousand young mamlūks and a multitude of porters to carry the red and gold palanquin of his kingship. Thus did the fireman become Sultān Zibl Kān al-Mujāhid and journey to Damascus with the wazīr Dandān and the amīrs Rustam, Turkāsh and Bahrmān.

The first care of the new Sultān was to arrange a splendid company to take the eight-year-old princess to Baghdād. He gave her ten young girls and ten negro lads for her own service, and heaped gifts upon her. These gifts consisted primarily of pure rose essence and apricot conserve sealed in great boxes against the damp, but there were also delicious interlaced pastries, so fragile that they were hardly likely to reach Baghdād in safety; twenty huge pots filled with crystallised dates in a syrup of cloves, and twenty chests of chosen sweetmeats ordered especially from the most cunning artists in Damascus. These things were loaded upon forty camels, together with large bales of silks and golden fabrics, with precious weapons and copper vessels damascened with gold.

The Sultān Zibl Kān also wanted to make a great present of silver to the wazīr Dandān, but the latter would not accept it, saying: 'O King, you are but newly set upon your throne and have better need of your money.' The caravan set out and came in a month by easy stages to Baghdād.

Dū al-Makān received young Power-of-Destiny with every manifestation of joy and gave her into the care of her delighted mother, Nuzhat, and of the chamberlain. He appointed the same teachers for her as for Kāna mā kāna, so that the two children became inseparable and loved with a love which increased as they grew older. Thus eight years passed away while King Dū al-Makān busied himself about the armaments which should resume the war against the perfidious Christians.

But, because of the fatigues and privations of his lost youth, King

Dū al-Makān daily diminished in strength and well-being. As his condition became worse, he called his wazīr Dandān, saying: 'O wazīr, I have a project which I wish to realise. Tell me strictly what you think of it. I have resolved to abdicate during my lifetime and to set my son Kāna mā kāna on the throne in my stead, so that I may rejoice to see his glorious reign before I die. Tell me what you think of this, O wazīr whose soul is steeped in wisdom.'

The wazīr Dandān kissed the earth between the King's hands, saying in a voice which quivered from emotion: 'Auspicious King, prudent and equitable Sultān, your project is neither profitable nor possible. For one thing, Prince Kāna mā kāna is much too young, and for another, it is certain that he who names his son to reign in his stead while he is yet alive, numbers his own days.' 'As for my life,' replied the King, 'I feel that that is over. As for the youth of my son, I will make the chamberlain, who is the husband of my sister Nuzhat, tutor to Kāna mā kāna as he reigns.'

The King called his amīrs and wazīrs and all the great ones of his kingdom and in their presence nominated the chamberlain as official adviser to his son, Kāna mā kāna, strictly commanding him to marry the young prince to Power-of-Destiny when they should reach a suitable age. 'I am overcome with honours and lost in the greatness of your generosity,' said the chamberlain. Then Dū al-Makān turned towards his son, weeping and saying: 'Dear child, when I am dead, the chamberlain will be your guide and counsel, but the wazīr Dandān will be your father in my place. I feel that I am about to journey from this unsubstantial world to a home which shall not pass away. Before I go I wish to hand on to you the one desire which yet remains in me, to take vengeance for the death of your grandfather, Umar al-Numān, and for your uncle, Sharkān, upon that evil and terrible old woman who is called Mother-of-Calamity.' 'Let your heart be at peace on that score, my father,' replied young Kāna mā kāna. 'Allāh will avenge you through my right arm.' Thereupon King Dū al-Makān felt a great peace descend upon his soul and he stretched himself contentedly upon that couch from which he was not to arise.

Not long afterwards King Dū al-Makān became, as every creature must, dust within the Hand which created him, and it was as if he had never been. For time reaps all and does not remember.

At this point Shahrazād saw the approach of morning and discreetly fell silent.

But when the hundred-and-thirty-eighth night had come

SHE SAID:

Time reaps all and does not remember; therefore let him who would know the fate which will befall his name in time to come, guard the fame of those who have passed before him into the room of death.

That is the tale of King Dū al-Makān, son of King Umar al-Numān, and brother of Prince Sharκān—may Allāh keep the three of them in His infinite mercy!

But to prove that the proverb does not lie which says: 'He who leaves children behind him does not die,' I will begin:

The Adventures of Young Kāna mā Kāna, son of Dū al-Makān

YOUNG Kāna mā kāna and his cousin Power-of-Destiny, yā Allāh! how beautiful they became! They grew in a harmony of fairness and early blossomed to perfection; they might be compared only to two boughs bearing remarkable fruit on one tree, or two moons shining in the same empty space. Power-of-Destiny had in her own person all that may make people mad. Beyond the reach of curious eyes in her royal solitude, her colouring had reached an excellent whiteness, her waist had become as slim as the letter alif, and her hips worthy of worship for their great heaviness. The water of her mouth. O milk! O wines! O sugar! where are you all? I can say nothing of her lips, which were pomegranate-coloured, but ripe fruit might tell you of them. Sad roses might inform you wistfully of her cheeks. A poet truly said of her:

> Get drunk, my heart, go mad, my eyes,
> For she was made in paradise,
> And is too good for paradise.
>
> No costly paint of kohl has shown
> Lids of so languishing a brown,
> The brownest eyelids ever known,
> So often seen, but never known.

The mild ripe grapes before they're pressed
Weep tears of sunny wine to rest
On their red skins, but it were best
To taste the wine her lips expressed
When 'But I love you' they expressed.

The palm-trees we discover where
Life is a dust and the sand bare,
Making a lonely shadow there,
Tall palm-trees loosing to the air
Their dark green fans: such is her hair,
The dim palm shadows of her hair.

Such was the young princess Power-of-Destiny, daughter of
Nuzhat. With Kāna mā kāna it was different. Hunting and riding,
tilting with the lance and javelin, shooting with the bow, and racing
on horseback had suppled his body and fortified his spirit, until he
had become the most accomplished cavalier to be found among the
Faithful. Yet the colouring of his face remained like that of a little
girl and his cheeks were more beautiful to see than roses or narcissus.
A poet said of him:

My love was hardly circumcised
When little downy hairs surprised
(Eh, but I'm drunk) his cheeks.

The smiles upon his countenance
Are little fawns at lonely dance
(Eh, but I'm drunk) in Spring.

The wine that flows below his skin
Is a publican to call us in
(Eh, but I'm drunk) to sing.

Of all the charms below, above,
Those small green silken moulds I love
(Eh, but I'm drunk) his breeks.

You must know that the chamberlain had already completely
usurped the kingly power, in spite of the remonstrances of his wife
and of all the benefits which he had received from Dū al-Makān.
He had even had himself proclaimed Sultān by a section of the people
and the army. There was, however, another party who remained

faithful to the lineage of Umar al-Numān, counselled to this duty by the old wazīr Dandān. Dandān himself had been obliged to leave Baghdād, owing to the threats of the chamberlain, and to establish himself in a neighbouring city, where he waited with assurance the time when Destiny should fight on the side of the orphan King.

The chamberlain, who had no one left to fear, had forced Kāna mā kāna and his mother to keep their apartments, and had forbidden his daughter to have anything to do with the young King. Mother and son lived in retreat, waiting until it should please Allāh to restore them to their rights.

But, in spite of the usurper's watchfulness, Kāna mā kāna was sometimes able to see his little cousin and to speak with her in secret. One day, when he could not see her and his heart was more wrung than usual by its love, he took a sheet of paper and wrote these verses to his friend:

> You walk in the garth and piqued roses adore you,
> Dropping their dry and coloured leaves before you.
> The silver lilies close their eyelids while
> The scented camomile
> And other red flowers dare not smile.
> When, fairest, when
> Shall the two dusty violets of my mouth
> Attain their cyclamen
> And slake their drouth?
> The lavender has said: 'Be apposite,
> O moon of white,
> But for one night!'

He sealed this letter and gave it to the eunuch on duty, who immediately carried it to the chamberlain. The latter foamed with rage when he read the declaration of this love, and swore that he would chastise the author of it. Presently, however, he thought better of his intention and determined to speak only to his wife, so that the affair should not be noised abroad. He found Nuzhat in her apartment and said to her. . . .

At this point Shahrazād saw the approach of morning and discreetly fell silent.

But when the hundred-and-thirty-ninth night had come

SHE SAID:

He found Nuzhat in her apartment and after he had sent little Power-of-Destiny into the garden to take the air, said to her: 'Young Kāna mā kāna reached the age of puberty some time ago; now he seeks to try his manhood upon our daughter. It is necessary therefore that they should be separated beyond any chance of meeting, for it is dangerous to bring wood and fire together. Your daughter must never leave the women's apartments and never uncover her face; she has reached an age when both these things may well be demanded of her. I charge you to prevent the two from holding any communication, for, on the least excuse, I will prevent that young man from ever having recourse to his instincts.'

Nuzhat wept and, as soon as her husband left her, called her nephew Kāna mā kāna and informed him of the chamberlain's anger. 'Yet you must know, dear child,' she added, 'that I will sometimes be able to manage secret meetings for you, if you can be content to speak through the door. Therefore be patient until Allāh has pity upon us.' But Kāna mā kāna felt his soul thrown into confusion by what he heard. 'I will not live for a moment longer in a place where my word ought to be the sole law!' he cried. 'The stones of this palace shall never again cast their shadows on my humiliation.'

Without an hour's delay he undressed, covered his head with a kalandar's bonnet, threw an old travelling cloak about his shoulders, and made his way to the gates of the city, taking with him only a single loaf which was three days old. He was the first to go out through the gates when they were opened; he walked with great strides, reciting these stanzas as a farewell to all he left behind him:

> I feared my heart,
> I do not fear it longer.
> Now let it ache
> Or break
> Apart,
> My soul is stronger.
>
> Heart fed on love
> And softened in the feeding,

Rides, for heart's dead,
My head
Above
Feeling and pleading.

If I'd remorse
To see heart when it languished
Or dying lust,
I must
Perforce
Have fallen vanquished.

I'll range the whole
Good earth until its ending
And the free wave
To save
My soul
Young and unbending.

Warring with men
Their valour shall renew me.
Walls of my home,
I'll come
Again,
You'll bow down to me!

While Kāna mā kāna thus fled from the city of his fathers, his mother vainly sought him everywhere. Then she sat down to weep and anxiously awaited his return. The second, the third, and the fourth day passed without tidings of him; she shut herself in her own apartments, wailing and saying: 'Where is my child? In what land may I look for him? Of what avail are these poor tears, my boy? Where are you, Kāna mā kāna? Oh, where are you?' The poor woman would neither eat nor drink, and her grief soon became known throughout the whole city, where it was shared by the inhabitants, who loved the boy as they had loved his father. All cried: 'Where are you, O Dū al-Makān, O just King? Your son is lost and none of those whom you so loved can find him. Woe, woe, there are none left of the race of Umar al-Numān!'

Kāna mā kāna walked all of the first day and only stopped to rest in the darkness of the night. For many days he went on, living upon the herbs which he gathered and drinking from rivers and streams, until, on the fourth day, he came to a valley filled with trees through which a sparkling river flowed. He halted amid the singing of birds and crooning of ringdoves, made his ablution and his prayer, and lay down under a great tree to sleep. At midnight he woke to hear a voice ringing through the silence of the valley. It sang from among certain rocks:

> To lighten my darkness
> I look for the red crescent of her lips,
> And if that comes not
> I look for the blue crescent
> Of the sword of death.
>
> Oh, joy of friends gathered upon the cool meadow
> To drink wine handed by white hands!
>
> Flowers of Spring on the meadow
> Between spread slim fingers!
>
> You sit drinking the tulip-coloured wine
> In the midst of this green earth
> With all her waters.

As this pleasing song mounted through the night air, Kāna mā kāna rose and tried to pierce the shadow in the direction from which the voice came. But he could see nothing save the dim trunks of the trees which overhung the river. He walked a little towards the sound, coming down to the banks of the water. The voice then became more distinct, singing this poem through the darkness:

> I left her with my tribe,
>   For love lines link us.
> Rich Taim is my tribe
>   And people think us
> Supreme in horses and in dark-eyed love.
>
> I left her with my tribe,
>   For vows have bound us:
> The dark tents of my tribe
>   Where dawn has found us
> Still thinking that the night stars shone above.

> Oh, breeze blow from my tribe
>   And cool my heartache,
> O Saad of my tribe,
>   Say does she partake—
> She with the horse which has the copper bells,
> She, scorpion of my tribe—
>   The bitten heartstring?
> Physicians of my tribe,
>   Oh, for my smarts bring
> The water of her lips and nothing else.

When Kāna mā kāna heard this second song, he tried to see the singer in the darkness. As he could not do so, he climbed a rock and cried at the top of his voice. . . .

At this point Shahrazād saw the approach of morning and discreetly fell silent.

But when the hundred-and-fortieth night had come

SHE SAID:

He cried at the top of his voice: 'O you who pass in the darkness of the night, I pray you approach that I may hear your story, which seems to be like mine. Thus will the time pass pleasantly.'

In a few moments the voice which had been singing answered: 'Who is that calling? Mortal or Jinnī from below the earth? If you are a Jinnī, continue on your way; but if you are a man, wait here till the coming of dawn, for the night is full of pitfalls and treachery.'

'It seems to me,' thought Kāna mā kāna, 'that the owner of this voice has led a life strangely like mine,' and he stayed where he was until morning.

With the first light he saw a man dressed as a desert Badawī, wearing a sword and carrying a shield over his mighty shoulder, come towards him through the trees. The two greeted each other, and the stranger asked in astonishment: 'Who are you, unknown young man? What tribe do you belong to? Who are your parents? You are not of an age to wander at night in places unpatrolled by soldiers. Tell me your story.' 'My grandfather was King Umar al-Numān,' answered the youth, 'my father was King Dū al-Makān, and I myself am that Kāna mā kāna who burns for love of his cousin Power-of-Destiny.' Then said the Badawī: 'If you are a king's son, how is it that you are dressed as a kalandar and journey without a worthy bodyguard?' 'I will make my own bodyguard in time,' answered Kāna mā kāna. 'If you wish, you can be the first member of it.' The Badawī laughed, saying: 'My child, you speak as if you were already a warrior, a hero accomplished in twenty fights. To show that you are far otherwise, I shall take you as my slave. Then, if your parents are royal, they will pay me a good ransom.' Rage beamed from Kāna mā kāna's eyes as he answered: 'As Allāh lives, I will pay my own ransom. Look out for yourself, O Badawī! When I heard your verses, I thought that you were a man of fair manners. . . .'

With that Kāna mā kāna hurled himself upon the other, who received him smiling, expecting but child's play. He was wrong. Kāna mā kāna set his feet solidly to the earth, as firm as if they had been mountains, as valiant as if they had been towers; then, when he was well fixed, he clasped the Badawī in such a grip that his bones seemed like to break and his bowels to gush from him. Suddenly the boy lifted him in his arms and ran towards the river. The Badawī, who was still amazed at finding such strength in a child, cried: 'What are you doing?' 'I am going to throw you into this river,' said Kāna mā kāna. 'It will carry you to the Tigris, the Tigris will carry you to the river Isā, the river Isā will carry you to the Euphrates, and the Euphrates will carry you to your own country, where your tribe may judge of its hero's valiance.' As the Badawī hung high in the air over the water, he cried: 'I conjure you to spare my life in the name of your mistress Power-of-Destiny! I will be the most submissive of your slaves.' At once Kāna mā kāna set him gently on the ground, saying: 'You have disarmed me.'

They sat down together on the river's bank, and the Badawī gave Kāna mā kāna barley bread and salt that their friendship might be established for ever. 'Tell me who you are, good companion,' asked Kāna mā kāna, 'for you know who I am.' The Badawī answered:

'I am Sabbāh ibn Rammāh ibn Humām of the tribe of Taim in the desert of Shām. This, in a few words, is my story:

'I was very young when my father died, and my uncle brought me up in his house with his daughter Najmah. We loved each other, and, when I was of marriageable age, I asked for her hand; but her father would not consent because I was poor. In spite of the remonstrances made him by the chiefs of our tribe, he swore that I might not marry her until I could give a dowry of fifty horses, fifty blood camels, ten women slaves and fifty measures each of corn and barley. Therefore I left my tribe for the purpose of attacking caravans and pillaging merchants, for that seemed to me my only means of collecting this dowry. That is the reason of my lying and singing in this place last night. But, O my friend, what are my songs compared with the beauty of Najmah! To see her once is to have the soul filled with benediction for the rest of life.'

'I thought that your story would be like mine,' said Kāna mā kāna. 'Let us henceforth fight side by side and win our mistresses with our swords.' As he was speaking a cloud of dust rose in the distance and came rapidly towards them; a horseman rode up out of it, whose face was yellow as death and his garments stained with blood. 'A little water for my wound, Believers!' he cried. 'Hold me up, for I am about to die! If you help me, my horse shall belong to you.' The Badawī, who understood horses very well, looked at the animal which the wounded stranger rode and found it to be un-equalled among all the steeds of the desert, perfect in a beauty which would confound the heart of any Arab. 'Indeed,' he exclaimed, 'it is such a horse as one sees no more in these days!' Kāna mā kāna took the rider gently in his arms and laid him on the grass, saying: 'Who are you, my brother, and what is the nature of your wound?' The rider opened his garments and showed that his back was one great hole from which waves of blood were pouring. The young King washed these wounds as best he might, and gently dressed them with fresh herbs. Then he gave the dying man water to drink, saying: 'Who has put you into this grievous state, my brother?' The man answered:

'Good helper of mine, the beauty of this mare has killed me. She belonged to King Afrīdūn of Constantinople, and her fame had gone forth throughout all the deserts. She was not the sort of animal which ought to stay in the stables of an unbelieving king. I was selected by my tribe to deliver her out of the hands of the soldiers who guarded her day and night. I came to the tent where she was lodged and scraped acquaintance with the guards. Wishing for my advice, they asked me to try the animal. I took advantage of this to lash her with my whip and gallop away. They pursued me on their horses with a cloud of arrows and javelins, many of which came to rest in my back; but the mare carried me away from them more quickly than a falling star and has borne me for three days without a stop. Now my blood is spent, and I feel death weighing upon my eyelids.

'You have helped me. At my death the mare belongs to you. Her name is Al-Kātūl Al-Majnūn, and she is the leader of all her people.

'But before you take possession of her, O youth with the poor clothes and noble countenance, I pray you carry me behind you to my own tribe that I may die in the tents where I was born.'

'Brother of the desert,' answered Kāna mā kāna, 'I also belong to a worthy house; therefore I am ready to do as you wish, whatever happens to the mare.' With that he began to lift the Arab, but the poor man gave a great sigh, saying: 'Wait a little, for perhaps my death is closer than I thought. I would bear witness to the Faith.' He half shut his eyes and stretched out his hand with its palm to the sky, saying:

'I witness that there is no God but Allāh. I witness that Muhammad is the Prophet of Allāh.'

Then, being prepared to meet his death, he sang this song:

> I have galloped the world bloodily on my black mare,
> Kātūl my mare,
> Spreading terror and carnage everywhere,
> Breaking down mountains to plant despair,
> Drying up rivers to leave blood there,
> Stealing all gold, debauching all fair,
> And I die as I lived in the open air.
> Passing, beside this river here,
> I have one regret and but this fear
> That you, young stranger I make my heir,
> Will not be worthy of my black mare,
> Kātūl my mare.

With that the Arab convulsively opened his mouth and gave the death rattle; then his eyes closed for ever.

Kāna mā kāna and his companion buried the dead man with suitable prayer and set off together to find their destiny upon the road of Allāh.

At this point Shahrazād saw the approach of morning and discreetly fell silent.

But when the hundred-and-forty-first night had come

SHE SAID:

Kāna mā kāna rode his new steed and Sabbāh walked faithfully behind, for he had sworn eternal fealty upon the Holy House of Allāh.

Then began a life full of adventure, of conflicts with wild animals and brigands, of hunting and travelling, of nights passed in hiding from savage beasts and days of fighting and collecting booty. At the peril of their heads, they amassed great herds with their keepers, horses with their grooms, and tents with their furnishings. Kāna mā kāna gave Sabbāh charge of all they took and spent his own time in fighting for more. Whenever they sat down to rest they spoke of Power-of-Destiny and of Najmah, consoling each other and exchanging hopes. Two years passed in this way.

Here is one of a thousand of Kāna mā kāna's exploits:

One day Kāna mā kāna was riding in search of adventure, preceded by his faithful Sabbāh. The latter walked with his naked sword in his hand, uttering terrible cries from time to time, opening his eyes like caves, and calling to the solitude of the desert: 'Make way there, make way!' They had just eaten a spitted gazelle and drunken from a little spring when they saw, at the bottom of the hill on which they sat, a pasture covered with camels and sheep, cattle and horses. A band of armed slaves sat under an awning and guarded the animals. 'Stay here,' said Kāna mā kāna to Sabbāh, 'I will capture all these animals and slaves myself.'

He galloped his horse down the hill, like the sudden thunder of a breaking cloud, and threw himself upon the slaves, shouting this warlike hymn:

> We are the blood of Umar al-Numān,
> We are the heroes big with fate.
> We are the driving head of the sword
> And the shield of those who call us lord.
> See, our enemies bow to us,
> Scarfed in red they bow to us,
> Bow and bow on the lance point—thus!
> We are the heroes big with fate,
> We are the blood of Umar al-Numān.

The terrified slaves began to call for help, thinking that all the Arabs of the desert had suddenly come upon them. At their calling three warriors ran from the tent and, leaping upon their horses, rode towards Kāna mā kāna, crying: 'Here is the man who stole the mare Kātūl! We have him at last! Down with him!' The young King whispered in Kātūl's ear, and she bounded forward like an ogre upon his prey. Kāna mā kāna's lance jested with the enemy. It passed through the belly of the foremost and came out at his back with a kidney on the end. The next two thrusts sought out two more kidneys, and the three warriors were dead. The victor turned toward the slaves, but they threw themselves face downwards on the ground begging for mercy. Then said Kāna mā kāna: 'Drive these beasts before me to such and such a place, where my people are.' Thus, with the new booty, he rejoined Sabbāh, who had not stirred during the fight.

As they went forward, they saw a cloud of dust raised by a hundred cavaliers armed in the fashion of Constantinople. 'Look after our prizes,' said Kāna mā kāna to Sabbāh, 'and I will deal with the Unbelievers.' The Arab drove their flocks and slaves behind a nearby hill, while Kāna mā kāna went forward to meet the horsemen, who soon surrounded him on all sides. Their chief addressed him thus: 'Sweet girl who rides a horse so charmingly, O tender eyes and flowering cheeks, draw near that I may kiss you and make you queen of all.'

Kāna mā kāna cried out in his shame: 'Dog, son of a dog, what is that you say? If my cheeks are hairless my arm is strong enough to teach manners to a lustful Christian. Do you not know the difference between a warrior and a girl?' The leader of the hundred drew near and saw that he had indeed to deal with a warrior whom it would be difficult to tame, however rose and white his cheeks might be.

So he cried out: 'Where are you going, you insolent boy? Yield yourself, or you are dead!' He ordered one of his men to bind the youth, but hardly had the horseman come near when Kāna mā kāna, with one stroke of his sword, divided turban and head, body, saddle, and horse into as many halves. A second, a third, and a fourth, threw themselves upon him and met the same fate.

The leader then ordered his men to retire and came near to Kāna mā kāna, saying: 'You are a true warrior, delightful youth. I am Kahrdāsh, known for my bravery through all the lands of Rūm, and I spare your life because of your beauty. Go your way in peace.' 'Whether or not you are Kahrdāsh is of little interest to me,' answered Kāna mā kāna, 'the thing which concerns me is that you should feel the point of my lance. For if you are Kahrdāsh, I am Kāna mā kāna son of Dū al-Makān son of Umar al-Numān.' Then said the Christian: 'Son of Dū al-Makān, I have fought against your father in many battles. You join his bravery to a beauty such as I have never seen. Therefore retire with all your booty, for it is my will.' 'It is not my custom to turn aside for any man. On guard, O Christian!' cried the young man, as he whispered to his horse. Kātūl understood the desire of her master and leapt forward with lowered ears and tail held high. The two warriors met like fighting rams or goring bulls. A few terrible passes were exchanged, and then Kahrdāsh swung his lance with all his force against Kāna mā kāna's breast. The youth saved himself, by swerving Kātūl aside, and ran the Christian through the belly so that hissing fire came out from his back. Thus Kahrdāsh ceased to be numbered among the hosts of the Unbelievers.

Seeing their leader fall, his knights fled as fast as their horses would carry them and disappeared in a mist of dust.

Kāna mā kāna wiped the point of his lance upon the bodies which lay before him and, signing to Sabbāh, continued upon his way.

It was about this time that the young man met the famous wandering negress of the desert, of whom he had heard much. She wandered from tribe to tribe, telling delicious tales in the tents and below the stars, and passed her life in this profession. Kāna mā kāna begged her to rest herself in his tent and to tell him some story which should pass the time and chase all melancholy thoughts away. The old wanderer sat down by his side on the mat and told him:

The Tale of the Hashīsh Eater

THE most delightful circumstance which I have yet heard, young lord, is an adventure which happened to a hashīsh eater.

He was a man who loved above all else the flesh of virgins. . . .

At this point Shahrazād saw the approach of morning and discreetly fell silent.

But when the hundred-and-forty-second night had come

SHE SAID:

He was a man who loved above all the flesh of virgins and occupied himself solely in the satisfaction of this appetite. Now such flesh, when it is carefully chosen, is very expensive and no fortune may suffice to buy enough of it. Therefore this man soon ruined himself by the intemperance of his tastes, for nothing is wrong unless it be carried to excess.

One day, as he wandered in rags and with naked feet begging his bread in the market, a nail entered his foot, and it bled exceedingly. As the blood continued to flow, even after he had tried to staunch it with a piece of linen, he went to the hammām and sat down in the common hall which, though reserved for the poor, was wonderfully bright and clean.

As he bathed his foot in the central basin, he noticed that a man who sat beside him and had already bathed, was munching something. Seeing this movement of the jaws, the wounded man was very anxious to eat also; therefore he asked his neighbour what he was chewing. The other answered in a low voice so that none might hear: 'It is hashīsh. I will give you a little if you like.' 'I would like it very much,' answered the man. So the eater took a piece from his mouth and handed it over, saying: 'May it lighten all your griefs.' Our hero took the piece and swallowed it whole; then, being unaccustomed to the drug, he burst into strange laughter and filled all the hall with his excessive mirth. A moment afterwards he fell back on the naked marble and became a prey to the following delicious visions:

He thought that he lay naked under the hands of a terrible rubber and two vigorous negroes, who had taken complete possession of his body. He was a plaything in their arms; they turned and moulded him in every way, and he felt their muscular fingers digging expertly into his flesh. He groaned beneath the weight of their knees upon his belly as they rubbed him skilfully, and then rejoiced as they bathed him from copper basins and rubbed him with vegetable fibre. At last the master rubber wished to wash certain delicate parts of his person, but, as this tickled him, he preferred to do the thing himself. When the bath was over, the rubber covered his body with three towels as white as jasmine, saying: 'The time has come, my lord, for you to enter to your bride.' 'What bride is that? I am a bachelor!' cried the man. 'Have you by any chance been eating hashīsh to make so great a mistake?' 'Do not jest with me, my lord,' said the rubber, 'but follow, for your bride is waiting you eagerly.' He threw a great veil of black silk about the man's shoulders and led the way, while the two negroes supported the bridegroom and tickled his bottom from time to time by way of jest, so that he laughed immoderately.

They brought him thus to a half-lighted hall, warmed and scented with incense, where he found a wide dish covered with fruits and pastries, sherberts and vases of flowers. The three attendants begged him to sit upon an ebony stool and then retired.

Soon a young boy came and stood before him, saying: 'O King of time, I am your slave.' The man gave a bellow of laughter and, quite disregarding the beauty of the boy, exclaimed: 'As Allāh lives, I think that everyone must have been eating hashīsh here! They are calling me a king now. Come here, my child, and cut me half of a red and juicy water-melon. That is the fruit I like best. There is nothing like a water-melon.' When the boy brought him the thing he desired cut into admirable slices, he said: 'Now begone, for you are not what I want. Run and fetch me my heart's desire. There is nothing like a virgin to take with water-melon.'

The boy departed and presently returned with a little girl, who advanced swinging her childish hips. The man snuffled with joy on seeing her; he took her in his arms and, holding her between his thighs, kissed her feverishly. He made her slip beneath him and, taking out his manhood, placed it in her hand. Other things were about to happen when he suddenly became very cold and woke from his dream.

He found himself surrounded by the bathers of the hammām, who were laughing at him with all their hearts and opening their mouths like ovens. They were pointing out to each other his naked zabb, which stood up in the air as far as was humanly possible, as great as that of an ass or an elephant. Some of them poured pitchers of cold water over this column, and all were making those jests which are customary when comparing matters in the hammām.

In his confusion the man replaced the towel over his thighs, and said bitterly to those who were laughing at him: 'Why did you take away the little girl, just as I was going to put things in their right places?' All the spectators rocked with joy and clapped their hands at this remark, crying: 'Are you not ashamed, O hashīsh eater, still to have such desires, when you have so thoroughly coupled with the air already?' Kāna mā kāna was convulsed with joyful laughter by this tale; he said to the negress: 'Hasten to tell me some more, for your tales are very good.' 'I have some, young master,' she answered, 'which will make you forget the one you have just heard, stories so pure and savoury and strange that the deaf rejoice at them.'

As the negress was preparing to continue, a man on horseback alighted at the tent door and wished Kāna mā kāna peace, saying: 'My lord, I am one of a hundred messengers sent in all directions by the wazīr Dandān, to look for young prince Kāna mā kāna, who has been absent from Baghdād for three years. The wazīr has succeeded in raising the army and the people against the usurper of the throne of Umar al-Numān, and has cast him into the lowest dungeon of the city, where he now lies dying of hunger, thirst and shame. I pray you tell me if you have ever met the prince, for he is called again to sit upon his father's throne.'

At this point Shahrazād saw the approach of morning and discreetly fell silent.

But when the hundred-and-forty-third night had come

SHE SAID:

When Prince Kāna mā kāna heard these unexpected tidings, he turned to his faithful Sabbāh and said in a calm voice: 'You see that everything comes upon its appointed hour, my friend. Let us rise up now and go to Baghdād.'

The messenger understood from this that he was in the presence of the new King, so he abased himself, while Sabbāh and the negress followed his example. 'You must come with me to Baghdād and tell me some more stories,' said Kāna mā kāna to the negress, while Sabbāh exclaimed: 'O King, let me run before you to Baghdād that I may announce your coming to the wazīr and the people.' The young King gave permission, and at the same time handed over to the messenger, as a gift for his good news, all the booty which he had taken in the three years which went before. Then he set out for Baghdād on Kātūl, followed by the negress on one of the camels.

Sabbāh journeyed a day ahead of the King and set the whole city of Baghdād in an uproar within a few hours of his arrival there. The people and the army went out, led by the wazīr Dandān and the three chiefs, Rustam, Turkāsh, and Bahrmān, to greet the King whom they had never hoped to see again. And, as they went, they called down blessing and honour upon the race of Umar al-Numān.

When Kāna mā kāna came in sight, swiftly galloping on Kātūl, thousands of voices of men and women hailed him as King. In spite of his great age, Dandān jumped nimbly from his horse and ran forward to swear fealty to the descendant of so many monarchs. He led Kāna mā kāna triumphantly into the city, while the negress on her camel told tale after tale to the assembled multitude.

Kāna mā kāna's first action was to embrace Dandān, who had remained faithful; his second was to kiss his mother, who sobbed with joy that she had found him again; and his third was to ask news of Power-of-Destiny. 'My child,' his mother answered, 'I can hardly tell you, for I have occupied myself with nothing but grief since you went away.' 'Then, dear mother,' said Kāna mā kāna, 'I beg you to go yourself and bring me word of my cousin and of my aunt Nuzhat.' His mother went to the apartment where the two women were sitting and brought them back into the presence of the King. Then was such a feast of joy as has never been equalled. A thousand songs were sung, and this was one of them:

> Water of smiles running among pearls,
> Rose and silver silk of the cheeks of girls,
>   And the kissing of them!
>
> Flashing as of steel, the blade is bright,
> The blade that does not rest, the blade of night!
>
> Black hair at dawn falling in broken glooms,
> Sweetly smoothed with living ivory combs,
>   And the kissing of them!

There is no need to say more, except that their joy was full. From that time misfortune ceased to perch above the posterity of Umar al-Numān, but flew off to fix her beak in their enemies.

The King passed many months of happiness in the arms of young Power-of-Destiny, whom he had made his wife. Then one day he called the chief people of his kingdom and the leaders of his army together in the presence of the wazīr Dandān, and addressed them in these words: 'The blood of my fathers still cries out for vengeance and the time has come. I have learnt that both Afrīdūn and Hardūb of Cesarea are dead. But old Mother-of-Calamity still lives and governs all the lands of Rūm. The new King of Cesarea is called Rumzān, and none know his father or his mother.

'To-morrow the war shall begin again against the Unbelievers. I swear on the life of Muhammad (upon whom be prayer and peace!) that I will never return to our city of Baghdād until I have crushed the life out of that calamitous old woman and avenged our race upon her.'

Next day the whole army set out for Cesarea. When they came below its walls and were preparing to reduce it to a pit of fire and blood, a young man as handsome as a king, followed by a woman with her face veiled, came towards the royal tent, where the wazīr Dandān and the Princess Nuzhat were sitting with their Sultān.

These strangers were granted audience. As soon as they came into the tent both the woman and Nuzhat uttered loud cries and fell fainting to the ground. When they came to, they threw themselves into each other's arms, for the woman was none other than Coral-Pearl, the faithful slave of Princess Ibrīzah.

Coral-Pearl turned towards the King, saying: 'My lord, I see that you carry a round white gem about your neck and that the Princess Nuzhat wears the same. Behold the third is here!' So saying she pointed to the third magic jewel which hung about the neck of the young stranger, and cried: 'This young man is the son of my poor mistress, Princess Ibrīzah. I have brought him up since birth, and he is now Rumzān, King of Cesarea, son of al-Numān. He is your brother, dear lady! He is your uncle, O King!'

The King and Nuzhat embraced Rumzān with tears of joy, and the wazīr Dandān embraced the son of his old master Umar al-Numān (whom Allāh keep in His infinite mercy!). Then said Kāna mā kāna to the King of Cesarea: 'My uncle, I see you reigning over Christians in a Christian land. Tell me, are you yourself an Unbeliever?' For answer Rumzān stretched out his hand and, raising his index finger, cried: 'There is no God but Allāh, and Muhammad is His Prophet!'

All who were in the tent rejoiced, crying: 'Glory be to Him who has chosen His own and reunited them!' Then Nuzhat asked: 'How came it that you were guided into the right way, my brother, among all these people who do not know God or His Prophet?' 'Coral-Pearl taught me the easy and excellent principles of our Faith,' answered the King. 'She embraced the Mussulmān religion when my mother did so, in the palace of Umar al-Numān at Baghdād. She has not only brought me up and been a mother to me, but she has made me a true Believer, whose destiny is in the hands of Allāh.'

Straightway Nuzhat made Coral-Pearl sit down on the carpet beside her and swore sisterhood with her, while Kāna mā kāna said to Rumzān: 'The Mussulmān throne belongs to you by right, my uncle. From this hour I number myself among your most faithful subjects.' 'Nephew,' answered the King of Cesarea, 'what Allāh has done He has well done. It is not for me to trouble His actions.' Here the wazīr Dandān interrupted, saying: 'O my Kings, the equitable decision between you is that each should reign on alternate days.' 'Your idea is an excellent one, O venerable wazīr of our father,' they answered in unison.

At this point Shahrazād saw the approach of morning and discreetly fell silent.

But when the hundred-and-forty-fourth night had come

SHE SAID:

The two Kings agreed to adopt Dandān's plan, and, to mark their amity, Rumzān re-entered his city and threw open the gates to the Mussulmān army. He proclaimed that, henceforth, Islām was the religion of the people of Cesarea, but that any Christians who liked were free to remain in their heresy. In spite of this clement clause, a thousand thousand new Believers proclaimed the act of Faith on that happy day. Glory be to Him who sent His Prophet to be a sign of Peace among all the peoples of the East and West.

The two Kings gave wonderful feasts of rejoicing and remained in Cesarea for a long time, ruling day and day about in perfect contentment.

While they were there, they concerted vengeance together against Mother-of-Calamity. Rumzān, with the consent of Kāna mā kāna, sent a messenger to Constantinople with a letter for Mother-of-Calamity, who knew nothing of what had happened and still thought that the King of Cesarea was a Christian like his maternal grandfather, Hardūb, father of Ibrīzah. The letter was couched in these terms:

'To the glorious and venerable Shawāhī Dhāt al-Dawāhī, the Terrible, the Victorious, the Acknowledged Scourge, the eye that watches over Christendom, scented with virtue and wisdom, smelling of the Supreme and Holy Incense of the Patriarchs, the Column of Christ in the midst of Constantinople,

'From Rumzān, Master of Cesarea, of the line of Hardūb the Great, whose fame has spread abroad over all the world:

'O Mother of us all, the Lord has made our arms to triumph over the Mussulmāns. We have destroyed their armies and taken prisoner their King, with his wazīr Dandān and the Princess Nuzhat, daughter of Umar al-Numān.

'Now we await your coming, that we may rejoice over this victory together and that you may see the heads of Kāna mā kāna and all his people roll before your sainted eyes.

'You may come quite safely to Cesarea, as the roads are now secure and the provinces lie in peace from Irāk to Sūdān, from Mosul and Damascus to the extreme boundaries of East and West.

'Do not forget to bring with you from Constantinople Saffīah, mother of Nuzhat, that she may rejoice to see her daughter again, whom we are keeping in our palace in as much honour as may be accorded to a woman.

'May Christ, the son of Mary, guard you and keep you as a pure essence which lies richly hid in unalterable gold.'

He sealed this letter with his royal seal and sent it by a swift rider to Constantinople.

Between this time and the arrival of that dreadful old woman to meet her well-merited fate, there passed several days in which the two Kings were able to settle some old accounts for good or evil. This was what passed:

One day, as the two were sitting with Dandān and Nuzhat (who never veiled her face in the presence of the old wazīr as she looked upon him as a father) and were talking over the chances of Mother-of-Calamity's arrival, a chamberlain entered and announced that he had without an old merchant, who had been attacked by robbers, and also the robbers themselves in chains. 'He solicits an audience, O Kings, for he has two letters,' said the chamberlain, and the Kings said: 'Let him enter!'

An old man with a saintly face came in weeping. He kissed the ground before the Kings, saying: 'O Sultāns, is it possible that a Mussulmān may be respected by Unbelievers, only to be attacked and robbed by the men of Islām?' 'What has happened to you, most respectable old man?' asked the Kings, and the merchant answered: 'My masters, I have about me two letters which have always made me respected among Mussulmāns and have served me as a safe-conduct, freeing me from all tax upon my goods. Also one of these letters has been a consolation during the loneliness of my travels, for it is written in exquisite verses and has become more precious to me than life itself.' 'Let us see this letter, good merchant, or read us its contents,' said the Kings. So the old man gave them two squares of paper with a trembling hand, which they themselves offered to Nuzhat, saying: 'You can read the most complicated writing and intone verse very pleasantly. We pray you therefore read these letters to us.'

Nuzhat opened one of the papers and cast a glance at it. Then she cried out and became as yellow as saffron and fell into a swoon. They sprinkled her face with rose-water, so that she came to herself and, springing to her feet, ran towards the merchant. With streaming eyes, she seized the old man's hand and kissed it. Those who were round could not speak for astonishment when they saw a thing happen so contrary to royal usage, while the merchant himself trembled and would have fallen had not Nuzhat held him up. She made him sit upon her own carpet, saying: 'Do you not recognise me, my father? Have I become as old as all that?'

The old man thought he was dreaming and cried: 'I recognise the voice, but my eyes are old and can hardly see.' Then said the queen: 'My father, I am that Nuzhat al-Zamān who wrote the letter in verse for you.' It was then the old man's turn to fall down in a swoon. While Dandān was throwing rose-water in his face, Nuzhat turned towards the Kings, saying: 'This is the good merchant who delivered me when I was a slave to the Badawī, who stole me in the streets of Jerusalem.'

The two Kings rose in honour of the merchant when he recovered from his swoon, and kissed him upon the brow; the old man himself bent over the hands of Nuzhat and the wazīr Dandān, and all who were concerned congratulated each other, giving thanks to Allāh for this reunion. The merchant raised his arms, crying: 'Glory be to Him who has made the hearts of men from mindful stuff, scenting them with the sweet incense of gratitude!'

The two Kings appointed him chief in general of all the khāns and markets in Cesarea and Baghdād, giving him free access to the palace by day and night. When they asked him how he had come to be attacked, he answered: 'As I went through the desert, some Arab murderers of a base sort, such as attack merchants when they are unarmed, surrounded me with a hundred men. Their chiefs were three, a terrible negro, a horrible Kurd and a mighty Badawī. They bound me to a camel and were leading me behind them, when Allāh sent your soldiers to capture them.'

'First bring in the negro!' cried the Kings. When he entered, they saw that he was more ugly than the bottom of an old ape and that his eyes were more wicked than those of a tiger. Dandān was just asking him his name and the reason of his brigandage, when Coral-Pearl, who had come in to speak to Nuzhat, saw the negro and uttered a loud cry. She threw herself upon him like a lioness and, digging her fingers into his eyes, pulled them out in one movement, crying: 'It is the negro Sullen, who killed Ibrīzah.' Casting on the ground the two bloodstained eyes which she had pressed like fruit-stones from the black man's face, she added: 'Blessed be the justice of the Almighty who has permitted me to avenge my lady with the same hands which held her as she died!' King Rumzān gave a sign to his executioner, and by a single blow there lay two negroes in the place of one. The eunuchs carried out what was left and threw it to the dogs which haunted the ruins beyond the city.

'Bring in the Kurd!' cried the Kings, and the Kurd entered. He was more yellow than a lemon, more scurfy than a miller's donkey, more verminous than a buffalo which has not plunged for a year. When the wazīr Dandān asked him his name and the reason of his brigandage, he answered: 'I was a camel-boy in Jerusalem. One day certain persons intrusted me with a sick youth to take to the hospital in Damascus. . . .' He had gone no further when King Kāna mā kāna, Nuzhat and the wazīr cried together with one voice: 'It is the traitor who left King Dū al-Makān on the pile of fuel by the hammām door!' Kāna mā kāna rose, saying: 'Evil must be paid with evil not once but twice, or the wicked would increase in number and the lawless multiply. There should be no pity for the evil-doer. That clemency which the Christians teach is but the virtue of eunuchs and sick men.' Then with his own sword, he made two Kurds lie where one had stood before, and commanded his slaves to bury the remains with the formal rites of religion.

'Bring in the Badawī!' cried the two Kings.

At this point Shahrazād saw the approach of morning and discreetly fell silent.

But when the hundred-and-forty-fifth night had come

SHE SAID:

No sooner had the Badawī put his head round the opening of the tent than Nuzhat cried: 'It is the man who sold me to the merchant!' 'My name is Hammād and I do not know you,' answered the prisoner. Nuzhat laughed and said: 'It is the same man, for there was never a fool like to him. Look at me, Hammād, I am the girl you stole in the streets of Jerusalem and so ill-treated.'

Then cried the Badawī: 'By my bonnet, it is the same woman! I think my head had better say farewell to its neck!' Nuzhat turned to the merchant, asking: 'Do you not recognise him now, good father?' and the old man replied: 'It is the same, a very mad fellow.' 'But in spite of all his brutal qualities,' said Nuzhat, 'this Badawī used to have one excellence, a love for beautiful verses and good stories.' 'By my bonnet, that is true!' cried Hammād, 'and I know a tale now of an adventure which happened to myself which is as strange a thing as you would wish to hear. If I tell it you and you are satisfied, I shall expect you to spare my life.' The tender Nuzhat smiled and said: 'Tell us your tale on that condition.'

Then Hammād said:

The Tale of Hammād the Badawī

I am a great robber, the crown of all robbers. The most surprising thing that happened in my life was this:

I lay alone in the desert one night near to my tethered horse; my soul panted beneath the weight of the wicked spells which the sorcerers who were my enemies had laid upon it. It was a terrible night for me; sometimes I cried like a jackal, sometimes roared like a lion, and then again complained like a camel. Trembling, I waited for the dawn. At last light appeared in the sky, and my soul grew calmer. To drive away the last smoke of my terrible dreams, I girded on my sword, seized my lance, and galloped forward on my swift horse.

As I rode I saw an ostrich standing straight ahead of me, looking at me and yet not seeming to see me. I was about to thrust at her with my lance when she turned with a great kick and, spreading her tufted wings, made off like an arrow across the desert. I pursued her at full gallop, until I came to a place of terrible solitude, filled only with bare rocks and the presence of God. I heard nothing but the hissing of vipers, the echoing calls of the Jinn in earth and air, and the howls of hunting Ghouls. The ostrich disappeared as if the earth had swallowed her up. I shivered throughout all my body, and my horse reared and halted in a sweat of terror.

In my fright I wished to return the way I had come, but my horse was exhausted and the midday heat made it impossible to move. A devouring thirst tortured me and made the belly of my horse open and close like a pair of bellows. 'O Hammād,' I said to myself, 'this is the place of your death. Here your body will nourish the children of the Ghouls!'

As I was about to make my confession of faith, I saw on the edge of sight a little green line of scattered palm trees; my horse neighed and set off of himself, so that a few minutes' riding brought me from the naked horror of the baking rocks into a sweet meadow, where a river ran at the feet of palm-trees, and a tent was pitched, beside which two splendid mares ate the moist grass.

I dismounted and watered my horse, whose nostrils were jetting fire, and then drank of the clear water until I could hold no more. I took a long cord from my saddlebags and fastened my horse in such a way that he could pasture at ease upon the green of the meadow; then I walked towards the tent, being anxious to see who was in it.

As I approached, I saw a smooth-cheeked boy sitting upon a white mat, as beautiful as the crescent of the young moon. On his right reclined a slim-waisted girl in the delicate splendour of her beauty. She seemed like the new-born branch of a willow.

I fell in love at that moment with a passion I had not yet known, and yet could not be sure which of them was the cause of this. Allāh alone knows which is more beautiful, the full moon or the crescent moon.

I called out: 'Peace be with you!' The girl covered her face and the boy rose, saying: 'Peace be with you likewise!' Then said I: 'I am Hammād ibn al-Fazarī of the chief tribe which camps by the Euphrates. I am an illustrious warrior, usually considered the equal of five hundred men. An ostrich led me hither. I beg for a mouthful of water.' 'Bring him meat and drink,' said the youth to the girl, and thereupon the maiden rose and walked towards the tent. She walked. I still hear the harmonious chinking of her gold anklets, I still see the heavy weight of her hair which her head carried like a burden. In spite of the looks of the young man, I kept my eyes fixed on the girl as she went, and as she came back balancing a cup of cold water on her right palm, and on her left, a tray with dates, curds, and steaks of a gazelle.

My passion was such that I could not stretch out my hand to take these things. Instead I constructed these verses on the spur of the moment and proclaimed them aloud:

> Your skin is snow,
> Your henna is wet-black still,
> As your fingers and palms will
> Show.
>
> It would pass all skill
> To render so
> On so small a page
> A black bird in an ivory cage.

The young man burst out laughing when he heard my poem and saw the fire of my regard. 'I can see,' he said, 'that you are a peerless warrior, a cavalier without rival.' 'I pass for such,' I answered. 'Tell me to whom I am speaking.' 'I am Ibād ibn Tamīm ibn Thaalaba of the Banū Thaalaba,' answered the youth, 'and this is my sister.' Then I cried: 'Make her my wife quickly, for I love her passionately and am myself a sufficiently good match.' 'Neither my sister nor I will ever marry,' he replied. 'We have chosen this calm green place within the desert to pass our life together, far from the cares and vexations of the world.' 'Nevertheless, I must have your sister as a wife,' I said. 'I will have her when you are dead.'

The boy leaped to the back of the tent, saying: 'Look to yourself, O traitor of hospitality, and may the best man win!' He took his sword and shield from their post, while I jumped into the saddle and made ready for the onslaught. The youth came out in arms and, having mounted his horse, was about to charge when his sister ran forth weeping and embraced his knees, crying:

> Brother, you fight for me,
>   Meeting a stranger.
> Is it not right for me
>   During your danger
>   To wound the listening air
>   With a well-balanced prayer
>   That Allāh may beware?

> I hurl a lance of faith
>   Up to the sky,
> Asking an equal death,
>   Swearing that I
> If you should come to scathe
>   Surely will die,
>   Trusting the sword of my
>   Infinite piety
>   To win you victory.

The young man leaned from his saddle and, raising the veil which covered his sister's face, kissed her between the eyes. Thus I saw her features for the first time. It was as if I watched from paradise the sun come suddenly from behind a cloud. The youth stayed his horse by his sister's side and answered her with these lines:

> Be still and watch the wonders of my arm,
>   The windy pattern of my lance,
>   My horse's leaping,
>   Keeping
>   From chance
> Of harm
> My sister.
>
> The circling birds of prey watch too,
>   A scarlet rapture in their hearts,
>   My lance point taking,
>   Breaking
>   His arts
> In two,
> My sister.

Then, turning to me, he cried:

> You, who would win to her when I am dead,
>   Shall earn a certain place in knightly story;
>   Not of the conqueror who has the glory,
> But of the needful man who dies instead.

With that he urged his horse against mine and sent my sword flying; before I had time to escape, he seized me with one hand and lifted me out of the saddle like an empty sack. Throwing me into the air like a ball, he caught me again on his left hand and held me thus at full stretch of his arm as one might sustain a captured bird upon a finger. I did not know whether to think that I was in a black dream or that this rose-cheeked boy was some Jinnī living in a tent with a hūrī. What followed did not help to resolve my difficulty.

Seeing her brother's triumph, the girl ran to him and, hanging joyously about the neck of his horse, kissed him upon the brow. Then she led the animal to the tent, while the young man followed, carrying me under his arm. Instead of crushing my head beneath his feet, he made me enter the tent, saying to his sister: 'This man is now our guest. Let us treat him with hospitality.' He made me sit down on the mat, and the girl put a cushion behind my head. Afterwards she returned her brother's weapons to their place and brought him perfumed water for his face and hands. She dressed him in a white robe, saying: 'May Allāh so whiten the honour of your exploit and place you as a beauty-spot upon the face of the tribes.' The boy answered:

> Sister, in whose veins run the pure red
> Of the Banū Thaalaba,
> I fight for the dark light in your eyes.

The girl said:

> Your bright hair makes a crown
> About your head,
> My brother.

He replied:

> Tell the lions
> To go behind their yellow hills.
> I would think shame to leave them
> Lying with the desert in their teeth.

Then cried the girl:

> This is my brother Ibād,
> The desert knows him,
> It were well to take another way.
>
> You have fought against my brother,
> My brother Ibād,
> And you saw death
> Darting like a snake out of the sand.

I was thrown into confusion by this exchange of verses and saw myself very small in my own eyes, recognising how ugly I was in comparison with these two charming people. The girl brought her brother a tray covered with meat and fruit, without casting so much as a glance at me, not even a scornful glance. It was as if I had been some dog, whose presence was known but not to be remarked. Yet I continued to find her lovely, and even thought her exquisite when she served her brother and neglected her own wants for him. At last the young man turned to me and invited me to share his repast, by which I knew that my life was safe. He handed me a bowl of curds and a saucer filled with a concoction of dates and aromatic water. I ate and drank with hanging head, swearing a thousand and five hundred oaths of servitude to my charming host. He smiled and made a sign to his sister, who straightway rose and opened a great chest. She took from it ten admirably beautiful robes of which she made nine into a packet, obliging me to accept it as a gift. The tenth, the sumptuous robe which I now wear, she made me assume on the spot.

On a second sign from her brother, she left the tent and returned to the door leading a she-camel, loaded with food and certain gifts which I have kept to this day. After so nobly rewarding my execrable conduct, they invited me to stay with them as long as I pleased. But for very shame I took leave of them at once, kissing the earth between their hands seven times. Riding on my horse and leading the camel by her halter, I journeyed across the desert by the way which I had come.

Thus it was that I became the richest man in my tribe and was able to have myself elected chief of an important band of high-waymen.

Such is the tale which I promised you. I think it fully deserves the remission of all my sins, which I venture to say are neither small nor unimportant.

When Hammād finished, Nuzhat said to the two Kings and the wazīr: 'I suppose that we ought to respect the mad. This Badawī has his head irrevocably put on the wrong way. I suggest that we pardon him because of his sensibility to poetry and his astonishing memory.' Hearing his pardon, Hammād fell down among the carpets, and the eunuchs came and carried him away.

At this point a messenger entered the tent, still panting from the exertions of his journey, and kissed the earth between the hands of the Kings, saying: 'Mother-of-Calamity is only one parasang from the city gates.'

The Kings and the wazīr were overcome with joy at receiving news for which they had so long waited. They asked details from the messenger, who answered: 'When Mother-of-Calamity opened the letter and saw the King's signature, she cried out for joy and made immediate preparations for departure. She sent me forward to announce her coming and to say that she brings with her Queen Saffīah and a hundred of the chief warriors of Constantinople.'

The wazīr Dandān rose and said to the Kings: 'It will be prudent for us to go out disguised as western Christians, and to take with us a thousand chosen soldiers dressed in the old uniform of Cesarea. We do not want any of her cunning shifts to save this terrible old woman.' His advice was so well followed that, when Nuzhat saw the expedition setting forth, she said: 'If I had not known you, I would have taken you for real Christians!'

When Mother-of-Calamity came in sight of those who had come to meet her, Rumzān and Kāna mā kāna told the wazīr Dandān to deploy his soldiers in a large circle and make them come in slowly on all sides. This he did that there might be no escape for the men of Constantinople. Then said Rumzān to his fellow King: 'Let me go forward first, as the wicked old hag knows me and will suspect nothing.' With that he set heels to his horse and in a few moments ranged up alongside Mother-of-Calamity.

He leapt from his steed, and the old woman did the same. They fell into each other's arms, and Rumzān, looking long into her eyes, hugged her so tightly that she let a ringing fart, which startled all the horses and sent pebbles jumping from the road into the faces of the warriors.

As if this had been a sign, the thousand horsemen galloped up and cried to the Christians to surrender. In the twinkling of an eye all were taken prisoner save Queen Saffīah, whom the wazīr Dandān greeted nobly and gently with a full explanation of what was happening. Mother-of-Calamity was heavily chained. She smelt that death was near and made great streams of water in her garments.

The Mussulmāns then left Cesarea and arrived without incident at Baghdād. The Kings had the whole city decorated and illuminated, and invited the people by public proclamation to assemble in front of the palace. When the whole place, and all the streets which converged upon it, were packed with men, women and children, a scabby ass was led forth from the great gate. Upside down upon its back appeared Mother-of-Calamity, her head covered with a red rag and crowned with dung. Before her walked a herald with a great voice, reciting the chief crimes of this old woman, who had been the most fruitful source of sorrow throughout East and West.

When all the women and children had spat in her face, she was nailed by the feet to the great gate of Baghdād. Thus perished, rendering her stinking soul through her anus to the hell which gaped for it, that disastrous stench, that fabulous farter, the cunning, the politic, the perverse Mother-of-Calamity. Treachery betrayed her as she had betrayed others, and her death was regarded as a presage that Constantinople would soon be taken by the Believers and that the arms of Islām should triumph in peace from end to end of the earth which Allāh made.

The hundred Christian knights preferred to embrace the Simple Faith rather than return to their own country.

The two Kings and the wazīr Dandān ordered the most able scribes in the palace to place on record all that had happened to the race of Umar al-Numān, that it might serve as a judicious example for future generations.

'Such, O auspicious King,' continued Shahrazād, 'is the excellent tale of King Umar al-Numān and his two wonderful sons, Sharkān and Dū al-Makān; of the three queens, Ibrīzah, Kudiya fa-Kāna the Power of Destiny, and Nuzhat; of the wazīr Dandān, and the Kings Rumzān and Kāna mā kāna!'

Then Shahrazād fell silent.

King Shahryār looked at his clever companion tenderly for the first time, saying:

'As Allāh lives, O Shahrazād, your little sister is right when she says that your words are delicious and savoury in their newness. I begin to regret having killed so many girls; it may even happen that I will forget my oath to make you share the fate of the others.'

Little Dunyazād rose from her carpet, crying: 'Dear sister, that was an admirable tale. I delighted in Nuzhat and the discourse which she gave, and the sermons of the five girls pleased me exceedingly. I confess that I rejoiced at the death of Mother-of-Calamity. I found all the details of your story marvellous in the extreme.'

Shahrazād smiled at her sister and answered: 'But what would you say if I told you something of the speech of beasts and birds?'

'Please do so, my sister,' replied Dunyazād, 'for their words should be charming, especially as reported by you.' 'With all my heart,' answered Shahrazād, 'but only if our lord the King still suffers from his sleeplessness.' King Shahryār said in some perplexity: 'But how can beasts and birds talk? What language do they use?' 'They speak verse and prose in the purest Arabic,' answered Shahrazād. 'As Allāh lives,' cried the King, 'I shall decide nothing concerning your fate until you have told me some of these things of which I was entirely ignorant. So far I have only heard men and women speaking. I shall not be displeased to hear the thoughts of those creatures which most of my subjects do not understand.'

As she saw that the night was far spent, Shahrazād begged the King to wait for the next day. In spite of his impatience Shahryār consented to do so and, taking her in his arms, lay with the beautiful Shahrazād until the morning.

But when the hundred and forty-sixth night had come

SHAHRAZĀD SAID:

The Delightful Tale of the Beasts and Birds

The Tale of the Goose, the Peacock and the Peahen

IT is related, O auspicious King, that there was once, in the antiquity of time and in the passage of the age and of the moment, a peacock who lived with his wife on the borders of the sea. They delighted to walk in the forest which stretched away from the strand, full of streams and the singing of birds. During the day they peacefully sought for their food, and at night the peacock chose them a perch in some shady tree so that no wanton neighbour might be tempted by the charms of his young wife. They lived thus in peace and happiness, blessing their benevolent Creator.

One day the peacock suggested to his wife that they should make an excursion, for change of air and scene, to an island which they could see from the shore. When the peahen answered: 'I hear and I obey!' they flew off together and soon came to the island.

They found the place covered with ripe fruit trees and nourished by a multitude of streams, so that they were charmed to walk about in the cool shadow and stop from time to time to eat the fruit and drink the clear water.

As they were thinking of returning to their own home, they saw a goose coming towards them, beating her wings in an ecstasy of terror. Tremblingly she asked for their protection, and both the peacock and his wife received her cordially. The peahen spoke soothingly to her, saying: 'Be very welcome. You will find in us a family.' The goose became a little calmer at these words, and the peacock, supposing that she had met with some extraordinary adventure, asked the reason of her fright. The goose answered: 'I am still quite ill with what has happened and the terror with which Adamkin has inspired me. Allāh keep us! Allāh guard us all from Adamkin!' 'Calm yourself, my good goose, calm yourself,' said the peacock who had been much upset by her words, and the peahen tried to console her, saying: 'How can Adamkin come to this island? He cannot jump, he cannot walk on the water!' Then said the goose: 'Thank you for the encouragement and peace which you have given me.' 'Dear sister,' urged the peahen, 'I pray you tell us the nature of your fear of Adamkin and what has happened.' So the goose recounted the following:

O glorious peacock and sweet hospitable peahen, I have lived on this island since I was a child, without experiencing either care or pain or ugliness. The night before last, however, as I was sleeping with my head beneath my wing, an Adamkin came to me in my dreams and would have entered into conversation with me. I was about to reply to his advances, when a voice cried: 'Take care, O goose, take care! Beware of Adamkin; his manners are pleasant and his tongue full of a sweet guile. Do not forget that the poet has said:

> Beware the sweet before the fox has sprung,
> The fox behind the honey of his tongue.

For know, poor goose, that Adamkin is so skilful that he can draw to himself ferocious monsters of the deep and those who live in the bosom of the waters; wings which sweep tranquilly above his head he can make fall in disorder with a ball of dried mud; though he is feeble, he is so wicked that he can overcome the elephant and tear away his defences to make things for his own use. Flee, goose, flee!'

I jumped up in my sleep and, without looking behind me, flew forward with stretched neck and beating wings. I hurried about and about until my strength failed me, and then alighted at the foot of a mountain, where I hid behind a rock with beating heart and a lively terror in my breast because of Adamkin. I had neither eaten nor drunken and yet I did not dare to move in search of food or water. Suddenly I saw appear in the entrance of a cave which was opposite my hiding place, a young and ruddy lion, whose virtuous and tender looks inspired me with both confidence and sympathy. He had already seen me and, now that I glanced at him, he showed signs of great joy because my timidity and expression had quite charmed him. He approached me, saying: 'Come hither, gentle child, and talk with me a little.' I felt honoured by his invitation and moved forward as modestly as I was able. 'What is your name, and to what tribe do you belong?' asked the lion, and I answered: 'My name is Goose, my tribe is the Birds.' Then said he: 'I see you all frightened and trembling, and yet I cannot imagine why.' I told him my dream, and he much astonished me by saying: 'Once I also had a dream like that, which I told to my father, who warned me most strictly against Adamkin and his treacheries. So far, however, I have never met the creature.' Hearing the young lion speak in this fashion, my fear grew greater and I exclaimed: 'There is no doubt as to what should be done! This scourge must be destroyed, and the glory of killing Adamkin suits with none so well as yourself, O Prince of Beasts. Your fame will go out through sky and earth and water when you have made an end of him.' I went on encouraging and flattering the young lion until he made up his mind to go out and seek our common enemy.

He left his cave, telling me to follow him, and we set forth, myself walking behind and the lion cantering in front, cracking his tail like a whip. I had some difficulty in keeping up with him. We went on and on until we saw a cloud of dust coming towards us and in the middle of it a naked and fugitive donkey who jumped, caracoled and even sometimes rolled in the dust with his four legs in the air. The lion was astonished at this sight, because his parents had hardly ever let him leave the cave before; he hailed the donkey, crying: 'Come here you!' The other obeyed, and my friend said to him: 'O beast of little sense, why are you behaving in this way? Who are you, and to what tribe do you belong?' 'Master, I am your slave the Ass, of the tribe of Asses,' answered the other, 'and I am come here to escape from Adamkin.' The lion laughed hugely, saying: 'What, is a beast with your shape and size afraid of Adamkin?' 'O prince,' replied the ass, shaking his head in a knowing fashion, 'I see that you do not know this terrible creature. I am not afraid of him because he can kill me, but because he can do worse. Let me tell you that he uses me to ride on; he puts something on my back which he calls a pack-saddle, he squeezes my belly with something which he calls a girth, and places below my tail a ring whose name I forget, but which cruelly wounds my most sensitive parts. He thrusts a piece of iron in my mouth, which makes my tongue bleed and which he calls a bit. When I am prepared in this way, he sits on top of me and pricks my neck and my behind with a sharp point to make me go faster than I can. If, when I am foundered, I show an inclination to go slowly, he curses and swears at me so terribly that I shiver, though I am only an ass. Even in front of other people he calls me: "Pimp! Son of a whore! Son of a bugger! Your sister's arse! Lover of women!" If, by evil chance, I wish to relieve my breast by passing air, his fury knows no bounds; it would ill become me to repeat in your presence what he calls me on such occasions. Alas, I can only relieve myself in my favourite way when I am far behind him or quite alone. And that is not all! When I am old, he will sell me to some water-carrier who will put a wooden saddle on me and load me with enormous water-jars on either side; at the end of certain months I shall die of ill-treatment and privation. Then my body will be thrown to the dogs who wander about the ruins. That, O King's son, is the fate which Adamkin reserves for me. Is there a more unfortunate creature in all the world? I pray you answer me, O virtuous and sensitive goose.'

I shivered with horror and pity, crying: 'Dear lion, the conduct of this ass is excusable. I have been almost killed by fright as I listened to him.' The lion, seeing the ass making off, called to him: 'Why are you in such a hurry, my friend? Stay with us a little; you have interested me very much and I would willingly take you as a guide to lead me to Adamkin.' 'My lord,' answered the ass, 'to my infinite regret I must confess that I would rather put a day's journey between myself and him. I ran away from him yesterday as he was journeying in this direction, and now I am looking for some sure hiding place which will protect me from his perfidy. With your permission, I will now enjoy myself for a short time, as I am quite sure he cannot hear me.' So saying, the ass brayed violently and followed this noise with a magnificent series of three hundred running farts. Then he rolled on the grass for quite a time. At last he rose and, seeing a cloud of dust on the horizon, stretched first one ear towards it and then another, looked fixedly at it, and finally cantered off.

Soon from out of the dust appeared a black horse with a silver spot like a new coin upon his forehead. He was a proud, beautiful and well-proportioned animal, having four crowns of white hair growing above his hoofs. He neighed most agreeably as he approached and, when he saw the lion, halted in his honour and would have withdrawn. But my friend, who was delighted with the newcomer's elegance, called out: 'Who are you, O beautiful stranger? And why do you run throughout this great solitude with so disquieted an expression?' 'O King of time,' the other answered, 'I am Horse, of the tribe of Horses, and I am fleeing before the approach of Adamkin.'

'Do not say such things, O horse!' exclaimed the astonished lion. 'Surely it is disgraceful for an animal of your shoulder-breadth and size to be afraid of Adamkin? You could destroy his wicked life with one blow of your foot. Look at me! I am not as big as you are and yet I have promised this gentle goose, whom you see trembling here, to kill and eat Adamkin, and thus free her from her fears for ever. After that it will be my duty and pleasure to return the poor child to the bosom of her family.'

The horse looked at my friend with a sad smile, and said: 'O King, I beg you not to entertain any such thoughts, or to over-estimate my strength and swiftness when matched against the cunning of Adamkin. When I am near him, he finds a way to tame me for his desire. He puts hobbles of hemp and hair upon my feet and fastens my head to a post fixed higher than myself in the wall, so that I cannot move or sit down or sleep. And that is not all. When he wishes to ride upon me, he puts a thing called a saddle upon my back and compresses my waist with two strong girths which hurt me very much; he places a piece of steel in my mouth and, pulling it about with reins, guides me in any direction he pleases. When he is on my back, he pricks me in the side with things called spurs until the blood runs down. When I am old and my back is not strong enough to bear him, my muscles too weak to carry him swiftly forward, he sells me to a miller who makes me turn his mill night and day for certain years, and then in his turn sells me to a knacker who cuts my throat and flays me. At the last, my hide goes to the tanner and my hair to those who make sieves and tammies and bolters. That is my fate with Adamkin!'

This recital disturbed the lion, and he said: 'It is quite certain that I must free creation from this disease which you call Adamkin. When did you see him last, good horse?' 'I ran away from him at noon. He is now pursuing me in this direction,' said the horse.

He had hardly finished speaking when yet another cloud of dust so frightened him that he ran away from us without waiting to say farewell. We held our ground and soon saw a camel coming towards us with great bounds, his neck stretched out and his throat bubbling for terror. Seeing so colossal an animal, the lion was quite sure that he was at last in the presence of Adamkin; therefore, without waiting for my advice, he leapt upon him and was about to strangle him, when I cried out: 'Stop, my King! that is not Adamkin, but a brave camel, the most harmless creature of us all. I am sure that he also is running away from Adamkin.' The lion stayed himself in time, and said in a concerned tone to the camel: 'O prodigious animal, are you also afraid of this creature whose face you could so easily tread into the dust with your great feet?' The camel shrugged his shoulders and answered sadly, with his eyes fixed as in a nightmare: 'Look at my nostrils, O King's son. They are gouged and split by a ring of hair which Adamkin has passed through them to tame me and lead me where he will. He fixes a cord to this ring and gives it to the littlest of his children who, by this means, can go mounted upon a tiny ass and control, not only me, but a whole file of us, one behind the other. Look at my back. It is humped with the burdens which Adamkin has placed on it throughout the ages. Look at my legs. They are calloused and foundered with forced marches over sand and stone. And that is not all! When I grow old through sleepless nights and days without repose, he takes no notice of my patience and my great age, but makes a little further profit by selling my old skin and venerable bones to the butcher, the tanner, and the webster. That is the usual way in which Adamkin treats my people.'

The lion's indignation knew no bounds. He roared and ground his jaws, stamping on the earth with vexation. At last he said to the camel: 'Make haste to tell me where you left Adamkin.' The other answered: 'He is looking for me, and may be here at any moment. I beg you to allow me to exile myself from this present company and to depart hurriedly into some other land than my own. For neither the solitude of the desert nor the difficulty of unknown places can hide me from his inquisition.' Then said the lion: 'Believe me, O camel, if you wait a little you will see me spring upon Adamkin, throw him to the earth, break his bones, drink his blood, and grow fat upon his flesh.' The camel, who trembled in great sheets all over his skin at these bloodthirsty words, replied: 'If you will give me leave, my lord, I would rather withdraw, for a poet has said:

> If in your own land and your pleasant tent
> A face appear which fills you with dislike
> Do not attempt to vanquish it but strike
> Your camp and change your very continent.'

The good camel kissed the earth between the lion's hands and departed in great haste.

As soon as he was gone, a little old creature appeared from I know not where. He seemed something like a debased man with a wrinkled skin, and carried on his shoulders a basket of carpenter's tools and eight large wooden planks.

I had not the strength to utter a single cry of warning to my companion, but fell paralysed to the ground, while the young lion went forward with an amused smile to examine this comic animal more closely. The carpenter fell on his face before my friend, smiling and saying humbly: 'O glorious King, O sitter upon the tallest throne under the sky, I give you good evening and beseech Allāh to increase you in fame and strength and virtue. I am an oppressed person who comes to beg your protection from his enemy.'

He wept and groaned and sighed so sadly that the lion made his voice gentle, and said: 'Who has oppressed you and who are you, most eloquent, most cultivated and, at the same time, most ugly of animals?' 'My lord,' answered the other, 'I am a carpenter of the tribe of carpenters and he who oppresses me is Adamkin, from whom may Allāh preserve my King. He makes me work from dawn till night, without payment and without food. Now I have revolted and fled far from the city where he lives.'

The young lion shouted in his anger. He leapt and foamed and shot sparks from his eyes, crying: 'Where is this calamitous Adamkin, that I may bray him between my teeth and avenge the multitude of his victims?' 'He will be here soon,' said the man. 'He is coming after me because he has no one to build his houses any more.' 'Where are you thinking of going to, O beast called carpenter?' asked the lion, and the other replied: 'I am looking for your father's wazīr, our lord the leopard. He has sent a command to me to build him a strong cabin against the assaults of Adamkin, who is rumoured to be coming into these parts. That is why I am carrying my tools and these planks.'

The lion felt himself inflamed with jealousy of the leopard, and said to the carpenter: 'It is extremely presumptuous of my father's wazīr to command things for himself before we have commanded them for ourselves. I bid you stay here and build the cabin for me. The wazīr can wait.' The carpenter pretended to make off, saying: 'O King's son, I fear the wrath of the leopard. But I will return as soon as I have executed his commission, and build you, not a cabin, but a palace.' However the lion would listen to no excuses and, as a jest, lightly struck the little man on the breast with his paw so that he lost his balance and fell with a clatter of tools and planks. The lion burst out laughing at the fellow's discomfiture, but the carpenter hid his anger, and set slowly to work with a fawning smile.

He took the lion's measure and, in a few moments, had constructed a solid box with a narrow opening, spiked with nails reaching through to the inside. He bored a few holes in the planks, and then respectfully invited the lion to enter his new house. 'It seems very narrow,' objected the lion, but the carpenter said: 'Crouch down and then leap in, for you will find it large enough when you are inside.' The lion lowered himself and slipped into the box, leaving only his tail outside. At once the carpenter twisted the tail, packing it in with the rest, and then, in the twinkling of an eye, nailed up the opening.

The lion tried to move, but the sharp points of the nails entered his flesh on all sides, so that he roared in pain and shame, crying: 'What is the meaning of this narrow house and these detestable points?'

The man uttered a cry of triumph and jigged on his feet with laughter, saying: 'Dog of the desert, those are the points of Adamkin who, although he is ugly and feeble, can triumph over all courage, strength and beauty.'

So saying, the horrible little man piled faggots round the box and set them alight with a torch. Lying unnoticed on the ground, I saw my poor friend burnt to death and Adamkin making off with cries of exultation. As soon as he was gone, I flew as fast as I could in the opposite direction, half dead from grief and fear. Thus it was that I met you, my good compassionate friends.

At this point Shahrazād saw the approach of morning and discreetly fell silent.

But when the hundred-and-forty-seventh night had come

SHE SAID:

The two birds had listened to this recital with every mark of consternation. When it was over, the peahen said to the goose: 'We are safe here, my sister; you may stay with us as long as you like, until Allāh sends you peace of mind, which is His greatest gift next to good health.' 'But I am very frightened,' said the goose, and the peahen replied: 'It is unnecessary for you to be frightened. Fear argues an attempt to escape from Destiny, and you must know that every debt shall be paid and the writing upon our brows fulfil itself to the last letter. It should console you to know that the Just Judge allows none of His creatures to perish until it has consumed that portion of happiness which is reserved for it.'

As they were talking in this way, a breaking of branches and sound of footsteps so frightened the goose that she flew off towards the sea, crying: 'Beware, beware, or your destinies will surely be accomplished!'

It was a false alarm, however, and soon through the parted branches appeared the head of a beautiful roebuck with moist eyes. 'Do not be frightened, my sister,' cried the peahen after the goose. 'Come back quickly, for we have a new guest. He belongs to the animal people, just as you belong to the bird people. He never eats bloody meat, but lives on herbs and grasses. If you allow yourself to be thrown into such perturbation, you will become ill.'

The goose returned, moving her hips, and the roebuck said with a bow: 'This is the first time that I have been here. Never have I seen more tempting vegetation or sweeter greenery. Allow me to stay with you and partake of the blessing of Allāh.' 'Be very welcome, urbane roebuck!' answered the three others, and for a long time this family stayed together, feasting and drinking the good air in company. They never neglected their morning or evening prayers, except the goose who, now that she felt herself in safety, forgot her duty towards the Giver.

Alas, she paid for this ingratitude with her life!

One morning a ship was wrecked on the island, and the sailors who came to shore hastened towards the unsuspecting group as soon as they saw it. The peacock and his wife fled into the tall trees, while the roebuck bounded into the forest and disappeared; but the goose stayed still in confusion, attempting to run first in this direction and then in that, until she was captured and eaten.

To their horror the birds saw the goose's neck being cut, then they went in search of the roebuck whom they easily found. They told him of the goose's fate, and all three congratulated each other on their own escape. They wept to remember their companion, and the peahen said: 'She was a modest, sweet and gentle goose.' 'That is so,' replied the roebuck, 'but she forgot Allāh during these last weeks and did not thank Him for His blessings.' Then said the peacock: 'Let us pray, O daughter of my uncle, and you, most pious roebuck.' They kissed the earth between the hands of Allāh, saying:

> Blessed be the Just and Good God
> Who has made each bird and beast to stand before Him,
> Who watches over
> And rewards the evil and good which we have done
> In due season.
> He has stretched out and lighted the heavens
> As a pool for some of us,
> He has robed the earth with her seas
> For some of us,
> Making all things beautiful.

Shahrazād paused for a moment when she had told this tale. 'Those animals are very intelligent and their prayer is excellent!' cried King Shahryār. 'But is that all you can tell me of the beasts, O Shahrazād?' 'Ah, that is nothing, my lord, to what I could tell you,' replied the girl, and Shahryār asked: 'Why do you not go on then?' 'Before telling you any more about the animals, O King,' said Shahrazād, 'I would like to relate a story which confirms the moral which you have just heard, that prayer is agreeable to the Lord.' 'Certainly!' said King Shahryār.

Then Shahrazād said:

The Tale of the Shepherd and the Girl

THERE was once, in the mountains of our country, a wise and holy shepherd, who lived at peace, sufficing himself with the milk and wool of his flocks. He was so gentle that the wild beasts never attacked his sheep, and would salute him from afar, when they saw him, with cries after their kind. One day, as he still lived in peaceful virtue caring nothing for the cities of the world, Allāh determined to try the depth of his wisdom and the reality of his faith by the beauty of woman. Therefore He sent down one of His angels, bidding her spare no pains to make the good man sin.

As he lay sick in his cave glorifying the Creator, he saw a black-eyed girl, almost a child, come smiling through the entrance. The cave became on the instant perfumed with her presence and the venerable flesh of the shepherd trembled. He raised his eyebrows and frowned from his corner, saying: 'What are you doing here, O unknown woman? I did not call you and I have no need of you.' The girl sat down close to the old man and said: 'Look at me. I am a virgin, not yet a woman, and I give myself to you for my own pleasure and on account of the great goodness which I have heard attributed to you.' 'Begone, temptress of hell!' cried the old man. 'Leave me to wear out my soul in adoration of Him who dies not.' The girl made all of her body move in a tempting rhythm, and sighed: 'Why will you not take me? I bring you a submissive spirit and a body melting with desire. Is not my breast whiter than the milk of your sheep? Is not my nakedness cooler and brighter than a spring breaking from the rocks? Feel my hair, how much more soft it is than the wool of a lamb that is not yet born. My thighs are small and refreshing in the first flower of my youth. My little breasts have hardly flowered yet, but a quick finger can give them ecstasy. Come! Here are my lips ready to crush your mouth! Come! My teeth can infuse the old and dying with new life, and all my flesh is ready to weep drops of honey by your side!'

'O devil, depart from this place, or I will set about you with my knotted stick!' cried the old man, while each hair of his beard trembled with anger. The girl madly threw her arms about his neck and murmured in his ear: 'I am tart fruit, hardly yet sweet. Eat and you shall be cured. The smell of jasmine is coarse to the odour of my virginity.'

'The perfume of prayer is the only one which does not pass

away!' exclaimed the shepherd, and he pushed her from him, crying: 'Begone, begone, seductress!'

The child rose and lightly undressed herself until she stood before him naked and white, bathed in the dark sea of her hair. Her silent invitation was more dangerous in that lonely cave than all the desirous cries which she had uttered before. The old man groaned and hid his face in his mantle, that he might not see this living lily. 'Depart, depart, O traitorous eyes!' called the old man. 'You have been our grief since the beginning of the world; you have destroyed men from the old times till now and have sown discord among the children of God. In gaining you, many a wise man has lost that infinite joy which comes after death.' With that the shepherd wound his head more closely in his garment.

'You speak of the men of old time,' answered the girl. 'Know then that the wisest of them loved me and the chastest of them sang my praise. My beauty never led them from the right way, but lighted their path for them, showing them the flowers beside the road of life. True wisdom is to forget all between my breasts; therefore be wise, for I am ready to teach you.'

The old shepherd turned his face to the wall, crying: 'Get you behind me, O wickedness! I abominate you and vomit from you! You have ever preserved the evil man and pulled the virtuous from his righteous seat. Your beauty is a lie; all beauty is a lie save that invisible grace which comes from prayer. Get you behind me, I say!'

The girl who had been sent from Paradise answered: 'O holy shepherd, continue to drink the milk of your sheep, to dress in their wool and to pray to our Master in solitude and peace!'

The vision departed and the wild beasts came from every ridge of the mountain to kiss the earth between the old man's hands and ask his blessing.

At this point Shahrazād fell silent, and King Shahryār said sadly: 'O Shahrazād, the example of that shepherd gives me matter for reflection. I think it might be better for me if I retired to a cave to escape the cares of my kingdom, and passed my life in tending sheep. But first I should like to hear some more about the beasts and birds.'

But when the hundred and forty-eighth night had come

SHAHRAZĀD SAID:

The Tale of the Tortoise and the Heron

IT is told in one of my old books, O auspicious King, that a heron stood one day on the bank of a river watching with stretched neck and vigilant eye the course of the water. For this was the business by which he honestly and industriously earned a livelihood for himself and his children.

As he was waiting for the least movement in the water, he saw the dead body of a man come down stream and fetch up against the rock on which he was standing. Seeing the traces of sabre and lance cuts all over the corpse, he thought to himself: 'This is some brigand who has been justly punished!' and raising his wings thanked Allāh, saying: 'Blessed is He who makes dead evil-doers profitable to the living virtuous!' He was about to tear strips from the body to carry to his children when he saw the sky obscured by a cloud of vultures and sparrow-hawks who were descending towards him in lessening circles.

Fearing to be devoured by these wolves of the air, he flew away as hard as he could and came, after a few hours, to a tree which grew on an islet at the mouth of the river. Here, while he waited for the corpse to be borne down to him, he began to consider the uncertainty of life and the inconstancy of chance, saying to himself: 'Behold, I am obliged to leave my own country and the bank where I was born, which shelters my wife and children. It is an empty world, and the more so for him who trusts in chance and does not put up provision for an evil day. If I had been wiser in this respect, the wolves of the air could not have troubled me. But let me be patient, for the wise always counsel patience in adversity.'

As he was occupied with these thoughts, he saw a tortoise swimming slowly toward the tree. She raised her head and, seeing him, wished him peace. 'O heron,' she asked, 'how is it that I see you so far from your accustomed bank?' The heron answered:

> 'If in your own land and your pleasant tent
> A face appear which fills you with dislike,
> Do not attempt to banish it but strike
> Your camp and change your very continent.

Good tortoise, I saw my bank encompassed by the wolves of the air, and rather than be disturbed by their unpleasant faces, I preferred to exile myself until Allāh shall have compassion on me.'

'If that is so,' replied the tortoise, 'I am ready to serve you devotedly and to be the companion of your exile, for I know how unhappy a stranger can be when he is far from his own country and how pleasant it is for him to find warm affection among unknown peoples. So far I have only known you by sight, but from henceforth I hope to prove a cordial and helpful companion.'

'Warm-hearted tortoise, O creature hard without but surely soft within,' answered the heron, 'I feel that I am about to weep because of your unstudied offer, which I accept with gratitude. You are right in all that you say concerning hospitality towards strangers. What would life be without friends, without the conversation of friends, without the laughter and singing of friends? He is a wise man who finds companions suiting with his own nature and does not frequent the society of the uncongenial as I have been compelled to do. My fellow herons are not only jealous of me, but are dull stupid fellows with nothing to talk about except their catches of fish. They occupy themselves with petty concerns, never thinking to lift up their hearts towards Allāh. Their beaks are turned to the ground and, though they have wings, they do not use them. They can only dive in the water, and often, for very foolishness, they remain lifeless upon the river bed.'

The tortoise, who had listened in silence, now cried: 'Come down, O heron, that I may kiss you.' The heron came down and the tortoise kissed him between the eyes, saying: 'My brother, you were not made to suit with birds of your own race, who have neither subtle perception nor charm of manner. Stay with me here, and life will pass pleasantly for both of us, shaded by this tree and soothed by the low singing of the river.' 'Thank you, thank you, my sister!' exclaimed the heron, 'but how about my wife and children?' 'Allāh is great and pitiful,' returned the tortoise. 'He will help us transport them here, so that we may all live together in security and peace.' On this the heron exclaimed: 'O tortoise, let us both thank the good God for having brought us together.' They both said:

> Praise be to Him whose deep design
> Has made your fortune equal mine;
> His poor are rich in smiles, and see
> His rich are poor in gaiety.

At this point Shahrazād saw the approach of morning and discreetly fell silent. Then King Shahryār said: 'O Shahrazād, your tales all combine to lead me into a milder way. And yet I should like to know if you are acquainted with any stories about wolves or other wilder animals.' 'That is the kind of tale which I know best,' answered Shahrazād, and Shahryār exclaimed: 'Tell me some of them at once!' Shahrazād promised for the next night.

And when the hundred-and-forty-ninth night had come

SHE SAID:

The Tale of the Wolf and the Fox

THE fox, O auspicious King, grew weary of the continued anger and cruelty of his lord the wolf, so he sat down one day on the trunk of a tree, his head filled with thoughts of those rights which had been taken away from him, and began to reflect. Suddenly he bounded joyfully in the air, for he had found a solution of his difficulties. He searched out the wolf and, when he had found him frowning and with his every hair bristling from bad temper, kissed the earth and stood before him with lowered eyes waiting to be spoken to. 'Son of a dog, what is it?' cried the wolf. 'Excuse my presumption, my lord,' answered the fox, 'but I have a plan to put before you and a request to make of you, if you will be so good as to grant me an audience.' 'Be less prolix,' snapped the wolf, 'say what you have to say quickly, or I will break every bone in your body.' Then said the fox: 'I have noticed for a long time, my lord, that Adamkin has been making relentless war upon us; the forest is filled with traps and gins and pitfalls. Soon it will be altogether uninhabitable unless all the wolves and foxes league together against Adamkin.' 'Miserable fox, foundered and evil beast,' cried the wolf, 'do you presume to alliance and friendship with me? Take that for your insolence!' And so saying, he gave the fox a kick which stretched him half dead upon the earth. The fox rose limping and, in spite of his anger, assumed his most smiling and apologetic air. 'My lord,' he said, 'I beg you to pardon your slave his lack of tact. He knows well that he has many faults, and even if he did not, the terrible and merited kick with which you have just gratified him, a kick which could easily have slain an elephant, would have taught him.' The wolf was a little soothed by the fox's attitude, so he said: 'Very well. Only remember

597

another time not to meddle with things which do not concern you.'
'You speak justly,' replied the fox. 'A wise man has said: "Do not speak till you are spoken to, do not answer until you are questioned. Mind your own business, and do not load with your advice those who cannot understand it, or those who will return evil for good." '

As he spoke the fox was thinking to himself: 'My time will come, and then this wolf shall pay to the uttermost farthing; pride, insolence and foolish conceit are always punished in this world. Let us be humble until we are powerful.' Then aloud he said: 'My master, you are not ignorant that justice is a virtue of the great and that to pardon is to follow the fair example of God. My crime is great, I know; but my repentance equals it. Your charming kick hurt my body, it is true, but it has cured and rejoiced my soul. A wise man has said: "There is some slight bitterness in the first taste of punishment, but the second taste is more delicious than clarified honey." '

'I accept your excuses and pardon the trouble you put me to in kicking you,' said the wolf. 'Now go on your knees with your head in the dust.' The fox obeyed and adored the wolf, saying: 'May Allāh strengthen your domination so that you triumph always.' Then said the wolf: 'Now I wish you to go before me as a scout and report any game you see.' The fox, answering 'I hear and I obey!' ran ahead into the forest.

He soon came to a place planted with vines, and remarked in it a dubious stretch of ground which suggested that there might be a pitfall concealed there. The fox made a large detour to avoid this path, saying to himself: 'He who does not look shall fall. I know something, by this time, of the snares of Adamkin. If I saw the effigy of a fox among the vines, I should surely flee, knowing it to be a trick of Adamkin; seeing an equivocal runway such as this, I am on my guard, for discretion is the better part of valour.' He advanced towards the suspected place very slowly and sometimes skipping backward; sniffing at every inch of the earth, he pricked his ears and went softly, so that at last he won past the equivocal path and was able to see a deep hole which had been covered with light branches and powdered with earth. 'Praise be to Allāh who gave me good eyes and a share of prudence!' cried the fox, beginning to dance with joy as if he had drunken all the grapes of the vine. He sang:

The trench is digged, the earth trembles to have
The great wild wolf, the proudest of the brave:
 Runner of girls, devourer of young men,
Shall eat my dung as I squat on his grave.

After that he rejoined the wolf, saying: 'Good news! Blessings rain upon you and are not weary.' 'Speak with less art!' cried the wolf, and the fox continued: 'To-day the vine is beautiful and the beasts rejoice because the keeper of the wineyard is dead and buried below branches in the place of his labours.' 'What are you waiting for then, vile pimp?' grumbled the wolf. 'Lead the way at once!' The fox led him to the middle of the vineyard, saying: 'Here is the place.' Instantly the wolf sprang upon the branches with a howl, and they gave under his weight. When the fox saw his foe rolling at the bottom of the pit, he recited these jubilant lines:

Rejoice, rejoice, for the green forest is mine,
 The beautiful vines and the plumpest game,
The marrow of the wild deer's chine,
  The fat of geese,
  The duck's elastic grease,
  The hen's soft bottom piece,
 And cock's head red as flame.

He jumped with a beating heart on the borders of the pit, rejoicing to hear the lamentations of the wolf. He himself began to weep and groan, and the prisoner lifted his head, saying: 'Dear friend, what is the use of weeping for me? I know that I have been hard on you at times, but now, for pity's sake, leave your tears and run to tell my wife and children of my danger.' 'Vilest of creatures,' answered the fox, 'are you foolish enough to think that I shed tears on your behalf? Know that I weep because you have lived so long, and bitterly lament because this fate did not overtake you years ago. Die, ill-omened wolf, and I will piss on your tomb, dancing with all the other foxes above your head!' The wolf said to himself: 'This is not the time for threats, since he is my only hope.' Then aloud he continued: 'Dear lad, it was only a minute ago that you swore fidelity to me in a thousand words. Why this so sudden change? I may have been a little short with you in the past; but do not bear malice. Remember the words of the poet:

> Let your seed fall even as the rain drop goes
> On every ground, and do not pass by those
>   Which seem to you the barrenest and least,
> For God shall gather more than you suppose.'

'O fool of wolves,' answered the fox snarling, 'have you already forgotten your insensate behaviour? A poet has said:

> If you offend a foe, and sleep;
> Your enemy will keep
> But one eye closed.
> It is to be supposed
> The other sees your crime—
> And God has both eyes open all the time.

You have oppressed me so long that I have a right to rejoice at your misfortune and eat your humiliation as if it were food.' 'O wise and subtle fox,' whined the wolf, 'you are only saying these bitter things in jest. But this is no time for joking. Rather fetch a cord and tie it to a tree, that I may climb up into safety.' 'Gently, gently, my wolf,' answered the fox laughing, 'your spirit may come out of the pit, but your body shall not. There are great stones which will effect this separation. Gross animal, heavy-brained tyrant, I am inclined to compare your fate with the tale of the Falcon and the Partridge.'

'I do not know what you are talking about,' whimpered the wolf.

Then the fox said:

Know, inauspicious wolf, that I was one day eating from the vines when I saw a great falcon drop from the air upon a little partridge. Somehow the smaller bird managed to escape the other's talons and hide himself in a small hole. The falcon stood at the narrow entrance of this place, saying: 'Sweet little fool, why do you fly from me? I wish you well and have taken much trouble on your behalf. I only wished to catch up with you because I knew you were hungry and wanted to feed you with corn which I had collected for you. Little partridge, gentle little partridge, come out without fear and eat the corn. My eye, my soul, my fair partridge, you will find it both pleasing and digestible.' The trustful bird came out in answer to this invitation and, in less time than it takes to tell you, lay all ripped open under the falcon's terrible claws. As she was dying, she said: 'O wicked traitor, may Allāh turn me to poison in your belly!' The falcon ate her in a single mouthful, but no sooner had he swallowed her than Allāh heard her prayer and destroyed him as if by an internal flame. He fell lifeless to the ground.

'And you, O wolf,' continued the fox, 'have fallen into this pit because you so humiliated me.'

'Have mercy upon me, old comrade!' cried the wolf. 'Forget the past, since I am well paid for it. I might easily have broken a leg, or put out both of my eyes. Try to help me; the finest friendship is that which shines brightest in adversity. Help me out of this and I will be your best friend, your wisest counsellor.'

The fox laughed heartily at this, saying: 'I see that you know nothing of the Words of the Wise.' 'What words and what wise?' groaned the astonished wolf. Then the fox said:

'Know, O ill-conditioned wolf, that the wise have taught us that people like you with ugly faces, coarse expressions, and malformed limbs have a soul to match their exteriors. I grant that what you have said about friendship is very fine, but you delude yourself in applying such excellent maxims to a traitor like yourself. Also, O stupid wolf, if you were wise enough to give me good counsel, would you not be wise enough to get yourself out of this hole? You remind me of the tale of the doctor.' 'Another tale,' whimpered the wolf, and the fox said:

'There was once a peasant who had a large tumour on his right hand which prevented him from working. He sent for a famous doctor, who came with one of his eyes bandaged. "What is the matter with your eye, good doctor?" asked the sick man, and the other answered: "I have a tumour there which prevents me from seeing." "You have a tumour and do not cure it?" cried the patient. "How then will you cure mine? Be off, and let me see your back."

'Before presuming to become my counsellor, you should find some way of leaving your present position and escaping that which will presently fall upon you. If you cannot do so, you had better stay where you are for ever.'

The wolf burst into tears, and said in his despair: 'Dear friend, I pray you stretch down your tail and pull me from this hole. I swear by Allāh that I will repent of my past cruelties. I will file my claws and break my great teeth that I may be no more tempted to attack my neighbours. I will indue the rough habit of an anchorite and pass my time in lonely penitence, eating the herbs of nature and drinking nothing but water.' The fox was not softened by this, but said: 'How can a creature change its nature? Wolf you are, and wolf you will be until the end of time. I have very little faith in such an apt repentance. Nor am I such a fool as to trust my tail to you. I wish to see you die, for a wise man has said: "The death of a sinner purifies the earth." '

At this point Shahrazād saw the approach of morning and discreetly fell silent.

But when the hundred-and-fiftieth night had come

SHE SAID:

The wolf bit his paw in rage and despair, and then made his voice sweet to say to the fox: 'Dear fox, your family is famous throughout all the world for its charming manners, its cleverness, its eloquence, and its benevolence. Remember your family, my boy; act up to its fine tradition.' This time, the fox laughed so heartily that he fainted away. When he came to himself, he said: 'I see that your education has not yet begun, and I have hardly time to undertake it now. Yet you might listen with advantage to these few precepts: There is a cure for everything except death: Corruption waits for everything except the diamond: We may escape all except our destiny.

'You spoke just now of rewarding me with your friendship if I helped you to escape. I very much fear that you are like the serpent in a story which, through your ignorance, you doubtless do not know.' The wolf was obliged to confess that the tale was unknown to him, so the fox said:

'A snake once escaped from a juggler's bag and, being cramped from long confinement, moved painfully along the ground. He would certainly have been either recaptured or crushed under foot, had not a charitable stranger seen him, imagined him to be ill, and lifted him up to warm him. The snake's first care, when he felt life returning to him, was to choose out the most delicate part of his preserver's body and fasten his fangs there, so that the man fell dead. Even before that time, a poet had written:

> If you must put a snake to school,
>   Teach him your tricks and dances while
>   He hisses at you: for his smile
> Means that the poison bags are full.

And another poet wrote:

> The gentle boy you spurned
> And put disgrace in;
> His strength to manhood turned,
> Will smash your face in.

'That you may have a foretaste of the sweet attentions and beautiful round stones which folk will presently shower upon your head, and before I freely water your tomb in my own way, lift up your head and look.'

So saying the fox turned his back, crouched on his two hindlegs over the pit, and did that on the wolf's face which wonderfully perfumed his last moments.

Then he climbed on a mound of earth and barked till the owners and keepers of the vineyard ran up to see what was the matter. The fox skipped off and hid himself in a place where he could see the great stones dropped upon his foe and hear the howling of his dying agony.

At this point Shahrazād paused for a moment to drink a glass of sherbert which little Dunyazād handed to her, while King Shahryār exclaimed: 'Ah, ah! I thought that the wolf would be killed. His death pleased me very much. But can you not now tell me some tale illustrating the evils of blind trust and thoughtlessness?' 'I hear and I obey!' said Shahrazād, and continued:

The Tale of the Mouse and the Weasel

THERE was once a woman whose trade was the husking of sesame. It happened that a customer brought her a measure of the finest sesame, saying: 'The doctor has instructed a sick friend of mine to eat nothing but this food; I have brought it to you that you may husk and prepare it carefully.' The woman set to work and by nightfall the sesame lay upon a tray in suggestive whiteness. A weasel who passed that way was tempted by the sight. She went that night to the place where the tray was hidden, and enjoyed herself so much that only a handful or so of the good food remained in the morning.

The weasel from her hiding place was able to see and hear the woman's astonished anger, and her cry: 'Those terrible mice! They have overrun my house since the cat died. If I saw one of them, I would make it pay for all the depredations of its tribe.'

The weasel said to herself: 'I must confirm this woman's suspicions of the mouse, if I wish to escape her anger. If I do not do so, she will break my back.' Therefore she went and found the mouse, saying to her: 'Dear sister, a neighbour has certain duties towards a neighbour. I know nothing more repulsive than a selfish householder who does not send to those houses which are near her own the best food which the women of the place prepare, and sweets and pastries on a feast day.' 'That is true, my good friend,' answered the mouse. 'I am gratified that you, who have only been in this neighbourhood a few days, should be so generous and obliging. Would that all neighbours were as punctilious as you are! I imagine that you have something to tell me?' 'The woman of the house has received a measure of the finest sesame,' announced the weasel. 'Her children have eaten so heartily of it that only a little remains, therefore I have hurried to tell you, before the little gluttons finish it all up.'

The mouse moved her tail and jumped with excitement. Instead of taking time for reflection, instead of noticing the hypocritical air of the weasel, instead of pausing to find out where the woman might be, instead of asking herself what could have caused a weasel to be so generous, she jumped into the middle of the tray and greedily filled her mouth with the white grains. At the same moment, the woman broke in her head, and she perished through not taking thought.

King Shahryār said: 'O Shahrazād, your tale has taught me a lesson in prudence. If I had known it before, I would not have trusted so easily in the wanton wife whom I was obliged to kill with my own hand and the black eunuchs who helped her in her treachery. Have you no story which illustrates a faithful friendship?'

Shahrazād said:

The Tale of the Crow and the Civet

IT is related that a crow and a civet were great friends and passed their time in games and conversation. One day they were talking of such interesting things that they took no notice of what was passing about them, until suddenly they were brought back to earth by the howling of a terrible tiger in the forest.

On this the crow, who was sitting on a tree trunk by the side of his friend, fluttered into the upper branches, but the civet did not know where to hide, as she could not make out from which direction the tiger's cries had come. 'What must I do, my friend?' she asked the crow. 'Have you neither advice nor help to give me?' 'What would I not do for you, dear friend?' replied the crow. 'I would confront the world, if that would aid you; but, before I bring help to you on this occasion, I would like you to hear these words of a certain poet:

> At last and first
> True friendship is a fighting thing,
> A headlong thirst
> To leap into the thick and swing
> Hot blows
> At your friend's foes.'

When he had made an end of these lines, the crow flew as fast as he could towards a passing flock of sheep who were guarded by dogs larger than lions. He came close and bit first one and then another of the dogs painfully in the head, so that the rest became disturbed and angry. Croaking in mockery, the crow hopped and fluttered just far enough ahead of all the dogs to escape their teeth, and led them, in a state of increasing fury, through the forest. When he considered that their baying had certainly frightened the tiger far away, he flew straight up into the air, leaving the dogs to make their way back grumbling to the flock. As soon as it was safe, he rejoined his friend the civet whose life he had so bravely protected, and the two lived together in peace and security.

Now, O auspicious King, continued Shahrazād, I will tell you without further delay:

The Tale of the Crow and the Fox

IT is related that an old fox, whose conscience was charged with many sins and depredations, had retired with his wife to a certain valley rich in game. He ravaged the smaller animals to such an extent that the mountain-side was soon depopulated, and he himself was obliged first to eat his own children and then treacherously to strangle and devour his wife in order that he should not go hungry.

He was too old to change his hunting-ground and was not quick enough to catch hares, or partridge on the wing. As he sat one day, brooding over his black destiny, he saw a tired crow come to rest on the branch of a tree. Thought the fox to himself: 'If I can persuade this crow to become friends with me, it will be a piece of good luck. His strong wings will be more useful than my poor crippled legs; he will bring me food and be a companion for me in this lonely place.' No sooner was this plan conceived than he put it into execution, bowing to the crow and saying: 'Sweet neighbour, one good Mussulmān must always have two qualities which appeal to a neighbouring Mussulmān: that he is of the Faith, and that he is a neighbour. I recognise these two merits in you, and all my heart has suddenly become filled with feelings of fraternal love towards you. Now tell me what you think of me?'

The crow burst out laughing and nearly fell from the tree, as he said: 'I must admit that I am surprised. Whence this sudden friendship? How comes sincerity into your heart, when you have ever before kept it on the point of your tongue? How can animals and birds live together, and how can you persuade me with all your eloquence that your race have ceased to be the killers and mine the killed? Does that astonish you? Wicked old fox, put your charming remarks back in your pocket and spare me this strange friendship.'

Then said the fox: 'I have no fault to find with your reasoning, O judicious crow, and yet there is nothing impossible to Him who made the hearts of His creatures and lit a sudden flame in my soul on your behalf. To prove to you that persons of a different race can get on wonderfully well together, I will tell you a tale which I once heard of a flea and a mouse.'

'If you talk of proofs,' said the crow, 'I am quite ready to listen to your tale of the flea and the mouse which I have never heard before.'

So the fox said:

Delightful friend, the wise, who have read books old and new, tell us that a flea and a mouse both lived in their own places within the house of a rich merchant.

One night the flea, being disgusted with sucking the bitter blood of the house cat, jumped on to the bed where the merchant's wife was sleeping. He entered among her garments and, slipping below her chemise, soon gained the delicate fold of her groin. He found the place soft and sweet and white, without rough redness or indiscreet hair, but far otherwise, dear crow, far otherwise. The flea set his feet strongly and sucked the woman's delicious blood until he could drink no more. He went so indiscreetly about his meal that the young woman woke and clapped her hand to the place where she felt the bit. The flea would certainly have perished if he had not slipped nimbly through the numerous folds of her drawers—that is a garment which women wear, O crow—and, jumping to the ground, hidden himself in the first sanctuary which came his way.

The young woman gave a cry of pain which brought all her slaves to her. They rolled up their sleeves and searched through her garments for the flea: two investigated her robe, one searched her chemise, and two others spread out the drawers, fold by fold, while the woman herself stood naked in the light of the torches, examining herself in front. Also her favourite slave investigated exhaustively behind. But, as you can suppose, none of them found anything.

'But I do not see any proofs in what you have told me,' objected the crow, so the fox hastened to say: 'We are just coming to them,' and continued: . . .

At this point Shahrazād saw the approach of morning and discreetly fell silent.

But when the hundred-and-fifty-first night had come

SHE SAID:

The hole in which the flea had taken refuge belonged to a mouse, who was extremely offended to see a stranger so calmly making free with her home. 'O parasitic flea, what are you doing here?' she cried. 'You are neither of my blood nor of my kind.' 'Hospitable mouse,' replied the flea, 'if I have acted with indiscretion, it was to save my life from the mistress of this house, who would have killed me for the matter of a little blood which I took from her. I grant you, however, that it was of the first quality, deliciously warm and sitting most comfortably on the stomach. I beg you of your known goodness to let me stay with you until the danger has passed. Far from tormenting you and driving you from your own home, I shall so serve you that you will thank Allāh for my presence.' Recognising the sincerity of the flea, the mouse answered: 'If what you say is true, O flea, you may share my hole and live in peace, dividing with me good and evil fortune. As for the blood from the woman's thigh, do not say any more about it. Digest it in peace, for Allāh has provided for each creature food after its kind and there is no disgrace in taking what He has given. If we criticised His designs and tried to better them, we should soon die of hunger and thirst. I once heard a santon say these words on the subject of simple diet:

> I have nothing, nothing,
> And my heart is light;
> A rag for clothing,
> No wife for loathing,
> Coarse salt for soothing
> Bread or dough thing,
> And then nothing—
> Do you wonder my heart is light?'

The flea was very much touched by the mouse's remark, and answered: 'O my sister, what a pleasant life we are going to live together! May Allāh hasten the occasion on which I may repay your kindness!'

The flea's prayer was heard. On that very evening the mouse, who was out hunting, heard a continuous metallic chink and, going to investigate the noise, saw the merchant counting many dīnārs contained in a little bag. When he had calculated his treasure, he hid it below the pillow and went to sleep.

The mouse ran and told the flea what she had seen, adding: 'This is your chance to repay me by helping me to transport these dīnārs to my hole.' The flea nearly fainted at the enormity of this request, and at last said sadly to the mouse: 'Do not you see my size? I could not carry a single dīnār on my back. Nay, a thousand of us fleas could not do so. Yet I think I can help you by getting rid of the merchant. I can drive him from the house, and you will be left alone to remove each coin as slowly as you like.' 'I had not thought of that, good flea, and yet it is an excellent plan!' cried the mouse. 'My hole is large enough to contain all the gold, and I have constructed seventy-two doors so that no one may shut me in and starve me. Let us hasten, O flea.'

In a few bounds the smaller animal reached the merchant's bed, and journeyed till he came to the man's backside, which he bit as never a backside has been bitten before. The sharp pain woke the merchant and he quickly slapped the part, but by that time the flea was far away and his victim had to be content with a thousand curses which echoed through the silent house. After tossing restlessly from side to side, the merchant tried to sleep again; but the flea returned to the attack, and bit the man with all his strength in that sensitive part which is called the perineum. The unfortunate man jumped howling out of bed and ran to the back of the house, where the wells were, to bathe himself in cold water. He did not dare to return to his room, but stayed on a bench in the courtyard all night.

In this way the mouse was able to carry the money piece by piece to her home. When the merchant returned on the morrow, not a single dīnār remained in the bag. Thus the flea repaid the mouse a hundredfold for her hospitality.

'And now, O crow,' continued the fox, 'I hope you will recognise how ready I am to repay you for the friendship which I have requested.'

'Your tale is hardly convincing, Fox,' replied the crow. 'After all, one is free to do a kind action or to refrain from it, if it seems likely to harm oneself. You have a great reputation for deceit and broken promises; how can you expect me to place confidence in one who betrayed and did to death his own cousin the wolf? He who would destroy one of his own race, almost of his own family, on whom he had fawned for years, is hardly the animal one would choose as an ally. There is a tale which illustrates our relative positions very well.' 'What tale is that?' asked the fox, and the crow replied: 'The tale of the vulture.' 'I do not know the tale of the vulture,' admitted the fox, so the crow said:

'There was once a vulture who surpassed all the tyrants of history by his cruelty, so that no bird, great or small, was safe from him, and the wolves of both earth and air so feared him that they would leave their prey and depart hurriedly when they saw his terrible beak and rampant feathers. The time came when old age weighed upon the vulture, making his head bald and his claws blunt, and joining with his past intemperance to rot his beak and wither up his wings. Thus he became almost an object of pity to his victims, who disdained to punish him with anything worse than contempt. At last he had to be content with scraps, which were carelessly thrown to him by those who had formed his food in the days of his wickedness.

'Like the vulture, you have lost your strength, O fox,' continued the crow, 'but you have not lost your treacherous habits. You wish to form an alliance with me, because by God's grace, I still have a vigorous wing, a sharp eye and a beak of steel. I advise you not to try to behave like the sparrow.' 'What sparrow?' asked the fox; so the crow said:

'It is related that a sparrow came to a field where sheep were grazing and walked behind them, gleaning unpleasant matters, until he suddenly saw a great eagle swoop from the sky and carry off a little lamb in his claws. Filled with pride at this exploit of his cousin, the sparrow said to himself: 'I can fly as well as the eagle, so I think I will carry off one of these great sheep.' He chose out the biggest in the flock, one whose wool was so long and old that it fell in a mass below his belly, stiff and clotted with his nightly urine. The sparrow leapt upon the back of this beast and tried to fly off with him, but instead he was taken prisoner in the tangles of the sheep's fleece. The shepherd ran up and, disentangling him, pulled out his wing feathers and fastened him by the leg with a thread. He gave him to his little children as a plaything, saying: 'Mark well this bird, for he tried to imitate one who was greater than he, and is now a slave.'

'O wreck of a fox,' said the crow, 'you wish to compare yourself with one greater than yourself, even as the sparrow did. My last word to you, old rascal, is a request that you show me the breadth of your back as quickly as possible!' Then the fox understood that it was useless to attempt to deceive so sharp and quick an individual as the crow. He ground his teeth with rage and broke the largest of them. 'I am glad that my refusal has broken one of your teeth,' mocked the crow, but the fox looked respectfully at him, saying: 'It was not your refusal that broke it, but my own shame at meeting one as wicked as myself.'

So saying, the fox made off as fast as he could.

'Such, O auspicious King, is the tale of the crow,' continued Shahrazād. 'Perhaps it has been a little long, but to-morrow, if Allāh spares my life, I will redeem that fault by telling you the Tale of the Fair Shams al-Nahār and Prince Alī ibn Bakr.'

'O Shahrazād,' cried King Shahryār, 'your tales of beasts and birds have charmed me very much, and have not seemed at all long. If you know any more you must tell them to me in the future. At present the title of the tale which you promise me pleases me so much that I am ready to listen to you.'

Shahrazād saw the approach of morning and begged the King to wait until the next night.

But when the hundred-and-fifty-second night had come

SHE SAID:

The Tale of Alī ibn Bakr and the
Fair Shams al-Nahār

IT is related, O auspicious King, that there was once in Baghdād, during the reign of the Khalīfah Hārūn al-Rashīd, a rich young merchant whose name was Abū al-Hasan. Of all those who sold in the great market he was the handsomest, most affable, and best dressed, so that the eunuchs of the palace chose him out when the King's favourites would buy fabrics or jewellery, and the women themselves trusted blindly in his taste and a discretion which had been proved in the course of many delicate commissions. It was his custom to give refreshment to the eunuchs who came to his shop and to make them presents according to their rank; therefore all the women and slaves of the palace loved him, and he even came to the notice of the Khalīfah himself. Hārūn al-Rashīd grew to admire him for his exquisite manners and calmly beautiful face, allowing him access to the palace at any hour of the day or night, and inviting him to a feast sometimes, that he might rejoice in those qualities of eloquence and fair singing which chiefly delighted him and which were the noticeable gifts of young Abū al-Hasan.

This youth's shop was famous among the young people of Baghdād, the sons of amīrs and the wives of chamberlains, and one of its chief frequenters was a handsome friend of the owner, a certain Alī ibn Bakr, of the line of the ancient Persian kings.

One day this prince, who was of great beauty, with perfectly drawn eyebrows, smiling teeth, and a voice like music's own, sat talking to his friend in the shop when there appeared ten girls, as it might have been ten moons entering the market, about an eleventh mounted on a mule with golden trappings. This damsel was concealed under an izār of rose silk, fastened to her waist by a very wide gold belt studded with diamonds. Her face was veiled only with transparent tissue through which her eyes beamed gloriously; the flesh of her hands shone like milk and her fingers showed slim beneath their weight of pearls. Certain hints allowed by the rose izār led the imagination to build wonderful dreams.

This young woman entered the shop and was greeted by Abū al-Hasan with every mark of respect. He arranged cushions on the couch for her, and stood back a little to wait her pleasure. She chose carelessly certain fabrics on a gold background, a few jewels, and some rare bottles of rose essence, lifting her veil the while to prove that she had no fear of the young merchant. At the sight of her face Alī ibn Bakr was thrown into a violence of passion. Yet, through delicacy, he was on the point of retiring when the girl, who had noticed him with the same interest, said with a sweet smile to Abū: 'I would not drive any of your customers away. I pray you request this young man to remain.'

Alī ibn Bakr was delighted and, not wishing to be backward in politeness, exclaimed: 'As Allāh lives, my mistress, if I was about to retire, it was not only that I feared to be in the way, but also that these lines came into my head on seeing you:

> You see the fire-gold sun high in a blue
> Space which your eyes else could not journey to;
>   Fool, do you think to reach him without wings
> Or hope that he will golden drop to you?'

Charmed by a compliment so sweetly spoken, the woman rewarded Alī with a laughing glance and asked the merchant in a whisper who his friend might be. 'He is Alī ibn Bakr, a descendant of the ancient Persian kings. His spirit is as fine as his face,' answered Abū. 'He is delightful,' said the young woman. 'You must not be surprised, O Abū al-Hasan, if I send one of my slaves back to ask both of you to visit me. I would like to prove to your friend that there is a palace in Baghdād fairer and having more beautiful women, more skilful entertainers, than may be found among the Persian kings.' Abū al-Hasan well understood her meaning. When he had bowed and thanked her, the girl replaced her veil and departed, leaving behind a fine scent of garments kept in jasmine and santal.

For a full minute Alī ibn Bakr did not know where he was; indeed he was so confused that Abū was obliged to warn him that people were noticing the strangeness of his look. 'My friend,' said Alī, 'why should I not look strange when my soul is seeking through my body for a way by which it may rejoin the spirit of that moon which has just departed? Oh, tell me who she is, for you seem to know her.' 'She is the favourite of the Khalīfah,' answered Abū, 'she is that Shams al-Nahār whom the Prince of Believers has set above his own wife, the lady Zubaidah. She has a palace to herself in which she is absolute queen; no eunuchs guard her because the King has faith in her. Indeed, for all her beauty, there is less scandalous winking in her regard than about any other woman in the palace.'

Abū had only just given this explanation to his friend when a little slave came up to him and whispered in his ear: 'My mistress Shams al-Nahār has sent for both of you.' Abū shut up his shop and, taking Alī by the arm, followed the slave, who soon introduced them into the King's own palace.

Alī thought that he had been transported into some realm of magic, for all about him was beauty, passing the compass of poetry. But the slave, without giving either of the young men time to express their satisfaction, clapped her hands for food to be brought. When the tray covered with meats and fruits whose perfume was a balm to the nostrils and the heart had been set before them, the slave waited upon them herself, gave them a golden vase holding scented water when they had eaten, poured a rose scent for their faces and beards from an ewer enriched with rubies, and perfumed their clothes with aloes burnt in a small gold brazier.

Then she opened a door and introduced them into a great hall having a dome held up by twenty-four pillars of transparent alabaster, whose bases and chapters were sculptured with gold birds. Upon a golden background inside the dome, lines of living colour repeated the designs of the wide carpets which covered the floor. Between the columns were vases of flowers, and empty vases too beautiful in their bright flesh of jasper, agate and crystal, to contain anything. The hall gave straight upon a garden, whose entrance path was ornamented with pebbles in the same colour and symmetry as the carpets and dome, so that all three made a harmony beneath the naked sky.

While Abū and Alī were gazing their fill upon these things, ten young women appeared before them and sat in a circle, with moving breasts, black eyes, and cheeks of roses.

At this point Shahrazād saw the approach of morning and discreetly fell silent.

But when the hundred-and-fifty-third night had come

SHE SAID:

Each of them had a stringed instrument in her hand, with which, at a sign from the little favourite slave, she joined in so sweet a prelude that Alī, dreaming of Shams al-Nahār, felt his eyes fill with tears. 'My heart is moved, my brother,' he said to Abū. 'This music speaks to me with a voice of weeping though I cannot tell why.'

'Do not be troubled, my lord,' answered Abū, 'let your soul float with the music, for it signifies that Shams al-Nahār will soon arrive.'

At this point the ten girls passed their fingers across the strings, the slaves shook their little tambourines, and all sang:

> All suddenly the blue air laughs,
>> The moon picks up her pale
> Silk mist, and coifs
>> Her hair as with a veil.
> The sun,
>> More moved than they,
> His shining work half done,
>> Flees darkling down the day.

Then one of the singers sang alone:

> Shams al-Nahār,
> Our moon, has come to her pavilion,
> And the young sun, whose ripe vermilion
> Lips ache to know her,
> Surely will show her
> All the delights there are.

Prince Alī, who was thus represented as the sun, saw a dozen young negresses come towards him, bearing upon their shoulders a silver throne on which was seated a veiled woman. These black slaves had naked breasts, and thighs which cinctures of gold and silk outlined to rich perfection. They set the throne down gently in the midst of the singers and retired among the trees of the garden.

A hand parted the draperies which floated about the throne, and the two eyes of Shams al-Nahār looked forth, as if they were two stars seen against the shadow of the moon. The favourite was dressed in a light mantle of blue on gold, pricked with a few selected and unpurchasable rubies. She bowed smiling to the prince, who sighed on beholding her. In a few seconds their eyes said more to each other than their lips could have framed in several meetings.

At last Shams al-Nahār with difficulty withdrew her eyes from her lover and ordered her women to sing. One of them tuned her lute and chanted:

> When two young lovers fair and fit
> Kiss each the other's soul into eclipse,

> Not they, but He who made their lips
> Shall answer it.

The lovers sighed, and a second damsel sang to a different rhythm:

> When it is dark
> The light splits into flowers which men call stars
> And which I call your eyes.
>
> When it is dark
> Your body distils a bright drink for my lips,
> A sweet wine for my mouth.
>
> When it is dark
> Beauty in moon-spun vests comes to my bed
> And whispers in my ear:
>
> 'When it is dark
> The God who made him puts fire in his kiss
> To sweeten a girl's soul.'

Alī ibn Bakr and the fair Shams al-Nahār looked long at each other, while a third singer murmured this:

> The green water changes
> To black and silver,
> To dark blue,
> To nothing as the moon sets.
> All lovers and their days
> So change, so pass.
> Oh, seize
> The young beauty of now,
> The little hour which seems to stay.

Prince Alī uttered a long sigh and wept, so that Shams al-Nahār wept also and retired towards the door in her emotion; Ibn Bakr ran in the same direction; they met behind the great curtain and embraced and fainted away. They would have fallen except for the women who held them up and carried them both to one couch, where they sprinkled their faces with water of flowers and held sharp scents to their nostrils.

Shams al-Nahār looked round her as she came to herself and smiled happily to see that her friend Alī lay so near. Then she asked anxiously for Abū al-Hasan, whom she could not see because he had retired discreetly and stood far off. He was in some anxiety lest this latest happening should be noised abroad in the palace. When he heard her asking for him, he returned to her and bowed respectfully. 'How can I ever thank you, O Abū?' cried the favourite. 'I would never have known but for you that the world held such a lover and such joyful minutes. You will not find me ungrateful.'

Abū thanked the girl, who turned towards Alī, saying: 'Now I have no doubt of your friendship, my master, even though it cannot equal mine. Alas, alas, that Destiny should have tied me to this palace and bound the feet of my love for you in chains!' 'Dear Mistress,' returned Alī, 'your love has so penetrated my soul that it has become a part of it; it shall not be unknitted even after death. Oh, how unhappy we are!' Both wept scalding tears, until Abū al-Hasan said to them: 'As Allāh lives, I do not understand your grief. What would happen if you were separated? Leave tears for then. The present was made for laughter.' On this the favourite dried her eyes and signed to one of her slaves, who hastened forward, followed by many servants bearing silver dishes on their heads, loaded with appetising dainties. When they had spread a cloth with these good things between Alī and his mistress, they withdrew and stood as still as statues against the wall.

Shams al-Nahār invited Abū to sit opposite herself and Alī, within reach of the carved gold plates which smiled with fruit and were ripe with pastries. She fed first her lover and then his friend with morsels in her own fingers, and, when they had eaten, caused perfumed water to be brought for their hands in basins of illuminated silver. The young negresses handed them old wine in cups of coloured agate on saucers of vermilion. The lovers drank slowly, draining each other's eyes above the cups, and then the favourite dismissed all her women except the singers and musicians.

Shams al-Nahār felt moved to sing, and commanded one of the damsels to test her lute for her with this composition:

> The mystery of my soul is scattered
> > For all to see,
> > > Seeking my lover.
> The proud defences of my heart are shattered,
> > Falling from me,
> > > Seeking my lover.

> My traitor tears—as if it mattered—
> Flow ceaselessly,
>   Seeking my lover.

Shams al-Nahār filled a cup and half drained it; then she gave it
to the prince, who set his lips upon the same place her lips had
touched and drank the rest.

At this point Shahrazād saw the approach of morning and discreetly fell silent.

But when the hundred-and-fifty-fourth night had come

SHE SAID:

The lutes trembled in love beneath the fingers of the lute-players.
One of them, at a sign from her mistress that something should now
be sung low and more tenderly, murmured almost in a whisper:

> My lips are wet with tears
> Again and yet again,
> My cup is filled with tears
> More often than with wine,
> And yet I think
> I ought to take this mingled drink
> Of mine;
> For it appears
> To fortify my heart for pain,
> Because the tears are from my soul
> And if I drink I shall be whole
> Again.

Shams al-Nahār was drunken with this song, she took the lute
and, half shutting her eyes, expressed her soul thus admirably:

> Young fawn with lighted eyes,
> When you come near
> It is as if my glances had drunken wine.
>
> The light breeze of the desert
> Is born scented, when you sigh
> At evening, at cool evening
> Under the palm-trees.

I am offended with the west wind
Because he kisses you
And refreshes the scarlet languor of your cheeks.

Jasmine of his belly under vests,
White jasmine
Milky as moonstones!

The crimson flowers of his lips
Are watered with the water of his mouth,
His eyes close after love.

My heart flutters like a moth
About his body,
Heedless of arrows.

The two young men nearly fainted away from ecstasy and then trembled with pleasure, calling out: 'Allāh, Allāh!' most fervently, laughing and weeping at the same moment. Prince Alī seized another lute and, handing it to Abū, begged him to play an accompaniment. Then, with his head on his hand, and his eyes half closed, he sang this song of his own country:

Listen, slim cup-bearer:

If I were king
I would account and sell my heritage
For a thing.

If I were king
I would banish crimson from the white page
And scarlet poppies from their pasturage,
The grapes' red and the roses' rage,
For a thing.

Alī ibn Bakr rendered this song admirably. Just as he had finished, the little favourite slave of Shams al-Nahār ran up trembling and said: 'My mistress, Masrūr is at the door with Afīf and the other eunuchs, demanding to speak with you.'

Alī and Abū were startled at these words and the slaves trembled for their lives, but Shams al-Nahār remained mistress of herself, saying with a calm smile: 'Do not be afraid.' Then she continued to her confidant: 'Beg Masrūr and Afīf to give me time to receive them according to their dignity.' When the doors and curtains had been closely shut, she left the two young men in the hall and herself went out with all her singers, locking the door behind her. Her silver throne was set under the trees of the garden and she took up a languorous pose upon it, ordering one of her girls to rub her limbs and the others to move to a distance.

Masrūr and Afīf with twenty eunuchs, great-belted and carrying naked swords, were introduced by one of the negresses. They bowed very low to the favourite, as she said to them: 'Allāh grant, O Masrūr, that you bring good news.' 'He has granted it, O my mistress,' answered Masrūr, approaching the throne. 'The Prince of Believers wishes you peace and says that he much desires to see you. The day began well and auspiciously for him; he would perfect its end at your side. He wishes to know your desires, and whether you will come to him or receive him here.'

Lovely Shams al-Nahār rose and kissed the earth to signify that the Khalīfah's request was a command. 'I am my lord's submissive and happy slave,' she said. 'I pray you inform your master that my palace will be illuminated by his coming.' Masrūr and his eunuchs returned in haste, but they had scarcely disappeared when the favourite ran back to the hall and threw herself weeping into her lover's arms. At last Prince Alī found voice to say to his beloved: 'Ah, let me hold you, let me feel you near me, let me adore the touch of your body against mine, for separation is at hand and my soul would carry away some sweet memory for the hours of darkness.' 'What will your grief be compared with mine,' she said, 'when I remain alone in this palace? You can go about the markets and find distraction in the little girls walking; their long eyes will make you forget me; the laughter of the sun upon their glass bangles will daze my fading image from your eyes. O Alī, how much easier it would be for me to shut myself in with my grief than to command my quivering lips to smile and sing for the Commander of the Faithful! What music or what laughter can any but you inspire in me henceforward? I will for ever be looking at your empty place; I shall die when I share the wine cup with another.'

As Abū al-Hasan was about to console the lovers and bid them be patient, the confidant ran up to warn her mistress of the King's coming. Shams al-Nahār gave a last embrace to her lover and said to the girl: 'Lead them quickly to the gallery which overlooks the Tigris on one side and the garden on the other. When the night is dark enough, you can guide them to the river bank.' So saying the poor girl conquered her tears and ran to meet the Khalīfah.

The confidant led Alī and Abū into the gallery and left them with many reassurances, locking the door behind her. At first they were in the dark, but soon they saw a great light shining through the guarded windows and, looking out to see, found that it came from lighted torches in the hands of the hundred young eunuchs and hundred old eunuchs who surrounded the King on his visit. The old eunuchs bore swords and marched before a group of twenty white slaves, who themselves clustered about Hārūn al-Rashīd. The torches and the jewels of the girls shone upon him as he advanced, and the lutes of the musicians encompassed him with music as Shams al-Nahār came and bowed before his feet. He helped her to rise and said in his happiness: 'For many days the cares of state have prevented my eyes from reposing themselves with your beauty, but Allāh has at last rewarded them with this evening.' He seated himself on the silver throne, and the favourite sat before him, while the twenty women made a circle about them and the players and singers stayed in a group round their mistress. The eunuchs, young and old, took their torches and scattered among the trees so that the Khalīfah might have the greater ease for his pleasures.

When all were disposed in this way, the Khalīfah made a sign to the singers, and one of them chanted this ode, which the King preferred to all others because of the rich beauty of its close:

> An early dew woos the half-opened flowers,
>   Wind of the south, dear child,
> Close clings about their stalks for drunken hours;
>   And yet your eyes, dear child,
>   Cool pools which rise, dear child,
>   High in the mountains of my soul,
>   These, these
>   The lips have drunken whole;
>   And yet your mouth, dear child,
>   Your mouth, dear child, is envied of the bees.

When these passionate words had died out in the evening air, Shams al-Nahār signed to her confidant, who, understanding that this song would hint at her mistress's love for Alī ibn Bakr, herself sang:

When the tall rider meets the Badawī,
She colours to a fire of laurel rose.
Quench that rose laurel quickly, Badawī,
Tall riders ride with love, and love is loss.

The beautiful Shams al-Nahār heard this song and fell fainting from her seat into the arms of her women, and Prince Alī, seeing her do so, and impelled by a secret sympathy, fell in a swoon into the arms of Abū al-Hasan.

At this point Shahrazād saw the approach of morning and discreetly fell silent.

But when the hundred-and-fifty-fifth night had come

SHE SAID:

Abū did not know what to do. He was hunting vainly for water in the dark, when one of the doors of the gallery opened and the confidant hurried in, saying: 'Follow me quickly, for all outside is in a confusion which bodes no good to any of us. Come with me, or we shall all be dead!' 'O girl in need,' said Abū, 'draw near and see the condition of my friend!'

When the slave came near enough to see Prince Alī lying in a faint upon the carpet, she ran to a table on which were certain flasks and chose a sprinkler charged with water of flowers. With this she refreshed the face of the young man until he came to himself. Then she lifted him by his feet, while Abū took his shoulders, and the two of them carried him to that bank of the Tigris which lay behind the palace. They set him down gently on a bench. When the young girl clapped her hands, a boat with a single rower came to them across the water. Without a word the oarsman took the prince in his arms and laid him down in the vessel. Abū followed, but the confidant excused herself from accompanying them further, wished them peace in a sad voice, and hastened back to the palace.

Alī ibn Bakr had quite recovered, owing to the cool wind and the water, by the time the boat reached the opposite bank. He was able to disembark, leaning on his friend's arm, but immediately sank down upon a mossy stone. 'Dear friend,' said Abū, 'pluck up your strength and try to walk. This place is infested with bandits, and you have only to reach the house of one of my friends which is quite near here. You can see the light from where we are.' With that he invoked the name of Allāh and, helping Alī to rise, led him to the house. The door immediately opened to his knock, although it was late at night, and both Abū and his companion were cordially welcomed. The merchant invented a story to explain their arrival at such an hour; and the two friends passed the night in that admirable house, where hospitality denied itself the joy of asking questions. They slept ill; Abū because he seldom lay away from home and feared that his folk would be anxious about him, Alī because he had ever before his eyes a picture of Shams al-Nahār lying pale and unconscious at the feet of the Khalīfah.

Next morning they took leave of their host and managed to reach the city, although Alī had great difficulty in walking. Abā's house lay first upon their way, and the merchant insisted on his friend entering, as he did not wish to leave him alone in so dolorous a state. He prepared the best bedchamber, stretching new mattresses which were kept rolled in the large cupboards for such an occasion. Prince Alī fell upon the bed and slept for many hours, as if he had been walking for whole days about the countryside. He made his ablution and his prayer on waking, and was dressing to go out when Abā al-Hasan prevented him, saying: 'Dear master, you must spend the whole of the day and night here, in order that I may bear you company and distract the gloom of your reveries.' After talking with his friend all day, Abū sent in the evening for the finest singers of Baghdād; but these only exasperated the prince with their songs, and he passed a worse night than before. In the morning his state was so grave the Abū thought it better to send for a mule from the prince's stable and conduct his patient to his own house. Thinking that, in the hands of his own people, Alī would lack for nothing, the merchant took his leave with a few words of encouragement, promising to return as soon as possible. He hastened to his shop and sat down to wait for customers. The first person who entered was the young slave, the confidant of Shams al-Nahār.

At this point Shahrazād saw the approach of morning and discreetly fell silent.

But when the hundred-and-fifty-sixth night had come

SHE SAID:

She wished him peace, and Abū felt his heart beat faster as he remarked the sadness of her expression. He hastened to ask her news of her mistress, but she begged him first to tell her of the state of Prince Alī. When Abū had given an account of his friend's sorrow and weakness, she became sadder than before and sighed, saying: 'Ours is an unhappy lot! The state of my mistress is even worse than that of her lover. Listen and I will tell you all that has happened since my mistress fell fainting at the feet of the Khalīfah:

'After leaving you two in charge of the boatman, I hurried back to Shams al-Nahār and found her lying pale and unconscious, with tears flowing drop by drop through her scattered hair. The Prince of Believers sat by her side, desolated that she did not come to herself in spite of the cares he lavished on her. The rest of us stayed in consternation and answered the questions of the Khalīfah only by tears and genuflexions, rather than run the risk of exposing our secret to him. At midnight, thanks to our application of rose water and the use of our fans, my mistress came to herself, but at once, to the stupefaction of the King, she shed a flood of tears.

' "Speak to me, light of my eyes, Shams al-Nahār," said the Sultān to his favourite, "tell me the cause of your trouble, because I greatly suffer from not being able to help you." My mistress tried to kiss his feet, but he prevented her with his hands and sweetly asked her again and again the reason of her fainting. At last, in a broken voice, she answered: "Prince of Believers, it is a passing trouble caused by the disagreement within me of certain things which I have eaten to-day. I took two unripe lemons, six green apples, a bowl of curdled milk, a great slab of katāif, a measure of salt nuts and pumpkin seeds, and several handfuls of sugared chickpeas hot from the oven!" "Imprudent little friend," cried the Khalīfah, "I am sure those things were very appetising, but you must control yourself and not gratify your stomach with all which your eyes desire. I pray you, as you love me, do not run such a risk again." Thereupon the King, who is as a rule most sparing of words and kisses with his women, petted my mistress and watched by her until the morning. Then, as she did not seem any better, he sent for all the doctors of the palace and the city. These were careful, for reasons of policy, not to diagnose the real cause of her trouble, which they could see was exaggerated by the constraint which the presence of the Khalīfah imposed on her. They contented themselves with making so complicated a prescription that, with the best will in the world, I cannot repeat a single item of it.

'The King and the doctors withdrew at last, and I was able to

approach my mistress and kiss her hands with words of encouragement and also with a promise, which helped her a great deal, that I
would contrive a second meeting with Alī ibn Bakr. I gave her a
glass of fresh water with a dash of flower essence, which brought
back the colour to her cheeks. Then I hurried hither at her orders to
find out news of her lover.'

'My girl,' answered Abū, 'as I have no further news to give you of
Alī, go back to your mistress and tell her how grieved I am to hear
what has happened. Say that I fully realise how hard a trial she is
undergoing, but that I exhort her to patience and silence, lest anything should come to the ears of the Khalīfah. Come again to my
shop to-morrow, and, if Allāh wills, I shall have better news for
you.'

As soon as the confidant had left, Abū al-Hasan shut his shop, at
an earlier hour than usual, and hurried to the house of Prince Alī.

At this point Shahrazād saw the approach of morning and discreetly fell silent.

But when the hundred-and-fifty-seventh night had come

SHE SAID:

He found Alī surrounded by friends, relations, and doctors without number. Some of them were feeling his pulse, and others were
writing out many and contrary prescriptions, which the old women
criticised in loud voices as they cast sidelong glances at the doctors.
So well was he being looked after that he had hidden his head under
the coverings, stopping his ears with his hands that he might hear
and see no more.

Abū pulled gently at the clothes and said with an encouraging
intonation: 'Peace be with you, Alī!' The prince showed his face,
saying: 'Peace and the blessings of Allāh be upon you, O Abū! May
He grant that your news be as fair and pleasing as your face.' Abū
contented himself with winking, and Alī sent away all his people at
this sign; then the merchant reported the news of the confidant,
adding: 'I am devoted to your cause, my brother. My soul belongs
to you entirely. It will take no rest until I have brought back peace
into your heart.' Alī wept from gratitude, saying: 'Put a crown upon
your kindness by staying with me to-night and distracting the
torture of my thoughts with your conversation.' So Abū stayed by
him, reciting poems and singing love songs in a whisper close to his

ear. Sometimes the verses were addressed to the poet's friend, sometimes to his mistress. Of a thousand which Abū sang, here is one:

> She has taken me with a single blow
> Of her eyes and their blue swords,
> With the arrow of musk which lies below
> The camphor of her chin.
> Yet I have seen carnelian change to pearl
> About this girl
> At a few words.
> She puts her hand to her bare left breast
> In all surprises,
> Five branches with red petals
> As the hand spreads and settles,
> A sixth as the nipple rises.
> There is no silver-bright
> Shield to save your sight
> Where the breasts begin.

and again:

> She is a golden table
> With two inverted silver cups,
> And he who sups
> Is able
> To find the scarlet seeds of the fable
> Of Allāh making the sunset.

When Abū saw his friend moved to tears, he said: 'Now I will sing you that song which you so love to whisper over to yourself in my shop. May it be a balm to your wounded soul, O Alī! Listen:

> I can see the gold
>   Under the jacinth wine,
>   O cupbearer;
>   There is no time where wine is.
>   Your hand can make this drink of mine
>   Stronger and rarer
> Than the untold
>   Age which the best of mine is.

Ah, who can unlock
  The secret of my heart,
    O cupbearer,
      With white angers as you can?
  But even you cannot well start
    The hidden rarer
Thought, as the shock
    Of this old crimson hue can.'

Prince Alī wept afresh at this song, because of the memories which it brought back to him; and Abū watched by him all night. In the morning he hastened to open his shop, which he had neglected for some time, and stayed there all day. At evening, as he was rolling up his fabrics and preparing to shut up his place of business, the young confidant of Shams al-Nahār came to him closely veiled, saying: 'My mistress sends peace to you and to the prince, and begs you to give her news of your friend's health.' 'Gentle child, do not ask me,' said Abū. 'My answer would be too sad, for our friend neither sleeps nor eats nor drinks. He lives upon verses and has become very pale.' 'That is distressing,' answered the slave. 'My mistress, who is no better herself, has charged me with a love letter which I have hidden in my hair. I am commanded to return with an answer. Will you not take me to him?' Abū consented to do so. He shut his shop and walked at ten paces in front of the confidant until they came to Prince Alī's house.

At this point Shahrazād saw the approach of morning and discreetly fell silent.

But when the hundred-and-fifty-eighth night had come

SHE SAID:

Abū requested the girl to wait at the entrance and, entering the prince's chamber, made a sign to him to dismiss those who surrounded his bed. Alī turned to them, saying: 'With your permission, I have a belly-ache.' As soon as the bedroom was empty, Abū introduced the confidant, and Alī felt himself better in health already at the sight of one who recalled his mistress to him. 'The blessing of Allāh upon you, O delicious comer!' he said, and straightway the girl thanked him and handed him the letter. Alī kissed it and then, being too weak to read, handed it to Abū, who found in it verses traced by the hand of the favourite which perfectly revealed all the great pain of love. The merchant gave only a cheerful condensation of what he had read, adding: 'I will write an answer which you can sign.' Upon this motto, which Alī gave him: 'If there were no grief in love, lovers would miss the joy of writing,' he composed an answer which Alī handed weeping to the confidant, who in her turn could not refrain from tears. Then the merchant and the slave left together, the one to return to his shop, the other to hurry to her mistress.

Abū seated himself upon a couch, thinking within himself: 'O Abū, this matter is getting serious. If the Khalīfah hears of it, what will happen? I love Alī ibn Bakr, and would lose one of my eyes for him. But I have a family, a mother, sisters and little brothers. What will become of them if I continue in my imprudence? No, no! Things cannot go on as they are. To-morrow I will beg Alī to rid himself of this fatal passion.'

Faithful to his determination, Abū visited his friend on the next morning and said to him: 'I have never seen, I have never heard tell of an adventure such as yours, nor have I known so strange a lover. You are aware that Shams al-Nahār loves you with a passion that equals your own, and yet you become iller every day. What would happen to you if she did not return your love? If she was like the generality of women and doted upon lies and trickery? Also, have you considered what misfortunes will fall upon us if the Khalīfah comes to hear of this intrigue? It is not at all unlikely that this will happen, because the coming and going of the confidant is bound to pique the curiosity of the eunuchs. Then Allāh alone knows how far we all may fall. Your love is a house without a door; if you persist in staying there, you will sacrifice yourself and your mistress with you. I say nothing of myself, who am likely to be utterly crushed with all my family.'

Alī ibn Bakr thanked his friend, but informed him that his will was no longer free and that, in any case, he would never forsake Shams al-Nahār, who was ready to risk her life for love of him.

Seeing that his words had been in vain, Abū left his friend and walked back to his house, revolving dark fears for the future.

Now the merchant numbered among his most intimate friends a certain young and discreet jeweller named Amīn, and this youth came to pay him a visit as he lay among his cushions trying to make up his mind what he should do. Amīn sat down by his side and, being to a certain extent in his confidence, asked: 'O Abū, how go the loves of Alī ibn Bakr and Shams al-Nahār?'

At this point Shahrazād saw the approach of morning and discreetly fell silent.

But when the hundred-and-fifty-ninth night had come

SHE SAID:

Abū answered: 'Allāh preserve us all, O Amīn! I feel that no good will come of it and, as I know you to be a friend, certain and discreet, I will tell you a plan which I have formed to extricate myself and all those who are dependent on me from this very dangerous situation.' 'You may speak confidentially, O Abū,' said Amīn. 'You may look upon me as a brother entirely devoted to your service.' Then Abū continued: 'I have determined to satisfy all my obligations in Baghdād, to sell my merchandise at a reduced price, and to depart to some place such as Basrah, there to await the outcome of this love affair in safety. Life in this place has become impossible for me. Day and night I go in terror of being accused by the Khalīfah as an accessory to this intrigue.'

Said Amīn: 'You have decided wisely, O Abū. May Allāh guide you in the sole possible path, the one which you have chosen! If it will help you to leave without remorse, I am ready to take your place and faithfully to serve your friend Prince Alī.' 'How can you do that, since you do not know the prince and are not acquainted with the ways of the palace or the Sultān's favourite?' objected Abū, but Amīn answered: 'I have often sold jewels within the palace, even to Shams al-Nahār herself. And, as for your other objection, I can easily get to know the prince and win his confidence. If that is all the difficulty you find, depart in peace. Allāh can open every door!'

At this point Shahrazād saw the approach of morning and discreetly fell silent.

But when the hundred-and-sixtieth night had come

SHE SAID:

Amīn took leave of his friend Abū al-Hasan for that occasion and, when he returned in three days to obtain news of him, found the house empty and shut up. When he enquired among the neighbours, they said: 'Abū al-Hasan has gone on a business journey to Basrah; he told us that he would only remain away a short time and that he would return when he had collected the sums due to him from his foreign correspondents.' Amīn understood that his friend had succumbed to his terrors, therefore he went immediately to the lodgings of Prince Alī and was introduced into his presence by the slaves. Seeing him lying very pale among his cushions, he said: 'Dear master, although my eyes have not had the pleasure of looking upon you until to-day, I trust that you will excuse my liberty in coming to ask after your health. It is my duty to tell you something which will perplex you and to announce in the same breath a remedy for the inconvenience I report. I am the confidential friend of Abū al-Hasan. For the last three days he did not come to visit me, as it was his custom to do every evening, so I went to his house and found that he had departed from it. Can you tell me why he has done this?'

Poor Alī ibn Bakr became even paler than before; he was just able to stammer: 'That is news to me also, and I can think of no reason for it. I will send one of my slaves at once to find out the truth.' A slave was despatched and soon returned, saying: 'The neighbours tell me that Abū al-Hasan has departed for Basrah. A young girl was making enquiry at the same time as myself. I have brought her to you as she is the bearer of some message.' 'Show her in at once!' cried Prince Alī.

The girl was brought in, and the sick man recognised her as the confidant of Shams al-Nahār. She went up to the young man and whispered something in his ear which brought alternate light and shadow to his face.

The jeweller thought that it was time to put in a word, so he said: 'Dear master, and you O young girl, before he went away Abū told me all and revealed to me his terror lest the Khalīfah should come to know of the business in which you are concerned. Now I, who have neither family nor dependants, am very ready to take his place as your assistant, since your unhappy loves, my lord, have touched my heart profoundly. If you do not refuse my help, I swear by our holy Prophet (upon whom be prayer and peace!) that I will be as faithful as al-Hasan and more courageous. If you wish to do without me, rest assured that I will keep your secret.'

At this point Shahrazād saw the approach of morning and discreetly fell silent.

But when the hundred-and-sixty-first night had come

SHE SAID:

Amīn continued: 'If, on the other hand, I have managed to persuade you that there is no sacrifice I would not contemplate, I am
ready to make my house a meeting place for you, my lord, and the
lovely Shams al-Nahār.'

Prince Alī felt strength return to him as he heard these words of
the young jeweller; he rose and embraced him, saying: 'Allāh has
sent you to me, O Amīn. I put my trust in you and calmly await a
perfect cure at your kind hands.'

Amīn tore himself away from the long thanks and joyful tears of
the prince, and conducted the confidant to his own house, which was
destined at length to serve their loves as well as those of the prince
and the favourite. Having learnt the way thither, the young girl
left the jeweller, saying that she was anxious to tell her mistress all
that had happened and promising to return on the morrow with the
answer of Shams al-Nahār.

Faithful to her promise, she came in the morning, saying: 'O
Amīn, my mistress was transported with joy to hear of your good
offices. She has sent me to fetch you that she may thank you, in her
own palace and with her own lips, for your disinterested generosity.'

Far from being delighted at these words, Amīn trembled and
became pale, saying to the girl: 'My sister, I see that Shams al-
Nahār has not reflected upon this step which she requires me to take.
I am a man of the people, without the intelligence and breeding of
Abū al-Hasan. I lack the assurance which would take him safely
among the eunuchs of the palace. How could I, who still shudder at
the tale he told me of his meeting with your mistress, dare such a
risk myself? My house would be a much better place of meeting.
If Shams al-Nahār will deign to visit me, we can talk without fear on
either side.' As he was so saying, the young man's limbs gave from
under him, even as the confidant was trying to persuade him to
follow her, and she had to help him back to his seat and give him a
glass of fresh water to calm his terror.

Seeing that nothing would be gained by insisting further, she
said: 'You are right, it would be better for all if my mistress came
here herself. I will try to persuade her and am certain that I shall
succeed. Wait here, O Amīn.'

The girl was well advised, for no sooner had Shams al-Nahār

heard the reasons of Amīn than she rose up, unmindful of her weakness, and, hiding her face in a veil, followed her slave to the jeweller's house. The confidant went in first, in order that her mistress might not be seen by any other person, and asked Amīn if he had sent away all the people of his house. 'I live here alone with an old negress who looks after me,' replied the young man, and the girl said: 'Even she must not be allowed to enter.' With that she shut all the doors herself and went to fetch her mistress.

The lovely lady entered the house, filling the halls and corridors with the perfume of her garments. Without a word or look she sat down panting upon the cushions which Amīn placed for her, and stayed still there for some minutes until she had recovered her breath. At last she raised her veil, and the jeweller thought that the sun had been brought into his house. She turned to her confidant, whispering: 'Is this the youth of whom you spoke?' and, when the other answered that it was, she said: 'How do you do, O Amīn?' 'I am well, thanks be to Allāh,' he answered. 'May He keep you and preserve you as a perfume hidden in gold.' 'Are you married?' she asked, and he answered: 'As Allāh lives, I am both a bachelor and an orphan. I have nothing to do but to serve you. Your least desires shall be upon my head and within my eyes.'

At this point Shahrazād saw the approach of morning and discreetly fell silent.

But when the hundred-and-sixty-second night had come

SHE SAID:

Amīn continued: 'I have an empty house opposite this one in which I live. I place it entirely at the disposition of you and Prince Alī ibn Bakr. I will at once furnish it worthily of you, so that you lack for nothing when you are my guest.' Shams al-Nahār thanked him cordially, saying: 'I give praise to my destiny that I have met you! Help given for friendship's sake is more useful than any other, it is a strip of green in the desert of suffering. Some day I hope that I may repay you. In the meanwhile, see how young and charming is my confidant. Though it will be great grief for me to part with her even for an hour, I make you a present of her that she may give you cool and luminous nights.'

When Amīn had assured himself that the girl was charming, with perfect eyes and thighs of satisfying excellence, Shams al-Nahār continued: 'I have unlimited confidence in this child, therefore do not scruple to inform her of all the prince says to you. I charge you to love her, since she has all those sympathetic qualities which refresh the soul.' With that Shams al-Nahār retired, thanking Amīn in her gentlest speech, and the confidant followed her, looking back with smiling eyes at her new friend.

When they had gone, the jeweller ran to his shop and fetched from it all his engraved bowls and silver jars. To these he added carpets borrowed from one friend, silken cushions from another, china from a third, dishes from a fourth, and precious ewers from a fifth. With such things he magnificently furnished his empty house.

As he was giving a last glance to his preparations, the little confidant entered, swinging her hips and saying: 'O Amīn, my mistress wishes you peace and sends you thanks for the consolation you have given her in the absence of Abū al-Hasan. She begs you to inform Prince Alī that the Khalīfah will be absent to-night and that therefore she will be able to visit him in this place. Tell him as soon as you can, for the news should have the effect of bringing him back to his wonted condition of health and laughter.' Then, taking a purse of gold from her bosom and holding it out to Amīn, she said: 'My mistress begs you to spare no expense in your preparations.' Amīn pushed away the purse, crying: 'Do I seem so small in her eyes that she gives me gold?' The young girl took back the purse and, rejoicing in the unselfish liberality of Amīn, ran back to tell her mistress that the house was ready. She helped her to bathe, combed her hair, scented her, and dressed her in her richest robe.

After he had filled the room which was to receive the lovers with fresh plucked flowers in vases, trays heaped high with meats and pastries, conserves and drinks, and musical instruments of all sorts, Amīn hurried to the house of Prince Alī. He found the prince already a little medicined by hope. When he was informed that he would soon see his mistress, his joy knew no bounds; he forgot his sufferings, his cheeks flowered into roses again, and his face became even more beautiful than before, owing to a certain added touch of sympathy.

He dressed himself magnificently and set out with the jeweller, as strong and springing upon his feet as if he had not been down to the doors of the tomb. When they came to the house, Amīn invited the prince to seat himself and, when he had done so, not only placed cushions behind him but set two crystal vases of mingled flowers to right and left of him and gave him a rose to hold between his fingers.

The two young men talked together until a knock was heard at the door and two women entered, one of whom was entirely concealed under a thick izār of black silk.

At this point Shahrazād saw the approach of morning and discreetly fell silent.

But when the hundred-and-sixty-third night had come

SHE SAID:

It was the time of the call to prayer. The ecstatic voices of the muezzin brought down the invisible benediction of Allāh upon the earth, as Shams al-Nahār opened her veil and looked into the eyes of Alī ibn Bakr.

When the two lovers saw each other, they fell on the floor without consciousness, and it was an hour before they opened their eyes and, as sole means of expressing their passion, looked at each other again. When they could speak, they exchanged such tender confidences that Amīn and the confidant could not but weep in their corner.

After a certain time Amīn, helped by the young girl, served his guests, first with agreeable scents which should make them hungry, then with the meats and fruits and pastries, and lastly with an abundance of wines. When they had well feasted, he poured water for them and handed them napkins fringed with silks. By this time the lovers had recovered from the depth of their emotion and were able to taste all the sweetness of their meeting. Shams al-Nahār said to the young girl: 'Give me a lute that I may try to play the divine passion out of my soul.' The confidant gave her an instrument on which she played, by way of prelude, a song without words. The lute sobbed or laughed under her fingers as the music came in smiles or sighs. Then, with her eyes lost in the eyes of her lover, Shams al-Nahār sang:

> My body turns transparent
> Waiting for him,
> The breeze of his coming
> Plays on the sand of my heart.
>
> O night beside him!
> O tired lips leeching wine,
> Achieving honey,
> Knowing at last Spring!

The three listeners rejoiced exceedingly at this song, crying out: 'Ah, the delicious words!'

Amīn was delighted to see the two lovers in each other's arms and thought that his presence was no longer necessary, therefore he withdrew discreetly, leaving them the house for their loves. He returned to his own home where he slept calmly, thinking of the pleasure of his friends.

When he woke in the morning, he saw the old negress by his bed, beating with her hands a face convulsed by fear. As he was about to ask her what had happened, she pointed silently to a neighbour who stood by the door waiting for the jeweller to waken.

At a sign from Amīn the man approached, saying: 'I come to mourn with you in your terrible calamity.' 'What calamity is that?' cried Amīn, and the man replied: 'As soon as you had returned home last night, certain robbers, well practised in their profession, who must have seen you carrying all those precious things into your house, broke it open and took everything of value, including your two guests, whom they have probably killed.'

'By Allāh, this is terrible!' cried the jeweller, lifting his hands to heaven. 'My valuables and those which I borrowed from my friends are lost for ever, but that is nothing to the fate of my two guests.' Dressed in his shirt and with naked feet, he ran to the other house, followed by his lamenting neighbour, and found it empty, pillaged of everything, even as the other had said. He gave up hoping against hope and burst into tears, crying: 'What must I do now?'

At this point Shahrazād saw the approach of morning and discreetly fell silent.

But when the hundred-and-sixty-fourth night had come

SHE SAID:

The neighbour replied: 'Your best plan is to wait until the thieves are captured, for the Governor's guards are pursuing them even now, not only for last night's robbery but for many others.' On this the poor jeweller cried: 'O wise Abū al-Hasan to have departed for the peace of Basrah! And yet . . . what is written is written.'

He made his way through a commiserating crowd to the door of his own house, where he saw a stranger waiting for him, who said: 'I have a secret message for your private ear.' Amīn would have led him into the house, but the stranger said: 'Let us go to your second property which lies opposite, for it is absolutely necessary that I should speak to you alone.' 'I do not know you. How is it that you know me and all my houses?' asked Amīn. The other smiled and answered: 'I will explain that to you and also, if Allāh wills, help you somewhat in your misfortune.' The two crossed the road to the second house, but there the unknown, showing Amīn that the door had been forced by the thieves and would no longer give them privacy for their conversation, said: 'Follow me, and I will lead you to a place which is discretion itself.' The two walked through street on street and market on market until at nightfall they reached the bank of the Tigris. 'We will be safer on the other bank,' said the unknown. As he spoke, a boat appeared from nowhere and into this he thrust Amīn before the jeweller had time to refuse. With a few vigorous strokes of the oars the stranger crossed the river. Then, helping Amīn to disembark, he led him through narrow lanes and closes until they came to a low iron door.

The man took a large rusty key from his belt and opened the door, which groaned upon its hinges. Amīn found himself in a low tunnel along which he was obliged to walk on hands and knees. Soon he came to a room lighted by a single torch, round which were sitting ten motionless men dressed in the same way, whose faces were so alike that they might have been one man repeated ten times in mirrors. Amīn, who was worn out by his walk, relapsed without further strength upon the floor. His guide sprinkled water upon his face and then sat down to eat with the other ten. With one voice the seated figures requested Amīn to join them in their repast and he, considering that they themselves would not eat if the food were poisoned, drew near and satisfied his great hunger.

When the last of the food had disappeared, the same unison of voices asked: 'Do you know us?' and, when Amīn denied, in Allāh's name, that he did so, continued: 'We are the thieves who broke into your house last night and bore away a young couple who were singing to each other. Unfortunately their servant escaped by way of the terrace.' 'As you hope for the mercy of Allāh, tell me, my lords, where you have hidden those guests of mine!' cried Amīn. 'Restore my soul with the sight of them, as you have restored my body with your generous food. Allāh will give you a great enjoyment of all those things which you stole from me.' At his words eleven arms were pointed with one movement to a closed door, and eleven voices said: 'Do not fear for them; they are as safe here as if they were in the Governor's house. We have sent for you to know the truth about them, for their obvious nobility so daunted us that we have not dared to question them ourselves.'

Amīn was relieved at this intelligence and said, hoping to win over the thieves altogether: 'My masters, if ever mercy and politeness seem to vanish from this world, yet men will be able to find them in your house. With folk as honourable as you it is best to tell the whole truth. Therefore listen to the extraordinary story of these two young people.'

With that the jeweller told the thieves every detail concerning the loves of Shams al-Nahār and Prince Alī ibn Bakr, but nothing would be gained by repeating them in this place. As soon as he had finished, the thieves cried: 'It has indeed been an honour for our house to harbour the beautiful Shams al-Nahār and Prince Alī ibn Bakr. Are you sure that you have spoken the truth?' 'I swear that I have done so!' cried Amīn, and on that the thieves rose as one man and, opening the door which they had pointed out to the jeweller, led out Prince Alī and the Sultān's favourite, saying to them with a thousand excuses: 'We beg you to pardon the ill taste of our conduct. We had not thought to take persons of your rank in a jeweller's house.' Then, turning to Amīn, they continued: 'We will at once return to you all the precious objects which we took from your house and only regret that we are unable to give you back the larger furniture which we have already sold by auction.'

(Narrative continued in the words of Amīn the Jeweller.)

They made up the booty into a large package and, when I had thanked them for their generosity, said to the three of us: 'We do not wish to detain you any longer unless you would care to honour us by staying. We only request that you will forget the past and promise not to inform against us.' As they led us down to the river bank, we thought that we were dreaming and did not dare to exchange a word with each other. They helped us with every mark of respect into their boat and rowed so strongly that we were at the other bank before we knew ourselves to be well embarked. Hardly had we set foot to ground than we were terrified to see ourselves surrounded by a troop of the Governor's guards. The thieves, however, who had stayed in the boat, immediately rowed off and escaped.

The chief of the guards asked us, in a threatening voice, who we were and whence we came; but our fear was such that we could not answer. Therefore his distrust of us increased and he cried: 'Unless you answer truthfully and at once, I shall have you bound hand and foot and taken to prison. Where do you live, in what street, in what quarter?' Hoping to save the situation, I answered: 'We are strolling musicians, my lord, and this woman is a professional singer. This evening we performed at a feast in the house of those persons who have just rowed away. We cannot tell you their names as, in our trade, we do not ask questions, but are content with a good price for our services.' 'You do not look like singers or musicians,' replied the lieutenant with a piercing look. 'You are too agitated for your story to be true. Also that woman has too many jewels to be what you say she is. You, there, take these three to prison!'

At this point Shams al-Nahār decided to interfere. She drew the lieutenant aside and whispered in his ear something which caused him to leap backwards and bow to the earth with a babble of compliments and excuses. He made his men fetch two boats, into one of which he conducted the favourite, placing the second at the disposition of Prince Alī and myself. While we rowed towards the city, the other vessel turned up stream, bearing Shams al-Nahār to her palace.

When we came to the prince's house, Alī fell unconscious into the arms of his slaves and the women of his home. He had finally lost hope of ever seeing his mistress again.

At this point Shahrazād saw the approach of morning and discreetly fell silent.

But when the hundred-and-sixty-fifth night had come

SHE SAID:

While the slaves and the women were doing all they could to bring Prince Alī round, his relations, supposing that I was the cause of his misfortunes, pressed me for details. I answered discreetly: 'Good people, that which has happened to Prince Alī is so extraordinary that only he could tell you of it.' Happily, while they were still insisting, my friend came to himself, and I was able to escape.

At my own house I found the old negress still lamenting and many neighbours gathered to condole with me on my loss. The woman threw herself at my feet, asking many questions, but I cut her short, saying that I had need of nothing but sleep. I fell heavily among the cushions of my bed and slept like a dead man until morning. When I woke, the negress came to me with more questions, but I sent her for a filled bowl, which I drained before I answered: 'That which has happened, has happened.' She retired and I fell asleep again, not waking for two nights and two days.

When I came to myself, I was so refreshed that I took a bath at the hammām and then went to visit my shop. As I was producing the key of it, a little hand touched me on the shoulder and a voice said: 'Greeting, O Amīn!' I turned and found myself face to face with the confidant of Shams al-Nahār.

This time I was not rejoiced to see her, but was thrown instead into a state of great fear lest the neighbours should see me in conversation with one who was known to be concerned with the Sultān's favourite. I returned the key to my pocket and made off as fast as I could, hurrying for hours up and down the city with the confidant at my heels. At last, coming upon a mosque which was very little used, I slipped off my shoes and rushed into the darkest corner of it. There I knelt in an attitude of prayer, marvelling at the good sense of my old friend Abū al-Hasan and swearing before Allāh, if I ever got free of this intrigue, nothing should persuade me into another such.

At this point Shahrazād saw the approach of morning and discreetly fell silent.

But when the hundred-and-sixty-sixth night had come

SHE SAID:

I was soon joined in my dark corner by the confidant, and this time I spoke with her freely, as there were no witnesses. She asked me how I did, and I replied: 'I am in good health, but would rather be dead than live in the midst of these alarms.' The confidant answered:

'Then what would you say if you knew the terrible condition of my mistress? I become weak when I call to mind how she looked when she returned to her palace. I had arrived there first, escaping from terrace to terrace out of your house, and jumping from the last building into the street. Who would have taken the face I then saw, pale as if it rose from the tomb, for the face of the luminous Shams al-Nahār? I threw myself sobbing at her feet, but she bade me rise and give a thousand golden dīnārs to the boatman. After that she fell swooning in our arms, and did not come to herself until we had placed her upon her bed, sprinkled her face with water of flowers, wiped her eyes, washed her feet, and changed all her garments. When we found that she was breathing again, I gave her rose sherbert to drink and made her smell an essence of jasmine, saying to her: "For Allāh's sake control yourself, my mistress, for He alone knows what will happen if we go on in this way." "Faithful girl," she answered, "I have nothing left to bind me to this earth; but before I die I would have news of my lover. I wish you to go and seek them from the jeweller Amīn, and at the same time to give him this purse of gold against the loss which he has sustained because of us." '

The confidant handed me a heavy packet, which I judged—and rightly as it turned out afterwards—to contain more than five thousand dīnārs. 'Now,' she continued, 'give me news, whether it be good or bad, of the young prince.'

I could not refuse a request so sweetly couched. In spite of all my resolutions, I told her to come that evening to my house for the latest tidings of Alī. I let the girl leave the mosque first, carrying the gold which she promised to leave at my house, and then departed myself, making towards the lodging of Alī ibn Bakr.

I found that the women and slaves had been waiting anxiously for me during the three days which had passed since my last visit, as they could find no way to calm their patient, who was for ever calling upon my name. Finding Alī more dead than alive, with the flame of life scarce flickering in his eyes, I wept and pressed him against my breast, vainly trying to console him with my words.

At this point Shahrazād saw the approach of morning and discreetly fell silent.

But when the hundred-and-sixty-seventh night had come

SHE SAID:

'Amīn,' he said to me, 'I feel that the vital part of me will not be here much longer and before I die I would give you somewhat in recompense for the losses I have occasioned you.' He signed to his slaves, who set before me in baskets jewels of great value, with vases and pots of gold and silver. These he begged me to accept, and sent his slaves straightway to carry them to my house. When we were alone, he said: 'Everything in this world has an aim or ending; woe be to him who misses the aim of love, for only the grave remains to him. If I were unmindful of the law of the Prophet (upon whom be prayer and peace!) I would ere this have sought death with my own hands, for you know not how deep my heart is drowned in pain.'

To distract him I told him that I had promised to send news to Shams al-Nahār, who had requested it. I left him after receiving a message that his only regret in dying would be the absence of his mistress.

I had hardly reached my house when the girl came as she had promised, but in so great a state of agitation that I hardly knew her. Through her tears, she exclaimed: 'All that we ever feared has come about! We are lost, for the Khalīfah knows all. The suspicions of the chief eunuch were aroused by the indiscretion of one of my lady's slaves, and he examined each of the women of her palace separately. They all denied the thing, but he was clever enough to piece together the truth by comparing the discrepant details which they gave him. He reported the matter to the Khalīfah who has sent a guard of twenty eunuchs to fetch Shams al-Nahār before him. All of us at the palace are in a state of the most miserable apprehension. I have stolen a few minutes to come here and beg you to warn Prince Alī.'

With that the poor girl ran off, leaving the world black about my eyes. 'There is no power or might save in Allāh!' I cried, and ran as hard as I could until I reached the bedside of the prince. 'O Alī,' I said, 'you must follow me at once, for the Khalīfah's guards are even now seeking you with death in their hands. We must flee, even beyond the frontiers of this kingdom!'

In the name of the prince, I ordered his slaves to load three camels with provisions and the most costly treasures of the house, and myself mounted with him upon the back of another camel. There was no time for Alī to say farewell to his mother; we set out on the instant and were soon crossing the desert beyond the city.

At this point Shahrazād saw the approach of morning and discreetly fell silent.

But when the hundred-and-sixty-eighth night had come

SHE SAID:

That which is written must come to pass. You may change the earth and sky but you cannot alter Destiny. We had left our sorrows in the city only to find greater in the desert. We had just come within sight of an oasis from which a minaret among the palm-trees looked out upon the sand, when we were surrounded by a band of brigands. Knowing that it would be fatal to resist, we allowed ourselves to be disarmed and spoiled. The vile fellows took our camels with their lading, and even stripped us of all our garments except our shirts. Then they rode off, leaving us to our fate.

My poor friend was so exhausted by the frequent emotions which he had experienced that he was like a lifeless puppet in my hands. I was able, however, to lead him very slowly to the oasis and aid him to enter the mosque, in order that we might pass the night there. He fell on the earthen floor, saying: 'This is the place of my death, for I know in my soul that Shams al-Nahār is no longer among the living.'

Now there was a man praying in that place, who, when he had finished, looked at us and said benevolently: 'Young men, am I right in thinking that you are strangers, and are going to pass the night in this place?' 'We are indeed strangers, O sheikh,' I answered. 'We have been despoiled of all we had by brigands in the desert; they have not left us even wherewith to cover ourselves decently.'

'Stay here, and I will return to you,' said the old man compassionately. With that he departed and came back, after a few minutes, followed by a child carrying a packet. This he opened, and gave us the clothes which it contained, saying, after we had dressed ourselves: 'Come to my house, for there you will be better off than fasting in this mosque.' He insisted on our going with him. But, when Alī came to the stranger's dwelling, he fell breathless among the carpets. As he lay there, there came with the breeze which sighed among the palm-trees the voice of some poor wandering woman singing this song:

> I wept a trifle, having lost my youth,
>   But then I dried my tears and kept them
> To weep love's little truth
>   And the hard master of the girl who wept them.
>
> Why should I mourn that death is nearer,
>   Seeing that I
> In death may find the meaning clearer
>   Of love and misery?

> If I had known that parting was so near
> I might have thought to take
> Food for the journey, glances bitter but dear,
> Dear for his sake.

When this song began, Alī ibn Bakr lifted his head and seemed to listen. When the voice died away, he fell back with a deep sigh. We came to him and found that life had departed with the song.

At this point Shahrazād saw the approach of morning and discreetly fell silent.

But when the hundred-and-sixty-ninth night had come

SHE SAID:

The old man wept with me all night, and, through my tears, I told him the story of Alī ibn Bakr. In the morning I begged him to guard the body, while I made my way as quickly as possible to Baghdād. Without waiting to change my clothes, I hurried to ibn Bakr's house and sadly wished his mother peace.

When the woman saw me without her son, she trembled with presentiment. 'Venerable mother of Alī,' I said, 'Allāh commands and the rest of us obey. When a letter comes from Him calling a soul, that soul must hurry into the presence of his Master.'

The prince's mother fell to the ground with a cry of pain, moaning: 'Is my son dead? Is my son dead?'

I lowered my eyes in silence, the poor woman fainted away, and I added my tears and lamentations to those which filled the women's quarter of the house.

When Alī's mother was in a state to hear me, I described the death to her, adding: 'May Allāh reward your merit, O mother of Alī, and comfort you with a great comfort.' 'Had he no message for his mother?' she asked, and I replied: 'He charged you to bring his body to Baghdād.' She tore her garments and promised me that she would set out at once with a caravan to bring back the corpse of her son.

I left her people at their preparations and returned home, thinking to myself: 'O Alī ibn Bakr, unhappy lover! Alas, alas, that you should have been cut down in such fair flower.'

As I was opening my door a hand touched me gently upon the arm, and I turned to see the confidant of Shams al-Nahār standing before me in mourning garments. I turned to flee, but she caught me by the robe and insisted upon entering my house. When we were inside, I started to weep, without very well knowing why, and said to her: 'Have you heard the sad news?' 'Which news, O Amīn?' she asked, and I answered: 'The death of Alī ibn Bakr.' She wept afresh; therefore I knew that she had not heard of it and told her how it had come to pass, answering her sighs with mine.

When I had finished, she said: 'And have you not heard of my grief, O Amīn?' 'Shams al-Nahār has been put to death by the Khalīfah?' I suggested, but she shook her head, saying:

'Shams al-Nahār is dead, but not in the way that you suppose. My mistress, oh, my mistress! When she came into the presence of the Khalīfah, he dismissed the twenty eunuchs and made her sit by his side, saying gently: "O Shams al-Nahār, you have enemies in the palace who have tried to blacken you in my eyes by relating things unworthy of either of us. I love you all the more, and to give the lie to their lies I have determined to increase your allowance and the number of your slaves. Therefore, I pray you cast aside these heavy looks, which weigh upon my spirit, and join me in a little feast I have prepared for you, with singers and flutes and pleasant things to drink."

'Scarcely had he spoken when the musicians and singers entered, followed by slaves bearing trays heavy with all manner of pleasant things. The Khalīfah sat down by the side of his favourite, the last resistance of whose heart was broken by so much goodness, and ordered music. One of the girls began this song:

> Tears falling so,
>   Ah, they discover
>   Secrets to all.
>   They fall and fall.
> If you must know,
>   I have lost my lover.

> Tears falling so . . .

At this point Shams al-Nahār gave a light sigh and fell back among her cushions; the Khalīfah bent over her, thinking that she had fainted, but he took her up dead.

'He threw his cup away from him and turned over all the dishes.

As he wept, he bade each be gone from the hall save me, after breaking the lutes. He took the body of Shams al-Nahār upon his knees and wept over her all night, without letting anyone approach him. In the morning he handed over his favourite to the mourners and washers, ordering that her funeral should exceed that of any lawful queen. Then he shut himself in his apartments, and has not since been seen of any.'

We wept together for the two lovers, and then I concerted a plan with the girl by which we were able to have Alī ibn Bakr buried in a magnificent tomb beside the one which the Khalīfah had raised for Shams al-Nahār.

Ever since then (concludes the jeweller) I and the confidant, who has become my wife, have not ceased at stated intervals to visit the two tombs and weep over the disastrous love of our young friends.

Such, O auspicious King, continued Shahrazād, is the sad tale of Shams al-Nahār, the favourite of Hārūn al-Rashīd.

At this point little Dunyazād burst into tears and hid her face among her carpets. King Shahryār said: 'O Shahrazād, your tale has made me very sad.'

'I told you that story, O King,' answered Shahrazād, 'though it is not of the same joyful kind as my others, firstly that you might enjoy the excellent poems which it contains, and secondly that it might prepare you for another tale which I am ready to tell you.' 'I pray you tell it, if it will comfort my sad heart. What is the title of it?' cried the King, and Shahrazād answered: 'It is the fairy tale of Princess Budūr, Moon of Moons.'

Dunyazād lifted her head, crying: 'Do begin at once, O Shahrazād!' But her sister answered: 'With all my heart and as in duty bound to our delightful King. Yet let it be for to-morrow night.' And, seeing the approach of morning, she discreetly fell silent.